# Encyclopaedia
## of Nationalism

### Encyclopaedia of Nationalism

**Editor:**
Dr. Athena S. Leoussi, University of Reading, UK

**Consultant Advisor:**
Professor Anthony D. Smith, London School of Economics and Political Science, University of London, UK.

**Editorial Assistants:**
Dr. Elisabeth Arweck, King's College, University of London, UK
Dr. Rachel Monaghan, University of Ulster, UK

**Editorial Advisory Board:**
Professor Michael Banton, University of Bristol, UK
Professor Martin Bulmer, University of Surrey, UK
Dr. John Hutchinson, London School of Economics and Political Science, University of London, UK
Dr. Obi Igwara, University of Hull, UK
Professor Paschalis Kitromilides, University of Athens, Greece
Professor David Marsland, Brunel University, UK
Professor George Schöpflin, School of Slavonic and East European Studies, University of London, UK

# Encyclopaedia
## of Nationalism

*Athena S. Leoussi*
*editor*

**Anthony D. Smith** consultant advisor

**Transaction Publishers**
New Brunswick (U.S.A.) and London (U.K.)

Library of Congress Catalog Number: 00-048403
ISBN: 0-7658-0002-0
Printed in the United States of America

Library of Congress Cataloging-in-Publication Data

Encyclopaedia of nationalism / Athena S. Leoussi, editor ; Anthony D. Smith, consultant advisor.
    p.  cm.
   Includes bibliographical references and index.
   ISBN 0-7658-0002-0
    1.  Nationalism—Encyclopedias.   2.  Nationalism—History—Encyclopedias.  I. Leoussi, Athena S., 1959-

JC311 .E499 2000
320.54'03—dc21                                          00-048403

# Contents

# Introduction

The image on the cover of this book is emblematic of the continuing and formative role of nationalism in the cultural and political history of the modern world. It also crystallizes in a synthetic image the fluidity of concepts of national culture and national solidarity. It shows the geopolitical maps of the new states of the Czech Republic and of Slovakia against the backdrop of an image of the older state of Czechoslovakia which they succeeded, personified as a young girl in folk, "Czechoslovak" costume. The two new states emerged on the political landscape of Europe on 1 January 1993. They were the result of the fragmentation of the larger state of Czechoslovakia, itself founded not so long ago, in 1918. That older state had united into a single "nation," and under a common political roof, the Czechs and Slovaks who, at the time, believed that they did, indeed, have a common identity—and that they therefore belonged together and apart from the even earlier, Austro-Hungarian Empire which they considered their "prison." Alphonse Mucha's image of young Czechoslovakia dressed in "national" costume and celebrating her tenth anniversary in 1928, reminds us of that earlier conception of national identity which gave rise to Czechoslovakia and which was to change within a period of seventy-five years into a conception of the distinctiveness of the Czech and Slovak "nations."

To say, as it has been said, that Czechoslovakia was, in actual fact, a *mariage de convenance* of Czechs and Slovaks does not adequately explain the divorce, nor indeed the wedding. Instead, it raises a fundamental issue, that of the role of culture in social relations and, as crucially, in political associations.

It was Emile Durkheim who saw most clearly that culture, which he called *conscience collective*, unites. If we were to accept Durkheim's observation that culture unites its adherents into a community called a "church," this sociological fact does not provide an adequate solution to the modern problem of state-formation which is the problem of political legitimacy—not only the legitimacy of governments, but also, the legitimacy of state borders. In relation to the latter—how should political communities be delimited?—the modern belief that a cultural community should define a state has thrown into high relief, first, the complexity of the notion of "culture"; and second, the relationship between "church" (in this wider sense of a moral community, a group of people holding the same moral values) and state as two distinct domains of human social organization and endeavor.

Although state-formation of the democratic variety includes some of the ingredients of Durkheim's "religious" community, a consensus on values, and some of the *tendresse* of its *Gemeinschaft*, it is not identical with it. Indeed, the modern, ideological and indeed liberal distinction between Church and State has to be maintained *analytically*, in order to obtain a clearer understanding of the cultural politics of our time—that is to say, an understanding of modern nationalism.

Wherever the link between culture and politics has been pursued in practice, it has led to some important theoretical as well as practical qualifications and words of caution. Firstly, and as Elie Kedourie has correctly observed, the "general will," in the sense of a common culture, is difficult to define. It is especially difficult to delimit the boundaries of a common culture and to do so for political use: for drawing the frontiers of states. Secondly, the nation-state often involves an element of cultural coercion. The assumption by the state of a cultural role involves, not only the protection by the state of a culture and its bearers, but also the imposition of this culture on a population which is not always culturally homogenous. This element of coercion is felt among national minorities and free-thinkers alike. The transformation of a particular culture into the culture of the state makes that culture compulsory and thus removes the element of freedom—the freedom of conscience and association—which characterizes all cultural communities. Thirdly, if culture means a variety of manifestations of the

# Introduction

mind, and at least language and religion, then as the historical record indicates, these two quite different phenomena are not always, either coextensive or harmonious from the point of view of their social bases. For example, linguistic communities have often been divided by religion and even *irreligion* (a secular cast of mind); and religion has often united linguistically diverse communities. Fourthly, a common language, as indeed a common religion, is neither necessary nor sufficient motivation for political association. And fifthly, the very concept of a common language is difficult to define not least because languages exist in different dialects. The disappearance of Czechoslovakia from the political map of Europe exemplifies all these problems. It also indicates the interaction between culture and other factors of common experience in forging bonds of national solidarity and hence states. The different political and economic histories of linguistically related communities may impede the growth of sentiments of 'national' solidarity and political commitment.

The visual consideration of the history of Czechoslovakia on the cover of this volume is also *in memoriam* of that great contemporary scholar of nationalism, the late Ernest Gellner (1925-1995) who was born in Prague, and returned there, after retiring from the University of Cambridge, to found a Centre for the Study of Nationalism. Gellner's place lies not above that of all others, but at the center of a community of many distinguished students of the subject all of whom have considered it necessary, if not imperative, to engage, at one time or another, in intellectual conversation with his thought, in either agreement or constructive opposition.

The dissolution of Czechoslovakia and its replacement by two new, independent, and just as "national" states, is not the only *raison d'être* of the present volume. In fact, the case of Czechoslovakia inscribes itself in a much wider politico-cultural transformation of our time, the dissolution of the USSR. The end of the internationalist Soviet experiment in 1989 and the resurgence of nationalism which succeeded it throughout the former Eastern bloc have given a new impetus to the field of nationalism studies. Until then and for almost exactly two hundred years starting with the French Revolution, the world had been faced with two options, two systems of political, cultural, and economic organization: liberal-democratic nationalism and socialist internationalism. For a while the choice was hard to make. It was not a choice between good and evil but a much more fatal choice as Isaiah Berlin has remarked, a choice between two goods—equality and freedom. In 1945, with the end of the Second World War, the world finally became divided, almost equally, between the two options, and politicians, the academy, and the press spoke of a new balance of powers: Eastern communism and Western liberal democracy. And the two worlds, East and West, appeared as *exempla virtutis*—each a typical embodiment of its chosen virtue and its path to economic prosperity for all. But when, in the 1950s and 1960s the evil of equality without freedom became obvious in the streets of Budapest and Prague and when, in the late 1980s it was whispered that in the shops of Moscow not only was there *almost* nothing on the shelves, but that there was *nothing* on the shelves, the balance tilted and the peoples of the East turned West. The "trial by growth" which is how Gellner described the criterion of success in the struggle between the two systems proved not only the inhumanity but also the poverty of communist internationalism. The years following the *annus mirabilis* of 1989 showed the full extent of the actual failure of an apparent success as Stevan K. Pavlowitch has so brilliantly demonstrated in the related case of the simultaneous collapse of the second Yugoslavia.

Between 1945 and 1989 students of nationalism had been visiting the peripheral regions of Western Europe and the new, post-colonial states of Asia and Africa trying to understand the nationalist option. Since 1989 they have been visiting or, as we should say, revisiting, Central and Eastern Europe and what is now the Commonwealth of Independent States. The year 1989 did not mark the end of history but the reclaiming of history in the post-communist world. This history was not one history, but many distinct, national histories and traditions of the peoples of the Eastern bloc which the communist system had attempted to obliterate. In actual fact, the communist system only managed to repress, in a quasi-Freudian sense, and then only partially, a national life which was lived, in both its content, and its form.

# Introduction

The return to Eastern Europe of scholars of nationalism who are now replacing the Sovietologists who, as Alexander J. Motyl has interestingly pointed out, had largely ignored the powerful undercurrent of national forms of existence in the former Eastern bloc, has combined with both historical and contemporary studies of nationalism in other parts of the world, including its European *locus classicus*, to produce a wealth of new and more refined concepts and theories of nationalism. The current concern in Western Europe and America with the politics of identity in the context of successive waves of mass immigration into the industrialized "West" and of intermarriage, has given further impulse to the development of an analytic vocabulary to understand such phenomena as the "hyphenated American" and the "hybridity" of national identities. These same experiences have also necessitated a reconsideration of concepts of "citizenship" and "nationality." Of course, as Anthony D. Smith and Steven Grosby have pointed out, the questions of personal identity and group membership are constitutive of humanity. We find these questions in that most moving and revealing passage in the Book of Ruth:

> And Ruth said, Intreat me not to leave thee, or to return from following after thee: for whither thou goest, I will go; and where thou lodgest, I will lodge: thy people shall be my people, and thy God my God...

However, modern "reflexivity" demands a systematic account of why we are the way we are and of our becoming. This *Encyclopaedia* is a response to this demand. It is an attempt to survey and inform this new *prise de conscience* in the sphere of modern nationalism. It offers an inventory of the analytical instruments which are currently available for an inter-disciplinary study of nationalism. It brings together leading scholars in nationalism studies many of whom have developed the very analytical instruments on which they were invited to write. The focus of the *Encyclopaedia* is thus theoretical and for this reason particular nationalist movements and national leaders are mostly treated as illustrative material within more general or typological entries.

The *Encyclopaedia* expresses no *parti pris*. Rather, it seeks to encompass the wide range of issues and debates in the field, including the latest debates on the nature of nations and nationalist movements, such as the postmodernist analyses of nationalism as a discourse; the role of ethnicity in shaping the foreign policy of democratic multinational states; and the role of the nation-state in an increasingly globalized world.

Of course, the result is inevitably incomplete as it was not realistically possible to go to the field and, in a Ruskinian way, select nothing, reject nothing. Nevertheless, this volume provides scholars and students of nationalism with a broad framework and a rich vocabulary for identifying and understanding this most complex and fundamental phenomenon of human experience, nationalism.

A special feature of this *Encyclopaedia* is its essay-long entries. The essay format allows succinct and at the same time in-depth discussions of issues. The entries are organised in alphabetical order. They span the whole field of nationalism and can be grouped into the following six broad categories:

- entries on the defining figures of nationalism in the eighteenth and nineteenth centuries, including Fichte, Herder, Renan, and Rousseau;

- entries on the diverse aspects, manifestations and types of nationalism, such as apartheid, assimilation, cultural nationalism, decolonization, diasporas, ethnic competition, ethnicity, genocide, ghetto, homeland, *indigenismo*, jingoism, multiculturalism, national identity, national symbols, race and racism, and xenophobia;

- entries on the relations between nationalism and other collective phenomena such as art, citizenship, class, immigration, language, music, state and youth;

- entries on the relations between nationalism and other ideologies, such as communism, cosmopolitanism, feminism and liberalism;

# Introduction

- entries on the various theories of nationalism such as ethnosymbolism, instrumentalism, kin selection, modernism, primordialism, and rational choice;

- and entries on the various accounts of the nation, including views of the nation as a civic community of citizens, an ethnic community of kin, an imagined community, an invented community and a modern industrial society.

The *Encyclopaedia* includes a general index of entry titles, an index of subjects, and three mechanisms of cross-referencing intended to alert readers to the further implications, complications and alternatives involved in a particular concept or theory. First, the general index. This consists of a complete list of entry titles accompanied, where relevant, by a "*see also...*" suggesting related entries. Second, the subject index. This is a list of subjects with instructions to readers as to the entry title under which a subject appears or the entry title which includes a discussion of that subject. Readers may find it useful to consult this index first, when looking for particular subjects or themes. And third, readers are referred to related entries through the capitalization of words with a separate entry in the text of each entry. Each entry is accompanied by a bibliography detailing the sources used in the essay and some additional sources for further reading.

As the editor of this *Encyclopaedia* I feel very proud of each and all the contributions of my *encyclopédistes,* all of whom are either already distinguished scholars in the field of nationalism studies, or are the bright new lights of a younger generation of thinkers on whom the past, present and future of this field of study most crucially depend.

I am also grateful to all the contributors for the enthusiasm with which they joined me in this project, their promptness in delivering their manuscripts, and the exceptional quality of their contributions. Quite early on in the course of this project I realized, to my delight, that I was in the company of friends all of whom, without exception, responded to their task with the utmost sincerity and excitement and to their editor with most obliging responsibility, consideration and many excellent ideas and suggestions. Indeed, it is a tribute to all the participants in this project that the initial model of the present volume evolved into a much richer and deeper consideration of the subject than was originally envisaged. This was a result of their personal, imaginative engagement with the whole problem of a theoretical survey of the phenomenon of nationalism rather than just with the part on which they were invited to reflect. I shall very much miss the deep satisfaction which I derived from the sense of participating in such an intensely collaborative, common endeavour.

My task was further facilitated by an excellent editorial advisory board who embraced this project with their usual warmth, expertise and professionalism: Professor Michael Banton, Professor Martin Bulmer, Dr John Hutchinson, Dr Obi Igwara, Professor Paschalis Kitromilides, Professor David Marsland, and Professor George Schöpflin.

I am especially grateful to my three wise men: Professor Anthony D. Smith, for being so much more than a consultant advisor; Professor Irving Louis Horowitz, to whose many talents I owe not only the publication of this volume, but also a major entry on ethnic politics; and Professor David Marsland not only for his contributions but for always being "there" for me. I am also especially indebted to my two handmaidens, my two editorial assistants, Dr. Rachel Monaghan and Dr. Elisabeth Arweck whose grace, intelligence, conscientiousness, hard work and commitment were crucial for the successful completion of this project. I extend my gratitude to Gordana Uzelac for making available to me, and without hesitation, her untiring and ingenious electronic expertise; and to Philippa and Leo Bernard for offering me, as always, inspiration.

Athena S. Leoussi
London
July 2000

# A

## Anti-Semitism

The term "anti-Semitism" ("*Antisemitismus*") was popularized by Wilhelm Marr in 1879 in order to differentiate modern, scientific attitudes towards the Jews from hatred of the Jews derived from old-fashioned religious prejudice. In popular usage, the term has come to mean any hatred or prejudice directed against Jews, irrespective of time or place. The assumption that it has always existed ("Eternal anti-Semitism"), implies that there is something innate in the Jews—be it vice or virtue—which produces a negative response from non-Jews. This is a fundamental proposition of the Zionist analysis of Jewish history which identifies the Jews' decisive shortcoming as lack of a homeland. This homelessness inevitably produced an abnormal relationship between Jews and Gentiles. The uncritical use of the term "anti-Semitism" has often led to a lack of proper differentiation between varieties of hostility towards the Jews.

Scholarly efforts to prove the "eternal" quality of anti-Semitism have cited hostility to the Jews in the classical world, before the emergence of Christianity. Episodes of hostility (the story of Haman in the Book of Esther, anti-Jewish riots in Alexandria in 38 A.D., hostile descriptions of Jews by the Roman historian Tacitus) are in fact typical of the interethnic, intercommunal and religious struggles of the day. It is noteworthy that the Romans gave Jews the privileged status of a *politeuma*, a community governed by its own practices and traditions. Some Roman pagan writers decried the "impiety" of the Jews, but military repression, featuring the destruction of the Second Temple and the expulsion of the Jews from Palestine in the aftermath of the Bar Kokhba Revolt (132-35 A.D.) was the inevitable Roman response to political opposition and revolt. Diaspora Jews developed practices, institutions and myths which allowed them to survive, as a self-aware community, under disparate forms of alien rule.

While the relations of Jews with the followers of the other Abrahamic religions were always problematic, those between Jews and Christians were especially fraught because both lay claim to an identical spiritual inheritance. The sacred writings of the Jews, "the Tanakh" (the Hebrew Bible) serve also as Christian prophetic texts: the "Old Testament" bears witness to and is fulfilled by the "New Testament." As Christianity evolved from a Jewish sect into a separate, universalized religion, the two religions remained locked in a fundamental debate over proof texts. Christians read Jewish texts to show that Jesus Christ was not only the Jewish Messiah (itself a much debated concept) but also the Son of God. Jews rejected both these claims. It was thus necessary for Christians to deny the Jewish interpretation of their own texts, and to lay claim to the status of God-elected or chosen people which the texts clearly attributed to the Jews. Christians became the "New Israel." The Christian scriptures, especially the Gospel of John which equated Jews with the Devil, and the letters of Paul the Apostle to emergent Christian communities, created a climate of hostility between devotees of the two faiths. There was an element of rivalry as well, in the form of Christian fear of Jewish proselytism, especially "Judaizing" among new Christian converts. Modern scholars tend to view skeptically the claim that Jewish instigation lay behind some Roman persecution of the Christians.

This essentially theological debate between pagans, Christians and Jews was transformed by the establishment of Christianity as the state religion of the later Roman Empire. Coercion became the handmaiden of religious polemic. In the ensuing Christian debate over the status of the Jews, two traditions emerged. That associated with the foremost father of the Eastern Church, John Chrysostom (c.347-407), associated the Jews with Satan's anti-Christian work. This link justified their expulsion or total exclusion from interaction with Christians. The tradition which emerged from the writings of the Western theologian, Augustine of Hippo (354-430), proved more influential and accommodating. Augustine offered an exegesis on the Genesis story of Cain and Abel. Just as Cain's treachery verified and exalted Abel's faith, so the skepticism of the Jews and their fall from divine favour, exemplified by the destruction of the Temple and their exile, reinforced the truth of Christianity. Jews, like Cain, were not to be killed, but to wander the world as proof of their rejected status. They could be tolerated, but they were never to have domination over Christians. Augustine also awarded Jews a vital role in Christian apocalyptic thought: the second coming of Christ would be accompanied by the conversion of the Jews and the end of their exile. This tradition inspired the caveat—often honored in the breech—that Jews were not to be forcibly converted.

Some scholars have argued that the period of the Church Fathers played a decisive role in assigning to Jews the mythic role of "Other," a status which forever objectified them in the Christian and post-Christian consciousness. Others have identified this moment in the thirteenth and fourteenth centuries when a number of grotesque and occult charges against the Jews gained wide acceptance. The Jews underwent a process of demonization, whereby they were directly equated with the Devil and his anti-Christian conspiracies. Demonic characteristics were attributed to the Jews—horns and a tail, a particular stench (the *feotor judaicus*), cloven feet, and swine's teeth. Jews were linked to anti-human activity in general—the poisoning of wells, black magic, and sorcery—as well as anti-Christian outrages in particular—ritual murder of Christian children and desecration of the sacramental bread. Gavin Langmuir contends that these motifs were a clear reflection of the insecurities of Christian society which transformed the Jews into a "chimera," a level of fantasy which projected all the insecurities of Christian society onto a powerless and subordinate out-group. The demonization of the Jews was accompanied by efforts to exclude Jews by special clothing or symbols, special places of residence (such as the Italian ghetto), or physical expulsion (England and southern Italy, 1290; France, 1306, 1394; the German lands, 1350; Spain, 1492; Portugal, 1497). The aftermath of forced conversions in the Iberian lands promoted the activities of the Holy Office, better known as the Inquisition, which acquired a sinister reputation for its efforts to identify and punish crypto-Jews. The Protestant Reformation forced a rethinking of the theological position of the Jews but, as the example of Martin Luther reveals, not always to the Jews' advantage. Luther's 1523 pamphlet, "That Jesus Christ Was Born a Jew," expressed sympathy for the Jews as a target of Christian persecution. Towards the end of Luther's life, disappointed in his hopes for the conversion of the Jews and fearing "Judaizing" among Protestants, he wrote crude and vulgar polemics, exemplified by "On the Jews and Their Lies," published in 1543.

The intellectual changes in European thought signalled by the French Enlightenment in the eighteenth century had two implications for Jews. The theory of a rationally apprehended Natural Law worked against the dogmas of revealed religion and Christian intolerance, while the Lockean concept of the *tabula rasa* implied the possibility of universal human improvement, Jews included. The assumptions of so-called Political Economy argued against restrictions on the Jews which conflicted with the economic interests of society. Taken together, these intellectual currents helped give rise to concepts of Jewish "emancipation" or "naturalization." Yet, parallel lines of Enlightenment thought viewed the Jews in negative terms by denying Judaism the status of a "Natural Religion," and seeing the Jews as a backward and obscurantist element. The Jews' traditional economic pursuits were often viewed as a threat to the national well-being. Most thinkers, especially Voltaire, viewed the Jews as corrupt and degraded, and disagreed only as to whether or not Jews were susceptible to improvement. Many thinkers subconsciously recast traditional religious prejudices against the Jews into secular or "scientific" form.

Emergent national states offered Jews varying degrees of acceptance. In return, or as a precondition, liberal statesmen demanded Jewish acculturation or assimilation. The movement of Jews into modern society, either as an identifiable sub-culture or, even more, as an invisible element, provoked a reaction. Some responses, such as the Prussian debate in the 1840s over the role of Jews in a Christian state, bore clear vestiges of religious prejudice. Whatever their underlying origins, however, most hostility toward Jews was presented as "modern" and rational. The European Left, represented by Bruno Bauer and Karl Marx, saw Jews as a remnant of obsolete socioeconomic systems, while others on both Left and Right, depicted them as the symbol of harmful economic change, the "Gold International" or the plutocratic "Kings of the Age."

Advances in the biological sciences were especially significant for views on the Jews. Anthropologists sought to differentiate the world's population into "races," to which concept a hierarchy of value was inevitably assigned. Jews were consistently seen as a distinct group or sub-group, the "Semitic race." The evolutionary theories of Charles Darwin, especially the concept of survival of the fittest within species, were applied to human beings. Social Darwinism had a special appeal for the ideologues of European imperialism, eugenics, and militarism. Racial mixing, warned pessimistic thinkers such as ARTHUR DE GOBINEAU, was a retrograde process, whereby the "higher" races were swamped by the "lower," a category which invariably included the Semitic Jews. This negative influence was not only biological, but cultural as well. Jews were denounced by authors like Richard Wagner as uncreative parasites, capable only of corrupting higher cultures.

Nineteenth-century anti-Semitism was thus a coat of many colors, albeit intimately linked to all the ideas of the "century of -isms." Scholars have detected, as the crucial aspect of anti-Semitism, its propensity to mirror the fears and discontents of the age. While there is disagreement over the objective or psychological sources of these obsessions, there is little doubt that for many thinkers, a subjective conceptualization of "The Jews" came to represent both the negative aspects of modern civilization as well as the archetypal "Other." For example, the Jews were linked to the spirit of revolution, despite the negligible role that they played in 1789, 1830, and 1848. In this way, they also became associated with the Freemasons who had been one of the original targets for those who sought a conspiratorial angle in the events of the French Revolution. Jews served as a symbol of emergent capitalism, and were blamed for its failures (particularly

the famous crash of 1872 in Germany, which followed a period of stock market speculation, the *Gründerzeit*). In France, the Dreyfus Affair (1894-1906) introduced anti-Semitism into the violent debates over the nature and future of the Third Republic.

Many students of nineteenth-century anti-Semitism have seen an objective foundation for its growth. Hannah Arendt famously linked the Court Jews of the early modern period with the modern banking system. Peter Pulzer points to the strength of the Jews in middle class activities in Germany and especially in the press in Austria-Hungary (Pulzer 1988). Albert Linderman has emphasized aspects of Jewish behavior which underlay notorious affairs such as the Dreyfus Affair and the Beilis ritual murder affair in Russia (1911-13).

On the other hand, the ease with which anti-Semitism was able to serve so many ideological masters, suggests deeper, non-objective roots. Jacob Katz, among others, has suggested that much of "modern" anti-Semitism is religious hostility transmuted into secular form (Katz 1980). Claims that Jews were objectified, demised, or made into a chimera in the premodern period, are all attempts to explain the enduring force of anti-Semitism in the nineteenth century and beyond. The ease with which mundane realities of Jewish life—the role of some Jews in the modern economy or in modern political life—were transformed into mythic forms—the international Jewish conspiracy envisioned by the *Protocols of the Elders of Zion*, the "Gold International," and so on—suggests a deep psychological source for modern anti-Semitism.

Anti-Semitism was a strong ideological current in the twentieth century, exemplified by the attempted extermination of the "Jewish race" by the followers of German National Socialism. While widely spread, however, most varieties of anti-Semitism did not lead logically to mass murder. "The Jews" in the guise of "Bolsheviks" were variously blamed for the rise of Communism or, as "international bankers," for the collapse of capitalism by a number of right-wing ideologues in Europe and the United States in the interwar period.

More substantial was anti-Semitism in the states created in the aftermath of the collapse of the Russian, Austro-Hungarian and German Em-

# Anti-Semitism

pires in 1917-8 (Klier 1995). State-building societies such as Poland and Romania were faced with the challenges of integrating national minorities, such as Ukrainians and Belorussians (Poland) and Hungarians (Romania), together with substantial Jewish minorities. Trianon Hungary, on the other hand, no longer required Magyarized Jews as a counterweight to non-Hungarian minorities, as had been the case before 1918. The role of Jews as a commercial element in primarily agrarian societies also created tensions, especially with the onset of the Great Depression. The growth of chauvinism and authoritarianism in Central and Eastern Europe threatened discrimination and mistreatment of Jewish minorities, but gave no hint of the Nazi experiment in genocide.

Anti-Semitism adapted easily to a variety of ideological systems, ranging from the embattled democracy of the French Third Republic (where the *Action Française* employed anti-Semitism), to the military authoritarianism of Poland, and the native fascism of Romania (the Iron Guard) and Hungary (the Arrow Cross). The absence of any anti-Semitism in the archetypal fascism of Italy suggests that anti-Semitism was at least in part a product of local conditions, rather than an inevitable ingredient of the fascist corporate state.

German National Socialism remains the special case. Anti-Semitism was an integral part of its *Weltanschauung* (if not the source of its widespread appeal) primarily because of its importance for Adolf Hitler. There is a substantial historical debate regarding the extent to which the physical removal of the Jews, by exterminatory force if necessary, was a specific long-term objective of Hitler and his movement (Kershaw 1993). Some scholars have seen it as inherent in *Mein Kampf* (1925), while others have argued that the resort to genocide was the outcome of the unique conditions created by the Second World War.

New forms of hostility toward the Jews emerged with the establishment of the State of Israel in 1948. Israel's Arab and Muslim enemies have always argued that their antipathy is directed against the "Zionist entity," and should be considered anti-Zionism, not anti-Semitism. Whatever the truth of this claim, there is no question that elements of Western anti-Semitism (i.e., the *Protocols of the Elders of Zion*) have been as-similated into anti-Zionism. Scholars such as Bernard Lewis argue that this is a late ideological borrowing and an aberration, pointing to the long centuries during which Jews were accommodated by Muslim communities (Lewis 1986).

Divergent forms of anti-Semitism appeared in the second half of the twentieth century. The last years of Stalin in the Soviet Union witnessed the linking of Jews to "Western imperialism," and anti-Soviet activities were attributed to Jewish charitable organizations, such as the American Joint Distribution Committee, which had been active in the USSR. Geopolitical considerations led the USSR to become a strong partisan of "anti-Zionism." These phenomena helped to undermine the status of Soviet Jews, and helped give rise to the Jewish emigration movement in the 1970s, and international campaign in support of "Refuseniks." With the collapse of the Communist system which had maintained a monopoly on anti-Zionism, a few new post-Soviet political movements incorporated anti-Semitic themes into their programs, although with little political success.

In the United States, African-American nationalist movements, exemplified by the Nation of Islam, have toyed with anti-Semitic themes. The extreme fringes of the radical Right in America have integrated anti-Semitic motifs (especially the threat of domination by a world state and Holocaust denial) into its paranoid world view.

From the above survey it is obvious that hostility to Judaism and Jews, whether derived from classical pagan or Christian sources, has been a recurrent theme in the western intellectual tradition. For convenience, the diverse forms of this hostility have been given the popular appellation of "anti-Semitism." Given its diversity, which is the product of differences in time and place, it is imperative that anti-Semitism never be treated as an unitary, internally consistent, phenomenon, but always placed into a broader historical context.

## Bibliography

Almog, Shmuel (ed.). 1988. *Antisemitism through the Ages*. Pergamon: Oxford.

Cohen, Jeremy. 1982. *The Friars and the Jews: The Evolution of Medieval Anti-Judaism*. Ithaca, NY: Cornell University Press.

Cohn, Norman. 1967. *Warrant for Genocide: The Myth of the Jewish World-Conspiracy and the Protocols of the Elders of Zion*. New York: Harper and Row.

Dundes, Alan (ed.). 1991. *The Blood Libel Legend: A Casebook in Antisemitic Folklore*. Madison, WN: University of Wisconsin Press.

Feldman, Louis H. 1993. *Jews and Gentiles in the Ancient World: Attitudes and Interactions from Alexander to Justinian*. Princeton, NJ: Princeton University Press.

Goldhagen, Daniel. 1996. *Hitler's Willing Executioners: Ordinary Germans and the Holocaust*. London: Little, Brown.

Graml, Hermann. 1992. *Antisemitism in the Third Reich*. Oxford: Blackwell.

Hertzberg, Arthur. 1968. *The French Enlightenment and the Jews: The Origins of Modern Antisemitism*. New York: Columbia University Press.

Jäckel, Eberhard. 1972. *Hitler's Weltanschauung*. Middletown, CT: Wesleyan University Press.

Katz, Jacob. 1980. *From Prejudice to Destruction: Antisemitism, 1700-1933*. Cambridge, MA: Harvard University Press.

Kershaw, Ian. 1993. *The Nazi Dictatorship*, third edition. London: Edward Arnold.

Klier, John D. 1995. *Imperial Russia's Jewish Question, 1855-1881*. Cambridge: Cambridge University Press.

Langmuir, Gavin. 1990. *Toward a Definition of Antisemitism*. Berkeley: University of California Press.

Levy, Richard S. 1975. *The Downfall of the Antisemitic Political Parties in Imperial Germany*. New Haven, CT and London: Yale University Press.

Lewis, Bernard. 1986. *Semites and Antisemites: An Inquiry into Conflict and Prejudice*. New York.

Madras, Ronald E. 1994. *The Catholic Church and Antisemitism in Poland, 1933-1939*. Chur, Switzerland.

Massing, Paul W. 1949. *Rehearsal for Destruction: A Study of Political Antisemitism in Imperial Germany*. New York.

Marrus, Michael R. 1986. *The Holocaust in History*. London.

Mosse, George L. 1978. *Toward the Final Solution: A History of European Racism*. London.

Nolte, Ernst. 1969. *Three Faces of Fascism*. New York: Mentor.

Parkes, James. 1934. *The Conflict of the Church and the Synagogue: A Study in the Origins of Antisemitism*. London.

Pauley, Bruce F. 1992. *From Prejudice to Persecution: A History of Austrian Antisemitism*. Chapel Hill: University of North Carolina Press.

Poliakov, Leon. 1974. *The Aryan Myth: A History of Racist and Nationalist Ideas in Europe*. London: Basic Books.

Poliakov, Leon. 1965-1985. *The History of Antisemitism*, 4 vols. London.

Pulzer, Peter. 1988. *The Rise of Political Antisemitism in Germany and Austria*, revised edition. London.

Rose, Paul L. 1990. *Revolutionary Antisemitism in Germany: From Kant to Wagner*. Princeton, NJ: Princeton University Press.

Trachtenberg, J. 1943. *The Devil and the Jews: Medieval Conceptions of the Jew and Its Relation to Modern Antisemitism*. London.

Vago, Bela. 1975. *In the Shadow of the Swastika. The Rise of Fascism and Antisemitism in the Danube Basin, 1936-1939*. Farnborough.

Volovici, Leon. 1991. *Nationalist Ideology and Antisemitism: The Case of the Romanian Intelligentsia in the 1930s*. Oxford: Oxford University Press.

Wilson, Stephen. 1982. *Ideology and Experience: Antisemitism in France at the Time of the Dreyfus Affair*. London: Associated University Press.

Wistrich, Robert S. 1990. *Anti-Zionism and Antisemitism in the Contemporary World*. Basingstoke.

Zimmerman, Moshe. 1986. *Wilhelm Marr: The Patriarch of Antisemitism*. Oxford: Oxford University Press.

John Klier

# Apartheid

The term is an Afrikaans one; its literal meaning is "separateness." It acquired domestic and pejorative international salience following the election victory of the Afrikaner National Party in South Africa in 1948 and the attempt to enforce a comprehensive policy of racial segregation. It is difficult to establish the provenance of the term, although there is a reference to apartheid in the Sauer Commission which reported to the National Party leadership in the mid-1940s, arguing "that the fundamental basis of [the party's] policy...is the maintenance and protection of the white race" (Price 1991: 16). Apartheid proved to be a potent weapon in the National Party's struggle to mobilize electoral support in the immediate postwar period. Indeed, articulation of the policy in the years of opposition in the 1930s and 1940s and its implementation in practice after 1948 contributed massively to the consolidation and development of Afrikaner nationalism. This ideology, based on the principle of racial exclusiveness, stressed the maintenance of white supremacy in the face of rising black numbers—especially in the urban areas—and the threat posed by its developing African counterpart.

Apartheid had deep roots in South Africa's past. The constitution of the Union of South Africa pro-

# Apartheid

mulgated in 1910 was based upon the principle of "white rule and black disenfranchisement." This remained unchanged and was thus the precondition, not the result, of apartheid. The particular contribution of the Nationalists after 1948 was the formalization, consolidation, and extension of the inconsistent and often ad hoc racist laws, customs and practices that they inherited, and the elevation of white domination to an official ideology (Schirire1991: 4). Or as Edgar Brookes, a distinguished South African liberal argued, "1948 is different, not only in degree but even in some measure in mind, from pre-1948 policies of separation....The men of 1948 set out to rationalize the prejudices of their fathers and to present apartheid as a moral principle. The doctrine of national self-preservation took on the overtones of a religious dogma" (Brookes 1968: xxvii-viii).

Thereafter, in terms of this doctrine, the government created an elaborate and highly bureaucratic system of social control to regulate the day to day lives of the African majority and effectively prevent any challenge to the maintenance of white and—more specifically—Afrikaner supremacy.

Thus, in the early years of National Party rule, the government concentrated on a host of measures enforcing separation "in all the spheres of living": in 1956 the franchise was removed from the small number of colored voters whose rights had been entrenched in the 1910 constitution; apartheid was also enforced in urban areas through the Group Areas Act (1950); in the workplace via the job reservation policy (Industrial Conciliation Act, 1956) as well as sexual relations across the color line (The Prohibition of Mixed Marriages Act, 1949; Immorality Amendment Act, 1957). Freedom of movement for blacks was rigorously enforced through the so-called Pass Laws (an inheritance from the past refined after 1948), university education was segregated (Extension of University Education, 1960), while there were severe legal limitations on black trade union activity. The linchpin of this gigantic effort of social engineering was the Population Registration Act (1950) which defined the individual's place in society strictly according to race and which reached Orwellian proportions in its bureaucratic scope and method as the following ministerial statement abundantly clarifies:

A population register is actually a book containing the life-story of every individual whose name is recorded on that register. It contains the most important facts relating to such a person. In some cases the life-story of the individual is very short. In the case of a stillborn baby it contains only one entry and one page. In other cases a long life-history has to be recorded in that book. All those important facts regarding the life of every individual will be combined in this book and recorded under the name of a specific person, who can never change his identity. It is only when the last page in that book of life is written by an entry recording the death of such a person that the book is closed and taken out of the gallery of the living and placed in the gallery of the dead. (Dr T. E. Donges, Minister of the Interior). (Brookes 1968: 21)

The phrase "can never change his identity" summarizes the essence of the apartheid doctrine. It is this crucial factor which distinguished South African policies in the eyes of its critics as a special case of human rights transgression and in large part explains the mounting internal and external pressures against the government over a period of four decades. These so-called "negative" aspects of apartheid were, however, always regarded as preliminary to a grand reconstruction of South African society based on the premise of "separate development" and the provision of *bantustans* (homelands) for the major ethnic groups constituting the African population as a whole. This was the creation of Prime Minister, Dr. Hendrick Verwoerd, an academic/journalist turned politician, and the major theorist of so-called "grand" apartheid.

This policy had intellectual antecedents which can be traced back to the 1920s and 1930s when Afrikaner nationalism was in the political wilderness and its leaders—churchmen, journalists, and academics—were in desperate search of a policy to underpin and give coherence to a burgeoning national identity. Its basic assumption was an explicit denial of the notion of an African nationalism cutting across ethnic boundaries; if the African was to achieve self-determination, ethnicity would have to be the basis for any claim made in the name of this principle. As one spokesman put it, "the aim is an elaborate process of separate nation-building...the development of several sovereign peoples...sovereign and democratically experienced in the full sense of the words" (Erasmus 1961: 24).

The territorial bases of the *bantustans* were to be the reserved areas (some 13 percent of the total area of South Africa) from which the urban workforce—especially on the gold mines—had been traditionally recruited and whose migration back and forth was elaborately controlled. In the mid-1950s, the government promised economic and political advancement for these territories and early in the 1960s the first of these *bantustans* came into being with the establishment in the Transkei of a constitution embodying provisions for a cabinet and parliament to be elected by the indigenous inhabitants, together with their ethnic counterparts living in the "white" urban areas. Ultimately, it was envisaged that as many as eight independent *bantustans* would emerge as the work of consolidating the scattered tribal areas into single coherent units was completed. The new "states" would provide a legitimate outlet for the political energies, not only of the rural population of each "homeland," but also those urbanized Zulus and Xhosas, for example, whose ethnic links ultimately derived—over however many generations of urban existence—from Zululand and the Transkei. Thus, the urban African, regarded as a "temporary sojourner," was denied any prospect of political and economic rights in the so called "white" areas.

The policy's failure to cater to the needs of the urban African was regarded by its critics as a major weakness compounded by the likelihood that the numbers of Africans living in the "white" areas (both urban and rural) would increase significantly over the long term. (Indeed, as long ago as 1954 a conservative projection put the size of the population living in these areas as 40 percent of the total African population or some six million persons by 1984). The government's traditional answer to criticisms of this kind was contained in the concept of "political independence and economic inter-dependence" between South Africa and its *bantustans*—the assumption being that political aspirations could be divorced from economic ones in both geographical and psychological terms.

The *Bantustan* policy might be regarded as "official" theory of social change designed to find a solution to the complex problems of a multiracial society in which the "liberal" ideologies of Western Europe with their emphasis on mass democracy and "one-man-one-vote" were regarded as a dangerous irrelevance. And this was precisely the view taken by the South African government in defending its domestic posture against the hostility of the outside world.

Throughout the 1950s and 1960s the National Party government relentlessly implemented the policy of grand apartheid and its supporting infrastructure of repressive legislation. The result was that black resistance to apartheid weakened as the African National Congress (ANC) and other organizations were—following the Sharpeville shootings of March 1960—banned, jailed, driven underground or into exile. The economy prospered in the 1960s with an annual growth rate of some 6 percent; the country remained politically stable and although external criticism at the U.N., in the Commonwealth and elsewhere mounted, Western governments and the international business community placed their faith in the long term liberalizing impact of economic development on apartheid structures.

The turning point came with the Soweto rebellion in 1976. The spectacle of black schoolchildren being killed by white policemen provoked extensive media coverage and although order was quickly restored, both the National Party government and its Western counterparts realized that apartheid in its pristine form would have to adapt or crumble under the weight of the bureaucratic and economic costs involved. Within the ruling elite a fierce debate began between so-called *verligtes* (the enlightened) who favored piecemeal reform and the gradual elimination of apartheid barriers especially in the economic arena, and *verkramptes* (hard liners) who were determined to maintain the legacy of Hendrick Verwoerd. Eventually, the *verkramptes* left the National Party in 1980 to form the Conservative Party, led by Andries Treurnicht, a former cabinet minister.

In the West there was a dawning recognition that change in South Africa could not be left to the impersonal forces of the marketplace; that a more proactive strategy was required. The result was a policy of "constructive engagement" designed to push South Africa's reluctant leaders into a reformist posture. At the same time, apartheid's critics abroad were pressing for full scale economic sanctions as a means of compelling the South Afri-

# Apartheid

can government to abandon apartheid in favor of root and branch reform. The ANC, from its bases in exile, was also mounting a sporadic military campaign within the country. In the 1980s this led to counterattacks by the South African military (by this time a powerful influence on government policy) on bases in neighboring states and the result was further condemnation by external critics.

The combination of these pressures forced a degree of sporadic change on the apartheid regime in the economic and social arenas. For example, the policy of job reservation began to erode as the demand for skilled labor to sustain an industrial economy effectively removed traditional racial barriers to advancement. This coincided with legislation to legalize the position of black trade unions and the right to collective bargaining. In the political arena, Prime Minister P. W. Botha established a tri-cameral parliamentary system in 1983, providing for separate representation for white, colored, and Asian communities. But the exclusion of the black majority from the new political dispensation provoked bitter opposition and the result was the formation of the United Democratic Front, a coalition of black organizations with close links to the exiled ANC. This opposition culminated in outbreaks of violent protest in September 1984 in the Witwatersrand area; a state of emergency was declared in July 1985 and the government's repressive strategy evoked a powerful external response in the form of the "private" sanctions of overseas banks and companies and the "public" sanctions of a wide range of governments and international organizations.

By 1989 the government was in serious difficulties. Unable to meet its foreign debt obligations, denied vitally important foreign direct investment, and faced with a rising tide of black militancy, the outlook seemed bleak. These constraints on state power together with a series of fortuitous events finally eroded government resistance to ending apartheid: the removal from office through illness of P. W. Botha; the forced withdrawal from Namibia; the ending of the Cold War and the elimination of the so-called "total onslaughts" of the Soviet Union against South Africa gave F. W. de Klerk, Botha's successor, room for political manoeuvre. The consequence was the announcement on 2 February 1990 of the release of Nelson Mandela and his colleagues from prison and the unbanning of the ANC and a number of other black organizations. Thereafter, negotiations began to create an apartheid-free constitution, culminating in South Africa's first fully democratic election in April 1994 and the establishment of a Government of National Unity.

To sum up: apartheid was designed to maintain white supremacy in South Africa by enforcing segregation through legislative means in "all the spheres of living." It was this emphasis on statutory discrimination which defined South Africa as unique in the international society of states. Moreover, apartheid was a virulent manifestation of an Afrikaner nationalism determined to safeguard its identity, and in its application over decades, it profoundly damaged the lives and aspirations of millions of black South Africans. Grand apartheid signally failed to meet the economic and political needs of the black majority while the barrage of repressive legislation that the policy engendered could not—in the last analysis—prevent the emergence of an African nationalism bent on removing the injustices of the past and the present.

True, the government in the late 1970s and 1980s attempted a more pragmatic version of the apartheid doctrine, but the reforms it spawned proved too little and too late to mollify both domestic and external hostility. De Tocqueville's famous dictum is pertinent in this context: "the worst moment for a bad government is when it embarks on a policy of reform." Yet, ultimately, South Africa was fortunate in producing two leaders—Nelson Mandela and F. W. de Klerk—who both, albeit for different reasons, realized that radical change was required, if disaster was to be averted. How far the current post-apartheid dispensation can heal the wounds of the past and create in the process a sense of national identity inclusive and liberal in ethos is a critical question both for practitioners and academic theorists alike.

## Bibliography

Brookes, E.H. (ed.) 1968. *Apartheid: A Documentary Study of Modern South Africa.* London: Routledge and Kegan Paul.

Erasmus, B. P. 1961. "The policy of apartheid," *African Affairs* 60, 238 (January).

Price, R. 1991. *The Apartheid State in Crisis: Political Transformation in South Africa 1975-1990*. New York and Oxford: Oxford University Press.

Schirire, R. 1991. *Adapt or Die: The End of White Politics in South Africa*. New York: Ford Foundation.

Spence, J. E. 1975. *The South African Republic*. World Survey No. 77. London: The Atlantic Education Trust.

J. E. Spence

# Art and Nationalism

Since their earliest formulations in the late eighteenth century, nations and nationalisms have always held a special attraction for writers, scholars, and artists, and nationalists in turn have always looked to artists and writers to celebrate the nation. In this connection, the role of the visual artist and musician has received much less attention than that of their counterparts. However, as Herder made clear, music, art, and the dance were crucial parts of the cultural heritage of "the people," and artists and musicians, from the *fêtes* of the French Revolution to the contemporary epoch, have played a vital part in the portrayal and representation of the nation.

The origins of this attraction may be traced to the Earl of Shaftesbury's cultivation of the artistic "genius of the nation"; and following him, to Montesquieu's and Rousseau's emphasis upon the virtues of national spirit (*esprit national*) and natural simplicity. The musical counterparts of Rousseau's "Spartan" virtues can be found in Gluck's reforms of opera drama, in the naturalism and solemnity of Mozart's *Magic Flute* (1791), and in Beethoven's heroic symphonic dramas. This same heroic "neo-classical" drama can also be found in French and British history painting and sculpture from the 1760s. Inspired by Johann Winckelmann's idealization of classical Greek sculpture which he linked to the liberties of ancient Greek society, and the discoveries at Pompeii and Herculaneum, painters like Anton Raphael Mengs, Joseph Vien, James Barry, and Benjamin West, and sculptors like Thomas Banks, John Flaxman, Antonio Canova, and Bertel Thorvaldsen sought to portray in a bold, austere style the *exempla virtutis* of ancient and medieval heroes and heroines for the emulation of posterity. Their didactic art was increasingly framed by a concern with archaeological verisimilitude, which found its perfect expression in the series of spare classical moral dramas on Greek and Roman heroes like Belisarius, Hector, Socrates, and Brutus, the first Roman consul, which Jacques-Louis David (1748–1825) painted in the 1780s. Each of these very public images was located in carefully reconstructed antique settings and was designed to depict an inspiring heroic virtue. The most celebrated of these *exempla* was *The Oath of the Horatii* (1784), which shows the (invented) moment when the father of the Horatii brothers makes them swear on his uplifted sword to fight or die for the fatherland, while on the right side of the painting their women faint in grief and fear. David has not sought to minimize the tragic costs of patriotism, yet it is clear he approves the brothers' resolve to fight the Curiatii, showing their interlocked arms united by a single electric impulse and stretched to the limit in a defiant gesture of war.

A more romantic vein of early nationalistic art can be found in Henry Fuseli's *Oath of the Rutli* (1781). This too shows a moment of defiant resolve when the representatives of the three cantons, Uri, Schwyz, and Unterwalden, swore an Everlasting Alliance in 1291 to defend their valleys against the Habsburg tyranny. Here the huge, elongated, mannerist figures which Fuseli took from Michelangelo, stand alone on a bare heath, signaling the "pre-romantic" *Sturm und Drang* current that was to usher in the medievalist revival and the "picturesque" movement. In this kind of art, influenced by English and German literary and philosophical Romanticism, historical setting, atmosphere and exotic drama took the place of the earlier stoic virtues of neo-classical romanticism, a current exemplified in Eugene Delacroix' contemporary dramas, *The Massacre at Chios* (1824) and *Liberty Leading the People* (1831), the latter showing Marianne in her Phrygian bonnet holding aloft the *tricolore* and leading the insurgents across the barricades in the July 1830 Revolution in Paris. The apotheosis of romantic medievalism can be found in the art of the Pre-Raphaelites in England and of Delaroche, Flandrin, and Ingres in France. In Jean-Louis-Dominique Ingres' *Joan of Arc at the Coronation of Charles VII* (1854), for example, the rich medievalist religious nationalism of mid-century France is embodied in the militant figure of a vic-

## Art and Nationalism

torious Joan, simple, pious, and heroic, as she stands before the altar in Rheims Cathedral with its gold vessels, holding the two-pointed *oriflamme*, and looking to heaven for national deliverance.

A similar romantic literary medievalism swept the musical world, from Berlioz' *Romeo and Juliet* and Liszt's *Mazeppa* to Wagner's *Die Meistersinger von Nurnburg*, Tchaikovsky's *Swan Lake* and Musorgsky's *Boris Godunov*. In each of these musical dramas, as in Romantic art, the people as a whole—their trials and triumphs, fears and joys— were vividly evoked, with a mass impact which was wider and deeper than most literary works, since they clothed the word in the immediacy and tangibility of sound and paint. This serves to correct Benedict Anderson's exclusive emphasis upon the printed word, and reveals the hidden quasi-religious dimensions of nationalism beneath its secular formulations. Not only were the "people" held up as exemplars of truth and noble simplicity in the art of Frederic Chopin, Antonin Dvorak, and Bela Bartok, and of Gustave Courbet, Ford Madox Brown, and Vincent van Gogh, but composers and painters increasingly sought out the deepest recesses of the "collective memory" in the myths and symbols of a hidden and distant past. In *Finlandia*, *The Swan of Tuonela,* and *Tapiola*, as in his symphonies, Jean Sibelius evoked the dark, mysterious forces of nature and the equally brooding shadows of the *Kalevala*, the Finnish national epic; Ralph Vaughan Williams returned to a specifically English Tudor polyphony, Ernest Bloch to a romantic Jewish and biblical heritage, Bedrich Smetana to the legends and folk dances of Bohemia and Moravia, while Manuel de Falla evoked the lush harmonies and popular dramas of his native Spain.

Musical nationalism was paralleled by artistic nationalism in both style and motif. There was the evocation of specifically English, German, and Russian ethno-scapes in the art of John Constable, Caspar David Friedrich, and Isaac Levitan, the triumph of the common people in the heroic dramas of Diego Rivera, Ilya Repin, and Stanley Spencer, the heroic deaths of fallen patriot-heroes like Wolfe and Marat in the art of Benjamin West and Jacques-Louis David, and the evocation of popular legends by Edward Burne-Jones in En-

gland, Ferdinand Hodler in Switzerland and Akseli Gallen-Kallela in Finland. In each of these representations, the idea of the nation and its glorious history and destiny formed the explicit or implicit basis for a deep communal attachment and pride. Until the mass slaughter of two World Wars extinguished the elation of heroic nationalist struggle, statues and monuments were erected throughout Europe and in the colonies to commemorate the heroic acts of soldiers in the many national wars fought to defend or aggrandize the father- or motherland; and allegorical female personifications of the nation like Marianne, Germania, and Britannia appeared in city squares and on coins in most countries. These were complemented by countless mausolea, temples, and assembly buildings, from the Capitol in Washington and the converted Pantheon in Paris—"aux grands hommes reconnaissante"—to the British and Hungarian Parliaments, designed in the neoclassical or Gothic styles deemed to convey the dignity of the reborn or newborn nation, and to impress the populace with the power and grandeur of their nations.

This suggests that we are dealing with much more than the simple portrayal and imagination of the nation. The nation of these icons and images is a deeply felt and willed community, in which the members enact their roles, as in a religious ritual. In the art, architecture and music of the nation, despite and perhaps because of the ethnic and regional variety among its citizens, lives the image of a sacred communion which continues to evoke powerful attachments to a homeland and to bind the otherwise fragmented and divided members of the community to a shared sense of collective history and destiny.

### Bibliography

Anderson, Benedict. 1991. *Imagined Communities: Reflections on the Origin and Spread of Nationalism*. London: Verso.

Rosenblum, Robert. 1967. *Transformations in Late Eighteenth Century Art*. Princeton, NJ: Princeton University Press.

Smith, Anthony D. 1993. "Art and national identity in Europe," in J. C. H. Blom *et al.* (eds.), *De onmacht van het grote: cultuur in Europa*. Amsterdam: Amsterdam University Press.

Vaughan, William. 1978. *Romantic Art*. London: Thames and Hudson.
Whittall, Arnold. 1987. *Romantic Music*. London: Thames and Hudson: chs. 7–9.

Anthony D. Smith

# Aryanism

As the most important brand of European racist thinking in the nineteenth and early-twentieth centuries, Aryanism expressed not simply the alleged superiority of the white peoples in general but, even more sharply, the supposed virtues of their finest branch in particular. These so-called "Aryans" were more truly the invention of philology than the product of biology. In the 1780s Sir William Jones, the celebrated English orientalist, had demonstrated that Sanskrit was related to the Persian, Greek, Latin, Celtic, and Germanic languages, and that they were all derived from a now unknown mother-tongue. Scholars were soon regularly labeling this in a way which reflected the fact that, long ago, the Sanskrit-speaking invaders of India and the Persian inhabitants of Iran had both referred to themselves as "Aryas."

As this term also carried connotations of "nobility," an advance from assertions of linguistic kinship to far bolder claims about shared possession of some superior racial essence was all the more easily effected during the first half of the nineteenth century. The process was further assisted by a romanticism which gloried in the exotic and encouraged the idea that the greatest civilizational achievements of Europe could be attributed to the stimulus of ancient Aryan tribal movements. The temporal and spatial patterning of these migrations—whether originating beyond the continent, or even possibly within it—became an issue of increasingly hot dispute during an epoch when various modern European populations were beginning to assert their particular national consciousness, and often their distinctive blood and soil. Historians seemed increasingly bent on discovering in each case a vigorous national past from which could be projected an even greater future. Scholars searching for Aryan pedigree also availed themselves of such newer disciplines as ethnology and anthropology. Even so, the greater the number of those who attempted to dissipate the mists shrouding the early history of this supposed race, the thicker did the fog become. By 1900 many different regions had been credited with the honor of having cradled the first Aryans. Although parts of Central Asia (especially the Hindu Kush) remained the most favored choice, arguments in support of direct European origins had also surfaced with respect to a series of locations falling virtually anywhere between the Black Sea and the Baltic.

The principal manifestations of "the Aryan myth" turned out to be those embodying forms of racist determinism which treated the Teutonic, Anglo-Saxon, or Nordic peoples as some kind of biological elite, superior not only to the "colored" stocks but even to the rest of the white or "Caucasian" breed. Much of the tone was set in the 1850s by the writings of GOBINEAU, and then consolidated in a less pessimistic vein by Houston Stewart Chamberlain at the end of the century. The latter's particularly emphatic polarization between the culture-creating talents of the Teuton and the culture-destroying forces of the Jew was something that, by the 1930s, Nazism would be exploiting to the utmost. As Hitler himself declared, "All the human culture, all the results of art, science, and technology that we see before us today, are almost exclusively the creative product of the Aryan." Such was the essence of the positive racist creed which he would use to justify Germany's expansion towards "living space" and which, in its negative aspect, he would no less powerfully employ to inspire the Holocaust. However, even if the genocidal assault upon the Jews proved to be the very worst consequence of Aryanism, this same belief-system was also fundamental to the still wider project of racial hierarchization which in the early 1940s the Hitlerian "New Order" and the Himmlerian "SS State" sought to impose upon the Slavs, and in varying degrees upon the rest of Europe's non-Germanic peoples.

## Bibliography

Poliakov, Léon. 1971. *The Aryan Myth: A History of Racist and Nationalist Ideas in Europe*. London: Sussex University Press and Heinemann Educational Books.

Michael Biddiss

**11**

# Assimilation

The term "assimilation" describes a process whereby members of an ethnic group take on the cultural and structural characteristics of another ethnic or national community. In the last instance, this results in the group exchanging its previous identity (in the eyes of self and other) for the new one. Hence assimilation is a broad term, covering many varieties of cultural change, and is thus applicable to individuals who "convert" to the cultures and identities of ethnic groups, civic nations and universalist cosmopolitanisms. On the other hand, assimilation is not the correct term for describing the kind of two-way cultural fusion characteristic of the melting-pot phenomenon.

The assimilationist perspective of the Chicago School tradition, which grew from liberal-progressive roots, informed ethnic relations theory in the United States from the 1920s until the 1960s (Park 1950; Laczko 1995: 32). However, prior to Milton Gordon's formulation of 1964, the term was rather loosely used by both professionals and the American lay public and covered a wide variety of processes, from acculturation to "melting-pot" fusion. In response to this terminological confusion, Gordon put forth a systematic seven-variable model of the assimilation process as it applied to the United States: cultural assimilation, the first stage, was followed by structural, marital, identificational, attitude receptional, behavior receptional and civic assimilation (Gordon 1964: 71).

The assimilation process is, to a great degree, universal, unlike the *melting pot*, examples of which are much more limited. For example, FREDERICK BARTH'S concept of the permeability of ethnic boundaries is implicitly grounded on the idea that migrants come to be assimilated into adjacent groups (Barth 1969). In the classical world, for instance, Romans assimilated members of many groups, especially the Gauls, into their ranks while Greece assimilated a great many Slavic migrants and invaders in the early medieval period (Deutsch 1966: 120; Smith 1986: 96). The Jews, Magyars, Zulus, and English are other examples of ethnies that have participated strongly in this process.

The direction of assimilation is also variable. For instance, Czechs tended to become Germans in nineteenth-century Bohemia, but the reverse occurred in the twentieth century (Deutsch 1966: 133). Karl Deutsch theorizes that the direction of assimilation is governed by six factors, chief among which is prestige. Other factors include similarity of communication habits, frequency of contacts, material rewards and penalties, the similarity of values and desires between groups, and the centrifugal/centripetal balance of symbols and social barriers (Deutsch 1966: 156–62).

In North America, the assimilation process dates to at least the mid-eighteenth century, when Benjamin Franklin and William Smith, alarmed at the growth and concentration of the German-speaking population of Pennsylvania, founded the Society for Propagating Christian Knowledge among Germans. The intent of the society, was, in their words, to "anglicize" or "anglify" the Germans (Kerman 1983: 8). The Americanization movement, which gained strength after the First World War, represented a continuation of these assimilationist ideals. However, assimilation, normatively associated with dominant-group conformity and theoretically linked with functionalism, experienced an ideological setback in the 1960s (Glazer and Moynihan 1963; Novak 1972; Birch 1989: 46). Notwithstanding these developments, the rapid rise in inter-ethnic marriage and the flattening of ethnically based income disparities (between most European and some Asian groups) in the U.S. since that period has led to a revival of assimilationist ideology in that country (Salins 1997; Fukuyama 1995: 320; Schlesinger 1991; Sollors 1986; Hollinger 1995). Assimilation theory has also returned to favour in American academic circles (Lieberson and Waters 1988; Battistella 1989; Alba 1990).

As in the United States, conflicts between the aims of multiculturalism and assimilationism (associated with monoculturalism) have erupted in western Europe (particularly France), Australia and Canada. The latter, for instance, has experienced patterns of cultural, structural and marital assimilation almost identical to those in the United States (Halli, Trovato and Driedger 1990). This in turn has led to criticism of Canada's official multiculturalism policy (Meghji 1991; Bissoondath 1994).

In summary, the debate between assimilation and ethnic persistence is as old as ethnicity itself.

Theoretically speaking, functionalists and classical liberals tend to favour an assimilationist model while conflict theorists and communitarians cleave to a more pluralist approach.

## Bibliography

Alba, Richard D. 1990. *Ethnic Identity: The Transformation of White America*. New Haven, CT and London: Yale University Press.

Barth, Fredrik (ed.) 1969. *Ethnic Groups and Boundaries: The Social Organization of Culture Difference*. London: Allen and Unwin.

Battistella, Graziano (ed.) 1989. *Italian Americans in the '80s: A Sociodemographic Profile*. New York: Center for Migration Studies.

Birch, Anthony H. 1989. *Nationalism and National Integration*. London: Unwin Hyman.

Bissoondath, Neil. 1994. *Selling Illusions: The Cult of Multiculturalism in Canada*. London: Penguin Books.

Deutsch, Karl. 1966 (1953). *Nationalism and Social Communication: An Inquiry into the Foundations of Nationality*. 2nd ed. Cambridge, MA: MIT Press.

Fukuyama, Francis. 1995. *Trust: The Social Virtues and the Creation of Prosperity*. London: Penguin.

Glazer, Nathan and Daniel Patrick Moynihan. 1963. *Beyond the Melting Pot*. Cambridge, MA: MIT Press and Harvard University Press.

Gleason, Philip. 1992. *Speaking of Diversity: Language and Ethnicity in Twentieth-Century America*. Baltimore, MD and London: Johns Hopkins University Press.

Gordon, Milton. 1964. *Assimilation in American Life. The Role of Race, Religion and National Origins*. Oxford: Oxford University Press.

Halli, Shiva S., Frank Trovato and Leo Driedger (eds.) 1990. *Ethnic Demography: Canadian Immigrant, Racial and Cultural Variations*. Ottawa: Carleton University Press.

Herberg, Will. 1955. *Protestant, Catholic, Jew: An Essay in American Religious Sociology*. Garden City, NY: Country Life Press.

Hollinger, David A. 1995. *Postethnic America: Beyond Multiculturalism*. New York: Harper Collins.

Kerman, Lucy Eve. 1983. *Americanization: The History of an Idea, 1700-1860*. Unpublished doctoral dissertation, U. C. Berkeley.

Laczko, Leslie S. 1995. *Pluralism and Inequality in Quebec*. Toronto: University of Toronto Press.

Lieberson, Stanley and Mary C. Waters. 1988. *From Many Strands: Ethnic and Racial Groups in Contemporary America*. New York: Russell Sage Foundation.

Lipset, Seymour Martin. 1990. *Continental Divide: The Values and Institutions of the United States and Canada*. New York and London: Routledge, Chapman and Hall.

Meghji, Al. 1991. "Multiculturalism in the New Canada," in J. L. Granatstein and Kenneth McNaught (eds.), *"English Canada" Speaks Out*. Toronto: Doubleday.

Novak, Michael. 1972. *The Rise of the Unmeltable Ethnics: Politics and Culture in the Seventies*. New York: Macmillan.

Park, Robert E. 1950. *Race and Culture*. New York: Free Press of Glencoe.

Salins, Peter D. 1997. *Assimilation, American Style*. New York, NY: Basic Books.

Schlesinger, Arthur M. 1991. *The Disuniting of America*. New York: W. W. Norton.

Smith, Anthony D. 1986. *The Ethnic Origins of Nations*. Oxford: Blackwell.

Sollors, Werner. 1986. *Beyond Ethnicity: Consent and Descent in American Culture*. New York: Oxford University Press.

Eric Kaufmann

# Authenticity

One of the key motifs of nationalist ideologies, the idea of authenticity can be traced to the influence of JOHANN GOTTFRIED HERDER (1744–1803). His "cultural populism" proposed, *inter alia*, that to be truly free, human beings must listen only to their own voice and obey only their inner dictates. Only in their own thoughts and experiences could true freedom be found, because we are only ourselves when we experience, act and think for ourselves. However, no person thinks and acts alone; the individual's experiences and thoughts are always social, they always form part of a wider network of group experiences. It is only in this "authentic" or genuine experience and thought that we can realize our true potential and freedom.

Combining these assumptions with Rousseau's call for a return to the simple, natural, and hence genuine life, untainted by urban luxury and corruption, German Romantics like Schlegel, Schiller,

# Authenticity

and Fichte elaborated an ethic of autonomy based upon Kant's ideal of the good will and on the need to recover authentic individual and collective experience through unhampered self-expression. Fichte, in particular, applied these assumptions to the cultural and linguistic units of population which, for Herder, formed the basic building-blocks of human experience. Only in and through these cultural nations could human beings, he claimed, recover their authentic soul and destiny; and only by striving for authentic experience and educating the young in the authentic vernacular culture of the nation could self-determination of the individual and the group be realized. The authentic "will of the people" and its "self-determination" became the touchstone for any genuine political action and any viable polity.

Under the influence of the German Romantics, the cult of authentic national experience and popular will spread first to Eastern Europe, then to Asia and Africa, and finally to all corners of the globe. Often combined with the call to return to nature and the simple life, the exaltation of authentic experience and the people's will has led to many movements of national purification and vernacular mobilization in the name of the uncorrupted "folk." Often allied to calls for religious purification and restoration, the cult of authenticity has been particularly prominent in the Islamic world and the Indian subcontinent, encouraging the mobilization of the masses and inspiring in them a righteous zeal against corruption and exploitation. Tilak's use of the "authentic" Hindu past, such as the ancient cults of Shivaji and Kali, and his patriotic reinterpretation of the Bhagavad-Gita are a case in point. So are the calls of the Russian Slavophiles for a return to the pure mores and authentic Orthodox faith of the pre-Petrine Russian people, sadly corrupted in modern times by the inroads of Western cosmopolitan "civilization." This drive to purify society and rediscover indigenous roots and vernacular "culture," in opposition to a corroding cosmopolitan "civilization," can easily spill over into a popular crusade against everything alien, and breed a sense of moral superiority that excludes minorities and foreigners by equating them with everything that is inauthentic and corrupt. In ethnic nationalisms, in particular, the invocation of the will of the people and the return to an authentic ethnic past and its "golden ages," become yardsticks for discriminating between the genuine national inner experience and the false cosmopolitan world outside, and between the true patriot and kinsman and the corrupt and sinister outsider. When such notions are allied to the quest for pure racial types, and a cult of violence, they can furnish the rationale for outbreaks of xenophobic violence and for the excesses of integral nationalism and fascism, such as we witnessed in Central and Eastern Europe in the interwar period, and to a smaller extent even today.

In more muted form, the ideal of authenticity continues to play an important part wherever the issue of national identity is contested. This is particularly true in plural nations where ideologies of multiculturalism are prevalent. The celebration of ethnic cultures in a liberal democratic national state requires an idea of the beliefs and practices that constitute genuine expressions of minority (and majority) cultures. This has become particularly important where identities appear to be more fluid, malleable and optional. Indeed, in a postmodern era of greater migration and intermarriage, the possibility of transcending authenticity in a cultural pastiche of hybrid identities has become attractive to many people, and this sometimes provokes a backlash on the part of the dominant ethnic majority intent on preserving the received traditions and narratives of their "authentic" and unmixed national identity.

## Bibliography

Thaden, E. C. 1964. *Conservative Nationalism in Nineteenth Century Russia*. Seattle: University of Washington Press.

McCulley, B. T. 1966. *English Education and the Origins of Indian Nationalism*. Gloucester, MA: Smith.

Barnard, F. 1965. *Herder's Social and Political Thought: From Enlightenment to Nationalism*. Oxford: Clarendon Press.

Berlin, Isaiah. 1976. *Vico and Herder*. London: The Hogarth Press.

Smith, Anthony D. 1994. "Ethnic nationalism and the plight of minorities," *Journal of Refugee Studies* 7, 2–3: 186–98.

Anthony D. Smith

# B

## Balkanization

Balkanization is a semi-colloquial, semi-technical term referring to the division of a larger state into smaller, mutually hostile states. The process which it describes and explicates has an important bearing on both the collapse and the creation of nation-states. Nationalist movements and feelings of pride in national identity play a large part in the process of balkanization.

It takes its origin from the area of southeastern Europe lying south of the Danube and Sava rivers. Ruled by the Byzantine emperors as part of the eastern domain of Christendom, it was invaded and settled from the third to the seventh century by waves of barbarian Slavs. With the fall of Constantinople to Islam in 1453, it was ruled for centuries by the Ottoman Turks until wars of independence began in the early nineteenth century. Independent states were established as a result in Greece (1830), Serbia (1878), Rumania (1878), and Bulgaria (1908).

With the Balkan Wars of 1912–13, involving Turkey and all the other states of the Balkan region, the Turkish Empire finally collapsed, and the region fell into the violent internecine conflict which characterizes "Balkanization" (Todorova 1997).

Politicians, political analysts, and especially journalists often warn about the dangers of balkanization in geographical and cultural contexts far removed from south-eastern Europe. However, the concept of balkanization relied on in these warnings is often a mere caricature, the process is typically over-generalized, and such predictions have usually been falsified (Goldsworthy 1998). There are, nonetheless, historical instances which both exemplify and are analytically illuminated by the concept.

Thus the decay of the Roman Empire produced a "balkanization" of Europe whose dynamic lasted through the chaos of the Dark Ages, the wars of the Middle Ages and the Early Modern period

conflicts between France, Spain, and England, to the two rounds of the twentieth century's European civil war in 1914–18 and 1939–45. The liberation of Latin America from Spanish rule provides perhaps a modest example. The splitting of India, occasioned by British withdrawal, into three independent states might be regarded as a species of slow-burning balkanization. Pakistan and India have been in a state of continuing conflict ever since, and now threaten each other with nuclear weapons.

In an arena where balkanization might have been expected, the collapse of the Soviet Empire after 1989 has been remarkably peaceful for the most part on its western flank, where Poland, Ukraine, Hungary, Estonia, and other states have established effective independence and mutual cooperation with apparent success (Pipes 1994). On the Soviet Union's southern borders, however, especially in Georgia, Armenia, and Azerbaijan, in eastern regions such as Tajikistan, and within Russia's own borders in Chechnya and in other ethnic enclaves, a process of balkanization is ongoing with fluctuating ferocity.

The former communist state of Yugoslavia—much of it geographically Balkan—has been in a state of radical balkanization, involving genocidal slaughter, large-scale ethnic cleansing, and mass migration ever since the late nineteen eighties (Malcolm 1994). Continuance of this process into Albania, Macedonia and perhaps beyond is at the time of writing highly probable. Once started, balkanization is hard to stop.

The major remaining arenas for balkanization are the communist empire of China and Africa. As the Chinese economy is liberalized, old warlord regions are beginning to reassert themselves and religious conflict threatens in Tibet and in Sinkiang. The possibility of political rupture and violent conflict cannot be excluded.

Fissiparous processes in African states are widespread and often violent. They have thus far, how-

## Barth, Frederick [Fredrik] (1928- )

ever, been largely contained without resort to open warfare, by means of *coups d'état* and a cynically Paretian circulation of elites. The major exceptions are in Nigeria, where Ibo insurrection was savagely suppressed precisely to prevent general balkanization of the country, and in the former Belgian possessions of the Congo, Rwanda, and Burundi, where splitting and conflict seem inevitable.

All states, whether imperial, national, or tribal, are inevitably subject to a recurring natural process of growth, centralization, rebellion, and division (Eisenstadt 1965; Mayhew 1982). Balkanization is an acceleration of part of this process. It appears to be explicable in terms of a combination of unjust and incompetent control by the center, internal or external threat to the power of the center, availability of alternative national or religious identities in the subordinate peripheries, and support by outside powers for the independence of newly balkanized entities (Horowitz 1985).

The threat of balkanization can be countered successfully in some circumstances by the devolution of central state power to autonomous regions. Contemporary Spain provides an important test-case, with Basque and Catalan claims for independence—earlier suppressed by force of arms by Franco—now addressed by constitutional reforms which have granted the regions a substantial degree of autonomy.

Where it works, autonomy (or home-rule in British terms) preserves the cultural distinctiveness of the regions, allows for a significant level of local political independence, secures the integrity of the larger state, and inhibits conflict. It looks as if this—essentially federal and typically American—model of political structure is being exported worldwide, to Europe and beyond, as a means of preserving the central state against nationalist challenges.

### Bibliography

Eisenstadt, S. N. 1965. *Modernization: Protest and Change.* Englewood Cliffs, NJ: Prentice Hall.

Goldsworthy, V. 1998. *Inventing Ruritania: The Imperialism of the Imagination.* New Haven, CT: Yale University Press.

Horowitz, D. 1985. *Ethnic Groups in Conflict.* Berkeley: University of California Press.

Malcolm, N. 1994. *Bosnia: A Short History.* Basingstoke: Macmillan.

Mayhew, L. H. (ed.) 1982. *Talcott Parsons on Institutions and Social Evolution.* Chicago: University of Chicago Press.

Pipes, R. 1994. *Communism: The Vanished Specter.* Stockholm: Scandinavian University Press.

Todorova, M. 1997. *Imagining the Balkans.* New York: Oxford University Press.

David Marsland

## Barth, Frederick [Fredrik] (1928- )

Educated at the University of Chicago, the London School of Economics (LSE), and the University of Cambridge, Frederick Barth was professor of social anthropology at the universities of Bergen (1961-73) and Oslo (1973-85). He remains active as a research fellow at Oslo. Few anthropologists can rival his extensive fieldwork record in Norway, Iraq, Pakistan, Iran, Sudan, New Guinea, Oman, Bali, and Bhutan. His range of substantive interests is equally wide, covering politics and leadership, economics and entrepreneurship, ritual and religion, cosmology, and ecology.

Barth's major theoretical influences appear to have been Chicago sociology and symbolic interactionism (particularly Goffman), the British LSE tradition of social anthropology (Malinowski, Leach, and Firth), and cybernetics and communications theory. However, Barth's own theoretical writings are important and original in their own right. His project has consistently been to explore patterns of social form as a cumulative result of the choices and decisions made by individuals interacting with each other, given the constraints and opportunities that they face (Barth 1959, 1966, 1981). He wants to understand how collective social forms can exist, given that the social world is—in the first place—a world of individuals.

Barth begins with individuals and their behavior; but he focuses on the processual generation of collective social forms—such as identities—as the unintended consequence of interaction. If a body of work of great substantive variety can be characterised by one theoretical keyword, "generative" would be appropriate: Barth does not suggest that "society" is merely the aggregate of individuals and their relationships. Another consistent theme of his work is the need to avoid reifying the complex fluidities of social life. He cautions us against the simplicity of identifying any locality in which we are interested as a "society" or a "culture." Along with the interactional production of social pattern and form, the lack of closure of social life is another consistent theme of his work. These theoretical themes can be seen at play in his seminal writings on ethnicity.

In 1969 Barth edited *Ethnic Groups and Boundaries*, a symposium on ethnic identity that was sub-titled "the social organisation of culture difference," indicating that ethnicity and cultural difference are connected, and that the social and the cultural are not separate domains. Barth's model of ethnic identity broke new ground for social anthropology, going beyond existing conceptualisations in depth and detail, and locating ethnicity within the broader theoretical framework he had already begun to develop in other contexts. He began his much-cited "Introduction" to this collection by observing that the persistence of differences between ethnic groups—indeed the groups themselves—had been taken for granted. Anthropology had not problematized how ethnic groups maintained their distinctiveness or were reproduced. He suggested that ethnic boundaries are not watertight, that groups persist despite a flow of members to and fro. Ethnic collectivities are thus independent of the individuals whose membership constitutes them. Members come and go, if only (but not only) as a consequence of mortality. An ethnic group can survive the fact that individuals in the course of their lives may change their ethnic identities.

Barth's model of ethnic identity has a number of core elements. Ethnic identities are ascriptions and self-ascriptions, held by actors, and produced and reproduced by actors in the course of social interaction. Processes of ethnic boundary maintenance and group recruitment—interethnic relations—are most important in this respect; among the most common contexts of inter-ethnic transactions are ecological and economic competition. Lastly, cultural commonality is a product of boundary maintenance, rather than a defining characteristic of group organisation and differ-

ence; there is no "one-to-one relationship between ethnic units and cultural similarities and differences" (1969: 14).

Barth has been criticised for means-ends voluntarism and a neglect of power, and for the individualism of his ideas about the transactional and situational flexibility of ethnic identity. There has also been a largely unproductive debate about situationalism versus primordialism. Nonetheless, Barth's social constructionist framework has become central to anthropological conventional wisdom about ethnicity (Eriksen 1993: 36-58; Jenkins 1997). As he himself has recently observed, it can be seen to have anticipated the postmodernist position on the construction of culture and difference (Barth 1994: 12).

The anthropological, social constructionist perspective is important. In its comparative global reach and its local-level research focus, in its emphasis upon cultural and social construction, and in its capacity to see individuals as well as collectivities, anthropology relativises our understanding of ethnicity and resists the naturalization or taking-for-granted of ethnic identity and nationalist ideologies. Frederick Barth's work continues to be central to that important task.

### Bibliography

Barth, F. 1959. *Political Leadership Among Swat Pathans.* London: Athlone.

Barth, F.1966. "Models of Social Organisation," Occasional Paper No. 23, London: Royal Anthropological Institute.

Barth, F. 1969. (ed.). *Ethnic Groups and Boundaries: The Social Organisation of Culture Difference.* Oslo: Universitetsforlaget.

Barth, F. 1981. *Process and Form in Social Life: Collected Essays of Fredrik Barth*, vol. 1. London: Routledge and Kegan Paul.

Barth, F. 1994. "Enduring and emerging issues in the analysis of ethnicity," in H. Vermeulen and C. Govers (eds.), *The Anthropology of Ethnicity: Beyond 'Ethnic Groups and Boundaries.'* Amsterdam: het Spinhuis.

Eriksen, T. H. 1993. *Ethnicity and Nationalism: Anthropological Perspectives.* London: Pluto.

Jenkins, R. 1997. *Rethinking Ethnicity: Arguments and Explorations.* London: Sage.

Richard Jenkins

# Berlin's Conception of Nationalism

Isaiah Berlin is one of the few contemporary thinkers to have a prescient understanding of the emerging importance of nationalism as a political and cultural phenomenon. He ends his essay: "Nationalism: Past Neglect and Present Power," with the following prophetic words: "It would not, I think, be an exaggeration to say that no political movement today, at any rate outside the Western world, seems likely to succeed unless it allies itself to national sentiment" (Berlin 1980: 355). "Nationalism," he writes in the early sixties, an age in which most Anglo-American philosophers were anticipating the emergence of a post-national world order, "seems to me the strongest force in the world today."

Berlin's attentiveness to nationalism is not surprising; his personal life experience as well as his philosophical approach led him to the conclusion that nationalism, in one form or another, is an essential component of the private and public life of modern individuals. An enquiry into Berlin's theory of nationalism must then be grounded in a general overview of his philosophy, and his personal biography. Berlin directs us towards the proper point of departure of such an enquiry: in order to grasp the ideas of a social philosopher, he argues, one should examine the conception of human nature that lies at its core. Following this lead, it is proper to start an analysis of Berlin's conception of nationalism with his view of human psychology, his understanding of the way individuals acquire knowledge, form beliefs and preferences, and structure their value-system.

The ideas of the Enlightenment, Berlin argues, are grounded in a shallow human psychology that disregards the social-communal aspects of human life and overemphasises their rational aspects. Men and women, he claims, are governed in their thoughts and sentiments by the customs, traditions and language in which they were nurtured, and not by rational principles. Vico was then right to assert against Descartes that natural languages, and civilization itself, are products of imagination, of a poetic invention and of metaphor, rather than of abstract reasoning and of clear and distinct ideas.

This inevitable contextuality of human life is attributed by Vico and Herder to the important role played by language "men necessarily think in words or other symbols; their feelings and attitudes [of] life are...incorporated in symbolic forms—worship, poetry, ritual...the entire network of belief and behaviour that binds them to one another can be explained only in terms of common, public symbolism, in particular language" (Berlin 1976: 165). The need to belong to a cultural community is not merely a psychological need to live in a close, affectionate community, nor is it solely a need for continuity, for finding a place for oneself, in the endless chain of being, but also an epistemological need for systems of meaning that will allow one to interpret the world and understand it, and a creative need for means of expression.

Belonging however, is but one component of an active, dignified life which is captured by nationalism, the need for status is another. Long before the present emergence of the "Politics of Recognition" Berlin acknowledged the motivating force of the search for status and recognition. The demand to be treated as equal lies at the heart of the social and national revolutions of our times, he wrote: "it represents the modern form of the cry for recognition— violent, dangerous, but valuable and just...The nationalism of the last two hundred years is shot through with this feeling" (Berlin 1996: 256). "The desire for recognition," he concludes, "is surely one of the greatest forces that moves human history" (Berlin 1996: 252).

The desire for status, the need to belong, to live in a community which is familiar and transparent are transformed from a psychological and expressive need to a political one by means of two related arguments. The first adopts the point of view of the individual; individuals, it argues, can feel free and secure and see themselves as self-governing only if they live in a social setting which is theirs. The second adopts the social perspective and argues that a free democratic society cannot be sustained unless its citizens belong to the same cultural-national community. If the freedom of individuals and the stability of democratic communities depend upon the formation of homogenous nation-states, then national heterogeneity may be rejected as an option on liberal-democratic grounds. Exclusion, expulsion, or even ethnic cleansing may be seen as the perverse, though logical, conclusions of liberal-democratic nationalism. The ugly faces of nationalism thus seem to find support in the corruption of a set of noble ideas: freedom, equality, democracy, and the search for recognition. A corruption generated by a tendency Berlin warns us against—to push ideas to their logical conclusions.

Berlin was well aware of the ideological and political transformations that led to the development of malignant types of nationalism. These, he argued, are often stimulated by social and political injustice. Peoples which have been victims of oppression and aggression or humiliation lash back like bent twigs at their oppressors, developing a defiant self-esteem and a violent self-consciousness which ultimately turns into burning nationalism and chauvinism.

For Berlin, then, zealot nationalism is the product of an injured pride. The reaction of a wounded nation can develop in two distinct ways: into "an anxiety to learn from the superior culture or nation, so as to emulate it and reach equality...[or] alternatively by means of resentful isolationism— a desire to leave the unequal contest and concentrate on one's own virtues which one discovers to be vastly superior to the vaunted qualities of the admired or fashionable rival" (Berlin 1996: 256). The distance from the latter kind of response to the most arrogant and violent forms of nationalism is short.

Nationalism is not the only possible repose to defeat and humiliation; Kantian rationalism is another kind of response. Despite appearances the two responses have more in common than meets the eye. The romantic, the national and the Kantian modes of thinking, Berlin claims, are all rooted in the need of the defeated Germans to develop a philosophy fitting their unfortunate conditions. A philosophy which purports that "political impotence means spiritual freedom: material defeat means moral victory. Since I cannot control the consequences of my acts, only that which I can control—my motives, my purposes, the purity of my heart—that alone counts" (Berlin 1996: 242). This austere self-insulation, the idea that freedom is being what you are, the veneration of integrity, Berlin argues, is the core

of both the Kantian and the Romanticism school of thought. In this respect, Kantian philosophy is a necessary, though by no means sufficient, step toward nationalism.

The move from Kant's position to Romanticism is accomplished in two successive steps: the first is a move from universal justifications to particular ones. According to Romantic thinking "when I act and live in the light of certain values, this is not because they are made or discovered by the reason that is present in all fully developed men, and therefore guaranteed by it and universally valid for all rational creatures. Rather, I do indeed live by such values...because they are my own, express my inner nature, the particular vision of the universe that belongs to me," a vision that belongs to me by virtue of my being a member of a particular group (Berlin 1996: 242-243).

The second move is from the individual to the group. It starts with Herder's claim that one ought to substitute Kant's autonomous self for the contextual self whose identity is determined by his social milieu, a product of social interaction and historical forces. It continues with Fichte's claim that the true self "is not the individual at all: it is the group, the nation," and ends with Hegel's veneration of nation, and his distinction between "historic" and "submerged" nations, coupled with the assumption that the more bellicose nations which are chosen to play a historic role by virtue of their superiority, had a historic right to absorb and dominate the unfortunate submerged nationalities. In this process the nature of the essential unit in which man's nature is fully realized shifts, from the individual or a voluntary association which can be dissolved or altered or abandoned at will, to the community of fate—the nation. The endurance and prosperity of that unit becomes paramount and the lives of subordinate units, the individual, the family, the tribe, the clan, the province, must be dedicated to its survival.

The two moves coupled with a belief in absolute truth, deeply rooted in the Enlightenment, cultivated the ground for the emergence of the most terrible kind of nationalism—organic, egoistic, xenophobic, sanctifying the glory of the nation, harnessing every possible means to serve its goals.

# Berlin's Conception of Nationalism

For Berlin, then, the history of nationalism is a peculiarly German history, not because of some unique feature of the German "national character" but because Germany was the twig that was bent time and again. Every additional bent lashed back in a more violent and dangerous form of nationalism.

Soberly analysing the transformation from abstract universal rationalism to xenophobic, ethnocentric nationalism, Berlin sees the danger embedded in attempting to sanctify either of these forms of thought. True to his distaste for all kinds of ruthless monism which eliminates all but one of the rival claimants, he opts for a messier position which acknowledges the value of nationalism without ignoring its bleak and dangerous aspects.

Berlin then is no enemy of nationalism as such. His sympathies lay with Herder's cultural nationalism. For Herder, a nation is not a state but a cultural entity of people who speak the same language, live on the same soil, and possess the same habits, a common past, common memories, and a hope for a common future. He attributes no significance to blood, biological continuity, or genetic features, his notion of belonging is cultural and spiritual. The proposition that "my nation is superior to yours," which is at the root of aggressive nationalism, is false for Herder. Every nation has a right to its own individual development. All the flowers in the human garden could grow side by side, different cultures can be stimulated by coexisting in creative harmony.

Like all those who experienced the horrors of our century, Berlin is much less optimistic than Herder. Nevertheless, even if he never explicitly said so, he seemed to believe that a mild form of nationalism could exist. At least this was his judgment of the early Zionists. His support for Zionism was grounded in the fact that the originators of Zionism were liberal, if not Herderian. They had a cultural mission; they wanted to establish a way of life which was culturally Jewish. Even those Zionist leaders who, like Herzl, wanted to go beyond cultural Zionism and establish a *Judenstaat*—a state of the Jews—dreamed of a liberal, bourgeois democracy, in which state and religion would be separated.

The Zionist claim, Berlin acknowledged, was grounded not merely in cultural demands but also in existential ones. Jews wanted a place where they could live a normal life without fear of persecution or discrimination; the history of the twentieth century proved that they desperately needed one.

Berlin's sympathy for nationalism is a sympathy for the nationalism of the *Risorgimento* and the European revolutionaries of 1848; it is a sympathy for the cultural, liberal form of nationalism of Verdi and Clemenceau, of Achad-Ha'am, Herzl and Weizman, rather than the militant nationalism of Treitschke, Barrès, or Wagner. Hence, even though he never produced a theory of nationalism of his own, it is quite clear that if he had produced one it would have been a theory of liberal nationalism; a theory which balances the needs of individuals with those of the community, the human aspiration for freedom, recognition, equality, with the aspiration for belonging and expressive creativity. A theoretically untidy, though a human kind of theory, the only kind of theory that could fit the "crooked timber of humanity."

## Bibliography

Berlin, I. 1969. *Four Essays on Liberty*. Oxford: Oxford University Press.

Berlin, I. 1976. *Vico and Herder: Two Studies in the History of Ideas*. London: Chatto & Windus.

Berlin, I. 1980. *Against the Current*. London: The Hogarth Press.

Berlin, I. 1996. *The Sense of Reality: Studies in Ideas and their History*. London: Chatto and Windus.

Gray, J. 1995. *Isaiah Berlin*. London: Harper Collins.

Yael Tamir

# C

## Chosen People

The idea of the "chosen people" signifies an intimate relationship between a people and its special deity, and can be found as far back as late Sumerian and ancient Egyptian times. In the Hebrew Bible, the relationship assumed the form of a "covenant" between God and His people and it became the pivot of a salvation history, insofar as God chose the Israelites and the Jewish people as His means of securing the redemption of the world. The Biblical doctrine was strictly conditional: Israel's status as a chosen people was assured only so long as it kept God's commandments. Backsliding and sin was to be punished by loss of protection by God for His people.

From the Old Testament, the doctrine of ethnic election entered into the religious belief systems of several other peoples, notably the Gregorian Armenians, the Monophysite Copts and Ethiopians, the Orthodox Greeks and Russians, and later the Catholic Franks and French and Irish, and the Protestant English, Scots, Ulster-Scots, Afrikaners and Americans. Though in many cases not as strict as the strong Jewish form of "covenantal" myth, the idea of the chosen people, with its belief in an ethnic mission entrusted to the community by the deity, was important in engendering, sustaining and directing ethnic identity over long periods.

It was this sustaining and directing quality that nationalism sought to emulate and, in many cases, to absorb. It found in the myth of ethnic election a powerful means of mobilizing the people and restoring their dignity and self-confidence. By appealing to the ancient ideal of chosenness, they could represent to their own people and the world the image of a once-great nation now subjected to oppression and even exile but soon to be restored to its rightful place in the moral economy of the world. We find examples of this process, not only in modern Zionism and Greek nationalism, but also in modern Irish, Swiss, Arab, Sikh, Hindu Indian, Burman, Sinhalese, and Japanese nationalisms. In this way, religious myths of ethnic election became important components of the secular nationalist salvation drama, and vital elements in forging the ideal of unique nations bent on rediscovering, preserving and expanding what Weber termed their "irreplaceable culture values."

### Bibliography

Akenson, D. 1992. *God's Peoples*. Ithaca, NY: Cornell University Press.

Armstrong, J. 1982. *Nations before Nationalism*. Chapel Hill: University of North Carolina Press.

Atiyah, A. S. 1968. *A History of Eastern Christianity*. London: Methuen.

Smith, A. D. 1992. "Chosen peoples; how ethnic groups survive," *Ethnic and Racial Studies* 15, 3: 436–56.

Anthony D. Smith

## Citizenship and Nationality

In the most basic sense citizenship has generally been understood to mean membership in a polity. Citizenship has therefore often been intrinsically linked to notions of territory. The interdependence between the concept of citizenship and the state has meant that as forms of rulership were questioned and overturned, so did the meaning of citizenship come to encompass both more, and, paradoxically, less, as a result of the dilution of the precisely defined role of the polity itself.

But what is the relationship between citizenship and nationality? The two concepts tend all too often to be confounded with each other. This is because today they almost coincide, due to the gradual democratization of politics during the last two centuries. Yet, both historically and conceptually nationality and citizenship are separable. Nationality has been acquired according to different criteria in different countries, depending

# Citizenship and Nationality

on their traditions and prevalent conceptions of nationhood. In some cases it is the principle of descent, the "*ius sanguinis*," that is the determining factor, whereas in other cases it is the principle of territorial affiliation, the "*ius soli*" (Brubaker 1992). The two different conceptions of nationality are related to the distinction between ethnic and civic nationalism, originally identified by Hans Kohn (although Kohn did not use these terms). Nationality having been determined and granted in one way or another, citizenship, on the other hand, was not automatically granted to all nationals. Historically, certain moral requirements were considered necessary for the responsible performance of the duties and the appropriate use of the rights related to citizenship. Thus, the status of citizenship was initially bestowed upon only to those nationals who were seen as possessing sufficient reason and property. As a consequence, minors, the mentally disabled, women, and all those who did not possess property were excluded from citizenship (as early as 1789, the French assembly which had equated the rights of the citizen with the rights of man in the Declaration of the Rights of Man and Citizen, nevertheless, decreed the payment of a poll tax to be a voting qualification). Besides the fact that the majority of nationals were thus excluded from citizenship, another illustration of how the two concepts were clearly distinct can be seen in the example of the French constitution of 1793, which authorised the national assembly to grant French citizenship to foreigners who "deserve[d] well" of humanity (in practice, intellectuals who sympathized with the French Revolution such as Tom Paine and Jeremy Bentham). Even today, despite the degree to which citizenship and nationality have come to coincide in terms of their membership, not all nationals are citizens: the mentally disabled and minors are not citizens, although they are nationals (Preuss 1995; Oomen 1997).

The beginnings of citizenship are usually traced to the sixth century B.C. Ideals of citizenship were for the first time fully expressed in Athens with Solon's laws (c. 594 B.C.), which gave all citizens the right and the obligation to participate in the affairs of the *polis*. Besides the practice of citizenship, Athens, and Greece more generally, in the two centuries following the promul-

gation of Solon's laws, gave the first brilliant examples of political thought on the idea of citizenship. In this context, Pericles's Funeral Speech as presented by Thucydides, a most eloquent panegyric to Athenian democracy, can be considered its first and fullest expression. The works of Plato and Aristotle perfected Greek thinking on the concept (Riesenberg 1992). The Greek city-states provide the first experiment in self-government based on participation in public matters. While the ideal of political participation dominated the concept of the citizen in the ancient Greek city-states, the necessity of protection which also animated conceptions of citizenship must not be forgotten. Political participation was held to be a citizen's primary obligation and expression of virtue, because it both exacted and promised service to the community. This service could take the form of political participation as reward for participation in the defense of the community or it could take the form of the defense itself. Thus, it must not be overlooked that citizenship in the Greek city-states was also largely based on the necessity and inevitability of war (Riesenberg 1992: 3-56).

Besides the Greek *polis* model, the other example of the development of citizenship in antiquity is afforded by Rome. The major difference between citizenship in Greece and citizenship in Rome was that in the case of Rome, there was a distinction between passive and active citizenship. Passive citizenship applied to Roman plebeians who were considered citizens, but were effectively barred from full participation in the life of the Republic. Active citizenship was a privilege reserved only for the other class of citizens, the patricians. Thus, for the plebeians, citizenship incorporated merely status, whereas for the patricians it incorporated both status and participation (Clarke 1994: 5-9). Some of the most distinguished expressions of Roman thinking on citizenship are to be found in Cicero's writings.

Classical ideals and practices of citizenship almost disappeared during the following centuries, when Christian notions of withdrawal from the affairs of this world and "the city" in favor of "another kind of city" prevailed. The most influential and characteristic work in this context was Augustine's *De civitate dei* (*The City of God*, 413-16 A.D.). The "inward turn" towards the Heavenly

City advocated by Augustine left little space for ideals of citizenship (Clarke 1994).

Classical ideals of citizenship re-emerged with the flourishing of city life in the Italian peninsula. During the Middle Ages and into the early years of the Italian Renaissance, the Italian city-states embodied a form of civic humanism which at its core combined the ideals of Aristotle and Cicero while adapting them to the necessities of mercantilism. Trade had taken the place of war as the organising principle of citizenship within a city-state.

Modern notions of citizenship emerged and developed gradually from the end of the eighteenth century onwards. Two developments were of particular significance: the American and the French Revolutions. These two events generated what can be termed a "universalist concept of citizenship" (Preuss 1995: 111-113) based on the premise that, all individuals being born free and equal, citizenship is constituted by the participation of these naturally free and equal individuals in a common enterprise, namely the constitution of a polity. The polity in question is based on a social contract. According to this understanding of citizenship, an individual can enter into the social contract and thus become a citizen on the basis of her/his human rights, rather than any pre-existing communal bond binding her/him with the rest of the social body, the fellow citizens. Such an understanding of citizenship presupposes a universalist and voluntarist definition of membership in the nation, such as that associated with the French Revolution.

This liberal conception of citizenship can be encapsulated in the ideas of such contemporary political theorists as John Rawls or Bruce Ackerman. According to these theorists, who hold minimalist versions of citizenship, the citizen is an abstract being and citizenship is a framework of rights and duties that leaves as much room as possible for each citizen's personal interpretation of the good life.

The opposite end of the continuum exhibits theories of citizenship which might be referred to as "thick" theories of citizenship—in a Geertzean sense. Such conceptions of citizenship take issue with what are perceived as narrow, liberal, procedural notions and replace them with more con-

textual, "communitarian" versions of participation and citizenship. A vision of political community such as Rousseau's, exemplifies this understanding of citizenship where the characteristics of a community, its values, beliefs, etc. inform the community's understanding of rights and duties. Thus, this vision defined the citizen not against a neutral backdrop of minimal rights and duties but against a rich—and perhaps cumbersome—backdrop of communal life suffused with ideals which require an allegiance to the community as a whole far more developed and complex than that required of the citizen in a strictly liberal conception of citizenship.

Furthermore, for these theorists, citizenship in each particular polity is based on the collective identity of the community in question, a collective identity which "presupposes a pre-political commonness of its members" and does not depend on the will or the choices of individuals (Preuss 1995: 113). Here, an individual's attachment to a specific community is pre-determined and inescapable since it partly defines the individual's personal identity and self. Rather than being a mere association of free individuals aiming at furthering their particular interests, the community itself has intrinsic moral value. Citizenship is an exclusive status, reserved for those who are already members of the community which exists before the polity comes into being.

Another meaning of the concept of citizenship, or perhaps a development of the concept to cover new fields, is the idea of "social citizenship," as developed by T.H. Marshall in his famous essay, "Citizenship and Social Class" of 1950. According to Marshall, citizenship had three different aspects: civil (referring to rights such as freedom of movement and liberty to make contracts); political (referring to the right to be elected to public office or to be an elector); and social (referring to the right to welfare provision and to share in the heritage of society). Social citizenship in Marshall's work was designed to combat social inequality which hindered the individual's participation in the social, cultural, and political life of the society in which s/he lived. According to Marshall, citizenship had to include "the right to share to the full in the social heritage and to live the life of a civilised being according to the stan-

# Citizenship and Nationality

dards prevailing in the society" (Marshall 1991).

Another concept of citizenship is the so-called "earth citizenship." Arguments related to the common stakes that all human beings have in the preservation of the natural resources of the planet and the environment are used in justification of the evocation of the concept (Preuss 1995). Other conceptions of citizenship are "cosmopolitan citizenship" or "world citizenship" (Linklater 1998; Habermas 1992). Perhaps the most influential contemporary advocate of world citizenship has been the German philosopher Jürgen Habermas. According to Habermas, "The arrival of world citizenship is no longer merely a phantom, though we are still far from achieving it. State citizenship and world citizenship form a continuum which already shows itself, at least, in outline form" (Habermas 1992). As Thomas Mertens has commented, "Habermas' central theme is both the sociological reality of the separation of citizenship and national identity and the moral need to do so" (Mertens 1996: 335). Thus, Habermas has argued strongly against the association of citizenship with national identity.

Besides advocating world citizenship, Habermas has been a supporter of the idea of European citizenship. It has been argued that his plea for European citizenship "must be regarded as an intermediary step towards world citizenship, where the ultimate disconnection between citizenship and national identity is attained" (Mertens 1996: 338). Habermas has offered a potentially useful conception of a European public sphere. For him, the public sphere "is a communicative network formed by different actors who engage in negotiations over particular aspects or contents of social and political life." But what is the meaning of European citizenship? The Treaty on European Union, signed at Maastricht on 7 February 1992 (known as "the Maastricht Treaty"), established the concept of European citizenship by introducing a "Citizenship of the [European] Union" (Article 8). According to the Treaty "[e]very person holding the nationality of a Member State shall be a citizen of the Union." The attributes of Union citizenship include, the right to move and reside freely within the territory of any of the Member States; the right to stand and vote in municipal elections and elections to the European Parliament in any state in the European Union; rights to consular protection in third countries; the right to petition the European Parliament and to apply to the Ombudsman established by the Treaty. These E.U. "rights" are in fact insignificant as compared with the rights attached to national citizenship. It is somewhat ironical that democracy in the E.U. is guaranteed, not through the European Parliament, but through the national parliaments. This is because there is no such entity as the European "people" or *demos*." The EU is constituted by the individual nations of the member states. The current equation of *"demos,"* a voting constituency, with an *"ethnos,"* understood in the more general sense of a (variously defined) national community, has been described as "the No Demos Thesis." This thesis is an important part of the debate regarding the necessity or otherwise of the existence of a single *"demos"* for the functioning of European democracy and European citizenship (Habermas 1992; Meehan 1993; Weiler 1999).

## Bibliography

Andrews, G. (ed.) 1991. *Citizenship*. London: Lawrence & Wishart.

Brubaker, Rogers. 1992. *Citizenship and Nationhood in France and Germany*. Cambridge, MA: Harvard University Press.

Clarke, Paul Barry. 1994. *Citizenship* (Reader). London: Pluto Press.

Habermas, Jürgen. 1992. "Citizenship and national identity: some reflections on the future of Europe," *Praxis International* 12: 1-19.

Linklater, Andrew. 1998. "Cosmopolitan citizenship," *Citizenship Studies* 2, 1: 23-42.

Marshall, T.H. 1991 (1950). "Citizenship and social class," in T. H. Marshall, *Citizenship and Social Class and Other Essays*. London: Pluto Press.

Meehan, Elisabeth. 1993. *Citizenship and the European Community*. London: Sage.

Mertens, Thomas. 1996. "Cosmopolitanism and citizenship: Kant against Habermas," *European Journal of Philosophy* 4, 3: 328-47.

Oomen, T. K. (ed.). 1997. *Citizenship and National Identity: From Colonialism to Globalism*. New Delhi: Sage Publications.

Preuss, Ulrich K. 1995. "Citizenship and identity: aspects of a political theory of citizenship," in Richard Bellamy, Vittorio Bufacchi & Dario Castiglione (eds.), *Democracy and Constitutional Culture in the Union of Europe.* London: Lothian Foundation Press.

Preuss, Ulrich K. 1996. "Two challenges to European citizenship," in Richard Bellamy and Dario Castiglione (eds.), *Constitutionalism in Transformation: European and Theoretical Perspectives.* Oxford: Blackwell Publishers.

Riesenberg, Peter. 1992. *Citizenship in the Western Tradition: From Plato to Rousseau.* Chapel Hill and London: The University of North Carolina Press.

Smith, Anthony D. 1991. *National Identity.* London: Penguin Books.

Weiler, Joseph H.H. 1999. *The Constitution of Europe: "Do the New Clothes Have an Emperor?" and Other Essays on European Integration.* Cambridge: Cambridge University Press.

Catherine Fieschi and Georgios Varouxakis

# Class and Nation

The concept of social class broadly refers to a category of people within a given society who possess a similar socioeconomic position, one which distinguishes them from other individuals in the same society. In its Marxist variant it refers to diametrically opposed positions in the process of production, and in its Weberian variant it refers to individuals with the same life chances. In contrast, nation refers to a political community of culture and to a claimed common ancestry, or in its North American variant, to a political community of citizens. Class is an internal category within a given society. This is because a class does not exist independently but by reference to another class or classes within the same society.

Nation, in contrast, is an external category to a given society because it often demarcates boundaries between societies. From this, one may conclude that the two concepts are different and that any overlap is implausible. Paradoxically, there is a remarkable link between the two concepts. Many revolutionary movements, particularly those informed by some version of Marxism, invoke the ideas of class and nation concurrently to enhance their ability to mobilize a population towards a revolutionary goal. The Cuban revolu-

tion invokes the ideas of the working class in struggle against Yankee imperialism and, simultaneously, the qualities of the Cuban nation as a guarantee for the defense of the revolution. Likewise, the twin calls of class liberation and national liberation are the central ingredients in the success of the Chinese Communist Party in defeating both the Japanese aggressors and the Kuomintang opposition. The same applies to the Vietnamese revolutionaries and even to the success of the Yugoslav communists in the aftermath of the Second World War. What all these movements have in common is the formulation of a strategic alliance of class and nation in their revolutionary rhetoric. Even today, many feminist and postcolonial theories invoke the narratives of race, class, gender, and nation to provide a discourse of resistance against globalization and the inequalities it generates.

The Italian Marxist revolutionary Antonio Gramsci provided a theoretical link between the notions of class and nation in his well-known concept of "national popular." Here Gramsci argues that given the cosmopolitan nature of the bourgeois class, the working class must become the national class by overcoming its narrow corporatist inclinations and build what he calls a "national popular historical bloc" to crystallize a national collective will. This is done by building a hegemonic collective will which encompasses other social strata under the national banner of the working class (Nimni 1994:110).

The second influential conceptual link between class and nation is provided by the prominent African revolutionary Frantz Fanon. In his influential work *The Wretched of the Earth* of 1963, Fanon was concerned that the colonized middle classes would not pursue the redemption of the nation in a postcolonial world, but would rather pursue the aims of colonialism by misusing the national culture. Thus, in his famous chapter "On National Culture" Fanon warned against such misuse of the national culture to further colonialist aims and explained that the culture of the nation could only retain its meaning if it echoed the revolutionary efforts of the oppressed, that is, of those who dream of class emancipation. In Fanon's words, "A struggle which mobilises all classes of the people and which expresses their aims and their impatience, which is not afraid to count almost exclusively on the peoples' support, will, of necessity, triumph" (Fanon 1967:198).

Outside the area of influence of the Red Army, class emancipatory movements succeeded only when ideas of class and nation were credibly combined. With hindsight, and on this issue at least, Gramsci and Fanon had a point.

### Bibliography

Fanon, Frantz. 1967 (1963). *The Wretched of the Earth*. Harmondsworth: Penguin.

Nimni, Ephraim. 1994. *Marxism and Nationalism: Theoretical Origins of a Political Crisis*. 2nd edn. London: Pluto Press.

Smith, A. D. 1991. *National Identity*. Harmondsworth: Penguin.

Smith, A. D. 1979. *Nationalism in the Twentieth Century*. Oxford: Martin Robertson.

Ephraim Nimni

# Communications Theories of Nationalism

The role of communication runs like a connecting thread through both modern nationalist thought and theories of nationalism. Although the communicative dimension most often operates in the *Hinterland* of theories of nationalism, there is a discernible line of argument that takes communication as of central importance. In this article, I offer a sketch of how communication and the nation are related in the work of Karl Deutsch, Ernest Gellner, Benedict Anderson, and Jürgen Habermas, pointing up the scope and limitations of their broadly shared framework of assumptions.

To Karl W. Deutsch goes the credit for attempting probably the first most explicit and wide-ranging theorization of the role of communication in nationalism in his book *Nationalism and Social Communication*, originally published in 1953, with a second edition in 1966, to which only a brief introduction was added. There is complementary material in Deutsch's *The Nerves of Government* (1966) and *Politics and Government* (1980, 3rd ed.), but the essentials of the argument do not change.

In his introduction to the second edition of *Nationalism and Social Communication*, Deutsch (1966: 4) highlighted a cardinal theme that remains pertinent for current debate: he observed that the nation-state was "still the chief political instrument for getting things done," and underlined his view that supranational integration had limits given the resilience of nationality. The key proposition of Deutsch's theory is this: "The essential aspect of the unity of a people ... is the complementarity or relative efficiency of communication among individuals—something that is in some ways similar to *mutual rapport, but on a larger scale*" (Deutsch 1966: 188, emphasis added).

Deutsch sees a "people" as providing the basis for the forging of a nationality. This, in turn, is distinct from nation-statehood, where political sovereignty is harnessed to the pursuit of a group's cohesion and the continuity of its identity. Hence, the exercise of national power relies upon "the relatively coherent and stable structure of memories, habits and values" which in turn "depends on existing facilities for social communication, both from the past to the present and between contemporaries" (Deutsch, 1966: 75).

"Social communication" is very broadly understood by Deutsch; it is akin to an all-embracing anthropological notion of culture that integrates a given people (Deutsch 1966: 96–97). It is otherwise represented as a principle of coherence for a community, and has its basis in the "facilities for storing, recalling, and recombining information, channels for its dissemination and interaction, and facilities for deriving further information" (Deutsch 1966: 75). It embraces the ways in which sociocultural groups cluster and their institutions and interactions. Such clusters have a key sociocultural significance. Deutsch (1966: 95) stresses the distinction between community and society, keenly aware that a society may contain quite different ethnocultural communities that cannot find a common, overarching code—or mode of social communication.

The argument is that nations and nation-states are strongly bounded by their socially communicative structures of interaction: "Peoples are held together "from within" by this communicative efficiency, the complementarity of the communicative facilities acquired by their members"

(Deutsch 1966: 98). Nationality is therefore an objective function of communicative competence and belonging. Although Deutsch acknowledges the analytical place of such ideas as "national consciousness" and "national will," the symbolic level of national self-awareness—or what today would be termed "national identity"—is seen as an outcome of the structural cohesion that comes about through social communication.

One key implication is that the communicative practices of nations lead to the exclusion of foreigners. "Ethnic complementarity" (which equates to nationality) sets up "communicative barriers" and engenders "marked gaps" in the efficiency of communication relative to other groups (Deutsch 1966: 100). Although some nations, those based on immigration and openness to assimilation, are well adapted to the integration of new members, others may throw the process into reverse by expulsion or even extermination.

A further consequence is that the creation of wider collectivities via, for instance supranational political arrangements such as federalism, is inherently difficult to achieve, especially where communicative complementarity is weak or does not exist. Deutsch is more struck by the likely persistence of the nation-state than by its disappearance. As he puts it, "the present distribution of sovereign states" is "necessary in its essential features, though not in its accidents" (Deutsch 1966: 187).

Deutsch's functionalist conception of cultural integration does have a decisive weakness when the level of analysis shifts outside the nation-state. It offers no general principle for analyzing the interaction between communicative communities—a matter of central concern to contemporary cultural and media studies—because that is not where the center of interest lies.

Deutsch's underlying conception of social communication—if not his theoretical idiom—lives on strongly in more contemporary work, such as, for instance, Ernest Gellner's noted *Nations and Nationalism* (1983). Most commentators, while justifiably analyzing the validity of Gellner's stress on the role of industrialization in creating nations, at the same time have tended to underplay how his theory is also crucially dependent upon the social role of culture and communication.

Gellner argues that the formation of nation-states is the inevitable outcome of industrialization, with its concomitant complex division of labor. The new social relations of industrial society mean that to function effectively one needs to be able to do anything, in principle, and that requires "generic training." This transmission of know-how necessitates a universal, standardized system of education, using a standardized linguistic medium. It is this process of making us into nationals that brings about an inevitable "deep adjustment in the relationship between polity and culture," namely nationalism, which is "the organization of human groups into large, centrally educated, culturally homogeneous groups" (Gellner 1983: 35). Gellner's theory, then, connects the explanatory motor of industrialization to a Deutschian conception of social communication.

Thus, for Gellner, culture refers to "the distinctive style of conduct and communication of a given community," which, in the modern world takes the modal form of a nation-state. For the members of such political formations "culture is now the necessary shared medium" and based in education and literacy (Gellner 1983: 37–8). Cultural boundaries, then, become defined by national cultures, in which the key agency is a national education system. The culture of a nation is broadly identified with official culture, and the theory is less interested in sources of internal differentiation and conflict than what makes the nation cohere. Like Deutsch's theory, Gellner's is mainly concerned with how a national culture comes to be created, rather than concerning itself with how it is maintained and renewed. And it also stresses the self-containedness of nation-state protected cultures.

Whereas contemporary media and cultural theories are especially concerned with cultural flows and relations of dominance within the global communications order, this is not a key interest for Gellner, any more than it was for Deutsch. Mass-mediated communication is dealt with in passing. Gellner (1983: 127) argues that it is not the content of such communication that matters, but rather

# Communications Theories of Nationalism

the media themselves, the pervasiveness and importance of abstract, centralized, standardized, one to many communication, which itself automatically engendered the core idea of nationalism, quite irrespective of what in particular is being put into the specific messages transmitted. ... The core message is that the language and style of the transmissions is important, that only he who can understand them, or can acquire such comprehension, is included in a moral and economic community, and that he who does not and cannot, is excluded.

The media, therefore, function as a categorial system: widespread public identification with the national space is an effect of this form of cultural organization. Media are boundary markers, intimately related to the "political roof" that caps a culture and makes it into a nation-state. It is their function in sustaining a political community that is of prime interest.

The communicative dimension also runs through another pivotal text of recent years, Benedict Anderson's *Imagined Communities* (1983). Since Anderson's work appeared, his title has turned from a pithy descriptor of nationhood into a sociological and journalistic cliché. In his account of the emergence of European nations, Anderson, like Deutsch and even more than Gellner, takes mediated communication to be of central importance in the formation of a nationalist consciousness (or identity):

> What, in a positive sense, made the new communities imaginable was a half-fortuitous, but explosive, interaction between a system of production and productive relations (capitalism), a technology of communications (print), and the fatality of human linguistic diversity. (Anderson 1983: 46)

Whereas for Gellner education takes center-stage, Anderson's key contention is that "Print-language is what invents nationalism, not a particular language per se" (Anderson 1983: 122). Thus, what is highlighted is the importance of the media of communication in the construction of an imagined community, given the appropriate material conditions.

According to Anderson, "print language" was the means whereby vernaculars became standardized, being disseminated through the market for books and newspapers. His account is resolutely Gutenbergian: the impact of electronic media is not addressed. Mechanically reproduced print

languages unified fields of linguistic exchange, fixed "national" languages, and created new idioms of power. The "nationalist novel" (its plot enacted in a socially recognized common space) together with the newspaper, with "calendrical consciousness" as its principle of organization, were, Anderson argues, the two key vehicles in shaping national consciousness. By co-ordinating time and space these could address an imagined national community even before it is formed into a nation-state.

Hence, the collective consumption of mediated communication serves to create a sense of national community. Like Gellner, Anderson understands the confines of the nation to be inescapably implicit in the way that media categorize reality, and address their audiences. Strikingly like Deutsch, who writes of "mutual rapport," Anderson speaks of the nation's "deep, horizontal comradeship" (Anderson 1983: 16).

Although (unlike Gellner) Anderson makes no reference to Deutsch's work, his approach is still unmistakably located in a social communications framework: the imagined community is situated within the sociocultural and communicative space of the nation-state.

Social communication theories, then, all share a broad concern with how nations speak to themselves, mark themselves off as different from others. This theme is also central to the work of Jürgen Habermas, whose work is widely recognized as premised on a theory of communication, but is less well understood to be also concerned with the nation addressed as a political community. Habermas's theory of *The Structural Transformation of the Public Sphere* (originally published in 1962; English translation 1989) has exerted a profound influence in the recent debate about the role and quality of political communication. The "public sphere"—another sociological trope of our time—refers to the whole domain of debate in an institutional space that exists outside the state, but which engages all who are concerned with matters of public interest. The existence of this domain is central to the freedom of expression commonly associated with democracy; it is necessarily a space in which communication takes place.

Whereas recent democratic and media theories have taken the theory of the public sphere as common ground, the co-extensiveness of that space with nation-statehood has been largely ignored. In fact, the formation of the classic public sphere coincided with the growth of nationalism and nation-state formation. And this theory stresses that public communication remains preeminently tied to the structures of meaning of nation-states—although these have long been open to global information flows. The boundaries of the public sphere therefore coincide with those of a political community conceived of as quintessentially national in scope. The nation-state, consequently, has provided the retaining wall, not only for the all-inclusive Deutsch-Gellner-Anderson conception of social communication as national culture but also for the more narrowly conceived Habermasian domain of political communication.

It could justly be said, then, that it is a sense of politico-cultural enclosure that is best conveyed by the social communications tradition. All the above theories share a notion of the prototypically modern—national—communicative community as strongly bounded. Deutsch's work emphasizes communicative "gaps" between peoples, this being the dark side of relatively cozy insider efficiency and complementarity. Gellner and Anderson too, stress the role of a common culture based in a standardized language and cultural institutions in making a common people, whereas Habermas sees national communicative space as, ideally, offering a forum for the exercise of political judgment.

Yet, the world of nation-states is interactive, and an ostensible communicative sovereignty has to face the reality of the global flows of cultural products that enter the national domain. This point has been latterly acknowledged in passing by Anderson (1994: 320–321), who recognizes the boundary-crossing impact of electronic media, although without explaining what that might be. For detailed explorations of the transnational potentialities of communication, we undoubtedly have to look to media theories rather than theories of nationalism, which remain deficient in their detailed institutional grasp of new developments. The sense that there are two quite distinct domains of theory remains strong (Schlesinger 1991), although it would be correct to say that of

late media and cultural theories have become increasingly oriented by the problem of national identity.

Communication theories of nationalism have yet to integrate the implications of a series of debates that have occurred over the past quarter of a century. There has long been a recognition in media theory and analysis of the transnational, latterly "global," framework as crucial for the analysis of communication. It is a commonplace that both states and media enterprises may operate at national and transnational levels (and must be analyzed accordingly) and that communicative links such as the Internet respect no boundaries.

The international context has been particularly relevant to communication studies since World War II. For example, there has been widespread official concern about national communication sovereignty in the face of transborder broadcasting, accentuated by satellite transmissions. Moreover, the transnational flow of media products has been a live issue in debates about political and economic dependency and neo-imperialism, as in Latin America, where, during the 1970s, the critique of U.S. cultural dominance via popular culture and consumerism led directly to the pursuit of developmental goals through national communication policies. A subsequent debate that lasted into the early 1980s concerned the possibility of creating a New World Information and Communication order, motivated by the desire to resist the unequal cultural trading relations between the core capitalist countries of the West and the Third World (MacBride 1980; Mattelart 1994).

More recently, the accelerating pace of "Europeanization" through the development of the European Union has had an increasing impact on media theory and its conceptualization of national sovereignty in the 1990s. In fact, the European Union offers a laboratory test for those interested in the communicative relations between nation-statehood and supranationalism. To what extent is the classical framework of communications theories of nationalism—focused, as we have seen, almost exclusively on the level of the nation-state—transposable to an emergent supranational entity?

## Communications Theories of Nationalism

Deutsch (1966: 3–4) doubted that a common communicative space could easily emerge in the then European Community because of the continuing strength of the nation-state. Thirty years later, in sharp contrast, Habermas (1994: 21) has maintained that the "classic form of the nation-state is presently disintegrating." For him, the European Union now offers scope for a new, wider, conception of CITIZENSHIP with a correlatively broader framework of public communication. He has thus transposed the national public sphere to the supranational level, assuming the diminished hold of the nation-state and nationality on collective loyalty and identification. By this account the eventual European political community would be linked not by means of common symbols but rather through a less emotionally compelling framework of rules—a challenge to nationhood as conceived by Deutsch, Gellner, and Anderson. Is such political rationality enough to make an extended and variegated collectivity cohere?

Theoretical arguments and contemporary policy developments inside the European Union are intimately connected. The E.U.'s attempts to define a "European" cultural identity and common communicative space in the 1980s and 1990s took place in the context of global industrial competition, most especially with the United States and Japan. Heightened invocations of a common European culture accompanied efforts to protect European audiovisual production from the impact of U.S. film and television imports during the concluding phase of the GATT negotiations in 1993 (Schlesinger 1997). The stress upon "Europeanness," and the need to treat films and television programs as protectable cultural goods, reflected governmental concern about the extent to which the globalization of communication had undermined the cultural sovereignty of nation-states, and, by extension, that of the intergovernmental European Union.

Parallel concern for the protection of collective identities has been aroused by trade liberalization on the other side of the Atlantic. The North American Free Trade Agreement (NAFTA), a regime regulating goods and services, like the GATT, contains specific reference to the cultural industries. As for the E.U., the cultural impact of economic relations with the U.S. was (and remains) a matter of concern both in Canada and Mexico, with specific exemptions sought to protect given sectors of cultural production. In each country, securing national cultural identity, as well as underpinning domestic cultural industries, were motive forces (McAnany and Wilkinson 1996). Plainly, such policy thinking has been premised on the functionalist assumptions of social communications theory.

In global cultural trade, the E.U. has made efforts to represent itself as a coherent cultural entity. However, that is only its outward face, since internally the E.U. demonstrates acutely the tensions between supranationalism and nationalism. Where diversity of language and culture are crucial symbols of collective identity, supranational Euro-goals encounter national resistances. To complicate things further, the E.U.-endorsed recognition of regional differences within member states—the "Europe of the Regions"—has reinforced autonomist, even secessionist, tendencies, particularly in the territories of stateless nations. Hence, not only state-endorsed national culture may contradict the demands of "Europeanization" but European nation-states may also simultaneously find themselves challenged by claims made for cultural and communicative recognition by national, ethnic and linguistic minorities. Theorising about communicative space inside the E.U. therefore needs to take serious account of at least three levels: the supranational, the nation-statal, and the sub-nation-statal. In other words, it needs to move theoretically beyond the existing tight, homologous coupling of social communication and nation.

But the European case simply underlines a broader lesson. Namely, that communication theories of nationalism now need to incorporate the theoretical insights and analytical findings of cognate media and cultural studies. For these have long dispensed with thinking about nation and communication as explicable purely in terms of a close functional fit.

This article is based on research carried out as part of the "Political Communication and Democracy" project in the ESRC's "Media Economics and Media Culture Programme" (Reference No. L126251022). The author is grateful to the Council for its support.

## Bibliography

Anderson, B. 1983. *Imagined Communities: Reflections on the Origin and Spread of Nationalism*. London: Verso.

Anderson, B. 1994. "Exodus," *Critical Inquiry* 20, 2: 314–327.

Deutsch, K. W. 1953 (1966, 2nd ed.). *Nationalism and Social Communication: An Inquiry into the Foundations of Nationalism*. Cambridge, MA. and London: The MIT Press.

Deutsch, K. W. 1966. *The Nerves of Government: Models of Political Communication and Control*. New York: The Free Press, London: Collier-Macmillan.

Deutsch, K. W. 1980 (3rd. ed.). *Politics and Government: How People Decide their Fate*. Boston: Houghton Mifflin.

Gellner, E. 1983. *Nations and Nationalism*. Oxford: Blackwell.

Habermas, J. 1989. *The Structural Transformation of the Public Sphere: An Inquiry into a Category of Bourgeois Society*. Cambridge, MA: Polity Press.

Habermas, J. 1994. "Citizenship and national identity," in B. van Steenbergen (ed.), *The Condition of Citizenship*. London: Sage.

McAnany, E. G. and K. T. Wilkinson (eds.) 1996. *Mass Media and Free Trade: NAFTA and the Cultural Industries*. Austin: University of Texas Press.

MacBride, S. 1980. *Many Voices, One World*. London: Kogan Page.

Mattelart, A. 1994. *Mapping World Communication: War, Progress, Culture*. Minneapolis, London: University of Minnesota Press.

Schlesinger, P. 1991. *Media, State and Nation: Political Violence and Collective Identities*. London, Newbury Park and New Delhi: Sage.

Schlesinger, P. 1997. "From cultural defence to political culture: media, politics and collective identity in the European Union," *Media, Culture and Society* 19, 3: 369–391.

Philip Schlesinger

# Communism and Nationalism

The outbreak of the First World War in August 1914 signalled the collapse of the Second International. Contrary to its intentions, workers fought for their countries, and socialists voted heavy war credits for their governments. The proletariat did have a fatherland—or fatherlands—and national unity triumphed over class solidarity. The war saw three great European empires defeated not by proletarian internationalism but by the idea of nationalism. East European nationalist leaders such as Jozef Pilsudski and Thomas Masaryk saw the War as a fight for the freedom of their nations. Ostensibly, at least, the victorious powers organized the post-1918 international order on the principle of national self-determination. Nationalism also prevailed as the most powerful European idea between the two world wars (Szporluk 1988: 226).

For Karl Marx, immunity to nationalism was the single most important defining characteristic of a communist (Connor 1984: 10–11). Communists flew the banner of proletarian internationalism. They regarded nationalism as a relic of a bourgeois society, as something to be destroyed, to be consigned to oblivion. The proletariat was an international force, and it would carry out a worldwide communist revolution. The triumph of the proletariat and communism would mark the defeat of the bourgeois ideology of nationalism, it would see the withering away of the state, and hostility between states would disappear together with the nations themselves.

In practice the communist regimes in the Soviet Union after the Bolshevik Revolution in 1917, and in Eastern Europe after 1945, pursued ambiguous policies. On the one hand they tried to stamp out nationalism; on the other they wished to harness it to the service of communist states, to confer on them a legitimacy that communism on its own never could. The precise reach of nationalisms in the territories comprising the Romanov empire at the time of the Bolshevik Revolution in 1917 remains to be established. What is known is that between 1918 to 1921 the Bolsheviks engaged in battle with nationalist forces in Armenia, Azerbaijan, Ukraine, and Georgia before defeating them and consolidating the power of the Soviet state (Pipes 1954). But Lenin realized that the victory of the Bolsheviks was incomplete. Nationalism had proved to be far stronger than expected, and it remained a force to be reckoned with. The political structures of the Soviet Union, most notably the establishment of Union Republics, having a constitutional right to secede, were intended to win over the vanquished nations.

## Communism and Nationalism

Chapter 3, Article 4 of the 1924 constitution gave Union Republics "the right to freely withdraw from the Union"; Article 17 of the 1936 constitution and article 72 of the 1977 constitution granted the same right. This was a mere gesture; in practice, Lenin did not envisage secession at all.

Having forged the Soviet state through civil war, the top priority of Soviet leaders was to preserve its territorial integrity. The Union Republics represented an acknowledgment of the national and cultural variety of the Soviet Union, but "democratic centralism" signified intolerance of political and intellectual diversity. Communism made no distinction between state and society, and it had no place for any idea of the separation of powers. The Soviets were determined to invent a single will and sought to do this by a combination of social and intellectual engineering.

Marxist-Leninists gave primacy to economic ideas, and held that the relationships of production constituted society's base. Soviet economic policies were intended to change the prerevolutionary social structures by redistributing political and economic power. Only in this way could society be modernized and the bourgeois relic of nationalism be wiped out. Collectivization was not just a means of reorganizing the society and economy by eliminating *kulaks* as a class; it was also a means of breaking the will of non-Russian peoples and guaranteeing their subjugation under Stalin's dictatorship. By the end of the 1930s collectivization had completed the process of destroying the old elites, and the constitution of 1936 boasted that the USSR was "a socialist state of workers and peasants." Rapid industrialization was achieved under the command economy, and the territories constituting the Soviet Union were wrenched out of economic backwardness. The country became a major industrial power, and the state introduced full employment, housing and social security for the whole population. But they were achieved at a low level of satisfaction, and at enormous cost in human and material terms. The successes of the command economy were temporary, and after the 1950s a plethora of economic problems contributed to the strengthening of the nationalisms which challenged the legitimacy of the Soviet state in the 1980s.

Religious, educational and linguistic policies were the instruments of social engineering. They were the tools with which the Soviet authorities tried to create a centralized educational system, and a single culture, identified with the state. The rapprochement or *sblizheniye* of nations would be followed by their *sliyanie* or assimilation. The tacit assumption was that assimilation would take place into the Russian culture, and that Russian would be the state language.

Political integration and social assimilation entailed the overcoming of religious and ethnic loyalties and the setting up of a uniform educational system. The Communist Party sought to erase the nationalist memory if it conflicted with the interests of the Soviet state; and to revive or shape it in a manner which shore up its appeal. Stamping out religion was a political task. It was necessary to destroy all class forces hostile to the Party. But the Communist leadership also took into account the extent to which religion could be made to suit their purposes. In Central Asia Union Republics were created to counter pan-Islamic and pan-Turkic sentiment (Hajda and Beissinger 1990: 255). In Russia, Soviet leaders from Stalin to Gorbachev made the Russian Orthodox Church serve the interests of the state. Moreover, official control over the mass media and culture would remove those vestiges of nationalism that the state deemed harmful to its interests from the popular consciousness. Official nostrums would dictate the personal values and commitments of Soviet citizens.

And yet, the combination of social engineering and the communist ideology was never enough to secure the legitimacy of the Soviet state. Stalin tried to graft legitimacy on to the Soviet state by identifying it with both the multinational Romanov empire and Russia. Great Russian nationalism was invoked in support of the Soviet state; during the Second World War Soviet citizens were exhorted to fight for their *rodina* (motherland). Russians were settled in non-Russian republics. Local communists were given party posts: the first secretary of a republican communist party belonged to the titular nationality. His influence was countered by the republican second secretary, who was always a Russian, reported direct to Moscow and wielded the real power. In the 1980s, confronted with a rising tide of nationalism, Gorbachev encouraged Russians in the Baltic republics to resist the claims to independence of non-Russians. The official association of Russia with the Soviet state lasted until the collapse of the Soviet Union, and it was encapsulated in Gorbachev's reference to "a state that is one thousand years old."

The result was that most non-Russians associated Russians with some of the worst excesses of the communist regime. The irony was that the equation of Russia with the Soviet state did not in the long run make Russians its guarantors. That Russians dominated the Communist Party of the Soviet Union cannot be doubted. But many Russians thought communism was an assault on Russian culture and the Russian Orthodox Church, and they saw themselves as victims of communism. It was left to Boris Yeltsin, between 1989 and 1991, to represent the idea that the Soviet state was unresponsive to Russia's interests, and that Russia was not at one with the Soviet state (Dunlop 1993). August 1991 found Russia in revolt against the Soviet state. Russia's disengagement from the Soviet Union called into question the common assumption that a state can moderate or pre-empt political opposition and survive by obtaining the support of linguistic, religious or ethnic elites (Inder Singh 1995).

The attempt to identify Russia with the Soviet state was also part of a wider policy of "divide and rule." The practice was based on the assumption that national division implied political division; thus it assumed the potential or existence of nationalism as a political force. The policy bore fruit, though not necessarily the one sought by Soviets. The post-1989 Abkhazian-Georgian and Armenian-Azeri conflicts can be traced to Stalin's policy of exploiting divisions between these communities. Because divide and rule cannot by its very nature forge consensus, it failed to sustain the Soviet state.

Communism also became "national" in other communist countries. In Eastern Europe communist regimes established themselves in the aftermath of World War II in Yugoslavia, Poland, Hungary, Bulgaria, Czechoslovakia, Romania, and Albania. Nationalism was woven into the communist ideology by communist rulers partly to bolster themselves domestically. But it also mirrored their resentment at Soviet domination.

Yugoslavia's rift with the Soviet Union showed that there was no single communist political and economic model, and that all communist leaders would not formulate their domestic and foreign policies in accordance with Soviet instructions. Communist nationalisms were a reality and they came into conflict with one another. In Romania, Nicolai Ceausescu espoused nationalist motifs and symbols, portrayed himself as a Romanian national hero, and condemned the Warsaw pact invasion of Czechoslovakia in 1968. However, a series of economic failures led him to arouse nationalist sentiment against Hungarian and Jewish minorities in Romania, on the grounds that Romanians must be masters in their own home. In Bulgaria virulent nationalism masqueraded as communism, as Turkish language schools were closed in the 1970s, Turkish removed from the national school curriculum, and officials denied the existence of Turks in Bulgaria. In 1984 Muslims were ordered to change their Turkic and Arabic sounding names to Bulgarian sounding ones. In Poland, Wladislaw Gomulka affirmed a national road to socialism. But scapegoats were needed to take the blame for the economic disasters under Polish communism. They were found in Poland's Jews, who comprised less than two percent of Poland's population. In 1968, an anti-Semitic campaign culminated in the expulsion of thousands of Jews from Poland. "Yugoslavia" was for both Croats and Serbs a symbol of domination by the other community. The outstanding fact is that no communist state was able to build consensus or to achieve lasting legitimacy, or even to secure the support of the majority community whose sentiments they exploited against minorities.

Communists never enjoyed the support of the majority of the populations over whom they ruled. Their failure to win more than a quarter of the seats to the Russian *duma* in 1905, only enhanced their dislike of democracy. In 1946 the Czech Communist Party won 40 percent of the vote in the free elections in the Czech lands; the Hungarian Communist Party won 17 percent of the popular vote in 1945. Between 1945–8 communist parties in many East European countries, supported by the Soviet Union, destroyed social democratic and peasant parties and established one-party dictatorships.

## Cosmopolitanism and Nationalism

The failure of communism to accommodate or to triumph over nationalism is evident at many levels. Communist parties themselves were never free of nationalism. Even as Leonid Brezhnev hailed the birth of a new Soviet Man in 1967, he deplored the prevalence of ethno-national challenges to the Soviet state. By the late 1980s, many communist leaders had jumped onto the nationalist bandwagon. All communist states which were constituted as "federations"—the USSR, Czechoslovakia, and Yugoslavia—disintegrated in the early 1990s. In the Soviet Union, secessionist nationalism had emerged in only six (Estonia, Latvia, Lithuania, Moldova, Azerbaijan and Armenia) of its fifteen union republics before August 1991, but the Soviet state was unable to accommodate even moderate demands for changes to its political structures which would have altered the balance of power between Moscow and republican capitals. An analogous situation prevailed in Yugoslavia, which dissolved into civil war in 1991. Czechoslovakia broke up by agreement between Vaclav Klaus and Vladimir Meciar. Contrary to the dreams of communists, nationalism did not wither away in any communist state; it contributed to their demise.

### Bibliography

Connor, Walker. 1984. *The National Question in Marxist-Leninist Theory and Strategy*. Princeton, NJ: Princeton University Press.

Dunlop, John B. 1993. *The Rise of Russia and the Fall of the Soviet Empire*. Princeton, NJ: Princeton University Press.

Inder Singh, Anita. 1995. "Managing ethnic diversity through political structures and ideologies," *Nations and Nationalism* 2, 2.

Hajda, Lubomyr and Mark Beissinger (eds.). 1990. *The Nationalities Factor in Soviet Politics and Society*. Boulder, CO: Westview Press.

Pipes, Richard. 1954. *The Formation of the Soviet Union: Communism and Nationalism*. Cambridge, MA: Harvard University Press.

Szporluk, Roman. 1988. *Communism and Nationalism: Karl Marx versus Friedrich List*. New York and London: Oxford University Press.

Anita Inder Singh

# Cosmopolitanism and Nationalism

The term cosmopolitanism derives from a double Greek root: the first component is *kosmos,* meaning world or order, applied by Pythagoras to the universe in order to stress the orderliness of creation. The second one is *polis*, meaning the city or city-state. Thus, in ancient Greece a *kosmopolites* was a citizen of the world (*polités,* meaning citizen). The term came to indicate someone who considered the entire humankind as more meaningful than his or her own city, group, region, or state.

The idea of a universal city and sense of belonging was first formulated by Stoic philosophers, at least since Zeno of Citium (c. 335-262) began to lecture about 300 B.C. The Stoics, like the Cynics, saw man as a rational agent, with universal rights and citizenship in a common *Kosmopolis* (Bracht Branham, and Goulet-Caze 1996). Happiness derived from observing the law of the universe and from the acceptance of personal and human destiny. The Stoic tradition lasted for about 500 years and the latest *stoa* flourished in Rome around the teachings of the former Greek slave Epictetus (55-135) of Hierapolis, of whom the emperor Marcus Aurelius Antoninus (121-180) was a disciple (Hadot 1998).

In Rome, Marcus Tullius Cicero (106-43 B.C.) deepened the Stoics' theory of justice by elevating the *jus naturale* (natural law) into a universal standard against which all particularistic civil laws should be adjudicated. This vision of a universal law was accompanied by a cosmopolitan emphasis on a universal commonwealth of all creatures possessed of reason and speech. Reason and language were central to this definition. Since Cicero was extensively emulated as a model of rhetoric and Latin style, his teaching became extremely influential in the Middle Ages and has been identified as the chain transmitting Stoic cosmopolitanism to the Church (Wood 1988).

However, universalism already permeated Christianity since its very inception. Indeed, nearly all religious and philosophical systems sharply demarcate humans from other living beings on the basis of their monopoly of speech and reason (*logos*). It is this common rationality which makes mankind predestined to share a common fate. Thus, the primary "oppositional" use of cosmopolitanism was to define humankind vis-à-vis other living beings, as well as against all forms of us-them dichotomies dividing humanity.

St. Augustine's (354-430) project of theocratic universalism (in his *City of God—De Civitate Dei*) reflected this vision. The medieval conception of natural law combined an apology for the papacy's temporal power with the defense of an international jurisdiction of the Church. This was framed within a cosmopolitan theory of the human condition which saw the papacy as the ideal candidate for a "world empire."

Notions of the universality of rights run parallel to the Medieval Church-centered international order. During the Crusades (1095 to ca. 1270), "cosmopolitan" appeals went from Gregory IX's (1227-1241) claim to the *imperium mundi* to the Canon Lawyers' matchlessly influential system of international jurisdiction (Muldoon 1998). The climax was reached in 1302, when Boniface VII (c. 1228-1303, pope from 1294) promulgated the bull (edict), *Unam Sanctam*, affirming the complete temporal and spiritual power of the papacy. In this, he declared that "it is absolutely necessary for salvation that every human creature be subject to the Roman Pontiff." In this sentence, we already have in embryo the clash between a sacred form of cosmopolitanism and the princes' sovereignty, from which national sovereignty would later emerge. Yet, as Hans Kohn has observed, "this radicalization of the doctrine of the universalism and supremacy of the Church was voiced at the very moment when its influence on the affairs of this world began to wane" (Kohn 1956: 88). At the time, however, even the critics of the temporal power of the popes wholly subscribed to and shared the same longing for an universal political order.

According to Dante Alighieri (1265-1321), humankind constitutes a single community (*humana universitas est quoddam totum*) whose aim is peaceful coexistence for all individuals. In *De Monarchia* (1310-13), Dante claimed that the "world is our fatherland" over and above specific dissimilarities, including differences of religious creed. Coexistence is not only natural, but imperative, and only through coexistence can man attain this-worldly happiness.

Some centuries later and in an even more secular mood, Gian Battista Vico (1668-1744) also viewed "the history of mankind as a unity following its providential course, subject to the same universal laws" (Kohn 1956: 502; Berlin 1976: 42-52). Of course, elements of cosmopolitanism richly permeated the writings of the major Enlightenment thinkers, who "viewed all races and all continents with the same human interest and concern" (Kohn 1955: 228). Montesquieu (1689-1755) wrote that "if I knew something useful to my fatherland which were prejudicial to Europe, or something which were useful to Europe and prejudicial to mankind, I would consider it a crime" (Kohn 1955: 228).

Enlightenment principles were unmistakably corrupted by the French Revolution which eventually restricted the idea of the "rights of man" to a limited number of individuals, those constituting the "nation." The movement away from cosmopolitanism was consummated in the revolutionary years once the national principle was glorified above everything else. Cosmopolitanism and nationalism shared the same intellectual foundations in the idea of natural rights, but, once applied to real life, their interests increasingly and inevitably diverged. For instance, Maximilien Robespierre (1758-94) interpreted cosmopolitan ideas about the universal rights of man quite selectively, emphasizing them only when they coincided with his view of the national interest (Rapport 1996). Finally, it was the invocation of war as an external pretext which forevermore replaced cosmopolitanism with chauvinistic (rather than liberal) nationalism. Imaginary threats of foreign conspiracies had been used in the past, but war itself created the conditions for turning cosmopolitan principles on their head and transforming them into xenophobic axioms. From then onwards, war "ensured that the more narrowly defined national interests...won over the universal application of the rights of man" (Rapport 1996: 333).

A similar route was followed by other European nationalist movements, for instance in Italy: "Through the French Revolution [Italian intellectuals] followed the road from a rational cosmopolitanism to a liberal nationalism: the *Risorgimento* fused the longing for human happiness and for the resurrection of ancient greatness into a modern nationalism" (Kohn 1956: 509). Giuseppe Mazzini (1805-1872) best exemplified this fusion of universal, romantic, modernist, and nationalist values. Yet, in less than half a century, what initially was an elitist liberal nationalism turned into a mass creed of radical intolerance.

Perhaps the country where the complex and peculiar relationship between cosmopolitanism and nationalism can better be observed is Germany. Liah Greenfeld's interesting point is that nationalism was a latecomer in Germany and that German intellectuals, followers of the *Aufklärung* (German Enlightenment) were cosmopolitan and anti-nationalist (or at least eminently indifferent to nationalism). When, as a consequence of the Napoleonic invasion (1806), nationalism first arose in Germany, the shift was sudden, radical and abrupt (Greenfeld 1992: 310-14 and 354-58). It was a leap forward from universal ideals to an exasperated mood which already contained the seeds of its xenophobic development. In the wake of war, the intelligentsia and the *Bildungsbürgertum* (the 100,000 strong "educated class" of university-trained commoners, often unemployed, and their families) suddenly moved from neo-classicism to romanticism (Greenfeld 1992: 296), and from the liberal cosmopolitanism of, say, Wilhelm von Humboldt (1765-1835) to the nationalist jacobinism of Johann Gottlieb Fichte (1762-1814)—the latter a fervent admirer of the French Revolution in his youth (Meinecke 1970).

The German philosopher who most unequivocally expressed a longing for cosmopolitanism would seem to be Immanuel Kant (1724-1804). Yet, Kant's insistence on a world government parallels his stress on individual self-determination, and this has led some scholars, such as ELIE KEDOURIE, to describe him, albeit quite controversially, as one of the inspiring lights of nationalism. Kant pledged for the abolition of national jurisdictions and their replacement by a universally applicable law. His project of "perpetual peace" was to be achieved under the auspices of an international government. Thus, it may come as a surprise to find some deeply rooted prejudices behind the sincere cosmopolitan creed of

many Enlightenment philosophers and their followers. For instance, Kant himself claimed that "the Negroes can become disciplined and cultured, but never civilized," and that "the Whites are the only ones who will always strive towards perfection." The private correspondence of Marx and, particularly, Engels is punctuated by similar statements addressed to variously despised nations, groups, and races (Connor 1984, Nimni 1993). Indeed, in the century of expanding European colonial empires (of which the independence movements in the Americas were but a phase), assumptions of racial superiority were the norm, rather than the exception.

The rise of internationalism as a distinctive concept has been ascribed to the emergence of the working class as an historical actor (Ishay 1995). In the nineteenth century, the working class was torn between national identification and internationalism. The first usage of the term "internationalist" comes from the members of the First International (International Association of Workingmen, founded in 1864 in London under the guidance of Karl Marx), while the idea of an "international solidarity among the proletarians of the world" dates back at least to Marx's and Engels's *Communist Manifesto* (1848), in which they asserted that "the working man has no fatherland" (Marx 1998; Connor 1984). Socialist illusions crumbled in 1914, when working-class organizations proved unable to prevent war and sided instead with their governments and their respective "nation-states"—thereupon capitulating to the nationalist imperative.

The study of the relationship between nationalism and cosmopolitanism raises more questions than it answers, because both concepts lend themselves to contradictory interpretations, lacking empirical—indeed, universal—clarity. Are nationalism and cosmopolitanism deeply opposed and inconsistent? Or, rather, are they mutually compatible? These questions are pointless if we employ the two terms too loosely. Unfortunately, they are often utilized as either eulogies or pejoratives, without specifying their contextual meanings. For instance, nationalists have often used the term "cosmopolitan" as an invective, while "cosmopolitans" have correspondingly abused and distorted the term nationalism. As personal ennoblement, cosmopolitanism implies an emphasis on sophistication, openness to other ideas and cultures, acquaintance with the ways of the world. As affront and offense, it implies lack of loyalty and aristocratic decadence. In a more neutral usage, a cosmopolitan is someone who regards the whole world as his/her native homeland. Ideally, a citizen of the world should be exempt from national prejudices.

Nationalists have often viewed cosmopolitan ideas with deep suspicion. Ernest Gellner mentions that nationalists have been hostile "not merely to rival cultures, but also, and perhaps with special venom, to bloodless cosmopolitanism, probably in part because they perceived it an ally of political centralism" (Gellner 1994: 112).

The multifaceted character of nationalism as a modern Janus makes it a double-edged ideology adaptable to multiple, often contrasting, purposes. One of nationalism's inherent dilemmas is the contrast between traditionalist and modernist trends in its midst. A parallel dilemma is nationalism's split between isolationists and cosmopolitans, which makes cosmopolitanism a potential ally of nationalism. A major difference is that cosmopolitanism is a personally held attitude rather than a political movement with a precisely framed programme, while nationalism is usually both. This may make their relationship occasionally congruous, even compatible. Indeed, Will Kymlicka argues that there is no meaningful opposition between "liberal" nationalism and cosmopolitanism (Kymlicka 1999). Citing the examples of Catalonia, Quebec, and Flanders, Kymlicka observes that many contemporary nationalists have also been liberal reformers. Their fight for self-government includes a fight to reform society in a liberal direction (Conversi 1997). However, it is important to recall that this may hold true today, but in the past it has often not been the case—and that even today nationalism is not always liberal, as Kymlicka recognizes. Both nationalism and cosmopolitanism refer to political power (the universal monarch, or the pope against the local prince), as well as to shared values (universal values and customs against specific or localized ones). But, since between power and values stands the law, the two terms also refer to different concepts of jurisdiction (universal as opposed to national or local jurisdictions).

Enlightenment thinkers not only espoused a deep appreciation of human diversity, but also, on occasions, seemed to conflate cosmopolitan and pro-nationalist attitudes. Thus, in 1778 Anne-Robert-Jacques Turgot (1727-1791) "protested against the domination of one people by another and maintained that a man oppressed by an unjust law could not be regarded as free" (Kohn 1956: 228-9). Was this an implicit advocacy of the principle of self-determination? Was his resistance to *etatist* oppression an appeal to the oppressed to constitute their own state(s)? Most likely it was not; yet, Turgot's claims can be interpreted otherwise and seen as perfectly compatible with aspirations for national independence. Other Enlightenment philosophers, from Rousseau to Voltaire, from Montesquieu to Diderot and Condorcet, have all made pronouncements that can eventually provide fuel for the nationalist fire. By the same token, it would be improper to infer that JOHANN GOTTFRIED HERDER (1744-1803) was a nationalist, even though his intuitions "laid the ideological foundation of nationalist doctrine" (Barnard 1965: 62). Herder can well be seen as a universalist preaching the rights of all human groups to exist, reproduce their culture and manage their own affairs. Herder's view is more a hymn to human creativity than cold reason.

Like nationalism, cosmopolitanism has to be seen in opposition to something else. Kymlicka rightly observes that "in the past, cosmopolitanism was a reaction against the privileging of the local city, class or religious sect. But in today's world, cosmopolitanism is almost always defined in contrast to nationalism" (Kymlicka 1999). Cosmopolitanism can also be opposed to localism, but in a complementary, more neutral, rather than judgmental, sense. For instance, Hannerz has observed that cosmopolitans still depend on the locals in order to be able to conceive themselves as cosmopolitans—and to be recognized as such (Hannerz 1990). Hence, cosmopolitanism can, at one and the same time ally itself with, and be opposed to, both localism and nationalism. Conversely, nationalism can find valid allies in both cosmopolitanism and localism.

One important critique of cosmopolitanism from the point of view of liberal nationalism has been the accusation that cosmopolitanism is a dis-

## Cosmopolitanism and Nationalism

guised tool for imperial aggrandizement and global oppression. According to this view, the function of cosmopolitanism has been that of providing imperial elites (from Alexander to the Roman Empire, from the popes to the expanding colonial powers and to present-day neo-colonial imperialism) with an ideological armor to mask their expansionist aims and other grand designs. For example, enthusiasm for cosmopolitanism has been associated with the expansion of the Roman empire and Rome's transformation from a city-state into an ever-conquering machine. Likewise, the very birth and spread of Stoicism has been described as unimaginable without Alexander the Great's (356-323 B.C.) parallel drive to rack up a "world empire"—quite a non-Greek endeavour (Kohn 1956: 12).

On the other hand, cosmopolitanism may involve the imposition of particularistic values, habits, language and norms upon the entire *oecumene* (inhabited earth). Indeed, cosmopolitanism has often been equated with Westernization. French cosmopolitanism of the age of the Enlightenment is a good example; for it was mostly the perception of a small portion of Parisian elites who, despite their sincere efforts to view with the eyes of the entire world, were still deeply imbued with French aristocratic culture. Thus, Condorcet's stress on the need for a universal language ended up with a reassertion of French as the ideal candidate for such a task (Kymlicka 1999). Its paradoxical corollary can be synthesized in an old Breton witticism: "if we really need a world language, well, so be it, but let it be Breton !" The Russian project to construct a new "Soviet man" also exploited this spirit.

The outright rejection of cosmopolitanism entails its own problems: the risk of total relativism and the denial of even the possibility of comprehension between mutually unintelligible communities. This attitude denies *au fond* the common humanity of mankind, and it is precisely this attitude which we find among illiberal nationalists. They have often denied the humanity of a specific target group.

Since cosmopolitanism arises out of a positive assessment of humanity as a whole, the doctrine of universal human rights constitutes its vital core. From this perspective, neither nationalism nor localism are to be considered the cosmopolitan's main antagonists. Rather, the adversary *par excellence* is state sovereignty. Cosmopolitanism relates to those norms, values and principles which are applicable throughout the entire *oecumene*. Hence, such norms necessarily infringe upon state sovereignty—which is the building block of international relations. Basic principles such as "non-intervention" are normally advocated by states wishing to be sheltered from all forms of criticism. Likewise, state sovereignty is seen as being inherently adverse to the ideas of both a world decision-making body (not necessarily a world government) and universal human rights. In this picture, nationalism plays a relatively minor role, since it is largely unthinkable outside the modern interstate system.

Another antagonist of cosmopolitanism is moral relativism. This is the view that when two sets of values clash, we should find an "equidistance." Moral relativism assumes that all views should be taken equally into account. Extreme forms of moral relativism would bring us to the conclusion that victims and aggressors are to be treated equally and, even more extremely, that all crimes are to be judged according to particularistic criteria, hence that no crime is such for the entire humanity. For the sake of precision, moral relativism should be distinguished from cultural relativism. Whereas moral relativism is the claim that there is no superior moral judgement and human beings should not adhere to the same values, cultural relativism is the claim that there is no superior culture and all cultures should be treated equally. Universal values—normally a selection of them—may be embraced, while at the same time propounding that each culture has the right to survive and none is intrinsically superior to any other. Moral relativism reflects instead a belief in the non-universality of human values, including human rights. In other words, cultural relativism does not inexorably result in moral relativism.

The cosmopolitan idea is about pacifying mankind through the development of a strong sense of moral obligation to human beings everywhere. But adherence to such a program implies a clear understanding of moral priorities. Hence, the most crucial question is: what really are these universal human values? Or, what are precisely those values which should be more strongly buttressed? Apparently there is no agreement on that. However, there are some basic human rights and values which transcend distinctions between different value systems. Genocide, for example, is a universally execrated crime against humanity. Yet, the fin-de-siécle cases of Rwanda, Bosnia, East Timor, Tibet, and several other instances of mass killings have shown that even the most basic universal principles can not be easily implemented in the age of globalization.

Cosmopolitan thinkers crave for a world organization in which universal values are protected and somehow enforced (Zolo 1997). The idea of a supra-national (i.e., supra-state) organization is not only deeply related to the prevalence of universal moral principles, but also to each state's acceptance of, and commitment to, these principles. Furthermore, it can be argued that a convincing cosmopolitan agenda can only be pursued by encompassing the human variety of local, national and universal ideals, making them compatible, rather than competitive (or mutually exclusive). And, if we accept that the common goal of humanity is peaceful coexistence (rather than destructive processes such as hegemony, obliteration or assimilation), then cosmopolitanism must be incompatible with homogenization and, indeed, with contemporary globalization.

## Bibliography

Barnard, F.M. 1965. *Herder's Social and Political Thought: From Enlightenment to Nationalism*. Oxford: Clarendon Press.

Benner, Erica. 1995. *Really Existing Nationalisms: A Post-Communist View from Marx and Engels*. Oxford: Clarendon Press/ Oxford University Press.

Berlin, Sir Isaiah. 1976. *Vico and Herder: Two Studies in the History of Ideas*. London: Hogarth Press.

Bracht Branham R. and Goulet-Caze, Marie-Odile (eds.) 1996. *The Cynics: The Cynic Movement in Antiquity and its Legacy*. Berkeley: University of California Press.

Connor, Walker. 1984. *The National Question in Marxist-Leninist Theory and Strategy*. Princeton, NJ: Princeton University Press.

Conversi, Daniele. 1997. *The Basques, the Catalans, and Spain: Alternative Routes to Nationalist Mobilization*. London: Hurst/ Reno: University of Nevada Press.

Gellner, Ernest. 1994. *Conditions of Liberty: Civil Society and Its Rivals*. New York: Allen Lane/Penguin Press.

Greenfeld, Liah. 1992. *Nationalism: Five Roads to Modernity*. Cambridge, MA: Harvard University Press.

Hadot, Pierre. 1998. *The Inner Citadel: The Meditations of Marcus Aurelius*. Cambridge, MA: Harvard University Press.

Hannerz, Ulf. 1990. "Cosmopolitans and locals in world culture," in Mike Featherstone (ed.), *Global Culture: Nationalism, Globalization, and Modernity*. London/ Newbury Park, CA: Sage Publications.

Ishay, Micheline. 1995. *Internationalism and its Betrayal*. Minneapolis: University of Minnesota Press.

Kedourie, Elie. 1993 (1960). *Nationalism*. London: Hutchinson.

Kohn, Hans. 1956 (1944). *The Idea of Nationalism: A Study in its Origins and Background*. New York: Macmillan.

Kohn, Hans. 1955. *Nationalism: Its Meaning and History*. Princeton, NJ: Van Nostrand.

Kymlicka, Will. 1999. "From Enlightenment cosmopolitanism to liberal nationalism," in Steven Lukes (ed.), *The Enlightenment: Then and Now*. London: Verso.

Marx, Karl. 1998. *The Communist Manifesto*. London: Verso.

Meinecke, Friedrich. 1970 (1907). *Cosmopolitanism and the National State*. Princeton, NJ: Princeton University Press.

Muldoon, James. 1998. *Canon Law, World Order, and the Expansion of Europe*. Aldershot/ Brookfield: Ashgate.

Nimni, Ephraim. 1993. *Marxism and Nationalism: Theoretical Origins of the Political Crisis*. London: Pluto Press.

Rapport, Mike. 1996. "Robespierre and the Universal Rights of Man, 1789—1794," *French History* 10, 3: 303-333.

Smith, Anthony D. 1976. "Neo-classicist and romantic elements in the emergence of nationalist conceptions," in Anthony D. Smith (ed.), *Nationalist Movements*. London: Macmillan.

Wood, Neal. 1988. *Cicero's Social and Political Thought*. Berkeley: University of California Press.

Zolo, Danilo. 1997. *Cosmopolis: Prospects for World Government*. Cambridge: Polity Press.

Daniele Conversi

# Cultural Nationalism

"Cultural nationalism" has as its primary concern the regeneration of the nation as a distinctive moral community. It is based on an organic conception, according to which the nation is a natural entity with unique cultural characteristics and homelands, so that to realize their humanity, its members must actively belong to their nation by participating in its distinctive way of life. Although JOHANN GOTTFRIED HERDER (1744–1803) is often cited as the intellectual founder of cultural nationalism, he cannot be regarded as a nationalist in any simple sense. It is safer to say that cultural nationalism can be seen as one manifestation of the emerging European romantic movement which propounded a novel historicist conception of the cosmos, nature and society, a cult of authenticity, and a restoration of vernacular cultures.

Scholars have tended to be dismissive about cultural nationalism which has often been equated with linguistic nationalism, and regarded as a surrogate statist nationalism, and as a regressive and transient movement, destined to fade away with full industrialization. More recently, there has been something of a reevaluation of the moral and symbolic dimension of cultural nationalism, which recognizes its distinctive communitarian ethos and politics, its socially innovative qualities, and its embeddedness in the modern world (Hutchinson 1987; Chatterjee 1993).

## Cultural Nationalism and Language

The idea that cultural nationalism as essentially a linguistic movement is pervasive in nationalist scholarship. ELIE KEDOURIE among many others traces this back to Herder, for whom allegedly language expressed the inner consciousness of the nation, its distinctive ethos, and continuous identity in history. The primary duty of nationalists was to defend the national language against foreign adulteration, otherwise moral degeneration would follow.

Cultural nationalism is much broader than this, and it is more true to say that it is through history that nationalists seek to rediscover the distinctive character of the nation. Language is only one of many symbols invoked as an incarnation of the collective experience of the nation. Even when it is the dominant symbol, it is never cited alone. Herder himself referred not just to language, but also to folk songs, dances and educational institutions. Cultural nationalists always employ multiple symbols and seek to make them consistent with each other with the aim of reviving the collective personality of the nation (its name, a sense of its unique origins, history, culture, homeland, and distinctive social and political institutions), and differentiating it from others. The key figures of cultural nationalists are historians, writers, painters, composers, folklorists as well as philologists. In Central and Eastern Europe where different ethnic populations are intermingled, this process of internal and external definition continues to have explosive consequences, giving rise to violent conflict.

## Cultural Nationalism and Moral Regeneration

It is often assumed that the underlying drive of nationalism is political, the ultimate realization of which is a sovereign state, and that the cultural projects of nationalists are only a means towards this end. Elie Kedourie (1960), for example, agrees that there have been two distinct varieties of nationalism: a voluntarist and republican form, which conceives of the nation as a body of individuals who have come together to decide on a form of government, and an organic version that perceives the nation as a natural solidarity with inherent unique cultural characteristics. But he argues that in practice the two versions converge in a statist doctrine that holds that each nation is culturally unique and must have a protective state of its own.

It is often difficult to distinguish between the two forms of nationalism since many individuals may adhere to both, and cultural institutions have acted as a cover for political revolutionaries as in the early nineteenth-century Habsburg Empire, where constitutional politics was severely restricted. Nonetheless, there are important differences between the "idea-worlds" of cultural and political nationalists, and they tend to give rise to the distinctive types of movements.

Political nationalists tend to define human beings in terms of their rationality which gives them the capacity to be self-governing. The social realization of this vision is of an independent and representative state founded on the consent of its members which will guarantee equal citizenship rights to all and which will promote continuous progress. Political nationalists tend to form legal-rational institutions which develop into centralized parties, and these parties seek to mobilize against the existing state as many groups as possible round a single objective: the achievement of a genuine nation-state. By contrast, for cultural nationalists the basis of the national solidarity is not reason but a passionate identification with its unique life-force. In this organic conception, the nation is not a construction of rational self-interest. It is rather a quasi-natural institution like the family which is composed of strongly differentiated individuals and groups, united by a love of its common historical achievements and an active participation in its way of life.

Although cultural nationalists may advocate an independent state, the basis of the nation is the community—the expression of its unique creative force which binds individuals to each other and gives them individual and collective purpose. What triggers them into collective action is evidence of social demoralization and conflict which they believe results from a loss of continuity with the national heritage and a subsequent adoption of foreign values. Forming historical and cultural institutions, they preach a moral regeneration of the national community by returning to the ideals of its ancient past. Invocations of the name of the nation, pilgrimages to "sacred" places, commemorations of heroes, the revival of the national language, these are just some of the rites by which cultural nationalism seeks to unite and mobilize its adherents into a community of sacrifice without a loss of their own individuality. Cultural nationalism then is an educational movement directed to inner reform. Because a national way of life is a spontaneous outgrowth of different individuals and groups, it cannot be constructed like a state from above. Cultural nationalist movements are, therefore, at least initially, decentralized movements which seek to build from below a common sense of values while respecting the regional and other diversities of the nation.

Such movements are usually small in size and scale, but at various times they may appeal to a rising generation of political leaders who feel excluded from positions of power and status by existing leaders and organizations. These activists, often journalists, then seek to broaden the cultural into a broader grassroots sociopolitical revival movement, by appealing to other excluded groups. They organize clusters of historical and language societies, dramatic groups, choral societies, publishing centres, agricultural co-operatives, credit societies, and political journals and parties to form a counter-culture to the dominant value system. In many countries such "counter-cultures" have had significant impact, socializing a dedicated elite of national activists who may mobilize should there be a systemic crisis. In Ireland the Gaelic revival furnished the activists who led the 1916 rebellion and the subsequent war of independence against Britain, and who after independence formed the governing class of the Irish nation-state.

### Cultural Nationalists as Moral Innovators

Cultural nationalism has been dismissed as a reactionary phenomenon which either seeks to block or which is irrelevant to modernization. In HANS KOHN's West/East typology of nationalism, there are two forms of nationalism—political and rational, and cultural and mystical—and the emergence of one or other as dominant is determined by the level of development of the community. Cultural nationalism, according to Kohn, arose first among the intellectuals of Central and Eastern Europe and Asia as a defensive and compensatory response to the prestige of the political nations of Western Europe. Aware of the social and economic backwardness of their largely agrarian peasant-based societies compared with the rationalist urban middle class societies of the West, cultural nationalists rejected the rationalist citizenship models of the latter in order to celebrate an ideal and ancient nation with a special mission founded on the superior organic bonds between peasant, land, religion, and community. These historico-cultural revivals nurtured the development of a patriotic public opinion, but, Kohn maintains, the

## Cultural Nationalism

revival they seek is of the nation as an archaic folk society.

This West/East dichotomy has been followed by recent "post-colonial" historians such as Partha Chatterjee (1993). But Kohn neglects the modernizing aspects of cultural nationalism, and the reformist nature of its core constituencies, and he fails to observe that cultural nationalism is also present in "advanced" countries, for example in England in the late nineteenth century. Its intellectuals are generally highly educated individuals, and may be drawn from many social strata. The golden age they evoke (for Indians, the founding Aryan civilization) is generally a time when the nation was a dynamic and integrated high culture in active contact with major world centres, and this golden age is used as a critique of a decaying tradition. Certainly, cultural nationalism has allied with neo-traditionalist religious forces to insulate the nation from foreign influences. But its underlying thrust is dynamic, to reform tradition and to articulate options by which modernization should be pursued.

Cultural nationalists act as moral innovators in providing new directions at times of social crisis, generated by the disruptive impact of modernization, when societies may be polarized between traditionalists and modernists (sometimes known as Westernizers). The golden age is used to transform the accepted meanings of tradition and modernity, and thereby persuade their adherents to ally in a common national project. Cultural nationalists seek to convert traditionalists to a version of modernization by arguing that the nation was in its heyday a dynamic civilization confidently exchanging ideas and technologies with other cultures. To modernists who uncritically admired foreign models, cultural nationalists argue that the greatest embodiment of a successful modernity was to be found in the golden age of their nation, which had instructed the then backward "West."

Such cultural nationalisms find their core constituency among religious and social reformers (e.g., the Grundtvig "meeting movement" of Lutheran peasant intellectuals in Denmark, the Bernacacina movement of Slovak lower clergy in the early nineteenth century, the Arya Samaj in late nineteenth-century India), and a young urban intelligentsia, who translate the cultural goals into a political self-help program and contribute their political drive, organizational skills and communicative abilities. The revivalism of folk cultures goes hand in hand with the construction of new standard languages as the medium of modern scientific discourses and schools of literature, and campaigns for an integrated national economy. In this spirit the leading organizations of nineteenth century Ukrainian and Latvian revivalism, the Shevchenko Scientific Society and the Riga Latvian Association, in constructing a modern vernacular literary and scientific culture out of a largely illiterate oral culture, have promoted a vigorous lay self-help movement among the peasantry, including an explosive expansion of libraries, agricultural and credit co-operatives, newspapers, and support for (in the Ukrainian case) a native university at Lemberg.

### Cultural Nationalism as a Recurring Movement

Finally, cultural nationalism has been dismissed as a transient force, whose romantic concerns about identity will fade away in favor of pragmatic questions about economic social progress as "rationalization" proceeds. Kosaku Yoshino, however, has shown how in the case of contemporary Japan cultural nationalist assumptions about Japanese uniqueness have become routinized to be consumed (often unselfconsciously) by different groups seeking to negotiate the problems of communication in an increasingly global environment. Even more, cultural nationalism has not just become routinized; it preserves its dynamic qualities as the current resurgence of cultural nationalist movements over much of the globe testifies in both "metropolitan" and "peripheral" political communities. Indeed, there is in many settings an alternating relationship between communitarian and legal-rational modes of politics in pre-independence settings.

After independence, although the state acts as the protector of the nation in a world of competing states, states are often denationalizing forces when in the pursuit of economic and social efficiency, they adopt the successful strategies of their rivals, intervening to restructure social institutions. Indeed, their very bureaucratic efficiency has produced an anomie that may lead to a search for roots in a restored national community, perhaps in alliance with a religious revivalism. For this reason, it is likely that cultural nationalism is a recurring force in the modern world, emerging at times of disillusion with statist and bureaucratic modes of development in favor of grassroots revitalization.

## Bibliography

Berlin, Isaiah. 1976. *Vico and Herder*. London: Hogarth Press.

Chatterjee, Partha. 1993. *The Nation and its Fragments*. Princeton, NJ: Princeton University Press.

Hroch, Miroslav. 1985. *Social Preconditions of National Revivals in Europe*. Cambridge: Cambridge University Press.

Hutchinson, John. 1987. *The Dynamics of Cultural Nationalism: The Gaelic Revival and the Creation of the Irish Nation*. London: Allen and Unwin.

Kedourie, Elie. 1960. *Nationalism*. London: Hutchinson.

Kohn, Hans. 1946. *The Idea of Nationalism*. New York: Macmillan.

Nairn, Tom. 1977. *The Break-up of Britain: Crisis and Neo-nationalism*. London: New Left Books.

Newman, Gerald. 1987. *The Rise of English Nationalism: A Cultural History, 1748–1930*. London: Weidenfeld and Nicolson.

Smith, Anthony D. 1986. *The Ethnic Origins of Nations*. Oxford: Blackwell.

Yoshino, Kosaku. 1992. *Cultural Nationalism in Contemporary Japan*. London: Routledge.

John Hutchinson

# D

## Decolonization

One of the momentous transformations of the postwar world was the final decline and fall of colonial empires, whose lineages trace back to the fifteenth century. The long cycle of European expansion which began with the establishment of Portuguese garrisons on the North African shore in 1415, led to the occupation of the entire Western hemisphere, most of South and Southeast Asia, Australasia and Oceania, then in a final paroxysm of imperial expansion the European partition of the African continent in the late nineteenth century. In the process, the political, cultural, economic, and religious geography of these vast regions was largely reconfigured.

The tides of empire first began to recede with the American Declaration of Independence in 1776, with much of Latin America following in the first part of the nineteenth century. At this early stage, the battle for decolonization was conducted by European settler populations. Elsewhere, however, empires seemed securely in place until World War I.

Anti-colonial nationalism began to appear as a significant force by that time in the Arab world, India, and Southeast Asia. World War II, however, sealed the fate and accelerated the decline of the colonial system. Dutch, French, American, and some British Southeast Asian colonial territories were under Japanese occupation for several years. Belgium, Netherlands, and France experienced humiliating German occupation at home, and Italy forfeited its colonies by fighting on the losing side. The mystique of the invincibility of the major colonial powers was thoroughly shattered.

Following World War II, the colonial order was on the defensive everywhere. Whereas the prewar international system was dominated by the colonial powers, especially Britain and France, the postwar world saw the emergence of a bipolar global order dominated by the United States and the Soviet Union; for different reasons, both superpowers favored an end to the colonial system. As the number of independent states in Asia and the Arab world increased rapidly, new voices spoke with growing force in the international forums demanding rapid liberation of the remaining colonized territories. The United Nations (U.N.), as the primary superstructure within which international norms were fashioned, became an important force in support of accelerated decolonization. Thus, the international system, which before 1945 regarded colonial empires as part of the natural order, became increasingly hostile to their perpetuation.

Another potent factor accelerating the dissolution of colonial empires was the appearance of armed guerrilla struggle as a possible strategic choice. First in Indochina and the Dutch East Indies, then in Algeria, subsequently in the Portuguese African colonies, Rhodesia and Namibia, insurgent armies demonstrated that independence could be achieved by protracted combat if the colonial adversary was unyielding. New doctrines of guerrilla warfare, associated with the Chinese and Vietnamese revolutions, defined strategies of prolonged struggle carried out from rural bases. Anti-colonial liberation movements could now count upon access to outside military supply, sanctuary in neighbouring independent countries, and deepening support from international public opinion. Outright military victory was not necessary, only the capacity to sustain insurgent action until the costs of an unending and fruitless military campaign became politically and economically unsustainable for the colonial occupant. Thus, the conviction took hold on all sides that liberation of colonial territories was an irresistible historical trend.

Anti-colonial nationalism provided a powerful doctrine around which popular support could be mobilized. The idea of nationalism which had taken form in late eighteenth-century Europe, was reinterpreted in its adoption. In the original European version, the "nation" was either a state claiming the collective attachment and loyalty of its citizenry, or an ethnocultural community asserting the right to define its own future. In the colonial territories, what defined the "people" was not necessarily shared culture or historical statehood, but rather the common bondage of alien rule.

Intimately joined to the idea of nationalism was the doctrine of self-determination, originating in the nineteenth century. A "people" possessed a sacred right to determine their own destiny. In the colonial empires the population carrying this right were the subjects within a particular colonial territory, however culturally diverse they might be. Thus, nationalism, in its anti-colonial usage was a largely territorial doctrine.

Its resonance was no less powerful among the subjugated. The litany of grievances evoked by colonial occupation was long, and woven into the message of nationalism: political oppression and exclusion; exorbitant economic benefits accruing to the colonial private sector; pervasive racism and cultural arrogance intrinsic to alien rule. Also central to the doctrine of anti-colonial nationalism was a promise of future prosperity; sweeping away colonial privilege, choosing a development strategy dictated solely by the interests of the new nation unlocked the keys to the kingdom of modernity. The veneer of alien culture imposed by the colonizer could be dissolved in favor of a recovered indigenous heritage.

Anti-colonial nationalism had somewhat different themes in the various regions where its message spread. The most venerable nationalist movements arose in Asia, especially India, where the Indian National Congress dated from 1885. Although the extraordinary diversity of India made impossible any claim that "Indians" were a single people, in the thoughts and writings of such nationalist heroes as Mahatma Gandhi and Jawaharlal Nehru, a remarkably sophisticated historical and cultural justification for Indian nationalism is found. In countries such as Myanmar (Burma) or Vietnam, anti-colonial nationalism could lay claim to the submerged rights of an historical state.

In the Caribbean, the carriers of anti-colonial nationalism were the descendants of slaves or indentured labor imported from Africa or South Asia. Thus, anti-colonialism could make no claim to cultural authenticity or historic restoration, but was rather formulated in terms of an inherent right to majority rule. A significant subtheme was the reaction to the racism of the colonial system, in the assertion of a redemptive solidarity of the black world.

In the Arab world and Africa, anti-colonial nationalism was at once territorial and pan-Arab or pan-African. For the eighteen nations of primarily Arab heritage, the dream of a vast political entity founded on a linguistic, cultural and (for most) religious zone stretching from Mauritania to Oman is as inspiring as it is elusive. Most of the Arab world experienced colonial subjugation, and nearly all the state boundaries were drawn by imperial powers. Abiding grievances over the Palestine question are also laid at the door of imperialism; thus, pan-Arab nationalism has an important anti-colonial component. Yet, in the end, the territorial units largely issuing from imperial partition prove amazingly resilient, and various experiments at even partial pan-Arabism through unification of some states, such as the short-lived United Arab Republic of Egypt and Syria, have invariably failed.

In the African case, the idea of Pan-Africanism extends back nearly a century; the first pan-African conference took place in 1900, with essentially Caribbean participation. Until 1958, denunciation of the arbitrary frontiers imposed by colonialism was standard fare at pan-African assemblies. The actual battle for independence, however, could only be conducted effectively against the specific colonial power within the particular geographic confines of a given territory issuing from the colonial partition. Thus, the nationalist struggle for African independence, at the hour of its triumph, became thoroughly territorialized. Once independent, new states invested considerable energies in promoting amongst their citizenry the concept that a destiny of nationhood summoned.

Thus, the doctrine of nationalism was essentially appropriated by the state system in the Arab and African worlds. These two visions of vast domains of possible unification overlapped across

## Diaspora Nationalism

the northern tier of Africa, geographically African but predominantly arabophone. The pan-African dream contained an underlying ambiguity as to its ultimate basis: a racial solidarity linking sub-Saharan Africa and the African diaspora in the Americas, or a continental destiny of geographic unification. Both pan-Arabism and pan-Africanism find contemporary structural expression in organizations which are devoted to interstate cooperation, the Arab League, and the Organization of African Unity.

Thus, the final legacy of decolonization is a vastly enlarged world state system, now numbering over 180 sovereign units, as measured by United Nations membership. The international legal doctrine of sovereign equality postulates them as equals, therefore each entitled to one vote in such world forums as the U.N. General Assembly. Sovereign equality does not confer equivalent weight or influence to the many small and impoverished states which have joined the global system of interstate relations, but the end of empire has nonetheless transformed the parameters of the international system.

Membership in a world system of nation-states connotes a vocation of "nation-building" for new states. The mere territorial juxtaposition of a culturally diverse citizenry does not naturally translate anti-colonial solidarity into a post-colonial allegiance (see also POST-COLONIALISM) of formerly subjugated populations to the new state, however indispensable the discourse of nationhood may seem as text of state legitimation. Herein lies one of the central challenges of the world beyond decolonization, and the source of internal conflicts which afflict a significant number of new states: how statecraft may be practiced, and the idea of nationalism may be interpreted, to assure inclusion of all ethnic, religious and racial components of the citizenry, and to accommodate their cultural diversity.

### Bibliography

Bethell, Leslie (ed.). 1984. *Colonial Latin America: The Cambridge History of Latin America*, vol. 2. Cambridge: Cambridge University Press.

Dominguez, Jorge I. 1980. *Insurrection or Loyalty: The Breakdown of the Spanish Empire*. Cambridge, MA: Harvard University Press.

Emerson, Rupert. 1960. *From Empire to Nation: The Rise to Self-Assertion of Asian and African Peoples*. Cambridge, MA: Harvard University Press.

Fanon, Frantz. 1965. *The Wretched of the Earth*. London: MacGibbon and Kee.

Gann, L.H. and Peter Duignan (eds.). 1970-1975. *Colonialism in Africa 1870-1960*. 5 vols. Cambridge: Cambridge University Press.

Gifford, Prosser and Wm. Roger Louis. 1988. *Decolonization and African Independence: The Transfers of Power, 1960-1980*. New Haven, CT: Yale University Press.

Nehru, Jawaharlal. 1946. *The Discovery of India*. New York: Meridian Books.

Young, Crawford. 1994. *The African Colonial State in Comparative Perspective*. New Haven, CT: Yale University Press.

Crawford Young

# Diaspora Nationalism

By "diaspora nationalism" we refer to the nationalism within ethnic groups living (voluntarily or involuntarily) in host countries, maintaining attitudes of loyalty and patriotism towards their original home countries and sometimes organizing themselves to this effect. Nationalist attachment to the home country is most frequently based on collective memory and is expressed by a sense of commonality of *ethnie* and culture, in the broadest sense. The main shared ingredients in the discourse of diaspora ethnic nationalism are language, history, and religion. Diaspora studies and other publications uncover facts or invent myths about a past and present common language, historical exploits, literary works, archaeological remains, art, music, and folklore. Past commonality in these and other areas serves as an argument for present and future national solidarity. Of these, a linguistic culture has increasingly become the chief bond between diaspora and home country. Identification with the home country has often created tensions between the diaspora and the host country's majority population which, in extreme cases, has accused the diaspora of disloyalty.

When Lord Acton wrote, in his *Essays in the Liberal Interpretation of History*, that "exile is the nursery of nationality," he might just as well have said "nationalism." Numerous nationalist ideologies were created and their organization initiated, at least in part, in the diaspora. Probably these were able to develop more freely in an independent atmosphere, unhampered by autocratic government or colonial rule; moreover, older brands of nationalism in the United States or Western Europe have often provided models for newer ones. Sun Yat-sen developed his philosophy of nationalism during his years in the United States, while Mahatma Gandhi developed his during his studies in England and his sojourn among his compatriots in South Africa. For both, the ambiance in Imperial China and British-governed India, respectively, was hardly conducive to nationalist activities.

A characteristic example of this process is the multiethnic, multilingual, and multireligious Ottoman Empire. Many of the nationalist ideologies and movements of its people were initiated, or at least developed, outside its territories. This occurred mostly during the last quarter of the nineteenth century and the early years of the twentieth, under the absolute rule of Sultan Abdulhamid II, who strove to quash any incipient nationalism which, as a fissiparous phenomenon, could endanger the integrity of his empire. As a result, organisations championing the nationalist hopes of various peoples within the empire were set up among diasporas abroad.

Jewish nationalism was born in the late nineteenth-century diaspora (*golah*) in Eastern Europe, with the intention of emigrating to Palestine (then under Ottoman rule), settle there and "return to work the land." Zionists in Western Europe, led by Theodor Herzl, searched for a political solution, a "charter" for a Jewish entity in Palestine. The subsequent fusion between the two trends shaped a nationalist diaspora movement for restoration of the ancestral home; Zionists who did not emigrate were consistently supportive of Palestinian Jews. The Zionist Organization of America's political intervention was crucial in recruiting United States support for the establishment of the State of Israel in 1948; other Jewish diasporas have combined to support Israel politically and financially.

The patterns of diaspora restoration are also noticeable in black African, Greek, Palestinian, and Armenian nationalisms. The Armenian dispersion (*ëspiurk*) remained as deeply attached to their land as the Jews to Palestine and shared the nationalist sentiments of their brethren in the Ottoman Empire and tsarist Russia. Although the first political party was set up in Van, Eastern Anatolia, its founder, Portukalian, soon left for Marseilles, whence he directed it and published its journal. The first revolutionary party, the *Hunchak*, was founded in Geneva, with agents canvassing the diaspora in Western Europe and the United States (in addition to the Ottoman Empire). Diaspora Armenians have lobbied for the Armenian cause. When Armenia became a Soviet republic, the diaspora maintained its ties through organized networks, chiefly the *Dashnaktsutian*. Later, ultra-nationalist diaspora groups, like ASALA, attacked Turkish diplomats. Following the breakup of the Soviet Union, nationalist sentiments were reinvigorated in the diaspora, which sent volunteers to independent Armenia in its war with Azerbayjan, served in its bureaucracy and assisted it financially and politically.

Several other diasporas have been involved, in varying degrees, in the nationalist politics of their home countries. In the years immediately preceding the First World War, well-known Syro-Lebanese patriots left their land to promote nationalist congresses in West European cities, aiming at the achievement of Arab autonomy or independence. Many Lebanese living abroad have continued to be involved in the struggles of their communities inside Lebanon. Others have adopted a diametrically opposed stance, strongly identifying with their host countries.

Diaspora nationalist identification with the home country has assumed many forms. A common one may be called "long-distance nationalism." Upon the large emigration following the 1846-1849 Irish potato famine, the Catholic Church created a far-flung network, whose Irish clergy fostered a distinctively expatriate culture. This, and similar networks, offered support for Irish nationalism in the twentieth century. Nowadays, many Irish Bostonians know little Irish literature, speak no Gaelic, play no Irish games, neither pay Irish taxes nor vote in Irish elections—but emphasize their nationalism, often more patriotically than the Irish of Ireland.

## Diaspora Nationalism

Some, indeed, continue to finance the Sinn Fein and the IRA.

Parallel symbolical attachments are felt by the Poles in Chicago and the Slovenes in Cleveland. Indeed, Irish-American and Polish-American groups have repeatedly argued that their support for their home countries' independence does not contradict their integration into the United States and indeed helps improve their standing in America. Polish-Americans' patriotism also induced them to quarrel with the neighboring German diaspora. Similarly placed Israelis abroad, accused at home of deserting their motherland, defend Israel's policies or send financial contributions, thus playing a sort of "hero's role" in their diaspora. The Philippine and Chinese diasporas, too, have assisted their home countries financially.

Sometimes, diaspora nationalist identification takes an irredentist or violent turn. While the long-established German diaspora in Russia and the more recent in Kazakhstan, have exhibited chiefly cultural identification with their homeland, the Sudeten Germans in Czechoslovakia between the two World Wars were so politically committed to an irredentist union with the *Vaterland* that they were expelled *en masse* after the Second World War. Parts of the Croatian diaspora had been actively involved, since the establishment of the state of Yugoslavia after the First World War, using violence to "liberate" Croatia. More recently, they have financed and armed Franjo Tudjman's breakaway state. The "Tigers" in Sri Lanka have been largely subsidised by Tamil communities abroad, while the Palestinian diaspora has fostered its own kind of nationalism, aimed at gathering in the exiles and founding their own state in Palestine, next to, or instead of, Israel. For an entire generation, this nationalism evolved, chiefly in Lebanon and Tunisia, along a double track: initiating violence against Israel from abroad and encouraging institution-building among the Palestinians locally. Later, it became a search for investors in the newly created Palestinian Authority.

In the examples given above two main factors have determined the nature and scope of diaspora nationalism and its involvement with the home country—language and religion. Looking at religion first, it has long been the most powerful bond between Jews in their dispersion, and an important, although not the only factor in their strong attachment to Palestine (Zionism has a powerful secular component). The Turkish diaspora in Western Europe is displaying signs of the increasing hold of Islam, hence some of its communal leaders use religion to buttress their identification with Turkey.

However, it is language— as the core of native culture—that has a prime share in the nationalist appeal. Many nationalist movements started with language congresses held abroad. The revival of Hebrew as a modern spoken language soon became a central factor in the Zionist call for "the return to Zion." Seven hundred thousand Magyars in the eastern province of Slovakia long resisted assimilation by striving to retain their culture, language, folklore, customs, and traditions. They set up societies to safeguard Hungarian against the intrusion of German or Slavic words. They published books, newspapers and literary magazines, also establishing cultural and scholarly organizations.

Near-unanimity in this case is uncharacteristic. A hotly debated issue among Turks living and working in Germany is the amount of Turkish that should be imparted to their children, to enable them to lead a normal life upon their hoped-for return to Turkey. Similarly, Greeks in Germany have obtained the right to sit for the *abitur* (school-leaving diploma) in Greek, so that they may continue their studies in Greece if they wish. North African Arabs living in France, chiefly comparatively new arrivals, are torn between patriotic feelings towards their nearby home countries, expressed by preferences for Arabic and Islam, and their desire for accommodation in their host country through extensive acculturation in French language and culture. The Cuban community in Florida and elsewhere in the United States insists on maintaining the study of Spanish as part of their hoped-for return in the post-Castro era. Similar attitudes prevail among other Hispanic groups in the United States. In the Chinese diaspora, the study of classical Chinese is perceived as an essential element in national identification with the culture of its home country.

A different stand was adopted by "autonomism," an early twentieth-century Jewish diaspora nationalist ideology. Formulated by the historian Simon Dubnov, it held that, in Jewish history, every diaspora served as its own natural centre, ensuring its national minority rights and defending its political interests. The autonomists maintained that "Jews should not be a state within a state, but a nation within a nation"—as a cultural historical entity based on spiritual factors. Cultural autonomy in each diaspora was perceived as the only viable nationalist solution, with Yiddish as the common language.

Pan-nationalism has been a common element in certain diaspora nationalisms. Pan-ideologies aim (often more intensely than mere nationalist ones) at promoting solidarity—and, sometimes, union—between a diaspora and its home country. They constantly emphasise kinship of language, race, tradition and (where applicable) geographical proximity. The more moderate elements usually strive for cultural solidarity, as in *Francophonie*, aiming at promoting French language and civilisation in the cause of closer cooperation between metropolis and diasporas. More extreme, politically motivated elements, are perceived by the diaspora as aiming at territorial union with the motherland, an objective sometimes supported by the home country (by the state, or, unofficially, by NGOs).

Pan-movements have often originated in the diaspora. Thus, pan-Slavism, as a nationalist idea, really started at the 1848 Prague Congress which was attended by delegates of Slav origins from various diasporas. After Russia's defeat in the Crimean War (1856), the movement was transformed into a militant version of Pan-Slavism; the second Pan-Slav Congress met in Moscow in 1867 and was controlled by Russians. Greek irredentism, characteristic of the *Megali Idea* of pan-Hellenism, was fostered by the Kingdom of Greece and by the diaspora in Russia, Crete, Asia Minor, and elsewhere. The case of Cyprus is instructive: the nationalism of the island's Greeks and Turks has been continuously nourished by their co-ethnic groups abroad, very often in terms of pan-Hellenism and pan-Turkism; indeed, certain groups in Greece are pressing for *Enosis*, or the political incorporation of Cyprus into the mainland.

Pan-Turkism, too, is an important instance of diaspora nationalism. Starting in the late nineteenth century among Turkic groups outside the Ottoman Empire, chiefly Tatars and Azeris, pan-Turkism proposed a *rapprochement*, cultural or political, between all Turkic peoples and their brethren in the Ottoman Empire. It was subsequently adopted by certain groups in the empire itself. Its spokesmen generally stressed commonality of language, culture, race and territory—sometimes playing these up into a version of "a Great Turkey." Nowadays, with five ex-Soviet Turkic republics in the Caucasus (Azerbayjan) and Central Asia (Uzbekistan, Kazakhstan, Kyrgyzstan, and Turkmenistan) attaining independence in 1991, pan-Turk propaganda is heard again. However, the new republics have their problems with nationalist issues in their own diasporas, such as Tajikistan's demands on Uzbekistan for "the return" of Bukhara and other Tajik-inhabited regions; or Azeri demands to unite with their people in the province of Azerbayjan in Iran.

Suddenly, the breakdown of the Soviet Union has created new diasporas—Russian minorities in most of the ex-Soviet states where, during the fifty years of the Soviet Union, they had been masters. With variations, conflicts occur over language, education, and strategies of developing a market economy. While some political leaders of these Russian diasporas are emotionally attracted to Russia, relatively few have moved there from what have become their host countries.

The revolution in mobility, transportation and communications is influencing diaspora nationalism in ways which cannot yet be gauged. Our generation has witnessed an international nomadism to wealthier postindustrial capitalist host countries. One result is the enlargement of existing diaspora communities and the creation of new ones. Various factors could conceivably influence the attachment to the original home. Many migrants can visit their home countries more cheaply and frequently than before. In many cases, they can listen to or watch programmes from their home countries in their native languages. Making no less an impact on a diaspora's subjective experience, perhaps, is reactive nationalism in the host country, such as Romania's restrictive policies against its Hungarian minority under Ceausescu.

## Discrimination

Radical xenophobic movements may oppose the inflow of "aliens" into the "demarcated homeland." Such are Le Pen's Front National in France (claiming that immigrant diasporas are unassimilable), and similar movements in Germany (where hate-groups use violence), the United Kingdom, and elsewhere.

### Bibliography

Chazan, Naomi (ed.). 1991. *Irredentism and International Politics*. Boulder, CO: Lynne Rienner Publishers.

Dubnov-Erlich, Sophie. 1991. *The Life and Work of S. M. Dubnov: Diaspora Nationalism and Jewish History*. Bloomington and Indianapolis: Indiana University Press.

Fishman, Joshua A. (ed.). 1993. *The Earliest Stage of Language Planning: The 'First Congress' Phenomenon*. Berlin and New York: Mouton de Gruyter.

Landau, Jacob M. 1995. *Pan-Turkism: From Irredentism to Cooperation*. London: C. Hurst & Co., and Bloomington and Indianapolis: University of Indiana Press.

Lemelle, Sidney and Kelley, Robin D.G. (eds.). 1994. *Imagining Home: Class, Culture and Nationalism in the African Diaspora*. London and New York: Verso.

Sheffer, Gabriel (ed.). 1986. *Modern Diasporas in International Politics*. London and Sydney: Croom Helm.

Smith, Anthony D. 1981. *The Ethnic Revival in the Modern World*. Cambridge: Cambridge University Press.

Jacob M. Landau

## Discrimination

The less favorable treatment of persons because they are thought to belong in a given social category. Discrimination is not necessarily either unlawful or immoral. For example, a film director making a film about the life of Martin Luther King or Nelson Mandela could lawfully limit selection to black actors of an appropriate age. Under some circumstances it may be both lawful and moral to show favor to members of a category that historically has been disadvantaged. To determine whether discrimination has occurred it is therefore necessary to decide whether someone has been treated less favorably than someone who did not belong to the same social category would have been treated. To determine whether the discrimination was unlawful it is necessary to decide either whether the action occurred in a protected field (e.g., in applying for a job, and not in inviting someone to a family party); and that it was unlawfully motivated (e.g., on the grounds of race or sex). These characteristics define direct discrimination. Alternatively, an action may constitute indirect discrimination if it occurs in a protected field and has the effect of disadvantaging members of a protected class of persons. To determine whether discrimination is morally appropriate, reference must be made to moral and not legal standards.

States which have ratified the International Covenant on Civil and Political Rights have accepted an obligation under Article 26 to prohibit discrimination "on any ground such as race, color, sex, language, religion, political or other opinion, national or social origin, property, birth or other status." The prohibition of discrimination on the ground of national origin should include discrimination on the ground of nationality, because national origin is determined at birth, whereas a person may change his or her nationality.

When a person is treated less favorably because he or she is thought to be of a particular national or ethnic origin this may be described as categorical discrimination (i.e., motivated by the belief that all persons belonging in a certain category should be so treated). This may be contrasted with statistical discrimination in which an employer, for example, knows that some job applicants from a certain category have the desired qualities but believes that since the average applicant of this background is less well-qualified it will save time and trouble to exclude such persons from the selection process. Whether the belief is justified or not is a separate issue. Stereotypes have been said to be guidelines in making statistical discriminations in situations of imperfect information.

For reasons of public policy some governments have chosen to favor candidates from particular ethnic groups as candidates for state scholarships, business licences, and appointments to posts in the civil or military services. Such policies of ethnic preference, or quotas, have been employed (e.g., in Malaysia and Sri Lanka) in order to achieve what the government regarded as a better ethnic balance. In India the government lost the election of 1991 because of its support for quotas to advance "backward castes." Preferential policies can be justified in international law only if they are objectively warranted and are not continued after their goals have been met. Some European countries restrict to their own nationals not only sensitive posts involving national security but mundane positions such as the delivery of letters; whether such restrictions can be justified is open to question. If not, a court might find them to be discriminatory.

### Bibliography

Banton, Michael. 1994. *Discrimination*. Buckingham: Open University Press.
van den Berghe, Pierre L. 1997. "Rehabilitating Stereotypes," *Ethnic and Racial Studies* 20: 1–16.

Michael Banton

# Dominant Ethnie

The concept of a "dominant ethnie" refers to either a nation's (a) politically dominant ethnic group or (b) its culturally/ontologically dominant ethnic group. The two are often, but not always, the same entity. This is easily discernible in cases where political dominance does not coincide with cultural dominance. Afrikaners, White Rhodesians, Alaouites, Americo-Liberians, and Tutsis provide but a few instances of politically dominant groups which are not culturally dominant.

These cases were especially pronounced in the colonial era and appear frequently in the early histories of settler societies like prerevolutionary Mexico. Minority nations' dominant ethnic groups (i.e., *ethnic* Basques, Catalans, Kurds or Scots) provide another complicating set of cases to the rule of political and cultural congruence. To complicate matters, there are also cases where dominance is economic, but not political or cultural (Anglos in pre-1960s Quebec). Hence the fact that economic, political and cultural factors are variable makes it imperative that the form of dominance be specified when using the term dominant ethnie. Perhaps the term "national ethnie" is

a more useful one in that it captures the concept which most users of "dominant group" seek to elucidate: namely, the ethnic group whose *mythomoteur* furnished the symbols, myths and narratives for the nation.

The ethnocentricity of most ethnic relations material, especially in the United States, has meant that little attention has been paid to majority groups. For instance, Donald Young's 1932 work, described as the first comparative volume in the field, was aptly titled *American Minority Peoples*. Later volumes in the United States either reinforced the idea of ethnicity as innately "foreign" or tended to ignore the "majority" question entirely (Warner and Srole 1945: 28; Bloom 1948; Rose and Rose 1953: v).

John Higham's *Strangers in the Land* (1955) did attempt to focus on majority attitudes, but failed to link American Anglo-Saxonism to any comparative model of dominant ethnicity. This was also a failing of Thomas Gossett, whose thesis (1953) and book (1963) on American Anglo-Saxonism reduced dominant ethnicity to "race." The publication of the late Digby Baltzell's *The Protestant Establishment* (1964) proved another important landmark, but again, little attention was paid to the "ethnic" quality of the "WASP" dominant group (Baltzell 1964: 321–3). Generally speaking, this situation has persisted, even though the existence of a majority group began to be discussed in the American literature by the 1970s (Schermerhorn 1970; Burkey 1978: 170; Feagin 1978: 50–76).

Within this discussion, the dominant ethnic group was given little attention, as the principal focus of inquiry remained centered on the "other." Moreover, as Ashley Doane comments, there was too exclusive a focus on the "superordinate" status or political dominance of the majority group, which, though important, is but one side of the dominant ethnicity coin (Doane 1997: 375). The development of the "ethnic" dimension of dominant ethnicity theory, on the other hand, has received scant attention in the ethnic relations literature of the past two decades (Greeley 1971: 35; Isajiw 1974; Glazer and Moynihan 1975; Burgess 1978; Schaefer 1979; Postiglione 1983; Gleason 1992).

The first attempt to probe the question of dominant groups' *ethnicity* appeared with A. D. Smith's

# Dominant Ethnie

(1971) discussion of "revivalist" nationalism as the alter-ego of reformist nationalism. Smith argued that the "Janus-faced" character of nationalism could either lead the nation outward toward "reformist" modernization in the pursuit of scientific legitimacy, or inward, toward its dominant ethnic (Smith didn't use this term) particularity, in search of spiritual legitimacy (Smith 1971: 246–54). Smith's investigation into the "revivalist" nature of dominant-group ethnicity has since been given a new interpretation by John Hutchinson, who postulates that dominant ethnic groups seek ethnic revival in response to what their intellectuals perceive as a weakening of the group's cultural self-awareness. Here again, however, no definition of dominant ethnicity was provided (Hutchinson 1987).

Orlando Patterson's *Ethnic Chauvinism* (1977) also warrants comment. Patterson put forth a six-category typology of ethnic groups that included "national" ethnic groups. France, Germany, Italy, Israel, Japan, Ireland and even Iran were given as examples. Patterson never, however, actually used the term "national ethnic group," always preferring "nation-state" as an expression of this idea (Patterson 1977: 106–7). He also failed to specify the exact nature of the link between ethnie and nation, postulating instead that there existed an Anglo-Saxon model of nationhood, territorially based, which differed from the more ethnic model to be found on the European Continent (Patterson 1977: 68). At this point, therefore, theoretical approaches to the "ethnic" dimension of dominant ethnicity remained under-systematized.

Also around this time, there appeared one of the few empirical case studies of a dominant ethnie, namely *Ethnic Russia in the USSR* (1980), edited by Edward Allworth. Yet despite a promising line of inquiry, the book was short on theoretical generalization and failed to develop a conceptual framework relating ethnie to nation. In fact, it was not until 1991 that the term "dominant ethnie" was first used—by Anthony Smith, who had refined the concept sufficiently to be able to provide its definition within the pages of his *National Identity* (1991). In this work, Smith emphasized that nations are built around "ethnic cores" or "dominant ethnies" which furnish the

nation with its legitimating myths, symbols and conceptions of territory. In Smith's words:

> Though most latter-day nations are, in fact, polyethnic, many have been formed in the first place around a *dominant ethnie*, which attracted other ethnies or ethnic fragments into the state to which it gave a name and cultural charter...since ethnies are by definition associated with a given territory...the presumed boundaries of the nation are largely determined by the myths and memories of the *dominant ethnie*, which include the foundation charter, the myth of the golden age and the associated territorial claims, or ethnic title-deeds. (Smith 1991: 39, emphasis added)

Beyond this discussion, however, there has been little explicit attention paid to dominant ethnicity in the European nationalism literature.

In the American ethnic relations literature, the past few years have witnessed a growth in the study of whiteness (Roediger 1994; Gallagher 1994; Delgado 1997). Yet, here again, a promising line of enquiry has fallen prey to the ethnocentric tradition of the discipline in the United States. Of all the recent writing about dominant group identity, only that of Ashley Doane has delved into the question of dominant ethnicity. Doane first defined the term in a 1993 conference paper entitled "Bringing the majority back in: towards a sociology of dominant group ethnicity." This was followed by a 1997 article on "Dominant group ethnic identity in the United States" which made explicit Doane's definition of the term "dominant ethnicity" and his concerns about the ethnocentric neglect of its study (Doane 1993; 1997).

Doane defined dominant ethnicity as follows: "a dominant ethnic group [is] the ethnic group in a society that exercises power to create and maintain a pattern of economic, political and institutional advantage, which in turn results in the unequal...distribution of resources" (Doane 1997: 376). Clearly, Doane's definition addresses the political dimension of dominant ethnicity while Smith's leans more heavily toward the cultural. In practice, the two facets often overlap, but, as mentioned earlier, the numerous exceptions to this relationship warrant a new terminological approach. As a preliminary suggestion, a distinction might be drawn between the *dominant ethnie*, which could refer to the nation's politically dominant group, and the *national ethnie*—which

## Bibliography

Allworth, Edward (ed.) 1980. *Ethnic Russia in the USSR: The Dilemma of Dominance*. New York: Pergamon Press.

Baltzell, E. Digby. 1964. *The Protestant Establishment: Aristocracy and Caste in America*. New York: Random House.

Bloom, Leonard. 1948. "Concerning ethnic research," *American Sociological Review* 13, 171–177.

Burgess, M. Elaine. 1978. "The resurgence of ethnicity: myth or reality?," *Ethnic and Racial Studies* 1, 265–285.

Burkey, Richard M. 1978. *Ethnic and Racial Groups: The Dynamics of Dominance*. Menlo Park: Cummings.

Delgado, Richard and Jean Stefancic (eds.) 1997. *Critical White Studies: Looking Behind the Mirror*. Philadelphia, PA: Temple University Press.

Doane, Ashley W., Jr. 1993. "Bringing the majority back in: towards a sociology of dominant group ethnicity," paper presented at the annual meeting of the Society for the Study of Social Problems, Miami Beach, FL.

Doane, Ashley W., Jr. 1997. "Dominant group ethnic identity in the United States: the role of "hidden" ethnicity in intergroup relations," *Sociological Quarterly* 38, 3, 375–397.

Feagin, Joe R. 1978. *Racial and Ethnic Relations*. Englewood Cliffs, NJ: Prentice-Hall.

Gallagher, Charles A. 1994. "White reconstruction in the university," *Socialist Review* 24, 165–187.

Glazer, Nathan and Daniel P. Moynihan. 1975. *Ethnicity: Theory & Experience*. Cambridge, MA: Harvard University Press.

Gleason, Philip. 1992. *Speaking of Diversity: Language and Ethnicity in Twentieth-Century America*. Baltimore, MD and London: Johns Hopkins University Press.

Gossett, Thomas F. 1953. *The Idea of Anglo-Saxon Superiority in American Thought, 1865-1915*. Unpublished doctoral dissertation, University of Minnesota.

Gossett, Thomas F. 1963. *Race, the History of an Idea in America*. Dallas: Southern Methodist University Press.

Greeley, Andrew M. 1971. *Why Can't They Be Like Us?: America's White Ethnic Groups*. New York: Dutton & Co.

Higham, M. John. 1955. *Strangers in the Land*. New Brunswick, NJ: Rutgers University Press.

Hutchinson, John. 1987. *The Dynamics of Cultural Nationalism: The Gaelic Revival and the Creation of the Irish Nation-State*. London: Allen and Unwin.

Isajiw, Wsevolod W. 1974. "Definitions of ethnicity," *Ethnicity* 1, 111–123.

Patterson, Orlando. 1977. *Ethnic Chauvinism: The Reactionary Impulse*. New York: Stein and Day.

Postiglione, Gerard A. 1983. *Ethnicity and American Social Theory*. Lanham, MD: University Press of America.

Roediger, David R. 1994. *Towards the Abolition of Whiteness*. London: Verso.

Rose, Arnold and Caroline Rose. 1953. *Minority Group Relations in the United States*. New York: Alfred A. Knopf.

Schaefer, Richard T. 1979. *Racial and Ethnic Groups*. Boston and Toronto: Little, Brown and Co.

Schermerhorn, Richard A. 1970. *Comparative Ethnic Relations: A Framework for Theory and Research*. New York: Random House.

Smith, Anthony D. 1971 (1983, 2nd ed.). *Theories of Nationalism*. New York: Harper and Row.

Smith, Anthony D. 1991. *National Identity*. London: Penguin.

Warner, W. Lloyd and Leo Srole. 1945. *The Social Systems of American Ethnic Groups*. New Haven, CT: Yale University Press.

Young, Donald Ramsey. 1932. *American Minority Peoples: A Study in Racial and Cultural Conflicts in the United States*. New York and London: Random House.

Eric Kaufmann

# Durkheim and Nationalism

Of all the great Continental classical sociologists, Émile Durkheim's work on community and religion bears most closely and profoundly on the issues of nations and nationalism. This, despite the fact that Durkheim never wrote directly on these phenomena, addressing them only briefly at the end of his life as his contribution to France's cause during the Great War. Nor did he give us an historical or comparative account of nationality such as was adumbrated by MAX WEBER. Nevertheless, it is possible to see in much of his major work on collective solidarity and on totemic religion the source and inspiration of a deeper sociological analysis of the roots of national identity and community.

Of course, Durkheim's work drew on a number of predecessors in this regard. His emphasis on the need for solidarity harks back to the radical tradition of Montesquieu and Rousseau, on the one hand, and to the conservative tradition of de Maistre and Bonald, on the other hand. More immediately, he drew on the ideas of Comte and Schaffle for his account of "mechanical solidarity" and the *conscience collective*. For Durkheim, this kind of solidarity is essentially tribal or ethnic; as he puts it in *The Division of Labour* which was first published in 1893:

> What brings men together are mechanical causes and impulsive forces, such as affinity of blood, attachment to the same soil, ancestral worship, community of habits, etc. It is only when the group has been formed on these bases that co-operation is organised there. (Durkheim 1964: 278)

The result of such mechanical forces is a similarity in the beliefs and sentiments of the members of a community, and a respect for traditions which form its *conscience collective*. These traditions change only very slowly, because of the veneration accorded to the past, and because of the tight solidarity built up on the resemblances between the members.

However, in the modern world, we witness the decline of both the mechanical type of solidarity and the *conscience collective*. In Durkheim's view, this is the result of population growth, the resulting "moral density" and the ensuing competition for resources. With urbanization, specialized labor, and secularism, respect for tradition declines, widespread mobility separates the generations and a new "organic" kind of solidarity based on the division of labor and mutual cooperation takes the place of the old. But not entirely. For Durkheim, even modern, contract-based societies are moral communities. They too require a measure of *conscience collective*, and even some kind of mechanical solidarity, albeit with a more restricted scope. To be sure, the modern cult of individual worth ensures much greater freedom for each member of society. Nevertheless, in the

last analysis, individuals continue to feel a degree of dependence on society; and even in modern, industrial societies, some element of moral consensus and some sense of belonging must be retained, if they are not to dissolve in *anomie*. In this "moral re-turn," this crucial shift in Durkheim's analysis of modernity, is foreshadowed the kernel of our latter-day understanding of the contemporary "ethnic revival" in West and East, namely, that ethnic ties have been revitalised by social mobilization and modernization.

Of course, there has been a fundamental change in the *content* of communal solidarity. In premodern epochs, it was essentially religious in character. It embodied a system of beliefs and practices which divided the world into sacred and profane things, and which bound those who observed them into a community of worshippers. Today, the totems, images and doctrines of the gods and forces which embodied society's sense of dependence, have lost much of their meaning; science has undermined traditional beliefs. Nevertheless, the *form* of communal solidarity remains. Worship continues, rites are still performed, collective sentiments are still regularly reaffirmed. Only today, society worships itself, under its particular totems—flags, anthems, holidays, and so on; the rituals of national commemoration are solemnly rehearsed in the funerals of the fallen, the ceremonies of remembrance, and the museums of memory; and the national identity is reaffirmed through festivals of liberation and solidarity. As an example of the latter, Durkheim twice cites the patriotic fervor generated during the French Revolution. The French Revolution was an example of society (the nation) setting itself up as a god, or creating its own gods:

> At this time, in fact, under the influence of the general enthusiasm, things purely laical in nature were transformed by public opinion into sacred things: these were the Fatherland, Liberty, Reason. A religion tended to become established which had its dogmas, symbols, altars and feasts. (Durkheim 1915: 214)

What Durkheim is arguing, and its relevance for the study of nations and nationalism is immediately apparent, is that "religion" in this broad, functional and social sense is "eternal." There is, claims Durkheim, no real difference between Christian or Jewish festivals and "a reunion of citizens commemorating the promulgation of a new moral or legal system or some great event in the national life" (ibid: 427).

Every society, be it never so free and individualistic, requires reunions and assemblies and rites; for before all, rites are means by which a social group reaffirms itself periodically (ibid: 387). This is why "there is something eternal in religion," which will survive all changes in beliefs and symbols: for "There can be no society which does not feel the need of upholding and reaffirming at regular intervals the collective sentiments and the collective ideas which make its unity and personality" (ibid: 427).

Throughout, Durkheim was concerned with the simplest and the most complex societies, contrasting primitive totemism with modern secularism. Yet, we have only to substitute the word "nation" for "society," and Durkheim's analysis fits the phenomena of nations and nationalism with far more ease than totemism. When Durkheim tells us, for example, that "before all else, a faith is warmth, life, enthusiasm, the exaltation of the whole mental life, the raising of the individual above himself" (ibid.: 425). Furthermore, when Durkheim uses the analogy of the soldier dying for his flag rather than his country, because the sight of the flag rekindles his collective emotions (ibid.: 220), we are easily persuaded of the striking aptness of his account for an understanding of the passions of nationalism. It is, indeed, strange, that Durkheim failed to draw this conclusion, and that like so many of the classical sociologists, he did not appreciate the force and ubiquity of nations and nationalism, because he has, almost unconsciously, provided vital concepts and tools for grasping their power and endurance. Perhaps, Durkheim's own fervent adherence to France, like Weber's to Germany,—and the influence of French nationalism on the Jews of France—prevented him from defining a separate (modern) type of society, the nation and its nationalism, and thereby detaching himself sufficiently from an equation of "society" with "nation." Be that as it may, the "communitarian" approach associated with Durkheim's sociology and Durkheim's own ideas about religion and society have provided powerful insights for an understanding of nationalism and laid the groundwork for "internalist" sociological approaches to national identities and communities.

## Bibliography

Durkheim, Émile. 1964 (1893). *The Division of Labour in Society*, trans. G.Simpson. New York: Free Press.

Durkheim, Émile. 1915 (1912). *The Elementary Forms of the Religious Life*, trans. J. Swain. London: Allen and Unwin.

Mitchell, Marion. 1931. "Émile Durkheim and the philosophy of nationalism," *Political Science Quarterly* 46: 87-106.

Steven Lukes. 1972. *Émile Durkheim: His Life and Work*. New York: Harper and Row.

Strenski, Ivan. 1997. *Durkheim and the Jews of France*. Chicago and London: University of Chicago Press.

Anthony D. Smith

# E

## Enlightenment and Nationalism

### Contrasts

The systems of ideas conventionally denoted by the terms Enlightenment and nationalism respectively, appear on the surface as diametrically opposed and incompatible with each other. The Enlightenment represents the values of universalism and reason, and extolls the rights of the individual and personal autonomy. Nationalism on the other hand negates universalism by projecting the particular, the specific and the local that define the content of the cultures of distinct groups and populations. Against the power of reason nationalism projects the appeal to the emotions and is captivated by the mystique of traditions and collective sentiments. Against individual rights and personal autonomy finally, nationalism deifies the values of the collectivity, insists on the absolute moral primacy of national goals and readily concedes the expendability of individual persons and human life for the sake of the fulfilment of national aspirations. The contrasts could be unnecessarily multiplied in illustrating the difference in outlook and in moral temper that separate nationalism from the Enlightenment. *Prima facie*, it appears therefore justifiable to refer to two incompatible philosophical and moral systems, respectively connected with visions of society and politics fundamentally divergent from each other: the Enlightenment appears to be associated with an individualist and liberal conception of society and politics, while nationalism presupposes a corporatist and collectivist vision with an immanent authoritarian logic built into it. On the level of conventional historical chronology—on a Eurocentric historical paradigm of course—the Enlightenment and nationalism appear associated with different epochs and with different points in the chain of historical cau-

sation: the Enlightenment is considered the hallmark of prerevolutionary eighteenth-century culture in Western Europe, thus defining the "age of reason" and contributing to the ideological and social fermentation leading up to the French Revolution. On the other hand, nationalism is connected with the nineteenth century, contributing to the temper of a "romantic era" which expressed the revolt of human sensibility against the tutelage of rationalism. Finally, in a perspective of European cultural geography, the Enlightenment and nationalism appear associated with different regions of the continent. The Enlightenment's flourishing is connected with Northwestern Europe and its weakness and failures with the "European periphery". The shades of geographical differentiation in connection with the Enlightenment's successes and failures begin in Central Europe and extend with increasing density to the East, South, and Southeast: the further away from the Northwestern core of European culture—located in a triangle defined by London, Paris, and Amsterdam—the weaker the Enlightenment tradition. This is almost a truism in the historiography of the Enlightenment. Conversely those outlying regions are connected with stronger and more extremist expressions of nationalism than the privileged core, whose nationalism is considered to have been temperate and "civic" minded. This view, in turn, gave rise, in scholarly literature, to typologies and classifications of "Western" and "Eastern" nationalism. All the above views, which illustrate the extent of the contrast between Enlightenment and nationalism prevailing in the conventional scholarly understanding of the two notions, have been propounded by often important scholars and supported by serious arguments and by evidence which cannot be easily dismissed. As it so often happens, such conventional views in scholarship are supported not only by the strength of set habits of thought and established standards of understanding, but also by bodies of evidence which it is necessary to reinterpet in convincing ways in order to bring about a sustainable revision of conventional wisdom. In the specific case of the relation between Enlightenment and nationalism, I do not think that it will be an easy task to bring about such an interpretative revision. It is possible, nevertheless, to produce a more complex and nuanced picture that will reveal deeper affinities and unexpected points of proximity between Enlightenment and nationalism. Methodologically, this could be done, at three levels of analysis. First, one could attempt to trace early conceptualizations of the idea of the nation in Enlightenment thought. This will elucidate the substantive contribution of certain strands of Enlightenment thought to the intellectual sources of nationalism. Secondly, an examination of the transition from the political thought of the Enlightenment to the politics of nationalism might illustrate the continuities as well as the breaks that place the two on an evolving continuum of secular European thought. Finally, the articulation of the eventual estrangement of nationalism from the Enlightenment tradition will perhaps contribute to an understanding of the origin of the contrasts between the two.

### Concepts

Another convention in the historiography of European political thought connects the emergence of the conceptualization of the idea of the nation with eighteenth-century thought, primarily with two names: JEAN-JACQUES ROUSSEAU and JOHANN GOTTFRIED VON HERDER. This is obviously true, but as it is usually the case with conventional wisdom it conveys only a partial picture. It is entirely true that the conceptualization of the idea of the nation as a primary agent of political life and the foremost, indeed the only locus of political legitimacy, is owed to Rousseau. It is due to his powerful rhetoric and to his seductive ability to argue by paradox that the concept of the nation acquired its intense political meaning and was set on its distinctly modern conceptual itinerary, as against the mediaeval connotations of its earlier uses. Rousseau's contribution to laying the groundwork for the theory of nationalism consisted primarily in the stress he put on the na-

tion as a community of active citizenship and moral sentiments, held together by a common will and shared purposes and transcending in its ethical hypostasis any kind of individual autonomy or value. From this point of view Book II of the *Social Contract* can be seen to possess the equivalent of biblical authority for nationalist thinking.

However, Rousseau's conception of the nation, despite its appeal to the Jacobins, remained abstract and outside a frame of concrete historical reference. His attempts to connect his ideas with the specific cases of Poland or Corsica, although greatly suggestive, remained theoretically rather feeble efforts. The nation was endowed with an emotively effective substratum and became a culturally recognizable personality thanks to the work of Herder on language, poetry, and the philosophy of history. Herder was a child of the Enlightenment, trained at Koningsberg by Kant in the thought of Montesquieu, Rousseau, and Hume. As he matured intellectually, however, and became aware of the complexity of the European cultural landscape following his travels in the 1760s and 1770s, Herder developed a quite critical perspective on the Enlightenment's abstract, universalist, and rationalist tenets and came to appreciate the appeal and evocative power of what is unique and specific in human cultural expression. This led him to recognize the centrality and value of history as a form of understanding and thus he came close to the intellectual heritage of Vico (Berlin 1976). It was upon this basis that Herder recognized the critical significance of language and the value of poetry as the characteristic expressions of the human spirit. In this connection communities of language, held together by the symbolic power of traditions of poetic expression came to be recognized as the naturally fulfilling contexts of human existence. The deeper meaning and purpose of history was, according to Herder in *Ideen zur Philosophie der Geschichte der Menschheit* (1784-91), the unfolding of the genius of individual national cultures, whose creative expression diversifies and enriches the aesthetic heritage of humanity as a whole.

Although Herder's politics diverged widely from Rousseau's ideas, the combined force of their respective conceptions provided the intellectual impulse for the subsequent growth of the theory of nationalism. Yet, besides Rousseau and Herder who first introduced the modern usage of the term nation into the language of politics and forged the term nationalism two other leading Enlightenment thinkers contributed in even more substantive—if rather indirect ways to the elaboration of the intellectual preconditions of nationalist thinking. These two thinkers were Montesquieu and Kant. In the profoundly divergent philosophical approaches of Montesquieu and Kant, as in the case of Rousseau and Herder, the theory of nationalism can trace its substantive intellectual and moral lineages, thus illustrating the multiplicity of its sources and the surprising heterogeneity of its origins. Montesquieu's contribution is the least recognized and understood because he does not discuss in any systematic way the concept of the nation. It is true that he does use the language of republican patriotism which he tries to adapt to his understanding of modernity and of the distinct meaning of liberty that it presupposes. These components of his argument were picked up by the French revolutionaries and other radicals around Europe (in Italy, Central Europe, and the Balkans), in order to sustain their own claims and visions. But it was not primarily this part of Montesquieu that provided a theoretical underpinning for nationalism. This can be found in his conception of society as a dynamic totality of interacting factors—physical, historical, institutional, and cultural. This sense of social totality to which Raymond Aron traced the origin of sociology, could be connected as well with the mode of thinking that produced nationalist thought later on (Aron 1967). Nations as social entities are organic totalities travelling in time and marked by their distinctive "spirit" which is a moral force encompassing but also going beyond conventional customs and traditions—how else could the most accomplished theoretician define the nation? This could be considered as a distinct contribution of the social thought of the Enlightenment to the intellectual heritage of nationalism. A final Enlightenment contribution to laying the intellectual groundwork for the future growth of nationalist thinking is connected with Immanuel Kant's critical philosophy. To connect Kant's name with the origins of nationalism certainly appears paradoxical. If

anything, he is the philosopher of moral universalism par excellence. Kant's search for a scale of ethical values that would establish a moral categorical imperative involving the recognition of persons as ends-in-themselves and his insistence on the need to transcend all forms of moral heteronomy in human action (be it religious, political or simply utilitarian), provided the philosophical foundation of the principle of moral and political self-determination. This concept, initially elaborated in connection with the principle of individual moral autonomy, was to prove of seminal significance for the future of political thought. Extended by Kant's German followers from the level of individual to that of collective claims and actions it became the fundamental aspiration of the nationalist movements that sought independent political status for the several cultural collectivities emerging in modern Europe in the wake of the French Revolution. This political dimension of Kantian ethical theory was first recognized with great ingenuity and perceptiveness by ELIE KEDOURIE, who ascribed to nationalist intellectuals the achievement of turning a principle of individual morality into a demand for mass movements, which, as a rule, in striving for national self-determination often suppressed and treated as readily expendable precisely that aspiration for individual autonomy for which Kant had sought to provide a philosophical foundation (Kedourie 1960).

### Transitions

The preceding survey of conceptual antecedents to nationalist thought in eighteenth-century philosophy illustrates the diversity and the divergent, occasionally contradictory, strands of thought that were interwoven in the rich texture of Enlightenment culture. The heterogeneity of its heritage is also reflected in the diversity and multiple antinomies that determined the outlook of nationalism as a theory of society, politics, and human action. Obviously, nationalism, despite the conceptual debts and affinities traced above, did not spring from the Enlightenment in a straight line of descent. It took the cataclysmic political and social changes associated with the French Revolution to bring about the transition from the culture of the Enlightenment to that of romantic nationalism as the prevailing Zeitgeist in Europe in the early part of the nineteenth century. Concomitantly, it took the theoretical redefinition and re-orientation of the Enlightenment heritage toward a new political agenda by the founding fathers of nationalist thought for the fully fledged outlook of nationalism to become articulated. This intellectual transition and transvaluation was the work of genuine epigones of the Enlightenment, steeped in its culture and learning, fully aware of its achievements and aspirations. Perhaps, the most representative among them were JOHANN GOTTLIEB FICHTE in Germany and Vittorio Alfieri in Italy, respectively a philosopher and a poet turned into prophets of the national regeneration of their peoples.

Fichte was Kant's disciple and initially shared his republicanism, his belief in freedom and the autonomy of the individual citizen. In response to the levelling of German freedoms by Napoleon in 1807, however, Fichte, in his "Addresses to the German Nation" transformed this Kantian heritage into a passionate argument on behalf of the integrity and freedom of the "German nation," a community whose moral status was, in his opinion, superior to any individual autonomy or purpose. Only by realizing oneself in this higher community and by extending one's freedom through immersion in the higher freedom of the nation could the individual citizen fulfil the teleological logic of human existence. Nations, their cultures, their collective purposes, their glory and immortality became the true ends of history. According to Fichte, nations were defined by their language and their organic original characteristics, and individual members of the national community ought to be guided by education and inculcation with national values in order to recognize their identity, be fiercely proud of it and ready to die for it. It was thus that nationalism as moral temper and intellectual outlook was born. Alfieri, a genuine exponent of Enlightenment classicism and republicanism, found in the civic humanist models of Renaissance culture the response to the demoralization, and tyranny that accounted for Italy's annihilation by Napoleon's armies. His belief in republican virtue and his hatred of despotism as expressed for instance in his treatise *Della tyrannide* (1777) and in *Del principe e delle lettere* (1785-6), were inspired by Montesquieu.

Combined with the patriotic readings of Macchiavelli in the pioneering phase of the *Risorgimento*, such arguments provided the moral stimulation for an Italian patriotism of a new, specifically modern kind. This was the threshold to nationalism. The vision of national unity and the quest for a powerful state to bring it about involved many sacrifices including the republican values of the original project. Individual liberty and personal choice were among the earliest victims of the new political logic dictated by the necessities of nationalism. This became clear in the middle of the nineteenth century with the revolutionary wave of the year 1848 and the politics of expediency that led eventually to national unification. The legacy of the Enlightenment appeared as good as spent.

### Negation

Despite its multiple conceptual debts to the Enlightenment and despite its close association with liberalism in the politics of opposition in Restoration Europe up to 1848, nationalism gave way to the dictates of a political logic that annulled its Enlightenment heritage. In the great cultural divides of European history the Enlightenment and nationalism often appear contiguous on the same side of symbolic polarities. They both represent expressions of the outlook of secularism against the religious and theocratic value systems of medieval culture. As such both Enlightenment and nationalism form integral components of the culture of modernity and share its primary belief in equality as against the hierarchical society of feudalism and medieval Europe. Nowhere is this clearer than in the historical experience of Eastern and Southeastern Europe, in short, of all the regions outside the "core" areas of the Enlightenment in Northwestern Europe. In these regions of the "other" Europe, the Enlightenment, as the aspiration for modernity and cultural change was identical with the origin of local nationalist movements that sought the political regeneration and emancipation of their peoples. The transformation of subject populations into free nations was a goal which both the Enlightenment and nationalism shared. These early movements of national assertion in Central, Eastern, and Southeastern Europe found in the culture of the Enlightenment their inspiration, their vehicle of expression and their hope for success. Yet, nationalism could be fully articulated as a doctrine by turning against certain fundamental principles that are integral to the Enlightenment. These central principles of the Enlightenment, in Isaiah Berlin's parsimonious formulation, universality, objectivity, rationality, had to be abandoned by nationalism primarily in order to achieve the psychological potency and effectiveness necessary for the promotion of its political goals. This pressure took nationalism a long way down the road of the romantic sensibility and eventually led it to a complete identification with the irrationalism, mysticism, and subjectivism that sprang from the temper of the Counter-Enlightenment.

However, through these means of communication and symbolic expression, it was easier to appeal and mobilize a mass following. In the logic of realpolitik, which does not have any qualms over means so long as it can further its ends, nationalism could feel no hesitation in working through such social sentiments in promoting its overriding political ends. For the independence and aggrandizement of the nation no price was high enough to pay, no scruple sufficiently binding to get in the way. The Kantian heritage belonged to a very distant and incomprehensible past.

## Bibliography

Aron, Raymond. 1967. *Les étapes de la pensée sociologique*. Paris: Gallimard.

Berlin, Isaiah. 1976. *Vico and Herder*. New York: Viking.

Berlin, Isaiah. 1981. *Against the Current: Essays in the History of Ideas*. Oxford: Oxford University Press.

Kedourie, Elie. 1960. *Nationalism*. London: Hutchinson.

Meinecke, Friedrich. 1970. *Cosmopolitanism and the National State*, translated by Robert B. Kimber. Princeton, NJ: Princeton University Press.

Thom, Martin. 1995. *Republics, Nations and Tribes*. London: Verso.

Viroli, Maurizio. 1995. *For Love of Country: An Essay on Patriotism and Nationalism*. Oxford: Clarendon Press.

Paschalis M. Kitromilides

# Ethnic and Civic Nationalism (Hans Kohn's Typology)

The concepts "ethnic" and "civic" nationalism are closely identified with the work of Hans Kohn, as published in his *The Idea of Nationalism* (1944) and his *Prelude to Nation-States* (1967). In his work, Kohn argued that there existed two brands of nationalism, one democratic and rational, that is, civic, and the other undemocratic and irrational, that is, ethnic. He did not actually use these terms as such, however, and that is where the problems begin. For Kohn claimed that there was "Western" nationalism, which was nice and civic, and "Eastern" nationalism, which was nasty and ethnic. Civic nationalism, in Kohn's view, was based on the state and citizenship, whereas ethnic nationalism drew on culture.

Any closer look at these distinctions shows that Kohn's attributions were arbitrary and clearly influenced by the time when he was writing, during the Second World War. Yet, the distinction is valuable and this is one of the paradoxes of Kohn's legacy, that he identified a central aspect of the modern nation, but then misunderstood its provenance.

In essence, all nations have both a civic and an ethnic dimension. The former is based on legal-rational institutions, whereas ethnicity is built on the traditions of culture and other usable materials possessed by a community. Crucially, ethnicity is not an attribute solely of the "east," but underlies the cohesiveness of the Western states. France, for example, the quintessential civic state, is permeated by French values that are derived from French culture of a very ethnic kind.

The Central and East European nations, on the other hand, were obliged to call themselves into existence without pre-national state institutions, to mobilise on the basis of culture—particularly language—and then underwent the imposition of communism that largely destroyed what civil society and other non-ethnic identities had come into being. The reception of nationalism in the east was, evidently, not a spontaneous development, but a response to the transformation of the power, and the cultural, as well as economic, eradiation, of the West.

As modernity, in the shape of much improved state capacity and military power impacted on

# Ethnic and Civic Nationalism (Hans Kohn's Typology)

Central and Eastern Europe, at the end of the eighteenth century, there was a real fear that unless these weak cultural communities began to reorganize themselves according to the new Western models, they would disappear. The example of partitioned Poland was there for all to see.

The new organizing principle of nationhood was taken over very rapidly, within the space of a generation, and those who were the agents of this reception gave it the shape that it would continue to have. Crucially, the period saw the rise of a modern, secular intellectual stratum—the descendants of the "republic of letters"—which saw in the ideal of the nation a means to mobilize their cultural communities. In this respect, the coming of nationalism was an emancipation.

The reason why the Central and East European nations assumed very different contours from those in the West is to be found in the social structure of the region. Whereas in the West, there was a fairly well developed society with growing literacy, including the rise of a civil society, with aristocracy, gentry, bourgeoisie, peasantry, and the beginnings of an industrial working class, the East had only an aristocracy and a peasantry, and sometimes only a peasantry. The arrival of the new intellectual stratum, therefore, impacted quite differently in the different parts of Europe. In the West, the ideas of nationhood were evolved through the complex interaction of the different social strata, whilst in the East, the intellectuals had the field to themselves.

They constructed an alliance with the local sub-elites, which needed their skills to take on the ruling empires in their struggle for power. This was the origin of the national movements that began to emerge in the first half of the nineteenth century and which the Holy Alliance was determined to block. Consequently, the national movements in the East had to rely on culture, history and memory for their mobilization, given that the legal-rational civic and state institutions were not in their hands. This weakness of the civic dimension has haunted Eastern nations ever since.

Hence, the supposed irrationality of "eastern" ethnic nationalism has its origins in the weakness of its civic institutions, a problem that the West has not had to face. The implication is that if civic institutions were to gain in strength, "eastern" nationalism would lose its irrational quality.

The distinction between the civic and ethnic dimensions of the nation has been one of the most fruitful in the study of nationhood. By looking at the civic side of the nation, one can identify the institutional underpinnings of the modern state, conceptualise the relationships formed by the exercise of power and see the sources of predictability that connect nationhood with democracy. In essence, the connection between the individual and the political power exercised within the state is acquired through membership of the civic nation. Citizenship, then, is intimately linked to civic nationhood.

Furthermore, for a nation to feel that power is exercised legitimately, it must have a sense that the overt rules of citizenship are stable, predictable, and accountable. The civic nation is the space where this provision is made most clearly. Where the citizenship is not a separate, autonomous entity with its own dynamic, and its purposiveness is weak or absent, then the relationship between the individual and state power will be obscure and a potential source of insecurity.

Ethnicity, on the other hand, while not necessarily a direct source of power, is one of the bases of identity. Crucially, the codes of solidarity and community which are encoded in ethnicity play a pivotal role in creating the growing inputs of consent that the modern state requires. Without this deep sense of community, the coherence of the state is more difficult to sustain, though it is not impossible (viz. Belgium, Switzerland). This is the sense in which both the civic and the ethnic dimensions of the nation are essential to its existence. Hans Kohn saw the nature of the problem, but was not able to press his analysis home.

## Bibliography

Brubaker, Rogers.1992. *Citizenship and Nationhood in France and Germany*. Cambridge, MA.: Harvard University Press.

Kohn, Hans. 1944. *The Idea of Nationalism*. New York: Collier Books.

Kohn, Hans. 1967. *Prelude to Nation-States: The French and German Experience, 1789-1815*. Princeton, NJ: Van Nostrand.

George Schöpflin

# Ethnic and Territorial Nationalism

Although nationalist movements the world over subscribe to the same basic tenets of nationalist ideology, demanding for their nation autonomy, unity and identity, their specific goals, contexts and bases of community vary considerably. For this reason, the study of nationalism has spawned a number of typologies of nationalist movements, ranging from HANS KOHN's (1944) well-known distinction between "Eastern" and "Western" nationalisms to the more complex typologies of Louis Snyder (1968), Konstantin Symmons-Symonolewicz (1970) and John Breuilly (1982).

One of the most important ways of differentiating nationalist movements lies in the bases of their claim to nationhood. On the one hand, we have movements that base their claim to constitute a nation on the territory and political institutions of the designated population. On the other hand, there are the many nationalisms that base their claims on the pre-existing ethnic and cultural identity of the designated population.

The first type of nationalism, called "territorial," invokes four criteria in support of its claim. The first is the clear territorial demarcation of the population who thereby constitute a recognized territorial and legal unit. This may be either a duly constituted national state, or a colony or trustee territory administered by another state. In the latter case, the claim to be a nation is based in the first place on the recognized borders of the territory and the sentiments of loyalty which derive from inclusion in a clearly delimited territory, with its own economic system and resources being administered on a territorial basis. The ideal of a fairly compact, well-defined territory in which people and territory, as it were, belong to each other, became integral to this kind of nationalism. Equally important are the sentiments evoked by the land itself. For, to evoke mass loyalty, the territory in question cannot be any stretch of earth; it must be, or be made to be, an "historic" territory and a "homeland," where the people fought and worked, lived, and died. Hence, a sacred quality is sought by territorial nationalisms in the land and in the popular memories that it evokes.

The second criterion is the legal unity and status of the territory and its population. This proceeds in part from the recognition accorded to the separate political status of the particular territorial unit, but also from the administrative centralization and jurisdiction of the political institutions of that territorial unit. Where that territory and its population enjoy sovereign independence, the political institutions constitute a national state. Where that territory and its population possess the status of a colony or trusteeship, the colonial political institutions receive direction from another source, namely, the authority of the colonizing (and often overseas) state, and the nationalist movement sees its primary objective in eliminating this foreign source of authority and "returning" that sovereignty to political institutions within the colonial territory and representative exclusively of its population. In both cases, legal equality of all members of the nation or nation-to-be, and a territory-wide and unified code of law applicable to all members, are assumed to be both bases and goals of a territorial nationalism.

Third, and springing from the preceding, is the ideal of citizenship of the nation, and of the citizen nation. Both ideals were fervently embraced and promulgated during the French Revolution, where they were opposed to the privilege and lack of political participation characteristic of the *ancien régime*. For the revolutionaries and for all subsequent territorial nationalisms, legal equality of citizens entailed identical rights and duties for all citizens, if they were to be true members of the *patria*. It also implied a single code of laws binding the rich and powerful along with the poor and weak citizens, animated by a "civic" ideal of fraternity (and sorority) which must override all sectional interests. In particular, the equality of civil and political rights entails a sense of inclusion in the national community and a correlative exclusion of those outside as "aliens."

The final criterion of a territorial nationalism is the establishment of a mass, public culture, based on common values, codes and traditions of the population or its "core" community. A territorial nationalism requires a sense of cultural community, with its common popular understandings, sentiments, and ideals. This is reinforced by a "civil religion" of the nation, an ideology and rituals of civic belonging, formally secular, but in practice retaining many of the sentiments, practices and beliefs of traditional religion in generalized form. The "American creed" is a good example of this nontraditional civil religion that nevertheless incorporates elements of Judeo-Christian beliefs and forms, and which offers to its citizens a sense of transcendental belonging to a "community of history and destiny." These ideals are reinforced through the mass media and mass education system which socialize successive generations of Americans into the territorial civil religion and public culture of their ancestors.

If an historic territory, legal-political unity, fraternal citizenship, and mass civic culture are the defining features of the territorial varieties of nationalism, genealogical and indigenous cultural dimensions delineate the ethnic forms of nationalism. Here, too, we can distinguish four main criteria. The first is the shared belief in common ancestry. For ethnic nationalists, the individual is first and foremost a member of the nation in virtue of his or her birth into a particular culture community. Even if the blood tie is entirely fictive, genealogy and the myth of descent provide the essential bonds between the citizen-members of the nation. This is essentially an organic conception of the nation. If in the territorial kind of nationalism individuals had to choose to belong to some nation but were free to choose to which nation they wished to belong, in the ethnic forms of nationalism they had no such latitude for choice: born into a particular nation, they remained members of that nation, however far they might travel, wherever they chose to reside, and with whomsoever they chose to live and consort. The members of the ethnic nation were stamped by the community of their birth. Small wonder, then, that family metaphors are most frequently invoked by ethnic nationalists; the nation is viewed as a kind of fictive "super-family," and any territorial claims it makes are interpreted in the light of historic proprietary rights of the genealogical community.

A second criterion of ethnic nationalism is its nativism, or emphasis upon indigenous history and traditions. The history of the nation is the history of a genealogical community; its value lies in the rediscovery of the roots and develop-

ment of the nation as seen and interpreted by the members of the community. This "insider" view of the ethnic past, or "ethno-history," which analysts must explore if they are to grasp the power of nationalism, is particularly marked in the case of ethnic nationalisms. Its importance is twofold. Nativism in this sense is valued for its "authenticity"; it expresses the "genuine" folk elements of the community and its pristine mores and virtues. It is also an important component of political and territorial claims, notably for the restoration of lands and populations to their "true" and rightful owners, the ethnic nation. Nativism supplies irredentism with much of its power and justifications; at the same time, it supplies vital weapons in the war against cosmopolitan "falsifications" of national history.

Closely related to nativism is the return to vernacular culture. Where territorial nationalists emphasized the need for unified laws, ethnic nationalism holds up vernacular languages and customs, as the repositories of authenticity and the definers of collective cultural identity. For ethnic nationalists, following HERDER, language, in particular, evoked the intimacy of the family and the private, expressive qualities of the community's culture. The vernacular language embodied and expressed the inner historical experiences of the nation, in contradistinction to the public and official language of the state with its dominant elite symbolism. Hence the importance accorded by ethnic nationalists to philology. Along with archaeology, ethnography, and folklore studies, philology enabled members of the community to recover their authentic past, which was often buried under centuries of "foreign" accretions.

Finally, ethnic nationalism was, at least in theory, fervently populist. In its drive to mobilize "the people," it went out of its way to exalt the life-style of the folk, together with popular culture and mores. Even if it was hell-bent on rapid industrialization, ethnic nationalism eulogized the peasantry as the repository of the genuine national virtues and the authentic spirit of the community. Like Levin in *Anna Karenina*, it was necessary to "return to the people" and learn the truth of the community from their simple, timeless ways. Moreover, the peasants were closest to the soil; even if most nationalisms originated in the towns and promoted urban progress, they looked to the folk as the embodiment of nature, and to the land itself as the essence of the spirit of the nation. Even if "going to the people" was more of a moral and rhetorical stance than a realistic political option, ethnic nationalism's appeal to the "will of the people" implied an important role for the common people as a device for "interclass" coordination of diverse sectional interests in the struggle against oppressors.

These two types of nationalism with their very different conceptions of the nation, have dominated the history of nationalism in every continent. If the territorial varieties have been prevalent in the West and in its colonies in Latin America, Africa, and Asia, ethnic nationalisms have predominated in Eastern Europe and the Middle East, and have latterly been gaining ground in the new "state-nations" of Asia and Africa. In fact, the two kinds of nationalism have often found themselves pitted against each other, particularly in the new states of Africa and Asia; hence the spate of separatist ethnic nationalisms claiming independence on cultural-historical grounds from the territorial units in which they had been incorporated as a result of colonial treaties and divisions. Hence, too, the various irredentist nationalisms from Italy and Greece to Kurdish, Palestinian, and Somali, where vernacular cultures and presumed genealogical ties form the basis for claims to territories and populations incorporated in "alien" states. Many of the more protracted and bitter conflicts in the contemporary world may be traced to the opposition between these two kinds of nationalism.

In addition, current debates about "civic" and "ethnic" types of national identity in the West have underlined the continuing relevance of the distinction between territorial and ethnic varieties of nationalism. Adherents of a civic type of nationalism have tended to adopt a territorial and political conception of the nation, in the hope of reconciling nationalism with the principles of liberal democracy. In their eyes, it is only the ethnic and genealogical varieties of nationalism that breed the kind of exclusive and superior attitudes on which racism and fascism feed, whereas the civic forms of nationalism which define member-

ship of the nation in terms of prolonged residence rather than birth can be justified in terms of a liberal ethic and their track record of tolerance to minorities and aliens. This may well overlook the intolerance to ethnic minority cultures built into the logic of civic nationalism; the collective public culture and civil religion of territorial nationalisms brook no rivals within and may well portray the tacit assumptions and attitudes of the dominant ethnic majority as the only legitimate culture of the national state.

This suggests that, in many cases, civic-territorial conceptions may be superimposed upon ethnic-genealogical ideas of the nation. In the East as well as the West, we find the two kinds of nationalism in often uneasy coexistence, with now one, and now the other dominating public affairs and policies. The distinction remains a crucial one, as the differences, for example, between the immigration policies of France and Germany attest; but the history of not a few national states may be written in terms of the oscillations and interplay between the civic-territorial and ethnic-genealogical kinds of nationalism.

### Bibliography

Kohn, Hans. 1944 (1967, 2nd ed.). *The Idea of Nationalism.* New York: Macmillan.
Snyder, Louis. 1968. *The New Nationalism.* Ithaca, NY: Cornell University Press.
Symmons-Symonolewicz, Konstantin. 1970. *Nationalist Movements: A Comparative View.* Meadville, PA: Maplewood Press.
Breuilly, John. 1982 (2nd ed.). *Nationalism and the State.* Manchester: Manchester University Press.
Smith, Anthony D. 1983 (2nd ed.; 1971, 1st ed.). *Theories of Nationalism.* London: Duckworth.
Smith, Anthony D. 1995. *Nations and Nationalism in a Global Era.* Cambridge: Polity.

Anthony D. Smith

# Ethnic Cleansing

The term was first used in a technical rather than a merely colloquial sense during the wars which accompanied the collapse of Yugoslavia in the 1990s. It refers to the deliberate and forced mass expulsion of ethnically defined groups from their home territories.

A wide range of diverse rationales for the policy have been offered by its perpetrators, including allegations of treacherous disloyalty and economic exploitation on the part of those expelled. However, the underlying motivation is usually provided by ultra-nationalist ideology rooted in a—sometimes more, sometimes less—well-justified collective inferiority complex in the face of the ethnic "OTHER." Conceptually, it comprises an intermediate level of hegemonic dominance between APARTHEID and GENOCIDE.

Widespread use of the concept since the Yugoslav wars is explained by the scale and intensity of ethnic cleansing in that context, with large-scale expulsion of Moslems from areas of Bosnia claimed by Serbs, of Serbians from the Krajina region of Croatia, and of ethnic Albanians from Kosovo. However, the phenomenon is commonplace throughout history and across the globe. Other contemporary instances are occurring at the start of the twenty-first century in many parts of Africa and in much of Asia, including in particular Indonesia. At an earlier period both Hitler and Stalin resorted to ethnic cleansing on a massive scale in combination with genocide, and the mid-twentieth century also saw huge forced expulsions of Moslems, Hindus, and others across the Indian sub-continent. Before that, reaching back through industrial modernity, feudalism, and the great civilizations, to the earliest barbarian invasions cleansing and counter-cleansing by ethnic groups have recurred.

Indeed, while ethnic cleansing is anathematized by international law and subject to extreme moral opprobrium by governing elites worldwide, it seems likely to continue until the salience of the ethnic component of NATIONAL IDENTITY is acknowledged by social scientists and realistically addressed by the United Nations and the world's great powers.

### Bibliography

Ahmed, Akbar. 1995. "'Ethnic cleansing': a metaphor for our time," *Ethnic and Racial Studies* 18, 1: 1-25.

Frost, Gerald. (ed.). 1997. *Loyalty Misplaced: Misplaced Virtue and Social Disintegration*. London: Social Affairs Unit.

Horowitz, Donald. 1985. *Ethnic Groups in Conflict*. Berkeley, CA: University of California Press.

Malcolm, Noel. 1994. *Bosnia: A Short History*. Basingstoke: Macmillan.

David Marsland

# Ethnic Competition

Competition should be distinguished from conflict. Competition is a form of struggle conducted according to rules. Athletics teams and individuals compete; if they are caught breaking the rules they may be suspended or eliminated from the competition. Manufacturing companies compete with one another, but are required to observe the law, which may include provisions about fair-trading; members of different national or ethnic groups may hate one another, but still feel that it would be wrong to kill their opponents, even though this feeling, and the implicit rule, may be suspended in times of riot. The classic example of human conflict is that of warfare, but conflict cannot be defined as a form of struggle governed by no rules since there are rules of war and after hostilities end there may be war crimes trials. The distinction between competition and conflict has therefore to depend upon the scope and effectiveness of the rules regulating struggle.

Competition arises from the processes by which individuals seek to attain their goals. Each individual has been socialized as a member of a variety of groups, starting with the family, and can develop human potentialities only in association with fellow group members. People can speak a language only with others who understand the same language. Through socialization most humans learn that one of their goals should be to help other members of their family; these sentiments of obligation and identification are then extended to larger groups, often including the nation. Individuals may compete with one another for personal satisfaction (e.g., that gained by winning a race) or to earn money for the benefit of their dependents. To attain certain goals they have to combine with others, at times in very complex organizations (e.g., the production of a new airplane may require large companies in different European countries to collaborate over several years to produce a machine to be marketed in competition with one produced in North America). Very rarely is there anything approaching perfect competition, especially when governments act to further what are seen as national interests.

When members of different ethnic groups have different goals they do not compete with one another and may live side by side for centuries without losing their distinctive characteristics (as was the case of the Greek communities living within the Ottoman Empire and still obtains for Gypsy— or Roma—groups in many countries). When members of one ethnic group immigrate into an industrialized society any differences between their goals and those of the majority diminish quickly in most fields except that of religious belief where change may be slower. Competition to attain the same goals makes them think and behave in similar ways. This generates processes of assimilation.

Competition has therefore been described as the critical process shaping patterns of ethnic relations. It varies in both form and intensity. Among the forms of competition an important distinction is that between individual and group competition. When members of groups encounter one another in new situations the boundaries between them will be dissolved if they compete as one individual with another, whereas the boundaries between them will be strengthened if they compete as one group with another. Variations in the intensity of competition are associated with the value placed on the goals for which people compete and the degree to which their energies are mobilized for competition.

The form taken by ethnic competition may be affected by the structure of the market in question, and, in particular, by the use of political and economic power to secure advantages for either sellers or buyers. The best-known form of imperfect competition is that of monopoly (one seller, many buyers), but monopsony (one buyer, many sellers) can also be important. For example, employers in the South African mining industry have always needed a supply of black labor. They chose not to bid against one another, which would have driven up the price, but established instead a common recruiting agency to enlist workers at a standard rate. White employers colluded to prevent any of their number paying wages above a certain minimum. There was a triangular relationship between the (white) employer, the higher-paid (white) section of the labor force, and the lower-paid (black) section which was forbidden under the APARTHEID regime to form trade unions. Because the higher-paid section had greater bargaining power it could get a bigger share of the employers' wages bill and therefore profit from its power position. Apartheid governments acted to prevent South Africans of different ethnic origin from competing with one another as individuals while trying to regulate group competition. They failed. But government policies encouraged competing nationalisms.

Powerful interests lay behind the structure of apartheid, but group distinctiveness can be maintained by less overt means. A striking example is that of the Burakumin, the "invisible minority" who comprise about 2 percent of Japan's population. In the seventeenth-century Japanese social structure developed in the direction of a caste system. The process was halted, but not before two outcast groups had been created. The lowest consisted of those who performed ritually polluting tasks including animal slaughter and the disposal of the dead. Though they are not outwardly distinguishable from other Japanese, their descendants are still shunned. Japanese parents will go to great lengths to ensure that their children do not marry partners of Burakumin descent, and employers try to avoid hiring them. In such ways competition is restricted and the minority is obliged to press as a group for political change.

The Burakumin are too small a proportion of the population, and too dispersed, to entertain nationalist aspirations. The black South African elites have cultivated an ethnically inclusive nationalism which may be compared with the cooperation between the Malay and Malaysian Chinese elites in Malaysia, and the situation in eastern Europe (such as in the former Czechoslovakia) where ethnic elites have competed with one another for power and have increased the separation of the groups they represent.

Examples abound of how different forms of competition have shaped ethnic relations but it is difficult to test the claim that competition is the critical process.

## Bibliography

Banton, Michael. 1983. *Racial and Ethnic Competition*. Cambridge: Cambridge University Press. Reprinted Aldershot: Gregg Revivals, 1992.

Michael Banton

# Ethnic Humor

Ethnic humor is based on ethnic "scripts," qualities that are humorously ascribed to different national, sub-national ethnic, regional and local groups as when the Ibos are depicted as canny, the Germans as militaristic, the Rashtis (from Rasht in Iran) as stupid, Essex girls as over-sexed, or Argentineans as conceited. Usually this humor is conveyed in a joke which may take either a narrative or a riddle form. The joke-tellers may or may not believe that the butts of their joke really do possess the quality that is humorously ascribed to them. The Quebecois tell jokes about the Italians being dirty but there is no evidence at all that they really believe this to be the case. By contrast, it is clear that many of those who told jokes about the Italians being cowardly during the Second World War saw the jokes as reflecting reality, for their actions and serious statements at the time were entirely congruent with the jokes they told.

Likewise, the joke-tellers may or may not feel hostile towards the butts of their jokes. There is no independent evidence, for example, to show that the French feel hostile towards the Belgians or Americans towards "Polacks" or Polish-Americans, even though both groups have been made the butt of thousands of French and American stupidity jokes respectively. Jewish ethnic jokes are often self-directed but it would be absurd to regard this as evidence of group masochism. At the same time these jokes can easily be adopted and retold with an identical content but in a different tone and context by hostile, anti-Semites. It is impossible to judge the feelings attached to a specific ethnic joke except in relation to a particular telling in a particular setting.

Ethnic jokes are a world-wide phenomenon to be found in every part of the world. There are Tongan jokes about Fijians, Indian jokes about Sikhs, Syrian jokes about Homsiots, Mexican jokes about Regiomontanos (from Monterrey), South African jokes about van der Merwe the Afrikaner, Greek jokes about Pontians (Black Sea Greeks).

The only part of the world where they are not found is northeast Asia for such jokes are not invented or told in Japan and it is uncertain whether truly ethnic jokes are to be found in China. It is a strange absence since the Japanese do have other forms of ethnic humor. The people of Tohoku in the far northeast of Japan, for instance, are very much the butt of Japanese television situation comedies but they do not appear in popular jokes. The Japanese do not appear to tell jokes about topics other than sex. In other countries too, sexual matters are the main subject of joking but in most countries ethnicity has been the second most favoured topic for humor, though often edged into third place by political jokes in authoritarian countries where political matters may not be discussed. Likewise attempts to censor ethnic jokes have led to their flourishing in the Netherlands in the 1990s, where they are very popular among the working classes, partly as a way of mocking the hegemonic political correctness of the Dutch upper-middle class.

Ethnic humor and ethnic jokes are also a very old phenomenon. Such jokes were popular in the time of the ancient Greeks and the Romans when they were told about the inhabitants of particular city states such a Cumae or Abdera and Egyptian jokes about Nubians seem to be several thousand years old. In mediaeval Europe every country had numerous fool towns whose inhabitants were the butts of jokes about stupidity. As local identity was replaced by ethnic identity in the modern world, so too these town or village jokes were replaced by ethnic stupidity jokes.

Ethnic stupidity jokes are easily the most numerous, geographically widespread and oldest of any ethnic jokes. Such jokes are inevitably told about a neighboring people who occupy a geographically, economically or culturally peripheral position in relation to the joke-teller at the center, as, for example, with the Pontians in relation to Greece, the Irish in relation to Britain, the

## Ethnic Minorities

Pastusos in relation to Colombia and Ecuador, the Sa'idis in relation to Egypt, the Newfoundlanders in relation to Canada or the Sikhs in relation to India and Pakistan. The second most common theme is the opposite of stupidity; it is canniness, the quality of being crafty, stingy, and too clever by half as found in jokes about the Scots, the Dutch, the Jews, the Paisas, the Regiomontanos, the Gujaratis, the New Englanders, or the Ibos. These two opposed qualities reflect the two ways in which it is possible to fail in a modern, impersonal, market and bureaucracy-based society. The stupid lose and the canny are trapped by their own ethic.

Other ethnic jokes seem to put qualities into pairs, so that we have the jokes about the stupid and the canny, the cowardly and the militaristic, the promiscuous, and the frigid. Such jokes make fun of excess in either direction, as if from the standpoint of Aristotle's golden mean.

Most ethnic humor exists in the form of jokes—there are tens of thousands of them invented and circulated not by script writers but by millions of ordinary people. As such they constitute a true popular culture and a vehicle for individual creativity in a way that is not true of, say, television sit-coms. Nonetheless, television relies heavily on ethnic humor as in such popular series on British television as *Dad's Army, Allo, Allo, Fawlty Towers,* and *Not the Nine O'Clock News.* Likewise, many of the great comic writers of the past such as Jaroslav Hasek, Phillip Roth, or Dylan Thomas have relied heavily on ethnic humor, often making fun of their own people's traits. Without ethnic humor both literature and popular culture would be greatly impoverished.

### Bibliography

Davies, Christie. 1990. *Ethnic Humor Around the World: A Comparative Analysis.* 2nd edn 1997. Bloomington: Indiana University Press.

Davies, Christie. 1998. *Jokes and their Relation to Society.* New York and Berlin: Mouton de Gruyter.

Oring, Elliott. 1992. *Jokes and their Relations.* Lexington: University Press of Kentucky.

Raskin, Victor. 1987. *Semantic Mechanisms of Humor.* Dordrecht: D. Reidel.

Ziv, Avner and Zajdman, Anat. 1993. *Semites and Stereotypes: Characteristics of Jewish Humor.* Westport, CT: Greenwood.

Christie Davies

## Ethnic Minorities

It is sometimes difficult to distinguish an ethnic minority from another kind of minority. About a person's nationality there can be little doubt because this is decided by entitlement to a passport. When a person who lives within one state but identifies himself or herself with the people of another state, and is so regarded by others, then that person can be considered a member of a national minority. There is no comparable criterion for determining membership of an ethnic minority.

In situations of conflict almost all persons may identify themselves continuously with an ethnic or national minority. In other situations identification is a variable operating in certain circumstances but not others. This variable is affected by group mobilization. A political entrepreneur or activist may succeed in mobilizing members of an ethnic or national minority in pursuit of common ends and in persuading them to show solidarity with other members.

In the former Yugoslavia there were people who were called, and called themselves, Albanians, Croats, Hungarians, Macedonians, Montenegrins, Muslims, Serbs, and Slovenes. These are all proper names. Some observers called all these groups ethnic minorities because they were constituted by common descent and shared culture. Many of them shared a common language (Serbo-Croat) with dialectic variations. Some groups had a distinctive religion, Croats being Catholic while the Serbs were Orthodox. The word *Narod* was officially used to identify five "nations"—Croats, Macedonians, Montenegrins, Slovenes, and Serbs with distinctive constitutional rights. The name "Muslim" was used to designate the majority group in Bosnia-Herzegovina, some, but by no means all, of whom were practicing Muslims. They were given the status of a nation after 1968. The word *Narodnost* was used for "national minorities" like the Albanians in Kosovo and the Hungarians in Vojvodina.

Little is to be gained by debating whether Albanians in the Yugoslav republic of Kosovo or in what is now the Former Yugoslav Republic of Macedonia (to use the U.N. name for the state that calls itself the Republic of Macedonia) are ethnic or national minorities or both. What should be recognized, however, is the difference between the application of the concept in Europe and in countries of immigration. The expression "ethnic minority" came into use in the United States as a name for "hyphenated" groups, like Italian-Americans and Greek-Americans. They were groups sharing a distinctive culture and descent that marked out their use of a private realm within the citizenship they shared with other ethnic minorities. There was no tension between their being members of an ethnic group and being U.S. citizens. In Australia there was a comparable readiness to see persons of Italian or Greek origin as forming distinctive groups within Australian society.

In Europe, however, the adjective "ethnic" was often used to identify a group membership that overlapped with nationality. Croats and Slovenes were members of groups recognized as nations within the Yugoslav federal state. In 1991 they became members of independent nation-states. So the word "ethnic" has been used to designate at least two different kinds of group, and it may be convenient to distinguish two kinds of ethnicity. Primary ethnicity is present when a shared self-identification as members of a group based on common descent and culture coincides with membership of a nation; secondary ethnicity is present when persons identify with a group based upon common descent and culture within a state. According to this usage, Croat and Slovene ethnicity changed from secondary to primary through political struggle.

Secondary ethnicity may be illustrated by groups such as Irish-Americans and Italian-Australians. In France and Germany young people of North African and Turkish origin may identify themselves with others of similar descent and may be culturally distinctive, but the national societies are less ready to recognize them as ethnic minorities. In France it has been declared unconstitutional to represent Bretons, Basques, and Corsicans as minorities—let alone North Africans. In Germany, most Turkish workers and members of their families remain Turkish nationals and there is no recognition comparable to that in the United

States and Australia, that citizens may be of different ethnic origin.

In Britain white people perceive persons of African or Asian appearance as ethnically distinctive but rarely think of themselves as possessing ethnic characteristics. Tariq Modood (1997) has described two dimensions of ethnic difference: behavioral and associational. The behavioral dimension is what people do, like speaking a particular language, attending a particular place of worship, wearing a particular kind of dress or celebrating a special holiday. The associational dimension is what people say or believe about themselves. Research workers found that for the first, or settler, generation, the two dimensions were closely related; but for the new generation the connections were looser. An ethnic element might be important to a personal sense of identity, but that sense was often affected more by the individual's own experiences of the majority society than by any influence transmitted through the individual's parents. Most members of both generations thought of themselves as being both British and members of a minority. This is a very different sense of ethnic minority membership than that reported from Bosnia.

### Bibliography

Banton, Michael. 1997. *Ethnic and Racial Consciousness*. London: Longman.
Modood, Tariq, Berthoud, Richard, et al. 1997. *Ethnic Minorities in Britain: Diversity and Disadvantage*. London: Policy Studies Institute.

Michael Banton

# Ethnicity

"Ethnicity" is a modern term, with Greek roots, referring to a phenomenon of near-universal applicability. The term is often joined with the term "RACE," but ethnicity is a concept distinct to that of "race" and with a wider remit. Almost all societies have ethnic groups identifiable within them, usually, although not always, as a minority of the population. The term "ethnic" group can be defined as a collectivity within a larger society which has real or imagined common ancestry, memories of a shared historical past, and a cultural focus

## Ethnicity

upon one or more common elements which distinguishes the members of the group from other members of the society. These distinguishing characteristics will include one or more of the following: area of origin, language, religion, nationality, kinship patterns, physical appearance such as skin color. Thus, people of Irish origin in Britain, Italian-Americans, Jewish-Americans and Indian-Americans, the Chinese minority in Indonesia, persons of Indian origin in Trinidad, Turkish people living in Germany, are all examples of ethnic groups. The existence of an ethnic group entails some recognition by the members of the group that they share ethnic group membership in common, which may be marked by symbolic acts and events.

The term "ethnicity," the character or quality of an ethnic group, derives from the Greek word *ethnos* (a people), but its application by social scientists in the sense defined above is modern, of recent origin, dating variously to the 1930s, 1950s or 1970s depending on the case to which one accords priority. The study of ethnicity has been pioneered by sociologists and anthropologists, but is now also pursued by political scientists, social geographers, cultural studies specialists and others. Although it is relatively easy to give a general sense of the phenomena with which the concept of ethnicity deals, it remains an elusive one in any precise definitional or theoretical sense, partly because it is an "essentially contested concept" about which contrasting theories of ethnicity have been constructed.

The mosaic of ethnic groups found within the same polity or the same society, has usually resulted from conquest, colonization, annexation, unfree or free migration, and even NATIONALISM. European imperial expansion brought white minorities to many parts of the world, and in some societies such as South Africa and Brazil created mixed-blood groups. Ethnic trading minorities were part and parcel of the imperial system. Societies of mass immigration such as the United States and Australia have many different ethnic groups within them as a result of cultural distinctiveness being maintained after migration. In Europe, conquest and annexation have been regular occurrences historically.

The relationship between ethnicity and nationalism is a complex one and can be close, but they are distinct concepts. The coming together of members of different ethnic groups within the same territory (for example, Serbs, Croats and Bosnians within the former Yugoslavia) may or may not lead to stability and co-existence. Nationalism can frequently have the effect of heightening ethnic consciousness and increasing divisions within political units. There is no necessary correspondence between ethnic boundaries and political boundaries, hence there is no necessary connection between ethnicity and the state. The political map of much of Africa (e.g., Nigeria) was constructed arbitrarily without reference to the location of different ethnic or tribal groups. Members of one ethnic group may be scattered across several political units (e.g., Kurds in Iraq, Iran, Syria and Turkey). Under certain conditions ethnicity may be transformed into citizenship. "Ethno-nationalism" can come into being where legal rights to citizenship are tied to membership of a particular ethnic group, as with the "*jus sanguinis*" in Germany recognising the rights of overseas Germans, and right of return granted to all Jews in the Israeli constitution, whilst denying the same right to Palestinian Arabs.

The relationship between ethnicity and "race" is perhaps closer, but these two concepts are also quite distinct. A racial group is composed of people who are believed to share a similar biological descent, usually identified in terms of skin color or body form. Even though it lacks biological or scientific validity as a category, the *belief* that such differences exist forms a basis for social action, and hence acquires social significance. By contrast, as was noted above, members of an ethnic group are distinguished by a variety of characteristics, singly or in combination, such as language, religion, geographical origin, kinship etc., which are cultural in character. In relations between groups identified as "races," there is more likely to be a dominant-subordinate relationship, in which members of the other "race" are subordinated and stigmatized. Relations between people identified as members of an "ethnic group" tend to be competitive in character (see also ETHNIC COMPETITION). In some situations, differences may be characterized as functional (e.g., a trading minority) and this may reduce ethnic antagonism; in others, ethnic differences may lead to a struggle for access to scarce social and economic resources (competition for positions in the labor market). There has been a marked tendency in social science to use "ethnicity" or "ethnic" in preference to "race" in recent years, and even to include "race" as a sub-category of "ethnic group." In addition, the analytical frame is affected by the society concerned. In North America and Britain it has been more common to juxtapose and contrast "race" and "ethnicity" than in France or Germany.

In the United States, theoretical contrasts have frequently been drawn between the mobility within an opportunity structure of white ethnic minorities such as Irish-Americans or Polish-Americans, and the blocks to upward mobility facing African-Americans, the descendants of slaves. Lieberson, among others, has argued that the experience of each group has been qualitatively different, so that the white ethnic minority member has not faced the entrenched inequality, and the justificatory beliefs to support that unequal treatment of members of subordinate "racial" groups, which black Americans have faced (Lieberson 1980). Indeed, other, non-European ethnic groups, such as Chinese- and Japanese-Americans, have been notably more successful in terms of educational mobility and employment than the average for the white population, so that ethnic group membership is seen as conferring advantage upon members of those groups.

What then explains the dynamics of the processes of ethnic group formation, and the consequences that it has for the integration of societies? Several distinct and contrasting theoretical approaches to the study of ethnicity may be distinguished. One set of theories start from the postulate that there is an objective basis in membership of the ethnic group through the common descent which the members share. Consanguinity with members of a group which is a more or less endogamous historico-cultural community is the basis of ethnicity. Such theories of the PRIMORDIALITY of ethnicity (sometimes also termed ascriptive theories) maintain that primary blood ties lead to overriding emotional attachments and allegiances (Shils 1995; Grosby 1995).

Ethnicity is ascribed, it is a "given," and as such transcends individual orientations and personal circumstances. It is a property of the group and of everyone born in the group. The strength of ethnic attachments in the modern world is thus explained by these blood ties and the emotions tied to them, which are far more intense than those pertaining, for example, to one's employment or one's support for a political party, about which rational judgement is exercised.

The conception of ethnic groups as makers and carriers of unique cultural values and the desirability of preserving these values as resources dates back to the German Romantics, particularly JOHANN GOTTFRIED HERDER. Herder stressed the importance of language as the vehicle of the distinctive systems of values whereby "nature" divided mankind into groups that we call "nations." The idea of the *Volk* played a central part in his theory, as unifying blood and soil, and through this notion explicit primordialism came to have a considerable influence upon Soviet ethnology. S. M. Shirokogorov in the 1920s defined *"ethnos"* as "a group of people speaking one and the same language and admitting common origin, characterized by a set of customs and a life style, which are preserved and sanctified by tradition, which distinguishes it from the others of the same kind." A stable core of ethnicity persists through all social formations. Walker Connor has explained the "national bond" as arising through ethnogenesis (Connor 1994). The fact that "People of the same blood attract!" is a fact of the unconscious, non-rational, emotional side of mankind.

A second theoretical approach, with affinities to functionalism, portrays ethnicity as part of MODERNIZATION. Claims to ethnicity, in this view, are a product of political myths, created and manipulated by cultural elites in their pursuit of advantages and power. Such INSTRUMENTALIST theories treat ethnicity as a remnant of the pre-industrial order, gradually declining in significance as the modern state and national integration advance, and the assimilation of ethnic minorities occurs. Marxist theorists anticipated that class would emerge as the dominant social cleavage. Such an approach was heavily influenced by American social science and the experience of the absorption of white ethnic groups into American society, culminating in ASSIMILATION. Modernity was expected to erode ethnicity as a principle of social solidarity and replace it with instrumental rationality.

In contrast to these two theories which emphasize the properties of the group and of the nation and society, a third theory, the constructivist or situational, puts the emphasis upon the ways in which people socially construct their ethnicity in a situational way. According to this view, what really matters, is that people define themselves as culturally or physically distinct from others. Shared descent is secondary, and may be manufactured or invented. Fictive kinship, invented blood ties, may serve their purpose as well as real ties. Social anthropologist FREDERICK BARTH has suggested that what is important is how members of an ethnic group define its *boundaries*, and defend these boundaries against incursions by others (Barth 1969). The ethnic boundary canalizes social life into networks of "us" which exclude "them." The content of ethnic claims is less important than the ways in which they are mobilized in real life. Ethnicity, in this view, necessarily implies a fluidity in the constitution of ethnic identity.

A fourth theory of ethnicity is couched in terms of RATIONAL CHOICE and seeks to show how individuals' preferences in social and economic behavior are constrained by the social structure in which they are situated. A rational person will only comply with group norms when there is a positive or negative sanction, or a selective incentive, for doing so.

None of the four theories is wholly compelling. MAX WEBER was of the view that the concept of ethnicity concealed very diverse phenomena behind a uniform term, and considered that it tended to dissolve when analysed rigorously. The first, primordial theory of blood ties, does not account for the fact that much "tradition" is invented, and that there is a large component of the "mythic" and "symbolic" in modern ethnicity (Hobsbawm and Ranger 1983). Myths of common origin may appeal to primordial traits, but they are often constructions after the event to justify subsequent actions. The second theory underplays the continuing strength of ethnic identification in the modern world, and as Herbert

Blumer has shown, there is no logic of industrialism which necessarily leads to the withering of such ties (Blumer 1965). Full assimilation of ethnic minorities does not occur—the melting pot fails to fuse—and class does not override ethnic ties. Constructivist theory gives too much emphasis to free will and group interaction, and neglects both the extent of constraint on the social actor, and the emotional power of ethnicity. However, some of the strengths of the constructivist approach are, first, that it can account for changing group boundaries and identifications; and, second, that it usefully shifts analytic attention from a single group by itself to the relations between ethnic groups. Finally, rational choice theory, in contrast to a primordial approach, seeks to reduce social action to the evaluation of action taken under external constraint, but fails to elucidate the internal aspect of action, and the extent to which non-rational orientations may enter into ethnic cohesion and identification, a possible strength of the first approach.

## Bibliography

Banks, M. 1996. *Ethnicity: Anthropological Constructions*. London: Routledge.

Barth, F. 1969. "Introduction," in F. Barth (ed.), *Ethnic Groups and Boundaries: The Social Organisation of Culture Difference*. Oslo: Universitetsforlaget.

Blumer, H. 1965. "Industrialisation and race relations," in G. Hunter (ed.), *Industrialisation and Race Relations: A Symposium*. Oxford: Oxford University Press.

Connor, W. 1994. *Ethno-Nationalism: The Quest for Understanding*. Princeton: Princeton University Press.

Grosby, Steven. 1995. "Territoriality: The transcendental, primordial feature of modern societies," *Nations and Nationalism* 1, 2: 143-162.

Guibernau, M. and Rex, J. 1997. *The Ethnicity Reader: Nationalism, Multiculturalism and Migration*. Cambridge: Polity.

Hobsbawm, Eric and Ranger, Terence. 1983. *The Invention of Tradition*. Cambridge: Cambridge University Press.

Hutchinson, J. and Smith, A. D. (eds.). 1996. *Ethnicity*. (Reader). Oxford: Oxford University Press.

Lieberson, S. 1980. *A Piece of the Pie: Blacks and White Immigrants Since 1880*. Berkeley: University of California Press.

Schermerhorn, R. A. 1978. *Comparative Ethnic Relations: A Framework for Theory and Research*. Chicago: University of Chicago Press.

Shils, Edward. 1995. "Nation, nationality, nationalism, and civil society," *Nations and Nationalism* 1, 1:93-118.

Martin Bulmer

# Ethnicity and Foreign Policy in Multi-Ethnic States: The American Model

Any attempt to define ethnicity raises at least three sociological problems: who is an ethnic; how can ethnicity be distinguished from other social variables and character traits; and what can ethnicity predict—what are its behavioral consequences, especially in the sphere of national policy formulation? Before coming to terms with the current ideological and political uses of ethnicity, it may be worthwhile to describe the ideological sources of the current celebration of ethnicity. The general characterization of ethnicity in the social science literature can be summarized under seven categories: (1) There is a strong tendency to describe ethnics in terms of whites living in the urban complex or in the inner city, in contrast to whites living in suburban or non-urban regions; (2) a distinction is often made between nativists and ethnics, that is, between people who have Protestant and English-speaking backgrounds and those with Catholic and non-English-speaking backgrounds, although in some cases (for instance, the Irish) ethnics may be identified solely on the basis of religion; (3) it is frequently claimed that ethnics are neither very rich nor very poor, nor part of either the ruling class or the under class. Rather, they are often identified with either the blue-collar working class or the lower-middle class; (4) the current literature presents highly selective idiosyncratic definitions of ethnicity. Jews and Japanese are often excluded by intellectual fiat from the ethnic category on the basis of their middle- or upper-middle class position and on the basis of their upward mobility through

education; at other times, they are included as a political category of an "anti-WASP" sort; (5) ethnicity within lower-class groups or racial groups such as blacks seems to be excluded from discussion. Thus, for example, distinctions and differences between East African blacks and Jamaican blacks are very rarely spoken of by those defining or employing the term "ethnicity"; (6) ethnics are said to have in common a vocational orientation toward education, in contrast to a liberal arts or humanities orientation. They tend to be non-academic, anti-intellectual, and highly pragmatic. Interestingly, although blacks are perhaps the best illustration of a vocationally oriented subculture, they are not generally categorized as ethnics; (7) ethnics are usually said to possess characteristics and attitudes identified with those on the political Right: strong patriotic fervor, religious fundamentalism, authoritarian family patterns, and so forth. Indeed, characterizations of ethnicity and conservatism show such a profound overlap that the only difference would appear to be the currently positive attitude toward such behavior on the part of the learned observers (Coles 1971; Namias and Coles 1992).

Determining who is an ethnic has more to do with sentiment than with science. The concept defines a new, positive attitude toward those who fit the model. One now hears "them" spoken of as middle class, lower-middle class, or working class in contrast to lower class. "They" are said to be part of a great new wave of populism: the struggle against opulence on the one hand and welfare on the other. As such, the concept of ethnicity claims a political middle ground. It does not celebrate a national consensus nor does it accept the concept of a class struggle. Its ideologists perceive of ethnics as a series of interest groups rather than a social class. There is an unstated kinship between classical liberalism and the ideology of ethnicity. It promotes the theme of cultural pluralism and cultural difference more distinctly than it does social change or social action. This helps to explain why dedicated civil libertarians have moved their attentions and affections from the black underclass to the white ethnic class (Novak 1993; Cottle 1982).

One of the more customary ploys in refocusing attention away from blacks and towards ethnics is to point to quantitative parity. The new ethnics take note of the fact that there are nearly as many Americans of Italian and Irish extraction as there are of African extraction. The supreme difficulty in this sort of quantitative exercise is the absence of the qualitative common sense that blacks have of a unique and special history in America that provides them with a solidarity and a definition quite apart from other Americans; whereas the Italians and Irish, and other ethnic groupings as well, have a far weaker sense of delineation and definition. The blacks (and this they share uniquely with the Jews) represent a group apart, while the new ethnics represent groups that would like the future pay-offs, but not the historic penalties, of becoming a group apart. It might well be the case that even blacks will be divided by sharpening class divisions to the point where racial commonalities dwindle. If this should be the case, then it is more likely that class factors rather than ethnic factors would become the beneficiary of economic cleavages (Wilson 1978).

### The Roots of Ethnicity

The rise of ethnicity as a separate factor reflects the existence of a cross-cutting culture that reduces any sense of common identity among those who comprise the 100 million members of the total working class in America of whom fewer than one-fifth are organized into unions. Observers have discussed the persistence of ethnic identity from this vantage point. Michael Parenti has observed that in a single weekend in New York, separate dances for persons of Hungarian, Irish, Italian, German, and Polish extractions are advertised in the neighborhood newspapers and the foreign language press. Others have noted the persistence of a tightly knit network of relationships among Italians living in Boston and in Chicago. Occupationally, the lower economic rung embraces secretaries and assembly-line workers, senior clerks, and cab drivers. Geographically, workers spread out over the South with its racially dominated politics, the Midwest where fear of communism is a serious sentiment, and the Northeast where problems of traffic congestion and state financial support for parochial schools excite political passions (Howard 1971).

Ethnicity thus refers to a cluster of cultural factors that define the sociogram of the person beyond or apart from the racial or class connections of that person. It defines the binding impact of linguistic origins, geographic backgrounds, cultural and culinary tastes, and religious homogeneity. In this sense, the concept of ethnicity is not only distinguished from class but in a certain respect must be considered its operational counterpart. It provides the cultural and theological linkages that cut through class lines and form new sources of tension and definition of inclusionary-exclusionary relationships in an American society grown weary of class perspectives on social reality.

The emphasis upon ethnicity signifies, in some measure, the decline of the achievement orientation and the return to an ascriptive vision. Generational success can no longer be measured in terms of job performance or career satisfaction. Therefore, new definitions of group membership are sought in order to generate pride. These often take the form of a celebration of ethnic origins and a feeling that such origins somehow are more significant to group cohesion than is class or race.

The notion of ethnicity, like other barometers of disaffection from the larger nation-state, is indicative of problems in self-definition. Americans have long been known to have weak class identification. Most studies have shown that class identification is weak because class conflict is thought foreign to American society—nearly everyone claims to be a middle-class member. Few see themselves at either end of the class spectrum. In fact, most analysts suggest that "The overwhelming bulk of Americans see themselves in the middle classes," and see class itself "of relatively meagre significance" (Wattenberg 1996). As a result, class as a source of status distinction is strong, but as a source of economic mobilization, it is weak. In a sense, the concept of ethnicity closely emulates the concept of race; for race, unlike class, is based upon ascription rather than achievement. However, ethnicity defines a community of people having national origin, language, religion, and/or race in common. For some, it further entails a commonality of tastes or "gut issues." For example, Poles and Italians share religious similarities, but they are not likely to share language identities. The Catholic Church has long recognized ethnicity on the basis of linguistic and national origin despite the formal universal ministerial claims of Catholicism. Determining the behavioral consequences of ethnicity entails the difficulty of establishing whether or not there are common political demands or even common economic conditions that all national and linguistic minorities share. Aside from the fact that a bare majority of ethnics participate in Democratic Party politics, there is little evidence that ethnics do in fact share common political goals. There seem to be greater gaps between first- and second-generation Irish and Poles than Irish and Poles of the same generation. Consequently, the actual power of ethnicity as an explanatory variable must be carefully evaluated and screened.

The new ethnicity often reflects rather than shapes the new politics. The present era represents a new kind of emphasis. The collapse of federalism, the strain on the American national system, and the consequent termination of the "melting pot" ideology has led to a situation where ethnicity, in a sense, fulfills the thirst for community—a modest-sized community in which the values of rural America as well as rural Europe could be simulated in the context of a post-industrial world, yet without the critique implied by the radical and youth movements (Glazer and Moynihan 1992). Disillusionment with the American system and its inability to preserve a universal series of goals has led to a re-emergence of community-centered parochial and particularistic doctrines. Indeed, the positive response of the American nation to the historic injustices heaped upon the black people has made it seem that ethnicity could achieve the same results by using a similar model of social protest.

The new emphasis on ethnicity is distinguishable from the old emphasis on minority groups in the United States primarily because it represents a repudiation of the "melting pot" ideology, but, more significantly, a breakdown in what used to be known as the majority. It is terribly difficult to have minority studies in a world where the major impulse is weak, nonexistent, or defined as another minority. Hence, the rise of ethnicity as a rallying point seems to be in inverse proportion to the decline of white Anglo-Saxon Protestant-

ism as a consensus framework. The latter, too, has turned ethnic. Ethnicity has become a relative concept instead of a subordinate concept.

With the shift of attitudes at the ideological level, what once appeared to be a minority problem with its attendant drives toward integration into the American mainstream has now become an ethnic problem, with its attendant drives toward self-determination apart from the American mainstream. This is the result of the erosion of that mainstream. With the existence of 20 to 30 million first- and second-generation Italian-Americans, 9 to 10 million Spanish-speaking Americans, some 15 million Irish-Americans (these often overlapping with 60 million Catholics), who, in turn, share a country with 6 million Jews and 30 million blacks, the notion of majority status for white Protestant America has been seriously questioned. The notion of the "WASP" serves to identify a dominant economic group but no longer a uniquely gifted or uniquely destined-to-rule political or cultural group. Ethnicity has served to express a genuine plurality of interests, without necessarily effecting a revolution in lifestyles or attitudes. Equality increasingly becomes the right to be different and to express such differences in language, customs, and habits, rather than a shared position in the white Anglo-Saxon Protestant ethos that dominated the United States up to and through the end of World War II and the Cold War period.

Ethnicity is also an expression of the coming into being of new nations throughout the Third World. As a consequence, this international trend toward diversified and separatist power bases has had domestic repercussions on minority standing in the United States. The external reinforcement of internal minorities has changed the self-image of these minorities. The new ethnics are (in part at least) the old minorities in an era of post-colonialism (Smith 1981).

## The Politics of Ethnicity

The amount of research and theorizing that has been produced concerning ethnicity is of such magnitude that one must wonder why so little has been done thus far on the impact of ethnic and national minority groups in the formation of U.S.

# Ethnicity and Foreign Policy in Multi-Ethnic States

foreign policy. Sometimes the most obvious aspects of an issue elude us precisely because of their *prima facie* character. In this instance, the overseas origins of most ethnics, and presumably their continuing concern with events taking place in the mother or father country of origin, in large measure explain the importance of the subject at hand: the impact of ethnic groups on U. S. foreign policy.

The consensus among researchers seems to be that the actual amount of impact has been minimal; far less than one would predict given the large number of immigrant peoples involved in gross aggregate terms. A number of research papers come perilously close to suggesting that the independent and dependent variables should be reversed: that U.S. foreign policy serves to galvanize ethnic sentiments as much, if not more, than the other way around.

If the impact of ethnics has been somewhat ambiguous in congressional quarters, there can be no ambiguity about the relative absence of ethnic impact at the judicial and executive levels. An extremely important point is what might be called the area of inter-ethnic group rivalries. Such rivalries tend to minimize any interest group impact by creating a cancellation or veto effect; that is, one ethnic group becoming hostile or remaining indifferent to the needs of another. For example, the specific demands for national independence and autonomy by Lithuanians, Latvians, and Poles are rarely, if ever, coordinated with demands for Jewish circles seeking to emigrate from the Soviet Union. Although they may have a shared animosity toward the Soviet system, and, although some leaders within these émigré groups have sought collaboration, at the same time they retain their own deep, inherited animosities towards each other. Similarly, differences between religious subvariables within ethnic groups may mediate or vitiate the impact of ethnic politics. In considering the extent to which the structure of Catholic churches in certain industrial parts of the United States are divided along national lines, that is, Italian Catholics, Polish Catholics, Irish Catholics, and so on, one can see what a formidable obstacle it is to generate ethnic politics that would have sufficient impact to moderate, much less cancel, established U. S. foreign policy. In short, when the aggregate numbers are further re-fined, we have a problem of a critical mass, an absence of a hegemonic standpoint that would make ethnics speak with a united voice towards common ends.

Another aspect that vitiates ethnic group politics is the complex nature of struggles being waged overseas. The conflicts between Biafra and Nigeria had the earmarks of a fundamental schism: Biafra asserting the right of each nation to self-determination, confronting Nigeria with its claims of the necessity of national cohesion over and against separatist demands. There are no absolute rights or wrongs at this level; just decisions and choices that American blacks had to confront and clearly did by choosing different sides of that struggle. Similarly, the Angolan struggle pitted the Cuban armed forces against military groups supported by the United States and South Africa. One might say that the blacks in America were caught between the devil and the deep blue sea: a choice between superpowers at one level and white satellites sending in guerrilla forces at quite another level—but such is the world of overseas conflicts. To make ethnic solidarity, even black solidarity on Third World matters obvious or *prima facie*, is to miss the complexity of real events. And when one examines a place like former Yugoslavia, in which at least six distinct ethnic groups were in extreme conflict, the question of policy choices becomes even more tangled and complex.

This would indicate that the ethnic variable, even at its more compelling levels, probably remains less unified to its adherents than other variables such as class, religion, or nation. It might be argued that a breakdown of perceived American interests has led to a return of pluralism—a pluralism emerging as a secular nationalism rather than a clerical theology. In the nineteenth century, pluralism really meant the proliferation of Protestant groups. The pluralism of the early twentieth century had meant the opening up of the economic valves to new groups, including new levels of mass participation in social movements aimed to stimulate the voluntary improvement of American life. One might say that the emergence of ethnicity represents a third-stage rocket in the take-off of pluralism: one that is based on the importance of secular national concerns in decision-making at personal levels, that is, marriage partners, work establishments, and so on. Again, such a pluralism, while strengthening the U. S. capacity to ensure its survival, even in the face of its current collective *anomie*, hardly adds up to a unified ethnic power bloc capable of influencing U. S. foreign policy.

There is a problem of strategy that is hidden behind the phrase "hyphenated peoples." How long, in spatial and temporal terms, is the hyphen between the terms Greek-Americans, Afro-Americans, and Jewish-Americans? Or, to be more specific, what weight does the ethnic factor prior to the hyphen assume in relation to the American after the hyphen? These questions involve strategic decisions that determine, in large measure, not only attitudes toward U. S. foreign policy, but ultimately issues of allegiance to America in a time of total conflict. We need only remind ourselves how rapidly support for German-American Nazi Bunds evaporated in 1940-41 once the United States entered World War II. Thus, even when ethnic groups in America receive strong overseas reinforcements and endorsements, when ethnicity appears to be a clear obstacle to U. S. foreign policy, it collapses under the weight of the national interest.

Political decisions involve not just a strident defense of overseas interests of ethnic groups, but also some careful calculations of what America means to these groups. To run the risk of complete isolation from a U.S. foreign policy context is to ensure ethnic defeats and frustrations. This is just as true for Afro-American groups who have to decide on the importance of African language, culture, and customs, vis-à-vis participation in American affairs, as it is for Jewish groups who, while seemingly having struck a balance between allegiance to the United States and commitment to the national goals and destinies of Israel, nonetheless, are constantly faced with pressure that at the very least weakens, if not entirely cancels, the impact of ethnic groups forging U. S. foreign policy. Even when there is relative solidarity in the goal orientation of such ethnic groups, only a concomitant drive by the national policy can effectuate changes in a desired way. Thus, we are faced with converting a problem of punctuation —the hyphen—into a problem of social science:

how do groups organize their politics in order to maximize both American and ethnic ends? Without showing what is in it for America, ethnic pressure groups are foredoomed to failure.

A critical factor is that ethnic politics have often involved generational solidarity. Common language, a shared culture, and a struggle to maintain and transmit that inheritance to subsequent generations born and reared within a strictly American context have provided the basis for ethnic solidarity. The problem here is nearly insurmountable. It involves the maintenance of dual cultures within a political and economic system that largely rewards high participation in the American culture and maximum utilization of the English language. There are so many cross-currents among the young that a considerable amount of ethnic politics is drained off in maintaining ethnic loyalties rather than extending such ethnicity to the policy-making arena. In this sense, the ethnic factor can be sharply contrasted to membership in the trade-union movement. There is no ethnic personage comparable to George Meany, nothing in ethnic politics that witnesses one leader coughing and 15 to 18 million members sneezing. That, in a sense, is exactly what the ethnic factor lacks in sociological terms, because the purpose of ethnicity is to distinguish not just the ethnic sub-culture from the larger culture, but the ethnic group from other ethnic groups. The search for distinction and distinctiveness serves to weaken, on sociological grounds, any overall political impact on international grounds.

The crossover points between religion and ethnicity also serve dramatically to weaken any direct ethnic impact on political affairs. The needs of a religious grouping are by no means isomorphic with those of an ethnic grouping. The Catholic Church, which often reveals clear lines of ethnic demarcation between Irish, Polish, Italian, and other ethnic forces, still registers a general orientation that overrides, to some extent at least, specific nationalities that the Catholic Church represents. This is true to an ever greater extent in the Greek community, where the power and potency of the Orthodox Church served to dampen, and in many instances still, opposition to the Greek military junta, despite the obvious sentiments of the Greek-American community for democratic government in the old country. Similarly, in the Jewish world, the pluralization process has gone on unabated. Orthodox, Conservative, Reform, and Reconstructionist temples and synagogues compete with each other for membership, loyalties, and affections. They provide a particularistic flavor to Jewish-American life that limits a singular Jewish impact on U. S. foreign policy, even with respect to Israel. Thus, the crosscutting impact of religiosity and ethnicity must be viewed as a major deterrent to an organized expression of ethnic politics in America.

There is a clear problem of organization involved in ethnic politics. In decades earlier in this century, and even in the mid-nineteenth century, ethnic groups were social rather than political in character. Their concerns were insurance policies, bank loans to the landsman, services to specialized charities that did not trust the larger culture, burial plots to ensure cultural continuity as well as eternal salvation. All of these activities were so worthwhile, but so readily absorbed by the general culture in more recent years. Jewish fraternal organizations, for example, can no longer compete with New York Life or Metropolitan Life in terms of insurance policy benefits. Hence, they are faced with either going out of business or finding new causes. Given Robert Michel's iron law of oligarchy we know that organizations do not voluntarily remove themselves from the world simply because they have no social function. What they do is find new functions. Chief among these are the causes of brethren less favored by fortune and fate, living in Europe, Asia, or Third World contexts. This clear differential permits the ethnic and fraternal societies and clubs to mobilize moral sentiments as well as muster economic support for these less fortunate ethnic kinsmen. In other words, what we have, in part at least, is a change in function in order to guarantee organizational continuity, and not simply a response to daily tragedy and travail taking place in an overseas context.

What we are witnessing in American society is, at the moment, a unique event. The end of the achievement society and the emergence of the ascription society is clearly upon us. As traditional forms of mobility begin to shut down, new forms of social distinction emerge. Social mobility comes upon the hard fact that the third- or fourth-generation daughter or son of a medical doctor, accountant, or engineer cannot aspire to anything more than their parental generation in economic terms. One might argue that the entire generational revolt of the 1960s was a backhanded recognition that going up on the occupational ladder of mobility no longer made sufficient sense to merit the effort. As a result, there has been a huge return to ascribed features of social life: to matters of race, sex, and religion, as well as to national origin. Ethnicity became a telling differentiation between people who in a previous generation were marked only by competing on the way up the occupational ladder of success. Now that the ladder has been opened wide, the bases of differentiation must clearly shift. It becomes pointless to discuss America in terms of the theory of the "melting pot" given the absence of achievement as the common denominator. The question becomes, in effect: what form of solidification remains to be tapped? This is an extremely important sociological aspect of the current ethnic revival, especially the search for ethnicity as a factor in the formation of interest group politics at home rather than abroad.

A serious factor inhibiting the expansion of ethnic politics is the potency of the United States as a centripetal force—even in the absence of older *Gemeinschaft* forms of authority. We must never ignore the "push" factors that led people out of their native lands as well as the "pull" factors that brought them to America. Ultimately, the passions for exercising a decisive influence in U.S. policy toward other nations are dampened by a foreknowledge that the country of origin was not so perfect when these people emigrated and is of dubious improvement years later. Often, the literature recites animosity for ethnics who have "forgotten" their ancestral hunting grounds. Regrettably, these same critics have more precisely forgotten the reasons for the century of immigration between 1850 and 1950. If America did not always turn out to be a promised land, there was little doubt in the minds of the émigrés that they were moving from lands often without the promise of equity, justice, or freedom. Thus, the limited capacity for impacting foreign policy is not necessarily a sign of confusion or weakness, nor the absence of will or interest on the part of the ethnic peoples to shape relevant policy.

In the act of forging pluralistic doctrines of political behavior, ethnic groups have carried over the ideology of pluralism to the inner workings of their own organizational life. In the very process of such democratization they have become linked with general American interests, norms, and values. As a result, ethnicity has probably contributed more to the forging of an American consensus than it has to the erosion of that consensus that seemingly characterizes other critical pivots such as class, race, and sex in the hierarchy of social stratification.

### Ethnic Interests and the National Interest

I have tried to illustrate the major series of dilemmas in efforts by ethnic nationals to overthrow or even alter American national policy. The main stumbling blocks are (1) the competition among and between differing ethnic groups; (2) rivalries within each of the major ethnic national clusters; and (3) specific resistance on the part of the national interest to limit and even cancel out ethnic nationalism. These are concerns that weigh heavily enough to merit books on each of the subjects, so all that can be done at the level of a brief essay is to highlight by some familiar examples, the limits to ethnicity in the formation of an overall American nationalism.

In considering the competition between ethnic nationals, one can readily cite the historic animosities of groups such as Greek-Americans for Turkish-Americans. What plays out on a smaller Cypriot canvas has ramifications throughout the United States. A similar situation obtains between Bosnians, Croatians, Serbians, and the other groups that constituted and destabilized former Yugoslavia. The cross-cutting purposes of these ethnic nationals on the American national scene are such as to make any substantial impact in changing United States foreign policy virtually nil.

Rivalries within each of the major ethnic national clusters, may be of such depth and intensity as to cancel out, or certainly limit the range of policy-making potentials on the host nation. The Israeli lobby is often cited as a model of a cohesive force capable of swaying American foreign policy with respect to military and social supports from the American nation as a whole. Yet, examined more closely, one can find ferocious debates and lobbying efforts against Zionism on the part of a small segment of Jews, and similar attempts to curb the propensity to seek foreign aid on the part of Jews favoring an emphasis on private sector and internal initiatives, rather than massive U.S. foreign aid. Other supposedly cohesive groups, such as the Pan-Arab bloc or the American friends of the Pan African Congress, also find themselves embroiled in profound differences within their groups: Hutus versus Tutsis, Christians versus Moslems, Francophones versus Anglophones, all find representation with the Black-Americans. Such extraordinary cross-cuttings, tend to minimize the involvement of these American groups in specific African causes. Similar conditions exist between different sects within the Moslem faith; near warlike conditions between Iraq and Iran and Libya and Egypt spill over into the manufacture of intense rivalries in an open, pluralist system such as the United States. Given such "pulls" and "pushes," what is amazing is the existence of any sort of ethnic politics as such.

Finally, we have reviewed circumstances in which powerfully orchestrated ethnic national movements are overcome by the larger national interest, such as the collapse of the German-American Bund, which achieved an amazingly high degree of cohesion between 1933 and 1941 but collapsed at once with the entrance of the United States into World War II on the side of the Allied Powers, indeed as leader of those powers. And when it was felt, even in the absence of much evidence, that a national group, such as the Nisei, or Japanese Americans might serve as a fifth column during wartime conditions in the Pacific theatre activities, the American government was not above illegal detainment through judicial order for much of the wartime period. In short, there are definite limits to nationalist or ethnic politics within the larger context of the American national interest.

All in all, the area of national identification and national rivalries within multi-ethnic societies is a fertile area for further and deeper investigation. Even if the power of ethnic nationals on the larger national scene is muted, the sheer size of these varied efforts are such as to command attention and examination. And as the American nation moves towards incorporating a notion of multi-culturalism in place of the "melting pot" hypothesis, one can expect such efforts to grow - if not directly to impact or change United States foreign policy, then at least to employ the politics of heritage as a mechanism to maintain relations to the origins of a people who otherwise have a brief, and at times even shallow, sense of history.

One important conclusion must be that democracy itself is a resilient as well as persuasive element in studying the interrelationship between ethnic interest groups and the national interest. Indeed, what has been often noted about the Jews: that a liberal tolerant society has had a greater impact on the peeling away of ethnic identification than centuries of oppressions, can be extended to many other groups as well—sometimes to the bane of ethnically oriented nationalists and secessionists. In this, we have an ultimate irony: that free societies seem better able to absorb the strains and tensions of separatist ethnic rivalries than those planned societies that tried desperately to bridle its ethnic minorities under the rubric of the national question. Seventy years of Bolshevism in Russia and half that amount of time in Eastern Europe, resulted in the fiercest suppression during Communist power and the most vicious rivalries afterward (Service 1998). What we have learned is not only the cross-cutting characteristics of ethnicity within larger national contexts, but also that the issue of interest group politics, and especially ethnic group politics, is not mitigated or overcome by instruments of state repression or mechanisms of planning that destroy native cultures.

### Bibliography

Berger, Peter (ed.). 1998. *The Limits of Social Cohesion: Conflict and Mediation in Pluralist Societies*. New York and London: Westview Publishers/HarperCollins.

Coles, Robert. 1971. *The Middle Americans: Proud and Uncertain*. Boston: Little, Brown.

Cottle, Thomas J. 1982. *College: Reward and Betrayal*. Boston: Little, Brown.

Glazer, Nathan and Daniel Patrick Moynihan. 1992. *Beyond the Melting Pot*. Cambridge, MA: The MIT Press.

Horowitz, Donald L. 1985. *Ethnic Groups in Conflict*. Berkeley: University of California Press.

Horowitz, Irving L. (ed.). 1971. *The Use and Abuse of Social Science*. New Brunswick, NJ: Transaction Books/E.P. Dutton.

Howard, John. 1971. "Public policy and the white working class," in I. L. Horowitz (ed.), *The Use and Abuse of Social Science*. New Brunswick, NJ: Transaction Books/E.P. Dutton.

Myrdal, Gunnar. 1996 (1944). *An American Dilemma: The Negro Problem and Modern Democracy*. New Brunswick, NJ and London: Transaction Publishers.

Namias, June and Robert Coles. 1992. *First Generation: In the Words of Twentieth-Century American Immigrants*. Champaign: University of Illinois Press.

Novak, Michael. 1993. *The Catholic Ethic and the Spirit of Capitalism*. New York: The Free Press/Macmillian.

Service, Robert. 1998. *A History of Twentieth Century Russia*. Cambridge, MA: Harvard University Press.

Smith, A. D. 1981. *The Ethnic Revival in the Modern World*. Cambridge: Cambridge University Press.

Wattenberg, Ben J. 1996. *Values Matter Most*. Washington, DC: Regnery Publishers.

Wilson, William J. 1978. *The Declining Significance of Race*. Chicago: University of Chicago Press.

Irving Louis Horowitz

# Ethnocentrism

The tendency to evaluate matters by reference to the values shared in the subject's own ethnic group as if that group were the centre of everything. The concept was coined by the Polish-born sociologist Ludwig Gumplowicz (1838–1909) when he compared the way in which the human sees himself as the center of the earth (anthropocentrism) with the way that every people sees itself as the foremost (ethnocentrism). The concept was subsequently popularized by William Graham Sumner. It has been utilized by psychologists for the study of attitudes towards other peoples. The distinction between ethnocentrism and racism has been blurred in recent years.

## Bibliography

Gumplowicz, Ludwig. 1881. *Rechtsstaat und Socialismus*. Innsbruck: Wagner.

Sumner, William Graham. 1940. *Folkways: A Study of the Sociological Importance of Usages, Manners, Customs, Mores, and Morals*. Boston, Massachusetts: Ginn.

Michael Banton

# Ethnonationalism

The category "ethnonationalism" emerged fairly recently, as a counterpart of the revived Greek term *ethnie*, used to designate a group with peculiar traits, above all language, the mother tongue, embodying the group's distinctive culture. Throughout most of history, such cultural groups rarely aspired to independent statehood, nor were they "mobilized" politically during the early stages of nationalism prior to the French Revolution or even immediately following that watershed in national consciousness. By the mid-nineteenth century, however, it became evident that a new type of nationalism was emerging in Central and Eastern Europe. It was commonly labelled "organic," with the term "ethnic" usually reserved for groups such as those in countries of immigration like the United States, which explicitly renounced nationalism in favour of purely cultural promotion. By the 1980s, however, a more succinct term was needed combining *ethnie* (as a cultural referent) with the political emphasis implied by "nationalism" (Breton 1981; Smith 1991).

To understand ethnonationalism, it is useful to recognize the typology of which it is a part. It is generally agreed that the earlier forms of nationalism arose in the most advanced and stable states of Western Europe, either England (as argued by Liah Greenfeld) or France (Greenfeld 1992). As the populist version of democracy upheld by the French Revolution spread in the established states of Western Europe, bureaucracies, still heavily influenced by aristocratic attitudes, used military conscription, print media, and mass education to instil concepts of state loyalty borrowing from earlier dynastic loyalty. Pride in "na-tional," that is, state accomplishments was emphasized, both for foreign affairs (military victories) and in constitutional provisions (written or unwritten). These were acclaimed for protecting individuals, maintaining stability, and promoting economic growth.

Usually, state loyalty was closely associated with use of a single national language, which had been standardized well before the period of populist revolution. Hence, elites could promote the established language in media and education as a matter of course, a prerequisite for social communication. Conversely, use of fine distinctions in pronunciation or grammar as shibboleths of class status was strongly fostered by institutions like the English public school and the École Normale. Only an insightful linguist like Antoine Meillet could penetrate the alleged instrumental nature of such institutional bias:

> [France] has a refined language made for an aristocracy, which can be fluently and correctly handled only by a small class of society... Like French, sometimes almost as much as French, English, Italian, Spanish, Portuguese, German and Polish are traditional languages created by elites for elites, which one can readily employ and write only at the price of a difficult apprenticeship and as part of a high culture. (Meillet 1928)

The principal, but unavowed effect of this "difficult apprenticeship," was to maintain class barriers, while suggesting a possible, but improbable route for individual social mobility. A more likely unintended consequence was to compel the socially mobile of non-standard ethnic origins to renounce those origins.

The mechanisms just mentioned were subtle. By stressing language and folkways as utilitarian forms of communication, social solidarity could be emphasized as instrumental for "national" well-being. However, as contact with colonial peoples increased and the European contest for state primacy intensified, stronger nationalist appeals appeared to be required. By the late nineteenth century, the pseudo-biological science of Social Darwinism attracted numerous disciples in Germany and the English-speaking countries through its preaching of survival of the fittest nations, in the first instance, at least, those who had already achieved the most. At the outbreak of

## Ethnonationalism

World War I, preservation of this status quo was widely acclaimed as meriting the ultimate sacrifice by men of the younger generation. Above all, a state was obliged to preserve its territory or, if feasible, to extend it for "security's sake." However, as the twentieth century reached its final decades, such appeals declined in effectiveness as casualties in obscure conflicts mounted.

In France, and some other countries of Roman Catholic tradition, Social Darwinist nationalism was less apparent; but the INTEGRAL NATIONALISM of Charles Maurras, ascribing transcendent value to national identity, and calling for quasi-Fascist measures to "protect" it, had similar implications.

Eventually, the Vatican excommunicated Maurras and his followers for placing nationalism above Christian principles; but somewhat less extreme nationalist versions have had wide currency in Christian societies. In effect, such manifestations of "religious nationalism" are frequent and strong enough to constitute a third type of nationalism. Thus Poland has been acclaimed as the Body of Christ martyred by Nazi and Soviet totalitarians. The Spain of Francisco Franco posed as a modern Crusader State defending the Church against "Red" assaults, while enforcing Nationalist (i.e., Castilian) unity against Basque Catholics and Catalan separatists. Similarly, ardent Orthodox believers relieved recently from Communist oppression have (in Russia and Serbia) vociferously posed as the successors of Slav front-line defenders of Christianity.

The most fervent opponents of these Christian myth themes, have been, understandably, Muslims. Yet, the concept of the *jihad*, holy war to defend *and* advance the faith, has often been the instigator of the Crusade complex. Today, in the absence of religious legitimization of separate national states as such, claims to *jihad* legitimacy tend to outweigh secular nationalist movements in many Islamic societies, and often call forth extreme terrorism.

The brief survey of civic and religious nationalisms helps to define the scope of ethnonationalism as it arose during the nineteenth century. On the one hand, ethnonationalist movements tended to replace or absorb religious identity as it declined during the age of secularism. Indeed, nearly all ethnonationalists at one period or another (usu-

ally during the early twentieth century) contained a hard core, often modelled on Maurras' *Action Française*, which deliberately flouted "clericalism." Still the appeal to intergenerational solidarity to some degree filled the need to confront the mortality, especially by the widespread cult of heroes.

Clearly, these cults, oriented toward the past and the future rather than the emphasis on the present in civic nationalism, are part of a syndrome of rebellion against the status quo by utilising the modern themes of "science" and populism. Such appeals were apparent in mid-nineteenth century "springtime of nations" which reached fruition in disunited Germany and Italy. Despite the high level of culture attained in both these regions (as yet hardly countries, much less states), early nationalist leaders in both were strongly motivated by *ressentiment*, that is, humiliation at the way in which France, particularly, had surpassed them politically and even culturally. Nevertheless, attainment of territorial unity during the mid-nineteenth century, introduced new elites to direct the process of cultural integration that, farther west, had been largely accomplished by bureaucracies imbued with old state traditions. Conversely, Italian and German elites continued to maintain a significant component of Romantic attachment to peasant populism as well as dissatisfaction with state frontiers. Hence the popularity of *völkisch* themes in Germany and *il sacro egoismo* in Italian nationalism.

In Central and Eastern Europe, under the rule of four empires (Prussia and its new successor the Second Reich; Austria-Hungary; Russia; and the Ottoman Empire) *ressentiment* directed at central authorities who increasingly based their bureaucratic rules on the linguistic and cultural patterns of dominant groups was more intense. Largely lacking local aristocracies (which earlier had adopted the standards of the imperial capitals), nineteenth-century aspiring elites in new occupations such as teaching and journalism, turned to their peasant heritage both as a refuge in a modernising society, and as a popular legitimization. The new "scientific" historiography (largely borrowed from Germans like Leopold von Ranke) and the "scientific," linguistics (borrowed from philologists like Jakob and Wilhelm Grimm) both encouraged a romantic attachment to the peasants.

At the same time, any claim for an independent nation, given the territorial criterion of the international order, required that a given peasant "nation," be delineated on the ground. The technique of mapping isoglosses, a new linguistic device for tracing speech patterns, often did not provide unambiguous criteria for such delineation even between solid settlements with transitional dialects, as in the lower Balkans and the Pripet marshes. Where peasant villages of widely differing dialects were intermingled, "scientific precision" on boundaries appeared possible only to the converted. In both cases, however, intellectual spokesmen for each nationalism insisted on versions favourable to the nationalism they had invented. Where (as among the South Slavs of the western Balkans) such linguistic differentials were clearly so minor as to be shibboleths, the new nationalist leaders eventually settled for a return to ancient religious criteria—even to the point of ethnic cleansing.

Lacking the considerable legitimization that claims for peasant attachments conferred in Europe, Islamic nationalisms have usually pursued rather different routes. Except for concepts diffused from Europe (particularly cogent in Anatolian Turkey where the peasantry was largely Turkicized before the modern era, and hence can be regarded as a conservative bulwark of popular nationalism), urban populations are the traditional Islamic source of rulers' legitimization. Moreover, the tradition of separate linguistic spheres for elite occupations, combined with widespread multilingual attainments, makes language claims (except vis-à-vis non-Muslims) less salient. As a result Muslim nationalist leaders commonly, as noted above, derive their legitimacy from roles as defenders of the Faith. Secondarily, they derive prestige from their genealogies that Mohammed counselled should be known to all, as contrasted to the peasant Babylonians and Nabateans who identified themselves by territorial attachments. Although these genealogies are (as in Europe) often fictitious, their assertion retains more significance throughout the Islamic world, and many other Asian and African cultures where nationalist concepts have taken root.

All the same, one should remember that even in England, respect for age-old peasant attachment to soil occurs, as in Rudyard Kipling's "Hobden the Hedger":

> His dead are in the churchyard—
> thirty generations laid.
> Their names were old in history
> when Domesday Book was made;
> And the passion and the piety and
> the prowess of his line
> Have seeded, rooted, fruited in
> some land the Law calls mine.

As one goes over the preceding pages, it is hard to avoid the conclusion that the boundaries between types of nationalism are as hard to set as those between *ethnies*—or their contemporary counterparts. This conclusion applies *a fortiori* to any judgments concerning their viability or their acceptability. Civic nationalism as it evolved after 1979 in the West European states certainly has many advantages, not the least being domestic tranquillity. Yet the resort to Social Darwinism as a legitimating ideology during the crisis of World War I and various lesser crises of expansion suggests that civic nationalism is *only* less vulnerable to hideous excesses such as ethnic cleansing than the ethnonationalisms heavily burdened by history. Often these were dealing *both* with cultural oppression in multiethnic polities ruled by elites drawn from a master group and simultaneously with alienation concomitant with secularization. One can see how they might seek security in allegedly primordial roots. Moreover, if fictitiously tracing ancestry to heroes of the remote past is dangerous, intergenerational community at a shorter range is neither bad nor avoidable. Still, the observer of varieties of nationalism, while trying to understand the myth themes that have increasingly displaced sober circumstances of contemporary life, is not obliged to treat myth, symbol, or even communication as sacrosanct. Even such distinctive forms as the "sacred" language are no more than human devices for coping with a difficult world.

### Bibliography

Armstrong, John A. 1982. *Nations before Nationalism*. Chapel Hill: University of North Carolina Press.

## Ethno-Symbolism

Barrington, Lowell W. 1997. "Nation' and 'Nationalism': The misuse of key concepts in political science," *PS: Political Science and Politics* 30, 4: 712-16.

Breton, Roland. 1981. *Les ethnies*. Paris: Presses Universitaires.

Greenfeld, Liah. 1992. *Nationalism: Five Roads to Modernity*. Cambridge, MA: Harvard University Press.

Haas, Ernst B. 1997. *Nationalism, Liberalism, and Progress*. Ithaca, NY: Cornell University Press.

LeVine, Robert A. and Campbell, Donald T. 1972. *Ethnocentrism: Theories of Conflict, Ethnic Attitudes and Group Behavior*. New York: John Wiley and Sons.

Lunt, Horace G. 1984. "Some sociological aspects of Macedonian and Bulgarian," *Papers in Slavic Philology* 5.

Meillet, Antoine. 1928. *Les Langues dans l'Europe nouvelle*. Paris: Payot.

Smith, Anthony D. 1991. *National Identity*. Harmondsworth: Penguin Books.

John A. Armstrong

# Ethno-Symbolism

"Historical ethno-symbolism" is the name given to an approach to the study of ethnicity and nationalism that emphasizes the role of myths, SYMBOLS, memories, values and traditions in their formation, persistence and change. It differs from other approaches in underlining the importance of subjective elements and of the *longue durée* in our understanding of ethnic groups and nations. It also differs from other perspectives in the weight it gives to popular cultures and practices and how these set limits to elite understandings and strategies.

In the study of ethnicity, two approaches have been dominant. The first, known as "primordialism," regards ethnicity as a given, a prior, constraining and overriding social bond, and hence nations as well as ethnic communities or *ethnies*, to use the French term, are seen as fundamental constituents of human history and society. Recently, primordialism has experienced something of a revival, both through sociobiology and in the formulations of Shils, Geertz, and their followers. Unlike the sociobiologists, the latter stress the affective ties and participants' popular attach-

ments that bind people and groups, and these are elements that ethno-symbolists have also adopted. In contrast, "INSTRUMENTALISM" points to the mutability and transformations of ethnicity and its "situational" variability. They argue that ethnic ties are always in flux; they are frequently malleable and plastic, even hybrid, especially in a modern world of large-scale migration and intermarriage. It is therefore more profitable to see in "ethnicity" an instrument to other ends: usually wealth, status, and power. Elites, locked in a competition for resources, use ethnic bonds to rally support for their strategies of wealth and power maximization exactly because, as Bell (1975) points out, ethnic groups combine "interest" with "affect" in a way that even class cannot.

These radically different approaches also feed into the analysis of nations and nationalism, especially the opposition between "PERENNIALISM AND MODERNISM." Primordialists are also perennialists; they see nations as underlying constituents of the human order. Instrumentalists also tend to be modernists; with their eyes on variability and change, they tend to see nations as products of modernity and of elite strategies of modernization. However, it is possible to regard nations as recurrent phenomena in every historical epoch, while adopting a broadly instrumental position; this is the approach taken by John Armstrong. In fact, he combines an instrumentalist definition of ethnicity with both a Barthian and an ethno-symbolic approach. Armstrong defines "ethnic identity" as a cluster of shifting attitudes, perceptions, and beliefs, which respond to changing circumstances. But he avoids the extremes of voluntarism and hybridity by emphasizing the durability of the social and cultural boundary between ethnic communities, based on the sense of the other, the outsider. Like Barth, he believes that the boundary, guarded by cultural symbols—of language, law, religion, dress, and the like—is crucial to maintaining ethnic communities which he equates with pre-modern nations. Ethnic communities are frequently combined with, or slide into, religious groups and classes; all three are marked by cultural border guards and boundary mechanisms of exclusion. Where Armstrong differs from Barth is in his evaluation of the role of ethnic "myth-symbol" complexes and their "codes of communication." For Armstrong, they play a crucial part in perpetuating ethnic communities and in differentiating them from their neighbors. Diaspora ethnic groups like the Jews and Armenians have been able to persist for millennia because of their powerful myth-symbol complexes and the religious codes and institutions—scriptures, liturgies, priesthoods, sacred scripts, education systems—that constantly reinforce and express these myths and symbols to the members of the community.

For Armstrong, there have been two major principles of human organization. The first is through kinship. Here tribal genealogies such as we find especially in the Middle East, form the classificatory basis of human association. In much of Europe, on the other hand, territorial propinquity and residence have formed the basis of human organization; the city-states of ancient Greece and Rome were the prime examples, and they have provided a vital legacy for Western Europe, despite the infusion of genealogical conceptions from the *Stamm* formation of Germanic tribes. In addition, human groups can be distinguished according to whether they are nomadic or sedentary: the ways of life associated with each contributes later to a powerful nostalgia that differentiates communities.

These differences provide very broad principles of human organization, insufficient on their own to account for the formation of ethnic groups. They need to be supplemented by other axes of differentiation, in descending order of inclusiveness. Of these, the most important are religious civilizations and imperial *mythomoteurs* (constitutive myths of a polity). Concentrating on Europe and the Middle East, Armstrong argues that medieval Islam and Christianity in the period of the Crusades formed large-scale ethnic identities, through the periodic conflicts that forged clear visions of the significant Other, as well as providing the cultural materials for smaller ethnic communities (see also NATIONALISM AND THE "OTHER"). The latter were formed in the first place through the impact of imperial *mythomoteurs* that defined and legitimated the various kingdoms and empires of Europe and the Middle East in terms of different models of the relations between monarchs and the gods. To these were added various other factors: different patterns of urban landscape, distinct types of legal code and

particular kinds of religious organization (centralized or dispersed). At the lowest, most exclusive end of the scale, language faults and fissures mark off the particular ethnic groups with which we are now familiar: the fault-lines of Germanic, Latin and Slavonic give rise to tribal associations, which are then subdivided by politics and religion.

In each case, Armstrong concentrates on the persistence through long time-spans of ethnic identities which undergo social and political transformations, and whose constitutive myths and symbols also slowly change but whose symbolic boundaries remain remarkably durable. It is this emphasis on the pre-modern nature of ethnicity and nationality, the long time-spans needed for a true understanding of these phenomena and the centrality of myths and symbols to their identity and persistence, that forms the core of an "ethno-symbolic" approach.

A similar concern with the role of myths and symbols and of long historical time-spans can be found in the work of others. John Hutchinson's study of the rise and development of Irish nationalism over two centuries emphasizes the role of recovered myths, shared memories and resonant symbols in the shaping of a modern Irish nation-state. The myths, memories, and symbols that the nationalists rediscover are often of great antiquity; they look back to the pagan and Christian golden ages of the early medieval epoch for visions of community which can help to regenerate Ireland and inspire Irish men and women with social solidarity and a sense of moral community. Hutchinson points to the way in which this CULTURAL NATIONALISM is recurrent: it is constantly needed to overcome the lethargy and moral despair consequent on the failure of political nationalisms to achieve their goals. More recently, Hutchinson has pointed to the problems inherent in the modernist and instrumentalist approaches to ethnicity and nationalism, and has adopted a position that stresses the importance of historical understanding and the *longue durée* without embracing any of the primordialist or perennialist assumptions.

A similar position has been adopted by Anthony Smith. Whereas his earlier work had stressed the importance of modernity and the "scientific state" in the genesis of nationalism, his later work focused on the pre-modern ethnic roots of modern nations and nationalisms. For Smith, ethnicity, although not primordial, is a worldwide and recurrent phenomenon. Rejecting both sociobiological and affective readings of ethnicity, Smith emphasizes the ubiquity of named groups possessing myths of common ancestry, shared memories and distinctive cultures linked to particular homelands. These constitute the defining features of ethnic communities, or what the French term *ethnies*. Ethnies can be found in every continent and period of history, emerging, persisting, changing, dissolving, as human beings evolve shared myths, memories, symbols, values and traditions associated with homelands. It is not even necessary for an ethnie to be in possession of the homeland, only to feel a bond with it, as have the diaspora communities for such long periods, such is the long-term power of symbolism.

Ethnic communities have often formed the basis of states in pre-modern periods. This was the case in ancient Egypt, Japan, and France. Alternatively, they may form wider cultural networks encompassing many smaller political units, like the city-states of Sumer, Phoenicia, and ancient Greece, or the cantons of medieval Switzerland. In these cases, ethnicity was separated from the polity, as it was in the many cases of ethnies included within much larger empires, like the Assyrian, Persian, Roman and Chinese empires which included a great variety of ethnic communities in their borders. Alternatively, kingdoms were formed on the basis of what may be termed "ethnic cores": dominant ethnies who provided the main support and personnel of the kingdom which included other ethnic minorities, as we often find in the medieval epoch.

Smith goes on to make a distinction between two kinds of ethnie, the one "lateral" and aristocratic, the other "vertical" and demotic. In the former, barriers are low, the population is dispersed, the boundaries are ragged and the ethnic culture is confined to high status groups, without penetrating to the middle or lower classes. In the latter, barriers to entry are high, the population is more concentrated, boundaries are compact and the ethnic culture tends to permeate all social classes. In the first type, we can find such ethnies as the Hittites or Normans, in the second such groups as the Irish or Armenians. These two types of ethnie afford two starting-points for the forma-

tion of nations, which are defined as named human populations occupying a specific homeland and sharing myths and memories, a mass, public culture, a single economy and common legal rights and duties. The first route is one of "bureaucratic incorporation": the rulers of the strong state built up by the aristocratic ethnie decide, for a variety of reasons, to spread their ethnic cultures and political myths and symbols downward to the middle classes and outward to outlying regions, thereby commencing the process of creating a territorial national sentiment and symbolic identity out of an ethnic heritage. The second route is one of "vernacular mobilization": the educated classes of vertical or demotic ethnies come into contact with western rationalism and romanticism, directly through colonialism or indirectly through reading and travel, and reacting against the imperial and cosmopolitan norms, often coupled with discriminatory practices, of the administrations of the polities in which their ethnies have been incorporated, they seek to rediscover their ethnic pasts and vernacular cultures and make them the basis for a new ethnically based nation. Here, too, myths, memories, symbols, and traditions play a critical role: it is exactly these elements that form the historical and social substance of the vernacular communicative codes of language and religion that set ethnies apart from each other.

Smith argues that as the result of this two-fold evolution there have emerged two symbolic conceptions of the modern nation. On the one hand, there is a more "civic-territorial" ideal of the nation, one which emphasizes the importance of long-term residence in a clearly demarcated territory, of the part played by unified law codes and legal institutions over the whole territory, of the equal and common rights and duties of citizenship in the territorial nation, and of the central role of a public, civic culture for all citizens which embodies the myths, memories and symbols of the nation. On the other hand, there is a more "ethnic-genealogical" conception of the nation, which stresses the importance of presumed ancestry ties and kin relatedness for citizenship, the crucial role of popular mobilization and a participant populace, the centrality of vernacular language, customs and culture, and the binding force of authentic, native historical memories of and in the homeland. Of course, for Smith as for others, there is considerable overlap between these two conceptions of the nation. Actual instances of the nation have both civic and ethnic components, and there is a constant oscillation and flux between the preponderance of civic or ethnic myths and symbols. The notions of a unified national identity, a homeland and citizenship play vital roles in both conceptions, and both insist on the importance of possessing a common and distinctive mass culture. Nevertheless, the difference between the two symbolic conceptions has had important consequences, notably for the treatment of immigrants and minorities within the national state. In addition, Smith points to the emergence of a third route to the formation of nations, and a third conception of the nation: the "pioneer-immigrant" route in which segments of ethnies left or fled their homelands to find a new life and community in a new "promised land," often across the seas, as in America, Canada, or Australia. Here a more "plural" conception obtains, one that seeks to celebrate the diversity of ethnic communities and identities in the national state, while binding them together through common legal institutions and a single overarching political culture in the public domain. How far the myths, memories, and symbols of the public domain, based as they are on the ethnic heritage of the founding and usually dominant ethnie, can be genuinely plural and/or stable enough to provide the national state with the necessary political solidarity remains to be seen.

In these authors, the emphasis is always on the need to understand modern nations and nationalisms as products of long-term historical processes. In contrast to the primordialists, ethno-symbolists regard ethnies and nations as historical phenomena, subject to the usual processes of flux and change. While they accept the durability of given historical examples of ethnic communities, they refuse to see these as "givens" of the natural order, or nations as natural components of history and society. In contrast to the instrumentalism and modernism, ethno-symbolists place the formation of nations in the context of broader historical processes, deriving many of their elements from premodern ethnic components. Similarly, ethnies they regard as recurrent phenomena in human his-

tory, to be found in every continent and age, thereby constituting the basis of nations and nationalisms. This is because the processes of myth-making, memorization, evaluation, symbolization, tradition, and communication are recurrent in all societies. Hence there is always a human propensity to form communities around clusters of the products of these processes over time, and thereby forge ethnies and, where conditions permit, as they do particularly in the modern epoch, nations. And this is why an approach that emphasizes the central role of myth, symbol, memory, and tradition could prove so fruitful in the understanding of ethnic and national phenomena.

**Bibliography**

Armstrong, John. 1982. *Nations before Nationalism*. Chapel Hill: University of North Carolina Press.

Bell, Daniel. 1975. "Ethnicity and social change," in Nathan Glazer and Daniel Moynihan (eds.), *Ethnicity: Theory and Experience*. Cambridge, MA: Harvard University Press.

Hutchinson, John. 1987. *The Dynamics of Cultural Nationalism: The Gaelic Revival and the Creation of the Irish Nation State*. London: Allen and Unwin.

Hutchinson, John. 1994. *Modern Nationalism*. London: Fontana Press.

Smith, Anthony D. 1986. *The Ethnic Origins of Nations*. Oxford: Blackwell.

Smith, Anthony D. 1991. *National Identity*. Harmondsworth: Penguin.

Smith, Anthony D. 1995. *Nations and Nationalism in a Global Era*. Cambridge: Polity Press.

Anthony D. Smith

# Everyday Nationalism

There is more to nationalism than organised, ideological, political projects. Looking at Mauritius and Trinidad, Eriksen (1993) compares formal nationalisms, ideologies of ethnic identification belonging to the institutional organisation of the state, with informal nationalisms, rooted in the daily round of civil society. Both exist in the context of the nation-state and may complement or oppose each other. Writing about Belize, Wilk (1993) contrasts official, governmental national-

## Everyday Nationalism

ism with the unofficial ideas and practices of nationalism revealed in beauty pageants or cuisine. Billig (1995) talks about banal nationalism: the everyday habits of social life, such as the routine flying of national flags, that remind citizens of their nation, of their place in it, and of its place in the world.

Well-worn distinctions between nationalism and national identity may also be relevant. For example, Borneman (1992), writing about Berlin, differentiates nationalism, a public ideology of identification with the state, from nationness, the implicit sense of being the kind of person, or living the kind of life, that is appropriate to membership in a particular state. This is broadly similar to what Cohen (1982) calls "belonging." Linde-Laursen talks about the nationalisation of trivialities (1993): national communities that are culturally similar, Danes and Swedes in this case, "do" everyday life—washing the dishes, for example differently, and use these distinctions to symbolize grander boundaries of identity. When Duara, talking about early-modern China (1993), contrasts the discursive meaning of the nation, located in ideology and rhetoric, with its symbolic meaning—found in "rituals, festivals, kinship forms, and culinary habits"—he seems to be addressing the same issues: the everyday life of civil society and the symbolic meaning of the nation for its members. All of these distinctions must be understood within the local context of the relationship between state and civil society (Jenkins 1997: 159-161).

These converging arguments and analogous distinctions remind us of the ethnic strands in nationalism and national identity. They also remind us of the importance of maintaining a his-torical perspective: the relationship between state and civil society is a product of history, and nations emerge, in part, out of that relationship. They also remind us that nations mean something to their members in the context of their routine daily rounds. "Everyday nationalisms" are local political narratives, by means of which people make sense of a complex and changing world. National identity is to nationalism, as unofficial, informal, everyday nationalism is to the official and the formal. National identity or nationness can exist in the absence of nationalism; nationalism without some everyday sense of the nation is unthinkable.

### Bibliography

Billig, M. 1995. *Banal Nationalism*. London: Sage.

Borneman, J. 1992. *Belonging in the Two Berlins: Kin, State, Nation*. Cambridge: Cambridge University Press.

Cohen, A. P. (ed.). 1982. *Belonging: Identity and Social Organisation in British Rural Cultures*. Manchester: Manchester University Press.

Duara, P. 1993. "De-constructing the Chinese nation," *Australian Journal of Chinese Affairs* 30: 1-26.

Eriksen, T. H. 1993. "Formal and informal nationalism," *Ethnic and Racial Studies* 16: 1-25.

Jenkins, R. 1997. *Rethinking Ethnicity: Arguments and Explorations*. London: Sage.

Linde-Laursen, A. 1993. "The nationalization of trivialities: how cleaning becomes an identity marker in the encounter of Swedes and Danes" *Ethnos* 58, 3-4: 275-293.

Wilk, R. R. 1993. "Beauty and the feast: official and visceral nationalism in Belize," *Ethnos* 58: 294-316.

Richard Jenkins

# F

## Fascist Nationalism

The understanding of fascist nationalism, as distinct from other forms of extremist nationalism, depends first of all on the definition of fascism. This is an extremely controversial problem, the subject of ongoing debate for three-quarters of a century. As distinct from broad and loose definitions which label as fascist any form of non-communist authoritarian nationalism, or at the other extreme the completely nominalist position which uses the term fascist only to refer to a specific political movement in Italy, a limited consensus has developed among scholars who specialize in the area. They conclude that the term "fascist" is most appropriate for a genus of revolutionary nationalist movements in interwar Europe whose members shared common characteristics which differentiated them from other political forces, even though at the same time the fascist movements in various countries often differed sharply among themselves.

The shared characteristic which set off fascist movements as a distinct genus of nationalist movement involved their common espousal of such goals and principles as simultaneous opposition to the existing political left, right, and center (though temporarily willing sometimes to ally with sectors of the right to gain power); charismatic leadership; extreme authoritarianism; a vitalist, non-rationalist, and anti-materialist philosophy and culture; statist domination of an economy still based on private property; an organic multiclass social policy; mass mobilization and creation of a "party army" of political militia; a highly positive theoretical evaluation of violence, together with the practice thereof; eager espousal of war and expansion; extreme emphasis on "virilism" or masculinity; exaltation of youth over other phases of life; and elaborate development of ultra-nationalist civic religion and political theater. Fascism may thus be described as a form of revolutionary ultra-nationalism for national rebirth that is based on a primarily vitalist philosophy, is structured on extreme elitism, mass mobilization and the *Führerprinzip*, positively values violence as end as well as means and tends to normatize war and/or the military virtues.

The ideological sources of fascist nationalism were in some respects similar to those of most European nationalist movements, stemming from the differentiation of national cultures in the era of the Enlightenment and the mobilization of nationalism during the French Revolution and the century that followed. What differentiated fascist nationalism from more moderate forms was the greater influence of the extremist and authoritarian aspects of the Enlightenment and French Revolutionary eras, and especially of the changes in Eurepean thought and values toward the close of the nineteenth century which comprised what some scholars have called the intellectual crisis of the fin-de-siècle.

These late nineteenth-century concepts rejected the liberalism, rationalism, and materialism which had been characteristic of most of the century in favor of idealism, non-rationalism and vitalism. New trends in sociology stressed the dominance of elitism, while the newer social sciences revealed a relativism in moral standards across cultures. Social Darwinism applied zoological concepts of competition to human society, which in extreme forms even encouraged military competition. Theoreticians of violence began to advance the notion that violence was not merely a grim necessity in certain situations, but positively desirable in and of itself for national cultures. In some countries new concepts of racial hierarchies—naturally privileging the home nationality—gained increasing influence, by the latter part of the century leading to the emergence of a "mystical racism" which affirmed a hierarchy of differences even between diverse European "races." In such countries a new form of racial

## Fascist Nationalism

ANTI-SEMITISM developed, in which Jews were no longer stigmatized for religious or cultural differences alone, but as a separate malevolent and unalterable "RACE," allegedly devoted to destroying the purity of other "races."

The precursors of fascist nationalism first emerged in the 1870s and 1880s, initially in France and then in Germany and greater Austria, but these initial expressions did not exhibit all the new characteristics which would be assumed by the fascist movements of interwar Europe. The new cultural trends that would encourage fascism were only beginning to develop in the late nineteenth century, and the exacerbation of nationalism which would eventually help to generate fascism had not yet taken place in Europe.

Fascist nationalism only clearly emerged in the form of significant mass movements after World War I, which not merely failed to solve the problems of the nationalism which had helped provoke the war, but exacerbated them, encouraging more extreme forms. Nonetheless, fascist movements only came to power in Italy and Germany, and aside from these two cases, significant movements only developed eventually in Hungary, Romania, and Austria, to which might be added the marginal cases of Spain and Croatia. Austrian National Socialism was only a variant of German Nazism, while the Hungarian Arrow Cross and Romanian Iron Guard enjoyed only transitory moments of power. The Spanish Falange became the state party of the Franco regime, but only after being merged with other forces; it was never permitted to dominate a system which was more right wing and Catholic than fascist. The Croatian Ustashi only achieved power in 1941 when Hitler awarded it to them after he had crushed and dismembered Yugoslavia.

Fascist nationalism did not constitute a single monolithic political type or form, for, beyond the common fascist minimum, considerable differences existed between fascist movements, reflecting national culture and political variations. Most important were the differences between Italian Fascism and German National Socialism. Italian Fascism produced a more moderate form of authoritarianism which permitted institutional semi-pluralism (even though it developed the abstract concept of "totalitarianism"), and prior to World War II Mussolini's regime only carried out nine political executions.

German Hitlerism was more extreme in every respect, producing a much more repressive one-man dictatorship, and developing a power dyarchy between state and party. RACISM was so fundamental to National Socialism that Hitler privately recognized that the Nazi movement was not simply nationalist in the normal sense, for a significant minority of the native German population was not of pure Aryan background, while in certain surrounding lands there existed certain purer Nordics or Aryans than might be found among a portion of the German population (see also ARYANLSM). The ultimate Nazi revolution would be a racial revolution to develop a purified Aryan master race. Not all Germans could ultimately participate in the final racial project, though pure Aryans outside Germany might in some cases be able to do so.

In general, fascist parties in western and northern Europe were weak, given the democratic traditions, greater prosperity, and satisfied international situation of the countries in this region. The small fascist parties in Northern and Western Europe also tended to be rather more moderate. Fascist movements in Central and Eastern Europe were intensely anti-Semitic, whereas some of those in Western Europe, like Italian Fascism for most of its history, were not anti-Semitic. In Northwestern Europe there were even "peace fascists," to the extent that Britain, France, Belgium, and Holland were satisfied colonial powers with large empires, which even their fascists did not propose to extend further through war.

The relationship of fascism to religion was ambivalent, at best. Its basic thrust was generally anti-clerical and anti-religious, seeking to create an alternative mystique of politics, culture and national identity. But in Eastern Europe, where national identity was closely bound to religion, hybrid "religious fascisms" developed, as was also the case in Spain.

The extremism of fascist nationalism deprived fascist movements of support in most countries, even though eventually there was a fascist-type movement in almost every European state and in most of those in Latin America and the Middle East. It was, however, only the great military power of Nazi Germany which made it possible for historians to speak of a "fascist era" from 1930 to 1945, for, generally speaking, anti-fascism was always a broader sentiment than pro-fascism.

To what factors can the relative success of fascist movements in a few countries then be attributed? To a large extent fascist nationalism developed in the "new nations" which had been formed during the 1860s and 1870s: Italy (1861), Germany (1871), Austria (1867), Hungary (1867), and Romania (1878).

The closest non-European analogue was Japan (1867). Nationalism was particularly intense in these countries not merely because independence or unification had been delayed, but because in most of these cases imperial expansion had consequently been handicapped and, most important of all, most of these states had either ended on the losing side in World War I, or were frustrated victors, like Japan, Italy, and Romania.

Fascist nationalism was a particular temptation in comparatively new states, not more than three generations old, and in which liberal democracy had existed for less than a generation. It developed strongly in countries in which it constituted the second or third generation of intense nationalism and was able to exploit the foundations laid by relatively influential nationalist precursors, and burgeoned in fragmented and unstable political systems. In most cases, a significant threat from the extreme left was also a factor of some importance, but even more basic was the existence of a national sense of status humiliation and the argument that a radical rebirth of nationalism, with or without allies, could overcome it.

Another factor of some importance was a strong impact from the cultural crisis of the fin-de-siècle and its vitalist philosophies, as well as strong challenges of new secularization. Fascist nationalism only developed in societies in which there was great economic stress and social dislocation, particularly in situations in which the economic crisis could seemingly be attributed to exogenous factors. Similarly, fascist nationalism only developed in societies in which the political party system representing the middle classes had begun to break down, and in which sizable sectors of farmers and workers did not feel themselves ad-equately represented. Only in countries where all, or nearly all, of these factors were combined were conditions fully encouraging.

Generally speaking, fascist nationalism and imperialism are usually credited with having been the main factors in unleashing World War II, and in broad terms this judgment is acceptable. One of the most unique features of fascist nationalism was its peculiar emphasis on the creative character of nationalist violence, and of the inevitability and indeed the desirability of war. Fascist philosophy was based on the rejection of rationalism and materialism, and in the approach toward war fascist non-rationalism reached its greatest extreme. The consequence was that by 1945 fascism had discredited itself to a greater extent than any other major political force in modern history, and in the process had been obliterated politically and militarily.

Efforts were made to imitate fascism outside Europe, but always fell well short of the Italo-German paradigm. In most countries of Latin America, for example, twentieth-century mass mobilization had not yet developed, nationalism generally was less intense and there was little sense of direct international threat or competition. The impact was somewhat stronger in South Africa, borne by racial doctrine and also by the fact that approximately one-sixth of the white population was of German origin. Nonetheless, two different political parties directly patterned on European fascism failed, and the system of racial APARTHEID (Separation) developed after World War II was led by the Afrikaner National Party, which largely maintained a "racial democracy" for the white population, guaranteeing for them parliamentary government and direct elections. Though undoubtedly influenced by European fascism, the South African system created a unique hybrid model of its own which lacked most of the special features of European fascism.

The non-European power which in the thinking of most analysts most nearly approximated fascist nationalism was Imperial Japan between 1937 and 1945. It developed its own form of Japanese ethno-racism, extreme militarism and imperial ambitions, and a political culture which fostered great discipline and unity for aggressive war. A number of small Japanese extremist groups were strongly influenced by European fascism—more by Germany than by Italy—and sometimes used concepts of "national socialism." Yet none of the petty proto-fascist groups attained the slightest degree of political power in Japan, which by the 1930s had scarcely attained the level of political modernization of the Germany of twenty years earlier. Rather than undergoing a fascist revolution, Imperial Japan was grounded in a radicalized neotraditionalism of emperor worship that was increasingly dominated by the military (like Germany after 1914). No new political system was introduced, though all the non-left parties were combined in an umbrella grouping in 1940. Regular competitive elections were maintained, and the nominal opposition registered a large minority of the vote in the parliamentary balloting of 1942. Japan lacked the preconditions for full fascism in terms of society, culture, economics, and political development, although, even without a full fascist-type ideology or a new political regime, it did provide the nearest functional equivalent to a fascist system outside Europe.

Though fascism ceased to exist as an historical force after 1945, certain fascist concepts survived in the political thinking of small minorities, to the extent that neofascism has been a permanent, if completely marginal, feature of the political landscape in the late twentieth century and probably in the early twenty-first century as well. Neofascism has, however, been completely unable to escape the "neofascist contradiction," which is simply that to the degree to which any neofascist party, cult, or splinter group seeks to become a genuine political force as distinct from a lunatic fringe, it must to an almost equivalent degree defascistize itself, at least to a certain extent. Genuine hardcore neofascist grouplets which maintain the pristine ideology have been doomed to isolation; conversely, those movements which have neared or broken the 5 percent electoral barrier have always adopted somewhat more moderate and post-fascist doctrines.

Political groups often called neofascist can be broadly divided into two general categories. The first consists of the more or less genuine neofascists or neo-Nazis, who subscribe to all or almost all of the original ideologies and exist as small sects in almost every country in the world.

There have been literally hundreds of them in the late twentieth century, and the general rule is that the greater the number of individual sects, the less significant they are as a whole, splintering into tiny mutually anathematizing rivals. The other and much more important category consists of the right-wing nationalist parties which propose corportatist or other hard-line changes in national policies of a greater or lesser confrontational or authoritarian character, but have dropped any categorical fascist minimum so as to attract broader support.

One feature of a significant number of neofascist groups has been their espousal of a broader Europeanist identity in distinction from the intense individual chauvinism of the historical movements. Most have not embraced a mystical racism similar to that of the former central European parties, although a minority have done so. Neofascist thought has not developed any major body of new doctrine or any noteworthy new political thinkers. Some neofascists preach a "left" fascism of social radicalism or revolution and semi-collectivism, though most maintain the principle of private property with a greater or lesser degree of state intervention.

Despite the fact that the historic example of fascism and certain aspects of fascist doctrine continue to attract small numbers of enthusiasts, it has been impossible to propagate the doctrines of fascism to any significant degree since 1945 because their form and content are severely dated and have had little appeal in the drastically altered cultural context of the later twentieth century. In the atomic era fascist concepts of violence made little sense, while the philosophy of vitalism and anti-materialism lacked broad appeal during the great era of economic expansion which followed World War II. The climate of culture and society turned toward ever greater individualism, shortcircuiting any possible attraction to fascist principles of group and racial identity and self-sacrifice. Knowledge of World War II and of the era of fascism also served as a source of inoculation.

Some of the specific individual ideas of fascism have lived on, however, and will perhaps be of some individual importance in the early twenty-first century, as well. These include such principles as extreme nationalism, charismatic leadership, political authoritarianism and statist economics, which, however discredited in Europe and the Americas, live on in certain other parts of the world. In no case, however, do non-Western nationalisms or regimes simply mimic the full ideology or systems of the historic fascist movements, for in every instance those individual features and doctrines which overlap with fascism are combined with more recent and indigenous characteristics, which in every case produce distinct morphologies.

Historic fascist nationalism was an epochal phenomenon of early twentieth-century Europe and cannot be specifically reproduced several generations later, for history never repeats itself exactly. There will be new authoritarian movements and regimes, but they will not have all or even most of the unique characteristics of European fascism. Fascism was a product particularly of the nationalist-imperialist conflicts of early twentieth-century Europe and of the ambitions of the newer states or powers formed during the third quarter of the nineteenth century. Its ideas had a clear genealogy, stemming remotely from aspects of the Enlightemnent and of Romanticism but drawing their specific form and content from the ideas and doctrines of the cultural crisis of the fin-de-siècle, catalyzed by the consequences of World War I and of the Great Depression. Though most early twentieth-century Europeans were not attracted to fascism, it was shaped by influences and attitudes found primarily in the culture of Europe during the era of world wars, and generated the most violent political forces of that singular age of conflict. It is unlikely that such a combined political and cultural constellation will reappear. The new forces of political violence and oppression of the twenty-first century will probably use some of the ideas of fascism, but will be unable to reproduce its full pattern, even should they so desire.

### Bibliography

Bessel, Richard (ed.). 1996. *Fascist Italy and Nazi Germany: Comparisons and Contrasts.* Cambridge: Cambridge University Press.

Birken, Lawrence. 1995. *Hitler as Philosophe: Remnants of the Enlightenment in National Socialism.* Westport, CT and London: Praeger.

De Felice, Renzo. 1977. *Interpretations of Fascism.* Cambridge, MA: Harvard University Press.

Gentile, Emilio. 1996. *The Sacralization of Politics in Fascist Italy.* Cambridge, MA: Harvard University Press.

Gregor, A. James. 1969. *The Ideology of Fascism: The Rationale of Totalitarianism.* New York: The Free Press.

Gregor, A. James. 1974. *The Fascist Persuasion in Radical Politics.* Princeton, NJ: Princeton University Press.

Griffin, Roger. 1991. *The Nature of Fascism.* London: Pinter Publishers.

Heinen, Armin. 1986. *Die Legion 'Erzengel Michael' in Rumanien.* Munich: R. Oldenbourg.

Jaeckel, Eberhard. 1972. *Hitler's Weltanschauung.* Middletown, CT: Wesleyan University Press.

Kershaw, Ian. 1993. *The Nazi Dictatorship: Problems and Perspectives of Interpretation.* 3rd edn. London: Edward Arnold.

Lyttelton, Adrian. 1987. *The Seizure of Power: Fascism in Italy, 1919-1929.* 2nd edn. London: Weidenfeld and Nicolson.

Milza, Pierre. 1987. *Le Fascisme français.* Paris: Flammarion.

Mosse, George L. 1978. *Toward the Final Solution: A History of European Racism.* London: Dent.

Nagy-Talavera, Nicholas M. 1970. *The Green Shirts and the Others.* Stanford, CA: Hoover Institution Press, Stanford University.

Nolte, Ernst. 1965. *Three Faces of Fascism.* London: Weidenfeld and Nicolson.

Payne, Stanley G. 1987. *The Franco Regime, 1936-1975.* Madison: The University of Wisconsin Press.

Payne, Stanley G. 1996. *A History of Fascism, 1914-1945.* Madison: The University of Wisconsin Press.

Roberts, David D. 1979. *The Syndicalist Tradition in Italian Fascism.* Manchester: Manchester University Press.

Sternhell, Zeev. 1974. *La Droite révolutionnaire: Les origines françaises du fascisme.* Paris: Éditions du Seuil.

Szollosi-Janze, Margit. 1989. *Die Pfeilkreuzlerbewegung in Ungarn.* Munich: R. Oldenbourg.

Stanley G. Payne

# Feminism and Nationalism

Women and men have experienced the nation and nationalism quite differently. Women have had a much more problematic relationship both to the idea and practice of "the nation." Feminist analyses of nationalism are motivated by the curiosity to know the causes of this uneasy relationship between women and the nation, and the consequences of this uneasiness. What feminists have been struck by is how seemingly uncurious most other analysts of nationalism have been in this respect. Supporters of non-feminist approaches to explaining nationalism appear either to assume (without testing their assumption) that women and men have identical relationships to nationalism, or to accept that men experience nationalism differently from women. Although this differentiation is correct and important, it is accompanied by an assessment (not based on evidence) of these differences as politically, economically, and socially trivial, inconsequential.

The seeds of nationalism were planted in the late eighteenth century during the French and American revolutions. In the middle of the nineteenth century, nationalism reached new heights in popular political thinking. During both periods, some women believed that the ideas about and movements advocating nationalism might allow women to claim a place in the public sphere as "citizens" since citizenship was so central to theories of the nation. Probably the most famous claimant was France's Olympe de Gouge. She and other members of the all-female Republican Clubs argued for a nation in which women were recognized as full citizens and not as simply members of families and dependents of male citizens. Of course, she was sent to the guillotine. For, not only in Italy and regions of the Habsburg Empire, but even in the most "universalist" states, the United States and France, male nationalists repeatedly took steps to shrink the notion of citizenship in order to keep women confined chiefly to the domestic sphere, suggesting that in reality the domestic sphere was central to the national life.

Most of the feminist theorizing about nationalism has been derived from empirical studies, charting the ways in which the idea of the nation has been constructed, how movements to promote the nation have been organized and how state policies to create and sustain the nation have been formulated, justified and implemented (Yuval-Davis and Anthias 1989). Out of this research has emerged a pattern: the very idea of what "the nation" should be has been repeatedly in the nineteenth and twentieth centuries constructed on a foundation of prescriptions of the ideal—and politically necessary—femininity and masculinity. That is, most nationalists in most eras and societies have acted as if the persuading of women to adopt a very particular form of femininity were crucial for the very making and sustaining of the nation. All of these nationalized notions of appropriate femininity have not been identical, some have pressed women to become more publicly participant than others. Thus, in the 1920s and 1930s China and Vietnam and in the 1940s and 1950s Indonesia, male nationalist leaders urged men to accept women's public activism because they considered it important for the achievement of national independence.

This mobilizing dimension of nationalism has been energizing for women in many societies. Yet, studies have revealed that, the participatory language notwithstanding, all too many male leaders of nationalist movements have not only been male, they have been masculinist. This means that they have held beliefs that ultimately privilege men in the construction and administration of the nation. Thus, while in the 1910s in Egypt women were among the principal activists for and articulators of a new Egyptian nation and the end of British colonial rule, they were shocked to discover that their male nationalist colleagues excluded women from the new constitution's voting public and from of its new representative legislature (Badran 1995). Likewise, Vietnamese women who began organizing to widen the public spaces in which women could operate in the 1920s were persuaded to meld their efforts in the 1930s with the new nationalist movement. However, they found that in this movement any women's concerns that were seen by male leaders to jeopardize the unity between men and women in the face of French colonial oppression were deemed concerns that should not be discussed (Tai 1992).

The idea of the "nation" has had particular appeal to many women in colonized and neo-colonized societies and in many ethnic and racial groups which have endured marginalization and oppression precisely because the nation seems to be so different from the state: less dependent on coercion; less hierarchical; less reliant on authority and formal structures of decision-making—that is, less patriarchal. The idea of the nation has also been porous enough to permit women to participate via avenues that are more broadly political: oral histories, cookbooks, non-state schools. But the very openness of nationalist movements to these new forms of political mobilization has frequently made women not the agents of nation-building strategies, but the objects. Thus, women's attire, women's reproduction, women's marriage choices, women's sexuality, each has been turned by some masculinized nationalist movements into a target of control, of political policing. If and when such a nationalist movement's leadership succeeds in taking over a state, then this patriarchal interpretation of what constitutes—or should constitute—the nation can lead to explicit policies to increase external control of women's lives. The experience of Eastern European women since 1989 in the policy realm of abortion rights curtailment is one vivid example.

An important concern of feminist theorists has been the idea of beauty. They have noted, first, that ideas about beauty tend to become feminized; and, second, that female beauty contests have become sites for nationalist politics (Cohen et al. 1996). A related point has also been noted, namely, that the nation is usually symbolized as a woman. One of the confusions one encounters when trying to unravel the gendering of most nationalist movements or state uses of nationalist rhetoric, is the classic combination of a symbolism that celebrates women—or "the woman"—with policies which insure that women are kept on the margins of political decision-making. Thus, for instance, while the nation is often represented as a woman in nationalist iconography, no women are elected or appointed to the executive of the nationalist party. Following the same logic, women are pressed by nationalist leaders, be they inside or outside the state, to consider themselves as

valuable to the nation because they can give birth to the nation's next generation; but this is frequently joined with policies which intimidate women who dare to marry and have children with men from "outside" the nation.

The relationship between women, religion and nationalism is of particular significance in this discussion. This is for two reasons, mainly: first, because virtually all of the world's major religious traditions have been interpreted as legitimizing women's subordination to men; and, second, because religious identities have been and today still are used by some (not all) nationalist leaders as one of the building blocks when constructing the nation. In this context, women, either as feminists or as believers in a secularized state, have found themselves contesting politicized religious doctrines in countries as varied as Ireland, the United States, India and Afghanistan. While some nationalists, such as Ho Chi Minh, have deliberately leaned toward a secular conception of the nation, others have claimed that it is a particular religion which not only distinguishes their community from the most significant oppressors, and/ or have claimed that religious beliefs have provided that community with such a strong sense of its collective self that imagining that nation without that set of religious beliefs (as determined by the leading nationalists themselves) would leave that nation nothing more than a hollow, soul-less shell. This has been the case among most Northern Ireland republican nationalists (though less and less so among Irish nationalists in the Republic itself), among 1990s Indian Hindu nationalists, and among Sri Lanka Sinhalese nationalists. In each instance, the nation is imagined as dependent for its social and cultural solidarity on very particular relations between women and men, in which men hold authority within the family, women are held to sexual standards more rigid than those to which men are held and women's roles as loyal wives and sacrificing mothers are the only legitimate bases for women's public or political activism. All these assertions are claimed to derive from specific and irrefutable religious teachings.

Feminist theorists have paid close attention to the responses of nationalist movements to women's organising to expand women's economic roles and legal rights. Sri Lankan feminist scholar Kumari Jayawardena was one of the first to monitor how male nationalists responded to women's advocates by claiming that such advocacy was "alien" to the nation (Jayawardena 1986). Since then, feminist historians, including those historians of the American and French revolutions, have detailed why and how Western nationalist theorists and activists have sought to portray women's efforts to change relationships between women and men inside the family and inside the political economy as allegedly "foreign" and thus worthy of suppression. Still, other feminist theorists have traced the policies and discourses which have enabled nationalist movements to become militarized in ways that have pressured women to see themselves chiefly as patriotic mothers (Enloe 1993).

The specific participation of women in warfare has not followed a uniform pattern. The leaders of both insurgent armies and state armies have repeatedly used ideas of "national loyalty" and "national pride" as resources for raising military forces. Usually, these ideas have been wielded to maintain the masculinization of militaries—women in wartime being encouraged to show their national devotion through supporting their sons and husbands as soldiers. But occasionally, when either insurgent or state militaries have run short of the men they consider trustworthy, they have enlisted women into their ranks. This has occurred in the following circumstances: first, and usually, women have been enlisted in feminized roles (clerks, nurses); and second, only in desperation, as combatants, for instance during the Israeli Jews' nationalist insurgency of the late 1940s and during the Soviet state's confrontation with Hitler's armies during the Second World War. When the military emergency recedes most military strategists try to reassert nationalist "normalcy" by demobilising almost all women and deploying those remaining in the military in jobs traditionally defined as "women's work."

The relationship between nationalism, women and feminist theory are fluid and dynamic. Among African Americans, Indian Hindus, Northern Irish Catholics, Japanese Okinawans, Zulu South Africans, British Scots and Kosovo Albanians there are public and private debates in progress concerning, first, what the proper relationship between women and men in the nation should be, and, second, what kind of masculinity and what kind of femininity best serve the best interests of the nation. While many feminist activists and thinkers have come to the conclusion that nationalism carries within it strong patriarchal tendencies and, therefore, that it should be avoided, other feminists have found nationalism valuable enough and sufficiently malleable to be worth engaging with, albeit critically (West 1997). What is clear is that nationalist movements, and nationalism as a package of ideas cannot be fully analysed without paying explicit attention to the politics of gender.

### Bibliography

Badran, Margot. 1995. *Feminists, Islam and Nation*. Princeton, NJ: Princeton University Press.

Cohen, Colleen Ballerino et al. (eds.). 1996. *Beauty Queen on the Global Stage*. London: Routledge.

Enloe, Cynthia. 1993. *The Morning After: Sexual Politics at the End of the Cold War*. Berkeley: University of California Press.

Jayawardena, Kumari. 1986. *Feminism and Nationalism in the Third World*. London: Zed Books.

Tai, Hue-Tam Ho. 1992. *Radicalism and the Origins of the Vietnamese Revolution*. Cambridge, MA: Harvard University Press.

West, Lois A. (ed.). 1997. *Feminist Nationalism*. London: Routledge.

Yuval-Davis, Nira and Anthias, Floya (eds.). 1989. *Woman-Nation-State*. London: Macmillan.

Cynthia Enloe

# Fichte, Johann Gottlieb (1762-1814)

German philosopher and patriot. Initially influenced by the critical philosophy of Immanuel Kant, Fichte later distanced himself from such ideas and, during his time as professor of philosophy at Jena, began to expound his own system of transcendental idealism. The Napoleonic victories over the Prussians in 1806 led him to deliver a series of fourteen lectures, the famous *Reden an die deutsche Nation* (*Addresses to the German Nation*) between 1807 and 1808. In these addresses, Fichte called on his fellow nationalists to assume the duty handed down to them from their German forefathers: that they should refuse to submit to foreign tyranny and that they should re-establish German freedom.

For Fichte, the world is divided into nations, with language constituting the most important criterion of a nation. "True" or "natural" nations are those language groups which are pure and devoid of external linguistic influences. The nation then is a unique and natural entity which stands over and above the individuals who are to be found within it. Such individuals possess common characteristics, and especially a common language, which distinguish them from other nations. The proof of this cultural individuality of "nations ordained by nature" is to be found in the manifest differences of language, history and custom which they exhibit. These external differences between nations lead to the development of a distinctive "spirit" of the nation whereby the individual's will is absorbed into that of the organic state: national self-realization through political struggle then follows.

Fichte believed not only that a German nation existed, but also that its preservation was worthwhile: "Our present problem is to preserve the existence and continuity of what is German. All other differences vanish before this higher point of view...It is essential that the higher love of Fatherland, for the entire people of the German nation, reign supreme, and justly so, in every particular German state. No one of them can lose sight of the higher interest without alienating everything that is noble and good."

### Bibliography

Fichte, Johann Gottlieb.1808. *Addresses to the German Nation*, trans. by R.F. Jones and G.H. Turnbull. 1979 reprint of the 1922 edn. published by Open Court Publishers. Westport, CT: Greenwood Press.
Kohn, Hans. 1949. "The paradox of Fichte's nationalism," *Journal of the History of Ideas* 10, 3.

Rachel Monaghan

# Foundation Myths

Stories about the origins and foundation of political communities are often regarded as serious talk, iterated through ritual, carried by myth and defended by religious or scholarly orthodoxy. One sociological reason for this is that we use language to cut up the continuum of time into meaningful categories which carry identity messages relevant to political mobilization. Where we choose our point of beginning can say much about who we see ourselves as and who we exclude from such a sense of communality. By establishing boundaries over the flux of time and space, meaning becomes possible and political allegiances and roles are defined and validated. Equally, however, other potentialities and identities become marginalized or invalidated.

Foundation myths are the stories of origin and arrival of peoples at their destinations. Such origins, journeys and destinations are rarely mere geographical constructions and are better understood as ontological statements in which spatial and temporal journeys iterate, realize and define communal identity. Foundation myths are not only stories that are told, but are often revisited on a regular basis as ritual since political communities are not only "imagined" but also enacted.

An elementary and universal form of foundation myth among agrarian peoples is genealogy. By exploring how genealogies work for the peoples who carry them we can discover some of the influence of foundation myths. Genealogies select from the vast potential array of biological ancestors an order based on socially selected structural principles (matrilines, patrilines, bilaterality) which relate to political and property relations (matrifocal, patrifocal). The genealogy becomes the mnemonic for the lineage. It selects and structures a past and shapes present and future socio-political arrangements. Genealogies regulate social relations and marriages and shape the boundaries of political groups and the social divisions within them. They are plastic political myths that can be arranged and rearranged to accommodate changing political alliances. This is so for, although the founders usually remain fixed as clan or ethnic badges, ancestor lineages beyond living memory are often telescoped or fused

97

## Foundation Myths

with elements from other clan lineages. Founders provide an ontological bridge from microcosm to macrocosm as gods, heroes, or totemic representatives.

One solution to the ontological problem posed by imposing beginnings on the continuum of time, much favoured by traditional communities, is that of autochthony. By asserting that the political group emerged with the land itself at the beginning of creation, political identity and political arrangements are given an anchor of cosmic validation. As Malinowski noted of the Trobriand Islanders, such myths can also function as charters. By "explaining" the relationships between clans, classes, age groups, or gender groups in terms of an overarching cosmological drama, a conservative ideology is reinforced as fate. The ancient Egyptians, the Japanese, some Australian aboriginal clans, the Athenians, and many native American peoples, such as the Incas of Peru, all promoted origin stories of this kind.

Perhaps the most ontologically complete foundation myth is where the people, their home, and the cosmos are ordered in harmonious relationship. The ontological centre is also the geographical centre. Peoples the world over seem to have attempted at times to replicate such a scheme architecturally, as with the circular cities of the ancient Middle East, the most famous of which, Ectbana, was set on a hill and surrounded by seven differently colored concentric walls of reducing height, symbolising the sun, moon and planets and thus the cosmos. In much of East Asia, agrarian civilizations focused around the person of the king, who was perceived to be the center of the universe, and a mediator with the heavenly realm. In the Indic cultures of classical Indonesia, such as Angkor, Pagan, and Majapahit in Central Java, the court was a copy of the cosmos, and the political community a copy of the court. The beginnings of states are often explained in terms of myths of these regnal founders. For example, in ancient Korea, where states were locked in rivalry until 676 A.D. the myths tend to be of two kinds; either the foundation story relates how the founder was born of a woman who became pregnant by a mystical light descending from heaven, or the founder of the dynasty descends from heaven onto mountain tops, forests and trees.

In contrast, many political communities have been shaped by foundation stories of ontological rupture. Here the original home has become separated from its people. In these circumstances the lost home can become a metaphor for ontological wholeness, to be reestablished by way of a journey. These are ancient patterns of thought with wide geographical distribution. For example peasant millenarian movements of China, as early as the second century BCE, have focused on the idealized realm of the Queen Mother of the West, a focus that has been accompanied by peasant uprisings through much of China's long history. On the other hand, ontological wholeness can be imagined as being entirely located in the future. From the new England Puritan John Winthrop's "city upon a hill" to the speeches of Martin Luther King there is a strong millenarian tendency in American political culture. Here, from the Great Awakening onwards, the geographical journey has also been westwards. As a companion to Alexis de Tocqueville commented during his visit in 1830, "it has something providential in it; it is like some flood of humanity rising constantly and driven by the hand of God."

Perhaps the three most influential foundation myths centring upon journeys are those of the Romans, the Israelites and the Mexica-Aztecs. Once shaped for the purposes of particular ethnic groups, each of these myths became a paradigm by which later political groups could forge allegiance and define a following.

By the time the Roman State, under Greek influence, had emerged with its own tradition of written historiography, two competing foundation myths were in the process of being synthesized into a common tradition. The older indigenous tradition of Romulus and Remus was a typical Indo-European foundation myth with alliterating twin founders one of which dies or is sacrificed. The more recent story with its journey theme was almost certainly borrowed from the Greek speaking world of the Eastern Mediterranean, where no less than seventeen Greek city states claimed descent from Troy. By this account, Romans were descended from the hero Aeneas, who escaped from the destruction of Troy with his father Anchises on his back, the latter clutching the family household gods in his hands.

For the syncretically minded Roman elites the separation of the foundation myth from the myth of origin does not have appeared to present ontological problems. On the contrary, the idea that the Romans had once been, or were essentially, Trojans, was embraced with enthusiasm and was seen to add to the splendour of their pedigree in their emergent Imperial identity in the Greek speaking world. This journey theme is transformed under the genius of Virgil to become a seminal model for later political cultures. Through their journey and trials the Trojan exiles forge a Roman identity, discover their Imperial destiny and win a homeland. There is no hint of nostalgia for a lost Trojan homeland. Nostalgia and the idea of ontological completeness are important for later Roman politics, but the golden age for Romans was firmly located in Rome itself, at the time of the Republic. The sense of the lost Republican ideals of simple, rural virtue was a mythological theme that shaped Roman political culture from Cato the elder to Juvenal, a period of some 350 years.

The Aztec-Mexica journey myth is part of a remarkable canon of migration myths of Mesoamerican peoples in which identities seem to be transformed and reestablished by ethnic name changes or new tutelary gods. Emerging from caves or springs these peoples are led by their gods and priests in search of their destined lands. There is strong nostalgia for the original home, Aztlan, "the white land" or "land of herons" in the Aztec-Mexica story. Huitzilopochtli, their god or leader, does not allow them to settle until through signs they find the place to recreate their original home, the lake garden paradise of their ancestors. The island city capital Tenochtitlan, in the middle of Lake Texcoco, as a recreation of the original home, is strictly aligned according to sacred geography and sacred time. The journey myth of the Aztec-Mexica not only establishes and explains political and gender hierarchies, by setting up spacio-temporal boundaries, it also explains political relations with geographically proximate peoples and seems to instil a tragic sense of fate.

Undoubtedly, the most influential foundation myth with a journey theme remains that of the Israelites. The ideas of chosenness, the promised land, covenant, and the New Jerusalem have been seeded in political cultures everywhere. To the ancient ideas of an ontological rupture to be counteracted by a journey, is added a strong ethical and, indeed, personal commitment. The journey myth reenacted regularly through ritual becomes both a collective quest for salvation and a personal affirmation. These myths sustain clear ethnic markers and have proved remarkably successful in consolidating and sustaining a following. Some of the oldest ethnic communities, including Jews, Armenians, Georgians, and Ethiopians have sustained political identity in this way. The separation of the myth of origin from the myth of foundation presents interesting ontological problems which the journey enacts and resolves. Abram's father Terah was from Haran in North-West Mesopotamia and a polytheist by faith. Abram became a Hebrew through his journey, by learning to listen to his unique tutelary god with whom he makes a covenant. This particular form of foundation myth is strongly oppositional and tends to be associated with identity markers of diet, hygiene, dress and communality against surrounding groups. The perceived danger is boundary crossing which would lead to backsliding and loss of identity. Whereas the Romans could cheerfully become Trojans when it suited them, the primordial influence of Mesopotamia seems to have been a constant fear and temptation to the Israelites, a temptation to which the "lost tribes" presumably succumbed.

The normal political community of the ancient world from Asia Minor through to Spain was the city-state. Here, foundation myths and rites were a central part of religious and political culture. Every city had its collection of heroes, ancestors and gods around which cults had formed, and the calendar was largely made up of festivals in their honor. The cities tended to evolve by a process of *synoecism*, the amalgamation of villages, clans, and townships into one religio-political community. Local gods and heroes had to be persuaded to join the wider state and festivals had to be established within the calendar to accommodate them. At times local cults were too prestigious or sacred to be moved, in which case as with the Lavinium for the Romans and Eleusis for the Athenians, processional routes and common sacrifices were arranged to link the two places. These festivals iterated and validated political allegiances

# Foundation Myths

and hierarchies through understood rules of commensalism and the gift exchange.

With the collapse of the Roman Empire the regnal community became the accepted political order in Europe, and genealogies the major validating mythological form. Nevertheless, the old learning was not entirely forgotten and the emerging Christian clerics, following Isidore of Seville, tried to amalgamate a unified past out of the book knowledge available to them. Saxon, British, and Frankish leaders and their peoples were given sequences of ancestors, that went beyond the Northern gods and heroes, that had originally served as ethnic badges, to include both Graeco-Roman and Old Testament figures. For example, the Germanic peoples that colonized southern Britain after the collapse of the Roman Empire produced rival alliterating twin hero founders. As Wessex came to predominate in the south, Hengest and Horsa, came to pre-eminence and, promoted by the church, eventually served as founders for the "English." That great rationalizer of English history, the Venerable Bede, computed a foundation date of the arrival of Hengest and Horsa in Britain (449 A.D.) and created an origin myth which includes a journey. He solved the ontological problem of separating origins from foundation by giving the Germanic settlers a backdated mythological charter to their Englishness. By Bede's account, the pagan invaders in their struggle against the (Christian) British are elected by God for His purposes and win a homeland. They become a covenanted people and a chosen people whose gift of the overlordship of Britain is contingent on their righteousness and missionary zeal, a chosenness that is recognized and promoted by both their founder saint, Augustine, but also Pope Gregory. This journey theme by which the English win a homeland becomes a focus for much Old English literature, so much so that in the Old English version of Genesis the desert journey of the Israelites to the promised land becomes represented as a long and arduous voyage by sea.

With the revival of trade in Western Europe in the Middle Ages, city states again produced lavish religious rites incorporating civic ceremonials focused on protecting saints, a tendency that was given new life by the Renaissance which rediscovered or reinvented festivals and rites of the Graeco-Roman world. But it is with the nationalist movements of the modern world that we see the most dramatic and far reaching attempts to define a particular past for particular peoples.

Since nationalism is based on the theory that the world is naturally made up of nations with territorial domains, one of the functions of much nineteenth-century historiography was to establish through foundation myths and origin myths charter rights of peoples to territories. Another was to explain favoured political and cultural trends in terms of ancient and accepted practices. The primordialism of historians, such as František Palacký for the Czechs or Eoin MacNeill for the Irish, and geographers, such as Friedrich Ratzel for the Germans, links imagined cultural, religious and even biological attributes to territory. In England, the myth of Anglo-Saxonism reached a mass audience through the popular writings of many talented historians and propagandists, including Macauley, Kemble, Green, Kingsley, Carlyle, and Stubbs. Echoing Wordsworth, the distinguished Anglo-Saxon scholar, John Kemble, in his book *The Saxons of England* (1849), provides us with both a clear example of and a definition of a foundation myth. In the preface he writes: "the subject is a grave and solemn one: it is the history of the childhood of our own age, - the explanation of its manhood." The problem is, of course, that the childhood that is selected predetermines the manhood (*sic*) that is favoured.

From a viewpoint of comparative mythography, one of the striking features of nationalist belief is its strong diachronic emphasis. A secular millenarian faith is conceptualized by the idea of "progress." The ancient paradigm of ontological rupture and a journey is influential, therefore, for nationalisms everywhere. From religious sectarian groups with political and territorial ambitions, such as the nineteenth-century Mormons, to border communities such as Serbs, Boers, Ulstermen, Israelis, and Georgians, journey themes have had a strategic significance in mobilising political groups. Settler communities, such as those of Canada, the United States and Australia, have attempted to galvanize support around journeys, as studies of their Centennial and Bicentennial celebrations have demonstrated. For Australians the ambiguous sacrificial journey of the Anzacs to Gallipoli has long been a source of powerful and ambiguous national feeling. But its "great narratives" that link territory, history, and suffering are still in the process of becoming. As Lyn Spillman notes in *Nation and Commemoration* (1997) of the Bicentennial celebration of the settlement of Australia by Europeans, the founding moment was repressed because of divisive ethnocentric connotations. Instead, activities seemed to focus around the "endless repetition of ... epic and unlikely circumnavigations, voyages and journeys."

## Bibliography

Heyden, D. 1989. *The Eagle, the Cactus, the Rock: The Roots of Mexico-Tenochtitlan's Foundation Myth and Symbol*. Oxford: B.A.R.

Hutchinson, J. 1994. *Modern Nationalism*. London: Fontana Press.

Kapferer, B. 1988. *Legends of People: Myths of State*. Washington, DC: Smithsonian Institute Press.

MacDougall, H.A. 1982. *Racial Myth in English History: Trojans, Teutons and Anglo-Saxons*. Hanover and London: University Press of New England.

Rehel-Dolmatoff, G. 1995. *Yupari: Studies of an Amazonian Foundation Myth*. Cambridge, MA: Harvard University Center for the Study of World Religions.

Reynolds, S. 1983. "Medieval *origines gentium* and the community of the realm," *History*, lviii: 375-90.

Rogers, G. M. 1991. *The Sacred Identity of Ephesos: Foundation Myths of a Roman City*. London and New York: Routledge.

Smith, A. D. 1992. "Chosen peoples: why ethnic groups survive," *Ethnic and Racial Studies* 15, 3: 436-456.

Spillman, L. 1997. *Nation and Commemoration: Creating National Identities in the United States and Australia*. Cambridge: Cambridge University Press.

Sebastian Garman

# Fuseli (Fussli), Henry (1741–1825)

Born in Zurich, the son of a painter, Fuseli studied under the Swiss nationalist intellectuals, Bodmer and Breitinger, who introduced him to Homer, Dante, Shakespeare, Milton, and the Nibelungenlied. In 1764 he went to London, took up art, and from 1770–78 stayed in Rome, imbibing the art of the antique, Michelangelo and Mannerism, and producing highly charged, romantic drawings and paintings on dramatic literary themes often drawn from Icelandic, Norse, Greek, and other mythologies. After a stay in Zurich, Fuseli returned to London where in 1799 he became Professor of Painting at the Royal Academy.

One of Fuseli's most overtly nationalist subject was a commission from the Zurich Rathaus to paint *The Oath of the Rutli* (1779–81) which still hangs there. It records the Swiss national foundation myth, when the representatives of the three forest cantons, Uri, Schwyz, and Unterwalden, met in 1307 (now redated to 1291) to swear a compact against their Austrian Habsburg oppressors. Fuseli depicts this theme in a symbolic and dramatic manner. In a barren setting stand three monumental neo-mannerist Roman heroes, their right arms swung passionately aloft to the sword of justice and freedom above their heads, their left hands conjoined in a tight knot in the center, symbolic of the indivisible Swiss fatherland.

Fuseli's *Oath* is one of a series of paintings of national and republican oaths by various artists of the period, starting with Gavin Hamilton's *Oath of Brutus* (1764) and including David's *Oath of the Horatii* (1784) and *Oath of the Tennis Court* (1791), all of which express the great wave of republican nationalism that swept Western Europe and North America in the late eighteenth century.

## Bibliography

Antal, F. 1956. *Fuseli Studies*. London: Routledge and Kegan Paul.

Pressly, N. 1979. *The Fuseli Circle in Rome*. New Haven, CT: Yale Center for British Art.

Rosenblum, R. 1961. "Gavin Hamilton's *Brutus* and its Aftermath," *The Burlington Magazine*, Clll, January: 8-16.

Tate Gallery. 1975. *Henry Fuseli, 1741–1825*. London: Tate Gallery Publications.

Anthony D. Smith

# G

## Gellner, Ernest (1925-1995)

Gellner's first systematic attempt to deal with nationalism came with *Thought and Change* (1964). Nationalism arises with the passage from agricultural religious society to industrial scientific society. It is a self-generated response to the modern need for a mobile labor force, which requires a common education in a common language. The role of mass education is related to the industrial need for a semi-skilled labor force that must be easily replaceable. By losing their traditional roles in pre-industrial societies, men (and later women) become available in the labor market as a uniform mass, rather than as individuals. The "standardization of expression and comprehension" leads to the capacity for context-free communication. With industrialism, peoples moved from a vertical status-centred social structure to a horizontal culture-centred social system, governed by individualistic and egalitarian principles.

Gellner's major target was ideological diffusionism, the vision that ideas have a power of their own, that they can indeed lead the world, and that nationalism is determined by the diffusion of ideas. In polemics with this position, personified by his colleague at the London School of Economics, ELIE KEDOURIE, Gellner wrote *Nations and Nationalism* (1983), a path-breaking critique of approaches to nationalism centred on the history of ideas. This, in itself, is certainly a major achievement on the part of a scholar trained in, and teaching, philosophy. One of Gellner's arguments against the role of ideas, is his claim that no major political philosopher has vindicated nationalism. For Gellner this was symptomatic of the intellectual inferiority of nationalist theories—and hence, a proof that ideas count for little. But, above all other considerations, *Nations and Nationalism* is a devastating attack on Western Marxism, with its still suffocating presence in British academia. To widespread Marxist clichés about structure and superstructure, Gellner responded with his own brand of labor-related and culture-tied determinism.

In the 1990s, his anti-ideological bent brought him into bitter polemics with the literary critic Edward Said in the pages of the *Times Literary Supplement* (Gellner 1994: 159-169). Nevertheless, the history of ideas was not totally alien to his views: for instance, in *Plough, Sword and Book* (1991), he concluded that the sixteenth-century *ex cathedra* acceptance of empirical evidence as the only yardstick for distinguishing veracity from deception—above the authority of Kings and Priests, represented the key breakthrough for the advent of industrial technology, and hence the beginning of modernity. The book's title implies a focus on production, coercion and cognition, which he sees as the crucible of all social transformations.

Gellner's interpretation of nationalism owes much to Émile Durkheim (1858-1917), and is influenced by both functionalism and modernization theories. Nationalism arises as a response to uprooting modernization which undermines traditional systems of ascriptive relations. Nationalism's historical mission is to dispense new forms of loyalty and identification with the nation-state. Hence, nationalism is a political response to a functional imperative: territorial and social mobility make necessary the construction of a collective identity which can operate for the uprooted individual as an anchor and steering compass. Gellner shared with modernization theorists the belief that there is a radical discontinuity between industrial and pre-industrial societies (1998b). This contrast is indeed at the centre of all his explanations of nationalism.

Following MAX WEBER (1864-1920), Gellner also focused on the bureaucratization of culture: "The state has not merely the monopoly of legitimate violence, but also of the accreditation of educational qualification. So the marriage of state and culture takes place, and we find ourselves in the Age of Nationalism" (1994: 107). However, state-enforced homogenization, metaphorically identified as the Empire of "Megalomania" (probably a reference to the Habsburg empire), provokes the reactions of those who have been either excluded, or have chosen to opt out in order to protect their own culture. These latter are bound to form their own national movements, in which a low culture is promoted and transformed into a high culture. Their political project is redefined as "Ruritania," the prototypical nationalist homeland (possibly, an allusion to his native Czechoslovakia).

In the homogenizing world of nation-states, human societies find themselves at a radical crossroads: they must either organize themselves on the basis of the nation-state model or perish. A nation is here defined as common membership in a shared high culture. According to Gellner, the high culture of the age of nations is the vehicle of industrialism. This is a mass, rational, and scientific-technological culture which is communicated by a standardized script in the "national" language.

In turn, nationalism is defined as "primarily a principle which holds that the political and national unit should be congruent" (Gellner 1983: 1). Weber's influence on Gellner is well illustrated by Nicholas Stargardt: "Quite simply, nationalism replaces Weber's 'Protestant spirit' as the ideology which legitimates the construction of the modern industrialized world. And the disenchantment is the same. The irony of history for Weber was that a world successfully built on the Protestant ethic was ultimately secular, materialist and irreligious...So for Gellner, the ultimate triumph of nationalism is also the signal for its dissolution...By fulfilling the nationalist goal of industrialising and creating a successful consumer society, public and collective values are inevitably replaced by private and individual ones" (Stargardt 1996: 186).

With a wealth of inventiveness, a taste for the paradoxical, and a never-failing trenchant humor, Gellner produced outstanding and entertaining metaphorical sketches of dramatic historical events, such as the famous contrast between Kokoschka's and Modigliani's pictorial styles, which he used to illustrate the shift from agricultural to modern society. The former was characterized by the coexistence and overlap of multiple color dots, the latter by sharply demarcated color fields which never intermingle (1983: 139-40). This penchant for analogy spiced with dry wittiness served to illustrate with captivating acumen some very simple models of social change. Nationalism, a bogey that had troubled so many scholars for nearly a century, was explained in relatively ingenuous terms, providing perhaps the best synthesis, still unequalled by other accounts.

Gellner believed that "Nationalism ... invents nations where they do not exist" (1964: 168) perhaps overstating the doctrine's arbitrary character—but without underestimating its creative potential. To the nationalists themselves, nationalism looks immemorial and ever-lasting. It is this doubly reassuring temporal projection towards the past and the future which explains nationalism's unfathomable force—but it also accounts for its simultaneous weakness. Indeed, there are far more potential nations in the world than there are actual ones. Nationalism is a powerful legitimizing force. However, its main legitimacy is grounded on the previous existence of a pluralist system of states. The multi-state system which emerged in northwestern Europe created the necessary preconditions for the advent of modernity. This is so, because a plural system supplies "a social variant of natural selection." In economic terms, this means that "production in a plural state system provides a better path to wealth than domination" (1994a: 74).

Gellner's only fieldwork—and subsequent anthropology Ph.D. degree of 1954—on the Berbers of the Central High Atlas (Morocco), provided the springboard for subsequent works and edited books on Islam, including *Arabs and Berbers* (Gellner and Micaud 1973), *Patrons and Clients in Mediterranean Societies* (Gellner and Waterbury 1977), and, most notably, his master achievement, *Muslim Society* (Gellner 1981). Here, he applied to Islam the same framework that he was applying to the study of nationalism. As he remarked elsewhere, "the mechanisms which underlie Muslim fundamentalism ... are similar to those which underlie modern nationalism: men

# Gellner, Ernest (1925-1995)

leaving, or deprived of places in a local social structure are attracted by identification with a community defined by a shared High Culture" (1994b: 179). His distinction between low Islam and high Islam reflects the distinction between low culture and high culture. "High" Islam (the creed of the *ulema*, the intellectuals) is characterized by puritanism, simplicity, scripturalism, lack of hierarchy, and other "Protestant ethic" features which, according to Gellner, are the basic requirements of modernity. In contrast, "Low" Islam is made up of the pluralistic folk practices of local communities. In the past, these two movements co-existed as two separate spheres, and such opposition often resulted in their mutual reinforcement. However, with industrialization and urbanization, uprooted peasant communities turned into a mass urban proletariat and lost their attachment to the old customs and practices. As a consequence, they became available to the new ideology of "social cohesion" supplied by the *ulema* (who, in that context, fulfilled the function of the nationalist intelligentsia of the Western world). For instance, the Islamic revolution in Iran displays all the hallmarks of a modernist revolution directed by the *ulema* and supported by disaffected, uprooted, anomic, recently urbanized youth in search of a new creed. In general, "new-style puritanism, with its elective affinity for social radicalism, prevails where colonialism had destroyed old elites and where a new one had come up from below, rather than from the outer wilderness" (Gellner 1981: 66). Or, as in the case of Iran, where ruthless Westernization plus elites' alienation from the masses challenged the rulers' legitimacy.

The fact that political Islam has emerged with particular strength in industrialized, urbanized, and Westernized societies, testifies to Islam's radical modernity. This is contrasted with the peaceful and balanced coexistence of high and folk religion in pre-industrial settings. Gellner's doctoral dissertation, published as *Saints of the Atlas* (1969), shows the crucial role of local Holy Men (intermediaries between high and low Islam, but only conceivable within the framework of folk practices) in maintaining harmony between the seasonally migrating shepherds and the sedentary, as well as among the nomadic communities

themselves. Twice a year over a million sheep and a hundred thousand people travel across the mounts into the hills and plains and vice versa, generating a gargantuan movement of mass dislocation. In these circumstances, the mediating role of the Saints is essential—considering also the shepherds' proud independent spirit and their anti-state sentiment.

Although Gellner's theory of nationalism is complete in itself, it is necessary to situate it within his critique of mainstream sociological, philosophical and literary approaches in order to grasp the author's message to the full. Among the philosophers, Gellner felt particularly close to David Hume (1711-1776) whom he had masterly compared to that "very great North African sociologist," Ibn Khaldun (1332-1406) (Gellner 1981). Immanuel Kant (1724-1804) was "the most heroic of philosophers" for his attempt to blend "enchantment" with external validation. His "unconstrained cognitive exploration" set the intellectual standard to be followed by subsequent generations (Gellner 1979: 8; 1995: 41).

His attacks on the orthodoxies of his time made him a unique, if not isolated, figure. He was a sworn adversary of fashionable dogmas swaying Western academia, chiefly relativism, feminism, post-modernism, psychoanalysis, "textism," neo-Marxism, and in general all "closed systems." He regarded psychoanalysis as another closed system—only matched in its closedness by Marxism—which "excludes critical assessment of itself by the implicit rules which succour-seekers must obey if the amelioration of their condition is to be attained" (Gellner 1993: 223). Psychoanalysis and nationalism share a common *Zeitgeist*: "The provision of human warmth and solace, much in demand in our society, is uncertain and precarious. In this situation, the vacuum principle operates: something must fill the crying need. It is psychologically impossible to tell the sufferer that no help is available, even if it is true" (ibid: 223). Consequently, psychoanalysis plays the same "filling" function as nationalism.

His relationship with religion was that of a fully-fledged secularist, but nevertheless one of empathy (Gellner 1974). Thus, he could understand the allure of Islam in the Islamic revival, while also recognising that the "secular *umma*" of communism could provide a similar sense of security to common people. Since Marxism offered a "moral order," its demise meant the collapse of that order, a void rather easily filled by nationalism (Gellner 1994b). Totalitarian socialism offered "total salvation" in a "naturalistic and sociological idiom," precisely as previous empires, founded on dynasty and religion, had offered salvation in a "transcendental" idiom. Behind a veneer of methodological Eurocentrism, his works evince esteem and even admiration for exotic cultures (Gellner 1975: 56-68).

Gellner remained close to social anthropology, especially to Bronislaw Malinowski (1884-1942) and, to a much lesser extent, to Sir James Frazer (1854-1941). Their influence is particularly felt in his writings on kinship systems (Gellner 1987). Of all the anthropologists, it was Malinowski who solicited his most devoted admiration. For the students of nationalism, Gellner "rediscovered" Malinowksi's late work, *Freedom and Civilization* (1944) which contained a number of important and very simple suggestions for policymakers in areas plagued by ethnic conflict. By rejecting both nationalism and cosmopolitanism, Malinowski continued the Central European heritage of "cultural autonomy" as a (never implemented) attempt to recognize and protect cultural differences within the existing political order. Gellner wrote some fine pages on Malinowski's own thought and his *Mitteleuropa* roots (Gellner 1994b: 74-80; 1998a). As for the general state of British social science, Gellner criticized what he recognized to be an ever-present concern, the "colonial sense of guilt." This sense of guilt misted all internal scrutiny like a malignant fog, hampering all possibilities of rational discussion.

Gellner's deeply-felt polemics against Marxism often expanded into a wider critique of the doctrinaire Left, but remained fair to those, innovative voices such as Tom Nairn, who attempted to rescue the ideology from its own fetters (Gellner 1978: 103-111, Nairn 1977). Paradoxically and provocatively, he preferred Soviet "Marxist" anthropology (with their cryptic and refined contributions) to the academic populism of British Marxists (Gellner 1988).

Gellner was much influenced by Karl Popper's (1902-1994) vision of an open society (Conversi

1999). But he also thought that it was necessary to protect citizens from the excesses of the market. For instance, he was aware that a relentless spread of the market model of universal competition would bring a social and ecological cataclysm: "Any unrestricted use of [technology] ... quite possibly will lead to a total disruption of the environment and the social order" (Gellner 1994a: 89). His exceptional interdisciplinary embrace meant that he brought insights from anthropology into philosophy, from historical learning into the social sciences and again into anthropology. This perhaps rendered him an isolated figure in the "compartmentalized community" of British anthropologists—reinforced by the fact that he did not engage in fieldwork after his doctoral research. By contextualizing, relativizing, and historicizing the discipline, he showed that anthropological problems could be solved with tools from other disciplines which experienced similar crises.

In 1993, and following the undoing of the Marxist "secular ideocracy" in Eastern Europe, Gellner moved to the newly established Central European University in Prague to direct, until his untimely death in 1995, the Centre for the Study of Nationalism.

Among possible critiques of Gellner's grand theory of nationalism, one is that it is too abstract to be applied to concrete examples of contemporary nationalism, particularly among stateless groups. The temptation, to which he tended to succumb, to pigeonhole ideas, movements and concepts has also been noticed (Tambini 1996, O'Leary 1997, Smith 1996). Roman Szporluk has rightly observed that Gellner's "own system, his grand vision of global scientific and industrial transformation, did not allow for the possibility of Auschwitz, or for the Gulag, and did not claim to have an ex-post explanation of that occurrence"(Szporluk 1999). Indeed, if the drive for total cultural homogeneity (hence for ethnic and racial purification) is assumed as a basic feature of modernity, then the alleged "ocean" separating 1789 (or 1848) from *Kristallnacht* may be no more than a rivulet. Once human beings become available for a homogeneous standardized high culture as interchangeable uniform mass, it is a short step from

# Gellner, Ernest (1925-1995)

transforming them into cheap flesh and blood for the new European conscript armies—a possibility first experienced in the French Revolution and its *levée en masse* of August 1793. The Nazi reintroduction of conscription in March 1935 is inconceivable without the homogenising idea of the unity of blood, language and destiny of the German *Volk*. The rise of uniform, assimilated, and uprooted "subjects" paved directly the way to all the major man-made tragedies in this century.

A related problem lies in Gellner's unorthodox method. The lack of an adequate bibliography and of an appropriate apparatus of footnotes which characterize his writings make his scholarship quite unique and entirely dependent on his syncretic genius. Moreover, most of his models, including his basic models of agrarian and industrial society, are ideal-types or reified categories rather than really existing social realities or historical events. Also, his approach is particularly competent in East European and Islamic matters but less so in West European matters. This may explain the fact that Gellner is one of the most popular theorists of nationalism in the ex-Communist world. However, when discussing Western Europe, he unconvincingly referred to the "lessening of the political salience of ethnicity."

Given Gellner's anthropological upbringing, one is struck by the glaring absence from his writings of the distinction between "ethnic boundaries" and "contents." The first scholar to formulate this distinction, FREDERICK BARTH, is mentioned only in relation to his Pathan fieldwork. Hence, cultural content seems to Gellner to be more important than the oppositional boundary that delimits one culture from another. This brings him dangerously close to the "Convergence Thesis." This is the view that, as advanced industrial societies come to resemble one another, conflicts diminish. However, in reality, the fact that "differences between languages become phonetic rather than semantic" (cultural convergence), has not been accompanied by the expected reduction in global conflict (political convergence). Even less realistic is the expectation that "generalized affluence diminishes intensity of hatreds" (economic convergence). As we know, economic welfare and development can, by themselves, bring peae and accommodation only in the short term.

Steeped in East European intellectual tradition and deeply rooted in its historical speculation, Gellner has failed to notice that a new chasm has arisen between high and low culture. This time, however, the low culture is simply the vast anonymous consumerist produce of the U.S.-led global village, while the "masses" no longer seem to yearn for an identification with a nationally defined high culture. This also accounts for the decline of the role of intellectuals, and their replacement by media pundits and rock stars. These use body-language direct semantics which replace lexical or morphological finesse and precision, and thereby fulfil basic needs through "neo-tribal" identification. Yet, globalization was not Gellner's concern. Refusing to conform to the post-modernist fad, Gellner seemed rarely concerned with contemporary developments. His past-oriented far-sightedness is not matched by a penchant for prognosis—nor did he probably wish it.

More generally, a form of "fatalism" underpins Gellner's approach to nationalism (Tambini 1996). His approach seems to suggest that things happen just because they have to. For instance, the idea that cultural homogeneity is a necessary concomitant of modernity has exposed him to charges of determinism, and can be easily counter-balanced by the opposite persuasion that multiculturalism is indeed a contemporary necessity dictated by the *force majeure* of globalization. This can be argued as follows: as states are inhabited by minorities, they can no longer impose a homogeneous culture with democratic means. In order to achieve a minimal degree of legitimacy, states have to stress pluralism and grass-roots participation, rather than a monolithic uniform culture.

Besides this modest criticism, **Gellner's** vision of nationalism (and of modernity in general) remains unsurpassed. No other scholar of nationalism has achieved such clear delineation of such a highly intricate phenomenon, sketching with masterly touches an extremely complex and changing world, while conveying the travail of an entire era with powerfully simple images.

## Bibliography

Conversi, D. 1999. "Ernest Gellner, open societies and the Central European legacy," *Nations and Nationalism*. 5,4:565-576.

Gellner, Ernest. 1964. *Thought and Change*. London: Weidenfeld & Nicolson.

Gellner, Ernest. 1969. *Saints of the Atlas*. London: Weidenfeld & Nicolson.

Gellner, Ernest and Charles Micaud (eds.). 1973. *Arabs and Berbers: From Tribe to Nation in North Africa*. London: Duckworth.

Gellner, Ernest. 1974. *The Devil in Modern Philosophy*. London: Routledge & Kegan Paul.

Gellner, Ernest. 1975. "The Kathmandu Option," *Encounter* 45, October: 56-68.

Gellner, Ernest and John Waterbury (eds.). 1977. *Patrons and Clients in Mediterranean Societies*. London: Duckworth.

Gellner, Ernest. 1978. "Nationalism, or the new confessions of a justified Edinburgh sinner," *Political Quarterly* 49, I: 103-111.

Gellner, Ernest. 1979. *Spectacles & Predicaments: Essays in Social Theory*. Cambridge: Cambridge University Press.

Gellner, Ernest. 1981. *Muslim Society*. Cambridge: Cambridge University Press.

Gellner, Ernest. 1983. *Nations and Nationalism*. Oxford: Blackwell.

Gellner, Ernest. 1987. *The Concept of Kinship*. Oxford: Blackwell.

Gellner, Ernest. 1988. *State and Society in Soviet Thought*. Oxford: Blackwell.

Gellner, Ernest. 1991 (1988). *Plough, Sword, and Book: The Structure of Human History*. London: Paladin Grafton Books.

Gellner, Ernest. 1993 (1985). *The Psychoanalytic Movement: The Cunning of Unreason*. London: Fontana Press.

Gellner, Ernest. 1994a. *Conditions of Liberty: Civil Society and its Rivals*. New York: Allen Lane.

Gellner, Ernest. 1994b. *Encounters with Nationalism*. Oxford: Blackwell.

Gellner, Ernest. 1995. *Anthropology and Politics: Revolution in the Sacred Grove*. Oxford: Blackwell.

Gellner, Ernest. 1998a. *Language and Solitude: Wittgenstein, Malinowski and the Habsburg Dilemma*. Cambridge: Cambridge University Press.

Gellner, Ernest. 1998b. *Nationalism*. New York: New York University Press.

Malinowski, Bronislaw. 1976 (1944). *Freedom and Civilization*. Westport, CT: Greenwood Press.

Nairn, Tom. 1977. *The Break-Up of Britian: Crisis and Neo-Nationalism*. London: New Left Books.

O'Leary, Brendan. 1997. "On the nature of nationalism: an appraisal of Ernest Gellner's writing on nationalism," *British Journal of Political Science* 27:191-222.

Smith, Anthony D. 1996. "Memory and modernity: reflections on Ernest Gellner's theory of nationalism," *Nations and Nationalism* 2, 2: 371-88.

Stargardt, Nicholas 1996. "Gellner's nationalism: the spirit of modernisation?," in Ian Jarvie and John A. Hall (eds.), *The Social Philosophy of Ernest Gellner*. Amsterdam/Atlanta, GA: Rodopi.

Szporluk, Roman. 1999. "Thoughts about change: Ernest Gellner and the history o f nationalism," in John A. Hall (ed.), *State of the Nation*. Cambridge: Cambridge University Press.

Tambini, Damian. 1996. "Explaining monoculturalism: beyond Gellner's theory of nationalism," *Critical Review* 10, 2: 251-70.

Daniele Conversi

# Gellner's Theory of Nationalism: A Critical Assessment

Whereas most theorists of nationalism base their observations on the words and actions of nationalists themselves, Gellner viewed nationalism through a vision of the entire history of humanity. As a historical sociologist, Gellner narrated mankind as a progressive adventure in which hunter gatherers evolved into agrarian societies, and then discovered modernity. He regarded modernity as a kind of miracle: mankind stumbled across the discovery that it could elicit the secrets of nature by scientific enquiry, and by exploiting this knowledge, could create a prosperous life for itself. Once the secret was out, it became irresistible to all the peoples of the world. Modernity is nothing else but the consequence of this achievement slowly spreading throughout the world. However much the religious may rail at materialism or conservatives yearn for the security of tradition, people will opt for modernity. Technology is the key to understanding our situation.

Nationalism, in Gellner's view, is functional to modernity. As towns and bureaucracies develop, peasants are forced to make cultural adjustments to this new form of productive life. Social location (as peasant, priest or lord) no longer determines the conditions of life; instead, education is the key to the new conditions. One reason for this is that education facilitates communication with strangers, and the peasant moving into this new world must learn how to deal with such unfamiliar people. It is no longer possible to live a life of warm communal familiarity. Another reason is that education provides the skill necessary for adapting to new tasks.

Education must take place in some specific language, and of available languages there is a great abundance (Gellner 1965: 160). The problem is: which languages shall become the vehicle of this advancing modernity? In empires—and for nationalists most political rule has hitherto been imperial—the dominant language will be that of the metropolis. The "peasant" (a term covering many actual forms of life) commonly adapts to the metropolis. Many peasants emigrate to more prosperous countries (such as the United States), where they will also have to learn a new language and culture. However, in some areas, intellectuals, responding to industrial transformation were able to turn the local language into a modernizing vehicle against the homogenizing power of the metropolis. The Czechs were able to resist the imposition of German, the Finns of Swedish and Russian, and so on. By doing this, the local intelligentsia acquired a monopoly of white-collar jobs. And where the metropolitan language did triumph—as in France or Britain—nationalism appears as the more or less hopeless attempt to resist by espousing the disappearing language of Celt, Basque, and so on.

This is a good story, and might suggest a kind of happy ending in which one language, ideal for world communication, ends by monopolizing the culture of the world. There are indeed hints in Gellner that some sort of world empire of modernity is where he thinks we ought to be heading. Why, then, we may ask, does the modernizing process not move more or less directly to one dominant world language? The reason is not to be found in any romantic attachment to one's own culture. Gellner has little patience with the view that cultural roots block the *telos* of one world, for "[c]hanging one's language is not the heart-breaking or soul-destroying business which it is claimed to be in romantic nationalist literature" (Gellner 1965: 165). The reason is that modernisation spreads *unevenly* through the world, and in specific conditions, an intelligentsia backed by a proletariat can succeed in setting up a limited, national, communication pool in which membership of the relevant culture will prove a practical advantage.

Gellner's view of nationalism has the advantage of distinguishing itself clearly from the assumptions of nationalism itself. He rejected, for example, the idea that national membership is a natural fact of life found in all humans. That would make nationalism a perennial fact of history rather than a response to historical circumstances. He rejected also the view that this natural fact explains all the conflicts of history. Nationalism, as Gellner understood it, is a specifically modern phenomenon. Like ELIE KEDOURIE, Gellner thought that nationalism has conditions, but (by contrast with Kedourie) he thought that these conditions were sociological. And that is where the problems begin.

Nationalism is in fact historically messy, cropping up in different forms all over the place. Gellner's nationalism is a highly rational response to a single abstract crisis. Eastern European nationalism can often be accommodated to the Gellnerian story, but what of Greek nationalism which long predated Greek modernization, or Irish nationalism which has continued long after it, in a form which has nothing at all to do with either communication or industrialisation? In responding to critics, Gellner has rejected the idea that his functional explanation reduces nationalism to a mere reflex of social circumstances. On the contrary, he insisted (Gellner 1996: 624), he was highly sensitive to the emotional vibrations of a romantic view of culture. Nonetheless, his explanation of nationalism bypassed the thoughts that people had in understanding their own situation, and invoked a standard human response to a specific *type* of situation.

Gellner dismissed the actual ideas of nationalism with disdain. Its "precise doctrines are hardly worth analysing" (Gellner 1983: 124). It follows that what nationalists are doing is actually different from what they think they are doing, at least at the level of conscious thought. Gellner's response to this was to equip his model with a set of standard thoughts: industrialisation produces a world in which human beings must either adapt or become "humiliated second class members," and nationalism is one form of adaptation (Gellner 1996: 627). But this defence against the charge of functionalism merely pushes the issue one stage further back: is it the case that people in these situations always interpreted their situation in this simple way? Like all forms of technological determinism (e.g., Benedict Anderson's emphasis on print technology), Gellner's reduces human autonomy and imagination to vanishing point.

### Bibliography

Gellner, Ernest. 1965. *Thought and Change*. London: Weidenfeld & Nicolson.
Gellner, Ernest. 1983. *Nations and Nationalism*. London: Oxford, Blackwell.
Gellner, Ernest. 1996. "Reply to critics," in John A. Hall and Ian Jarvie, *The Social Philosophy of Ernest Gellner*. Amsterdam and Atlanta, GA: Rodopi.
Minogue, Kenneth. 1996. "Ernest Gellner and the dangers of theorising nationalism," in John A. Hall and Ian Jarvie, *The Social Philosophy of Ernest Gellner*. Amsterdam and Atlanta, GA: Rodopi.

Kenneth Minogue

# General Will and National Interest

*The Social Contract* by the French-Swiss Jean-Jacques Rousseau (1712–1778) would more aptly have been entitled *The General Will*. Certainly it does mention a social contract. But for Rousseau this was a theoretical fiction rather than a putative historical fact. His own novel, characteristic and enormously influential idea was that of the general will.

He starts from a problem so stated as necessarily to be insoluble through the give and take of any ordinary contract. It is: "to find a form of association which will defend and protect with the whole common force the person and goods of each associate, and in which each, while uniting himself with all, may still obey himself alone, and remain as free as before" (1 [vi]). The clauses of this fictitious social contract:

> may be reduced to one—the total alienation of each associate, together with all his rights, to the whole community; for, in the first place, as each gives himself absolutely, the conditions are the same for all, and, this being so, no one has any interest in making them burdensome to others. ... Each of us puts his person and all his power in common under the supreme direction of the general will, and, in our corporate capacity, we receive each member as an indivisible part of the whole. At once, in place of the individual personality of each contracting party, this act of association creates a moral and collective body, composed of as many members as the assembly contains voters, and receiving from this act its unity, its common identity, its life, and its will. (1 [vi])

Thus, from the admitted fiction of a contract between all the separate individuals comprising a political society Rousseau develops his brilliantly paradoxical rationale for the total, unlimited power of the collective. It must, it seems, be in the interests—the *true*, the *real* interests—of any recalcitrant and dissenting individuals to be coerced by the general will: "In order then that the social compact may not be an empty formula, it tacitly includes the undertaking which alone can give force to the rest, that whoever refuses to obey ... shall be compelled to do so... This means nothing less than that he will be forced to be free" (1 [vi]).

It is clear that the general will, so defined, must necessarily accord with the interests of all, with the public interest, the national interest. Yet how in practice is it to be discovered? Rousseau himself felt the force of this objection, even though he never found any theoretically satisfactory answer. About representative democracy—seen as the English system—he had no good to say at all. Plebiscites perhaps might serve, so long as the questions set were suitably general: "Does it please the Sovereign to preserve the present form of government?" and "Does it please the people to leave its administration in the hands of those who are presently in charge of it?" (III [xviii]).

# General Will and National Interest

Here readers cannot but be reminded of General de Gaulle. It is, however, to those who see themselves as members of an elite "party of the vanguard" that Rousseau's ideas have had, and continue to have, the greatest appeal. Precisely as members of such a party they can have no doubts but that theirs are the policies expressing the interests, and hence the true general will, of the people or—later—the class of which they claim to be the vanguard. Again, those craving revolutionary change resonate to the essentially dynamic stress on will, and its suggestion of unlimited, all-transforming state action.

The first such party was that of the Jacobins. Prior to 1789 *The Social Contract* had been among the least read of Rousseau's writings. But subsequently that and his other political writings acquired among Jacobins a quasi-Scriptural status. Passages from them were even read at street corner meetings.

It was thanks to Rousseau's ideas that Robespierre and Saint-Just were able to see even their reign of terror as constituting the promotion of virtue. For Rousseau actually defines "virtue" as conforming with the general will. Thus, in the *Discourse on Political Economy* he gives instructions to his Legislator: "If you would have the general will accomplished, bring all the particular wills into conformity with it; in other words, as virtue is nothing more than the conformity of the particular wills with the general will, establish the reign of virtue."

In this context one has to mention the provisions in *The Social Contract* for the establishment of what is called Civil Religion: "There is therefore a purely civil profession of faith of which the Sovereign should fix the articles, not exactly as religious dogmas, but as social sentiments without which a man cannot be a good citizen or a faithful subject" (IV [viii]).

These "not exactly ... religious dogmas" could have provided the Jacobins with a justification for their persecution of the Roman Catholic Church. For after listing as "The existence of a mighty, intelligent, and beneficent Divinity, possessed of foresight and providence, the life to come, the happiness of the just, the punishment of the wicked, the sanctity of the social contract and the laws" as the "few, simple, and exactly worded ... positive dogmas" Rousseau concludes: "Its negative dogmas I confine to one, intolerance, which is a part of the cults we have rejected." For although "tolerance should be given to all religions that liberate others ... whoever dares to say: 'Outside the Church is no salvation,' ought to be driven from the state" (IV [viii]).

The nearest themes to Rousseau's Civil Religion to be found in our century are perhaps the official and seemingly always secular ideologies of some one-party states. Something like Rousseau's distinctions between the general will and the will of all or the will of a majority could, in the heyday of the self-styled People's Democracies, be found in the statements of their rulers. Thus, Janos Kadar, addressing the Hungarian National Assembly on 11 May 1957, one year after the tanks of Russian imperial "normalization" had installed him in office explained that

> The task of the leaders is not to put into effect the wishes and will of the masses ... The task of the leaders is to accomplish the interests of the masses. Why do I differentiate between the will and the interests of the masses? In the recent past we have encountered the phenomenon of certain categories of workers acting against their interests.

Again, consider the statement made by Abdul Kharume, first vice president of Tanzania on 7 July 1967 at the anniversary celebrations of the ruling and only legal party on the Tanzanian mainland. The government of which he was a member had recently rounded up everyone in Dar-es-Salaam without visible means of support, and driven them out into the countryside. The first vice president was apparently perplexed, and protested:

> Our government is democratic because it makes its decisions in the interests of, and for the benefit of, the people. I wonder why men who are unemployed are surprised and resentful at the Government ... sending them back to the land for their own advantage.

## Bibliography

Rousseau, J. J. 1973. *The Social Contract and Discourses*. Translated and introduced by G. D. H. Cole, revised and augmented by J. H. Brumfitt and John Hall. London and Melbourne: J. M. Dent and Sons.

Talmon, J. L. 1952. *The Origins of Totalitarian Democracy*. London: Secker and Warburg.

Nisbet, Robert. 1974. *The Social Philosophers*. London: Heinemann. (See the essays on "Rousseau and the General Will" and "The French Revolution and the Jacobins.")

Antony Flew

# Genocide and Nationalism

The United Nations Convention on Genocide (1948) defined genocide as, any of the following acts committed with intent to destroy, in whole or in part, a national, ethnical, racial or religious group, as such:

* Killing members of the group;

* Causing serious bodily or mental harm to members of the group;

* Deliberately inflicting on the group conditions of life calculated to bring about its physical destruction in whole or in part;

* Imposing measures intended to prevent births within the group;

* Forcibly transferring children of the group to another group.

This remains the only international standard of genocide and for this reason remains significant despite the many criticisms that have been levelled against it. Although there are no definitive statistics for deaths caused by genocide in the twentieth century, figures range from 120 million (Horowitz 1989: 2) to 170,000 (Rummel 1997: 94). With the burgeoning of nations and nationalisms in the twentieth century, it appears that the two phenomena might interrelate in direct and crucial ways.

There are two general perspectives to explain this interrelation. The first of these holds that since most genocides are instituted and executed by states, they are rationally decided policy. This perspective places great emphasis upon the historical circumstances in which a genocide occurs, both within the state and internationally, upon the decisive role of national leaders and upon the importance of nationalist ideology. In most cases, genocide is preceded by a period of intense national crisis in which the existing social, political, economic and cultural structures which give shape to the society, and which provide order and meaning to individuals and groups, break down. This creates a wide-ranging and deep vacuum which can affect the development of a genocidal situation in two ways. Firstly, the sudden disappearance of a meaningful social order gives rise to great uncertainty and creates a situation of mass *anomie*. Displaced, people revert to earlier identities and forms of order. This can occur where the modern nation-state fails to deliver the democracy it has promised, and gross inequalities remain in the distribution of justice and resources between ethnic groups. The result is escalating polarization and resentment between ethnic groups which can lead to growing cycles of violence and retribution, culminating in genocide (Ahmed 1995). It can also occur in post-colonial states where processes of democratic nation-state building are frustrated by a two-tier structure of political dominance (pre-colonial domination of one ethnic group over a second ethnic group; colonial domination is superimposed on top of this). Democracy crumbles as old enmities re-emerge—the dominant ethnic group seeks to reinforce its pre-colonial ethnic supremacy, and the ethnic groups without recourse to state power seek to gain political equality with their former rulers. Examples can be found in the genocides of Rwanda and Burundi (Kuper 1984). In both cases, nationalism is understood to have failed.

The second effect of the national crisis is the emergence of a leader or group who seeks state power. They are armed with a persuasive nationalist ideology with which they seek to reassert order upon the disparate mob. In order to seize state power and sustain control, the new ideologies must ensure that the population is obedient to the elite since it is through this power relationship that they can claim their legitimacy in office. Obedience is ensured through the immediate and harsh punishment of transgressors, which serves as an example to the rest of society, and which instills fear amongst the population. It is also ensured by the partial diversion of attention from the perception of the state leaders as the enemy of the people or as the locus of more potential failure, to a group of people who are defined within the nationalist ideology as enemies of the nation. Such a definition need not reflect any his-

# Genocide and Nationalism

torical reality, although the groups so identified have commonly been subjected to a history of persecution and massacre. The two most obvious instances of this are the genocide of Armenians by the Young Turks, 1915-1923, and the Jewish Holocaust, 1939-1945. In the former, Armenians had suffered massacres in 1894, whilst the nationalist ideology of the Young Turks portrayed Armenians as the most "deadly threat" to the integrity of the Turkish nation (Melson 1992:155). Jews had suffered large-scale massacres particularly in the eleventh and thirteenth centuries and were subject to centuries of prejudice and discrimination prior to the Holocaust itself. Nazi ideology portrayed Jews as a biological threat to the German nation and the Aryan race—they were "vermin" and an internal "disease" of German society. Jews were also depicted as a landless race who sought to dominate others, to transgress national boundaries by embracing communism and conspiring to rule the world, and as such they were considered to be profoundly anti-national.

In these instances, the new exclusionary nationalism of the new state elite urges genocide to unite the newly defined nation against a "threatening" non-national group that is located within the nation's territory. It also serves as the foremost example of the power of the new national elite, and warns against disobedience from within the nation.

The international situation may also fuel a genocide, by failing to intervene to prevent or halt it, or by exacerbating the nationalist claims of the perpetrator state. An example of the latter is the Young Turks' fear that the Turkish Armenians would seek support from the Armenians of the Russian Empire, or side with Russia against the Turkish authorities. The annexation of Turkish Armenia was symbolically loaded as the territory was considered to be the "heartland" of the Turkish nation.

A second path of inquiry into the domestic situation which also stresses the role of the nationalist leader, emphasises the development of highly ordered, hierarchized institutions. Bureaucracies, states and the armed forces operate to emphasise the highly mechanistic manner in which policy is implemented. Each top-level decision is constantly broken-down into minute details which are routinely carried out, and which are so small that the operator cannot see the whole picture. Instead, he does them because he has been authorized to do so. According to this view, the order for genocide (made within the context of a new national elite and an exclusionary nationalist ideology) need only to be made at the highest level for the machinery of bureaucracy to be put into motion (Bauman 1989; Kelman 1973).

There are two main problems with this perspective. First, it overemphasizes genocide as a process of systematic decision-making, planning and execution by state institutions. Society is overly portrayed as highly mechanistic. Secondly, it cannot explain the passion with which most genocides are carried out—it avoids the issue of emotional intensity. It also reduces nationalism to an elite construction which can be imposed upon the population, and ignores the strong emotions that people invest in nationalism.

This leads to the second general perspective of the interrelationship of genocide and nationalism. Here, genocide is understood to be the excessive manifestation of a specific type of nationalism—ethno-cultural nationalism. Ethno-cultural nationalism is seen to be emotive, non-rational, passionate instinctual, eruptive and exclusionary. It is counterpoised to civic nationalism, which is rational, inclusive, democratic, concerned with issues of equality and which is commonly upheld to be the best insurance against the emergence of genocide.

Ethno-cultural nationalism is organic—members are considered to be born into their nations, and it is extremely rare, as well as supremely difficult, for individuals to transgress borders of national identity. National members feel a sense of being "ancestrally related" to one another, and the nation represents a form of extended family, a group united by blood ties. Nationalism is concerned with both "blood loyalty" and deep subconscious psychological feelings of attachment to other members, and of detachment from non-members. In extreme situations the emotionally laden call of nationalism which resonates deeply within each individual, urges blood sacrifice to protect the nation-as-family. It is thus that ethno-cultural nationalism may ignite a genocide which is characterized by the willing and zealous participation of the masses. Two of the most likely situations in which this can occur is, firstly, within an ethnically heterogeneous state where two or more ethnic groups fight for the exclusive right to secure nation-state status. The conflict is zero-sum—only one group can win. The second is in the breakdown of order following a national crisis where the old moral constraints which operated through society to prevent a genocide from occurring, are demolished. With no moral boundaries, people are not only more likely to revert to barbaric behavior, but also to emotionally charged ethno-cultural national identities which are steeped with primal undertones. Such explanations have been used to understand the wide-scale participation in the recent genocides of Rwanda and the former Yugoslavia.

It remains to be stressed, however, that these two perspectives are not necessarily exclusive. They are, perhaps, at their most explosive when they occur simultaneously.

### Bibliography

Ahmed, Akbar. 1995. "'Ethnic cleansing': a metaphor for our time?" *Ethnic and Racial Studies* 18, 1:1-25.
Bauman, Zygmunt. 1989. *Modernity and the Holocaust.* Cambridge and Oxford: Polity Press.
Fein, Helen. 1979. *Accounting for Genocide: National Responses and Jewish Victimization during the Holocaust.* New York: The Free Press.
Fein, Helen.1990. "Genocide: a sociological perspective," *Current Sociology* 38: 1-126.
Horowitz, Irving Louis. 1989. "Counting bodies: the dismal science of authorized terror," *Patterns of Prejudice* 23, 2: 4-15.
Kelman, Herbert C. 1973. "Violence without moral constraint," *Journal of Social Issues* 29, 4: 25-61.
Kuper, Leo. 1981. *Genocide.* Harmondsworth: Penguin Books.
Kuper, Leo. 1984. *International Action Against Genocide.* London: Minority Rights Group, Report No.53.
Melson, Robert.1992. *Revolution and Genocide: On the Origins of the Armenian Genocide and the Holocaust.* Chicago: University of Chicago Press.

Rummel, R.J. 1997. *Power Kills: Democracy as a Method of Nonviolence.* New Brunswick, NJ: Transaction Publishers.

Alison Palmer

# Geography and Nationalism

As our world has been radically transformed over the past decade or so two key elements which had been oddly overlooked or downplayed during the ideological reductionism of the long Cold War, have reappeared on the scene—nationalism and an awareness of places, regions and homelands, or in a word, geography.

This new world of ours is clearly being shaped by the conflicting concepts of globalization and the power of identity, which have always existed in creative tension within the ancient discipline of geography. The recent powerful upsurge of national, regional and ethnic identities has upset the received wisdom of both classical-liberal and Marxist thought, which held, more or less consistently during the "modern" period that, in the context of the interdependent and homogenising world of economics and communications, such bourgeois anachronisms as nations, homelands and regional loyalties would inevitably wither away. Similarly, the ideological imperative tended to pre-empt the geographical dimension of world affairs, with its vivid particularities of place so close to the heart of actual communities, thereby ironing out the wrinkles of the real world. Now the belated return of geography as well as history signals a counterbalance to the pervading process of globalization with which the latter will increasingly need to reckon.

### The Geographical Dimension

Identification with the shared experiences of like-minded groups, or cultures, within a familiar and relatively stable territorial setting, has been a natural and continuous process in the history of human settlement. Communities have come to inhabit particular places and, over the centuries of occupation, have gradually come to identify with their regional environments, often perceived as archetypal, endowed with love and celebrated in song and poetry, as well as understood in terms

# Geography and Nationalism

of appropriate land use, and economic development. Thus the link between nationalism and geography can manifest itself in various ways, as in the proprietary claim to a particular landscape, conceived as personifying the nation and which is to be defended, and even died for. This ferocity can be enhanced if the "national" environment is seen as having been despoiled by "others" such as an overbearing outside power which has been a major factor in the independence movements of the former Soviet Union and Eastern Europe which marked the 1990s. Further, the physical landscape itself is sometimes even conceived as having "determined" the character of the national identity, such as the open grassland "frontiers" of America or Russia, or the Alps of Switzerland. Naturally, such ideas are subject to change and re-interpretation but they are still powerful as visual, conceptual underpinnings of national sentiment. The fact that the rallying image of a combined natural-national framework may be contrived and patently man-made, as in the case of the domestic rural landscape of southern England, does not reduce its power to move people and help to build national feeling. The regions of France were described by Vidal de la Blache, the founder of the French school of geography, as "medals stamped in the image of a people," but still very much retaining their natural elements that give them their original distinctiveness. The resurgence in the last quarter of the twentieth century of Catalonian patriotism is inseparable from its association with its loved and familiar landscapes, constantly nurtured by a tradition of "hiking clubs." Whereas in Europe it is almost always "humanized nature" which is being perceived, in larger and newer countries like Canada, Russia, Australia, or Brazil, the supposedly pristine, or almost pristine image, of the "outback," wilderness or frontier, may be a more telling and majestic national symbol. But even in these cases the long-term vision is usually tied up with concepts of human relativity, such as environment, resources, and geopolitical expansion. Geography has always been basically a humanistic science but, as its etymology implies, grounded in real places and regions on the earth and preserving a global framework throughout.

## Geography and Nationalism— A Natural Symbiosis

Ways of thinking systematically and geographically about the world—the categories, concepts and terminology—date back to the ancient Greeks and prevail in many ways to this day. Similarly, incipient nationalities were recognized and described by the Greeks from their travels, whether primordial or "imagined" as they might have been.

However, geography became institutionalized as a formal discipline in universities only in the last third of the nineteenth century, first in Germany and then in other countries of Europe, Russia, and the United States, at a time of competitive imperialism, mass emigration, free trade, urbanization, and universal education, stimulated by the world views of intellectuals such as Darwin, Marx, Adam Smith, and Malthus. It was also the age of resurrected or created nationalism, especially following the unification of Germany and Italy and the rise of the Russian and American empires to challenge the older Atlantic empires. This encouraged the mobilization of national cultures and the "state idea," and even the most impartial and idealistic geographers, proclaiming allegiance to an objective global view, were inescapably caught up with the particular preoccupations and priorities of their home country as they attempted to rejuvenate the thought-structure of their "new" discipline.

Thus an essential foundation for each emerging national movement was the promotion of knowledge and patriotic love of its national geography, ranging from natural history and environment to the population, power, resources, and geopolitical standing of the state.

Geographical education therefore was seen as an essential part of the construction of each nationalist ideology. In general, this was a benign influence, but that it was vulnerable to distortion was demonstrated by the sprouting of the tendentious, expansionist ideology of *Geopolitik* in Hitler's time, building on Ratzel's concepts of *Lebensraum* (living-space) and the organic theory of the state. Needless to say, such distortions continue to this day.

The simultaneous collapse of the empires of Russia, Austria and Germany in 1918 and the pursuit of "self-determination" released a plethora of nascent or submerged national identities in Europe, each intent on characterizing its distinctive geography, among other things, which stimulated local studies (*heimatkunde*). Most of these countries were trampled over by the expansion of Germany and Russia and many stayed effectively stifled for another half-century. Meanwhile, the former colonies of the Western powers, still imprisoned within their arbitrary, often quite irrational, boundaries, commonly felt it necessary to fashion their geographical, as well as their cultural identity.

After 1991 the equally arbitrary "republics" of the former Soviet Union, with boundaries gerrymandered by Stalin, have had to define themselves *de novo*, to accord with an urgent necessity to project themselves on the world stage. Ancient heroes and myths were exhumed, reconstructed, and pressed into service to bolster claims to an authentic national identity and hopes for emerging viability. The new national units of the Central Asian region of the old Russian Empire and Soviet Union, notably Uzbekistan and Kazakhstan, exemplify the felt necessity to justify a given geographical space as an ethnically legitimate and coherent sovereign state. Many new African states had to grapple with similar problems under the simultaneous global pressures of post-colonialism and the Cold War.

### The Overturned World of the 1990s

In addition to the perennial strivings of national population groups to identify themselves with distinctive natural environments and landscapes, and the perceived need to demonstrate how they had been developed (in the photographic sense) from a national "negative," an equally fundamental geographical element is that of relative location in relation to the ever-changing global geopolitical framework. To illustrate how dynamic this is, we have only to compare the worlds of 1988 and 1998.

In 1988 the world structure was still imperial in a real sense. The superpower stand-off was perceived as intact and all-pervading, with an expensive arms race and a line-up of client states. In the Soviet Union, the Gorbachev revolution (with its watchwords *perestroika* and *glasnost*) was being seen as in some sense a shaking up of the sclerotic Brezhnev regime, with the prospect of a strengthened and rejuvenated country which could be celebrated anew on its seventy-fifth birthday in 1992. Apart from some stirrings in Poland, the "Soviet bloc" still seemed solid as it faced NATO across the continuing reality of an Iron Curtain. Behind that curtain the European Community was looking forward to 1992, when the triumphant consummation of a carefully prepared integration of its constituent states and a substantial surrender of national sovereignty was to take place. The continuing conceptual dominance of the Europeanization of the world was illustrated by the fact that, for instance, Australia was celebrating the bicentenary of the arrival of its first "white settlers," with scant regard for the people who had previously inhabited that land for 40,000 years. Similarly, the quincentenary of the landfall of Columbus in the New World was being eagerly anticipated in the Americas.

When 1992 actually arrived the mighty Soviet Union was astoundingly dead, Germany unified, and Eastern Europe in a state of euphoric, often bewildered deliverance from bondage. Moreover, in an unanticipated irony, the ideal of European Union had become deflated and replaced with anxiety and confusion, with many newly liberated states eagerly pushing from the East at the Golden Doors. Even the new Germany was souring into a heavy, perplexing burden. The much-heralded Maastricht treaty had lost its magic and restrictive nationalism reared its head again, with doubts about the feasibility and desirability of a common currency and the whole integration venture itself. In the United States, the Columbus anniversary in the event fell rather flat amid an upsurge of multiculturalism and the aborigines of Australia, Canada and other places made significant gains in power. Other national states, like China, Japan, and those of South East Asia, underwent radical changes and even convulsions in these few years, as the end of the Cold War radically altered global geographical perceptions and relationships everywhere.

**115**

### Conclusion

It does appear that the geographical dimension of nationalism has been relatively neglected in comparison with the sociopolitical, ideological, and even historical approaches to this extraordinarily important continuing phenomenon in our world from its various angles—environmental, spatial, regional, and geopolitical, amongst others. At various scales, from the local to the global, it cries out to be kept in mind and applied, whenever the myriad cases and aspects of nationalism are explored. The geographical dimension, it should go without saying, is increasingly and ultimately inescapable, to be ignored at our peril and can be colourful, illuminating, and thoroughly enjoyable.

### Bibliography

Castells, Manuel. 1997. *The Power of Identity* (Vol. II of *The Information Age: Economy, Society and Culture*). Oxford: Blackwell.

Braudel, F. 1989. *The Identity of France.* Vol. I. *History and Environment.* London: Fontana.

Brubaker, Rogers. 1996. *Nationalism Reframed: Nationhood and the National Question in the New Europe.* Cambridge: Cambridge University Press.

de la Blache, Vidal. 1979. *Tableau de la Géographie de la France.* Paris: J. Tallandier.

Glacken, Clarence. 1967. *Traces on the Rhodian Shore: Nature and Culture in Western Thought from Ancient Times to the End of the Eighteenth Century.* Berkeley, CA: University of California Press.

Greenfeld, Liah. 1992. *Nationalism: Five Roads to Modernity.* Cambridge, MA: Harvard University Press.

Hobsbawm, Eric. 1993. *Nations and Nationalism since 1780: Programme, Myth, Reality.* Cambridge: Cambridge University Press.

Hooson, David (ed.) 1994. *Geography and National Identity.* Oxford: Blackwell.

Livingstone, David. 1992. *The Geographical Tradition: Episodes in the History of a Contested Enterprise.* Oxford: Blackwell.

Lowenthal, David. 1985. *The Past is a Foreign Country.* Cambridge: Cambridge University Press.

Lowenthal, David. 1996. *Possessed by the Past: The Heritage Crusade and the Spoils of History.* New York: The Free Press.

Meinig, Donald. 1993. *The Shaping of America: A Geographical Perspective on 500 Years of History.* Vol. 2. *Continental America 1800— 1867.* New Haven, CT: Yale University Press.

Schama, Simon. 1995. *Landscape and Memory.* New York: Alfred A. Knopf.

Smith, Anthony D. 1995. *Nations and Nationalism in a Global Era.* Cambridge: Cambridge University Press.

Smith, N. and Godlewska, A. (eds). 1994. *Geography and Empire.* Oxford: Blackwell.

Stoddart, David. 1986. *On Geography and its History.* Oxford: Blackwell.

David Hooson

# Ghetto

A term derived from the Italian, initially indicating urban quarters where Jews were obliged to live. It came to indicate both the physical location, as well as the Jews' response to a hostile environment ("ghetto mentality"). The term has expanded to denote any settlement of a minority, whether coerced or voluntary. During the Second World War, closed sections of cities where the Nazis concentrated the Jewish population were given this designation (i.e., the Warsaw ghetto).

The archetypal Italian ghetto was created in Venice in 1516, and gave its name to the phenomenon. In mediaeval Germany and central Europe, separate quarters (the *Judenstadt* in Prague), closed Jewish streets (*Judengassen*) and walled ghettos (Frankfurt am Main) were formed both to segregate Jews and, upon occasion, to provide them with security. In Eastern Europe, Jewish settlement was sufficiently large to work against ghettoization, although the right of some Polish cities to ban Jewish settlement resulted in adjacent Jewish suburbs (Kasimierz outside Cracow). A central feature of Jewish ghettoization was the existence of autonomous Jewish communal life (the *kehillah*). The process of Jewish legal emancipation and acculturation in the modern period has been called "deghettoization."

During the Second World War, the Germans concentrated the European Jewish population in "ghettos" in Central and Eastern Europe where they were exploited and, ultimately, murdered.

The Germans created Jewish administrative bodies for these ghettos, but their sole function was to fulfil German demands.

In contemporary American usage, the term ghetto designates the African-American residential section of cities (Chicago, Detroit), even when they are not deprived areas (Watts in Los Angeles).

### Bibliography

Bonfil, Robert. 1989. *Rabbis and Jewish Communities in Renaissance Italy*. Oxford: Oxford University Press for the Littman Library.

Gutman, Yisrael. 1982. *The Jews of Warsaw, 1939-1943: Ghetto, Underground, Revolt*. Bloomington: Indiana University Press.

Katz, Jacob. 1973. *Out of the Ghetto: The Social Background of Jewish Emancipation*. Cambridge, MA: Harvard University Press.

Osofsky, Gilbert. 1966. *Harlem, the Making of a Ghetto: Negro New York, 1890-1930*. New York: Harper and Row.

Rose, Harold M. 1971. *The Black Ghetto: A Spatial Behavioral Perspective*. New York: McGraw-Hill.

Ruderman, David B. 1992. *Essential Papers on Jewish Culture in Renaissance and Baroque Italy*. New York: New York University Press.

Zangwill, Israel. 1977. *Children of the Ghetto: A Study of a Peculiar People*, facsimile reprint of third edition. London, 1893. Leicester: Leicester University Press.

John Klier

# Gobineau, Arthur de (1816–82)

Gobineau, a French diplomat and largely self-taught polymath, is now widely known as one of the nineteenth century's principal proponents of the belief that racial differences, and indeed inequalities, constitute the principal determinants of political and social development. Notwithstanding that concentration upon race, it must be emphasized that the links which have often been made between his own writings and the encouragement of nationalism are largely the product of distortion by others. During the early 1840s, when working as a Parisian journalist, Gobineau undoubtedly had a youthful enthusiasm for the received ideas of romanticism which prompted him to comment quite sympathetically on the revivals of national spirit then particularly apparent in Greece and Germany. However, the demagoguery of the European revolutions of 1848–9 shocked him deeply. Those events prompted a change in the pattern both of his employment and of his thinking. Henceforth, while following a career in the diplomatic service, he would expound ideas centered on a racial determinism that became ever more bleakly pessimistic and reactionary.

The experience of his initial posting in Berne (1849–54), shortly after the war of the *Sonderbund*, led Gobineau to condemn amongst the Swiss what he perceived to be a dangerous frenzy of populist nationalism. This was also the crucial period during which he composed in a similar antidemocratic spirit the bulk of his most celebrated work, the *Essai sur l'inégalité des races humaines* (4 vols., Paris, 1853–5). The book took the form of a global history which argued for the political, cultural, and moral superiority of the white peoples over those both of the negroid and of the mongoloid stocks. Within the first of these three racial categories he laid much stress on an "Aryan" elite. He wrote of that particular breed:

> Everything great, noble, and fruitful in the works of man on this earth, in science, art, and civilization, derives from only one starting-point, develops from the same seed, is the result of a single thought, and belongs to one family alone, whose different branches have dominated all the civilized countries of the globe.

Starting from Central Asia, this outstandingly creative race of Aryans had moved from India to Egypt and Assyria; it had fostered the Alleghanian, Mexican, and Peruvian cultures of America, as well as that of China; and it had also underpinned the glories of Greece and Rome, before manifesting itself finally in the medieval Teutonic realms.

The *Essai* did not, however, preach any simple theory of racial purity. The tragic element in Gobineau's drama derived from the assertion that civilization arose only through mixture between the Aryans and some modicum of alien blood. By the nineteenth century, he argued, the cumula-

# Gobineau, Arthur de (1816–82)

tive effects of such miscegenation had produced nothing less than a scene of irreversible racial exhaustion. He did concede, on an essentially supranational basis, the existence of a few pockets of vestigial vigor (such as he himself claimed to embody as a self-styled "Count" descended from Viking warriors). However, these pools of "ethnic persistence" remained far too insignificant to shake his conviction that all the countries of modern Europe, as well as the U.S., were now in rapid and unstoppable decline. He claimed that mass mediocrity had triumphed, and indeed that one of its chief symptoms was the kind of nationalism which served merely to arouse the mob. During the last thirty years of his life, and especially after the Franco-Prussian War of 1870–1, this kind of lamentation constantly recurred within the many other works which he went on to publish, whether in the form of travel writings (such as *Trois ans en Asie* of 1859) or in the mode of imaginative fiction (for example, his novel of 1874 entitled *Les Pléiades*). For the purposes of social analysis his own strengths, as he saw them, lay in diagnosis—and definitely not in the prescription of remedies for a terminal condition of racial degeneration.

That conclusion turns Gobineau's eventual fate into something highly paradoxical. Here was an author whose gloomy racism, despite being largely neglected in his own lifetime, would become the object of an important posthumous cult amongst later and more optimistic German nationalists of an extremist persuasion. The key to this shift lies in the friendship which Gobineau had formed during the later 1870s with Richard Wagner. After the latter's death in 1883, his widow Cosima used the formidable resources of her Bayreuth Circle to promote the Frenchman's work as an adjunct to the more general cultivation of the composer's political as well as musical legacy. In this process, Gobineau's praise for the Aryan vigor of the ancient Teutons became distortively extended so as to apply to the modern Germans as well. Such was the context and spirit in which Ludwig Schemann founded the "Gobineau Vereinigung" (1894), and in which Wagner's son-in-law, Houston Stewart Chamberlain, remolded the Aryan myth to sustain the revivalist thesis of his own *Grundlagen des neunzehnten Jahrhunderts* (2 vols., Munich, 1899). Thus, from the epoch of the Pan-German League to that of the Nazis, the name of the author of the *Essai* remained firmly associated with an activist "Gobinism" which, in its promotion of an essentially regenerative form of Teutonic racial nationalism, amounted essentially to a betrayal of his own fundamentally pessimistic thinking.

## Bibliography

Biddiss, Michael. 1970. *Father of Racist Ideology: The Social and Political Thought of Count Gobineau*. London and New York: Weidenfeld and Nicolson.

Biddiss, Michael (ed.). 1970. *Gobineau: Selected Political Writings*. London and New York: Cape.

Michael Biddiss

# H

## Habsburg Empire and Nationalism

Following the acquisition of Bohemia and Hungary in 1526-7, the multinational character of the Habsburgs' central European empire was to remain its defining feature. Acquired by a mixture of conquest and marriage, the enormously diverse empire was held together by little more than the often questionable loyalty of its subjects to the ruling dynasty. Frontiers changed frequently, but by the end of the Napoleonic Wars the Habsburgs ruled about one seventh of Europe's population. These subjects belonged to a vast array of linguistic and ethnic groups. Besides the German-speaking Austrians, and the Magyars, there was a substantial Slav population (composed of Croats, Slovenes, Serbs, Poles, Ruthenes, Ukrainians, Czechs and Slovaks), as well as Italians, Romanians, and significant numbers of gypsies and Jews.

For much of the early-modern period the various component parts of the empire had on occasion sought to throw off Habsburg domination. This was particularly true of Hungary which saw a number of conspiracies and insurrections, and even co-operation with the Ottoman empire. Although these could be seen as early expressions of Hungarian nationalism, in most cases the motive seems to have been the personal ambition of individual magnates or the protection and pursuit of privileges within the imperial structure, rather than a desire for national independence. Indeed, while relations between the Habsburgs and their subjects were often strained, it was not until the first half of the nineteenth century that nationalism came to be seen as a threat to the integrity of the empire. The rise of national sentiment was closely linked to a growing interest in an often mythologized national past, and in the history of national languages, culture, and traditions which had its roots in the romantic movement. Works such as Josef Jungmann's *History of the Czech Language*, Frantisek Palacky's *History of Bohemia*, or the epic poems of the Magyar writers Mihály Vörösmarty and János Arany helped stimulate a sense of patriotic pride. This in turn combined with dissatisfaction at the shortcomings of rule from Vienna, to generate incipient nationalist movements. Czech, Magyar and even "Illyrian" nationalism became increasingly vocal in the 1830s and 1840s. In Italy, too, Austria's hegemonic position was widely criticized by patriots anxious to see an end to Habsburg rule in Lombardy and Venetia. Nationalist propagandists such as Giuseppe Mazzini also vilified Austria's interference in the peninsula in states beyond Austria's own imperial frontiers. Similarly in Germany some nationalist rhetoric (particularly from Protestant areas) called for the exclusion of Austria from German affairs, and the creation of a *Kleindeutschland* (lesser Germany) free from Habsburg influence.

Such sentiments played a pivotal role in the outbreak of revolutions across the empire in 1848. However, it is misleading to see the demands of the revolutionaries as purely nationalist. The primary cause of the revolutions was socioeconomic distress brought about by harvest failure. Significantly many of the revolutionary leaders had no desire to establish independent nation-states, but simply sought reform within the empire. Others were quite clearly not nationalist in any modern sense of the word. For example, the Venetian revolution led by Daniele Manin aimed initially at the recreation of an independent Venetian republic. Only belatedly did the Venetians appeal to Italian nationalism as a means of protecting the gains made by casting off Austrian rule. Moreover, the threat of German nationalism and the discriminatory policies adopted by Lajos Kossuth at the head of the Hungarian revolution soon demonstrated that the empire could provide a protective fold for less powerful ethnic groups.

**119**

## Habsburg Empire and Nationalism

The nationalities question did not disappear in the aftermath of the revolutions of 1848-9. On the contrary, the creation of a united Italy and a Prussian-dominated Germany from which Austria was excluded intensified the problems faced by the Habsburgs. On the one hand the emergence of two new nations made it clear to the various subject nationalities that the creation of independent states was a real possibility. On the other it forced the Habsburg administration to explore new ways of attaching the various nationalities to the imperial structure. The most radical attempt to solve the nationalities question came with the so-called *Ausgleich* (or "balancing") of 1867. This concession of a high level of autonomy to the Hungarian part of the empire succeeded in satisfying the demands of all but a handful of the most fervent Hungarian nationalists. However, this dualist solution brought with it other problems. The Magyars (who did not even constitute a majority in Hungary) took advantage of their newfound freedoms to persecute the various minorities within their half of the empire, pursuing energetic policies of Magyarization. Such policies proved counter-productive, merely fomenting nationalist sentiment among their victims. In the Austrian section of the monarchy language and education laws were generally less insensitive. For example, the so-called Stremayr ordinances introduced in the early 1880s guaranteed that all state officials in Bohemia and Moravia had to use the language of the person with whom they were dealing. This not only gave Czech an equal status to German, but also meant that the vast majority of government posts within these regions were occupied by native Czech speakers among whom there was a much higher level of bilingualism than among the large German-speaking minority. Nevertheless, Czechs in particular resented the privileges conferred upon the Magyars, and all the subject nationalities included elements who sought either complete independence or a radically altered position within the imperial structure. Even among the German-speaking Austrians there emerged radical German nationalists (centered on the anti-Semitic Georg von Schönerer) who sought closer links with the newly created German Reich, and an end to the polyglot nature of the empire.

Yet despite the emergence of a variety of nationalist groups, resistance to Habsburg rule was relatively weak. In part this must be attributed to the divisions of opinion within each subject nationality. For example, Czech nationalists were divided into a number of different movements with extremely varied programs, some seeking a reestablishment of ancient privileges, some total independence, and many merely a greater degree of autonomy within a federal empire. Such problems were further complicated by rivalry and tension between the different nationalities. Even among the Slavs, who might have been expected to make common cause against the German Austrians and the Magyars, there were long traditions of rivalry making it well-nigh impossible to appeal effectively to pan-Slavist sentiment. Occasionally individual leaders were able to transcend such tensions—Thomas Masaryk, for one, showed himself capable of appealing to both Czechs and Slovaks—but such instances tended to be the exception rather than the rule. Galician Poles were suspicious of Ruthenes, and reluctant in all but a few cases, to look to Russia as a possible protector. Similarly, among the South Slavs religious differences helped reinforce the divide between Croats and Serbs, undermining Serbian pan-Slavic irredentist claims. Faced with legion ethnic divisions, and wildly differing aspirations, the vast majority of Habsburg subjects remained fundamentally loyal to the empire if only because it was seen as providing a protective umbrella. Indeed, the widespread support for the dynasty at the outbreak of the First World War rivaled patriotic and nationalist outbursts in any of Europe's nation-states. Only among the Czechs was it seen as an opportunity to push for independence. It was the disastrous consequences of military conflict that brought the empire to its knees rather than the force of nationalism. Moreover, the successor states which were built on the ashes of the old empire were to face many of the same difficulties as the Habsburgs: they too tended to be multinational and polyglot rather than genuine nation-states.

### Bibliography

Kann, Robert A. 1974. *A History of the Habsburg Empire 1526-1918*. London and Berkeley: University of California Press.

Evans, R. J. W. 1979. *The Making of the Habsburg Monarchy 1550-1700: An Interpretation.* Oxford: Clarendon Press.

Ingrao, Charles. 1994. *The Habsburg Monarchy 1618-1815.* Cambridge: Cambridge University Press.

Bérenger, Jean. 1997. *A History of the Habsburg Empire 1700-1918.* Trans. C.A. Simpson. London and New York: Longman.

Sugar, Peter, Peter Hanák and Tibor Frank (eds.). 1990. *A History of Hungary.* Bloomington: Indiana University Press.

Macartney, C. A. 1968. *The Habsburg Empire, 1790-1918.* New York and London: Weidenfeld and Nicolson.

David Laven

# Herder's Theory of the Nation

If it were not for those arresting descriptions of what can legitimately be understood as "national culture" or "national spirit" that are occasionally found in various works ranging from Herodotus' *The History* (8.144) to Edward Gibbon's *The History of the Decline and Fall of the Roman Empire* (vol. 1, ch. 2, "Division of the Latin and the Greek provinces"), then credit for these analytical concepts—central for both the *Geisteswissenschaften* and the study of the nation—would rightly and exclusively belong to Johann Gottfried von Herder. While the concepts "national spirit" and "cultural spirit," or notions similar to them, appear explicitly and earlier in, for example, Giambattista Vico's *The New Science* and J. G. Ritter von Zimmermann's *Essay on National Pride*, it is in the work of Herder—especially in his youthful and provocative *Auch eine Philosophie der Geschichte zur Bildung der Menschheit*, but also in his later, more extensive and somewhat more measured, influential *Reflections on the Philosophy of the History of Mankind*—where these concepts are brought forth with such forcefulness and compelling suggestiveness that they quickly became and today remain central features of our cultural discourse and indispensable for understanding better human cognition and action.

It is in Herder's work where we find repeated use of such terms as *Geist* (as in the "unique spirit of the time, of the land, of the stage of the human race," *Auch* 485); "national spirit," "national character," "national mentality" (*Nationaldenkart*), "soul (*Seele*) of a nation," "national language," and occasionally "nationalism." Nationalism, for Herder, represents the narrow, vulgar conflict between two nations (*Auch* 510); thus, it is never to be confused with his use of the concept "nation," the latter being a kind of organic, social-psychological entity with its own language, land, customs, and religion. It is in Herder's work where we find the idea of an ineffable, spiritual core constitutive of and unique to a particular time and place, to a particular nation, whose unfolding is manifested in the literature, art, music, law, customs, and religion of that nation. It is Herder's work (especially his *Plan for the First Patriotic Institute to Foster a Common Spirit in Germany*) that surely served as the inspiration for Johann Gottlieb Fichte's *Addresses to the German Nation*. It is, above all, Herder's work, specifically Book 15, *Humanity the End of Human Nature*, of the *Reflections* (where Herder generally substituted the emanation and development of "reason" for his earlier use of spirit or soul as the core of a nation), that served as the model for Georg Wilhelm Friedrich Hegel's *Philosophy of History*. Finally, it is in the work of Herder—work also responsible in large measure for the subsequent emergence of anthropology (see, for example, *Reflections*, Book 7, *National Genius and the Environment*) and comparative philology (*Essay on the Origin of Language*)—where we find formulated, more suggestively than precisely, the methodology of *verstehen*: in order to understand even a single aspect of a national culture that is distant in time and place from one's own, one must first have a "sympathy" with that nation (*Auch* 502–3) by "feeling one's way into" (*sich einfühlen*) the entire character of the national soul that pervades and shapes every undertaking of the nation.

According to Herder, each nation has its own center of happiness within itself, just as each sphere has its own center of gravity (*Auch* 509); that is, each nation is a distinct, individual entity with its own unique, spiritual, quasi-Leibnizian "monad" at its core. This perceived uniqueness of the individual nation and its culture was based, at least in Herder's early work, on an explicit recognition of the Protean character of human nature:

> Human nature knows no absolute standard of unchanging happiness, as the philosopher defines it ... for it is made of such malleable clay that it shapes itself to varying circumstances, requirements and obstacles. The very concept of happiness changes with each situation and each region of the world (*Auch* 509).

Thus, Herder thought that every nation, as it modifies itself according to time, place, and its internal character, bears within itself the standard of its own perfection, entirely independent of all comparison with that of other nations (*Reflections* Book. 15, ch. 3). Indeed, any comparison between nations was distasteful (*misslich, Auch* 509). It was precisely because of the incomparable uniqueness of each national culture that *Einfühlung*—"to feel one's way into," "to sympathize with"—was necessary to understand even the slightest expressions of that inner spiritual core: for Herder, the distasteful comparison of one nation to another through employing the philosopher's arid, categorial generalizations (e.g., "virtue") only obscured the reality to be understood; rather, the task was to pursue and understand, with sympathy, the historical, anthropological, and linguistic details that were necessarily unique to a particular nation.

This historicist rejection of comparison and, indeed, generalization (*Auch* 501–2) in favor of the uniqueness of the individual nation and its culture has, with justification, been viewed by subsequent generations as a decisive point in the Romantic criticism of the Enlightenment. Here are to be found, for example, the arguments against the enlightened conceit of the philosopher who glorifies the present by condemning the past (*Auch* 507). It was a conceit based, so Herder argued, on the mistaken belief in the progressive perfectibility of humanity. "Thus, one [the philosopher of the Enlightenment] has created the fiction of the universal, continuing improvement of the world, which no one has ever believed, certainly not the true student of history, of the human heart" (*Auch* 511). Such an improvement is not possible; for man is incapable of perfection because as he advances, he must necessarily loose something precious that is unique to an earlier time and place.

However, other elements of Herder's thought appear to require that the certainty of such a conclusion about the romanticism of his thought be tempered, given, for example, his acknowledgment, in his early work, of (to be sure, a conceptually imprecise) developmental Providence, and, in his later work, of laws of nature, of the progress of natural science, and of the unfolding of redemptive reason. Indeed, his very insistence on *Einfühlung* undermines, as we shall see, the naive historicism of his early work. Nonetheless, while agreeing with Friedrich Meinecke that one must be wary of subjecting Herder's misty and fluctuating thought to too precise a conceptual analysis, the romanticism of Herder's early work is unmistakable: his rejection of the philosopher's "idolatry of human reason" (*Auch* 530–31); his denunciation of the age of cosmopolitanism as "already sick, bloated, and marked for death" (*Auch* 510); and his plea for "heart, warmth, blood, humanity, life" (*Auch* 538) in the face of the spiritual enervation of a putatively skeptical, mechanical age.

Similar to Leibniz's conception of the monad, the spiritual or symbolic core of potentiality constitutive of and unique to each nation was understood by Herder as a manifestation of God. Thus, each nation and its culture were ends unto themselves. It could be said, based on such a recognition, that Herder was a cultural pluralist. He was, once again, opposed to any expression of political nationalism, where political action is taken on behalf of one national culture against another. To do so would, for Herder, have meant to employ political power against a manifestation of God. There is neither an admiration for power politics nor an idolatry of the state to be found in Herder's thought.

While recognizing that each nation was an end unto itself, Herder also thought that each nation was a means in the development of humanity. In his early work, this development is the result, certainly not of the progressive refinement of reason, but of the inscrutable ways of Providence (*Auch* 559–60), described by Herder in terms of a biological metaphor of the aging of a human being:

> Yet it did not matter that the boy [Egypt] was repelled by the infant [the Patriarchal Orient, that is, Israel] in

diapers, and that the adolescent [Greece] detested the narrow walls of the boy's classroom, because each nation had to grow out of the preceding one. ... The very fact that they did detest each other shows development, progress, steps on the ladder. (*Auch* 489)

After the infancy of Israel and childhood of Egypt came the adolescence of Greece, followed by the adult maturity of Rome. Herder's use of the ideas of "progress" and "maturity" in this biological metaphor must not obscure for us the fact that, for Herder, childhood, for example, contains its own unique standard of happiness, incomparable to that of either the adolescent or the adult.

The combination of these two elements, the historically unique individuality of each nation and the historical development of humanity, are found in Herder's later work as well; but the relation between them is no clearer. Indeed, the relation is perhaps even more obscure because of Herder's use of the cunning of reason in place of inscrutable Providence. Reformulating his earlier recognition of incomparable individuality, Herder states that "All of the works of God have their stability in themselves, and in their beautiful consistency." However, in the later work, this unfolding of a multitude of historically unique standards of perfection appears to be subordinated to the developing cosmopolitanism of reason.

Still, human reason pursues her course in the species in general; she invents, before she can apply; she discovers, though evil hands may long abuse her discoveries. Abuse will correct itself; and, through the unwearied zeal of ever-growing reason, disorder will in time become order. By contending against passions, she strengthens and enlightens herself: from being oppressed in this place, she will fly to that, and extend the sphere of her sway over the earth (*Reflections* Book 14, ch. 5).

To be sure, this is still not the reason of the philosopher's generalization, for it is a reason that expresses itself through tradition (*Reflections* Book 14, ch. 5). Nonetheless, Herder's turn to reason in his later work appears to represent a qualification of his earlier view of human nature as "malleable clay."

Such a qualification to the putatively Protean nature of man is, as was subsequently clear to Hans Freyer and Joachim Wach, necessary if one insists on the methodological necessity of "feeling one's way into" the details of another national culture in order to understand it. If, in fact, human nature were entirely Protean, adapting itself, each time in a unique way, to varying circumstances, then *Einfühlung*, or any understanding of an alien national culture, indeed history itself, would not be possible. In his *Reflections* (Book 14, ch. 5), Herder appears to have realized this; for what he once thought was irretrievably and completely lost as one nation cedes its place to another, now is no longer:

> But history in a certain degree unlocks to us this arbour of pleasing conservation and intimacy with the intelligent and just of all ages. Here Plato stands before me: there I listen to the friendly interrogations of Socrates, and participate in his last fate. When Marcus Antoninus confers in secret with his own heart, he confers also with mine.

However great the cultural distance between a Plato, Socrates, or Marcus Antoninus, on the one hand, and a Herder, on the other, it is still one human mind speaking to another.

Meinecke thought that Herder's lasting contribution to the study of nations was that he recognized the existence of a national spirit as a real mental or social-psychological entity; that a nation was a structure constituted by central formative forces, working out a satisfactory solution to the problems connected with them. The task of clarifying Herder's concept of the spirit of a nation; of stripping away its mystical overtones; of elucidating the nature of those central formative forces, their relation to one another, and the problems that confront them—these tasks, made possible by Herder's accomplishments, have fallen to others to undertake.

### Bibliography

Berlin, Isaiah. 1976. *Vico and Herder: Two Studies in the History of Ideas*. New York: Viking.

Ergang, Robert Reinhold. 1966 (1931). *Herder and the Foundation of German Nationalism*. New York: Octagon Books.

Freyer, Hans. 1998 (1928). *Theory of Objective Mind: An Introduction to the Philosophy of Culture*. Translated and with an introduction by S. Grosby. Athens: Ohio University Press.

Herder, Johann Gottfried von. 1877-1913. *Herders Sämtliche Werke*. Edited by B. Suphan, 33 vols. Berlin: Weidmannsche Buchhandlung.

Herder, Johann Gottfried von. 1774. *Auch eine Philosophie der Geschichte zur Bildung der Menschheit*. Vol. 5 of the B. Suphan edition. (Cited page numbers refer to the page numbers of that edition.)

Herder, Johann Gottfried von. 1986 (1772). *Essay on the Origin of Language*. Translated by John H. Moran and Alexander Gode. Chicago: University of Chicago Press.

Herder, Johann Gottfried von. 1966 (1788). *Plan for the First Patriotic Institute to Foster a Common Spirit in Germany*. Abridged English version in R. R. Ergang: 129–33.

Herder, Johann Gottfried von. 1968 (1784-91). *Reflections on the Philosophy of the History of Mankind*. Abridged and with an Introduction by Frank E. Manuel from the Translation of T. O. Churchill. Chicago: University of Chicago Press.

Herder, Johann Gottfried von. 1968 (1774). *Yet Another Philosophy of History for the Education of Humanity: A Translation with a Critical Introduction and Notes*. Translated by Eva Herzfeld. Doctoral Dissertation, Columbia University.

Meinecke, Friedrich. 1972 (1959). *Historism: The Rise of a New Historical Outlook*. London: Routledge and Kegan Paul.

Vico, Giambattista. 1968 (1744). *The New Science*. Translated by T. G. Bergin and M. H. Fisch. Ithaca, NY: Cornell University Press.

Wach, Joachim. 1933. *Das Verstehen*. Tübingen: J. C. Mohr (Paul Siebeck).

Zimmermann, J. G. Ritter von. 1799 (1758). *Essay on National Pride*. New York: H. Caritat.

Steven Grosby

# Historicism and Nationalism

Few academics would deny that the ongoing investigation into the nature, origins and dynamic of nationalism has often been hampered by a lack of specialist consensus in defining the vocabulary of the debate. Literally, no term has caused more confusion than "historicism." A random trawl of dictionary definitions of "historicism" include: "a strong or excessive respect for the past"; "the theory that all sociological phenom- ena are historically determined"; "interpretations of history that purport to show the existence of fixed laws of historical development"; and "the principle that historical phenomena should not be judged teleologically but can only be evaluated by the standards of their own unique chronological context." It is not unnecessarily defeatist to assert that so disparate and indeed contradictory are the definitions enjoying current usage that no definitive account of "historicism" and nationalism can presently be attempted.

Nationalism is typically an ideology of the present geared to an action programme for the future predicated upon the moral authorisation of the past. As a consequence, nationalism has made history more fundamental to its self-perception and self-projection than any other modern ideology. If nationalism at its most reductionist is the pursuit of the nation-state, proponents of nationalism recognize no new nations, only new states. All nations worthy of the name are essentially primordial, differing only in the time-scale of their implementation of nation-statehood. While some nations achieved, then retained or lost early statehood, others suffered centuries of frustration before the nineteenth century ushered in an invigoratingly fresh political climate of revival or indeed resurrection (*Risorgimento*). Oppositional nationalists quickly developed a perception of fixed and generalized "laws of history" promoting an inevitable (albeit chronologically contingent) progression from cultural nationhood to political nation-statehood. Hijacking the popular fable of the "Sleeping Beauty," which was so familiar to the mobilizing classes of society targeted for recruitment, nineteenth-century nationalists identified three phases in the career of the typical nation: an early cultural flowering or "Golden Age" establishing communal identity; a transitional period of military conquest, political subjugation and cultural coma at foreign hands; and eventual self-emancipation from alien domination as a nation-state in the modern era. The fate-determining consensual factor which both sustained the nation in times of repression and galvanised the nation in times of opportunity was the legitimizing sense of historical validity and manifest destiny.

Critics of nationalism have naturally had a field day attacking such perceptions as politically formulaic and historically Procrustean. The fiercest contemporary opponents alleged that nationalists claiming such historical authorization were either fools or knaves. Some were harmless eccentrics carried away by their own enthusiasm, who lost all sense of historical proportion to inhabit a fantasy-land of their overheated imaginations. Others went so far as to invent a glorious national past which had never existed in order to buttress their political claims and ambitions with a spurious historical legitimacy. For all their trumpeted respect for history, nationalists have often (and deservedly) been pilloried for calculated perversion and disingenuous falsification of a defenseless past. The most uncharitable critics have gone so far as to claim that nationalism is less a natural, spontaneous and organic "secular faith" than a cynical, artificial and self-interested exercise in "ideological idolatry": nationalist movements cultivate the mass worship of a false "god" concocted by a manipulative elite of heretical "priests."

Switching to a variant interpretation of "historicism," many later critics have employed metaphors drawn from medicine to explain the historical role of nationalism in societal development, based upon the premise that nationalism is an illness afflicting the body-politic. What ailment is diagnosed reflects the optimism or pessimism of the critic. To Albert Einstein, nationalism was a regrettable "infantile disorder" which maturing nations happily grew out of entirely naturally. To others, nationalism was like political acne, briefly disfiguring "adolescent" societies but generally symptomatic of healthy development and therefore transitory. To still others, nationalism could be seen as political malaria: there was no inevitability about a society "catching" nationalism; but once contracted, nationalism could never be eradicated but remained in remission, awaiting the stimulus to course once again through the bloodstream of the infected body-politic.

To champions of nationalism, however, such metaphors of disease and dysfunction represent mere antinationalist rhetoric seeking vainly to discredit nationalism's rationale and legitimacy. While conceding the crudity of some nineteenth-century propaganda, twentieth-century nationalists have reaffirmed the fundamental or-

ganic relationship between national history and nationalist ideology: providing that its propagation is not anachronistic but coincides with the appropriate juncture in the nation's career path, history uniquely furnishes the crucial self-confidence to enable the nation to make the all-important shift from passive identity to voluntarist endeavor.

The question of "historicism," in all its manifestations, naturally featured prominently in the burgeoning academic debate about the nature and dynamic of nationalism which followed the Second World War and has assumed an even higher profile since the disintegration of the Soviet Bloc. In particular, historicism became a burning issue, often even the touchstone of debate, in the ongoing confrontation between the "PRIMORDIALIST" (or "ethnicist") and "INSTRUMENTALIST" (or "MODERNIST") camps. "Primordialists" insist that recent experience only reinforces the classic conclusion that ethnic identity combined with historical pedigree remain essential to modern nationalism. "Instrumentalists" counter that the nation-state is less an organic body-politic than an artificial construct responding to (and therefore dependent upon) the needs and resources of the societal moment, a sociopolitical precipitation which relegates past history to the minor function of retrospective Romantic rationalization.

The explicitly or implicitly adversarial nature of disputation about the origins and dynamics of nationalism should not, however, be allowed to obscure the significant measure of rapprochement that has recently emerged. Indeed, the long-running debate has promoted both a greater sophistication of argument and a general rejection of polarisation between the extremes of fanatical "primordialism" and extreme "instrumentalism." An agreed specialist definition of "historicism" to curtail current semantic confusion would immeasurably advance and enrich future scholarly debate on the historical significance of nationalism.

### Bibliography

Gellner, Ernest. 1983. *Nations and Nationalism*. Oxford: Blackwell.

Hobsbawm, Eric. 1990. *Nations and Nationalism since 1780*. Cambridge: Cambridge University Press.

Hutchinson, John. 1994. *Modern Nationalism.* London: Fontana.

Popper, Karl. 1957. *The Poverty of Historicism.* London: Routledge and Kegan Paul.

Smith, Anthony D. 1986. *The Ethnic Origins of Nations.* Oxford: Blackwell.

Raymond Pearson

# Hobsbawm's Theory of Nationalism

The central proposition of Hobsbawm's theory of nationalism is that the nation is "a very recent newcomer in human history," apparently no older than the eighteenth century. There are two corollary propositions to this central one. The first is that the nation is a product of the industrial revolution. The second is that nations are "artificial constructs" or inventions, "deliberately engineered" in a historically unique way by the "ruling classes" to serve their need "to compete for the loyalty of the lower classes." Since, according to these assumptions, the nation is some kind of ideational and intentional construct, there is no clearly developed distinction in the analysis between the ideology of nationalism, which, for Hobsbawm, is primarily a principle of the ruling elites that holds that the political and national unit should be congruent, and the temporally deep, social relation of territorial kinship of the nation. As a consequence, Hobsbawm insists that "nationalism comes before nations," that is, nationalisms make nations. The nation itself is defined by Hobsbawm as being "a social entity insofar as it relates to a certain kind of modern territorial state."

The use of the verb "relates" in Hobsbawm's definition of the nation is most suggestive, for it points, however ambiguously, to the image of a temporally deep territory as the necessary referent in the collective self-consciousness that is constitutive of the social relation of the nation. The theoretical problem is to understand better what is involved in the relation between "social entity" and territory such that a nation exists; above all, why "territory" is so significant to human beings such that throughout history collectivities of various kinds and of the utmost importance have been formed around it. While

Hobsbawm avoids the pressing task of understanding better this relation, the other propositions of his theory are dealt with in some detail.

The evidence initially appealed to by Hobsbawm in support of the putative novelty of the nation is an analysis of the history of the use of the term "nation" which concludes that "the modern sense of the word [nation] is no older than the eighteenth century." For example, to underscore how recent the understanding of "nation" as a relation between social entity and territory is, Hobsbawm points to earlier, shifting meanings of the term by noting that, according to the *Dictionary of the Royal Spanish Academy*, before 1884 the word *nación* simply meant "the aggregate of the inhabitants of a province, a country or a kingdom," but also "a foreigner"; or that "in medieval Low German the term (*natie*), insofar as it is used . . . does not yet have the connotation *Volk* (people), which it only begins to acquire in the sixteenth century. It means, as in medieval French, birth and descent group (*Geschlecht*)." Putting aside that the modern use of the term nation still refers to a descent group, the accuracy of Hobsbawm's examination into the history of the use of the word nation has been called into question by the findings of the multi-volume series *Nationes: Historische und philologische Untersuchungen zur Entstehung der europäischen Nationen im Mittelalter*. Moreover, irrespective of how the term nation may have been employed at any particular point in time, more relevant for understanding the nation would be an analysis of the use and changing reference of such terms as "France" and "Poland" from the twelfth to the nineteenth centuries, or "Hellenes" during the fifth century B.C., or "all Israel," `am, and *gôy* from the ancient Near East. Whether or not such terms indicate the existence of nations is a matter of legitimate dispute; nonetheless, they indicate, from various historical periods, forms of kinship or descent constituted through a recognition, with varying degrees of salience, of a territorial relation. To be sure, such terms and the structures of kinship to which they refer exhibit variation; but is not variation characteristic of all forms of social relation constituted, as they are, among living human beings? Is it not wrong to expect, as Hobsbawm does, the territorial relation of nativity that we call the nation not to exhibit variation, as if it were entirely objectivated like a sculpture fixed in stone? Finally, should one conclude, as Hobsbawm does, that because nations exhibit variation, for example, while many nations have a common language, some, like Switzerland, do not, that the category of the nation is suspect?

The nation, according to Hobsbawm, is not only "a very recent newcomer in human history"; but it is also "the product of particular, and inevitably localized or regional, historical conjunctions," of a "particular stage of technological and economic development." The conjunction or stage that is responsible for the emergence of nations is the development of industrial capitalism during especially the eighteenth and nineteenth centuries in Europe. This historicist perspective, where the nation is understood to be unique—"a product of particular, and inevitably localized or regional, historical conjunctions"—prevents one from undertaking theoretically productive comparisons of modern nations with other territorially relatively extensive collectivities from different historical periods and civilizations. This insistence on historical uniqueness also prevents analyzing the nation with other ideal-typical interpretative categories, for example, as a structure of kinship. Instead, according to Hobsbawm, nations began to take shape during the eighteenth and nineteenth centuries with the rise of industrial capitalism, reached their apogee during the first half of the twentieth century, and, now, given the existence of an international market, are no longer "a feasible prospect."

The development of industrial capitalism during the eighteenth and nineteenth centuries required a literate population and the captive market of the modern national state. Hobsbawm goes on to argue that modern means of communication such as newspapers and later radio and television, and policies made possible by these technological innovations such as language and educational reform have contributed mightily to the dispersion of literacy, hence the creation of a relative cultural uniformity throughout a population. Indeed, it was this dispersion (and all that is implied by it, for example, the stability of a territorially relatively extensive, uniform language) that made possible the very existence of a "people,"

that is, a nation. Thus, according to Hobsbawm, the national state is primarily a market-driven phenomenon.

The merit of this "functionalist" understanding of the nation with its dispersed and relatively uniform literacy—that it was required by industrial capitalism—exists in the recognition of how the dispersion of non-material elements, that is, tradition in all its changing forms (language, history, literary works, etc.) from the center of a society to its periphery facilitates the existence and stability of a territorially relatively extensive structure of relation, of kinship. Nonetheless, one must proceed cautiously in evaluating this putatively historically unique development of cultural dispersion because territorially extensive, cultural dispersions are found throughout history, for example, in antiquity, the spread of Christianity throughout the Roman empire, or the existence of a common culture, hence a relatedness of varying degrees of salience, throughout otherwise politically distinct areas as the city-kingdoms of ancient Sumer and Greece—a bounded cultural dispersion that led Friedrich Meinecke to employ the category of *Kulturnation* as distinct from *Staatsnation*. Moreover, and this is of the utmost theoretical importance, such a functionalist understanding of the nation offers little insight into either the existence of already present, to be sure often ill-defined, boundaries that distinguish certain, for lack of a better term, environments, for example, the early medieval linguistic differentiation between the area that was to become Germany and the area that was to become France (areas whose symbolic, constitutive elements are the prerequisites for the subsequent emergence of modern national states); or why individuals consider the nation—its people and its territory—as their own, even to the point of sacrificing their lives for it.

These latter two existential aspects of nationality (first, past collectivities and, above all, the not necessarily factually accurate memories of them as referential elements of the somewhat fluid, current collective self-consciousness constitutive of a nation; and second, the nation as an element of the image one has of oneself: elements of temporal depth characteristic of consciousness) raise a number of perplexing theoretical problems. Why

## Hobsbawm's Theory of Nationalism

do some elements of the past persist as referents in the consciousness of the present, both for the individual and the nation? Why does the attention of the individual and the shared attention of the collectivity focus on some symbolic elements, but not others? Why the variation in significance?

To these questions Hobsbawm responds by noting that traditions and the symbolic complexes that bear them, for example, language, are not platonic forms, floating changelessly above reality. In fact, argues Hobsbawm, the memories of the past that are referents of the shared image constitutive of the nation are inventions; that is, symbolic configurations, for example, the memory of a historical event or even language, are artificially revived, manipulated, or even invented by the elites to "inculcate attachment to a new form of civic loyalty," the nation-state. In support of this analysis of the invention of tradition, Hobsbawm points to the example of language itself: the development respectively of French as the national language of France after 1789, or Italian for Italy after 1870, or, as the dramatic example, Hebrew for the modern state of Israel. Thus, for Hobsbawm, France as a nation could only come into existence after 1789, Italy only after 1870, Israel only after 1948. One wonders, however, if such an analysis ironically views the nation as a kind of platonic form, as it seemingly either jettisons any consideration of why the past exists as a current object of attention at all, or fails to take into account the existence of heterogeneous, centrifugal forces (of which there are always some) within the nation by insisting that in order for a nation to exist it must both miraculously spring forth fully formed and be unrealistically homogeneous.

Such arguments about the invention of tradition, while often exaggerating the degree of "conscious and deliberate ideological engineering," do rightly draw one's attention to the importance of historically contingent decisions in the further development of a nation, for example, the decision to adopt Hebrew and not Yiddish as the language of modern Israel. Nevertheless, these arguments evade the pressing theoretical problem of how to understand the bearing of the past on the present, in particular, how the past provides a context for those contingent decisions. Clearly those who have written thoughtfully on tradition and

its reception, for example, Ernest Renan, T.S. Eliot, and Edward Shils, recognized the contingent character of that reception; namely, that each generation must affirm anew (and, by so doing, change) its not necessarily factually accurate memories of the past, its traditions. We are still left with the problem of why some symbolic complexes persist, of course with change, while others fade away; why some complexes, above all territorial location, attract our attention, while others do not. Indeed, as if to undermine his own argument, Hobsbawm admits, albeit fleetingly, that a language can be a "part of popular reality." What this admission amounts to is a hesitant recognition that language is neither just a utilitarian vehicle for communication nor an artificial, ideological construct; but that it may be viewed as significant, existentially so, by those who speak it; and, as such, may be a criterion to distinguish those who speak that language from those who do not.

Despite such hesitant admissions, Hobsbawm repeatedly denies any existential aspect to the nation. Presumably, Hobsbawm denies these existential elements because they are evidently not "real." Apparently all that is real are the economic relations that have, according to Hobsbawm, dictated the formation of the national state. But then what is one to make of the seemingly resilient attachments to the nation and its territory by the members of the nation? To this problem, Hobsbawm stresses again "the element of artefact, invention and social engineering which enters into the making of nations." What can this mean? It means that one's memories of the past, one's recognition of one's language, homeland, and countrymen as one's own, and the significance assumed by such attachments are somehow not "real"; that they are some kind of artificial concoction socially engineered by the so-called elites for the purpose of economically exploiting a people the very existence of which is taken for granted, but whose existence is the problem requiring explanation in any analysis of the nation. And because, according to Hobsbawm, the nation is primarily an artefact, a socially engineered invention, then nationalism—the artificial, ideational vehicle for the invention—must exist prior to it. Thus, one does not find in Hobsbawm's analysis any sustained attempt to distinguish the millenarian, quasi-manichaean ideology of nationalism that might be held by certain members of the nation from the temporally deep, territorial collectivity of nativity, namely, the nation itself. Indeed, there is no attempt to distinguish nationalism from patriotism, except for a factitious equation of patriotism with socialism.

If this brief summary of Hobsbawm's theory of nationalism were complete, then the theory would amount to yet one more Marxist analysis of a reality that the analysis, from the start, assumes does not exist. However, what is interesting is that Hobsbawm seems to realize the lack of seriousness of such an analysis when he states his desire to eschew what he calls "vulgar materialism." This desire apparently leads him to the recognition of what he calls "proto-national bonds," "supra-local forms of popular identification"—language, religion, kinship of various kinds, and an existing polity—that are "capable of eventual generalization, extension and popularization." One observes the theoretical difficulty that this appropriate recognition poses for Hobsbawm when he backtracks by admitting that such bonds, in particular language, are, in fact, not "artificial" but "semi-artificial." For example, while a particular language may be influenced greatly by the activity of a single individual (perhaps the classic examples are Luther's contribution to the formation of High German, or the creation of an Armenian script after 400 A.D.), obviously no language is the "invention" of either a single individual or a single moment. Moreover, as we saw, Hobsbawm admits that language can be a part of popular reality. But, then, why use such terms as artificial, albeit semi-artificial, or "imaginary" to describe these "proto-national bonds" at all? His disavowal aside, the use of such terms betrays a fidelity to a materialism that not only seeks to avoid the reality of nationality, but denies that the actions of human beings are often influenced by ideas, that is, the ideas constitutive of those proto-national bonds. Of course, languages, religions, and extensive territories are the creations of the mind; but that certainly does not mean that they are imaginary. Unfortunately, Hobsbawm lacks the theoretical apparatus to distinguish between qualitatively different orders of creation of the mind, between something that is imaginary,

for example, a unicorn, and a configuration of the imagination, for example, a language, religion, territory, or nation.

Hobsbawm's understanding of the nation and nationalism is deeply indebted to that of Ernest Gellner, as it embraces the latter's historicist and materialist analytical framework. While offering directly little theoretically to the understanding of the nation, Hobsbawm's analysis is, nonetheless, indirectly of interest because it reveals the different ways in which the nation poses profound theoretical difficulties for those who operate within that analytical framework.

### Bibliography

Eliot, T.S. 1950. "Tradition and the individual talent," in *Selected Essays*. New York: Harcourt, Brace and Company.
Gellner, Ernest. 1983. *Nations and Nationalism*. Ithaca: Cornell University Press.
Grosby, Steven. 1991. "E. J. Hobsbawm, *Nations and Nationalism since 1780*" *Ethnic and Racial Studies* 14, 3:418-20.
Hobsbawm, E. J. 1990. *Nations and Nationalism since 1780: Programme, Myth, Reality*. Cambridge: Cambridge University Press.
Meinecke, Friedrich. (1963), 1970. *Cosmopolitanism and the National State*. Princeton, NJ: Princeton University Press.
*Nationes. Historische und philologische Untersuchungen zur Entstehung der europäischen Nationen im Mittelalter*. Sigmaringen: Thorbecke Verlag.
Renan, Ernest. (1882), 1896. "What is a nation?" in *The Poetry of the Celtic Races and Other Studies*. London: W. Scott.
Shils, Edward. 1981. *Tradition*. Chicago: University of Chicago Press.
Weber, Eugen. 1996. "What Rough Beast?," *Critical Review* 10, 2:285-98.

Steven Grosby

# Homeland

It is likely that there is a behavioral component to the constitution of both home and homeland. In contrast to other mammals, human beings are instinctually or organically ill-adapted, that is, biologically undetermined, to survive in their environment. Negatively formulated, man is a deficient being (Gehlen 1950). Positively formulated, man is world-open (Scheler 1928). To be open to the world means that man has not only developmentally foregone physiological adaptation to a specific environment but also can disengage himself from the stimuli of the immediate environment through acts of the imagination. This lack of organic ties to a specific environment and openness to the world constitute a great burden of anxiety; for man, as a consequence, is continually confronted by a seemingly limitless array of stimulation (Gehlen 1950: 24–31). This burden is further heightened by man being conscious of that openness, of having to choose among the objects of stimulation (Eisenstadt 1992). One way that man finds relief from this burden is through limiting the field of stimulation by creating his own bounded environment of familiarity, the home. The home limits the potential for unexpected stimulation by providing a spatially differentiated structure necessary for habits to take shape—habitual activity offering further relief from the burden of constant choice. Thus, there appears to be a behavioral component in the orientation of human action toward spatial heterogeneity, specifically, the distinction between the inside, the locus of familiarity, and the anxiety-provoking outside. Home and homeland thus share characteristics of a behavioral "habitat" (Smith 1981), although the consciousness of the distinction between inside and outside, that is, the element of "free" choice in the creation of home and homeland (hence, the historical variability of their structures) made possible by the mind's openness to the world, indicates the inadequacy of deterministic explanations for their existence. In any event, our primary interest is in the meaning attributed to spatial delimitation as a part of one orientation of social action.

The mind, through its imaginative capacity, creates and participates in symbolic complexes whose jurisdiction, when territorially delimited, is more extensive than the locus of sight and touch of the familial home. As the mind of the infant develops into that of an adult, these territorially extensive, yet bounded complexes (e.g., language, customs) constitutive of larger collectivities become integral, hence familiar, to the patterns of cognition and action of the individual as the mind necessarily participates in them, that is, acquires

them, through the acceptance, modification, and rejection of various traditions. Thus, distinctive and substantive patterns of conduct are constitutive of both the larger area of familiarity—the homeland—and, to some degree, even the character of the individual such that not only the home of the family but also the territory of the larger collectivity is perceived to be his or her own. Thus, the acquisition of traditions with territorial reference, through which the cognitive extension of the mind develops, indicates that, while the familial home and the national homeland are structures distinct from one another, an absolute separation can not be drawn between the familiarity of the home and that of the more extensive homeland (the latter sometimes thought to be less real because it can not be tactually or visually experienced by the individual) (Tuan 1974).

These observations on familiarity—variations on Hume's (1777) and Hegel's (1821) criticisms of the contract theory of the state and the image of the isolated individual on which it rests—contribute to understanding how an extensive territory shares some of the properties of a home as it also is a locus of familiarity, one's own, and, as such, may be an object of intense attachment as a homeland. This is part of the significance of homeland. Nevertheless, as there are many complexes of meaning and orientation that are familiar to one and some that are not territorially delimited, the distinctiveness of homeland must be further specified.

While the inside of both home and homeland is where are found, indeed it is constituted by, patterns of activity whose meaning is familiar to one and, as such, is one's own, both home and homeland are also where one's life and the life of one's family is propagated, sustained, and transmitted (Grosby 1995). Perhaps the spatial reference in these processes of life accounts for the attribution of relatedness to those who dwell within that national territory perceived to be a home(land). In any event, home and homeland are not merely spatial settings; they are also spatial structures of vitality, hence objects of primordial forms of social relation by which individuals classify and evaluate one another as residents (members) of the home and homeland.

The house shelters the life-creating power of the family from potential disruptions of the outside (van der Leeuw 1933); the state shelters the existence of the family, nation, and the land necessary to sustain both from external forces that may threaten their destruction. These are also elements of the meaning attributed to the spatial settings of home and homeland, to which, because of their bearing on the existence of life, sacrality is attributed. Thus, the spatial distinction between inside and outside may also be one of religious reality (Cassirer 1955). Standing the logic of the opening paragraphs on its head by now positing meaning, instead of behavioral response, as initial, we entertain the possibility that the relief-providing focus of familiarity may at times be a consequence of the perception of spatial structures that bear, and are constituted by, the significance attributed to the generation, transmission, and protection of life.

The existence of homelands of varying spatial dimension is historically ubiquitous (Smith 1994; 1986), although the boundaries of the territories of ancient Asian societies were often geographically more imprecise (Loewe 1994; Tonnesson and Antlšv 1996) than those of the generally more territorially extensive modern national states. The *locus classicus* of the image of a homeland within the Occident is the life-sustaining promised land of ancient Israel (Grosby 1993a; 1993b; 1991). Intense attachment to a territorially extensive homeland is clearly found in modern times as witnessed by the continuing existence of patriotism.

### Bibliography

Cassirer, Ernst. 1955 (1925). "The articulation of space in the mythical consciousness," in E. Cassirer (ed.), *The Philosophy of Symbolic Forms, vol. 2.* New Haven, CT: Yale University Press.

Eisenstadt, S. N. 1995 (1992). "Action, resources, structure, and meaning," in S. N. Eisenstadt (ed.), *Power, Trust, and Meaning.* Chicago: University of Chicago Press.

Gehlen, Arnold. 1950 (1988). *Man, his Nature and Place in the World.* New York: Columbia University Press.

Grosby, Steven. 1995. "Territoriality: The transcendental, primordial feature of modern societies," *Nations and Nationalism* 1, 2: 143–62.

Grosby, Steven. 1993a. "Kinship, territory, and the nation in the historiography of ancient Israel," *Zeitschrift fÿr alttestamentliche Wissenschaft* 105, 1: 3–18.

Grosby, Steven. 1993b. "Sociological implications of the distinction between locality and extended territory with particular reference to the Old Testament," *Social Compass* 40, 2: 179–98.

Grosby, Steven. 1991. "Religion and nationality in antiquity: the worship of Yahweh and ancient Israel," *Archives Europ•ennes de Sociologie* XXXII: 229–65.

Hegel, W. G. F. 1821 (1952). *Philosophy of Right.* Oxford: Clarendon Press.

Hume, David. 1777 (1987). "Of the original contract," in S. Warner and D. Livingston (eds.), *David Hume: Political Writings.* Indianapolis: Hackett Publishing.

Loewe, Michael. 1994. "China's sense of unity as seen in the early empires," *T'oung Pao* LXXX: 6–26.

Scheler, Max. 1928 (1961). *Man's Place in Nature.* Boston: Beacon Press.

Smith, Anthony. 1994. "The problem of national identity: ancient, medieval and modern?" *Ethnic and Racial Studies* 17, 3: 375–99.

Smith, Anthony. 1986. *The Ethnic Origins of Nations.* Oxford: Blackwell.

Smith, Anthony. 1981. "States and homelands: the social and geopolitical implications of national territory," *Millennium* 10, 3: 187–202.

Tonnesson, Stein and Hans Antlšv. 1996. *Asian Forms of the Nation.* Richmond: Curzon Press.

Tuan, Yi-Fu. 1974. *Topophilia.* Englewood Cliffs, NJ: Prentice-Hall.

van der Leeuw, G. 1938. "Sacred Space," in G. van der Leeuw (ed.), *Religion in Essence and Manifestation.* London: George Allen and Unwin.

Steven Grosby

# Hybridity Theory of Nationalism (Homi Bhabha on Nationalism)

Homi Bhabha's approach to nation and narration is an original contribution to the study of nationalism. Bhabha points out the highly ambivalent nature of the idea of the nation and explores its

**131**

consequences for the symbolic construction of the national community through cultural representations. More specifically, he highlights the impossible unity of the nation as a symbolic force and investigates the expressions of such discontinuity and (dis)unity in national culture(s). He argues that "the nation, as a form of cultural *elaboration* (in the Gramscian sense), is an agency of *ambivalent* narration that holds culture at its most productive position, as a force for "subordination, fracturing, diffusing, reproducing, as much as producing, creating, forcing, guiding" (Bhabha 1990a: 3–4, italics in the original).

In his view, national culture is neither unified nor unitary; it contains Others within. Thus, one has to study nationness as a cultural space that is internally disruptive and ambivalent and whose boundaries are transgressive. Bhabha casts light to "the complex strategies of cultural identification that function in the name of 'the people' or 'the nation' and make them the immanent subjects and objects of a range of social and literary narratives" (Bhabha 1990b: 292). He points to the fact that these cultural and discursive strategies have a political edge because they are related to questions such as those asked by Edward Said: "When did we become 'a people'? When did we stop being one? Or are we in the process of becoming one? What do these big questions have to do with our intimate relationships with each other and with others?" (Said 1986: 34).

Bhabha highlights the fact that narrating the nation involves the transformation of a specific territorial space into a place of historical life. However, constituting the nation as a subject, through such narratives, brings about the diversity and inequality within it: this is what Bhabha calls dissemi-Nation (Bhabha 1990b: 299). As a matter of fact, his position is anti-essentialist. To him, "the political unity of the nation consists in a continual displacement of its irredeemably plural modern space, bounded by different, even hostile nations, into a signifying space that is archaic and mythical" (Bhabha 1990b: 300).

This view of cultural difference within is illustrated by post-colonial national narratives that are critical of the fixed and stable forms of western nationalist discourses. The cultural representations of post-colonial nationalisms show the prob-

lematic character of a national will that is totalizing. The Otherness within the national boundaries can also be seen in "the encrypted discourse of the melancholic and the migrant," the discourse of the wandering peoples, the discourse of the diaspora and its return (Bhabha 1990b: 300).

The ambivalence of the national narrative is illustrated in Geoffrey Bennington's study of the postal services as a cultural expression of the pairs of opposites that are included in the idea of the nation (such as its desired autonomy and its necessary dependence on other nations or its function of closure and its necessary opening and communication with Others) (Bennington 1990). Indeed, the very meaning of national ambivalence can be understood if we look at the Social Contract as a letter that is sent by the citizen as sovereign to the citizen as subject.

Moreover, the ambivalence of the nation as a *topos* of culture and identity is investigated through the study of literary texts. Martin Thom in his review and critique of Renan's lecture of 1882, *"Qu'est'ce qu'une nation?"* points to the plurality of views that characterise French national historiography in the eighteenth, nineteenth and early twentieth centuries (Thom 1990). By means of contrasting Renan's Germanist approach to the formation of the French nation with the classicism of Carlo Cattaneo and the *Année Sociologique*-Durkheimian school of thought, Thom highlights the diversity of intellectual traditions that may exist within the historiography of one nation.

In line with Bhabha's arguments, Timothy Brennan looks at the development of imaginative literature in conjunction with the idea of the nation and the emergence of the nation-state. More specifically, he argues that "nations, then, are imaginary constructs that depend for their existence on an apparatus of cultural fictions in which imaginative literature plays a decisive role" (Brennan 1990: 49). One important type of literature that historically has accompanied the rise of nations is the novel (Anderson 1983). The novel may be seen as the rhetoric of nationhood, that substitutes for the epic, as a form of national myth and symbolizes equality within the nation. Brennan concentrates his research on the post-colonial novel and its ambivalent nature, which includes discourses of both exile and nationalism. Simon During proposes the notion of "Civil imaginary," namely "prose writings which provide representations of social existence from the beginning of the eighteenth century through the period of the classic realist novel and beyond" (During 1990: 142) as an analytical tool which may be useful for the study of post-colonial novels.

The view of the novel as a cultural representation of the nation is confirmed by Doris Sommer who discusses the intertwining between novel and nation formation in the Latin American context. Sommer argues that there is often an erotic coding for political factors in Latin America which makes it hard to distinguish between romance and epic (Sommer 1990: 82). Within the same line of research, David Simpson studies the unitary representation of the American nation by the patriot-poet Walt Whitman and criticizes his neglect of racial, ethnic, and cultural diversity among Americans (Simpson 1990). Rachel Bowlby, on the other hand, points to the internal divisions of the American nation as these are represented in Harriet Beecher Stowe's *Uncle Tom's Cabin* and explores the ambivalence of Stowe's own discourse (Bowlby 1990). Bruce Robbins's analysis of Dickens's *Bleak House* shows the intertwining of national and imperial discourses in Britain and highlights the ambivalent and complex ways in which Dickens deals with the relationship between local constituencies and international problems (Robbins 1990). Finally, Gillian Beer explores the symbolism of the island in English literature, in the work of Virginia Woolf in particular, where the island represents a compact unit, such as the family or the nation, a place that is safe because isolated, a society in its closedness and hierarchy. The airplane, in contrast, is the symbol of freedom, equality, playfulness, the symbol of decline of the English national tradition, because it deprives the island from its insularity (Beer 1990) .

John Barrell examines the grounds on which a culture can be called "national" and looks at the relevant discourses within which such a claim can be made. In this context, he illustrates the difference between a view of the artist as a member of a specific nation, someone inspired by her/his local-national customs and the artist as a universal man, expressing general-universal ideas and principles (Barrell 1983; 1990). Similarly, Francis Mulhern investigates the role of the literary critic as the preserver of continuity. He points out that such a view implies a particular conception of history and culture that is dominated by a subject: "the people" and, hence, the view of culture as "national" culture (Mulhern 1990).

Sneja Gunew explores the issue of a post-colonial Anglophone national culture such as that of Australia where literary production will become truly multicultural, only if it includes the "dangerous supplement" deriving from the third or half of the population that is of non-Anglo-Celtic background (Gunew 1990: 100) and overcomes the dominant literary and cultural divide between Anglo and Celtic. Within the same research stream, James Snead discusses the interplay between African literature "contaminated" by European culture and African literature deemed to be close to its African source (Snead 1990). He explores the ways in which African writers have played with European cultural notions and their "contagion" by them. Thus, he highlights the possibility of a nonexclusive cultural contagion, that is, of a non-nationalist, in European terms, use of language, in its wide sense, in literature. In other words, he suggests that there is a black notion of universality, which allows for constituting the local-national in alternative ways.

All the scholars mentioned above share with Homi Bhabha an awareness of the complexity and ambivalence of nationalist narratives and explore their implications for the symbolic construction of the nation as a united and a unitary community. They show that the nation as a cultural force is constructed not only through totalizing discourses of community and similarity but also, and perhaps mainly, through narratives that transgress boundaries and are internally disruptive, complex and hybrid. Only through the analysis of these narratives in their fullness will we be able to understand that modernity is transnational in that "the 'other' is never outside or beyond us, it emerges forcefully, within cultural discourse, when we *think*, we speak most intimately and indigenously 'between ourselves'" (Bhabha 1990a: 4, italics in the original).

# Hybridity Theory of Nationalism (Homi Bhabha on Nationalism)

## Bibliography

Anderson, B. 1983. *Imagined Communities*. London: Verso.

Baker, Houston. 1987. *Modernism and the Harlem Renaissance*. Chicago: Chicago University Press.

Barrell, John. 1983. *English Literature in History, 1730-80*. London: Hutchinson.

Barrell, John. 1990. "Sir Joshua Reynolds and the Englishness of English art," in H. Bhabha (ed.) *Nation and Narration*. London: Routledge: 154–176.

Beer, Gillian. 1990. "The island and the aeroplane: the case of Virginia Woolf," in H. Bhabha (ed.) *Nation and Narration*. London: Routledge: 265–290.

Bennington, Geoffrey. 1990. "Postal politics and the institution of the nation," in H. Bhabha (ed.) *Nation and Narration*. London: Routledge: 121–137.

Bhabha, Homi. (ed.). 1990a. *Nation and Narration*. London: Routledge.

Bhabha, Homi. 1990b. "DissemiNation: time, narrative, and the margins of the modern nation," in H. Bhabha (ed.) *Nation and Narration*. London: Routledge: 291–322.

Bowlby, Rachel. 1990. "Breakfast in America—Uncle Tom's cultural histories," in H. Bhabha (ed.) *Nation and Narration*. London: Routledge: 197–212.

Brennan, Timothy. 1990. "The national longing for form," in H. Bhabha (ed.) *Nation and Narration*. London: Routledge: 44–71.

During, Simon. 1990. "Literature-Nationalism's other? The case for revision," in H. Bhabha (ed.) *Nation and Narration*. London: Routledge: 138–153.

Gunew, Sneja. 1990. "Denaturalising cultural nationalisms: multicultural readings of Australia", in H. Bhabha (ed.) *Nation and Narration*. London: Routledge: 99–120.

Mulhern, Francis. 1990. "English reading," in H. Bhabha (ed.) *Nation and Narration*. London: Routledge: 250–264.

Robbins, Bruce. 1990. "Telescopic philanthropy: professionalism and responsibility in Bleak House," in H. Bhabha (ed.) *Nation and Narration*. London: Routledge: 213–230.

Said, Edward. 1986. *After the Last Sky*. London: Faber.

Simpson, David. 1990. "Destiny made manifest: the styles of Whitman's poetry," in H. Bhabha (ed.) *Nation and Narration*. London: Routledge: 177–196.

Snead, James. 1990. "European pedigrees/African contagions: nationality, narrative, and communality in Tutuola, Achebe and Reed," in H. Bhabha (ed.) *Nation and Narration*. London: Routledge: 231–249.

Sommer, Doris. 1990. "Irresistible romance: the foundational fictions of Latin America," in H. Bhabha (ed.) *Nation and Narration*. London: Routledge: 71–98.

Thom, Martin. 1990. "Tribes within nations: the ancient Germans and the history of modern France," in H. Bhabha (ed.) *Nation and Narration*. London: Routledge: 23–44.

Anna Triandafyllidou

# I

## Idealist Theory of Nationalism

The idealist theory of nationalism is associated with the work of ELIE KEDOURIE. Kedourie first explained his theory in his highly acclaimed study of 1960, *Nationalism*. This was followed by several studies of Middle Eastern politics and nationalism, notably *Afghani and Abduh* (1966) and in 1971, by his anthology of nationalist writings, *Nationalism in Asia and Africa*, to which he wrote a long sociohistorical introduction.

Kedourie eschewed social scientific explanation, preferring to analyze ideas and events in their specific historical context. But this did not mean that his work is devoid of theory. On the contrary, it is possible to extract a remarkably coherent and clear statement of his general views on nationalism. For Kedourie, nationalism represented a fanatical vision and a dangerous opiate by which intellectuals and others are destroyed. It was, in the first place, an early nineteenth-century invention of European, mainly German, philosophers and historians, who, taking their cue from Kant's radical epistemology and his ethics of the determination of the good will, had fashioned an impious and heterodox doctrine of human perfectibility by preaching that the correct education of the national Will and its deployment in political struggle was necessary to realize human freedom and happiness. Second, by marrying Kant's ethical ideal of the good will as the autonomous will to Herder's belief in cultural diversity and authentic linguistic community, German Romantics like Fichte, Schlegel, Arndt, Muller, and Jahn had forged an illogical and incoherent doctrine which saw man's highest good as his self-realization through the struggle for national self-determination and his submission to the state which represented each autonomous language community.

For Kedourie, nationalism was a species of the revolutionary European ideal of progress. It attempted to attain the impossible, by seeking perfectibility in an imperfect world and certainty in a world of doubt. Guilty of both pride and falsehood, it gave political form to the optimistic rationalism of the Enlightenment which had succeeded in undermining formerly stable traditional communities like the family, the neighborhood and the religious community. Given the universal need to belong to a stable community, the nation appeared to offer a viable solution to the ensuing widespread malaise, especially for restless and discontented intellectuals who, as in Germany and Italy, felt excluded from the seats of bureaucratic authority. But in practice, the nation could only be implanted where fanatical acts of terror and mass destruction had uprooted populations and destroyed former ways of life, especially in ethnically mixed areas such as the Balkans and eastern Europe.

Outside Europe, too, nationalism was seized upon by restless and marginalized intellectuals for their own ends. Through reading and travel and study in the West, small groups of intellectuals in the colonies of Asia and Africa imbibed the European ideals of progress, aided by Western scholarship and the efforts of imperial colonialism to regiment indigenous societies, undermine their economies and disseminate literacy and ideals of justice and fair play. When their paths into the upper reaches of the colonial bureaucracies were blocked, the intellectuals sensing discrimination, turned against their colonial mentors in the name of the indigenous people and the ethnic cult of the "dark gods." In their eyes, only a millennial solution like nationalism, one that like its medieval forbears offered an immediate kingdom of justice on earth through the swift expulsion of the foreign ruler, sufficed to eradicate a personal injustice that through the "pathetic fallacy" was felt to be simultaneously a communal grievance. Hence the violence and terror of Bengali, Kikuyu, Arab, and all manner of chiliastic nationalisms that seek to destroy the barriers between private and public domains and institute a morality of absolute purity and brotherly love on earth.

Kedourie's views echo the fears of a century which has indeed witnessed nationalist violence on an unprecedented scale and which sees in its potential for international destabilization a dangerous and uncontrollable energy. If his definition of nationalism as a German Romantic doctrine is too restrictive, and his concentration of the plight of thwarted intellectuals too one-sided, his unusual capacity for plumbing and conveying the emotions of nationalism, and his deep insight into the predicaments of nationalists caught between tradition and modernity, West and East, give his perspective an immediacy and biting edge that other theories lack. While his attempt to derive nationalism from the heterodox millennialisms of the Middle Ages, his diffusionist and psychological explanations, and his Actonian conservatism may not have won the assent of many scholars, Kedourie's penetrating and original accounts of some of the sources of nationalist doctrine, and his profound understanding of the dilemmas of non-Western intellectuals, have proved seminal influences for the study of nationalism and landmarks of scholarship in the field.

### Bibliography

Hutchinson, J. 1987. *The Dynamics of Cultural Nationalism.* London: Allen and Unwin.

Kedourie, E. 1960. *Nationalism.* London: Hutchinson.

Kedourie, E. 1966. *Afghani and Abduh.* London: Cass.

Kedourie, E. (ed.). 1971. *Nationalism in Asia and Africa.* London: Weidenfeld and Nicolson.

Smith, A. D. 1983. *Theories of Nationalism.* London: Duckworth.

Anthony D. Smith

# The "Imagined Communities" Theory of Nationalism

The phrase "imagined communities" was coined by the British social anthropologist Benedict Anderson in his book *Imagined Communities: Reflections on the Origin and Spread of Nationalism,* first published in 1983. It can mean at least three things. Firstly, that the nation is an "imagined community." In this sense, the phrase has proved remarkably popular. Indeed, since the first publication of the book, the phrase "imagined community" has gained such an impressive currency, that many scholars of nationalism have felt obliged to pay at least some lip service to it. Furthermore, and as a result of its "appealing metaphorical reach" (Judt 1994: 45n) the phrase has been used time and again with explicit or implicit approval by scholars in different disciplines, often without any reference to the rest of Anderson's theory. Many historians for example, such as Eric Hobsbawm, would declare that the nation "is, in Benedict Anderson's useful phrase, an 'imagined community'" (Hobsbawm 1992: 46). The term has even been used to characterize other communities besides the nation, such as "classes." This use is consonant with Anderson's own statement that "[i]n fact, all communities larger than primordial villages of face-to-face contact...are imagined" (Anderson 1991: 6).

Secondly, no less popular has proved the overall definition of the nation offered by Benedict Anderson in the first—introductory—chapter of his book (Anderson 1991: 5-7). Thus, Linda Colley has spoken of "Benedict Anderson's admittedly loose, but for that reason invaluable definition of a nation as 'an imagined political community'" (Colley 1992: 5). In introducing his definition Anderson suggested that, rather than unconsciously hypostasizing "the existence of Nationalism-with-a-big-N" and then "classify[ing] 'it' as *an* ideology," it would "make things easier if one treated it as if it belonged with 'kinship' and 'religion,' rather than with 'liberalism' or 'fascism.'" (Anderson 1991: 5). He thus proceeds, as he puts it, "[i]n an anthropological spirit," to propose the following definition of the nation: "[The nation] is an imagined political community—and imagined as both inherently limited and sovereign....It is *imagined*," he explains, "because the members of even the smallest nation will never know most of their fellow-members, meet them, or even hear of them, yet in the mind of each lives the image of their communion." (ibid.: 6). He goes on to clarify this assertion, by way of criticizing a particular formulation by Ernest Gellner:

With a certain ferocity Gellner makes a comparable point when he rules that "Nationalism is not the awakening of nations to self-consciousness: it *invents* nations where they do not exist." The drawback to this formulation, however, is that Gellner is so anxious to show that nationalism masquerades under false pretences that he assimilates "invention" to "fabrication" and "falsity," rather than to "imagining" and "creation." In this way he implies that "true" communities exist which can be advantageously juxtaposed to nations. In fact, all communities larger than primordial villages of face-to-face contact (and perhaps even these) are imagined. Communities are to be distinguished, not by their falsity/genuineness, but by the style in which they are imagined. (Anderson 1991: 6)

Thirdly, the "imagined communities" theory of nationalism refers to the particular account of the origin and subsequent spread of nationalism offered by Benedict Anderson. This has not been as enthusiastically received as Anderson's phrase and its definition. Although not a wholly original account of the origins of nationalism, Anderson's theory has been a healthy antidote to the Eurocentrism characteristic of much of the literature on the subject. At the same time, and as Anderson himself has remarked, his emphasis on the New World origins of nationalism has been "largely ignored" in most reviews of the first edition of his book (Anderson 1991: xiii).

In accounting for the origins of nationalism Anderson begins by stressing the cultural roots of nationalism. He asserts that we can understand nationalism by aligning it, not with "self-consciously held political ideologies," but rather with "the large cultural systems that preceded it, out of which—as well as against which—it came into being" (ibid.: 12). The two relevant cultural systems were the religious community and the dynastic realm. Both of these, in their heydays, were "taken-for-granted frames of reference, very much as nationality is today" (ibid.: 12). Religious communities, such as the Ummah Islam, Christendom (by which Anderson usually means Western Christendom), and the Buddhist world, were "imaginable," according to Anderson, "through the medium of a sacred language and written script" (Church Latin, Qur'anic Arabic, or Examination Chinese). In this context, a crucial role was played by the relationship between the (bilingual) *literati* and their respective societies. The great religiously imagined communities started losing their unselfconscious coherence after the Middle Ages (ibid.: 16). Among the reasons for this decline Anderson stresses two as being most relevant to his enquiry. First, there was the effect of the explorations of the non-European world (ibid.: 16). These led to the "relativization" and "territorialization" of the imagined community (ibid.: 17). Second, there was a gradual demotion of the sacred language itself. In Europe, this development was well under way by the sixteenth century, and Latin had come to be replaced by the vernacular languages by the second half of the seventeenth century (ibid.: 18). Thus, "[i]n a word, the fall of Latin exemplified a larger process in which the sacred communities integrated by old sacred languages were gradually fragmented, pluralised, and territorialised" (ibid.: 19). Around the same time, similar developments were undermining the aura of the dynastic realm and, during the seventeenth century, the "automatic legitimacy of sacral monarchy began its slow decline in Western Europe" (ibid.: 21).

To these processes one should add the crucial changes in people's apprehension of time: "Beneath the decline of sacred communities, languages and lineages, a fundamental change was taking place in modes of apprehending the world, which, more than anything else, made it possible to 'think' the nation" (ibid.: 22). The notions of "simultaneity" and "homogeneous, empty time" are crucial here, as the old, religiously structured, cycles of time lost their credibility. Anderson demonstrates why this transformation was important for the birth of the imagined community of the nation by considering the basic structure of two "forms of imagining which first flowered in Europe in the eighteenth century": the novel and the newspaper (ibid.: 24-25). Novels and newspapers were crucial engines in the development of national communities because they managed to reach large numbers of people. This they did thanks to a combination of technological advances in print, which had begun in previous centuries, with the advent of capitalism and its impact on the printing enterprise. The development of print capitalism lies at the heart of Anderson's theory. For Anderson, it was, above all, "print capitalism, which made it possible for rapidly growing numbers of people to think about themselves,

# The "Imagined Communities" Theory of Nationalism

and to relate themselves to others, in profoundly new ways" (ibid.: 37). As Anderson puts it, "the convergence of capitalism and print technology on the fatal diversity of human language created the possibility of a new form of imagined community, which in its basic morphology set the stage for the modern nation" (ibid.: 46).

Besides this insistence on the crucial role of what he calls "print capitalism," another original feature of the book is Anderson's assertion that nationalism first appeared in the New World, in the Americas, and that the European nationalist movements, from the 1820s onwards, came to imitate models already available thanks to the experience of the "creole pioneers" (ibid.: 47-65). A crucial part in the plausibility of this assertion is played by Anderson's notion of the "pilgrimages" made by the creole officials of the imperial regimes. These were "white" men who were born in the Americas and who therefore shared what Anderson calls the "fatality of trans-Atlantic birth." The career of a creole functionary was circumscribed by the geographical limits of the imperial administrative unit in which he found himself. He had no general authority over Spain's Latin American dominions, to say nothing of metropolitan Spain itself, where only *peninsulares*, that is, men born in Spain, could be appointed to official positions. Consequently, for a creole functionary of imperial Spain, "the highest administrative centre to which he could be assigned," was the capital of his administrative unit. This professional climb included appointments in different provinces of that colonial unit. Thus, in the course of their career, creole functionaries undertook journeys which Anderson calls "pilgrimages" because, according to Anderson, they were the secular equivalents of the religious pilgrimages of faithful seekers to a sacred centre. In time, Anderson claims, three circumstances led the "pilgrim creole functionaries" of different colonial units to break away from the metropolis and create independent states in Spanish America: first, their common experience of the professional pilgrimage; second, their common language, which was the language of the imperial state; and third the emergence of a "consciousness of connectedness" as "travelling companions ("Why are *we...here...together?*").)" These cir-

cumstances united the creole functionaries against the *peninsulares* and led them to "imagine" their particular administrative units as their respective nations. The result of this imagining was the creation of independent states in Spanish America corresponding to these administrative units (ibid.: 64-65).

Of great importance to the whole argument of the book is the claim that the nation emerged in the Americas and became a model outside that region: "[T]he independence movements in the Americas became, as soon as they were printed about, 'concepts,' 'models,' and indeed 'blueprints.' ... Out of the American welter came these imagined realities: nation-states, republican institutions, common citizenships, popular sovereignty, national flags and anthems, etc., and the liquidation of their conceptual opposites: inherited nobilities, serfdoms, ghettoes, and so forth" (ibid.: 81). Thus, by the second decade of the nineteenth century, "a 'model' of 'the' independent national state was available for pirating."

According to Anderson, from about the middle of the nineteenth century, "there developed what Seton-Watson terms 'official nationalism' inside Europe." Anderson maintains that these nationalisms were "historically 'impossible' until after the appearance of popular linguistic-nationalisms," because, he argues, they were but "*responses* by power-groups—primarily, but not exclusively, dynastic and aristocratic—threatened with exclusion from, or marginalization in, popular imagined communities." Such official nationalisms were "conservative, not to say reactionary, *policies*, adapted from the model of the largely spontaneous popular nationalisms that preceded them." These nationalist movements were not confined to Europe, or, indeed, the Levant. In the name of imperialism, "very similar policies" were pursued by the same sorts of groups in the vast Asian and African territories which were subjected in the course of the nineteenth century. Finally, "refracted into non-European cultures and histories, they were picked up and imitated by indigenous ruling groups in those few zones (among them Japan and Siam) which escaped direct subjection" (ibid.: 109-110).

In the revised and expanded second edition of the book of 1991, the author added two new chapters. The last chapter, entitled "Memory and Forgetting," offers an imaginative and original treatment of the oft-discussed issue of the importance of selective memory in nation-formation.

Anderson's analysis of nationalism is greatly indebted to Hugh Seton-Watson's own study of European nationalisms, a debt that Anderson readily acknowledges. While, Anderson's own claim that the existence of an elite literary or administrative language was important as an element of proto-national cohesion, has been amply praised by Eric Hobsbawm (Hobsbawm 1992: 59). Even its most severe critics have found great merit in much of Anderson's account of the rise and spread of nationalism. Yet, many scholars have also raised serious objections to it. The most serious objections can be classified into three main categories. First, there are the criticisms raised, most notably, by Anthony D. Smith. Smith stresses the older ethnic ties which, he argues, are at the root of the most successful enterprises of "nation-formation" in modern times. From this perspective, Smith is critical of both the MODERNIST and the INSTRUMENTALIST aspects of Anderson's thesis—the former referring to the argument that nations first came into being in the eighteenth and nineteenth centuries; and the latter to the closely related assertion that nations are in fact artificial constructions, products of the imagination and consciousness of elites, intellectuals, and administrators who somehow fabricated national ties in the interests of their own political and economic ambitions (Smith 1986, 1991, 1992).

Second, Anderson's account has been criticized by modernist scholars of the nation and nationalism. While sharing Anderson's dating of the rise of nations, these scholars have criticized him for having neglected or underestimated the role of the modern state that they consider crucial in the emergence of nationalism. Among the most convincing of such objections have been those voiced by John Breuilly, who argues that Anderson has underplayed the political factor (Breuilly 1996).

Third, a number of critics, while conceding the value and plausibility of a great part of Anderson's theory, object, not only to its sweepingness—arguing that it works better for some cases than for others—but also to its historical weaknesses.

These have led critics to comment that this is "a book whose metaphorical reach exceeds its historical grasp" (Judt 1994: Breuilly 1996: 159-60; Balakrishnan 1996).

**Bibliography**

Anderson, Benedict. 1991 (1983). *Imagined Communities: Reflections on the Origin and Spread of Nationalism*. London and New York: Verso.
Balakrishnan, Gopal (ed.) 1996. *Mapping the Nation*. London and New York: Verso.
Breuilly, John. 1996. "Approaches to Nationalism," in Gopal Balakrishnan (ed.), *Mapping the Nation*. London and New York: Verso.
Colley, Linda. 1992. *Britons: Forging the Nation, 1707-1837*. New Haven, CT and London: Yale University Press.
Hobsbawm, Eric. 1992. *Nations and Nationalism since 1780: Programme, Myth, Reality*. Cambridge: Cambridge University Press.
Judt, Tony. 1994. "The new old nationalism," *New York Review of Books* XLI, 10: 44-51.
Smith, Anthony D. 1986. *The Ethnic Origins of Nations*. Oxford: Blackwell.
Smith, Anthony D. 1991. "The nation: Invented, imagined, reconstructed?" *Millennium: Journal of International Studies* 20, 2: 353-68.
Smith, Anthony D. 1992. "Nationalism and the historians," *International Journal of Comparative Sociology* 33, 1-2: 58-80.

Paschalis M. Kitromilides
and Georgios Varouxakis

# Immigration and Nationality

Immigration and nationality define and challenge each other in complex ways. In Western Europe there were, in 1997, about 18 million foreign residents lawfully present, most of them immigrants. Of these, over half were from outside Europe. Their preferences, needs and demands, fortified in many cases by strong feelings of ethnic solidarity and firm adherence to religions new in the West, now have considerable influence in re-defining the nations of Europe, their self-perception and the concept of their nationality. Immigrant ethnic and religious self-confidence has diversified European national behavior and institutions in a post-modern period when the coherence of those

# Immigration and Nationality

institutions, and faith and confidence in them, has already been weakened by two other processes.

Externally, by the advance of European Union institutions; and internally, and more generally, by the gains of "human rights" notions, especially in societies and media where the assertion of local national or traditional values is being discredited.

Before investigating the relationship between immigration and nationality, we must first consider what is meant by these terms, as they are used in a number of senses.

## Definitions

"Nationality" is sometimes used as a synonym of legal citizenship. This is a formally defined and unambiguous characteristic of an individual acquired by birth or naturalization. Another use of the term "nationality," also of a categorical nature, is frequent in Central and Eastern Europe, in the former Soviet Union and in today's Russian Federation (in the census, and on internal passports). In this usage, the term describes a formal, often registered status, which is akin to the categories of "ethnic origin" or "ancestry," used in the U.K., the U.S., and other English-speaking countries. These categories which indicate an individual's association with an ancient indigenous national community, such as "Ruthenian," "Tatar," or "Ukrainian," do not designate citizenship, although citizenship of that name may also exist elsewhere. These categories are not internationally recognized. The indigenous *Volksgruppe* of Austria (Gypsies, Slovenes, etc) are less formal categories of a similar sort.

"Immigration" has at least two manifestations. First, the demographic concept of (international) migration, less formal, is concerned with the physical movement of people into and out of independent states on a medium or long-term basis, therefore affecting the size, age-structure and composition of the population of these states.

Second, the United Nations definition of international criteria migration, which formalizes these demographic criteria: "the movement of persons into (or out of) a country intending to remain in (or leave) that country for at least twelve months, who have been absent from (or resident in) that country for at least twelve months." This definition recognizes the often temporary nature of migration and its potentially repeated quality. Its reasonable arbitrariness in defining migration as a year's residence or absence, is a compromise between short international trips with little or no residential settlement intentions, and journeys intended to be one-way and leading to permanent settlement.

The element of intent is important, although uncertain, precisely because intent is reversible. All migration flows generate a return flow. The huge transatlantic migrations of the nineteenth and twentieth centuries are seen as permanent settlement. But at least one third of those 54 million people eventually returned to their countries of origin, and of those return migrants, a proportion would have repeated the journey back to the Americas. This remains true in the "countries of immigration" today (U.S., Canada, Australia).

Some labor migration is explicitly temporary, such as the seasonal or one-year labor migration to Switzerland and Austria. But the German "guest-worker" experience has shown that few things are more permanent than "temporary" labor migrants. In many countries, such as the U.K., non-European Union workers enter for a fixed term under work permit, and may then be allowed to settle. Yet, other migrants enter on some temporary pretext and switch—through marriage, asylum claiming or illegal overstaying—to a more permanent category of residence. Statistical incorporation of those entering the U.K. on various short-term pretexts, and who then claimed asylum or secured residence by marriage, for example, have almost tripled estimates of net immigration in the mid-1990s from about 60,000 to 178,000 in 1998.

Partly in response to fraudulent claims, some countries' control systems (e.g., U.K.) have done away with "permanent" immigration on arrival, instead accepting most intended immigrants provisionally, and then giving them the right of permanent residence only after the fulfilment of some condition. In the U.K., for example, almost all "acceptances for settlement" in recent years (93 percent in 1993) have been of persons already in the country, admitted earlier on a limited basis as workers or intended spouses. These qualities of migration ensure that statistics relating to it are often poor, indirectly estimated and difficult to compare.

## Immigration and Nationality

So far it has not been necessary to introduce the notion of "nationality" to the discussion of international migration. However, this notion is in some ways central to the issues of immigration and emigration. The United Nations definition given above pays no attention to whether migrants are nationals of the country of migration or foreigners. Neither is it concerned with whether their arrival or departure was by regular or illegal means. It is possible to imagine a situation where all migrants were nationals of the country concerned, a position almost achieved with the very limited and controlled migration flows of communist countries in the Soviet era, but otherwise highly unusual.

More generally and realistically, migration as an issue is popularly perceived as a movement of foreigners into a country. Inward movement of citizens is not regarded as problematic and of course is not (usually) subject to any control (it may comprise half or more of the total migration movements). Emigration of citizens in large numbers can cause concern, of course, if that is regarded as representing a vote of "no confidence" in the country's future or as a harmful loss of talent or "brain drain."

The issue of foreigners takes us to the heart of many migration controversies. Non-citizens or foreigners are inevitably regarded in a different light to citizens: less easy to deal with because of differences in language, culture and values; inclined, through self-segregation to create enclaves of settlement which are out of communion with the rest of the country and its citizens, and uncommitted either to national values or to the national polity. These considerations and feelings are made more salient if foreign immigrants are racially as well as culturally different from the host populations, as has been the case with much of the mass migration to the West since the 1960s.

## Immigration and Nationality

### Nationality as a Criterion for Immigration

Nationality status is the cornerstone of national and international immigration regulation. Citizens can usually move freely into and out of their homelands, at least in Western countries. Accordingly, most migration statistics are immigration statistics based on the immigration of foreigners, not of citizens, or are based on changes in the annual numbers of resident foreigners, as in Italy and Austria and most other OECD countries.

Citizens of member states of free travel areas (E.U., European Free Trade Area [EFTA], Common Nordic Labour Market, European Economic Area [EEA]) and their dependents, have unqualified right of entry to other member states to live and work there. With the E.U., this principle represents a substantial and growing abandonment of national control over borders in the context of a supposed "E.U. citizenship." The European Commission claims further that the Single European Act of 1985 (effective 1992) obliges E.U. member states to admit legal residents of other member states even if they are not citizens of any E.U. country ("third country" residents). In 1993 the E.U. countries and EFTA, except for Switzerland, created the European Economic Area (EEA) to broaden these privileges of entry, residence and work. Freedom to migrate and work now applies between almost all countries of Western Europe (in its Cold War definition). The absence of such barriers within Europe, and their preservation between Europe and other countries, increasingly defines the relations between the Western European countries and the rest of the world.

The Schengen agreement (Convention on the Application of the Schengen Agreement, 19 June 1990) between a number of E.U. states is intended to speed up trade and travel further, while uniform procedures of control will be applied at the external borders of "Schengen-land." Intended to be effective from 1 December 1993, its implementation was repeatedly delayed and was far from working perfectly when it began on 26 March 1995. Some existing states remain opted out, not trusting the effectiveness of other countries' border controls with the non-European world (the former emigration countries of Southern Europe, especially Italy, still have weak controls, mostly

# Immigration and Nationality

evaded). Countries joining the E.U. in future will have to sign up to it.

Nationality in the broader, ethnic sense, is an important element in determining rights of entry to some countries. Germany, Greece, and a few others grant entry and immediate access to citizenship to "ethnic return migrants" born abroad but claiming ancestry from that country, often from several generations past. These movements arise, at least in part, from the rise of nationalism earlier this century (in the case of the Pontic Greeks); or more recently, from the freedom to escape from an increasingly uncomfortable position in the newly independent former Soviet republics (*aussiedler*, i.e., ethnic Germans), following the end of the Cold War. In an unexpected development, but through a not dissimilar process, Russia became the biggest immigration country in Europe in the early 1990s. This was due to the return to the Russian Federation of over two million out of the 25 million persons of Russian "nationality" (in the old Soviet sense) who had lived (often for some generations) in the now independent Republics of the Commonwealth of Independent States (CIS). Some have had a hard time; up to a third are regarded as forced migrants.

## The Weakening of Nationality through Immigration and Other Processes

Within the E.U. the privileges of citizenship are being weakened as criteria for entry, for work, for access to welfare and the housing market. It was once thought proper that citizens should have priority in such matters. Now, the rights to "integration" of foreign immigrants take precedence over the privileges of citizens, following decisions of the European Court of Human Rights, pressure from the Council of Europe and the harmonizing tendencies of the European Union, in its attempts to minimize the status of nation-states. Relatively unqualified rights of family re-unification for both sexes, once strongly opposed, have had to be accepted as a "right." Consequently, migration for family re-unification (almost always in the host, not the sending country), and, more recently, for marriage, has become the single largest component of legal migration into Europe, and is much abused for purposes of migration.

The privileges of citizenship are also eroded by the rights of resident immigrants. The right to vote, once a defining element of citizenship, is increasingly extended, through E.U. and other pressures, to non-citizens. E.U. citizens who are immigrants in another E.U. country already have the right to vote in the local and E.U. elections of that country. There is pressure to go further to extend the right to all elections and also to all long-term residents or "sojourners," irrespective of nationality.

Extension of rights to non-citizen immigrants erodes the meaning and value of nationality in its

Table
**Persons Admitted through an Ancestral Connection with the Country (Diaspora Return)**

| Country | Grounds |
| --- | --- |
| Estonia | ancestry |
| Finland | ancestry: Ingrians |
| Germany | ancestry: *aussiedler* (persons of German origin in Eastern Europe and former Soviet Union) |
| Greece | ancestry: "Pontic" Greeks |
| Hungary | national origin |
| Israel | Jews or close relatives |
| Lithuania | those who have kept right to citizenship |
| Poland | ancestry |
| Russia | Russian "nationality" in the Soviet sense |
| Turkey | ancestry |
| U.K. | "patrials"; persons with at least one grandparent born in the U.K., irrespective of nationality or ethnic origin |

citizen sense, and is making the concept more diffuse in its ethnic sense through the spread of MULTICULTURALISM as an engine of "integration." The United Kingdom and its citizenship provides an unusual example of the interaction between nationality and immigration. Here the definition of "citizenship" was, for most of the twentieth century, confused by the joint status of "British subject," shared by citizens of the United Kingdom with other residents of the former Empire. Until 1981 there was no unique "British" citizenship, only citizenship of the U.K. and Colonies. In 1913, the right of all British subjects to enter the U.K., previously informal, was defined in law. All British subjects (now called "Commonwealth citizens") also had, and retain to this day, the right to vote in all U.K. elections if resident in the U.K.

In a crucial step, when the old colonies became independent after the Second World War, the British subject status of their citizens was continued in 1948 as long as they remained within the Commonwealth, and the right of all British subjects to free entry to the U.K. was confirmed. This made possible a substantial immigration of non-European population from the poorer countries of the New Commonwealth. By creating an ethnic minority population, now grown to 3.5 million, this wave of immigration has radically altered the British national scene. Legislation in 1962 and 1971 progressively imposed on British subjects the same controls on entry as those which had applied to "foreigners" since 1920. By that time, however, over a million Commonwealth immigrants were living in the U.K.

Only in 1981 did new legislation bring British Citizenship in line with the new realities of immigration control, confining citizenship to those with a substantial connection with the U.K. But the privileges of citizenship were not restricted to the possession of citizenship. The old entitlement of non-citizens from Commonwealth countries to vote in all elections was retained, a situation unique in the industrial world. This has had important electoral consequences, reinforcing the claims of immigrants and their pressure groups for multicultural entitlements and muting attempts to make immigration controls more effective. Also unusually in the industrial world, the British census has not included a question on citizenship since the census of 1961, as it was (then) allegedly too confusing.

## Immigrant and Foreign Populations

The categories of "immigrant" and "foreigner" or non-national often do not coincide. Most continental countries cannot provide statistics on the number of "immigrants" in the demographic sense, only data on "foreigners" in the nationality sense. These are not the same thing. Many of the immigrants are not foreigners, either because they are return-migrant citizens or because they have naturalized. Many of the foreigners, in countries such as Germany which follow the *ius sanguinis* and which do not automatically confer citizenship on persons born on their territory, are not immigrants.

Ethnic return migrants, not being "foreigners," are not counted in the total of German foreign population. In the U.S., Canada, Australia, and New Zealand, data on persons from abroad relate more to immigration status (birthplace) than to citizenship, although the latter are also published. U.K. data on "foreigners" are not comparable with those of other European countries, because they exclude many immigrants who have, strictly speaking, that is, legally, never been "foreign," and because Commonwealth citizens were able, until 1987, to acquire U.K. citizenship by registration after one year's residence.

## Changing Nationality: How Immigrants Become Citizens

Naturalization is an important non-demographic aspect of this process. Naturalization procedures reflect a country's view of its own nationality. In France, until recent years, it was open and inclusive for those who could show a desire to adopt a new identity. In the U.K., naturalization has been nearly automatic for birth in this country and open for adults, largely because of a lack of conviction as to the distinctiveness of citizenship. In Germany, it was restricted and only granted after a strict test of assimilation, reflecting a more "ethnic" idea of what it means to be a citizen of that country. Some countries, such as Belgium, Austria, and Germany are moderating naturalization requirements to make the process easier, including permitting dual nationality.

Two viewpoints are apparent. One, in the ascendant and favored by the Council of Europe and other "human rights" bodies, is that naturalization is more or less a right for established immigrants and its early grant is an aid to "integration." The other is that citizenship is, first, a privilege to be earned by demonstrating knowledge of and sympathy for the culture of the host country; and, second, a reward for a degree of assimilation and of commitment. In this, latter sense, naturalization is a form of adoption, almost a sacrament, whereby the (perhaps diminishing) privileges of nationality are all instantly conferred on the recipient: right of abode, entry, voting, and some obligations of service.

The ease of access to naturalization itself has consequences. One of the most immediate of these is to obscure the demographic effects of immigration when population of non-national origin is counted according to citizenship criteria, not birthplace or ethnic criteria. Over 2 percent of the approximately 16 million foreign nationals in Western European countries were naturalized each year in the 1990s; about 350,000 people. Despite eight years of substantial net immigration, the pace of naturalization in France is so fast that the 1990 census actually recorded fewer foreigners than in 1982. In fact, even the figures on naturalization understate the process, because until recently all children of foreign parents were automatically naturalized (except for objectors). On the other hand, the size of populations of foreign origin in countries such as Austria and Germany is somewhat exaggerated because the children of immigrants do not acquire nationality automatically through their birthplace.

Few studies seem to have been done on the extent to which naturalized citizens really assimilate to, identify with or are committed to the country of their adoption. In cases where naturalization is hard, new citizens may be more committed to a new life; where it is easy, it may seem more natural to continue to live, as before, as members of a foreign community, but with new privileges. It seems unlikely that the remaining non-native characteristics of the naturalized, in values, preferences, demographic behavior and in life-style

in general, will disappear as a result of naturalization. What is more likely is that, with sufficiently rapid levels of immigration and rapid naturalization, the idea of what constitutes a particular nationality (in its more ethnic sense) may change as the criteria of citizenship widen and as the privileges of citizenship gradually cease to be exclusive but are more and more shared with other long-term residents.

## Conclusions

The immigration process, together with a particular interpretation of "human rights," is driving changes in the concepts and the realities of nationality and citizenship. Some of the pressures arise from the sheer volume of immigration since the 1960s and particularly since the mid-1980s. The consequence of this large-scale immigration, for Europe and for the countries of immigration overseas, has been a new form of large-scale diversity in the characteristics of the residents of these host countries and increasingly of their citizens. This, in turn, has forced some re-definition of the national community in almost every country of the free world. Other pressures, of a different sort, come from international human rights organizations and from the E.U., to whom, for diverse reasons, the pretensions of country level nationality are unwelcome. Such pretensions stand in the way of the realization of a larger supra-national identity and a broader citizenship of the E.U. Cultural resistance to these changes, as well as economic arguments, are behind the attempts made by European countries to contain the increase of immigration, during the 1990s.

## Bibliography

Fassmann, H. and Munz, R. (eds.). 1994. *European Migration in the Late Twentieth Century*. Aldershot: Edward Elgar.

Jacobson, D. 1996. *Rights Across Borders: Immigration and the Decline of Citizenship*. Baltimore, MD: Johns Hopkins University Press.

King, R. (ed.). 1993. *The New Geography of European Migrations*. London: Belhaven.

Moynihan, D.P. 1993. *Pandaemonium: Ethnicity in International Politics*. Oxford: Oxford University Press.

OECD. 1999. *Trends in International Migration: SOPEMI.* 1999 edition. Paris: OECD.

ONS. 1999. *International Migration 1997.* Series MN No. 24. London: The Stationery Office.

Tribalat, M., Garson, J.-P., Moulier-Boutang, Y. and Silberman, R. 1991. *Cent Ans d'Immigration: Étrangers d'Hier, Français d'Aujourd'hui.* Paris: Presses Universitaires de France.

David Coleman

# Indigenismo

The ancient indigenous diversity of Latin America is normally perceived as a contradiction of the modern project of nation formation. From the first half of the twentieth century the Latin American states have resorted to *indigenismo* to resolve a dilemma posited by the persistence of ethnicities and by the goals of official nationalism seeking homogenisation and linguistic unity. At the center of *indigenismo* lies the division between the "living" Indian and the "dead." The "living" Indian is constituted by the ethnic peoples of contemporary Latin American societies who are regarded as the main impediment to cultural and linguistic homogeneity. This, together with their geographical isolation, create underdeveloped poles and delay the creation of a united nation, a situation which is regarded as necessary for modernisation. On the other hand, the vast richness of Mesoamerican and Andean history and culture constitutes the "dead Indian." This is the Indian of archaeological sites and museums who has been widely interpreted, variously reconstituted and used by intellectuals and artists in their search for a unique national identity.

*Indigenismo* in Latin America is a formal policy of acculturation coordinated by federal governments. In 1940 a strategy of integration was agreed (First Indigenist Interamerican Congress) among seventeen countries of the continent resulting in the creation of ad hoc institutions. These indigenist policies which were oriented towards reshaping the sociocultural life of Latin America had three specific goals: firstly, the fabrication and inculcation of a shared national culture. This would have Hispanic/Portuguese and Catholic orientations; secondly, the integration of the in-

digenous peoples into national life; and thirdly, the introduction of developmental programs aimed at improving the living standards of the indigenous population.

The contribution of social scientists to the identification and implementation of these goals through specific policies was considerable. For example, in Mexico, *indigenismo* made use of anthropological research in its proposals for "cultural change." While in Peru, the leftist writer José Carlos Mariátegui, argued that Indian marginality was due to exploitation and prevailing socioeconomic conditions and land distribution unfavorable to Indian peoples.

Manuel Gamio (1883-1960), a leading founder of *indigenismo*, in his book, *Forjando Patria* (*Forging the Patria*) of 1916, proposed ways of eliminating or transforming the "great heterogeneity" of the multiethnic population and recommended a program of assimilation conducted by the state. Gamio argued that if a country has a uniformity of civilization or a common cultural type, then this was a sign of progress. The means and mechanisms of developing such a massive "cultural change" were mainly through the creation of an infrastructure, and especially through the development of communications, the creation and expansion of educational programs and institutions such as the *Instituto Indigenista Interamericano* (1940), the *Instituto Nacional Indigenista* which found its national incarnations in Bolivia and Ecuador (1941), Peru (1946), and Mexico (1948), and the *Fundacion Nacional del Indio* (1967) in Brazil. Social scientists were summoned to participate in such "development" projects, by, for example, coordinating the displacement and resettlement of populations, researching the effects of "planned acculturation," and analyzing and recording cultures which were only "tolerated inside museums."

The familiar contradiction of nationalism, with its search for both authenticity *and* "national" unity, produced a crisis in the culture of indigenism and a critical reappraisal of the enterprise became necessary. In the case of Latin America, nationalism sought to find a national culture in the "positive values" of Indian cultures, while at the same time promoting their disappearance in the name of national unity.

# Individual Choice vs. Ascribed Status in Nationalist Theories

Indigenism, nationalism, and anthropology were in crisis in as much as they insisted on utilising Indianness to forge national cultures in Latin America. The policy of respecting the culture of the Indian while at the same time promoting the assimilation of the Indian into the realm of Hispanic/Portuguese culture became such an ideological paradox that it provoked considerable academic criticism. One of the critics of *indigenismo* argued that the construction of an "authentic" nation could be enriched by the rich "mosaic of the different ethnic and regional cultures of the country" (Stavenhagen 1988). Another view insisted on the "autonomous development of the original culture of the Indian peoples" (Bonfil 1991). *Indigenismo* has also been criticized by indigenous organizations from all over the continent, especially since 1970.

With the upsurge of the Zapatista revolt in 1994 in the southern state of Chiapas demanding autonomy for indigenous peoples, together with the gradual democratization of Mexican politics, *indigenismo* has visibly declined as an official policy and ideology aimed at the regulation of indigenous ways of life by the central state.

Equivalents of the Latin phenomenon of *indigenismo* can be found in Australasia and Africa.

## Bibliography

Aguirre, Beltran Gonzalo.1957. *El Proceso de Aculturación*. Mexico: Universidad Nacional Autónoma de México.

Benítez, Fernando.1968. *Los Indios de México*. Mexico: ERA.

Bonfil, Batalla Guillermo. 1987. *México Profundo, una Civilización Negada*. Mexico: CIESAS-SEP.

Brading, David. 1988. "Manuel Gamio and Official Indigenism in Mexico," *Bulletin of Latin American Research* 7, 1: 75-89.

Comas, Juan.1953. *Ensayos Sobre Indigenismo*. Mexico: Instituto Indigenista Interamericano.

Gamio, Manuel. 1916. *Forjando Patria, Pro-nacionalismo*. Mexico: Porrúa.

Knight, Alan. 1990. "Racism, Revolution and Indigenism: Mexico 1910-1940," in R. Graham (ed.), *The Idea of Race in Latin America*. Austin: University of Texas Press.

Mariátegui, José Carlos. 1970. *Siete Ensayos de Interpretación Sobre la Realidad Peruana*. Mexico: ERA.

Stavenhagen, Rodolfo and Nolasco, Margarita. 1988. *Política Cultural Para un País Multiétnico*. Mexico: Secretaría de Educación Pública.

Urban, G. and Scherzer, G. (eds.). 1991. *Nation States and Indians in Latin America*. Austin: University of Texas Press.

Natividad Gutiérrez

# Individual Choice vs. Ascribed Status in Nationalist Theories

Many theorists take the position that nationalism, though a modern phenomenon, began several centuries ago. Almost all students of nationalism agree that the decades after the French Revolution were a period of qualitative change in nationalist arguments. Hence, it seems worthwhile to begin the present discussion by citing two prominent exponents with diametrically opposed positions. In his book *Géopolitique*, the French geographer Jacques Ancel defended plebiscitary choices (after World War I) for German-speakers residing in western frontier districts, on the ground that freedom of choice (*Plébiscite de tous les jours*) was a historic principle of republics (Ancel 1936). Conversely, the German geopolitician Karl Haushofer (a supporter of the Nazi regime who later became its victim) argued that "the prerequisite for such boundary studies is that one has absorbed the necessities ...of the life form to which he belongs to such an extent that violence and mutilation of it pain him as much as though they were inflicted on his own skin."(Dorpalen 1948: 23). Hence, no aggregate of individual choices should be determinative.

An irony of this exchange is that the Versailles Treaty returned the German-speaking province of Alsace to France without a plebiscite, while German-speaking areas within 1914 Germany were transferred to Belgium by a plebiscite permitting dubious freedom of choice. More generally, many members of nationalist movements, especially leaders, have vestigial attachments, either genealogically or by prolonged residence, to the disputed areas where separation is said to mean "violence and mutilation," a fate which neither linguistic science nor common experience in large countries like the United States and Russia supports. Nevertheless, *some* individuals even in countries historically known for large-scale and rapid population movements, do experience renunciation of their ethnic, and especially ethno-religious identity, as traumatic. Extensive biographical investigation, in a franker mode than was customary in earlier generations, might go a long way to determining the costs of severing ties with one's early identity, as well as motivations for such a drastic step.

Recently, a powerful argument, clearly detached from claims for organic or primordial origins for national identity, has been advanced by political science professor Vernon Van Dyke. He points out that international covenants providing for self-determination emphasize the individual right to "freely determine their political status." Van Dyke urges, however, that "I think it clear that ethnic communities and peoples, may have collective interests, and that some of them are of fundamental importance and so general (universalisable) that they are and ought to be called rights" (Van Dyke 1965). In effect, some rights can be exercised only by collectivities. He cites the state-supported separate Protestant and Catholic schools in Canadian provinces, and broader provisions for religious and linguistic distinctions in public education within the European Community. Discussing quotas for ethnic minorities, Van Dyke argues that even in the United States, where recognition of group rights is rare, "first one should develop an intellectually and morally defensible position and then face the constitutional problem."

Recent political developments in the United States suggest how strongly entrenched is resistance to group rights, notably quotas thinly disguised as "affirmative action." In 1979 this position was strongly advanced on an international basis by Dov Ronen: "my thesis is that the 'self,' in self-determination is the singular, individual human being and not any aggregation of human beings...it is only because the institutionalization of individual self-determination is not (or not yet) possible that the *aggregate* of 'Is' the

'us' is substituted." He continues that the only basic human entities are individuals and humanity, apart from the mother and her new-born child, and self-determination is only in the eyes of the beholder (Ronen 1979).

Certainly, Ronen's position seems to contradict not only Wilsonian principles, but widely supported recent declarations such as the Final Act of the 1975 Conference on Security and Co-operation in Europe. Still, close reading suggests internal contradictions in this document. Paragraphs 58 and 59 of Part viii explicitly require respect for self-determination, "all peoples have the right, in full freedom, to determine, when and as they wish, their internal and external political status, without external interference," yet refers to "territorial integrity of states" as a conditioning factor. Elsewhere the Helsinki Act (Part iv, Paragraph 35) has the participating states promising to refrain from any act (or, in Paragraph 32, even any demand) "against the territorial integrity, political independence or the unity of any participating State" (Maresca 1985). Unofficially, some U.S. delegates to Helsinki have conceded that the intent was to give priority to territorial integrity over any secessionist demands. Just before the break-up of the Soviet Union, major leaders including President George Bush, appeared to be acting on this principle, as well as the more obvious concern for disrupting relations with President Mikhail Gorbachev.

Prescinding from the basically authoritarian nature of the Soviet state, and the question of the degree to which this changed in 1991, one must confront the practical extent to which any compact minority with a highly distinctive history and culture can function without a large measure of territorial independence. Most poignantly, this issue has arisen for Estonia and Latvia since their attainment of legal independence. Whereas Lithuania has an overwhelming native ethnic majority, the other two Baltic republics include slight indigenous majorities, with the vast majority of the remaining population consisting of ethnic Russians. In particular, Estonia, that had few Russian settlers after centuries of tsarism, faced after 1939 a settlement of a Russian minority of one-third injected under the Stalin and post-Stalin dictatorship without real consultation with Estonians. The European Community, for which Estonia is a leading candidate, has exerted pressure to secure citizenship for most of the Russians there, regardless of the circumstances of their arrival. In contrast to most other nations, Estonia can claim to be restoring a society unjustly incorporated in the Soviet Union under the Molotov-Ribbentrop Pact. While avoiding precipitate actions like expulsion, Estonian nationalists argue that secure control of the institutions of their small country is the only guarantee for preserving a culture that has demonstrated its ability to foster economic standards far superior to the nearby Slavic countries. A similar argument was persuasive as a justification for Slovenia's insistence (1991) on separating from Yugoslavia.

Even when they are couched in theoretical terms, the sharply contending views just summarized really rest on ethical or legal principles. Moreover, even a cursory historical review indicates that contenders' actions often contradict their principles. Under the circumstances, clear-cut preference for either "theoretical" position would be misplaced. Instead, one may suggest that wise statecraft should at times prefer primarily pragmatic solutions concerning self-determination, taking into account considerations that far transcend the particular nationalist situations at issue.

### Bibliography

Ancel, Jacques. 1936. *Géopolitique*. Paris: Delagrave.
Armstrong, John A. 1990. "Contemporary ethnicity: the moral dimension in comparative perspective," *Review of Politics* 52, 2: 163-88.
Dorpalen, Andreas. 1948. *The World of General Haushofer: Geopolitics in Action*. New York: Farrar and Rinehart.
Maresca, John J. 1985. *To Helsinki: The Conference on Security and Cooperation in Europe, 1973-1975*. Durham, NC: Duke University Press.
Ronen, Dov. 1979. *The Quest for Self-Determination*. New Haven, CT: Yale University Press.
Smith, Anthony D. 1986. "History and liberty: dilemmas of loyalty in Western democracies," *Ethnic and Racial Studies* 9, 1: 43-65.

Van Dyke, Vernon. 1965. *Human Rights, Ethnicity, and Discrimination*. Westport, CT: Greenwood Press.

John A. Armstrong

# Instrumentalist Theories of Nationalism

In philosophy instrumentalism is the doctrine that scientific theories are not true descriptions of an unobservable reality but simply useful instruments which enable us to structure and interpret the observable world. In the social sciences, similarly, instrumentalism is the doctrine that ideas can primarily be explained by their uses for their beneficiaries, rather than by their accurate representation of truth or reality. So, in our field, instrumentalist theories explain both the genesis and maintenance of nationalism by the interests it is alleged to serve. They represent a sharp contrast to other explanatory theories which focus on the identities and ideas that nationalism expresses, protects, or represents.

Instrumentalist theories of nationalism are trivially true in one respect: no political phenomenon is likely to survive indefinitely if it is entirely useless to all conceivable human collectivities or individuals. However, most instrumentalist theories extrapolate well beyond this safe and uninteresting claim. They tend to become reductionist or simply false. They share an entertaining and at times a biting, debunking, flavor that seeks to expose the vested interests behind nationalism. They are, therefore, the favored theories of anti-nationalists. Instrumentalist theories of nationalism presently come in three packages, each of which is generally lacking in respect for the others. They are the sociobiological, the sociological and the individualist. The SOCIOBIOLOGICAL THEORY is well represented in the work of Pierre van den Berghe (1987). In sociobiology nationalism is a form of ethnic identification, a group-interest motivated belief, similar to xenophobia. Nations are extended families, really so, or imagined as such (in an important qualification); and people are said to be naturally disposed towards ethnic nepotism, selection in favor of their own kin.

Sociobiologists tend to debunk what nationalists say about their own nation or nationalism. For example, they interpret allegedly altruistic nationalist behavior, such as sacrificing oneself for one's nation, as driven, at some deeper level, by the imperatives of reproductive success. Or, they diagnose the language of "kin" and "kinship" regularly invoked by nationalists, as direct evidence for their theses. Their political vision is bleakly "realistic." Most sociobiologists generally adhere to what Steinberg (1981) has dubbed the "iron law of ethnicity," namely the belief that where there is group difference, especially difference based on kin, there will be ethnic conflict. Ethnocentrism, prejudice, and national and ethnic conflict are seen as natural outcomes of conflicts of group interest, deriving from kinship identity and belonging, part of the competitive world of nature.

There are many problems with sociobiological instrumentalism (for a general critical overview of sociobiology see Kitcher 1985). Critics focus on three. First, in so far as sociobiological instrumentalism relies on interests to do explanatory work it is interests at the subhuman level, amongst genes and more mysterious "gene pools." Here rational choice instrumentalists part company with their sociobiological cousins, maintaining that only individuals can have interests, even if genes can be modelled as having interests. Pop sociobiology, in any case, fails to demonstrate linkages between any given and presumably unmodifiable "nationalist" gene(s) and any nationalist behavioral trait(s). Sophisticated sociobiologists, by contrast, do not make the error of linking any specific gene with nationalist phenomena. They see their task to be that of disclosing the functional significance, defined by reproductive success, of nationalist behavioral traits or of nationalist cultural and political organizations. They have not had much success in persuading their colleagues in the social sciences of the merits of their insights. Second, while sociobiological instrumentalism may provide an (arguably) convincing account of (some of) the interests at stake in a lineage group, it is not obvious that this account can be successfully extrapolated to "the nation," a much higher or at least larger level of group-aggregation in which any

sense of hereditary kinship is, as sociobiologists concede, much more imagined. Third, critics maintain that while the sociobiological approach may be evolutionary, it is ahistorical. Whatever traits we have inherited from our early ancestors in savannah environments could not have been nationalist ones. Our stone-age ancestors, foragers and hunters, were not nationalists because without states there can be no nations. Modernists insist that nationalism is only coherently defined as a political doctrine—one that affirms the legitimacy of national self-determination, and maintains that nations should be the rightful cultural boundaries for state formation or organization (e.g., Gellner 1983; O'Leary 1997). Nationalist doctrine, in other words, is only conceivable after the formation of states, and only likely to be widespread in the post-caste conditions of modern industrialized and communication-intensive societies. All that sociobiologists do is to provide a bare account of why humans might have evolved group-interested identifications and behaviors; what they cannot convincingly do is to explain why these have taken a nationalist form in modern conditions. Their political vision has also been contested by egalitarian pluralists: for example Steinberg (1981) correctly maintains that the connection between ethnic and kin difference and conflict is not as inevitable as sociobiologists suppose: "If there is an iron law of ethnicity, it is that when ethnic groups are found in a hierarchy of power, wealth, and status, then conflict is inescapable... where there is social, economic, and political parity ... ethnic conflict, when it occurs, tends to be at a low level and rarely spills over into violence."

Sociological instrumentalism comes in two principal varieties: from Marxists and elite theorists. They share the view that nationalism, like several other belief systems, doctrines, and ideologies, is used and abused primarily by ruling classes or power elites, and, by rival or aspirant ruling classes and power elites. Their perspective is like that of Voltaire's on religion: a superstition, which serves the interests of its propagators. No enlightened person, they believe, could be a nationalist because, in Eric Hobsbawm's view, it requires too many beliefs in what is not so (1990).

# Instrumentalist Theories of Nationalism

One school of elite theorists suggests that elites use and abuse the identities and ideas of the masses on behalf of, and because of, the interests of elites, especially through the "invention of traditions" (Hobsbawm and Ranger 1983). Paul Brass's work on India is an exemplary illustration of this school of thought paying especial attention to political elitism choices of linguistic and cultural markers to build political coalitions in favor of territorial autonomy or employment preferences (Brass 1991). Brass's work is sophisticated, but does not deal with two matters satisfactorily: why and when elites choose ethnic or national identities for mobilization rather than other identities, for example, class or religious identities, and whether elites are constrained either by their national and ethnic formation, or that of their followers. Brass's position must be differentiated from an even stronger brand of elite theory which holds that elites both construct and then use and abuse the national identities and "ideas" of the masses—whose identities and ideas are therefore plainly inauthentic, and whose cognitive capacities are thereby seen as seriously challenged. Although the expression "false consciousness" is rarely heard these days it is plainly signalled in this pattern of thought. It is difficult to convict real academics of displaying this argument but it is the principal burden of John Breuilly's (1985), and of Eric Hobsbawm's work (1990). It must be noted, however, that, although Hobsbawm follows Ernest Gellner, nevertheless, he seeks to explain why ethno-national identities might have appeals rooted in the life-experiences rather than the vulgar interests of what he scornfully calls the "lesser examination passing" classes.

Elite theorists and Marxists jointly recognize that the interests pursued by nationalists only make sense in modern conditions (Hechter 1975; Schwartzmantel 1992). For elite theorists the modern state, with its extensive surveillance, regulatory and policy-making capacities, is the chief object of political mobilization because it is rationally perceived as a site of power and opportunities. Nationalism's social power derives from the ability of motivated elites to use cultural appeals to cloak their ambitions to capture state power or a share of state resources. For Marxists, by contrast, the power of nationalism is ultimately rooted in the capitalist economy and the interests to which it gives rise.

Instrumentalist Marxists portray the bourgeoisie and the petty bourgeoisie, in particular, as likely carriers of nationalist ideologies because nationalism successfully masks their class interests as universal interests, and because they have much to lose from the erosion of local cultures—allegedly unlike the proletariat. The historical account that Marxists give is simple enough: the bourgeoisie invite the masses as co-nationals to defeat the aristocracy, and thereby prize open the state apparatus to bourgeois as opposed to landed interests; and, subsequently, through the state apparatus, they promote the development of integrated national markets based around a common national language, or culture from which they benefit. In neo-Marxist argument nationalism in advanced countries is seen as a response to uneven economic development (Nairn 1977) or internal colonialism (Hechter 1975) on the part of a coalition of classes led by an aspirant national bourgeoisie. In this respect, Marxist thinking still owes much to Lenin's and Trotsky's portrayal of national liberation movements in the third world as cross-class coalitions organized against the imperialism of the metropolitan centres of advanced capitalism.

There are at least four core difficulties with both Marxists' and elite theorists' instrumental accounts of nationalism. The first is that elites and dominant classes, as much as the masses or subordinate classes are constrained by their ethno-national identities—and not just motivated by their interests. Although these identities themselves may be capable of slow and occasionally sudden shifts, it is not easy to restructure one's linguistic or cultural identity even when it is in one's interests narrowly conceived. In different ways and with different methodologies this argument is made by Walker Connor (1994), Donald Horowitz (1985), and by Anthony D. Smith (1986). The second is that it is difficult to dispute that the masses or subordinate classes have both genuine interests as well as their own identities at stake in "their nations," so that instrumentalists are wrong to see nationalism largely as a manipulative discourse imposed from on high, and oddly insensitive to the interests of those lower in social hierarchies—which they see as entirely saturated with wishful or foolish thinking. Mass hysteria and mass stupidity are, of course, regular features of human history, but working classes and petty bourgeois are not irrational or hysterical to support nationalist programs that offer them citizenship or better prospects of social mobility for their children. The third is that like all interest-based accounts in the social sciences such instrumentalist reasoning gives insufficient weight to the independent impact of ideas and doctrines in persuading people of what is right, independently of what their particular interests are, and without which they might have no recognizable sense of what their interests were. Lastly, these accounts reduce identities to interests. This is arguably a philosophical category mistake which conflates what people want to be with what they want (Ringmar 1996).

Marxists, of course, have separate difficulties all of their own (Connor 1984), to which most of them now are acutely sensitized (Moore 1975; Nimni 1993). The workers have displayed throughout this century in multiple milieux that they have fatherlands and motherlands, and that for them nation often trumps class in its appeal, both as an identity and as a perceived collective interest, and as a reason for fighting defensively or offensively. Marxist regimes in power have not, as they proclaimed, "solved the national question." Where Marxists won state power it was often as nationalist movements rather than as proletarian socialist internationalists. When they exercised state power they managed nationalism through repression or control, but failed to eliminate it. Indeed, failed Marxist regimes, such as Yugoslavia and the USSR, are perhaps the greatest living proof of the difficulties regimes have in trying to engineer anti-nationalist sentiments. This failure, in turn, casts some doubt on the heroic assumptions about the socialization powers of states, or of political elites, a point which is tacitly assumed in instrumentalist theories of nationalism.

The third large instrumental school is individualist, and today goes by the title of RATIONAL CHOICE (see e.g., Hechter 1986; Banton 1995; Hardin 1995). Theorists within this tradition work with a stylized model of a rational person who is narrowly motivated by self-interest, forward-looking, and maximizes expected utility subject to preferences and constraints on the feasibility of those preferences. Thus they see nationalism as a collective good, to which people will calculate their appropriate contributions on a cost-benefit calculus. They analyse, in particular, problems of nationalist mobilization which they typically see as a problem of collective action. A problem of collective action arises when what should be in the interests of all is not in the interests of each individual to contribute towards because they would benefit more from free-riding, or letting others provide the good or service in question. In these circumstances individuals are only likely to contribute if the probability that their own contribution will be decisive is very high, or if they are subject to a range of "selective incentives." Nationalism, however, seems to be less plagued by free-riding than other political movements—a matter to which rational choice theorists devote insufficient attention. Rational choice theory is usually espoused by liberals and libertarians (e.g., Banton), but there are also ex- or post-Marxist rational choice theorists (e.g. Hechter).

Rational choice accounts are often ingenious (see e.g., the contributions in Breton et al. 1995, or Laitin's account of language strategies by political elites and citizens in multilingual societies, Laitin 1992). However, they suffer from several recognized difficulties. First, although they may be able to account for individual nationalist conduct, for the conduct, for example, of politicians, bureaucrats, teachers or voters, given that they have nationalist preferences, instrumentalists are much less capable of explaining why people have nationalist preferences in the first place; or of explaining why such preferences are more frequent and intense in modern times than in the agrarian past. Second, rational choice theorists tend to reduce identities to interests. They assume that behind people's desires to be or become French, for example, there must lie an interest in French jobs, French pensions or French welfare benefits. However, historical experience should teach us that identities are much less elastic with regard to incentives than interests, and that people are culturally differentiated by their overt responsiveness to incentives. Third, rational choice theorists are often only pseudo-empirical, and their arguments are not amenable to testing. What rational choice theorists tend to do is to provide rational accounts of why so-called "choices" might have been rational. They very rarely probe deeply to see whether other accounts of the phenomena they seek to explain might be better. Lastly, ingenuity in this tradition is achieved by providing a rational account of what may otherwise appear manifestly irrational. Many features of nationalism, sunk costs in past traditions, the tapping of the emotions as well as interests, and its expressive attributes, seem invulnerable to the ingenuity of rational choice theorists. Perhaps this is the tradition's most important contribution, namely, to show the limits of rationality and choice when it comes to the examination of nationalism.

The instrumentalist habit of thought is found amongst "primordialists" (e.g., sociobiologists) as well as "modernists" (e.g., Marxists), so the temptation to equate modernist theories of nationalism with instrumentalism is false. All instrumentalist theoretical traditions have their place in any attempts to explain nationalist phenomena. This is so, as long as they are accompanied by accounts, which give due weight to the independent consequences of ideas and identities in shaping human conduct. It is possible, after all, to believe in the importance of both ideas and interests, or to believe in the importance of both interests and identities, or to believe in the importance of ideas and identities, and, lastly, to accommodate all three explanatory sources of the appeal of nationalism (ideas, interests and identities).

## Bibliography

Banton, M. 1995. "Rational Choice Theories," *American Behavioural Scientist* 38, 3: 478-97.

Brass, P. 1991. *Ethnicity and Nationalism: Theory and Comparison.* New Delhi: Sage.

Breton, A., J.-L. Galeotti, *et al.* (eds.). 1995. *Nationalism and Rationality.* Cambridge: Cambridge University Press.

Breuilly, John. 1993 (1982). *Nationalism and the State.* Revised edition. Chicago: University of Chicago Press.

Connor, W. 1984. *The National Question in Marxist-Leninist Theory and Strategy.* Princeton, NJ: Princeton University Press.

Connor, W. 1994. *The Politics of Ethnonationalism.* Reno: Nevada University Press.

Gellner, E. 1983. *Nations and Nationalism.* Oxford: Basil Blackwell.

Hardin, R. 1995. *One for All: The Logic of Group Conflict.* Princeton, NJ: Princeton University Press.

Hechter, M. 1986. "Rational choice theory and the study of race and ethnic relations," in J. Rex and D. Mason (eds.), *Theories of Race and Ethnic Relations.* Cambridge: Cambridge University Press.

Hechter, M. 1975. *Internal Colonialism: The Celtic Fringe in British National Development.* London: Routledge and Kegan Paul.

Hobsbawm, E and Ranger, T. (eds.). 1983. *The Invention of Tradition.* Cambridge: Cambridge University Press.

Hobsbawm, E. 1990. *Nations and Nationalism since 1780: Programme, Myth, Reality.* Cambridge: Cambridge University Press.

Horowitz, D. 1985. *Ethnic Groups in Conflict.* Berkeley: University of California Press.

Kitcher, P. 1985. *Vaulting Ambition: Sociobiology and the Quest for Human Nature.* Cambridge, MA: MIT Press.

Laitin, D. 1992. *Language Repertoires and State Construction in Africa.* Cambridge Studies in Comparative Politics. Cambridge: Cambridge University Press.

Moore, C. 1974-5. "Were Marx and Engels Racists? The Prolet-Aryan Outlook of Marxism," *Berkeley Journal of Sociology* 19: 125-56.

Nairn, T. 1977. *The Break-Up of Britain: Crisis and Neo-nationalism.* London: New Left Books.

Nimni, E. 1993. *Marxism and Nationalism: Theoretical Origins of the Present Crisis.* London: Pluto Press.

O'Leary, B. 1997. "On the nature of nationalism: A critical appraisal of Ernest Gellner's writings on nationalism," *British Journal of Political Science* 27, 2: 191-222.

Ringmar, E. 1996. *Identity, Interest and Action: A Cultural Explanation of Sweden's Intervention in the Thirty Years War.* Cambridge: Cambridge University Press.

Schwartzmantel, J. 1992. *Socialism and the Idea of the Nation.* New York: Harvester.

Smith, A. D. 1986. *The Ethnic Origins of Nations.* Oxford: Basil Blackwell.

Steinberg. S. 1981. *The Ethnic Myth: Race, Ethnicity, and Class in America.* New York: Atheneum.

van den Berghe, P. L. 1987. *The Ethnic Phenomenon.* New York: Praeger.

Brendan O'Leary

# Integral Nationalism

The concept of integral nationalism was used for the first time by Charles Maurras in an article entitled "Le Nationalisme intégral" that appeared in *Le Soleil* of March 2, 1900. In that article Maurras wrote that "Royalism corresponds essentially to the diverse postulates of nationalism: it is itself integral nationalism" (Buthman 1970: 111). Maurras explained that "In the days of yore, to serve the king was to make oneself useful to the *Patrie*; to-day, inverting the expression, to make oneself useful to the *Patrie* is really to serve the cause of the king" (Buthman 1970: 112). He argued that, in France, nationalism without royalism was a logical fallacy and that royalism completed nationalism, "since the monarchical institutions alone satisfied all the national aspirations, all the national ends, as the integral reproduced the sum of all the values of an algebraic function" (Buthman 1970: 269).

Integral nationalism explains that the origins of decay, decadence and disunity in a nation are linked to the dangerous Enlightenment ideas of humanism and idealism. In practice, this form of nationalism represents a forceful attack on liberal and republican ideas, that, in turn, evokes emotions for a nostalgic return to the ancient glories of the past. Integral nationalism is also a longing for absolutism and totality, a call to regenerate the nation as whole through collective patriotic action.

The nation, in the integral nationalist paradigm, is a racially, ethnically, and culturally distinct entity, and must be preserved as such. Integral nationalism demands the total subjection of the individual to the nation, and argues that the well-being of the individual is dependent on the well-being of the nation. An irrepressible sense of pride and a deep longing for the past results in a strong sense of loyalty to the culture of the nation and the political ideology of the state. The cru-

dity and vulgarity of the New Order with its secular and liberal democratic theories and practices, violently threatens sacred traditions, the cultural and political values of the Old Order.

Both absolutist and totalitarian governance are defended as aesthetic expressions of patriotism. A nation is born because patriots help shape the humanity of the nation with its heroes, martyrs and saints. Humanity does not exist in itself, the nation is its essence!

The patriotic war at home must be waged against "foreign" intellectuals who popularize antipatriotic politics at home. Putative adversaries are vital to mobilize the masses in defense of the nation. Integral nationalists were highly effective in their attacks against the Jews, as usurers, parasites, dangerous humanists and cosmopolitans, who undermined the moral and cultural fabric of the nation. The Jews, in the integral nationalist paradigm, also became the personification of revolutionary radical humanism and idealism that destroyed divine rule and order.

For instance, during the 1880s, the time of the French Third Republic, Édouard Drumont (1844–1917) published anti-Semitic books and articles that held Jews responsible for the emergence of a liberal and blasphemous status quo and the downfall of the Second Empire. In 1894, when Captain Alfred Dreyfus was sentenced to life imprisonment for allegedly supplying Germany with military secrets, Drumont and his followers argued that Jews were a suspect race most capable of treason. Maurice Barrès (1862–1923) and Charles Maurras (1868–1952), founders of *Action Française*, continued the anti-Semitic hysteria of Drumont and helped integrate anti-Semitism into the nationalism of *Action Franéaise*. Whereas Barrés favored a dictatorship, Maurras fervently argued for hereditary monarchy in order to purify French culture and society.

To Italian patriot Gabriele D'Annunzio (1863–1938), mystic patriotic festivals, national monuments and sacred objects would not only regenerate the aesthetic of politics in Italy, but they would also activate a militant nationalist political style. D'Annunzio popularized the poetic symbolism of the flame as the source of life, beauty and power, and also as the symbol of death and destruction. The flame became the symbol of fascism in Italy and was worn as the emblem of the storm troopers of Benito Mussolini, the Arditi.

The integral nationalist mystique advanced by Drumont, Barrès, Maurras, D'Annunzio and articulated by many other intellectuals at the turn into the twentieth century was based on an emotional attachment to the nation, its history, geography, art and language. Their nationalism proscribed internal opposition and dissent and separated itself radically from the type of nationalism which underscored the importance of individual rights and liberties. In terms of its *locus classicus*, integral nationalism is linked to fascism and anti-individualism where the state is the expression of the conscience and will of all the citizens. The tragic climax came during the 1930s and 1940s in Europe, when Nazi politics used integral nationalism to justify its horrific crimes. The love of nation as expressed through integral nationalism had clearly emerged as a love reduced largely to hate.

### Bibliography

Buthman, William C. 1970. *The Rise of Integral Nationalism in France*. New York: Octagon Books.

Curtis, Michael. 1959. *Three Against the Third Republic: Sorel, Barrés, and Maurras*. Princeton, NJ: Princeton University Press.

McClelland, J. S. (ed.) 1971. *The French Right*. New York: Harper and Row.

Mosse, George L. 1980. *Masses and Man: Nationalist and Fascist Perceptions of Reality*. New York: Howard Fertig.

Mosse, George L. 1964. *The Crisis of German Ideology: Intellectual Origins of the Third Reich*. New York: Grosset and Dunlop.

Nolte, Ernst. 1966. *Three Faces of Fascism: Action Franéaise, Italian Fascism, National Socialism*. New York: Holt, Rinehart and Winston.

Smith, Anthony D. 1971. *Theories of Nationalism*. London: Duckworth.

Smith, Anthony D. 1986. *The Ethnic Origins of Nations*. Oxford: Blackwell.

Sutton, Michael. 1982. *Nationalism, Positivism and Catholicism: The Politics of Charles Maurras and French Catholics, 1890–1914*. Cambridge: Cambridge University Press.

Robert Hazan

# Intellectuals and Nationalism

Different conceptions of "the intellectual" and of "nationalism" result in a variety of approaches to this topic. The term "intellectual" may be used to mean "philosopher" at one extreme or, if conflated with "intelligentsia," may denote a separate social stratum. Similarly, by "nationalism" might be meant a full-blown *Weltanschauung* or a set of motifs and sentiments.

Earlier historians of nationalism such as Carlton Hayes (1931) and Hans Kohn (1946) attributed an importance to nationalism as a cultural system by elucidating its ideology and symbolism in different contexts. Philosophers, however, with some exceptions have regarded nationalist thought as too intellectually primitive to study (in contrast with the considerable attention to rival secular ideologies such as liberalism and Marxism). One can identify many major figures as founding influences (Montesquieu, Burke, Herder, Kant, Rousseau, Fichte, and Mill), but their primary significance as thinkers does not lie in their nationalism. Benedict Anderson (1983) speaks for many in suggesting that nationalism should be understood as a style of imagining (like kinship) rather than an intellectual system.

One influential exception to this is ELIE KEDOURIE (1960) who has traced the origins of nationalism to a crisis within Enlightenment thought. The philosophers' rationalist conceptions of human autonomy had undermined religious ideas and the traditional political systems. The problem was that they were unable to reconcile their meliorist ideas of progress with the existence of evil and suffering in human history. Two German thinkers, Kant and HERDER, "solved" this problem by arguing that History demonstrated that folly and evil were necessary to test the individual and collective will and to spur future action. This historicist solution had revolutionary consequences, for the people, defined in linguistic terms, rather than God, now became the proper object of individual and collective devotion. Kant and Herder gave rise to different versions of the nation—the former to a voluntarist and civic conception and the latter to an organic and ethnic conception, but Fichte fused them to form the mature doctrine, according to which individuals must actively identify within their "natural" polities, defined by their objective cultural characteristics.

Kedourie argues that, although false, this German-based doctrine, once formulated, has had immense potency, and spread worldwide. History now replaced religion as the teacher of humanity, the interpretation of which was the preserve of a new stratum of secular intellectuals. This gave legitimacy to the leadership aspirations of these intellectuals who, feeling slighted at their exclusion from power, have everywhere challenged religious and dynastic authority in the name of the people and sought to establish on abstract principles a utopian state. Their ideas appealed to all those who feel a need to belong as a result of the erosion of traditional meaning and social structures by secular modernization. Recruiting first the educated young, nationalism has mobilized the masses into a millenarian crusade. But the fantasies of the intellectuals have resulted in totalitarian tyrannies, civil strife and war.

Kedourie's interpretation, which emphasizes the irrational and manipulative aspects of modern intellectuals, and their psychological vulnerability to "slights," has been influential, resonating with many characterizations of "third world" national regimes (see Kautsky 1962). His history of ideas approach has, however, been widely criticized. Its idealist focus on great texts makes the popular appeal of nationalism difficult to understand. Kedourie (1971) qualified this emphasis by introducing the modern state as causal factor, which undermines traditional social orders and thereby creates a crisis of identity, but he retained his diffusionist assumption of a single source to which all nationalisms are indebted. This is unconvincing because nationalist ideas emerged simultaneously in many centers, and the extended struggles of nationalist movements militate against any mechanical account of diffusion. His depiction of nationalism as millenarian is at variance with the stability of nation-states.

Few have followed Kedourie in attributing an independent status to the intellectuals, though many might share his scorn for nationalist politics. The dominant tradition, as elaborated in the famous study of Miroslav Hroch (1985), has focused on the social bases of nationalist movements. The role of intellectuals as "inventors of tradition" is recognized in the interpretations of ERNEST GELLNER (1983) and ERIC HOBSBAWM (1983), but as mere handmaidens of industrialization: their construction of new symbolic forms (of anthems, flags, vernacular languages, dress, literatures, and histories) enables the emergence of large economic and political units. But a focus on symbols rather than cognitions and loyalties provides a limited perspective. There is little attention to how nationalism as a meaning system establishes itself against its competitors, religious and secular, or how a novel cultural framework shapes actors' responses to modernization.

John Breuilly (1982) has analyzed the historicist vision of the intellectuals and the role of national symbols. He argues that nationalism offers a solution to a growing conflict between claims of state and civil society, by identifying the authentic state as that which forms organically from its society, and nationalist ideology and symbols serve to legitimize, co-ordinate, and mobilize social groups in their campaigns against the state. However, he also maintains that nationalism offers opposition elites powerful resources by which to seize state power, although it cannot provide the basis of a successful modern society, for history offers no authoritative guide to the relations between the state and society. The cohesion of nation-states is built not on intellectual blueprints but on the pragmatic processes of economic and political development (the territory-wide formation of markets, party-systems, forms of citizenship, etc.).

A more substantial role is given to intellectuals in the revisionist (Gramscian) Marxian approach of Tom Nairn (1977). Much of his study focuses on the contribution of novelists, poets, historians, and linguists to the formation of a national culture. Like Gellner, he argues that the ideology of nationalism is embedded in the unevenness of capitalist development. Whereas Gellner treats romantic nationalism, with its cult of authenticity, creativity, and the subjective will, as an epiphenomenon, Nairn understands it as a powerful ideology of development. Nationalism, Nairn maintains, emerges amongst the conscious section (the intelligentsia) of the indigenous bourgeoisie of relatively backward societies who, fearing the threat of more powerful industrial states, realize they had to overthrow traditionalist rulers and secure an effective rational state capable of protecting their markets and creating an educated personnel. Aware that they could not follow the model of the dominant states, since they had few native resources other than the people itself, they formulate a nationalism that emphasizes the individuality of peoples, the latent energies contained in their cultures, and their capacity for autonomous development. Constructing a hegemonic national culture out of vernacular cultures and popular historical memories, they seek to mobilize the masses in a multi-class alliance round the political goals of the modernizing bourgeoisie and to divert potential class antagonism outwards to foreigners.

Nairn offers a political-economic approach to nationalism and uses it to explain the lack of dynamism of Scottish romantic nationalism. Because Scotland during the eighteenth century was already economically and culturally advanced and because its intelligentsia found the union with England opened alternative avenues of social and political mobility, romanticism took on a conservative nostalgic character. His interpretation, however, has limitations in those many countries where nationalism predates the threat of an "external" capitalism, and where nationalism is often focused not on the creation of a modernizing state, but on the moral regeneration of the community. It is questionable, too, to tie the intelligentsia to bourgeois interests, since the bourgeoisie are notable absentees in many "third world" contexts, and to explain their cultural activities by the requirements of mass mobilization, because many nationalisms look first to social elites. Others have found it useful to treat the intelligentsia as a distinct social stratum by virtue of their educational qualifications, whose tendencies to radicalism may have political rather than economic motivations.

This is the thrust of Anthony Smith's model (1981; 1991) which highlights the rise of the modernizing state in the genesis of nationalism. Because of his conception of nationalism as primarily a form of culture (rather than of politics), Smith attributes great importance to the intellec-

tuals and the intelligentsia, but, unlike Nairn, distinguishes between their distinctive roles. Intellectuals are defined not as a social category but as individuals from any social background who are governed by a concern for meaning; whereas the intelligentsia are a modern social stratum, defined by their education and professional qualifications, and trained in the application of specialist knowledge to practical problems.

The intellectuals (Mickiewicz, Palacky, Mazzini) in this interpretation are the creators of the nationalist vision, languages, myths, and symbols, and they are significant in the early phases of nationalist movements. This vision is historicist, insisting on national identity as a dynamic creative force which must be reinterpreted for each generation. Those whom he sees as central are romantic intellectuals—historians, archaeologists, writers, painters, musicians, philologists—who look back to the past to reconstruct the authentic nation in all its dimensions and then project it as a living and dramatic force into the present. It is they who continually "recreate" the national character, whereas the social philosophers, Rousseau, Jefferson, and Burke, associate the nation with ideas of collective liberty and popular sovereignty.

What drives the intellectuals to nationalism is a recurring crisis of identity to which there is no final solution. This is generated by the increasing and unpredictable impact of a "scientific state" (a state in which scientific techniques are steadily incorporated into its bureaucratic apparatus) on traditional religious belief systems which formerly legitimated individual and social identities. The scientific state, by promising a secular solution to the problem of evil and suffering undermines the cognitive claims of religion and increasingly intervenes in the realms of social existence formerly regulated by religion. This produces what Smith calls "a dual legitimation crisis" in which individuals are faced with choosing between two antithetical worlds—religion and science. Like Kedourie, Smith relates the rise of nationalism to secularization, but his is a sociological rather than an intellectualist thesis. To this crisis of authority come three responses (secular modernism, religious reformism, and neo-traditionalism) which offer different and partial solutions, each of which breaks down and engenders nationalism. Modernists are associated with an aggressive secular political nationalism, hostile to tradition; reformists who look to ethnic history to find a communal model when religious principles harmonized with secular principles contribute to a regenerative cultural nationalism; and neo-traditionalists turn to ethnic tradition in order to mobilize the masses to shore up religious authority against a profane and materialist world, endowing nationalism with an authoritarian and puritanical fervor. The particular weighting of these three elements, which are in tension with each other, strongly influences the character of nationalist movements.

Nationalism, for Smith, is an episodic "wave-like" phenomenon, and although the intellectuals provide the vision and programs, what is crucial to its recurring formation as a movement is the attraction of the intelligentsia to become the cadres of nationalism, responsible for disseminating the ideas to a wider educated public and transforming it into a multi-class movement. They are a relatively new social stratum, substantially created by the secular educational systems and the mobile career structures of the "scientific" state. By dint of their rationalist training and qualifications, they are critical of received traditions and imbued with an ethos of meritocracy and a sense of elitism, justified by a claim of service to the community. Smith explains their attraction to nationalism as a result of two factors. Firstly, as a novel stratum they are set against tradition, but also feel a desire for rootedness in a community. Secondly, they look to the state as the engine of social improvement, but periodically they experience "blocked mobility" when there is an oversupply of aspirants to available positions, and this produces a crisis of function and a sense of resentment against the state. At this point of frustration, the nationalist vision of the intellectuals supplies them with a new identity and political function by promoting the rising educated classes as the necessary regenerators of the nation.

It is the rediscovery of roots and purpose in the historical community that explains the intelligentsia's turn to vernacular cultures rather than a quest to mobilize the masses. In many cases the intelligentsia direct their message initially to

social elites as the most effective means of permeating the community, and the switch to populist strategies may come only after they have been spurned by the gentry and upper middle classes. These movements may remain tiny, and fizzle out repeatedly before the power of the state. But what can sustain these projects over long periods of "foreign" rule is the institutionalization of national memories, particularly when based on popular traditions. In Smith's model such premodern ethnic memories have the capacity to channel nationalist movements and even nation-states.

### Bibliography

Anderson, Benedict. 1983. *Imagined Communities*. London: Verso.

Breuilly, John. 1982. *Nationalism and the State*. Manchester: Manchester University Press.

Gellner, Ernest. 1983. *Nations and Nationalism*. Oxford: Blackwell.

Hobsbawm, Eric and Terence Ranger (eds.). 1983. *The Invention of Tradition*. Cambridge: Cambridge University Press.

Hroch, Miroslav. 1985. *Social Preconditions of National Revivals in Europe*. Cambridge: Cambridge University Press.

Kautsky, John H. 1962. *Political Change in Underdeveloped Countries*. New York: John Wiley.

Kedourie, Elie. 1960. *Nationalism*. London: Hutchinson.

Kedourie, Elie (ed.). 1971. *Nationalism in Asia and Africa*. London: Weidenfeld and Nicolson.

Kohn, Hans. 1946. *The Idea of Nationalism*. New York: Macmillan.

Nairn, Tom. 1977. *The Break-up of Britain: Crisis and Neo-nationalism*. London: New Left Books.

Smith, Anthony D. 1981. *The Ethnic Revival*. Cambridge: Cambridge University Press.

Smith, Anthony D. 1991. *National Identity*. Harmondsworth: Penguin.

John Hutchinson

# Internal Colonialism

The idea that the term colonialism need not be confined to an overseas imperial system emerged, somewhat ironically, out of the post-Second World

# Internal Colonialism

War debates about the future of British and other European colonies. The United States, from a mixture of motives—a genuine belief in the right of peoples to self-determination, as well as a desire to gain commercial access to the European imperial markets in Africa and Asia—argued strongly in favour of de-colonization. In retaliation, the British delegates at the United Nations pointed to the systematic discrimination suffered by African-Americans and native Americans in the United States, which constituted, in their judgment, a situation tantamount to "internal colonialism." Despite a measure of validity to this "salt-water paradox"—that colonialism could take a continental as much as a maritime form—the struggles for independence in the Third World continued apace. The transfer of power took place in 1947 on the Indian sub-continent, and continued a decade later in Africa, following the example of Ghana under the leadership of Kwame Nkrumah.

The subsequent use of the term re-emerged in the 1960s and 1970s, when the winds of change in Africa combined with the Civil Rights struggle in America to produce strongly anticolonialist imagery and rhetoric. Several prominent scholars started to apply the colonial analogy to a wide variety of situations: Robert Blauner (1969) to blacks in the United States; Michael Hechter (1974) to the "Celtic Fringe" in the United Kingdom; and Elia Zureik (1979) to the Palestinians in the Middle East.

Blauner argued that domestic colonialism in the United States shared a number of characteristics with classical colonialism that made the label both appropriate and useful in understanding the special dynamics of black-white relationships in North America. The unique experience of involuntary migration, combined with the brutality of slavery, set African Americans apart from other migrants to the United States who had encountered far less traumatic disruptions. Only native Americans faced similarly destructive conditions on a sustained and inter-generational basis. Such policies set out quite deliberately to destroy the distinctive cultures, languages, and social traditions of the indigenous peoples and vigorously undermined any attempts to organize leadership or resistance. This strategy was administered by members of the dominant racial group

and the whole system was legitimized by an ideology of racial and cultural superiority. In some respects, internal colonialism was even more destructive than the external form, as in many of the European colonies the indigenous peoples had managed to sustain their cultures and social structures to a greater degree. Otherwise the comparisons were quite illuminating as the forces of the dominant white society administered and policed the inner-city ghettos, ran the educational and welfare systems and controlled most of the economy.

There were, of course, a number of academic critics of this approach who argued that the analogy was misleading. Nathan Glazer (1971), for example, suggested that the opportunities for leaving the inner-city ghettos were considerably greater than the internal colonial model implied and that the gradual increases in the black professional and other middle-class occupations attested to this trend. Significant African-American successes indicated that the community should be seen as conforming to the general pattern of ethnic group integration into American society despite an admittedly more disadvantaged history. Writing some twenty-five years later, Glazer was to modify this position and recognize that the stubborn persistence of black disadvantage did signify that this group had a unique legacy of social, economic and political oppression that should not be underestimated (Glazer 1997). Thus the language of black nationalism, and the identification of some radical African-American leaders with the independence struggles of the Third World, were not entirely without substance.

Another application of the internal colonial model can be found in writings about native peoples in Canada (Boldt 1981; Frideres 1988). Many features of the Canadian encounter between Indian groups and the considerably more powerful French and British colonial regimes fit the model quite well. There is the systematic destruction of indigenous economic and social systems, and the assault on traditional religious and cultural values. This was followed by the consolidation of political control by the settler societies and the familiar pattern of economic dependency. A separate administration of "Indian Affairs" and the exclusion of native peoples from full citizenship rights—such as voting in federal elections, freedom of movement, and restrictions on the consumption of alcohol—underpinned growing disparities in income, wealth, and the quality of welfare and other social services. The whole system was then legitimized by an ideology of racism promulgating a set of beliefs about biological inferiority which was then used to justify further suppression and exploitation.

Such an approach has been criticized from a variety of perspectives: some critics suggest that it posits an undifferentiated view of "natives" and "whites" that ignores important internal divisions in both categories; others claim that it plays down the active role of dominated groups in resisting oppression; still others that it privileges, if not reifies, spurious concepts like "race" and ignores class differences; and, finally, some argue that while it may be an appropriate way to characterize conditions on reserves or rural areas, it cannot adequately conceptualize the position of native peoples forced to participate in an industrial capitalist sector. Many of the criticisms come from scholars in the neo-Marxist or political economy tradition whose focus on classes and modes of production lead them to exaggerate the extent to which the internal colonial model necessarily ignores the economic dimension of exploitation (Wolpe 1975; Satzewich and Wotherspoon 1993). In addition, the concept of internal colonialism has been used to analyse some of the conflicts within Marxist states, such as those between Croatia, Serbia and other ethnonational units in the former Yugoslavia (Karlovic 1982; Vukovic 1987), although opinions varied widely on its applicability.

The internal colonial analogy was also employed in an attempt to explain the regional disparities found in many of the Western European states which were highlighted by the separatist movements that became increasingly salient in the 1970s. Hechter's study of the Celtic fringe in Great Britain was particularly seminal and stimulated attempts to apply the perspective by many other social scientists writing about societies as far apart as Alaska and Romania, Italy and Finland. In his original formulation of the thesis, Hechter had noted a close association between capitalist industrialization and the development

of ethnic separatist movements. Critics observed that many of the important nineteenth-century separatist movements in Eastern Europe had arisen prior to any significant capitalist penetration of largely rural areas; that capitalist exploitation and development has not always followed cultural cleavages; and that the theory did not easily account for the uneven incidence of separatist sentiments and, particularly, why they should arise in those regions that were "over-developed." Recognizing these shortcomings, Hechter and Levi (1979) proposed a modification to the original formulation of a hierarchical cultural division of labor that tended to promote what Hechter had called "reactive" group formation in internal colonies, peripheral regions largely excluded from the benefits of industrial development. However, in some situations where distinctive local institutions and a cultural elite managed to preserve a measure of autonomy, a different pattern often seemed to prevail. This typically produced a segmental dimension to the cultural division of labor, resulting in "interactive" group formation, a rather less politically unbalanced process found in societies like Scotland, Catalonia and the Basque country.

In this way, a more nuanced formulation of the variety of internal colonial experiences might more satisfactorily explain differential rates of ethnic mobilization. In addition, Hechter and Levi stressed the power of the state to respond to separatist challenges, as well as the impact of international politics which could lead one state actively to encourage a separatist movement in a hostile or competitive neighbour. This external state might prevent ethno-national insurgents from receiving outside support if the movement appeared to be potentially destabilizing for the region as a whole, or a possible threat to the state itself in the long run. The experience of the various Kurdish national movements is a classic example of the overwhelming importance of geo-strategic calculations by multiple state actors including Iran, Iraq, Turkey, and Syria, as well as the wider world community.

Such attempts to refine the theory of internal colonialism to account for the social roots of ethno-regional movements are necessary to explain why some social movements are aimed at achieving material benefits while others are much more concerned with cultural goals. It is also important to understand marked geographical disparities in ethno-national feelings—anomalies such as the contrast between significant ethnic mobilization in Brittany, but little in Normandy—to account for the different intensity of various movements, and the timing of ethno-national conflict. Hechter's subsequent focus on formulating theories of group solidarity based on rational choice assumptions, perhaps reflects the limitations and rather specific relevance of the internal colonial model. Nonetheless, it has proved to be a provocative analogy, even if it has not developed into a general theory of the origin and dynamics of ethno-nationalism.

### Bibliography

Blauner, Robert. 1969. "Internal colonialism and ghetto revolt," *Social Problems* 16: 393-408.

Boldt, Menno. 1981. "Social correlates of nationalism: a study of native Indian leaders in a Canadian internal colony," *Comparative Political Studies* 14, 2: 205-231.

Frideres, James. 1988. *Native Peoples in Canada*. Ontario: Prentice-Hall of Canada.

Glazer, Nathan. 1971. "Blacks and ethnic groups: the difference and the political difference it makes," *Social Problems* 18: 444-61.

Glazer, Nathan. 1997. *We Are All Multiculturalists Now*. Cambridge, MA: Harvard University Press.

Hechter, Michael. 1974. *Internal Colonialism: The Celtic Fringe in British National Development, 1536-1966*. London: Routledge & Kegan Paul.

Hechter, Michael and Margaret Levi. 1979. "A comparative analysis of ethnoregional movements," in *Internal Colonialism,* a special issue of *Ethnic and Racial Studies* 2, 3: 260-74.

Karlovic, N. L. 1982. "Internal colonialism in a Marxist society: the case of Croatia," *Ethnic and Racial Studies* 5, 3: 276-99.

Satzewich, Vic and Terry Wotherspoon. 1993. *First Nations: Race, Class and Gender Relations*. Toronto: Nelson.

Stone, John (ed.). 1979. *Internal Colonialism,* a special issue of *Ethnic and Racial Studies* 2, 3.

Vukovic, Branislav. 1987. "Neither internal colony nor external coloniser: a reply to Karlovic," *Ethnic and Racial Studies* 10, 1: 96-109.

Wolpe, Harold. 1975. "The theory of internal colonialism: the South African case" in I. Oxaal, T. Barnett & D. Booth (eds.), *Beyond the Sociology of Development*. London: Routledge & Kegan Paul.

Zureik, Elia. 1979. *Palestinians in Israel: A Study in Internal Colonialism*. London: Routledge & Kegan Paul.

John Stone and Susan Trencher

# The Invention of Tradition

Nationalism has been the subject of study of various disciplines including sociology, political science, anthropology and not least history. Among historians who have made a contribution to the study of nationalism, ERIC HOBSBAWM holds an outstanding position. Hobsbawm has written extensively on European history (1962; 1975; 1987; 1994), providing thus indispensable background material for sociologists who investigate the development of European nationalism. Moreover, in a recent book (1992), he examined the myths and realities of nations and nationalism in Europe since 1780. Nonetheless, his foremost contribution to the study of nationalism may be identified in his development of the concept of "invented traditions."

In his own words (Hobsbawm 1983a: 1), the term "is taken to mean a set of practices, normally governed by overtly or tacitly accepted rules and of a ritual or symbolic nature, which seek to inculcate certain values and norms of behaviour by repetition, which automatically implies continuity with the past." In other words, invented traditions are traditions which have been devised at a recent time to respond to new situations by means of appealing to a historic past and thus, through repetition, provide for a stable pattern of social relations in a changing reality. The link between invented traditions and a supposedly immemorial past is largely fictitious, however.

Such traditions must be distinguished from customs because the latter are more flexible than the former: their aim is to guarantee social continuity and mark any social change with the sanction of precedent. In this sense, customs, unlike invented traditions, cannot be invariant. Moreover, a distinction between tradition and convention or routine ought to be made. The latter consist of repetitive social practices whose scope is technical rather than ideological, and as such cannot fulfil the functions of tradition. Finally, invented traditions should be also distinguished from rules of games or other patterns of social interaction whose scope is to meet specific practical needs.

According to Hobsbawm (ibid.: 4–5), the invention of tradition occurs mostly in societies that undergo a period of rapid transformation during which old traditions no longer hold and, at the same time, old institutional carriers of such traditions are weakened or even eliminated. Under such circumstances, the formalization of new traditions is a strategy of adaptation of old uses in new conditions and may involve the use of old models for new purposes. Indeed, during the past 200 years, modernizing societies have often had to seek recourse to invented traditions in order to cope with rapid social change.

Invented traditions may consist of ancient materials assembled in a novel way and given a new meaning in order to serve novel purposes. In this case, we may talk of literally invented traditions, in that their continuity with the past is based either on fiction or on forgery. However, invented traditions may also serve in covering a break in social continuity by abridging antiquity with novel conditions and needs. Furthermore, "it may be suggested that where [traditions] are invented, it is often not because old ways are no longer available or viable, but because they are deliberately not used or adapted" (ibid.: 8).

Three types of invented traditions may be identified: (a) those establishing or symbolizing social cohesion or the membership of groups; (b) those establishing or legitimizing institutions, status or relations of authority and (c) those whose main purpose is socialization into a given system of beliefs, values, and conventions of behavior (ibid.: 9). In other words, invented traditions often offered the means of symbolizing inequality and led to specific socializations of different social groups in modern political communities of legal equals, where superior or inferior status could not be introduced directly.

The student of nationalism may however ask what the purpose of studying the invention of tradition is. Three main benefits have been identified by Hobsbawm (ibid.: 12): first, invented traditions are important indicators of social problems that might otherwise not be identified. They are evidence of developments which might have been difficult to follow though historical inquiry. Second, they cast light on the relationship between a society and its uses of history as a legitimator of action and the basis of social cohesion. Third and most important, invented traditions help us in analyzing the social engineering that takes place often in a deliberate and, however, always in an innovative way to bring about nationalism and its related phenomena: the nation-state, national symbols, historical pasts and myths of descent.

Having thus summarized the background and purposes of the invention of tradition as an analytical category, a number of examples of invented traditions will be presented in order to highlight their nature and functions as well as their proliferation during the past two centuries. In the volume edited by Hobsbawm and Ranger, Hugh Trevor-Roper (1983) investigates the emergence of Scottish traditions and their use in the Scottish nationalist movement. Through careful and detailed historical investigation, Trevor-Roper demonstrates that traditions that are today believed to be authentic and linked to the historical past of the Scottish nation are largely the product of invention through "usurpation of Irish culture and the re-writing of early Scottish history" (ibid.: 16), the artificial creation of supposedly genuine ancient traditions—for example, the kilt as the distinctive national costume and the specific tartans associated with Scottish clans—and, finally, the transfer of these traditions from the Highlands to Lowland Scotland and their adoption as the national tradition.

Prys Morgan (1983) sets out to analyze the course of Welsh nationalism and its invention of a romantic national mythology concentrating mainly on cultural matters and reconstructing the decaying and rapidly disappearing old way of life into a "new Welshness which would instruct, entertain, amuse and educate the people." By means of an historical analysis, Morgan shows how the decadence of the Welsh historical traditions was overcome through the rediscovery and reconstruction of the remote past of the Druids and the Celts. Moreover, he discusses how the mythical and romantic Wales, which had a healing effect by allowing the Welsh people to "forget" their immediate past and rediscover a new, more positive version of it in the arts and literature, was later replaced by the radical and non-conformist Wales, which suited better to the needs of a rapidly modernizing and developing society.

Another striking example of the role of invented traditions is that given by David Cannadine in his study of the role and meaning of the ritual and pageantry associated with the British monarchy, from the 1820s until the late 1970s. Cannadine argues that royal ceremonial should be seen in its context in order for its role to be correctly interpreted. Thus, he identifies four distinct historical periods in which royal ceremonial was developed and invented as a tradition. The first period, extending from the 1820s until the 1870s, was characterized by ineptly managed rituals performed within the context of a largely provincial, pre-industrial British society. During the second period (1877–1918), old royal rituals were improved and new ceremonies were consciously invented. Royal pageantry acquired thus a new meaning: "in an age of change, crisis and dislocation, the preservation of anachronism, the deliberate, ceremonial presentation of an impotent but venerated monarch as a unifying symbol of permanence and national community became both possible and necessary" (Cannadine 1983: 122). From 1918 until 1953, argues Cannadine, royal ritual became an invented tradition properly speaking, because it was taken as a distinctive feature of British tradition: the British were inclined to believe that they were good at it because they had always been. In other words, the royal ceremonial came again to symbolize continuity and stability in a period of unprecedented change. Finally, during the fourth and last period, which runs from Queen Elizabeth II's coronation until 1977, royal ritual acquired a new meaning, providing, as it were, a sort of compensation to the British for their loss of world-power status.

The role of a ritual idiom in representing authority and symbolizing stability and power is investigated by Bernard Cohn with regard to Victorian India. He investigates the construction by the British of a new ritual idiom by which their authority was to be represented to Indians and which came to substitute for traditional Indian ceremonial and ritual practices. This idiom was imposed in India through specific processes such as the formalization and rationalization of the Indian system of social hierarchy by means of ranking Indian royal titles, just like British titles were ranked in an orderly, linear manner; the institution of new royal orders following the English model and its feudal accoutrements; the reconstruction and standardization of the Indian cultural heritage according to what British experts thought it was worth preserving; and, finally, through the Royal Titles Act of 1876 and the Imperial Assemblage in 1877, by which the British ritual idiom was institutionalized in India:

> the main things which Lytton [viceroy and governor general] and his associates wanted to accomplish through the assemblage... was to represent the nature of British rule as they conceived it, and this was what the camp represented in their own ruling theory, order and discipline, which was in their ideology part of the whole system of colonial control. (Cohn 1983: 198)

The invention of tradition as a sociopolitical phenomenon can also be identified in colonial Africa (Ranger 1983). Here one may distinguish different types of invented traditions which played different roles. First, there was the invention of a gentlemanly tradition for European settlers, involving the creation of public schools and the redefinition of the social status of certain occupations so as to support their white elite status, despite their low social background in Europe. A second set of neo-traditions was related to the European invented traditions of command and subordination which were introduced into the colonial African context in order to ensure the voluntary obedience of the indigenous populations to the colonial authority. A number of specific subordination traditions are identified by Ranger (ibid.: 223): the hierarchy of the great house; the restructuring of the African armies following the European regimental tradition; the locally invented rituals in which British royal authority was invested; and the education of African youth following the public school tradition. A third set of invented traditions were the European neo-traditions incorporated into the African context and manipulated by locals to their own interest. Thus, titles and symbols of the European neo-traditional monarchy were used by local kings to gain authority. Moreover, educated Africans adopted European invented traditions and sometimes outdid colonial whites in their loyalty to the crown or in their involvement in churches, clubs and societies, striving to secure their position as members of "the nineteenth century British liberal universe" (ibid.: 238). Finally, Africans manipulated the traditions which the Europeans invented and defined as "African" in an effort to gain political advantages: "Africans wanted effective units of action just as officials wanted effective units of government. Europeans believed Africans belonged to tribes; Africans built tribes to belong to" (Iliffe cited in Ranger 1983: 252).

Hobsbawm (1983b) emphasizes that the invention of tradition took place within a changing society in which new methods of ruling and new forms of social cohesion were required. Invented traditions had a particular role to play in the political life of the nineteenth century in which nationwide politics were gradually established leading to the convergence of state, nation and society. He investigates the invention of mass-producing traditions on the part of the state in France, Germany and the United States and identifies similarities and differences between them (ibid.: 269–283). However, he also identifies traditions invented by organized mass movements, quite independently from state governments and chooses as an eloquent example of the politics of that period the socialist labor movements and the rituals, ceremonials and myths they created (e.g., May Day). Nonetheless, traditions were invented also by the emerging middle-bourgeois strata which sought thus to differentiate themselves from the working-class and the upper bourgeois elite. They created rituals, myths and patterns of social interaction which helped "establish an identity and a presence for the relatively large mass of those who neither belonged to the elite nor the masses" (ibid.: 291). In other words, the role of invented traditions in late nineteenth and early twentieth-century Europe can be analyzed at two levels: first, with regard to their contribution to nation formation and, second, with reference to their role in enhancing class divisions.

Despite the interesting overview of invented traditions provided by Hobsbawm and Ranger (1982), a number of related issues remains to be explored. These include the role of invented traditions as identifiers of national or class consciousness, their temporary character or their establishment as permanent ritual idioms and practices and, last but not least, the relationship between invention and spontaneous generation, namely the extent to which the invention of tradition can be manipulated (ibid.: 303–7).

## Bibliography

Cannadine, David. 1983. "The context, performance and meaning of ritual: the British monarchy and the "invention of tradition," c. 1820–1977," in E. Hobsbawm and T. Ranger (eds.), *The Invention of Tradition*. Cambridge: Cambridge University Press.

Cohn, Bernard S. 1983. "Representing authority in Victorian India," in E. Hobsbawm and T. Ranger (eds.), *The Invention of Tradition*. Cambridge: Cambridge University Press.

Hobsbawm, Eric. 1962. *The Age of Revolution: Europe, 1789–1848*. London: Weidenfeld and Nicolson.

Hobsbawm, Eric. 1975. *The Age of Capital, 1848–1875*. London: Weidenfeld and Nicolson.

Hobsbawm, Eric. 1983a. "Introduction: inventing traditions," in E. Hobsbawm and T. Ranger (eds.), *The Invention of Tradition*. Cambridge: Cambridge University Press.

Hobsbawm, Eric. 1983b. "Mass-producing traditions: Europe, 1870–1914," in E. Hobsbawm and T. Ranger (eds.), *The Invention of Tradition*. Cambridge: Cambridge University Press.

Hobsbawm, Eric. 1987. The Age of Empire 1875–1914. New York: Pantheon Books.

Hobsbawm, Eric. 1992 (2nd ed.). *Nations and Nationalism since 1780: Programme, Myth, Reality*. Cambridge: Cambridge University Press (first edition, 1990).

Hobsbawm, Eric. 1994. *Age of Extremes: The Short Twentieth Century 1914–1991*. London: Michael Joseph.

## The Invention of Tradition

Hobsbawm, Eric and Terence Ranger (eds.) 1983. *The Invention of Tradition*. Cambridge: Cambridge University Press.

Morgan, Prys. 1983. "From a death to a view: the hunt for the Welsh past in the Romantic Period," in E. Hobsbawm and T. Ranger (eds.), *The Invention of Tradition*. Cambridge: Cambridge University Press.

Ranger, Terence. 1983. "The invention of tradition in Colonial Africa," in E. Hobsbawm and T. Ranger (eds.), *The Invention of Tradition*. Cambridge: Cambridge University Press.

Trevor-Roper, Hugh. 1983. "The invention of tradition: the Highland tradition of Scotland," in E. Hobsbawm and T. Ranger (eds.), *The Invention of Tradition*. Cambridge: Cambridge University Press.

Anna Triandafyllidou

# J

## Jingoism

Jingoism is a term of opprobrium used by "peace-parties" to condemn what, from their point of view, are policies expressive of blustering and extravagant patriotism which advocate war.

The concept—based on a mild oath used by conjurors in the seventeenth century—is derived from the nickname "Jingo" given to supporters of Disraeli's dispatch of the British fleet to contain Russian expansionism in 1878. It was popularized by its use in a contemporary music-hall song: "We don't want to fight, yet by Jingo! if we do, We've got the ships, we've got the men, we've got the money too."

Situations of tension between states, especially where one or more of the states involved is sufficiently democratic and liberal to allow resistance to preparations for war, typically generate mutual accusations by opposed factions of "appeasement" on the one hand and "jingoism" on the other. Objective adjudication between the two cases is rarely possible without the benefit of hindsight.

Thus the appeasers of Hitler successfully maintained their criticism of Winston Churchill as a belligerent jingoist right through the 1930s and up until 1940, when Hitler's aggressive ambitions became undeniable. Again, Margaret Thatcher's resistance to the Argentinian junta's invasion of the Falkland Islands in 1982 was condemned in Britain as blatant jingoism before and during—but rarely after—the victorious British counter-attack.

The concept is largely restricted to the United Kingdom and the other English-speaking democracies, where the culture is so liberal as to legitimate criticisms of patriotism even in the most dangerous of military circumstances (Mercer 1986). However, *chauvinism*—now more commonly used to refer to excessive loyalty to gender rather than to nation—is a French near-equivalent, derived from the name of a Napoleonic veteran popularized in a play of 1831.

The phenomenon is common wherever freedom of expression is effectively institutionalized. Thus the peace-party of fifth-century Athens condemned Pericles' ambitions for the expansion of the city-state's influence in terms precisely echoed in the concept of jingoism, and was in turn accused of traitorous appeasement. Jingoism is currently the best—if clearly inadequate—concept available to define the fine line between patriotic loyalty and weak-kneed treachery. A more adequate appreciation of this important domain of the theory of nationalism awaits follow-up developments of the careful conceptual analysis of patriotism provided by Hastings (1997).

### Bibliography

Hastings, A. 1997. *The Construction of Nationhood: Ethnicity, Religion, and Nationalism.* Cambridge: Cambridge University Press.
Mercer, D. 1986. *The "Peace" of the Dead*. London: Policy Research Publications.

David Marsland

# K

## Kedourie, Elie (1926-1992)

Professor of politics at the London School of Economics from 1965 to 1990 and prolific writer on the politics and history of the Near and Middle East in the twentieth century, Elie Kedourie can be considered one of the foremost scholars who have contributed to the development of a critical study of nationalism in contemporary scholarship. He was born in Baghdad under the British mandate and was educated in local French and English language schools and was married there in 1950 to Sylvia Heim. In 1947 he went to study at the London School of Economics where he received his BSc. in economics. From 1950 to 1953 he was a senior scholar at St. Anthony's College, Oxford where he was initiated in the distinguished tradition of Middle East scholarship associated with that institution. In 1953 he was appointed to the faculty of the London School of Economics where he became Professor of Politics in 1965. In the teaching of the history of political thought he closely collaborated with Michael Oakeshott. Kedourie had a distinguished academic career which was marked by many visiting appointments in leading American, Australian, and Israeli universities and fellowships at prestigious institutes for advanced study. He was elected Fellow of the British Academy in 1975, appointed Commander of the British Empire in 1990, and awarded an honorary doctorate from Tel Aviv University in 1991. From 1964 onwards he played a leading academic role in the field of Middle East research as editor of the journal *Middle Eastern Studies* which he founded. His impact on scholarship, however, came through his many books, original research monographs, collections of articles, and anthologies. His outlook on the subject is most authoritatively conveyed in two monographs which have achieved the status of classics in the historiography of the Modern Middle East, *En-*

*gland and the Middle East* (1956) and *In the Anglo-Arab Labyrinth* (1976).

His interest in Middle Eastern history and politics naturally directed his attention to the major force shaping the destinies of the region in the contemporary period, nationalism. In the field of the study of nationalism Kedourie made a lasting contribution with the publication of the concise but dense monograph *Nationalism* (1960) and the anthology *Nationalism in Asia and Africa* (1971). His major accomplishment in the book *Nationalism* involved his removal of the study of nationalism from the rather simplistic intellectual history where HANS KOHN had left it and from the behaviorism with which Karl Deutsch had attempted to connect it (see COMMUNICATIONS THEORIES OF NATIONALISM). Kedourie gave a new direction to the subject by turning it into a part of social and political philosophy. That he himself had intended his project to be philosophical rather than political or historical—*prima facie* paradoxically so since the rest of his work is primarily concerned with political and diplomatic history—is made clear by one characteristic fact: among the issues raised by the criticism of *Nationalism* the only one to which he chose to respond in the "Afterword" to the revised edition (1985), concerned his interpretation of Kant whose philosophy of self-determination Kedourie considers the philosophical source of modern nationalism. The connection of Kant, the philosopher of Enlightenment universalism *par excellence*, with the philosophical origin of nationalism is Kedourie's distinct contribution to the study of the doctrine. Yet, he is careful to distinguish between, on the one hand, Kant's philosophical position and his understanding of self-determination as a necessary corollary of individual moral autonomy, and, on the other, the ideological uses to which this view was put by nationalist intellectuals in Germany and elsewhere. Methodologically, *Nationalism* is an essay in the history of ideas in the A. O.

Lovejoy mould and this reveals Kedourie's deeper Crocean belief that all philosophy is essentially historical. At the core of *Nationalism* is the dialectic between the two conceptions of the nation held by Kant and Fichte—or more simply the uses of Kant's ideas by Fichte.

The philosophical dimension of the book singled it out in the professional literature and it was certainly its philosophical reflectiveness which marked it with a deep, yet restrained and often delightfully understated, critical tenor. Kedourie sets before his reader an interpretative study of nationalism as social philosophy and yet through the lines of his interpretation flows an undercurrent of criticism which is difficult to miss. Indeed, in order fully to appreciate Kedourie's analysis of nationalism the reader must be aware of the gradual development of Kedourie's thinking on history and politics which reaches its climax in this book. Failure to appreciate this wider framework leads to a misunderstanding of the significance of this book. Furthermore, Kedourie's views on nationalism can be fully understood and appreciated in the light of such other writings on the Middle East such as his monograph on *Afghani and 'Abduh: An Essay on Religious Unbelief and Political Activism in Modern Islam* (1966) or the essays "Minorities" (1952) and "Religion and Politics," both included in the collection *The Chatham House Version and Other Middle Eastern Studies* (1970, reprinted 1984). These studies of the intellectual and ethical character of nationalism as manifested in concrete historical contexts, reveal the deeper antinomies and moral dubiousness associated with it and can explain Kedourie's critical perspective.

Kedourie's deeper philosophical interests are revealed in his posthumously published lectures on *Hegel and Marx* (1995). This work reveals yet another dimension of the theoretical framework that Kedourie brought to the consideration of nationalism as part of a tragic human predicament, inexorably tied to the culture and moral temper of modernity.

### Bibliography

Kedourie, Elie. 1985 (1960). *Nationalism*. London: Hutchinson.

Kedourie, Elie. 1984 (1970). *The Chatham House Version and Other Middle Eastern Studies*. Hanover: University Press of New England.

Sylvia Kedourie (ed.). 1998. *Elie Kedourie CBE, FBA 1926-1992: History, Philosophy, Politics*. London: Frank Cass.

Paschalis. M. Kitromilides

# Kin Selection

The concept of kin selection was first worked out in quantifiable form by W.D. Hamilton (1964) in a long article generally accepted as the main theoretical foundation of the paradigm shift in ethology generally called "sociobiology" (after the classic 1975 E.O. Wilson book), or, more recently "behavioral ecology," for those who want to avoid the political controversies associated with the term "sociobiology." The idea of kin selection remained arcane to social scientists until the publication of Wilson's 1975 compendium, R. Dawkins' popularized account, *The Selfish Gene* (1976), and others that quickly followed (e.g., D. Barash 1977, 1979).

The theoretical conundrum of biology was how to explain the apparent altruism of some organisms, assumed by classical Darwinian natural selection theory to promote their self-interest. "Group selectionist" explanations (e.g., Wynne Edwards 1962) were long accepted, namely that organisms could be self-sacrificing "for the good of the group," or even "of the species." Sociobiology provided a more parsimonious and reductionist explanation, namely that the main unit of natural selection was ultimately the gene, and not the organism. An organism is merely a temporary assemblage of genes, programmed by these genes to reproduce successfully, not so much the organisms themselves, but copies of their constituent genes. An organism, (especially a diploid one, which can only pass on half of its genome to its offspring) is merely a gene's way of replicating itself in the next generation.

Consequently, the most successful genetic programme is one which predisposes an organism, not to be ruthlessly selfish at the organismic level (e.g., by eating its children for breakfast), but to behave nepotistically. What looks like altruism at the level of the organism (e.g., the sui-

## Kin Selection

cidal bee sting) is easily reducible to ultimate genetic selfishness. Hamilton's (1964) formula, which neatly predicts such apparent altruism, is:

$$K > \frac{1}{r}$$

where K is the ratio of benefits accruing to the recipient of such apparent altruism to costs to the seeming altruist, and where r is the coefficient of relatedness, that is, the proportion of genes shared by common descent between "altruist" and recipient. (In sexually reproducing, diploid species, the coefficient of relatedness is exactly 1/2 between parent and offspring, on average 1/2 between full siblings, 1/4 between grand-parents and grandchildren, half-siblings, parents' offspring and parents' siblings; 1/8 between offspring of siblings, and so on.)

Put in common language, social organisms can be expected to "select kin," that is, to behave beneficently toward genetically related organisms, graduating their beneficence by degree of relationship, but only insofar as the cost of such beneficence to themselves is smaller than the benefits to kin, adjusted by degree of relationship. Thus, my sibling must get more than twice as many benefits from my "altruism" as it costs me, because we only share half of our genes. A first cousin with whom I only share 1/8 of my genes by common descent, must receive more than eight times as many benefits as my largesse costs me for my genes to be ahead of the game of pursuing their self-interest.

The ultimate measure of biological success is, of course, *reproductive* success, what biologists call "fitness," since the process of natural selection is driven by *differential* reproduction between organisms. Organisms are programmed to behave in ways conducive to their own reproduction first, but their *genes* will maximize *their* fitness best if organisms are also programmed selectively to help kin reproduce. If, say, I am sterile (as nearly all females in tens of thousands of species of social insects such as termites, bees, ants and wasps are), I can expect to do my best to help my mother and my siblings reproduce.

This simple model of kin selection or nepotism has successfully explained and predicted much animal sociality in thousands of species covering the entire phylogenetic spectrum from invertebrates to birds and mammals. (Alexander 1979; Barash 1977; Daly and Wilson 1978; Symons 1979; Wilson 1975). Although human sociality exceeds in complexity that of other species, its underlying basis in kin selection is identical. Social scientists cannot afford to continue ignoring the biological roots of human sociality, however much they delight in the diversity of social arrangements in our devilishly complex species. True, kinship for humans is socially constructed, and often extends beyond biological relationships. Indeed, we inject a social construction into everything we do or say. But no human society has ever successfully *ignored* biology (van den Berghe 1979). The few that tried, either quickly had to change their tune, or did not exist long enough to tell their disembodied tale.

### Bibliography

Alexander, R. 1979. *Darwinism and Human Affairs.* Seattle: University of Washington Press.

Barash, D. P. 1977. *Sociobiology and Behavior.* New York: Elsevier.

Barash, D. P. 1979. *The Whisperings Within.* New York: Harper and Row.

Daly, M., and Wilson, M. 1978. *Sex, Evolution and Behavior.* North Scituate, MA.: Duxbury.

Dawkins, R. 1976. *The Selfish Gene.* Oxford: Oxford University Press.

Hamilton, W. D. 1964. "The Genetical Evolution of Social Behaviour," *Journal of Theoretical Biology* 7: 1-52.

Symons, D. 1979. *The Evolution of Human Sexuality.* Oxford: Oxford University Press.

van den Berghe, P. L. 1979. *Human Family Systems.* Westport, CT: Greenwood Press.

Wilson, E. 0. 1975. *Sociobiology:The New Synthesis.* Cambridge, MA: Harvard University Press.

Wynne Edwards, V. C. 1962. *Animal Dispersion in Relation to Social Behavior.* New York: Hafner.

Pierre L. van den Berghe

# L

## Language and Nation

There are three important matters to be discussed here—language, nation and the relationship between them—and each possesses a large and complex literature. A large literature, because each has an importance that extends well beyond the academic cloister; a complex one, because definitional problems abound, because vital concepts continue to be argued over, and because language and nation are often invoked and discussed in heavily value-laden ways. They are the stuff of "blood and belonging," to cite the title of a recent popular treatment of nationalism.

What is a language? One approach is to consider what objective characteristics languages are seen to possess, how they differ from other varieties of communication (dialects, for example) and—most importantly, for present purposes—their symbolic or subjective value.

There have, of course, been many more or less objective definitions offered of language; a recent composite definition suggested that

> the essence of human language is a communication system composed of arbitrary symbols which possess an agreed-upon significance within a community. Further, these symbols are independent of immediate context, and are connected in rule-governed ways (Edwards 1994: 19).

Without going into too much detail, one can see that the "symbols" here are words or other meaningful utterances, that we can use them to discuss things not immediately present, and that it is a language's grammar which provides the rule-book—essential, of course, for an infinite creativity based upon a finite number of constituents. Different languages vary one from another, then, in that the communicative elements they use differ, as do their grammars; that is to say, different language communities have evolved different sets of "agreements" about which sounds, and combinations of sounds, are to be meaningful—this is

why the word "arbitrary" appears in the definition above.

Languages are often said to be mutually unintelligible communication systems, unlike dialects. These are sub-varieties within a given language, which possess distinctive vocabulary, grammar and pronunciation (accent) features—but which are not so markedly different from each other that mutual intelligibility is lost. It is readily apparent, however, that the criterion of *intelligibility* is not perfect. For example, most people have come across dialects of their own language that are virtually impossible to understand. Or, consider a continuum of (say) four geographically-based dialects: speakers of A can easily understand B, can just about follow C, but cannot comprehend D. If we took dialects B and C out of the picture, as it were, could we then consider A and D as separate languages?

If dialects are supposed to be mutually intelligible (if, occasionally, with some difficulty), but sometimes are not, it is also the case that supposedly mutually unintelligible languages can sometimes be understood by each other's speech communities. Here, we see that the dominance of political concerns over purely linguistic ones dictate that Norwegian and Danish, Serbian and Croatian, Hindi and Urdu, Flemish and Dutch, and so on, are to be seen as separate languages. We also see in such cases a clear demonstration of the symbolic value that languages can possess for the identities of speech communities, of the important linguistic element in ethnicity and nationalism. In this sense, Max Weinreich's famous observation—that a language is a dialect that has an army and navy—often proves more important than anything else. We should also remember that distinctions between languages and dialects are essentially of a temporal nature: French, Italian, Romanian, Portuguese, and Spanish all began their lives as dialects of vulgar Latin. The central point here, then, is that any linguistic variety—

**169**

language or dialect (or, indeed, accent)—is at least potentially a carrier of group identity and, therefore, of powerful symbolic value.

How can we best understand group identity? As with language, there are many definitions of ethnic and NATIONAL IDENTITY, many debates over distinctions between the two, and many arguments about the birth and growth of each. (Readers will no doubt discover a great deal about these matters elsewhere in this book.) If we first consider ethnic identity, a working definition could run as follows:

> Ethnic identity is allegiance to a group—large or small, socially dominant or subordinate—with which one has ancestral links. There is no necessity for a continuation, over generations, of the same socialization or cultural patterns, but some sense of a group boundary must persist. This can be sustained by shared objective characteristics (language, religion, etc.), or by more subjective contributions to a sense of 'groupness', or by some combination of both. (Edwards 1994: 128)

This definition draws particular attention to these assertions: (1) that *everyone* is a member of an ethnic group (i.e., ethnicity is not something associated only with small or powerless minority groups); (2) that a sense of identity rests upon subjective understanding as well as upon more objective "markers"; (3) that the continuation of group identity (which is, after all, but another way of talking about the preservation of culture and tradition) is more a matter of *boundary* maintenance than anything else. This last point is based particularly upon the influential work of FREDRICK BARTH (1969), whose reasoning was that the cultural "stuff" which boundaries enclose may change, but the group boundaries themselves can survive. This is clearly of importance in understanding the sense of ethnic continuity which connects (for example) first-generation and fourth-generation immigrants in a country like the United States: obviously, the cultural content within perceived ethnic boundaries is eminently mutable; or, to put it another way, different cultural markers can, at different times, act as boundary supports. For example, the loss of an original group language and the adoption of another variety represent a change in cultural content, but they do not necessarily signal the disappearance of

boundaries. Other supporting markers, tangible or psychological, may assume greater relevance in group definition; the new language may itself come to possess ethnic-marker status (particularly if it is used in a way distinctive of the group); the original language may retain a powerful symbolic status (indeed, in some cases this symbolic value may be reinforced by the loss of the communicative and instrumental roles); and so on.

Nationalism, like ETHNICITY, is essentially a manifestation of group identity; the main difference between the two is one of scale. Nationalism is ethnicity writ large, in which the desire for political autonomy, for self-government, is added to the belief in shared characteristics. As with ethnicity, national group boundaries can be supported by a variety of objective and subjective "markers," but many have seen the linguistic criterion as the most important way of delineating nations. Given the relationship between ethnicity and nationalism, and given what has already been said here about boundary maintenance, it is clear that a distinctive language is not, in fact, an essential requirement for national identity. This does not, however, alter the fact that it is often seen as *the* pillar of groupness.

It was JOHANN GOTTFRIED HERDER (1744–1803) who initially made this point most forcefully, in modern times at least, and it is to Herder that language revivalists and other linguistic nationalists often still appeal. Speech communities, according to Herder, survive as discrete entities only as long as they preserve their language. In post-Enlightenment romanticism, the group's language was viewed as "its collective treasure," the touchstone of its spiritual existence. "Has a nation," asked Herder, "anything more precious than the language of its fathers?"

Studies of Herder suggest that the philosopher was nationalistic without being chauvinistic, that he claimed that "ours is ours" and not "ours is best," that he did not fall prey to what might be called the excesses of nationalism. It is certainly true that Herder was less strident than some of his followers—notably JOHANN GOTTLIEB FICHTE—but he was quite capable of national prejudice; he told Germans, for instance, to "spew out the ugly slime of the Seine." The interesting point here is that Herder himself, the high priest of Cultural and linguistic nationalism, could exemplify the dark face of the phenomenon. That is, while logic does not require that nationalist fellow-feeling be accompanied by a disdain for others outside the group, most historical (and, indeed, contemporary) examples of the former show all too much evidence of the latter (see Edwards 1985 for a more detailed discussion).

In any event, Herder's influence on modern nationalism has been considerable, and Anthony D. Smith summarized it as follows: "The notion that nations are really language groups, and therefore that nationalism is a linguistic movement, derives from Herder's influence" (Smith 1971: 182). In fact, the strength of the commonly held linkage between language and nationalism is such that it has emerged, in many contexts, in epigrammatic form. Consider these sorts of statements:

"Language is the spiritual exhalation of the nation" (Wilhelm von Humboldt 1797).

"A people without a language of its own is only half nation" (Thomas Davis 1843).

"The care of the national language is at all times a sacred trust" (Friedrich von Schlegel 1815).

As well, even more motto-like equations have been made between language and nation. Thus

"Sluagh gun chanain, sluagh gun anam" (Gaelic: "A people without its language is a people without its soul").

"Hep brezhoneg, breizh ebet" ("Without Breton there is no Brittany").

"Gyn chengey, gyn cheer" (Manx: "No language, no country").

It is interesting to consider just *why* there should be such a strong popular association between language and national identity. The first reason—and the one that is naturally cited by nationalists themselves—is simply that, as the expressions above suggest, the ancestral group language is *necessary* for a continuing identity. We have already seen that theoretical work (like that of Barth) implies that the only necessity here is that of boundary maintenance, and that the cultural "stuff" which is contained within the group

borders, and which sustains them, is mutable. Beyond that—and beyond the transgenerational maintenance of ethnic identity (in immigrant settings, for example) which such work explains—we also have, at the level of nationalism, actual evidence that possession of the original group language is not always required for a strong and unique identity. The Irish (and other Celtic peoples) and the Austrians, for example, can lay claim to a distinctive national identity, but its linguistic component is shared with other nations (although locally contextualized at the levels of dialect and accent). None of this denies, of course, that continued possession of the ancestral variety is a strong national marker—the point is, rather, that a shift away from that variety, or the "shared" use of a variety, does not necessarily herald a broader assimilation.

Other arguments for a strong language-identity linkage include the symbolic power of an ancestral variety as a nationalistic rallying point, the obvious visibility of a language (as opposed, say, to what may be a psychologically real but intangible sense of belonging), the view that different languages imply different conceptions of the world, and the link to history, to tradition, to culture, which continuation of the original language facilitates. It is important to realize that—as with other ethnic or national markers—an emphasis upon language often *follows* the development of nationalistic awareness; it does not necessarily suggest or create it. (This is in line with modern conceptions of ethnic group and nation as, above all, psychological entities—IMAGINED COMMUNITIES, as Benedict Anderson [1983] has observed.) To cite Smith once more: "Linguistic studies, like historical, become an often unselfconscious means of justifying their prior nationalist conviction—to themselves as well as others ... nationalist movements, therefore, even in Europe, are not linguistic movements" (Smith 1971: 149).

Indeed, the power of nationalism per se—and not just of its linguistic elements—provides an excellent example of what is, perhaps, the single major contribution of psychology to human understanding: our *perceptions* of what is or was, or what ought to be, or what might be, are much more important than anything else. While RENAN

## Language and Nation

(1882/1947), in his famous "*Qu'est-ce qu'une nation?*," was able to note (in a manner foreshadowing the observations of Anderson) that "une nation est une âme, un principe spirituel ... la possession en commun d'un riche legs de souvenirs" (p. 903), he also felt obliged to touch upon historical selectivity: "l'essence d'une nation est que tous les individus aient beaucoup de choses en commun, et aussi que tous aient oublié bien des choses" (1892).

Drawing upon the simple (and often simplistic) linkage between language and national identity, we can better understand important linguistic and socio-linguistic phenomena. Given, for example, a passionate belief in the central importance of the ancestral variety, it is not difficult to understand the depth of commitment to *language maintenance*, nor the dismay over *language shift*. That is, we can now see that what is being protected is not simply a particular means of communication—an instrument—but also a symbolic system which connects child to mother and individual to group, which is the unique and precious transmitter of culture and tradition, which—in fact—embodies a community's "hoarded dreams" (see below) and its own unique sense of the *logos*, the *Word*. (The connection between language and religion is deliberate here, reflecting an historically powerful alliance.) Even more poignant, perhaps—for obvious reasons—are the feelings associated with attempts at *language revival* (see Edwards 1994).

As well, we can more easily comprehend the activities of institutions charged with language protection or purification—language academies, for example, such as the Académie française (Paris), the Accademia della Crusca (Florence), or the Real Academia Española (Madrid)—if we appreciate the potency of the language-identity relationship. After all, given the passionate belief noted above, what could be more natural than the desire to keep the linguistic wellspring undefiled, to reject foreign-language interference, to standardize and elaborate one's own variety? The most important aspect of the language academy, then, is not a *linguistic* one—it is, rather, *psychological* or *sociological*, and reflects underlying concerns for maintaining in some desired form the language which is, itself,

seen to be an essential component of the nation's collective identity.

Finally here, an awareness of the allegedly central connection of language to nationalism helps in understanding the ambivalence over translation—a necessary exercise, no doubt, but also a worrying one. As George Steiner pointed out in his *After Babel* (1975/1992), "there is in every act of translation ... a touch of treason. Hoarded dreams, patents of life are being taken across the frontier" (p. 233). The old Italian proverb is blunter: *traduttori, traditori*. Translation is the revealing of deep matters to others outside the group, and the translator—the one whose multilingual facility permits the straddling of boundaries—is a type of quisling. Many writers (including Wittgenstein in the *Tractatus*) have referred to the importance of language as a concealing, disguising medium co-existing with, and perhaps surpassing, its more obvious communicative role. As well, the construction of fictionalized myths, legends and stories is both important for internal group coherence and threatened by translation. One modern manifestation here is the "appropriation" of native stories by outsiders, for in many cultures—particularly ones with powerful and rich oral traditions—stories *belong* to the group or, indeed, to some designated story-teller.

All of these aspects of language are, as noted, better understood if we appreciate the links between language and nation. In addition, they illustrate and help to explain those very links.

It is unlikely, for the reasons noted above, that the common perception of language as the principal bulwark of the nation will change—until, that is, the conception of the nation itself alters. If, for example, we embraced the idea of so-called *civic nationalism*, and gradually de-emphasized *ETHNIC NATIONALISM*, then the centrality of language to "groupness" could lessen. However, civic nationalism seems little more than citizenship renamed, and a strong argument can be made that ethnic nationalism is, in fact, the only kind. And, if we move beyond the academic cloisters where such debates occur, we see that there is—for better or worse—plenty of life left in nationalism as it is historically understood. This means, in turn, that the language-nation linkage continues to thrive.

Contact and conflict between "small" languages and large ones are, however, also continuing and—particularly where English is involved—languages and their speakers are facing unprecedented pressures. This poses very obvious problems for those who associate language shift with loss of national identity. If, as some contemporary linguists believe, many existing languages are now virtually doomed to extinction (in any normal communicative sense, at least), then the outlook for that diversity of group identity which has so enriched the world is indeed gloomy. On the other hand, if the point made in this article—that identity boundaries can survive cultural alteration within them—has any validity, then the picture is not quite so dark.

### Bibliography

Anderson, B. 1983. *Imagined Communities: Reflections on the Origin and Growth of Nationalism.* London: Verso.

Barth, F. 1969. *Ethnic Groups and Boundaries.* Boston: Little Brown.

Edwards, J. 1985. *Language, Society and Identity.* Oxford: Blackwell.

Edwards, J. 1994. *Multilingualism.* London: Routledge.

Renan, E. 1882/1947. "Qu'est-ce qu'une nation?" in H. Psichari (ed.), *Oeuvres complètes de Ernest Renan.* Paris: Calmann-Lévy.

Smith, A. D. 1971. *Theories of Nationalism.* London: Duckworth.

Steiner, G. 1975/1992. *After Babel: Aspects of Language and Translation.* Oxford: Oxford University Press.

John Edwards

# Liberalism and Nationalism

The philosophical connection between liberalism and nationalism goes back to the work of JOHN STUART MILL. Mill was perfectly consistent in praising both diversity and homogeneity. For if disagreement is not to get out of hand, regulative rules of the game are absolutely necessary; differently put, the deepest bonds are needed if we are to change fundamental values peacefully. Whilst most of the details of the homogeneity that Mill as social engineer demanded—sobriety, endorsement of the laws of political economy,

altruism—are not relevant here, one central claim does matter. Mill insisted in *Considerations on Representative Government* that "it is a necessary condition of free institutions, that the boundaries of governments should coincide in the main with those of nationalities" (Mill 1960: 384). But this raises a serious problem. ETHNIC NATIONALISM's search for social homogeneity scarcely looks liberal. Purportedly morally superior civic nationalism, where choice replaces blood so as at least to allow the possibility of integration, may well be no better: both American and French revolutionary nationalisms brutally assailed minorities and expelled their enemies. Of course, these considerations in a sense make Mill's point: it is the initial absence of a settled frame which seems to debilitate liberalism. Still, how homogenous need we be in national terms? Must we agree about everything? Or is it possible to imagine a civil nationalism, allowing for the recognition of diversity within a more neutral frame?

One way of stressing the urgency of the last question is to note the entirely honorable split that developed within the thought of the late ERNEST GELLNER. The descriptive sociology of this great scholar insisted that the industrial mode of production of modernity demands national homogeneity (Gellner 1983). But Gellner's own background made him well aware that homogeneity can often only be achieved brutally, by mass population transfer, forced integration, ethnic cleansing, and genocide, making it all too possible that the postcommunist world will face a repeat of the type of politics that dominated the "new Europe" created at Versailles. This is most certainly not what Gellner wanted, and he accordingly came to stress the need for political centralization in tandem with varied national cultural flourishings (Gellner 1994: chapter 6). But this hope goes against his analysis: it demands something like Austro-Hungary whose fated demise is the base of his descriptive theory.

What seems to matter most of all in the first creation of nations is not industrialization but state competition. As the social reach and financial burden of war intensifies, so does national homogenization. It is in the administrative and fiscal interests of a state to have a single *lingua*

**173**

*franca,* and to these ends a language is selected and endorsed—and injunctions often issued against any continuing use of alternates. Coercion is not, however, everything: adaptation to an official language brings the benefits of law, whilst its use in any case initially only concerns the few (Laitin 1992: chapter 1).

Relations between geopolitics and nationalism have continued to matter a very great deal, not surprisingly since modernity comprises states as much as industry. But the form of the state has as much sociological impact as does its sheer presence. Hitler's Germany and Milosevic's Serbia have suggested an absolute equation of nationalism with viciousness. But the earliest nationalist leaders were equally involved in struggles for popular representation, not surprisingly given that eighteenth-century geopolitical-national struggles occasioned very significant increases in taxation. Still more important in the context of this essay is the reverse, that is, the way in which the liberalism of a regime impacts upon national sentiment. This crucial consideration is best approached by first examining what happens in the absence of liberalism, before then noting the way in which its presence affects the character of nationalist politics.

France and Britain, and to a lesser extent Spain, sought to increase their powers by means of societal rationalization. But dynastic extension was an alternative to bureaucratic intensification. Thus, composite monarchies were aggregations, with rulers promising to obey rather than to change the customs of distinct areas (Koenigsberger 1991). The presence of historic rights of this sort underpinned famous aristocratic revolts, notably those in the United Provinces in the late sixteenth century and in Hungary in the mid-nineteenth century. But where revolts did not take place, imperial but composite *anciens régimes* continued to dominate a set of societies, often themselves made hugely diverse both as the result of nomadic pasts and imperial policies. How did the composite empires manage when they were faced in the nineteenth century with the need to modernize?

The most interesting case is that of the HABSBURG empire, the territory of classical separatist nationalism. The phenomenology of the

movements is often understood in terms offered by Hroch (1985), according to whom everything is played out in a three stage movement—from folklorists to intellectuals to a mass movement seeking its own state. Gellner describes substantially similar processes, especially in his brilliant mythic history of the Ruritanians of Megalomania (1983: 58-62), stressing that nationalism is caused by the unevenness of industrialism, that is, that the most powerful social mobilization results from the interaction of social inequality and cultural marker.

There is truth to this interpretation, not least for Bohemia on whose experience both authors draw. Certainly, industrialization provided the conditions, most obviously that of mass schooling, in which national awareness could spread just as it created issues on which it could feed. Still, the wholly socioeconomic nature of this account is open to question, as thereby is the classical definition of nationalism in terms of "one nation, one state." Most immediately, the move from cultural to political nationalism occurred when Vienna insisted on imposing German as the official language of state. When this was rescinded, most of the peoples of the empire sought their historic rights rather than separation. Differently put, as long as reform within the empire was possible, the preservation of national identity within the empire remained attractive: the presence of voice undermined the option of exit (Hirschman 1970). In a nutshell, nationalism looks as if it is best explained in political terms.

The nationalities problem was never solved by the Austrian monarchy because it was not prepared to stick to a liberal line. It remained an empire, whose concern with geopolitical glory and territorial aggrandizement led it to avoid federal and consociational arrangements. Even so, the nationalities did not break up the empire; rather, they occupied the vacuum created by defeat in war. But the "new Europe" created at Versailles failed. The principle of national self-determination did not bring peace, as Wilson had expected, since the newly independent states sought to deal with their own minorities by means of the crudest nationalising practices. Forcible homogenization of this sort fuelled irredentist passions and helped ensure geopolitical disaster (Brubaker 1996).

Quite obviously, one of the key questions of *our* "new Europe" is the extent to which this disaster will be repeated. Despite the horrors of the Balkans, limited optimism is possible. For one thing, several countries have become homogeneous, thanks to the actions of Hitler and Stalin. For another, the amount of bloodshed following from the collapse of the Soviet Union has been surprisingly limited. Inside Russia many agreements with nationalities have been brokered, and these have allowed national identities to be preserved without secession. If the treatment accorded to the Volga Tatars had been offered to the Chechens, they might not have sought separation. *Pace* Gellner, the best formula seems to be genuine liberalism, that is, the devolution of powers more weighty than the cultural: if this means letting some secede, it remains the most likely way to ensure territorial continuity—a point much reinforced by considering the nationalist revivals of the advanced West.

The most prominent neo-nationalisms have been those of the Catalans and Basques, the Walloons, the Bretons, the Scots, the Quebecois, and the Lombard League. Their demands are often interpreted in economistic terms, as the desire of, mostly, rich regions to hold on to revenues that redistributive states seek to take from them. There *is* some truth to economistic considerations: secessionist leaders have to demonstrate that independence will not lead to penury, and this normally entails free trade attitudes that are the exact opposite of interwar nationalism—that is, a desire to remain part of the single market, whether of Europe or of North America. Nonetheless, a political account has greater explanatory power. It seems perfectly possible for states to make deals, federalist and consociational in character, with national minorities, as has occurred in post-Franco Spain. It is the absence of such political openings that underwrites separatist nationalism. For example, support for Quebecois nationalism has fluctuated in conjunction with political events, peaking during conscription crises and as the result of "the slap in the face" received when the rest of Canada refused to endorse the Meech Lake Accord. But cases such as Quebec and, also Scotland, are exceptions. Geopolitical calm has allowed most states to devolve powers, and thereby to assuage national sentiment. And any secession

would not matter much given the generalized desire to remain part of a larger system, something which ensures in the European case protection for minority rights.

It is worth noting that Gellner's position allows for an interesting objection to be raised against the central claim that has been made, namely that liberalism helps contain nationalism—or, differently put, that multinational states are viable. Gellner's emphasis on nationalism as the result of the combination of social inequality and cultural marker leads naturally to the hope that something of its bite will be lost within settled industrial society (Gellner 1983: ch. 8). Amongst the rich, Gellner seems to be saying, some degree of diversity may indeed be possible since politics no longer have an all-or-nothing quality. But what is possible in Canada or Great Britain may have no meaning in Rwanda or Burundi.

In the functionalist view of nationalism, present in Gellner's account, homogeneity is necessary for industrial society. It may be well true that the prior possession of homogeneity lends advantage. But there is everything to be said against the view that forcible nationalising practices help industrialism. Attempts to homogenize African societies have led to civil wars, to the export of refugees, many of them talented, rather than that of products. Given that forced homogenization is now likely to breed ferocious reactions, the better part of wisdom may be to seek development by means of diversity.

The argument can best be summarized by returning to John Stuart Mill. There is some justification to his insistence that liberalism flourishes most easily when there is no problem of nationality, although it should always be remembered that many homogeneous societies are not at all liberal. Homogeneity can further be seen as an aid to—that is, in Gellner's sense, functional for—economic growth. But certain conclusions do not follow from this. One is that the cause of nationalism is not to be found in industrialization per se. To the contrary, nationalism is often directed against authoritarianism—making it possible that liberalism can contain secessionist demands and that it can do so even in poorer countries. Secondly, processes of state and NATION-BUILDING in the modern world are fundamentally different from those of the past. Homogenization in the past could be slow, and relatively pacific. In modern circumstances, homogenization is likely to be very violent, in largest part because mass education has ensured that nations have attained consciousness. Whilst such violence can be seen in the contemporary world, there is equally evidence of an alternative policy option at work in which cohesion is sought by means of a shared liberal frame within which difference can exist.

## Bibliography

Brubaker, Rogers. 1996. *Nationalism Reframed.* Cambridge: Cambridge University Press.

Gellner, Ernest. 1983. *Nations and Nationalism.* Oxford: Blackwell.

Gellner, Ernest. 1994. *Encounters with Nationalism.* Oxford: Blackwell.

Hirschman, Albert. 1970. *Exit, Voice and Loyalty.* Cambridge, MA: Harvard University Press.

Hroch, Miroslav. 1985. *Social Preconditions of National Revival in Europe.* Cambridge: Cambridge University Press.

Koenigsberger, Hans. 1991. "Composite monarchies, representative institutions and the American Revolution," *Journal of Historical Research* 62, 148: 135-53.

Laitin, David. 1992. *Language Repertoires and State Construction in Africa,* Cambridge: Cambridge University Press.

Mill, John Stuart. 1960. *Three Essays.* Oxford: Oxford University Press.

John A. Hall

# M

## Melting Pot

Melting pot describes a model of ethnic relations in which a nation-state's constituent ethnic groups engage in a process of reciprocal fusion. This can take either of two forms: (1) all ethnic groups acculturate to a universalistic set of values and symbols with no ancestral connotations, or (2) there is two-way influence between ethnic groups in the society such that no ancestral group achieves symbolic dominance.

The melting pot process should not be confused with one-way assimilation to an ethnic core. In effect, its *telos* admits of no less than a fusion of all the groups known to mankind through "democratic association," Talcott Parsons' highest evolutionary universal (Parsons 1964: 353–56). The agent of dissolution of ethnic bonds is typically liberal individualism, although the socialist melting pot of Soviet Man would qualify as would the melting process that occurred within religious sects like the Druze (during their dynamic phase) and the Mormons (Rasiak 1980: 161; Smith 1986: 111–12). In addition, periods of ethnic fusion and fluidity—such as those which preceded the emergence of the Mestizos, Japanese, Central Asian Turks or English, may be classified as instances of the melting phenomenon (Akiner 1997).

With regard to empires, the usual pattern is ethnic hierarchy, though some Imperial civilizations, like the Assyrian or late Roman, appear to have been more universalistic, and hence more similar to the ideal-type of the melting pot. Finally, religious civilizations like Christendom or the Dar-ul-Islam may also be considered melting-pots, albeit at the elite level (Smith 1990: 4).

The term "melting pot" was first introduced in 1908 in a popular play by Israel Zangwill, a British Jew. Zangwill, a confirmed internationalist, worked with the International Territorial Association to resettle Russian Jews in the United States. His ideas were in turn shaped by the internationalist Jewish thinking of the late nineteenth century that pre-dated Zionism and found its most clear American exponent in Felix Adler. Adler, a lapsed rabbinical candidate who later taught at Columbia University, formed the Ethical Culture Society in 1876 which called for "a new religion where we may all grasp hands as brothers united in mankind's common cause." His work went on to influence the Liberal Progressive caucus of the Americanization movement, which included such figures as John Dewey, Jane Addams, and W. I. Thomas (Lissak 1989).

When Zangwill's play was first introduced to American audiences, the idea of the United States as a universal melting pot was virtually non-existent, even though American liberals like Emerson or Jefferson had made rhetorical use of universalist statements in earlier eras (Harper 1980). After Zangwill's play, the term "melting pot" began to gain currency but it was basically taken to refer to anglo-conformist assimilation, and several have commented that the term actually came to describe a "transmuting pot" rather than a melting pot (Gordon 1964: 89; Herberg 1955: 34). With respect to the American case, therefore, the term has served as a receptacle for a wide variety of paradigms, from the dominant conformist to the pluralist (Gleason 1992: 15).

In structural terms, the American melting pot certainly did not come to fruition until the decade of the 1960s, when the immigration quota system was removed, African-Americans achieved civil rights, electoral districts were reapportioned and Anglo-conformity subsided. Since then, progress towards a melting pot in the United States has been rapid: interethnic marriage has become a national norm (except with respect to African-Americans and *some* Asian and Hispanic groups), and most ethnic groups have achieved socioeconomic parity with British Americans. The demographic data on interethnic marriage has also breathed new life into melting-pot *ideology* since the 1960s, particularly among American neo-conservatives, but also among liberals opposed to multiculturalism in education, government and the universities (Salins 1997; Fukuyama 1995: 320; Schlesinger 1991; Sollors 1986; Hollinger 1995).

This is not to say that the melting pot is the dominant ideological or heuristic paradigm in the United States. Political opponents of the idea, whether of the neo-nativist right or communitarian left, are especially scathing in denouncing the abstract, cultureless society that the concept may bring forth (Novak 1972; Bellah 1985; Brimelow 1995). Scholarly critiques, meanwhile, have tended to emphasize resistance to the melting pot from ethnic elites and social movements. They also point out that intermarriage does not necessarily eliminate ethnic boundaries and practices (Gans 1979; Waters 1990).

### Bibliography

Akiner, Shirin. 1997. "Melting-pot—salad bowl—cauldron? Manipulation and mobilization of ethnic and religious identities in Central Asia," *Ethnic and Racial Studies*, 20, 2.

Bellah, Robert N. 1985 (1996, 2nd ed.). *Habits of the Heart*, London: University of California Press.

Brimelow, Peter. 1995. *Alien Nation: Common Sense About America's Immigration Disaster*. New York: Random House.

Fukuyama, Francis. 1995. *Trust: The Social Virtues and the Creation of Prosperity*. London: Penguin.

Gans, Herbert. 1979. "Symbolic ethnicity: the future of ethnic groups and cultures in America," *Ethnic and Racial Studies* 2: 1–20.

Gleason, Philip. 1992. *Speaking of Diversity: Language and Ethnicity in Twentieth-Century America*. Baltimore, MD and London: Johns Hopkins University Press.

Gordon, Milton. 1964. *Assimilation in American Life. The Role of Race, Religion and National Origins*. Oxford: Oxford University Press.

Harper, Richard Conant. 1980. *The Course of the Melting Pot Idea to 1910*. New York: Arno Press.

Herberg, Will. 1955. *Protestant, Catholic, Jew: An Essay in American Religious Sociology*. Garden City, NY: Country Life Press.

Hollinger, David A. 1995. *Postethnic America: Beyond Multiculturalism*. New York: Harper Collins.

Lissak, R. S. 1989. *Pluralism and Progressives*. Chicago: Chicago University Press.

Novak, Michael. 1972. *The Rise of the Unmeltable Ethnics: Politics and Culture in the Seventies*. New York: Macmillan.

Parsons, Talcott. 1964. "Evolutionary Universals in Society," *American Sociological Review* June: 339–357.

Rasiak, Ruslan O. 1980. "'The Soviet People': Multiethnic Alternative or Ruse?'" in E. Allworth (ed.), *Ethnic Russia in the USSR: The Dilemma of Dominance*. New York: Pergamon Press.

Salins, Peter D. 1997. *Assimilation, American Style*. New York: Basic Books.

Schlesinger, Arthur M. 1991. *The Disuniting of America*. New York: W. W. Norton.

Smith, Anthony D. 1986. *The Ethnic Origins of Nations*. Oxford: Blackwell.

Smith, Anthony D. 1990. "The Supersession of Nationalism?," *International Journal of Comparative Sociology* XXXI: 1-2, 1–25.

Sollors, Werner. 1986. *Beyond Ethnicity: Consent and Descent in American Culture*. New York: Oxford University Press.

Waters, Mary C. 1990. *Ethnic Options: Choosing Identities in America*. Berkeley: University of California Press.

Eric Kaufmann

# Mill's Theory of Nationality and Nationalism

British political thinker, philosopher, logician, economist, and political activist, John Stuart Mill (1806-1873) was probably the first major liberal theorist (and, at any rate, the most influential) to engage directly with the problems posed to liberalism and liberal politics by the existence of nations and nationalism. He did not use the word "nationalism" itself. Instead, like most of his contemporaries, he talked of "nationality" and of "patriotism." Mill used the term "nationality" in at least two senses. First, to designate a group of people constituting a nation; and second, nationality was used to designate what is called today "nationalism" (nationalist feeling or attachment, nationhood).

In the bulk of the literature he has been presented as strongly sympathizing with early nationalist movements, and as having offered the most influential theoretical justification for such movements from a liberal viewpoint. His theorising on these issues decisively influenced British and American liberal attitudes for several decades after his death, including American President Woodrow Wilson's views on nationality.

Mill's oft-quoted statements on nationality are to be found primarily in chapter XVI of his book *Considerations on Representative Government* (1861). That chapter was entitled, "Of Nationality, as Connected with Representative Government" (Mill 1963-1991, XIX: 546-52). Mill's definition of nationality was as follows: "A portion of mankind may be said to constitute a Nationality, if they are united among themselves by common sympathies, which do not exist between them and any others—which make them co-operate with each other more willingly than with other people, desire to be under the same government, and desire that it should be government by themselves or a portion of themselves, exclusively." This feeling of nationality "may have been generated by various causes," none of which were "either indispensable, or necessarily sufficient by themselves" (ibid.: 546). He then stated his now familiar principle: "Where the sentiment of nationality exists in any force, there is a *prima facie* case for uniting all the members of the nationality under the same government, and a government to themselves apart." This is merely saying, he went on to assert, "that the question of government ought to be decided by the governed. One hardly knows what any division of the human race should be free to do, if not to determine, with which of the various collective bodies of human beings they choose to associate themselves." Alfred Cobban interpreted Mill's principle of national self-determination as "merely a statement, in different terms, of the principle of democratic, or at least representative, government" (Cobban 1969:131). However, Mill's argument was not simply, or even mainly, based on the identification of the principle of national self-determination with the democratic principle of popular sovereignty. For he went on to present more compelling reasons: "But, when a people are ripe for free institu-

tions, there is a still more vital consideration. Free institutions are next to impossible in a country made up of different nationalities" (Mill 1963-1991, XIX: 547). Among a people without "fellow-feeling," especially if they read and spoke different languages, the "united public opinion, necessary to the working of representative government," could not exist. Their mutual antipathies were generally much stronger than "jealousy of the government." And, above all, "the sympathy of the army with the people" was wanting in the case of such a state. In such a state, soldiers of one nationality would regard members of the other nationalities which composed the state not just as strangers, but as enemies. And Mill went on to comment on the state of things he had just described:

> If it be said that so broadly marked a distinction between what is due to a fellow-countryman and what is due merely to a human creature, is more worthy of savages than of civilised beings, and ought, with the utmost energy, to be contended against, no one holds that opinion more strongly than myself. But this object, one of the worthiest to which human endeavour can be directed, can never, in the present state of civilisation, be promoted by keeping different nationalities of anything like equivalent strength, under the same government (ibid.: 548).

From the above considerations he concluded that "it is in general a necessary condition of free institutions, that the boundaries of governments should coincide in the main with those of nationalities." This statement figures in every account of his views on nationality. Most of them, however, fail to refer to the sentence which immediately followed and qualified it: "But several considerations are liable to conflict in practice with this general principle." Mill explained at length the difficulties that precluded the application of his principle of national self-determination in a great variety of cases. "[G]eographical hindrances" were among such considerations which obliged people of different nationalities "to make a virtue of necessity, and reconcile themselves to living together under equal rights and laws" (ibid.: 548-9).

Other, more important, considerations were moral and social. Experience proved, he asserted, that it was possible for one nationality to merge

**179**

# Mill's Theory of Nationality and Nationalism

and be absorbed in another. And "when it was originally an inferior and more backward portion of the human race, the absorption is greatly to its advantage." Thus,

> Nobody can suppose that it is not more beneficial to a Breton, or a Basque of French Navarre, to be brought into the current of the ideas and feelings of a highly civilised and cultivated people—to be a member of the French nationality, admitted on equal terms to all the privileges of French citizenship, sharing the advantages of French protection, and the dignity and *prestige* of French power—than to sulk on his own rocks, the half-savage relic of past times, revolving in his own little mental orbit, without participation or interest in the general movement of the world. The same remark applies to the Welshman or the Scottish Highlander, as members of the British nation.

This is followed by an emphatic declaration:

> Whatever really tends to the admixture of nationalities, and the blending of their attitudes and peculiarities in a common union, is a benefit to the human race. Not by extinguishing types, of which, in these cases, sufficient examples are sure to remain, but by softening their extreme forms, and filling up the intervals between them. The united people...inherits the special aptitudes and excellences of all its progenitors, protected by the admixture from being exaggerated into the neighbouring vices. (ibid.: 549-50)

Such statements do not represent attempts by a British imperialist to legitimize his country's rule over other nations, as has sometimes been suggested. Mill had a genuine and earnest desire to see different national and ethnic groups merge their best qualities in the interests of the improvement of mankind. This son of a Scottish father (James Mill) and an English mother had spent much of his energy, during at least three decades (1820s-1840s), trying to bring home to his fellow-countrymen what he saw as the advantage of combining different national and cultural traits pertaining to different "national characters," to use the vocabulary of his time, in order for a better national character to be attained. No other manifestation of this attitude is more striking than his almost life-long efforts to bring the British and the French closer to each other and to merge the best qualities of "Celt" and "Anglo-Saxon" in an improved hybrid national character.

In fact, the same desire to combine informed his views regarding the continuation of the union

between the Celtic peoples and the English in Great Britain. While he had ample praise for some qualities in the "character" of the Anglo-Saxons, few British thinkers have ever been so critical of the English character, which he criticized at least as often as he praised it. His wish was to see it improve through contact and fusion with what he considered to be the character best designed to correct it, the Celtic—in which he included the French as well as the Celts of the British Isles (Varouxakis 1996).

Many subsequent scholars who wrote on nationality or nationalism, including Lord Acton himself writing a year after the *Considerations* were published, felt obliged to comment on Mill's views. Some of these scholars criticized what they saw as Mill's naiveté or lack of perspicacity, especially by comparison with Acton's purportedly prophetic warnings against nationalism (Acton 1922; Kohn 1946: 35-38). Others, on the contrary, have seen Mill as a precursor of liberal notions of nationalism and nationality (Tamir 1993; Miller 1995), of "patriotism" (Viroli 1995: 185 and epigraph), or of what they see as the sober and balanced approach to nationalism characteristic of ISAIAH BERLIN's liberalism (Gray 1995: 99-100). ELIE KEDOURIE regarded Mill's position as having been most characteristic of what he called "the Whig theory of nationality": "This theory assumes not so much that humanity ought to be divided into national, sovereign states, as that people who are alike in many things stand a better chance of making a success of representative government" (Kedourie 1985: 131-3).

Almost all the scholars who have discussed Mill's contribution to debates on nationality based their commentary on chapter XVI of his *Considerations*. However, Mill had dealt with the issues he was to address there in a number of earlier writings, and did so most explicitly in 1849, in his "Vindication of the French Revolution of February 1848" (Mill 1963-1991, XX: 317-63). It was in the "Vindication" that Mill first formulated the idea that the main justification for "nationality" was its potential conduciveness to free representative government. This text shows beyond doubt that Mill was by no means blind to the contradictions and dangers involved in many nationalist movements. And he condemned in the strongest terms what is often called today "TRIBALISM" (Mill 1963-1991, XX: 347-8).

The reason why Mill was favorably disposed towards many movements of national liberation was his belief that the specific nation-states that would arise from the success of such movements were more likely to lead to the attainment of freedom than the multi-ethnic empires of Austria, Russia, and Turkey (see, e.g., Mill 1963-1991, XXV: 1203). At the same time he was conscious of the difference and tension between, on the one hand, national liberation (the attainment of "nationality," in the language of the time), and liberty within a state, on the other, and he endorsed the former only in so far as it seemed to be a necessary condition of the latter. This is clearly stated in a letter to the Italian patriot, Pasquale Villari (28 March 1859): "I would understand that at a certain point in time one could put nationality before liberty, I could even forgive it, because liberty often needs nationality in order to exist" (author's translation from a French original. Mill 1963-1991, XV: 610-1). Unlike the nationalist thinkers of his time, Mill accepted nationality only as a means to other ends. Therefore, he did not attach any intrinsic value to nationality *per se* or to the preservation of *national* cultures.

Mill's attitude with regard to nationalism was informed by his paramount commitment to rationality. He went as far as to fall out with a friend and fellow-thinker whose political views he found very congenial in most other respects, Alexis de Tocqueville. On the occasion of a Franco-British crisis, Mill deemed Tocqueville's stance to have been too prone to irrational, "low and grovelling" nationalism (Varouxakis 1998).

Yet, while he condemned nationalist sentiment as it manifested itself in Eastern and Central Europe, as well as in France, at his time, and while he discarded excessive particularistic attachments as retrograde and impeding the advance of civilization, Mill was acutely aware of the need for cohesion in a society. He was also sensitive to the need for the replacement of the more tangible attachments which had held people together under older social and political arrangements (local feudal institutions, religious attachments, etc.) with a form of solidarity adapted to the revolutionary changes that had taken place during the late eighteenth

and early nineteenth centuries. In his two reviews of Tocqueville's *Democracy in America* (1835 and 1840) Mill exhibits a sharp understanding of the changes entailed by the advent of modernity as far as people's allegiances were concerned (Mill 1963-1991, XVIII: 61-3, 83, 87, 182, 195n). In a passage in his 1843 work *A System of Logic* (book vi, chapter 10) he included in his three conditions of political stability "a strong and active principle of cohesion among the members of the same community or state." But he hastened to declare:

> We need scarcely say that we do not mean nationality in the vulgar sense of the term; a senseless antipathy to foreigners; an indifference to the general welfare of the human race, or an unjust preference of the supposed interests of our own country; a cherishing of bad peculiarities because they are national or a refusal to adopt what has been found good by other countries ... We mean a principle of sympathy, not of hostility; of union, not of separation. We mean a feeling of common interest among those who live under the same government, and are contained within the same natural or historical boundaries. We mean, that one part of the community shall not consider themselves as foreigners with regard to another part; that they shall cherish the tie which holds them together; shall feel that they are one people, that their lot is cast together...and that they cannot selfishly free themselves from their share of any common inconvenience by severing the connexion. (Mill 1963-1991, VIII: 923; and X: 135-6)

This sounds like a very sober patriotism indeed. It is a call for public spirit based on enlightened self-interest, rather than for nationalist attachment and sentimental particularistic preferences.

Mill should not be seen as a precursor of "liberal nationalism" or of any other type of nationalism. Rather, he should be seen as an advocate of enlightened patriotism, understood as a sense of civic spirit. In fact, and although this may appear as a contradiction in terms, Mill advocated a cosmopolitan patriotism. His ultimate goal was "the improvement of mankind," and he clearly believed that the best practical way for an individual to serve this goal was through active and conscientious participation in the affairs and common concerns of one's own political community. A major part of this active involvement which Mill demanded from the individual was a dedicated alert-

# Minorities

ness to the behavior of one's political community *as* a community vis-à-vis other communities, in other words, an attention to its foreign policy. He wrote some extremely powerful passages calling on his compatriots to see to it that their government follow a moral and even-handed foreign policy. And he did not mince his words when it came to admonishing them, each time he thought that they failed in the performance of that duty, or when the British government was behaving in a selfish manner dictated by a narrowly conceived national interest—as was the case of British policy towards the construction of the Suez Canal (Mill 1963-1991, XXI: 109-24).

Mill, like Jeremy Bentham before him (Rosen 1997), supported nationalist movements only to the extent that they would lead to the amelioration of the political arrangements under which those concerned would live. By amelioration he meant the attainment or better functioning of free representative government. While recognizing the political significance of nationalist attachments when they existed, and the need to accommodate them whenever possible, Mill would very much rather that people did not succumb to irrational sentiments such as those generated by nationalist attachments. Yet, nationalist attachments seemed inevitable facts of life that could not be explained away, so he tried to adapt his thinking to their existence, without ever according them an intrinsic ethical value. To use Bentham's felicitous bifurcation, in the case of nationalism Mill never confused what "ought to be" with what "is."

## Bibliography

Acton, First Baron, John Emerich Edward Dalberg-Acton. 1922. "Nationality," in J. Figgis and R. Laurence (eds.), *The History of Freedom and Other Essays*. London: Macmillan.

Cobban, Alfred. 1969. *The Nation State and National Self-Determination*. London: Collins.

Gray, John. 1995. *Berlin*. London: Fontana Press.

Kedourie, Elie. 1985 (1960). *Nationalism*. London: Hutchinson.

Kohn, Hans. 1946. *Prophets and Peoples: Studies in Nineteenth-Century Nationalism*. New York: Macmillan.

Mill, John Stuart. 1963-1991. *The Collected Works of John Stuart Mill*, 33 vols. Toronto and London: University of Toronto Press.

Miller, David. 1995. *On Nationality*. Oxford: Clarendon Press.

Rosen, Fred. 1997. "Nationalism and early British liberal thought," *Journal of Political Ideologies* 2, 2: 177-188.

Tamir, Yael. 1993. *Liberal Nationalism*. Princeton, NJ: Princeton University Press.

Varouxakis, Georgios. 1996. "The public moralist versus ethnocentrism: John Stuart Mill's French enterprise," *European Review of History-Revue Européenne d'Histoire* 3, 1: 27-38.

Varouxakis, Georgios. 1998. "Nationalism, patriotism and liberalism: A debate revisited," *Contemporary Political Studies* II: 1085-1096.

Viroli, Maurizio. 1995. *For Love of Country: An Essay on Patriotism and Nationalism*. Oxford: Clarendon Press.

Georgios Varouxakis

# Minorities

For over fifty years U.N. organs have tried, without success, to agree on a definition of a minority. Their experience demonstrates that the purpose of a definition must be settled first, and that one suited to the purposes of international politics may differ from the definitions useful to scholars.

The international protection of minorities can be traced back to the Treaty of Westphalia in 1648, but for present purposes it is more important to distinguish minorities resulting from incorporation and from immigration. Among the groups which have been incorporated into states, the special position of indigenous peoples should be acknowledged; their representatives maintain that indigenous peoples are not minorities. These peoples have in many cases found themselves incorporated into states by processes of treaty-making with parties of much greater power (as in North America), or by force (as in Australia). In some cases they have found themselves incorporated into several different states (as the Sami in northern Scandinavia). Invading minorities have sometimes been incorporated in a similar way, as in the case of Canada where there were two invading nations, French and British. Members of the indigenous and invading groups have been able to lay claim to group rights because the treaties had been contracted between representatives of their groups. Also, as a result of war, some old states have disappeared, new ones being put in their place; this sometimes imposed a common nationality upon ethnic communities which saw themselves as separate and incorporated them into states dominated by members of other ethnic communities. As a result of the redrawing of boundaries, whole groups of this kind have been transferred from one state to another. This is to distinguish situations in which the people have remained in the same place and the boundary has been moved, from those in which people themselves have left one state and crossed a boundary to enter another one. Persons who belong to groups affected by changes in state boundaries have historical rights of a collective character which cannot be claimed by migrants who have moved voluntarily.

Before the First World War about half the population of Europe lived as members of minorities. Boundary revision after the war reduced the proportion in that position to about one quarter, and the League of Nations sponsored a series of treaties in the attempt (largely unsuccessful) to protect the rights of many of these minorities. The dominant conception at this time was of a minority as a political group possessing collective rights. In sociology it was reflected in an influential essay of Louis Wirth and in an approach which insisted that a demographic majority could still be a minority (as in the case of blacks in South Africa).

After the Second World War, the U.N. sponsored the International Covenant on Civil and Political Rights which acknowledges the special position of minorities which have been incorporated into states by the moving or imposition of boundaries but recognizes only individual and not collective rights. Its Article 27 states:

> In those States in which ethnic, religious, or linguistic minorities exist, persons belonging to such minorities shall not be denied the right, in community with other members of their group, to enjoy their own culture, to profess and practice their own religion, or to use their own language.

This article is open to different interpretations depending upon the definition of a minority. The Human Rights Committee (the U.N. body which monitors the implementation by States of their obligations under the Covenant) stated in paragraph 5.2 of its General Comment 23 that "The existence of an ethnic, religious or linguistic minority in a given State party does not depend upon a decision by that State party but requires to be established by objective criteria." This does not exclude the possibility that Article 27 might also at some time be applied in the case of minorities that have arisen as a result of immigration.

The language of Article 27 is repeated in the U.N. Declaration on the Rights of Persons Belonging to National or Ethnic, Religious and Linguistic Minorities adopted in 1992. This states that "Persons belonging to minorities may exercise their rights individually as well as in community with other members of their group," but the Declaration also provides that

> States shall take measures to create favorable conditions to enable persons belonging to minorities to express their characteristics and to develop their culture, language, religion, traditions and customs, except where specific practices are in violation of national law and contrary to international standards.

The last clause restricts the kinds of claims that can be entertained. Representatives of a minority might well contend that if they are to maintain their language there needs to be a television channel transmitting programs in that language. Such a channel might well require a substantial subsidy paid, ultimately, by members of the majority as well as the minority, and therefore be politically contentious. Some of the provisions of this declaration should also be read in conjunction with those in the Declaration on the Elimination of All Forms of Intolerance and of Discrimination Based on Religion or Belief.

In 1995 the Council of Europe adopted a Framework Convention for the Protection of National Minorities which lays down a number of principles which ratifying states agree to implement through legislation or policy. According to Article 5(1) "The Parties undertake to promote the conditions necessary for persons belonging to national minorities to maintain and develop their culture, and to preserve the essential elements of their identity, namely their religion, language, traditions and cultural heritage." The Convention does not define "national minority."

For the purposes of social science it is simplest to define a minority by a numerical criterion, as a sub-class comprising less than half of a class of persons. An adjective can then identify the characteristic by which it is distinguished: national, ethnic, linguistic, religious, or any other feature. The same set of persons may then constitute both a national and an ethnic minority, or both a national and a religious minority, and so on.

### Bibliography

Cholewinski, Ryszard. 1997. *Migrant Workers in International Human Rights Law: Their Protection in Countries of Employment*. Oxford: Clarendon Press.

Thornberry, Patrick. 1990. *International Law and the Rights of Minorities*. Oxford: Clarendon Press.

United Nations. 1950. *Definition and Classification of Minorities. Memorandum Submitted by the Secretary-General*. New York: United States.

Michael Banton

# Modernization Theories of Nationalism

Most theories of nationalism assert the modern character of the phenomenon and account for its appearance and development by reference to a variety of factors associated with modernity. While some authors, like John Armstrong and Anthony D. Smith, contend that nations precede nationalism and that there is a continuity between old and modern nations (in that medieval or even ancient ethnic communities are often a springboard for the modern nation), only primordialists and sociobiologists consider the nation as perennial, that is, as an entity which has existed throughout human history.

In general terms, modernization theories maintain that nationalism emerges as a result of the process of transition from traditional to modern society. Some of these theories focus more specifically on the spread of industrialization, whose socioeconomic, political, and cultural conditions

they functionally associate with nationalism. They thus present industrialization as the main cause for the development of nationalism.

The ideological roots of modernization can be found in the Renaissance, the Scientific Revolution, and the Enlightenment. At the economic level, modernization began with the development of trade and commerce, and continued with the process of industrialization. At the political level modernization involved the appearance of the modern national state—a centralized, bureaucratic, territorial, sovereign polity. When applied to non-Western societies some features of modernity such as commercialization, bureaucratization, secularization, urbanization, mass communications, literacy, and so on may be present, while industrialization is often absent.

Modernization theories of nationalism come under different guises. Scholars of nationalism do not always fit easily into rigid typologies. Furthermore, in the course of their work they may have shifted their theoretical position substantially. With all these provisos in mind we can distinguish three major types of modernization theories:

1. Social communication theories (Deutsch, Rustow, Rokkan, Anderson)

2. Economistic theories:

    2.1. Marxist-inspired economistic theories.

        2.1.1. Classical

        2.1.2. Internal colonialism (Hechter)

        2.1.3. Uneven development (Nairn)

        2.1.4. World-system (Wallerstein)

        2.1.5. Hroch

    2.2. Non-Marxist inspired (Gellner)

3. Politico-ideological theories (Breuilly, Giddens, Brass, Mann)

### Social Communication Theories of Modernization

A pioneering study of the effects of modernization on nationalism was Karl Deutsch's *Nationalism and Social Communication* (1953). It deals with the growth of nations and nationalism in the context of the transition from traditional to modern societies. Deutsch emphasized the centrality of COMMUNICATION in the making of national communities: a nation is a group of people who communicate more effectively and intensely with one another than with people outside the group. By using a variety of data from economic history and demography, Deutsch pointed to the massive social mobilization which went along with the processes of commercialization, industrialization and urbanization, as well as with the growth of general literacy and mass communications.

The theory predicted that an accentuation of social mobilization would enhance the importance of language and culture and hence of nationalism. However, the theory did not specify which groups would develop nationalist tendencies. This is an important issue because, according to Deutsch's theory, modern nation-states are likely to absorb the languages and cultures of the subordinated ethnies or national minorities within their borders. Even allowing for some exceptions, it was clear for Deutsch that the general trend was for the disappearance of these entities.

We know at present that this prediction has been proven wrong. The intensification of the different processes of communication in recent years has not only consolidated cultural and linguistic differences, but has also produced autonomist and separatist movements in the West, the Third World and the ex-communist bloc.

Another author who has insisted on the connection between modernization and nationalism is the American political scientist Dankwart Rustow. In his book *A World of Nations* (1969) he pointed out that "the essential link between modernization and nationhood consists of course in the need for an intensive division of labour" (1969: 30). Other features such as equality and loyalty which are essential to the nation also emerged from the modernization process.

Rustow admitted that some traditional societies were possibly nations and that emerging modernization has also taken place without a sentiment of nationhood. However, the historical process has shown that modernization and nationhood are closely related and that the most appropriate political structure for the achievement of modernization is the nation-state. Furthermore,

national identity is best fostered and preserved in the context of modernization.

Stein Rokkan, who followed in many respects Deutsch's ideas, presented a much more complex and comprehensive model of nation-states in Western Europe (1983). His framework proposes a *longue durée* which locates some important variables in the medieval and early modern periods. As to the modern situation he accounted for accelerated nation-building in the nineteenth and twentieth centuries by reference to six variables: two economic (the combination of rural and urban resources, and the spread and localization of industrialization); two territorial (the pressures towards centralization and unification; and the pull of imperialist tendencies); and two cultural ones (the tensions between centre and periphery resulting from ethnic/linguistic mobilization, and the conflicts between state and Church).

Although Rokkan applied his model to Western Europe, there is no reason why most of the variables which he identified could not be used to analyse the emergence of the nation-state in other parts of the world. Unfortunately, Rokkan is mostly concerned with the formation of nation-states and pays little attention to other aspects of nationalism.

Benedict Anderson's *Imagined Communities* (1983) also stresses the issue of social communication in the early modern period of the development of modernity. Anderson's definition of the nation as an "imagined political community— and imagined as both limited and sovereign" (1983: 15) has had an extraordinary appeal. His argument about the origins of nationalism led him to focus on the tremendous consequences of print capitalism. The book was, after all, the first commodity produced *en masse*. According to Anderson, book selling was one area in which early capitalists, using the new technology of production available, were able to make great profits. Having exhausted the market in Latin, capitalists turned to the vernaculars.

The effect of print-language on national consciousness was to create a unified language that allowed a large part of the population to read the same texts and identify with each other. Furthermore, by giving fixity to language it was possible to develop the idea of the antiquity of one's nation.

# Modernization Theories of Nationalism

Anderson concluded that "what made the new communities imaginable was a half-conscious, but explosive interaction between a system of production and productive relations (capitalism), a technology of communications and the type of fatality of human linguistic diversity" (ibid.: 46). At a later stage in history, state consolidation both at home and, in the case of imperial states, in their colonies, created groups of people who felt politically and culturally excluded. These groups, by imagining themselves as communities, were able to shake off alien rule.

## Economistic Theories of Modernization

### Marxist-Inspired Economistic Theories of Modernization

*Classical.* The starting point of the economic conception of the nation is the assumption that national consciousness is fundamentally a type of false consciousness. By claiming that underneath the idea of the nation lie economic interests, this theory reduces nationalism to an ideology of the ascending bourgeoisie.

Economism is an extremely popular form of explanation and, as such, it is favored by Marxists and non-Marxists alike. In the modern literature this explanatory framework appears in different guises, but in the final analysis their common denominator is that they deny the specific character of the national fact.

Marxist theories regard nationalism as a modern phenomenon and posit a more or less explicit causal connection between the development of capitalism and the appearance of nationalism. The founders of historical materialism were certainly well aware of the nationalist phenomenon. As politically committed young intellectuals, Marx and Engels lived through the troublesome 1840s—a period in which nationalist struggles challenged the European political status quo. In their formative years, then, Marx and Engels had to confront the nationalist demands of a variety of European peoples. In order to understand the attitude of these thinkers towards nationalism, it is essential to note that they subordinated the survival of nations to the progressive march of history: some peoples were fossils from a long-gone past and were therefore objectively counterrevo-

lutionary. These reactionary nations had to be sacrificed on the altar of the mightier national states. In the articles written by Marx and Engels for the *Neue Rheinische Zeitung* (1848-1849), the national question was often discussed as part of their political scenario, but there was no attempt to explain the phenomenon except perhaps in terms of crude stereotypes of national character. It is obvious that for Marx and Engels the nation was not a central category of social existence, but rather a transitory institution created by the bourgeoisie, hence the passage in *The Communist Manifesto* declaring that the "proletariat has no fatherland."

At the turn of the century the vindication of the rights of nations changed the political panorama so radically that, even the Marxists of the Second International made the national question central to their political agenda. However, it was only within the Austro-Marxian tradition that a serious attempt was made to come to terms with the theoretical problems of the nation. Otto Bauer's *Die Nationalitätenfrage und die Socialdemocratie* (1907) presented a theory of nationalism based on the ideas of national character and national culture, although he also used the dubious idea that nations have an historical destiny to fulfil. A much better known and more influential contribution to the Marxist debate on the nation from this period is, of course, Stalin's *Marxism and the National Question* (1913).

In his definition of the nation, Stalin required the simultaneous coalescence of four elements (language, territory, economic life and psychic formation) in a historically constituted community of culture. As for Lenin, he adopted a more flexible definition of the nation, and, although he was in favor, like most Marxists, of the creation of large political units, he endorsed the principle of self-determination of oppressed nations, at least in theory.

In the 1970s a number of attempts were made to develop a theory of nationalism along modified Marxist lines. Among the most prominent approaches one should mention the following: INTERNAL COLONIALISM, uneven development and world-systems.

*Internal Colonialism.* Internal colonialism aimed originally to explain ethnonational movements within a state. The theory is a variant of older, Marxist-inspired imperialist and dependency theories. However, its most immediate antecedents, can be traced back to the Latin American literature of the 1960s. In a nutshell, the idea that states exhibit strong internal inequalities based on ethnic lines (Indians in Latin America, blacks in the U.S.) was transplanted to Europe where it received a regional basis. In his classical study of the United Kingdom, *Internal Colonialism* of 1975, Michael Hechter maintained that industrialization aggravated an already existing situation of economic dependency and inequality of the Celtic fringe (Scotland, Wales, and Ireland) vis à vis England and this manifested itself, at first, in differential political behavior and later in ethnonational movements. Hechter also emphasized the unequal development of industrialism within states. He suggested that in each country there is a region which is favored by capitalist development, while the others are subordinated.

Furthermore, Hechter defended the idea that, instead of a national culture, what we have is a core culture that dominates the others by establishing ethnic boundaries. The key feature of Hechter's theory is the idea of a cultural division of labor existing between the core and the periphery. A system of stratification develops by means of which the dominant group at the core is in a position to monopolize social positions with high prestige in the society, while the members of the peripheral cultures are assigned social roles which are considered inferior. As industrialization advances in its uneven way, the internal differences between these groups become more accentuated. Ethnonationalism emerges as a response to a situation of perceived dependence and exploitation.

Hechter's intention was to articulate a model valid not only for the U.K., but for Europe as a whole. It is unclear whether he intended it to have an even wider application, outside Europe. Even as a limited theory of ethnonationalism, mainly applicable to the European situation, Hechter's theory was plagued by glaring anomalies. A well-aired criticism against Hechter's approach has been that his theory was unable to account adequately for major ethnonationalist movements like the Scottish one, and even less for the Basque and Catalan variants which actually developed in the most industrialized areas of Spain. Hechter and Levi (1979) tried to counter some of these criticisms by putting forward a modified theory of internal colonialism which incorporated within it the notion of a cultural division of labor: the idea of a segmental division. In their own words: "the members interact wholly within the boundaries of their own group" (1979: 263) and an elite manages to monopolize the key positions in the social structure. It is arguable how far this modified approach, which also gives greater prominence to the role of the state, can be seen as a retreat from the original idea that the uneven development of industrialism was the primary factor in the development of ethnonationalism.

According to Anthony D. Smith (1983), one of Hechter's major critics, in spite of the amendments, Hechter's theory is still "flawed by its reductionist assumptions that cultural cleavages and ethnic sentiments can be wholly derived from purely economic and spatial characteristics" (1983:xvi). Other critics, like A. W. Orridge and C. Ragin are less negative, accepting that uneven development has played an important role in the genesis of many forms of nationalism, while admitting that in other instances it was, at most, a subsidiary factor (e.g., Ragin 1987).

*Uneven Development.* The contribution of Tom Nairn to a general theory of nationalism is essentially contained in chapter nine of his book, *The Break Up of Britain* (1977). Stemming from a Marxist tradition, but acknowledging that Marxism had little to offer to the analysis of nationalism, Nairn insisted that only by focusing on the ravages and contradictory effects of uneven development, could we hope to understand nationalism. Capitalism may have unified mankind, but at the price of great disequilibria and tremendous antagonisms which have triggered off a process of socio-political fragmentation, affecting even the Old Continent. Nationalism is the result of certain features of the world political economy in the modern era. It is a way that peripheral countries found to defend themselves against the core. This was done by an interclass mobilization on the basis of a different identity from that of the alien dominating state (1977: 340). Nationalism has had, of necessity, to express itself through the cultural peculiarities of each area. In conclusion, for Nairn, nationalism is the sociohistorical cost of the accelerated implantation of capitalism at a world level. It is arguable how reductionist Nairn's theory is, although in Anthony D. Smith's study of theories of nationalism, it is classified as "an economistic model of nationalism" (1983: xvi). Nairn, himself, maintains that nationalist phenomena cannot be reduced to economic trends, but rather, that the former are given real force by the latter.

*World-System.* In the wealth of writings that Wallerstein has dedicated to the world-system, he has occasionally touched upon the national question. However, in so far as a theory of nationalism presupposes a conceptualization of the nation, Wallerstein's theory is seriously defective. This is the result of his failure to consider in depth the cultural aspect of the modern world-system. So, if a theory of the nation involves a theory of culture, and if a theory of the nation can be deduced from Wallerstein's writings, then Wallerstein's theory can only be described as reductionist.

In his book, *The Modern World-System II*, Wallerstein defines cultures as "the ways in which people clothe their political interests and drives in order to express them in space and time, and preserve their meaning" (1980: 65). Like many other social scientists, Wallerstein does not make a clear-cut distinction between state and nation, although he is aware of the differences between the two notions. For him, the only possible relationship between state and nation is that the nation equals the nation-state.

An interesting development in Wallerstein's work is his attempt to graft onto the world-system theory a modified conception of the Weberian distinction between class and "status group" (*Stand*), in order to account for the existence of ethnicity/nationalism. According to Wallerstein, Weber's trinity of class, status group and party should not be seen as three different, and sometimes overlapping groups, but as three different existential manifestations of the same underlying reality. The problem is to determine when a stratum embodies itself as class, status, or party.

The strong Wallersteinian theory of nationalism maintains that within the capitalist world-system two phenomena can be observed: first, that classes can be reduced to material interests; and, second, that status groups and parties are blurred, often false, collective representations of classes. In situations of acute class conflict the status group lines tend to coincide with class lines. The weak Wallersteinian theory of nationalism maintains that ethnic consciousness is an assertion in the political arena of cultural and/or economic interests. And here culture is to be understood in terms of language, religion, history, life-style, etc. or a combination of these in so far as they are used to define the boundaries of a group. From these premises it follows that Wallerstein's failure to provide an explanation of nationalism is due, first, to the economistic, or at best, politico-economic, reductionism which pervades his conception of the capitalist world-system; and, second, to his inadequate conception of the nation.

In general terms, Wallerstein insists, like E. Hobsbawm and T. Ranger (1983), on the invented or constructed character of the nation. In his own words: "the nation hinges around one of the basic structural features of the world economy," that is, "the political superstructure of this historical system, the sovereign states that form and derive from the interstate system" (Wallerstein 1987: 381). Thus, for Wallerstein, the nation "derives from the political structuring of the world-system" (ibid.: 383). In other words, "statehood preceded nationhood"(ibid.: 384). Consequently, for Wallerstein, the nation is "in no sense a primordial stable social reality, but a complex clay-like historical product of the capitalist world-economy" (ibid.: 387).

*Hroch.* An original Marxist approach is that of Miroslav Hroch. In his seminal book, *Social Preconditions of National Revival in Europe* (1985), Hroch proposed a class analysis of the origin of the modern nation, which, at the same time included the role of cultural developments. The book is based on the comparative study of the social and territorial composition of the early nationalist movements of seven stateless nations (Czechia, Lithuania, Estonia, Finland, Norway, Flanders, and Slovakia).

Hroch distinguishes three main stages in the development of modern society. In the first stage, the transition from feudalism to capitalism takes place. This stage also comprises the fight against absolute monarchies and the unfurling of revolutions of a bourgeois type. The second stage coincides with the victory and consolidation of capitalism as well as the appearance of an organized working class movement. Thirdly, and finally, during the twentieth century, there is a process of world-wide integration and an unprecedented development of mass communications. At the cultural level each nationalist movement also goes through three phases: Phase A (the period of scholarly interest), Phase B (the period of patriotic agitation), and Phase C (the rise of a mass national movement).

The Marxist tradition has been, on the whole, extremely suspicious of nationalism, although for tactical reasons they have often made use of national sentiments to achieve socialist objectives. In any case, within the Marxist general framework, the nation is not a significant concept that can help us explain the dynamics of modern history. In fact, one must agree with Tom Nairn's sweeping statement that the "theory of nationalism represents Marxism's great historical failure" (1977: 329), a point which has been disputed by Benner (1995). The events of the 1960s and 1970s when socialist countries fought bitterly against each other along nationalist lines opened the eyes of some Marxists to the reality that national interests were, in the final instance, more important than socialist internationalism. With the collapse of the Soviet bloc in 1989 and the disintegration of the Soviet Union in 1991-92, these issues have come to the forefront. At present few believe that Marxism can provide a genuine theory of nationalism.

*Non-Marxist-Inspired Economistic Theories of Modernization*

At first sight it may be surprising to include ERNEST GELLNER among the proponents of a theory of nationalism anchored on the uneven development of (industrial) capitalism, that is, on an economistic approach. For one thing, Gellner avoids the expression "capitalism" (he prefers "industrial society" or "industrialism"). And, secondly, and more importantly, his theory has been labelled culturalist or linguistic (Smith 1983).

While Gellner is in no way a Marxist, he maintains that nationalism is the unavoidable outcome of an industrial society that requires a spatially ductile labor force (Stokes 1986: 594). In this sense he qualifies as an economistic theorist of nationalism, although this statement will have to be nuanced below.

Gellner's first major and influential statement on nationalism can be found in chapter seven of his *Thought and Change* (1964). There, he stressed that nationalism could only be understood in the context of industrialization, the competition between classes in the newly created industrial stratification, and the integrating effects of language and education. The process of industrialization undermined the traditional social structures and gave primacy to cultural elements (essentially communication). The identity of the individual was no longer defined in terms of his position in a hierarchical social structure, but in terms of his culture. And culture and nationality are closely related. Only the nation-state could provide, through the educational system and the official language, the kind of "cultured" persons which the process of industrialization requires.

According to Gellner, modernization and industrialization spread in an uneven fashion. This created a new system of social stratification—a class system—which was felt to be unacceptable, illegitimate. If this class system, overlapped with cultural differences, then an uneasy alliance between a culturally displaced intelligentsia and an overexploited proletariat often developed and led to national secession.

In 1983 came the publication of Gellner's definitive statement on nationalism in the form of a slender volume entitled *Nations and Nationalism*. The book did not represent a major theoretical shift, but rather Gellner's attempt to account for the more disruptive aspects of nationalism (separatism, violence) which he had neglected in the past. The major thrust of his theory was still very much that "it was social chasms (doubled with cultural differences) created by early industrialism, and by the unevenness of its diffusion, which made it [nationalist conflict] acute" (1983: 121). And he stated once again that "the specific roots of nationalism are found in the distinctive structural requirements of industrial society" (ibid.: 31).

## Modernization Theories of Nationalism

The Gellnerian model of nationalism strongly emphasizes that nationalism has its roots in the new industrial order, and that nothing before this period—Gellner's agrarian society—can be equated with nationalism because political units were not defined in terms of cultural boundaries. For Gellner, nations can only be defined in terms of the age of nationalism; therefore, he cannot conceive of the nation as an imaginative vision created by intellectuals in order to legitimize the medieval (agrarian) state (monarchy) of Western Europe. Besides industrialization, Gellner's second emphasis is on modernization (population explosion, rapid urbanization, labor migration, penetration of local economies by a global economy). Following Weber, he admits that the Protestant Reformation must have had an impact on nationalism; so did colonialism and imperialism. As far as the nation is concerned, Gellner's view is that nations are invented. For him, the notions of ethnicity or ethnic pasts are just raw material of limited if any importance.

Gellner's theory fails completely to account for nationalist movements in Western Europe. These were largely present prior to industrialization and, in any case, most followed a different pattern from his predictions. In the final resort, his approach cannot escape the constraints of its economistic scaffolding, and this is why Gellner cannot understand what motivates nationalists, what makes them vibrate emotionally, except maybe socioeconomic mobility.

In Gellner's later work (1994; 1997), there are no major theoretical changes, except for a refinement of his typology of nationalism. Gellner distinguished five stages in the evolution of nationalism in Europe, and four European time zones. The five stages in the evolution of nationalism were beginnings, nationalist irredentism, nationalism triumphant, totalitarian nationalism, and tamed nationalism. The four European time zones marking the regions where particular types of nationalism made their appearance were: Atlantic sea-coast, Holy Roman Empire area, Mitteleuropa and the ex-Soviet Union.

Both evolutionary and geographic ideal-types are rather rigid, and although they account for some cases, they leave out a lot of anomalous cases. For example, the Atlantic seacoast covers Portugal, Spain, France, the United Kingdom, and Scandinavia. According to Gellner, this is an area mostly bereft of "ethnographic nationalism." This is true for Portugal, but it is hardly applicable to Spain and the U.K. Even the French case is not so clear-cut as Gellner makes it.

Anthony D. Smith criticized Gellner's view of nationalism by indicating the ethnic antecedents of modern nationalism. Smith did not deny the modern character of nations and nationalism, but remarked that "we find in pre-modern eras, even in the ancient world, striking parallels to the 'modern' idea of national identity (...) and we find movements that appear to resemble modern nationalism" (Smith 1986: 11). An interesting and challenging turn to Gellner's theory that modernization creates nations is Liah Greenfeld's detailed defence of the opposite thesis, namely, that it is modernity that is defined by nationalism (1992: 11).

Gellner always rejected the accusation of being an economic determinist, although in the *Festschrift* in his honor (Hall and Jarvie 1996) a number of authors (Anderson, O'Leary) insisted on using this label.

### Politico-Ideological Theories of Modernization

In this final section I shall consider four authors: John Breuilly, Anthony Giddens, Paul Brass and Michael Mann. A common feature of the work of all these authors is the prominent role they give to the state in the development of nationalism in modernity.

In his *Nationalism and the State* of 1982, John Breuilly accepted the existence of nations and national sentiments in medieval Europe, but restricted nationalism to the modern period. Breuilly explained nationalism as a consequence of the development of the modern state and of the international state system. As he put it, "nationalism should be understood as a form of politics that arises in close association with the development of the modern state" (Breuilly 1993: xii). Breuilly recognized that in some cases economic interests do play a role in nationalism, but excluded a class-based or economistic explanation of nationalism, because of the diversity of nationalist movements.

According to Breuilly, the advent of nationalism is related to the first wave of modernization which started in sixteenth century Europe. Breuilly's attention is focused on the formation of the Western European states in the context of the religious and political struggles that characterized the early modern period. Throughout its history, the modern state has shaped nationalist politics and has been central to the making of nationalism.

Anthony Giddens examined the nationalist phenomenon in his two volume work, *A Contemporary Critique of Historical Materialism* (1981; 1985). According to Giddens, nationalism is "the existence of symbols and beliefs which are either propagated by elite groups, or held by many of the members of regional, ethnic, or linguistic categories of a population and which imply a community between them" (Giddens 1981: 190-1). For Giddens, nationalism is a basically modern phenomenon stemming from the French Revolution. Its association "in time and in fact with the convergent rise of capitalism and the nation-state" (ibid.: 191), is not sufficient ground for assuming that it is an excrescence of the nation-state and that the latter is a by-product of capitalism.

For Giddens, European nationalism is a world of its own and therefore it is not possible to generalize from the European experience to other parts of the world. Interestingly enough, however, the connection between capitalism and nationalism, which Giddens rejected at the economic level, is re-introduced at the psychological level. In this context, nationalism can be regarded as a response to certain "needs and dispositions" which appeared at a time when, as a result of the commodification of time and space, the individual had lost his ontological security (ibid.: 193-4). It must be noted, however, that Giddens did not deny that nationalism is connected with class domination, and that the uneven development of capitalism strongly influenced the "origins of oppositional nationalism" (1985: 220).

In his book *Ethnicity and Nationalism* of 1991, Paul Brass criticized perennialism, insisting that ethnicity and nationalism are the products of modernity. He further emphasized their constructed character. Cultures are fabricated by elites who use raw materials from different groups to create *ethnies* and nations. By using these representations, elites aim at securing for themselves economic or political advantages. Brass's theory states that ethnic identity and modern nationalism arise out of specific types of interactions between the leadership of centralizing states and the elites of non-dominant ethnic groups (1991:9).

Finally, Michael Mann sees himself as a modernist, although he accepts the existence of more or less conscious *ethnies* and protonations before modern times. In the second volume of his work, *The Sources of Social Power*, Mann maintained that any account of the development of nationalism must include all four sources of social power: economic, political, ideological, and military (1993). In the first phase, which began in the sixteenth century, ideological power dominated. This took the form of religion and generated such protonations as Protestant England. The second phase commenced in 1700 and can be described as a "commercial-statist" phase. This was characterized by a further diffusion of proto-national identities; it corresponds roughly to Anderson's idea of print capitalism. In the third phase, military power dominates and it propels nationhood. By the beginning of the nineteenth century most Western nations were already in full sight. The fourth and final phase is "the industrialist phase of the nation." This "encouraged three types of nation: state reinforcing, state creating and state subverting" (ibid.: 731).

For Mann it is obvious that nationalism appeared heavily mediated by the role of the state. In his contribution to a *Festschrift* in Gellner's honor Mann concludes that "industrialisation was not the principal cause" of nationalism; in fact, "it arrived too late." And he adds, "There were two principal causes: on the one hand, the emergence of commercial capitalism and its universal social classes; on the other, the emergence of the modern state and its professional armed forces and administrators. Conjoined by the fiscal-military pressures exerted by geopolitical rivalry, they produced the politics of popular representation and these formed several varieties of modern nationalism"(1992: 162).

In conclusion, there seems to be a general consensus among scholars that mass nationalism is a modern phenomenon. However, the assumption

## Multiculturalism

that it is the (uneven) development of industrialism that causes the appearance of nationalism and of nations cannot be accepted as a general proposition. Two arguments may be used to counter this proposition. Firstly, nations precede nationalism. Indeed, many modern nations are the result of a long historical process which finds its roots in the Middle Ages. Secondly, techno-economic or economic explanations of nationalism may account for *some* aspects of nationalism or some nationalist cases, but they are inadequate for a general, or even regional (European), theory of nationalism.

### Bibliography

Anderson, B. 1983. *Imagined Communities*. London: New Left Books.

Benner, Erica. 1995. *Really Existing Nationalisms: A Post-Communist View from Marx and Engels*. Oxford: Clarendon Press.

Brass, P. 1991. *Ethnicity and Nationalism*. New Delhi: Sage.

Breuilly, J. 1982 *Nationalism and the State*. Manchester: Manchester University Press.

Deutsch, K. 1953. *Nationalism and Social Communication*. New York: MIT Press.

Gellner, E. 1964. *Thought and Change*. London: Weidenfeld and Nicolson.

Gellner, E. 1983. *Nations and Nationalism*. Oxford: Blackwell.

Gellner, E. 1994. *Encounters with Nationalism*. Oxford: Blackwell.

Gellner, E. 1997. *Nationalism*. London: Weidenfeld and Nicolson.

Giddens, A. 1981. *A Contemporary Critique of Historical Materialism*. London: Macmillan.

Giddens, A. 1985. *The Nation-State and Violence*. Cambridge: Polity Press.

Greenfeld, L. 1992. *Nationalism: Five Roads to Modernity*. Cambridge, MA: University of Harvard Press.

Hall, J. A. and Jarvie, I. C. (eds.). 1996. *The Social Philosophy of Ernest Gellner*. Amsterdam: Rodopi.

Hechter, Michael. 1975. *Internal Colonialism*. London: Routledge and Kegan Paul.

Hechter, Michael and Levi, Margaret. 1979. "The comparative analysis of ethnoregional movements," *Ethnic and Racial Studies* 2, 3: 260-74.

Hobsbawm, E. and Ranger, T. (eds.) *The Invention of Tradition*. Cambridge: Cambridge University Press.

Hroch, M. 1985. *Social Preconditions of National Revival in Europe*. Cambridge: Cambridge University Press.

Llobera, J. R. 1994. *The God of Modernity: The Development of Nationalism in Western Europe*. Oxford: Berg.

Mann, M. 1992 "The emergence of modern European nationalism," in J. Hall and I. C. Jarvie (eds), *Transition to Modernity*. Cambridge: Cambridge University Press.

Mann, M. 1993. *The Sources of Social Power II*. Cambridge: Cambridge University Press.

Nairn, T. 1977. *The Break-Up of Britain*. London: New Left Books.

Ragin, C. 1987. *The Comparative Method*. Berkeley: University of California Press.

Rokkan, S. et al. 1983. *Economy, Territory, Identity*. London: Sage.

Rustow, D.1969. *A World of Nations*. Washington, DC: Brookings Institution.

Smith, A. D. 1981. *Ethnic Revival*. Cambridge: Cambridge University Press.

Smith, A. D. 1983. *Theories of Nationalism*. London: Duckworth.

Smith, A. D.1986. *The Ethnic Origins of Nations*. Oxford: Blackwell.

Stokes, G. 1986. "How is capitalism related to nationalism?" *Comparative Studies in Society and History*, 28: 591-8.

Wallerstein, I. 1974. *The Modern World-System I*. New York: Academic Press.

Wallerstein, I. 1979. *The Capitalist World-Economy*. Cambridge: Cambridge University Press.

Wallerstein, I. 1980. *The Capitalist World-System II*. New York: Academic Press.

Wallerstein, I. 1987. "The construction of peoplehood: Racism, nationalism, ethnicity," *Sociological Forum* 2: 373-88.

Josep R. Llobera

# Multiculturalism

The term multiculturalism may be used with differing degrees of precision in both popular political debate and in social science. In its loosest usage it refers to any society in which different groups are distinguishable by their physical appearance and culture. In this sense there are few who would disagree that European societies have, in recent times, become multicultural. From the point of view of comparative sociology or political science, however, the term refers to one possible policy which might be adopted to incoming immigrant ethnic MINORITIES, the others being racist exclusion, assimilation, and the guestworker system.

The notion of a multicultural society need not involve the idea of equal treatment of minorities. Many critics of societies purporting to be multicultural have pointed out that groups may be recognised as different so that they can receive unequal treatment or be manipulated for purposes of political control. Such criticisms have been made by democrats in Germany, the Netherlands, Sweden, and the United Kingdom which are often referred to as representing the multicultural alternative. In these circumstances it becomes necessary to distinguish another ideal which might be pursued by democrats and by minority groups. The British Home Secretary, Roy Jenkins, suggested this possibility when he defined "integration," "not as a flattening process of uniformity, but cultural diversity coupled with equal opportunity in an atmosphere of mutual tolerance."

The structural spelling out of this ideal seems to imply two separate cultural domains, two sets of institutions or two forms of social bonding. On the one hand there would be a shared public political culture based upon the notion of equality for all individuals; on the other there would be the cultures of distinct ethnic communities based upon their separate languages, religions, and family customs. The culture of the host society as well as those of immigrant groups would be a communal culture of this sort, quite distinct from the shared political or civic culture based upon the idea of equality.

Some radical advocates of multiculturalism go beyond this. They envisage the merging of separate communal cultures in a new hybrid amalgam which would modify or replace the culture of the host society. They would point to the existence of such a new hybrid culture as being exemplified in literary and artistic products of both an elite and a popular kind as well as in the obvious matter of changing cuisine.

As against this radical view, the more moderate concept of an egalitarian multicultural society accepts that the host society's communal culture as well as its institutions will continue to

exist with relatively little change. It simply argues that all of these institutions should be subject to the idea of equality.

Faced with institutions of this kind, immigrant minorities will accept that they have to live within an established institutional framework in matters of law, administration, and the economy. They have to become capable of living successfully in two worlds. This is one of the costs of migration.

The most difficult area of interaction is that of the school system. Schools bridge the two domains of the private and the public. They are concerned with primary socialisation, sharing this task with the family, but they also have to prepare students to operate in the more impersonal world of the economy and the polity. Since immigrant groups are concerned that their members shall have equality they would not want the kind of multicultural education which prevents their learning the necessary skills and competences to obtain jobs, although it is possible that some groups may feel that the impersonality required in the public sphere threatens their basic communal values. There are likely to be many disputes in the schools about the balance which should be struck between these conflicting goals.

So far as the public civic culture of equality is concerned, many of the most important issues have been discussed in the terms suggested by T. H. Marshall (1951). Marshall, in discussing the incorporation of social classes, suggests that in the past the working classes obtained first legal and then political rights, but they only obtained full citizenship when they achieved social rights through obtaining at least a minimum equal standard of life. It is only insofar as this occurs that citizenship is likely to become a more important focus of loyalty than social class. What was true for the process of incorporation of the working classes is equally true for immigrant communities.

Turning to the question of why, given that a society permits equality of opportunity it should still allow space for more private communal cultures, there appear to be two major reasons. One is that, individuals in a modern society still need a moral and emotional home standing between the family and the state. The other is that the maintenance of community creates the sort of solidarity necessary for collective political action.

## Music and Nationalism

To say this, however, is not to say that we should adopt an essentialist view of immigrant ethnic minority culture. It is true that one point of reference is the culture of the homeland, but even this homeland culture is changed by the influence of migrants. Even more important, however, is the fact that the minority's culture changes and develops in response to the challenges of the land of settlement and to the pull of possible further onward migration. When we speak of minority culture, therefore, we are speaking of a complex and changing entity that has to engage with the host society.

Two other final points may be made about the settlement of immigrant minorities in modern nation-states. One is that minorities may find allies in the host society who help them in the achievement of their political aims even though they may take care to defend their own interests within these alliances. The other is that over time the descendants of immigrants might defect from their own culture and it may well be that, if there is no new immigration, the problem of multiculturalism may be a three or four generation problem only.

### Bibliography

Durkheim. E. 1933. *The Division of Labour in Society*. Glencoe, IL: Free Press.

Guibernau, M. and Rex, J. 1997. *The Ethnicity Reader*. Cambridge: Polity Press.

Marshall, T. H. 1951. *Citizenship and Social Class*. Cambridge: Cambridge University Press.

Rex, J. 1996. *Ethnic Minorities in the Modern Nation State*. London: Macmillan.

Rex, J. and Drury, B. 1994. *Ethnic Mobilisation in a Multicultural Europe*. Aldershot: Avebury.

Schierup C.-U. and Alund, A.1990. *Paradoxes of Multiculturalism*. Aldershot: Gower.

John Rex

# Music and Nationalism

A part of the Herderian legacy has been the quest for the expression of the national culture in music. The proposition that the purest values of a nation are to be found in the "uncorrupted" traditions of the countryside led many protagonists of nationhood to look at all aspects of rural culture, including folk music, as encapsulating something profound and specific to the national "soul."

The practical articulation of this, broadly speaking, was a four- or maybe five-stage process. The first was the rediscovery of folk music by urban ethnographers, the recording of a vanishing past and establishing a frequently impressive record of village musical life and manners. The second stage was the transformation of this database into "high cultural" music, whereby the nation in question would be enabled to take its place among the high cultural national communities of Europe (where the movement had its origins and strongest protagonists).

This is the music that is customarily seen as "nationalist." It is marked by melodies that have or acquire powerful emotional resonance because they refer to their folk music origins and are, therefore, said to be the projection of that nation in musical terms. National-patriotic music of this kind has various themes, notably war, village life, the native hero against alien treason and so on. What is crucial to this music is that its mythic element is native and not taken from the standard mythopoeias, like the Greek, the Christian, the mediaeval, or the Romantic. In that sense and to that extent it underpins the national self-awareness and is, in effect, saying, "pay attention to us, we have just the same heroes and traditions as you." It is a way of placing one's high culture on the map.

The movement began on the margins, and, especially in Central Europe, at the moment when urbanization had already begun to erode the archaic ways of the countryside, and then, in a third stage, reacted back on the developed West. In this way, the national movement in music acquired a canonical character. Among the best known-figures composing national music were Dvořák and Smetana (Czech lands), Bartók and Kodály (Hungary), Enescu (Rumania), Borodin, Rimsky-Korsakov, and Musorgsky (Russia), Sibelius (Finland) Vaughan Williams (England). Less well known, but clearly having a place in this list are Suchon (Slovakia), Ciurlionis (Lithuania), or Szymanowski (Poland). Arguably, one can place third-stage composers like D'Indy and Canteloube (France), Ives and Copland (U.S.),

Grieg (Norway), Alfven (Sweden), and Granados and Falla (Spain) into this category. Wagner, as in so many things, is in a category of his own. He directly created his own mythic images and a musical language in which to express his idea of Germany in *Der Ring des Niebelungen* but he by no means restricted himself to a German idealism, so that it is not wholly accurate to regard him as a German nationalist composer pure and simple.

A possible fourth phase, some considerable distance from the original impulse, was constituted by those who used the folk motifs of another culture, thereby implying the assumption of the concept into the European mainstream. Brahms, Debussy, and Ravel are evidently in this category.

The unusual aspect of this entire process is that, throughout the period in question, very roughly from 1850 to 1950, one particular national tradition was never regarded as such, but was accepted as the canon: Germany-cum-Austria. Thus, the use of folk motifs by Schumann or Strauss, or of the *Ländler* by Mahler have never been seriously counted as "nationalist" music.

Some might see a fifth phase in the folksong revival of the 1960s and after, not least because in places it had an explicitly ethno-national character and was intended to underpin the national revival on the European periphery in the West. The Celtic fringe, Occitania, Catalonia and elsewhere all took part in this mode of self-articulation. It is noteworthy in this connection that this fifth-phase revival remained at the popular level and had almost no influence on "high cultural" music.

There were some parallels to this under communism in Central and Eastern Europe. Probably the best known example is the "Singing Revolution" in Estonia, where the role of popular choirs singing folksongs was seen as central in underpinning a national consciousness and encouraging the movement towards independence. In Hungary, the so-called "dance-house movement" of the 1970s and after drew heavily on the folk music of the Hungarians of Rumania, attained considerable popularity and was generally understood as an expression of solidarity with the Hungarians of Rumania.

Interesting in this context was that in the Czech lands it was jazz that acquired the role of being the focus of protest against communism. The Jazz Section of the Musicians' Union and the band the "Plastic People of the Universe" attracted considerable following because they were seen as defying the communist authorities. By the 1990s in Central and Eastern Europe, folk music had been reabsorbed into popular music and had given rise to a folk-influenced pop music with something of a national character.

In terms of content, "nationalist" music varies from what is little more than the reiteration of folksongs in, say, orchestral guise to the radical restructuring of folk motifs to produce a wholly new musical language. Arguably, Janáček and Bartók were the two most outstanding exponents of the latter. Although their musical expression was very different, they both wrote music in which the original folk element had been recast and was barely recognizable to the untutored ear. Another path was to compose music influenced by the folk tradition, in which the composer no longer used direct quotation but wrote music that was permeated by that tradition; or the two could be combined.

The broader social and cultural context of national music can be understood in the light of center-periphery theory. The national cultures of the European periphery felt themselves to be "incomplete" if they did not possess what they regarded as the full European cultural tradition. This tradition was identified variously with France or Germany or England. Completeness was defined, therefore, in an evidently abstracted way and certainly without any serious study of the roots, including the rural roots, of these "complete" canonical cultures. The idea of completeness was simply projected onto them and the definitions of Europeanness used on the periphery could never be more than a form of cultural appropriation.

Underlying this appropriation was a twofold response. There was fear that without completeness the nation in question would not be able to ensure its uninterrupted cultural reproduction. And, linked to this, was the fear that without a complete culture, the nation in question would not be recognized as fully European and thus possessing "moral worth."

Moral worth was measured by reference to the West which was seen as the "center." The agendas and schemata into which the Central and East European periphery wished to fit were defined by an interactive process between East and West. Thus, the protagonists of the cultures of the periphery felt that they were working in traditions that had to "catch up." In order to do so, they would have, as it were, to make a forced march through history and attain standards that the center was already seen as having reached. Hence, a spurt was needed and, if successful, within a generation, that culture would gain the desired accolade of universal European recognition. In reality, this never quite happened as its protagonists had hoped. This was because a single, universal European standard—in music, as, indeed, in any other field of cultural endeavor—had never really existed.

Besides, the entire project had two not wholly reconcilable aims—one political, the other cultural. The political aim was to ensure the untroubled cultural reproduction of the nation in question, to gain sufficient political power to secure the national community from its real and imagined enemies. Excessive emphasis on this goal would result in the politicization of art. Admittedly, this was more difficult to achieve in music than it was in literature or the theatre. Furthermore, a politicization of music would undermine its aesthetic value and weaken its claim to Europe-wide recognition. The cultural objective was to realize the aesthetic criteria of the "center." However, as noted above, the "European standard" was, in this sense, always more vague, more fluid than it had appeared from the periphery.

This process of cultural elevation was further complicated by the tendency to regard the work of one or other national composer who was successfully received in the West as an indication of mainstream taste. However, from the Western, supposed mainstream perspective, such positive reception depended primarily on aesthetic grounds. But from the standpoint of the periphery culture, it was a political and cultural success, which served the cause of the nation. Time and again, the playing of the music of this or that composer from the periphery was seen there as the assimilation of the music into mainstream culture, even when it might have been little more than a particular event, perhaps a brief excursion into exoticism.

At heart, those on the periphery never understood that critical opinion in the West was moved not by an abstract (and nonexistent) European aesthetic standard, but by local elements into which local ethnic elements might well have intruded. What has always been very difficult to see from either center or periphery has been the reciprocal quality of the European musical tradition, that throughout Europe individual composers and musicians might take over elements from another tradition on an *ad hoc* basis without ever being driven by a notional transcendental European standard.

Within national cultural communities, the discovery, identification and definition of folk music as national music has had a paradoxical result. Folk music began as the unself-conscious expression of a particular community living in particular social and economic conditions, with the music serving purposes of entertainment, ritual or just spontaneous expression proper to that community. Folk music then comes to be defined as the representation of the ethnic element of a particular community that is wider and different from the rural community in which it originates. But given modern communications, the now redefined music acquires a life of its own and impacts back on the rural community, which then reacts by reformulating its musical tradition, because it lives in its own center-periphery relationship with the ethnic center. Hence, the very purity that the national movement is so anxious to safeguard is automatically diluted.

Further, once folk music is identified and defined and placed as such into the public sphere, the national community in question will absorb it and regard it as its own, authentic form of ethnic self-expression. In this way, the appropriated folk elements are transmuted into an articulation of the redefined national character and, it is important to stress this, acquire a wholly new authenticity that has little or nothing to do with the rural world from which it sprang and everything to do with the modern or modernizing environment in which that music is now used. Thus, far from being a reflection of the "national soul," national music actually shapes that "soul."

Here is a concrete example. Before the coming of modernity in Hungary, Hungarian folk musicians used a somewhat crude double-reed wind instrument known as the *tarogato*. The *tarogato* became a national emblem in the nineteenth century, because it was seen as the truly authentic Hungarian musical instrument, and various urban patriots sought to play it (it is said to be quite difficult). By doing so, they contributed to the creation of an (admittedly short-lived) *tarogato* playing culture which became a strong expression of Hungarian nationhood; Hungarians saw their national identity as partly expressed in their playing of the *tarogato*. They played it and were made Hungarian by so doing. This shaping could only take place after the appropriation was finished; it was, of course, inconceivable for a genuine *tarogato* player to be invited into the elegant drawing rooms of upper middle-class Budapest society—there were limits to patriotism. This example could be parallelled by countless others from different cultures.

Overall, the trajectory of national and nationalist music can be seen as having started from the poorest and least modernized sections of the rural population, was appropriated by other social groups to strengthen national feeling, found expression in high culture, then faded until it was revived once more at the street level among the descendants of the marginal peasantry.

### Bibliography

Hughes, Gervase. 1967. *Dvořák: His Life and Music*. London: Cassell.

Karolyi, Otto. 1994. *Modern British Music*. London: Rutherford.

Millington, Barry (ed.). 1992. *The Wagner Compendium: A Guide to Wagner's Life and Music*. London: Thames and Hudson.

Whittall, Arnold. 1987. *Romantic Music*. London: Thames and Hudson.

George Schöpflin

# Myth and Symbolism Theory of Nationalism

It is a salutary challenge to present one's own theory in a limited space. But the task is difficult, especially when one's writings, beginning with a 1949 M.A. thesis on *The Baltic Nationalities between Germany and Russia*, span five decades.

Clearly an autobiographical approach, addressing theoretical positions in consecutive writings, would be inappropriate. All the same, the reader deserves, from time to time, some indications of continuity and change in the author's theoretical positions. It is important to stress that these positions constitute a "work in progress," which will probably never be complete. For example, as late as 1992, I expressed the view that more critical analysis of the Anglo-American version plus extended biographical studies was required before a comprehensive theory of nationalism could be attempted (Armstrong 1992a: 32, 37). But less than three years later, I concluded that "my assessment of the rocky road to theory may have been somewhat too pessimistic" (Armstrong 1995). Both rapid changes in the nationalist environment, notably in Eastern Europe, and the development of nationalism studies, led to this altered position. In these circumstances, the best approach at present appears to be to take up major theses, suggesting for each my own position, and briefly noting where appropriate, how each position has changed.

My first publications on nationalism contained extended references to religion: the roles of the Uniate Ukrainian Church and its Orthodox counterparts were essential components of Ukrainian nationalism (1955) and religious roles were even more salient in the comparative article, "Collaborationism in World War II: The integral nationalist variant in Eastern Europe" (1968a). Subsequent familiarity with the impressive sociological work by Peter L. Berger and Thomas Luckmann enabled me to show more clearly how nationalism, as a type of identity, "shelters the individual from ultimate terror," that is, death as "the most terrifying breakdown of identity" (Berger and Luckmann 1966: 46, 96). To a believer such as myself, universal religions (particularly those of the "Peoples of the Book," Muslims, Jews, and Christians) remain more satisfying than nationalism. But, as will appear later, in a secularized world, reinforcing combinations of national and religious identity occur frequently. In the worst circumstances, the combination may lead to extreme violation of justice; in better cases, religious concern for justice for all humanity may curb the excesses of nationalism (Armstrong 1997).

# Myth and Symbolism Theory of Nationalism

Because religion (often the mould of civilizations) is so salient in my interpretation, it is important at the start to stress that most of the following remarks apply primarily to nationalist movements in Europe. At various crucial points I shall point out how Islam differs. Initially, this difference arises from the distinct manner in which this religion differs from Christianity and most other world religions. Ideally, the *Dar ul'Islam* (House of the Faith) should constitute a single entity, with the identity of all believing rulers who protected that Faith of minor concern to the mass of believers. After some centuries of limited unity, the *de facto* fragmentation of the House induced most Islamic religious leaders to adopt a doctrine resembling the "king by Grace of God" principle among Christians, that is, acceptance of the ruler who had seized and maintained power, regardless of the extent or ethnographic character of his realm. In the current populist age, rulers (elected or usurpers) tend to be judged more severely on their ability to defend the Faith, domestically and from non-Islamic enemies. Except in the most stable polities (Turkey, Egypt, and perhaps Iran), religious considerations continue to trump ethnic claims of nationalism (Hodgson 1965).

As Berger and Luckmann pointed out over thirty years ago, in some sense, all human institutions are social constructs; more recently, specialists on nationalism like Eric Hobsbawm and Benedict Anderson, have emphasised that nationalism (and even the nation as such) was "invented," or "imagined" (Hobsbawm 1990; Anderson 1985). This position, which entails the conviction that no particular nation is "primordial" but that all originated from human agency at specific times and places, is widely held by nationalism specialists, Steven Grosby being a notable exception (Grosby 1994; 1996). In general, I share this consensus, while stipulating that *nations*, but no particular nation of the modern type, and certainly not *nationalism* existed before the sixteenth century. In my early works I was strongly influenced by the view, most cogently expressed by Hans Kohn and Carlton J. H. Hayes, that nationalism arose during the era of the French Revolution, and diffused in expanding circles to overseas countries of European origin, to Eastern Europe, and eventually to Asian and African countries

(Kohn 1944; Hayes 1933). Both these pioneers regarded nationalism as the product of specific intellectual and organizational activities of elites, primarily those directing the French Revolution. Indeed, Hayes tended to relate both democracy and nationalism to the Industrial Revolution (Hayes 1935). In contrast, I describe industrialisation as a "high human adventure not so closely linked to either democracy or nationalism" (Armstrong 1973). Moreover, recent research indicates that nationalism was produced in France several centuries earlier than the Revolution, or, according to Liah Greenfeld, in sixteenth-century England (Greenfeld 1992).

Such issues of timing and agency are very important to my theory, for my methodological preference is for intensive employment of historical data over the *longue durée*. I have consistently rejected "evolutionary theory" and its biological ontology, and even structural functionalism insofar as its organic model tends to reject human agency (Armstrong 1973). Instead, I favor multifactorial interpretations that leave a considerable scope to individual and group initiatives.

The premodern social formations that I treat in *Nations before Nationalism* (1982) and elsewhere, although the analysis is basically similar to that of modern nationalism, require an approach rather less specific in terms of the time and place of the genesis of national ideas (for example, see my study of Ukrainian national consciousness, in Armstrong 1992b). Fundamental themes are myth, symbol, and communication, especially as they relate to boundary mechanisms of a psychological rather than territorial nature. The French writer who observed that the "mythic past cannot be dated, it is a part before time or, better, outside time," had in mind the myths associated with the French Revolution as much as those relating to the ancient Gauls (Armstrong 1982). It is precisely the timelessness of myth, rather than its degree of truth content, that characterises myth as opposed to history. It is important to know whether a nationalist myth was initiated by obscure people and propagated only by word of mouth, or was deliberately constructed by self-conscious elites. However, persistence and dissemination are far more significant than genesis. For the symbols that commonly convey the myth, often in a subliminal manner, identifiable initiation is often more frequent than in the case of the myth itself, although the latter is far more complex. For example, innumerable folk traits, including elaborate costumes as well as linguistic devices, can be shown (as in the Scottish clan tartan) to have been invented by enterprising merchants; but perpetuation over centuries is commonly the work of elites interested in bolstering identity as well as those seeking commercial gain. Clearly elite perpetuation depends on manipulation of communication channels, whether early reliance on religious networks or contemporary resort to mass education and electronic media.

Consequently, while genetic explanations are relatively useful in explaining origination and persistence of elite institutions like governing bureaucracies, it is often not possible to trace many nationalist ideas that aim at popular audiences (Armstrong 1973; Greenfeld 1992). Because elites seeking to employ myth themes and symbols wish to influence such audiences, elites (like contemporary public relations specialists) eagerly scan the fund of popular beliefs and slogans for elements that can be incorporated in a mythic structure. As a result, not only is the myth structure complex; much of its substance, as well as many of its symbols originated in a truly "popular" form, taken out of context and often subtly altered to attract a mass audience. To some extent, therefore, the contours of the myth do include "primordial" elements. For example, many twentieth century Germans, even those well-educated, continue to believe that contemporary *Stämme* (e.g., Schwaben, Bavarians, Saxons) are direct descendants of the conquest agglomerations of the "barbarian invasions" or even Tacitus' vivid description of "tribes" centuries earlier. Scholarship has demonstrated, however, that *Stämme* identities were drastically altered during the late Middle Ages to correspond to the interests of rulers of emerging territorial states (Armstrong 1982). Nevertheless, present-day politicians occasionally resort to stereotypes derived from the "primordial" *Stämm* characterisations, to flatter their constituents. Ordinarily, such German rhetoric is no more dangerous than U.S. politicians' resort to football tropes such as "On Wisconsin" or "Anchors Aweigh." However, a clever demagogue like Hitler could manipulate the stereotypes with disastrous results.

The preceding discussion suggests that I accept the premise of elite predomination in the process of manipulating the dissemination of nationalist ideas. In fact, two of my books, *The Soviet Bureaucratic Elite* (1955) and *The European Administrative Elite* (1973) explicitly endorse the elite premise for a wide range of social communication and institutional activity that is only peripherally related to nationalism. But preceding paragraphs have also suggested restraints on elite influence. Other limitations demand at least passing notice. Most elite members, while often masters of rhetorical persuasion, are far from sophisticated thinkers. In propagating notions like nationalism, their expression is often unconsciously ideological, that is, it is imbued with what Karl Marx in one of his most trenchant observations termed "false consciousness." In Marx's doctrinaire system, the term implied furtherance of unacknowledged class interests. More broadly (and I think more fairly) construed, false consciousness is present when any person or group employs arguments that, often unconsciously, mask self-interest, material or psychological. Because nationalist arguments are frequently taken over by groups whose perceived status interests differ sharply from the originators', the ideology is especially susceptible to change in intensity or even direction, as analysis of totalitarian systems (which has occupied me throughout much of my career) demonstrate. Thus, the relatively mild pseudo-ethnic stereotypes of the nineteenth century became (as the preceding paragraph mentions) a potent Nazi tool, while Lenin's extreme adaptation of Marxism, although nominally tolerant of national diversity, became a legitimization of ethnic cleansing under Stalin.

While recognizing the key role of elite interests in the spread of nationalism, I sharply reject the notion that material interests consistently predominate. Whereas writers like Benedict Anderson appear to me to privilege working-class interests by exempting them from identification as "ideology," many other analysts of nationalism identify the material interests (in jobs as teachers, journalists, etc.) of nationalist leaders. To me, such search for material incentives, although pertinent, is often one-sided. More often, status incentives, which include a range of psychic satisfactions are more influential, as Liah Greenfeld has argued in her finding that *ressentiment*, directed at exclusive claims by representatives of a dominant culture (domestic or foreign), constituted the principal impetus to nationalism.

One reason elite interests in nationalism, consciously perceived or not, shift readily, is that the ideology is manipulated by social "outsiders" (whether motivated by material or *ressentiment* concerns) who must reach a broader audience to have a chance of prevailing. In the nineteenth century and in many regions during the twentieth century, this *populist* strategy has entailed three crucial arguments. One is glorification of the peasants. Even when, as is often the case today, these constitute a distinct popular minority, the intergenerational nostalgia common in nationalism assures that this glorification will have a wide resonance. Second, the occupation of the soil by peasant farmers commonly constitutes the basis for boundary claims. These claims are asserted in terms of peasant speech patterns (isoglosses), wherever these can be determined on the ground "scientifically," that is, wherever "ETHNONATIONALISM" predominates. Third, even where linguistic experts recognise that linguistic divisions between peasants in transitional regions like the Pripet marshes (Ukrainian-Belorussian) and Macedonia (Serb-Bulgar) are necessarily arbitrary, conflicting ethnonationalist claims often remain ardent (Lunt 1984).

Because Islamic myths, derived from the nomadic and urban environments of the originators of the religion and their most successful political and military epigones, treat peasant traditions as secondary or even inferior, the peasant of ethnonationalism is usually weak in Muslim societies (although it exerts some force in agrarian lands like Egypt). Where historic population intermixtures prevail (often in Balkan and Caucasian regions at one time under Muslim rule), the peasant myth component is especially vivid among contemporary Christian populations. In the absence of clear linguistic demarcations, however, the isogloss boundary is often replaced, with tragic consequences, by "ethnic cleansing" based on "historic" or "religious" affiliations (Armstrong 1988).

The preceding discussion suggests that nationalists, regardless of their personal motivations usually acquire an interest in maximising territory. Given the centrality of their objective of founding or expanding a national state in the international system as it has existed since 1648, such a *geopolitical* concern, one type of material interest, has been unavoidable. Given the assumptions of the system (at least until recently), defensible frontiers and a considerable measure of autarky have been indispensable in Europe. In Islam, on the contrary, the shaky legitimacy of any polity (see above) has made such concern with stable frontiers and autarky less salient among *soi-disant* nationalists. Even in such a linguistically and religiously distinctive polity as Iran, finding a base for restoring Islamic legal and social institutions as widely as possible, seems to take precedence over securing a territorial state.

The considerations just advanced—which derive both from the historical record interpreted in *Nations before Nationalism* and from observation of recent developments—point to the limitations of the nationalist state. In European "Christendom" (if such an entity can be posited after 1648) a major legitimisation for each absolutist entity was its "Christian mission," derived both from Biblical interpretations and from the historical perception (a quasi-national heritage) of Islam as the overweening threat. When, during the nineteenth century, this mission eroded during secularisation, it was replaced by Social Darwinism which elevated nationalist egoism to an extreme. In some non-European cultures—notably Japanese—such a radical national egoism also predominated. Islamic nationalism often embraced a radical version of the *jihad* precept, which (in conflict with religious counsels to respect non-Muslims) justified almost any means to attain the end of communal ascendancy. Reactions, notably among Hindus, contributed to an ascending spiral of violence.

In nominally Christian polities, diasporas, originating as non-Christian (Jews, certain Muslim elements) or from dissident Christian churches (Armenians, some Calvinist sects) have, for many centuries, provided bases, often economically and culturally fructifying, for non-territorial ethnic attachments (Armstrong 1987). More recently, the territorial autarky that characterised the most successful national states inherited from European absolutism, has been eroding. Technological innovations, especially in COMMUNICATIONS, followed by changes in corporative structure, have not only reduced the physical capacity for autarky, but have lowered the salience for personal identity of the national state. In his very recent book, Ernst Haas finds this identity transfer especially strong (as contrasted to the English-speaking countries) in France and Germany, pillars of the new European Community (Haas 1997). Yet, the paroxysm of Social Darwinist nationalism in Nazi Germany, the distortion of Marxism by Lenin and his epigones, and savage ethnic cleansing in Caucasia, the Balkans, and Africa render prediction of the end of nationalism dubious. Moreover, it is uncertain that the latter's role in promoting international pluralism is obsolete. The nation-state order defeated two totalitarian attempts at world empire. One is obliged, given the fragility of civil society, to ask whether a supranational order averting violence will feel compelled to promote social conformity; nor is it clear how regions where freedom is established could, without a measure of nationalist self-confidence, coexist with countries where the *cycle of ETHNOCENTRISM* is still peaking.

As noted at the start, the myth and symbolism theory of nationalism which is outlined in this article is a work in progress. Consequently, pessimistic as the last paragraph may appear, it is subject to revision as long as one is able to observe the impact of extreme nationalism, as a *cyclic* phenomenon, on world events. But this qualification merely emphasises that the study of nationalism, in all its complexity, merges with the study of world civilisations, as manifested in their material accomplishments, their psychological tensions and satisfactions, and ultimately, their spiritual achievements.

## Bibliography

Anderson, Benedict. 1985. *Imagined Communities*. London: Verso.

Armstrong, John A. 1968a. "Collaborationism in World War II: the integral nationalist variant in Eastern Europe," *Journal of Modern History* 40, 1: 396-410.

Armstrong, John A. 1968b. "The ethnic scene in the Soviet Union: the view of the dictatorship," in Erich Goldhagen (ed.), *Ethnic Minorities in the Soviet Union*. New York: Frederick A. Praeger. Reprinted in *Journal of Soviet Nationalities* 1990, 1, 1: 1-13.

Armstrong, John A. 1973. *The European Administrative Elite*. Princeton, NJ: Princeton University Press.

Armstrong, John A. 1980. "Administrative elites in multiethnic polities," *International Political Science Review* 1, 1: 107-28.

Armstrong, John A. 1982. *Nations before Nationalism*. Chapel Hill: University of North Carolina Press.

Armstrong, John A. 1987. "Mobilized and Proletarian Diasporas," in Helen Fein (ed.)., *The Persisting Question: Sociological Perspectives and Social Contexts of Modern Antisemitism*. Berlin: Walter de Gruyter.

Armstrong, John A. 1988. "Toward a framework for considering nationalism in East Europe," *Eastern European Politics and Societies* 2, 2: 288-89.

Armstrong, John A. 1990a (1955). *Ukrainian Nationalism*, third edition. Englewood, CO: Ukrainian Academic Press.

Armstrong, John A. 1990b. "Contemporary ethnicity: the moral dimension in comparative perspective," *Review of Politics* 52, 2: 163-88.

Armstrong, John A. 1992a. "The autonomy of ethnic identity," in Alexander J. Motyl (ed.), *Thinking Theoretically about Soviet Nationalities*. New York: Columbia University Press.

Armstrong, John A. 1992b. "Myth and history in the evolution of Ukrainian consciousness," in Peter J. Potichnyj (ed.), *Ukraine and Russia in their Historical Encounter*. Edmonton: Canadian Institute of Ukrainian Studies Press.

Armstrong, John A. 1992c. "Nationalism in the former Soviet Empire," *Problems of Communism* 41, 1-2: 121-131.

Armstrong, John A. 1994a. "National liberation and international balance," *Nationalities Papers* 22, 1: 11-26.

Armstrong, John A. 1994b. Review Esssay of *Nationalism: Five Roads to Modernity* by Liah Greenfeld, *History and Theory* 33, 1: 79-96.

Armstrong, John A. 1995. "Toward a theory of nationalism: consensus and dissensus," in

## Myth and Symbolism Theory of Nationalism

Sukumar Periwal (ed.), *Notions of Nationalism*. Budapest: Central European University Press.

Armstrong, John A. 1997. "Religious nationalism and collective violence," *Nations and Nationalism* 3, 4: 597-606.

Berger, Peter and Thomas Luckmann. 1966. *The Social Construction of Reality*. Garden City, NY: Doubleday.

Greenfeld, Liah. 1992. *Nationalism: Five Roads to Modernity*. Cambridge, MA: Harvard University Press.

Grosby, Steven. 1994. "The verdict of history: the inexpungeable tie of primordiality," *Ethnic and Racial Studies* 17, 2: 164-71.

Grosby, Steven. 1996. "The category of the primordial in the study of early Christianity and second-century Judaism," *History of Religions* 36, 2: 139-63.

Haas, Ernst. 1997. *Nationalism, Liberalism and Progress: The Rise and Decline of Nationalism*. Ithaca, NY: Cornell University Press.

Hayes, Carlton J. H. 1933. *Essays on Nationalism*. New York: Macmillan.

Hayes, Carlton J. H. 1935. *A Political and Social History of Europe*. New York: Macmillan (see esp. vol. 2, part IV, "Democracy and Nationalism").

Hobsbawm, Eric. 1990. *Nations and Nationalism since 1780*. Cambridge: Cambridge University Press.

Hodgson, Marshall. 1965. *The Venture of Islam*, 3 vols. Chicago: University of Chicago Press.

Hroch, Miroslav. 1985. *Social Preconditions of National Revival in Europe*. Cambridge: Cambridge University Press.

Kohn, Hans. 1944. *The Idea of Nationalism*. New York: Macmillan.

Lunt, Horace. 1984. "Some sociological aspects of Macedonian and Bulgarian," *Papers in Slavic Philology*.

Seton-Watson, Hugh. 1977. *Nations and States*. Boulder, CO: Westview Press.

Smith, Anthony D. 1991. *National Identity*. London: Penguin Books, 1991.

Young, M. Crawford. 1976. *The Politics of Cultural Pluralism*. Madison: University of Wisconsin Press.

John A. Armstrong

# N

## "Nation": A Survey of the Term in European Languages

Nothing connected with nations is simple or unproblematic and terminology is not an exception. Although the word "nation" is used all around the world every day, it is questionable whether we speak about the same thing. Scholars, too, are unable to come to an agreement about a working definition of the nation and often give up trying to define the term. Instead, current scholarly discourse tends to concentrate on the analysis of nationalism. This is just an illusory solution to the problem.

The term "nationalism" is a derivative of the term "nation" which has had in various times and cultural-linguistic milieux different meanings and connotations. The classical dichotomy of "Western" and "Eastern" nationalism as elaborated by Hans Kohn (1945), and still influential in its more recent modifications of "civic" and "ethnic" nationalism, appears insufficient in addressing the variety and changes of the concepts of nation. Varying definitions of the nation are not merely a product of theoretical reflections and political ideology, but they result also from the development of individual languages, rooted in particular social, political, and cultural contexts. Therefore, even when dealing with typologies of nationalism it may be useful to take into consideration the semantic differences implied in the term "nation" in individual languages.

Our aim is neither to discuss different scholarly definitions of the nation nor to address the dispute between the "primordialists" and the "modernists" concerning the origins of nations. Our starting point is the undisputed fact that by the nineteenth century the majority of the European population had acquired the awareness that they belonged to a large community which they called nation, "*la nation*," "*die Nation*," "*nemzet*," "*nasjon*," "*narod*," and so on. However, while

outside Europe—and the countries sharing its cultural and political background—the terminological development followed rather different paths, the semantic sources of the concept of nation in European languages can be traced back to the medieval period.

This article concentrates on the changes in the understanding of the term "nation" and its equivalents from the Middle Ages to the early modern period and the age of nationalism. For the premodern period, this involves two interconnected issues: the evolution and modification of the meaning of the term "*natio*" and its translations in individual European languages and, second, the development of other terms denoting a community, whether existing or invented, for which in the nineteenth century the term "nation" was used retrospectively. This survey should help English-speaking students of nationalism realize that the terms considered as equivalents of the English word "nation" may have somewhat different connotations in other European languages.

The origin of the term "nation" as it is currently used in most European languages can be traced back to the Latin word "*natio*," derived from the verb "*nascor*," I am born. In ancient Rome, "*natio*" designated a group sharing a common origin, a kind or a race, and was mostly applied to foreign peoples and tribes. While in this sense it was sometimes used as a synonym of "*gens*," it often referred to more distant and barbarous peoples and thus had a somewhat derogatory connotation. For themselves, Romans reserved the term "*populus*" which meant the citizens, the plebeians and the people as the source of sovereignty.

In medieval Latin, "*natio*" preserved its meaning of a group related by birth or place of origin. Initially, it designated a foreign, heathen people, but gradually it lost its derogatory connotation. It was used, for example, for foreign merchants and particularly for members of universities who were divided into "*nationes*" according to their

# "Nation": A Survey of the Term in European Languages

birthplace or language. By the early fourteenth century the concept had found its way to the councils of the Catholic Church whose members voted as representatives of "*nationes*."

These semantic shifts are sometimes interpreted as changes in the concept of nation from a group of foreigners to a "community of opinion and purpose" in university disputations, and later, in the councils, to "representatives of cultural and political authority" or an elite (Greenfeld 1992: 4-5). At the same time, although the delimitation of these "*nationes*" was generally vague and imprecise, language played an important role. At the council of Constance in 1415, for example, Hungarians, Czechs, Poles, Danes, and Swedes were connected to the German "*natio*" while the delegates of Savoy, Provence, and parts of Lorraine voted as members of the French "*natio*" on the basis of their French language. It is worth noting that the English "*natio*" in Constance in particular stressed the importance of the ties of blood and common language (Kemiläinen 1964: 22).

Apart from these international occasions, local sources such as chronicles, also indicated a certain awareness of cultural-linguistic ties in the late Middle Ages. This community was rarely called "*natio*." Instead, it was sometimes referred to by the term "*gens*," which had originally meant foreigners as in ancient Rome, or "*lingua*" and its translations, which among other things, designated a group of people using the same language (Du Cange 1885: 116).

However, it was the Latin term "*natio*" which became the basis of the new terminology in national languages in the sense in which it is used today. These terms were either loanwords from Latin, as the French or English "nation," or calques, translations of the original Latin meaning of "being born," like the Czech "*národ*" or the Hungarian "*nemzet*." Not infrequently, both the calque and the loanword existed and, at least temporarily, were used simultaneously, for example, "*naród*" and "*nacja*" in Polish and "*narod*" and "*natsiya*" in Russian.

By the sixteenth and seventeenth centuries, and in some cases even earlier, the Latin term "*natio*" possessed its equivalents in most European languages. In French the word "*nation*" (or "*nascion*") appeared already in the twelfth century, though up to the seventeenth century, it was not precisely defined and was applied particularly for university divisions or foreign merchants as in medieval Latin (*Trésor de la langue française* 1986: 2-3 ; Godechot 1988: 13-14). The late thirteenth-century Italian "*nazione*" was later reintroduced after it ceased to be used in the fifteenth century (Cortelazzo and Zolli 1983: 796). The Czech word "*národ*" can be found in the early fourteenth century, but its meaning then vacillated between anything born, a kind, kinship, gender, and a group of people of a common origin (Gebauer 1970: 492-493).

The early modern period also witnessed the identification of the concept of nation with the emerging political community. In this sense, England is often mentioned as the first and unique example where the term "nation" gained the meaning of the people as a repository of sovereignty and a basis of political solidarity (Greenfeld 1992: 6-7). By the early seventeenth century, "the nation" designated the whole people of a country (Onions 1970: 1311). At the same time, other interpretations, including common origin and even blood, survived.

In parts of Central and Eastern Europe the term also acquired a political content somewhat different from that of England. The Latin word "*natio*" was introduced for a political nation, in the sense of elites—the estates, and particularly the nobility. The concepts "*Natio Polonica*" as well as "*Natio Hungarica*" did not have an ethnic connotation, at least not in this period, and were connected with the state and its ruling classes. Thus, "*Natio Hungarica*," the nation of Hungary (not the Magyar nation), meant privileged estates, in contrast to their subjects, the "*plebs*." This political and territorial concept included the nobility living within the limits of the Hungarian Kingdom, regardless of their ethnic origin and even knowledge of the Hungarian language (Islamov 1992: 166).

"*Natio Polonica*" had a similar political implication of the estates. The nobility defined itself through the state in which it ruled. At the same time, two Polish expressions existed which today signify "nation." The older word "*naród*" was still used in the sixteenth century, with a lack of precision, in the sense of estate, generation, group of people etc. (Linde 1857: 274). The term "*nacja*" was introduced in the second half of the sixteenth century and applied more specifically to a large group of people, either foreign or Polish.

In German, the term "*Nation*" appeared alongside the older term "*Volk*." Originally denoting a medieval regiment of warriors, the latter gained the meaning of a group of people connected by certain ties, like members of a family or a profession. By the sixteenth century, "*Volk*" denoted a community of people sharing the same origin, country, language, and laws, or the inhabitants of a country under one ruler, sometimes with the connotation of the lower classes, the common people (Grimm 1951: 453-471). The German word "*Nation*" was an equivalent of "*Volk*" in the sense of a people with a common origin and territory. However, already in the sixteenth century, "*Nation*" also referred to the estates, representatives of the people. In this latter sense, the term was used by Luther who, in his *An den Christlichen Adel Teutscher Nation* used the terms "German nation" to refer to bishops and princes ruling over the people, "*Volk*," and protecting it (Luther 1898: 223).

Apart from the spread of the term "nation" in national languages, the medieval terms indicating ethnic ties such as "*lingua*" or "*gens*," together with the Latin "*natio*," survived in Central Europe. According to Johannes Calvinus' *Lexicon Juridicum* from the seventeenth century, "*natio*" and "*gens*" were synonymous, but "*natio*" implied a common country while "*gens*" referred to a series of ancestors (Kemiläinen 1964: 23). The Czech scholar Jan Amos Komenský who, in his earlier Czech works, used the words language (*jazyk*), nation (*národ*) and people (*lid*) indiscriminately, in his Latin work *Gentis Felicitas* from 1652 defined "*Gens, seu Natio*" as "a number of people originating from the same tribe, living in the same place in the world (as if in the same house which they call "Country"), using the same language, and thus connected by the same ties of common love, unity and effort for the common welfare" (Komenský 1972: 259).

The eighteenth and nineteenth centuries saw further shifts in the understanding of the term "nation" accompanying an increasing national awareness, although the ambiguity of the terminology as well as the older meanings of the word were preserved. Even in English, "nation" was used in the eighteenth century for races, tribes, ancient and modern peoples, countries, and groups without a state. The Scots, for example, were considered a separate nation as well as forming one nation with England. However, the main characteristics of the nation were seen in a common country and government, especially when referring to England. Nation and country were often used as equivalents. At the same time, the concept of the nation had strong political connotations. In the nineteenth century, Gladstone identified the nation with the electorate ruling the country; Disraeli claimed that to destroy the political institutions meant destroying the nation. More than in any other language, the term "nation" acquired in English the meaning of the state-nation or even the state itself (Kemiläinen 1964: 32-36; Deutsch 1953: 7-8).

In France, the Enlightenment philosophers still used the term "nation" inconsistently, often interchangeably with "*peuple*" (people). Sometimes, the latter had a connotation of common people or the electorate while nation implied, among other things, a distinct character. ROUSSEAU's idea about the "*peuple*" as a collective body with a common will and as the source of sovereignty was taken over by the French Revolution, although the word "*peuple*" was replaced by "*nation*." The Revolution thus spread a new concept of nation encompassing the whole people as the bearer of sovereignty and an ideal worth any sacrifice. The nation, as a person with a distinct character, conscience and will, was regarded as separate from the state and independent of it; it could exist prior to the state or when the state did not exist any more. However, although the nation was not identified with the state, the state could be considered to form one of the characteristics of the nation, together, for example, with the laws, and sometimes with the language. Diderot's *Encyclopédie* defined the nation as a large number of people inhabiting a certain territory and obeying the same government. On the other hand, the Dictionary of the French Academy spoke in 1694, as well as in 1798, about the inhabitants of a single State who live under the same laws and

# "Nation": A Survey of the Term in European Languages

speak the same language, while in the following edition of 1830 the language was not mentioned. Similar definitions, including the state, or the language, or both, appeared in other dictionaries both before and after the Revolution (Kemiläinen 1964: 25-31; Godechot 1988: 13-15).

In the Italian and German cases, the understanding of the nation as a community of origin and cultural values was interwoven with the political claim for statehood. Under the impact of the French revolutionary concept, the Italian term *"nazione"* was connected, in the political discourse, with civil rights. During the *Risorgimento* the state was regarded as a "legal organization of the nation" (*Enciclopedia Italiana* 1934: 471).

In nineteenth-century German, the parallel use of the words *"Nation"* and *"Volk"* persisted. The terms were not entirely synonymous; their meanings overlapped when *"Nation"* was understood as a community characterized by common language and origin (Grimm 1881: 425). At the same time, in the political discourse of the first half of the nineteenth century, *"Nation"* was sometimes connected with the state—namely the Prussian, the Bavarian and other *"Nationen."* Some liberals defined the "modern nation," apart from the language, also by equal civil rights and liberties. However, the revolution of 1848 revealed that in German language usage the concept of the *"Nation"* as a community of culture and common origin was dominant. When politicians claimed the need for a national state, this was not an extension or modification of the definition of the nation, but the state was seen rather as a general precondition for the full existence (and even mission) of a nation, defined by common language and origin.

Norwegian patriots who in 1814 created the Norwegian constitution and asked for the independence of their country used the term *"nasjon"* to designate all citizens living on the Norwegian territory. They determined this territory by historical-geographical criteria and not primarily by language; the literary language of the country was Danish while the population of the countryside spoke a number of rather different Norwegian dialects. Only later generations inserted the unity of language into the definition of Norwegianness (Fure 1989: 38, 76).

The dichotomy of the nation-state and stateless nation is exemplified in the terminological development of modern Greek, marked by a transition from the word *"genos"* to the term *"ethnos."* Up to the early nineteenth century, *"genos,"* which in classical Greek denoted race, kin, clan, family, generation, and so on, prevailed. On the eve of the Greek war of independence, it gained also the meaning of a nation, including the Greeks, and was used simultaneously with the word "ethnos," although the former was more popular. Adamantios Koraes, one of the founders of the Greek national ideology, made a distinction between the two terms: he applied the term *"ethnos"* to those nations which had a state of their own while he used the term *"Genos"* when speaking about the Greeks. Today, the Greek word for nation is *"ethnos,"* or *"Ethnos"* when applied to the Greeks themselves (Xydis 1969: 208-209).

In Poland, on the other hand, the late eighteenth and early nineteenth centuries brought a shift from a political definition of the nation which had prevailed until the division of the Polish state to an ethnic concept. The first step in this direction was the provision of the constitution of May 1791, according to which, Polish was proclaimed the official language of the Polish state. After the dissolution of this state in 1795, Polish politicians faced the question whether the destruction of the state meant also the end of the Polish nation. In this debate, the leader of liberal patriots, writer and historian Hugo Kollataj, described an ideal nation as a community of people knowing their equal rights, including all the estates of the free people and sharing the same language and culture. The persistence of the political concept was manifested in the Constitution of the Grand-Duchy of Warsaw from 1807 which still mentioned only the state, not the nation. Several decades later, Linde's dictionary reflecting the new language usage, defined *"naród"*—as a synonym of *"nacja"*—as a group of people of one language and common customs living in the same territory (Linde 1857: 274). Despite the emphasis on ethnic features, the idea of the Polish state-nation including also the non-Polish population never completely disappeared.

In Czech, the term *"národ"* had been long connected with a language and cultural community.

Therefore, it seemed natural and generally acceptable that in 1806, in the early stage of the Czech national movement, one of its leaders, the linguist Josef Jungmann, defined the nation primarily by language and common past (Zelený 1873: 66-68). In the 1840s, the idea that the characteristics of the modern nation included also the civil liberties and equality of all Czech-speaking inhabitants of the country, appeared. A major mid-nineteenth century encyclopaedia insisted, in almost Gellnerian terms, that "the nation and the state should be one" and that any other situation was unnatural (Rieger 1866: 644). This, however, has not changed the culturally based understanding of the nation; the state was considered a goal, not a feature of the nation.

The Finnish national movement also defined the nation primarily by ethnic features. Two terms existed for this community: the Swedish term *"nation"* and the Finnish *"kansakunta,"* the latter used in this sense already in the late eighteenth century. Unlike other languages, the Finnish term was not a calque of the Latin *"natio"* but a compound, consisting of *"kansa,"* which, since the sixteenth century meant "people," and *"kunta,"* signifying community.

Although the Russian case stands somewhat apart from the major trends outlined above, at least some points of contact can be mentioned. Leaving aside the complex and ambiguous term *"narodnost,"* two expressions for "nation" existed in nineteenth-century Russian: the older *"narod"* which today means "people" and which has a similar etymology as in other Slavic languages, and the recently introduced loanword *"natsiya."* In the mid-nineteenth century dictionaries, *"narod"* was defined as a population of a country or a state, speaking the same language, born on the same territory and living under the same government; as a language, tribe, or as the lower estates—the common people (*Slovar' tserkovno-slavyanskago i russkago yazyka* 1867: 836; Dal' 1865: 1050). *"Natsiya"* was often regarded as a synonym of *"narod."* However, it could also have the connotation of the French *"nation."* One of the dictionaries even gave among its meanings that of "all estates" (*vse sosloviya*), a content which was foreign to the prevailing concept of the nation in Russia (Dal' 1865: 1080).

In the period of emerging nationalism, the new concepts of nation took over the terminology which had earlier developed in individual languages—together with the established connotations of the terms. The emphasis on the different meanings of the term "nation" in various languages is not an end in itself. These differences can help us understand some aspects of the nation-forming processes and are relevant to the current scholarly discourse on nationalism.

Where an old state tradition existed, the concept of nation was related to the state, although the identification of the nation with the state was nowhere as complete as in English language usage. On the other hand, especially when nation-formation occurred in a situation without statehood, the concept of nation emphasized such features as language, culture, or common origin. The nation-state could be a supreme goal, but was not necessarily a criterion of the existence of a nation. Similar differences concern also the derivatives from the term "nation" and particularly "nationalism" which, in some languages, do not naturally imply statehood.

As long as the concept of nation is connected to the state scholars tend to consider the nation-formation processes completed only after/if (independent) statehood has been achieved. The ethnic group and the nation are regarded as separate. A national movement in the framework of such a state-nation is easily classified, and dismissed, as an example of mere "regionalism." Although the importance of the political aspects of the concept of nation vary, the differences cannot be explained by a division of "Western" and "Eastern," "civic" and "ethnic," "democratic" and "undemocratic" nationalisms. The situation is much more diverse. Finally, if the term "nation" and its equivalents in European languages are derived from the common root of the Latin *"natio,"* then it follows that it is necessary to be very careful when using the term for non-European civilizations with a completely different language and cultural social development.

The research for this article was made possible by a grant from the Research Support Scheme of the Open Society Institute/Higher Education Support Programme.

### Bibliography

Cortelazzo, Manlio and Zolli, Paolo. 1983. *Dizionario etimologico della lingua italiana* [Etymological Dictionary of the Italian Language], vol. III. Bologna: Zanichelli.

Dal', Vladimir Ivanovich. 1865. *Tolkovyj slovar' zhivago velikoruskago yazyka* [Dictionary of the Living Great-Russian Language], vol. II. Moskva: Obshchestvo lyubiteley rosiyskoy slovesnosti.

Deutsch, Karl. 1953. *Nationalism and Social Communication: An Inquiry into the Foundations of Nationality.* Cambridge, MA: Harvard University Press.

Du Cange, Carolus du Fresne. 1885. *Glossarium mediae et infimae latinitatis*, 2nd edition, vol. IV. Niort: Léopold Favre.

*Enciclopedia Italiana.* 1934, vol. XXIV. Milano: Rizzoli.

Fure, E. (ed.). 1989. *Eidsvold* 1814. Oslo: Dreyer.

Gebauer, Jan. 1970. *Slovník staročeský* [Old Czech Dictionary], vol. II, 2nd edition. Praha: Academia.

Godechot, Jacques. 1988. "The New Concept of the Nation and its Diffusion in Europe," in O. Dann, O. and J. Dinwiddy (eds.), *Nationalism in the Age of the French Revolution.* London and Ronceverte: The Hambledon Press.

Greenfeld, Liah. 1992. *Nationalism: Five Roads to Modernity.* Cambridge, MA: Harvard University Press.

Grimm, Jacob and Grimm, Wilhelm. 1881. *Deutsches Wörterbuch* [German Dictionary], vol. VII. Leipzig: S. Hirzel.

Grimm, Jacob and Grimm, Wilhelm. 1951. *Deutsches Wörterbuch*, vol. XII. Leipzig: S. Hirzel.

Islamov, Tofik M. 1992. "From *Natio Hungarica* to Hungarian Nation," in R. L. Rudolph and D. F. Good (eds.), *Nationalism and Empire: The Habsburg Empire and the Soviet Union.* New York: St. Martin's Press.

Kemiläinen, Aira. 1964. *Nationalism: Problems Concerning the Word, the Concept and Classification.* Jyväskylä: Kustantajat Publishers.

Kohn, Hans. 1945. *The Idea of Nationalism.* New York: Macmillan.

Kollataj, Hugo. 1954. *Listy Anonima* [Anonymous Letters]. vol. I. Warszawa.

Komenský, Jan Amos. 1972. "Štěstí národa" ["Good Fortune of the Nation"], in J. Polišenský and J. Brambora et al. (eds.), *Vybrané spisy Jana Amose Komenského* [Selected Works of Jan Amos Komenský], vol. VI. Praha: Státní pedagogické nakladatelství.

Linde, Samuel Bogumil. 1857. *Slownik jezyka polskiego* [Dictionary of the Polish Language], vol. III., 2nd edition. Lwów: Zaklad narodowy imienia Ossolińskich.

Luther, Martin. 1898. "An den christlichen Adel Teutscher Nation" ["To the Christian Nobility of the German Nation"], in *Werke* [Works], vol. I. Berlin.

Onions, C.T. (ed.). 1970. *The Shorter Oxford English Dictionary on Historical Principles*, 3rd edition. Oxford: Oxford University Press.

Rieger, František Ladislav (ed.). 1866. *Slovník naučný* [Encyclopaedia], vol. V. Praha: I.L. Kober.

*Slovar' tserkovno-slavyanskago i russkago yazyka* [Dictionary of the Church-Slavonic and Russian Language]. 1867, vol. I. 2nd edition. Sanktpeterburg: Imperatorskaya Akademia nauk.

*Trésor de la langue française* [Thesaurus of the French Language]. 1986, vol. XII. Paris: Gallimard.

Xydis, Stephen G. 1969. "Modern Greek Nationalism," in P. F. Sugar and I. J. Lederer (eds.), *Nationalism in Eastern Europe.* Seattle and London: University of Washington Press.

Zelený, V. (ed.). 1873. *Život Josefa Jungmanna* [Life of Josef Jungmann]. Praha: Matice česká.

Miroslav Hroch and Jitka Malečková

# Nation-Building

The term nation-building has been used to describe the process whereby a nation integrates new populations into its official culture and national *conscience collective*. In the process, people come to identify with the nation's history, boundary symbols, language and territory. According to Ernest Gellner, this "garden culture" consists principally of the official language, which tends to crowd out or extinguish the folk-based languages and "wild cultures" of ethnic and regional minorities (Gellner 1983: 50–52). Symbols of the nation-state, like a national anthem, flag or public monument, constitute another arm of the nation-building process, and are typically transmitted to the young via the state school system and state-run media (Birch 1989: 41). John Breuilly is especially emphatic about the role played by elites, whose mobilization of the population to achieve state power is seen as the engine behind nation-building (Breuilly 1982: 20).

Of course, since the nation is constituted not merely by the state, but by the private sector and civil society, nation-building also occurs in the realm of private communicative action. For instance, in the decentralized United States of the early nineteenth century, national symbols like Greek Revival architecture, the national flag or Washington's portrait found their way onto (or into) private homes, consumer products and private buildings (Zelinsky 1988). Another private force underlying nation-building, as Benedict Anderson persuasively argued, is modern print-capitalism, with its common stock of geographic and historical references. This process worked to codify vernacular languages (eliminating many others) and gave them, and by extension, their nations, a fixity previously unknown (Anderson 1991). A more recent exposition of this theme as it pertains to the modern media may be found in Billig (1995).

It is also important that the process of nation-building be distinguished from related social phenomena. For instance, if we accept, as do most theorists of nationalism, that nations are modern constructs, it becomes imperative to differentiate nation-building from expansionist ethnicism. The latter phenomenon, for instance, describes the pattern to be found after 987 in Capetian France, among the Zulus of the nineteenth century and among lateral-aristocratic ethnies like the Greeks (Smith 1986: 141–2; Smith 1991: 57; Francis 1976: 28–31). The spread of ethnic consciousness within these pre-modern populations sprang from the efforts of clerics, monarchs, warrior bands or wandering performers, whose activities lacked the intensity, coordination or precision that is associated with *nation*-building (Armstrong 1982). Here, however, it must be noted that this distinction presents a fine line that is a matter of debate between "perennialists" and "modernists."

Similarly, *ASSIMILATION*, which describes a process applicable to both ethnic communities (pre-modern or otherwise) and modern nations does not exhaust all possible meanings for the term nation-building. Nevertheless, nation-building very definitely does have an assimilationist component which proceeds from the corpus of myths and symbols with which the national elite attempts to integrate its population. Thus we find a similarity between Birch's typology of social, economic and political integration and Gordon's typology of assimilation, which encompasses cultural and structural realms (Gordon 1964: 71; Birch 1989: 51).

A further point concerns the relationship between European and Third-World nation-building. Some, for example, argue that centralizing developments on the western and eastern edges of the old Roman Empire facilitated the later emergence of successful nation-states there. By contrast, they add, nation-building in the post-colonial world has often lacked a basis in pre-modern ethnic state-building, which in turn has contributed to instability (Emerson 1963: 95–116; Rokkan 1975: 597). This problem is especially acute in Africa and on the Indian subcontinent, where borders were drawn up, often arbitrarily, by colonial powers (Emerson 1963; Smith 1983: 27, 124).

## Bibliography

Anderson, Benedict. 1991 (1983). *Imagined Communities: Reflections on the Origin and Spread of Nationalism*. Revised edition. London and New York: Verso.

Armstrong, John. 1982. *Nations Before Nationalism*. Chapel Hill: University of North Carolina Press.

Billig, Michael. 1995. *Banal Nationalism*. London: Sage.

Birch, Anthony H. 1989. *Nationalism and National Integration*. London: Unwin Hyman.

Breuilly, J. 1982. *Nationalism and the State*. Manchester: Manchester University Press.

Emerson, Rupert. 1963. "Nation-building in Africa," in K. W. Deutsch and William J. Foltz (eds.), *Nation-Building*. New York: Atherton Press.

Francis, E. K. 1976. *Interethnic Relations: An Essay in Sociological Theory*. New York: Elsevier Scientific.

Gellner, Ernest. 1983. *Nations and Nationalism.* Oxford: Blackwell.

Gordon, Milton. 1964. *Assimilation in American Life. The Role of Race, Religion and National Origins.* Oxford: Oxford University Press.

Kerman, Lucy Eve. 1983. *Americanization: the History of an Idea, 1700-1860.* Unpublished doctoral dissertation, U. C., Berkeley.

Rokkan, Stein. 1975. "Dimensions of state formation and nation-building: a possible paradigm for research on variations within Europe," in C. Tilly (ed.), *The Formation of National States in Western Europe.* Princeton, NJ: Princeton University Press.

Seton-Watson, Hugh. 1977. *Nations and States: An Enquiry into the Origins of Nations and the Politics of Nationalism.* London: Methuen.

Smith, Anthony D. 1983. *State and Nation in the Third World.* Brighton: Harvester Press.

Smith, Anthony D. 1986. *The Ethnic Origins of Nations.* Oxford: Blackwell.

Smith, Anthony D. 1991. *National Identity.* London: Penguin.

Weber, Eugen Joseph. 1976. *Peasants into Frenchmen: The Modernization of Rural France, 1870–1914.* Stanford, CA: Stanford University Press.

Zelinsky, Wilbur. 1988. *Nation into State: The Shifting Symbolic Foundations of American Nationalism.* Chapel Hill: University of North Carolina.

Eric Kaufmann

# National Autonomy

In a world of nation-states, national autonomy refers to the attribute of a national or ethnic community of being self-governing, especially when this attribute of self-government is accorded as a right or by a treaty, or as the outcome of a bilateral agreement. More specifically, national autonomy refers to a situation when a national or ethnic minority proclaims or is accorded, the right to maintain some degree of organizational difference and self-governance within the broader framework of an existing state.

The connection between nation and state is expressed, in its conventional interpretation, in the principle of national SELF-DETERMINATION and sovereignty. This convention suggests that sovereign governments and national cultures should be congruent within the boundaries of independent territorial states. The product of this admixture, the NATION-STATE, is conventionally understood to be the main protagonist in the international system.

This arrangement, however, assumes that the citizens of nation-states are nationally homogeneous, something that is at odds with the reality of most contemporary nation-states. In theory, the nation-state and ethnic diversity are diametrically opposed, and on many occasions nation-states have attempted to solve the problem of ethnic diversity by the elimination or expulsion of ethnic groups.

The discrepancy between the mono-national theory of the nation-state and its multi-ethnic and multinational reality, sets the background for tensions and, occasionally, virulent conflicts. Here, the model of national autonomy offers a possible solution to these seemingly intractable conflicts.

Ethnic and national diversity is a form of social complexity found in most contemporary states. Ethnic and national groups are some of the most resilient social formations, even if they are subjected to continuous internal and external mutations. Frequently, they cannot be surgically isolated to make up separate monocultural territorial states. The unprecedented pattern of contemporary migration further dilutes the cultural homogeneity of most nation-states. In settler societies, the demands of indigenous peoples challenge the myths of openness and equity of those nation-states. Consequently, for the nation-state, national and ethnic minorities are "problems" (Eriksen 1993:122). They are dislocating "others" that interrupt the consummation of the perfect match between a nation and a state.

Likewise, the condition of being an ethnic or national minority is dependent on the expectation that nation-states are ruled by sovereign national or ethnic majorities. Without this comparative referent, the notion of "MINORITY" is meaningless. National minorities are collectivities that possess the attributes of nationhood, but do not possess an independent state (Jackson-Preece 1998:17). Often, the same principle that legitimizes the existing nation-state—the principle of self-determination—is then used by disaffected minorities to demand a state where they could become a majority. Thus, many contemporary nation-states are under the threat of dismemberment by the very same principle that sustains their claim to separate existence.

However, in many cases it is not practical or possible to dismember existing national states, or, as it often happens, the territorial mixes of populations makes it impossible for disaffected minorities to build territorial states that will enable them to become majorities. Under these circumstances, the principle of national autonomy can provide political recognition to the demand of national and ethnic minority groups for self-determination.

An early form of national autonomy was provided by the Ottoman Empire's *millet* system. The idea originates in the Islamic tolerance of "the people of the book" (Jews and Christians). In the Ottoman Empire, a *millet* was an autonomous, that is, self-governing community normally led by a religious leader and practicing its own laws. The leader (a Patriarch, Ethnarch or Chief Rabbi depending on the group) was responsible to the Ottoman government for the performance of the *millet*'s responsibilities and duties. These comprised almost exclusively the payment of taxes and loyalty to the Sultan. Once these two conditions were fulfilled, each *millet* was allowed to perform a wide range of social and administrative functions without interference from the Ottoman state. Membership of the *millet* was personal and not territorial. Individuals of the same ethno-religious group formed a *millet* regardless of their place of residence. Ethno-religious mixture within a territory was not an impediment to the exercise of this form of autonomy.

In sharp contrast to the *millet* system, is territorial autonomy. Most modern forms of national autonomy are territorially based, as in the federal system, which is the most common form of territorial autonomy. Another form of national autonomy is home rule. It is a form of restricted self-government that is granted by a central authority to one or more of its political dependencies. Home rule mainly occurs in multinational empires like the Roman or British Empires. This system provides some recognition of minority cultures, if autonomous populations remain loyal to the imperial government.

The autonomous governments within the Spanish state are yet another form of national autonomy. Here the Spanish constitution stipulates a distinction between "historical" and "non-historical" autonomous regions. The historical autonomous regions are those that were autonomous before the Franco dictatorship. These are usually regions with a strong ethno-national identity (Catalonia, the Basque Country and Galicia).

In the Soviet model, national autonomy reached levels of unprecedented complexity. The Soviet Union defined itself as a multinational state, and granted different levels of national autonomy to its large collection of ethnic and national minorities. In contrast to the *millet* system and like the federal system, the principle of autonomy was applied to territorial administrative districts organized on an ethno-national base. Here, over 100 different national and ethnic minorities were given differing levels of cultural autonomy in their historic territories. Those who did not have one, such as the Jews, were simply administratively allocated one. The largest units, the "titular" Republics, were given the formal right to secede from the Union in the Soviet constitution, despite constitutional cast iron safeguards to prevent secession. The idea was that every nationality should have its own territorial base from which it could develop its cultural life. This was considered a necessary prelude to the ASSIMILATION of all nations into a Soviet higher unit. The result was, paradoxically, the reaffirmation of national differences, for this was the only feature of Soviet political life that escaped rigid centralization. The Soviet model is still used in China, which defines itself as a "multinational unitary state." In theory, ethnic minorities are granted the right to express their cultural differences within the strict confines of regional autonomy.

The Yugoslav model of COMMUNISM developed into a system that allowed an even greater degree of territorial national autonomy. Yugoslavia was more decentralized and the constituent autonomous republics had more autonomy than their Soviet counterparts. Yet, with the collapse of communism, the autonomous federal system became the basis for the disintegration of the federal state. The burning desire to create ethnically based independent nation-states in place of the autonomous republics led to unparalleled acts of brutality and ethnic cleansing.

The Communist system's recognition of national and cultural autonomy for minorities is not incompatible with the authoritarian character of the Soviet Regime. Cultural autonomy is a collective, not an individual right, and can be granted to ethnic and national communities that do not enjoy liberal democratic freedoms. The *millet* system was highly authoritarian, yet it granted minorities an unparalleled degree of national-cultural autonomy.

In contrast, liberal democracies have considerable difficulties in coming to terms with national autonomy. Classical liberalism has difficulties in recognizing national autonomy because it is committed to privileging equal individual representation and individual autonomy above any other right. Likewise, the liberal normative tradition is always suspicious of collective rights. As mentioned earlier, national autonomy is a collective demand, one that demands special and differentiated rights for a national minority. Often, demands for national autonomy clash with basic liberal beliefs in freedom and strict political equality of all individual citizens. Quebec, for example, enjoys considerable autonomy within the Canadian State. It enacted legislation requiring the compulsory use of French in the public domain, and required from French speakers and immigrants to send their children to French schools. The Chibouks government sees Quebec as a threatened linguistic island in an Anglophone sea, and considers that Chibouks culture will disappear if it is not protected. Here the compulsion to speak French in the public domain is considered a matter of cultural survival. Yet, this expression of national autonomy violates the liberal principle that requires freedom of choice and political equality for all citizens of Canada.

Affirmative action principles are not of much help here. In the case of women and other minorities, such principles and policies are designed ultimately to erase differences based on sex, gender, and ethnicity. In sharp contrast, demands for national and cultural autonomy are designed not to erase, but, on the contrary, to maintain and legitimize difference. These demands clash with

versions of liberalism that are, according to Charles Taylor (1994: 60), inhospitable to difference.

The demands of indigenous peoples in settler liberal democracies dramatically highlight the problem. Indigenous groups invoke centuries of displacement, settler invasion, cultural destruction, and often genocide to justify their demands for national and cultural autonomy with differential rights. As Sir James Anaya (1996: 3) argues, compelling evidence makes it difficult to deny the systemic maltreatment of indigenous peoples and their severe disadvantage.

In spite of this, indigenous demands for self-determination and sovereignty stretch to the limit the ability of liberal democracies to integrate aggrieved minorities who demand autonomous rights (Eriksen 1993:126; Reynolds 1996:175). Indigenous groups rarely demand separate nation-states. In states that often are the result of alien and violent intrusions into the ancestral HOMELANDS of indigenous populations—an intrusion that made them scattered minorities—indigenous peoples demand national autonomy and public recognition of their way of life. Paradoxically, when indigenous peoples demand separate nation-states, their demands are better understood. Since this is usually not practical or possible, indigenous peoples demand national autonomy, and their demands generate almost impossible dilemmas and cracks in the discourse of freedom and equity of liberal democratic nation-states. The plight of indigenous peoples highlights one of the greatest difficulties facing liberal democracies: how to recognize politically ethnic and national autonomy while preserving the integrity of the state and equal rights for all citizens.

Liberal democratic states deal comparatively well with "MELTING POT" situations. These are situations in which members of minorities, usually immigrant minorities, simply want non-discrimination to allow for full integration and assimilation into the national majority. In this situation the issue is not autonomy but individual choice, something that liberal democracies are particularly well suited to handle. However, problems arise when minorities demand not only individual non-discrimination or formal equality, but also the recognition of their specific collective identity in the public domain, demanding rights and autonomous arrangements that are not applicable to the national majority. Here the issue is of recognition of segmental and differentiated collective rights, something that violates the liberal notion of a sovereign and unencumbered individual. Demands for segmental collective rights violate liberal assumptions on strict political equality between citizens, and liberal philosophical assumptions about the liberation of the individual from subservience to a group.

This problem was resolved in an ingenious way in the declining years of the Austro-Hungarian empire, by the theoreticians of Austrian Social Democracy, Karl Renner and Otto Bauer. They proposed the principle of "cultural-national autonomy." The model separated sharply the idea of national autonomy from territorial self-determination.

The model of cultural-national autonomy is based on the premise that ethnic and national communities can be organized as autonomous units in multinational states without taking into consideration the residential location of their members. The model contrasts with most theories of national autonomy. In most conventional theories, national autonomy requires a territorial base for the autonomous national community or, at least, the aim is to build some kind of "autonomous homeland" that will serve as the territorial base. Bauer and Renner's theory differs in that it rests on the idea of "non-territorial national autonomy." This means that autonomous communities are organized as sovereign collectives whatever their residential location within a multinational state. As in the *millet* system, peoples of different ethnic identities can co-exist in the same territory without straining the principle of national autonomy. The crucial difference with the *millet* system is that the autonomous communities are organized democratically, based on individual consent to belong, and internal democracy.

The analogy used by Renner is that of religious communities. Much in the same way as Catholics, Protestants, and Jews can coexist in the same city, Renner argued, so members of different national communities can co-exist with their own distinct institutions and national organizations, provided that they do not claim territorial exclusivity. The model for national-cultural autonomy acknowledges that national communities require recognition of their specificity and difference in the public domain, and this is achieved through the existence of legally guaranteed autonomous and sovereign organizations. Unlike more conventional forms of autonomy and self-determination, this model rejects the idea of ethnic or national exclusive control over territory. In this way, it differs sharply from nation-states and other federal and confederal arrangements.

The model proposed by Renner and Bauer was the result of reflections on the social and political circumstances of the Austro-Hungarian Empire before the First World War. The collapsing Empire experienced in the late nineteenth century a process of rapid industrialization and urbanization that resulted in a significant internal migration to cities and industrialized areas. This migration took place concurrently with struggles for democratic rights. The net effect was the revival of ethnic and national identities and a fierce linguistic competition between Czechs, Germans, and others. This led Viktor Adler to argue sardonically that the naming of a railway station was considered a matter of absolute principle.

Internal migration had two effects: it diluted the ethnic and national homogeneity of the most developed areas of the Empire, and it created a fierce antagonism between different nationalities over access to resources. This paralyzed the political system. The Austrian socialists were the only truly multinational organization in the Empire, and from the start they devoted considerable energies to resolving the intractable nationalities problem. The disintegration of the Empire into separate nation-states was bound to cause considerable upheaval because of its population mix, something similar to the former Yugoslavia's tragedy in the 1990s. Unlike the warring factions in former Yugoslavia, the socialists saw the economic advantages that would flow from maintaining the Empire united as a single political entity. The problem was how to convert a decaying empire of squabbling national communities into a democratic federation of nationalities in which every national community would find its place. They thought that the solution was the model of national-cultural non-territorial autonomy or the "personality principle."

The system was called the "personality principle" because it referred to the personal choice of its members to be part of a particular national association. This was contrasted by Karl Renner with the "territorial principle," which is the characteristic of the modern nation-state. The territorial principle is described by Renner in the following way: "If you live in my territory you are subjected to my domination, my law and my language" (Renner 1994:29, author's own translation). This, according to Renner, suggests domination and not equality of rights. It suggests the dominance of one ethnic group over another, the dominance of settled populations over immigrants, the dominance of settlers over indigenous peoples. Renner then compares this to the religious wars that plagued early modern Europe, when absolutist German states after the Peace of Augsburg imposed a particular religion on its subjects. Here the organizational principle *cuius regio illius religio* (in whose region that religion, or, who governs the territory decides its religion) decided religious beliefs and this led to countless wars. The problem was settled according to Renner, when religion was separated from territorial sovereignty and the right of religious groups to co-exist side by side became the norm. In the modern nation-state, however, Renner argues, the organizational principle is *cuius regio illius lingua* (in whose region that language, or, who governs the territory decides the language). However, the personality principle, according to Renner, favors religious freedom, and separates the question of governance from the protection of national and cultural identities.

The model of national autonomy requires from all citizens to declare their nationality as they reach voting age. Members of each national community regardless of territory of residence will form a single public body or association which is endowed with a legal status and sovereignty and competent to deal with all national-cultural affairs. For example, this corporate body will organize the educational system of its members, the legal system, and all other issues that are national in character (Macartney 1968:149). The idea here is to eliminate competition between national communities as there is here a strict separation of competences. The weakness of the model is that Renner and Bauer do not clarify how the model can deal with issues that concern the bilateral relation between national communities, and how litigation will be dealt with when the parties belong to different national communities. The problems are not insurmountable, but require a careful balance of different cultural priorities and criteria. This model is based on the premise that the most controversial issues in the relationship between ethnic and national groups are issues concerning language, education and the recognition of cultural rights in the public arena.

The national-cultural autonomy model is controversial, not because of its ideological radicalism (many Catholic-conservative politicians in Austria supported this model even though it was originally conceived by socialist thinkers), but because it calls into question the main assumptions of the contemporary world of nation-states. These assumptions are that sovereignty is one and indivisible, that the self-determination of nations requires the constitution of separate nation-states, and that nation-states are the only legitimate international players. It does, however, have two important advantages: first, it addresses a key weakness of other, territorial models of autonomy: national territorial boundaries always create minorities and propensities for ethnic discrimination. The contemporary Western European experience shows that in a world of migration and differential development, territorial boundaries are porous, and population movements tend to upset neat schemes for fortress states. This situation inevitably leaves ethnic and national minorities as unwelcome pockets in any autonomous or sovereign territory. And the second advantage of the model is that it does away with the concept of national minority and the need for specific minority protection. As argued earlier, the status of national minority is the by-product of a national state that has a sovereign national majority. In Bauer and Renner's model, even if the citizen lives in a territory where the majority belongs to a different national group, in questions of national and ethnic interest, citizens of different ethnies are not subject to the cultural practices of the majority, but can rely on their own, trans-territorial national organization that has the status of a public corporation with sovereign areas of competence (Kann 1951:244).

The model proposed by Renner and Bauer was never put into practice because the Empire disintegrated into nation-states at the end of the first World War. The model was also branded as utopian by many critics of the Austrian socialists, including Lenin, Stalin, and the Bolshevik party. In a period when the nation-state was the uncontested and preferred form of political organization of nations, an idea that attempted to replace the nation-state by a transnational state organization was condemned to failure. Interestingly enough, the model was criticized for being both too nationalistic, as it created the conditions for the survival and cultural reproduction of national communities, and not nationalistic enough, since it did not produce a nationally homogeneous territorial state (Nimni 1994:143).

In response to their left-wing critics, Bauer and Renner emphasized that internationalism did not imply a-nationalism, least of all anti-nationalism. For Bauer, internationalism presupposed the existence of and continuous unfolding of nations and ethnies. Internationalism aims to regulate the relations between nations in a more even and balanced manner (Schlesinger 1945:218).

National autonomy is considered by a menaced group an essential guarantee of its survival, a way of securing access to resources, language, education, political representation and the recognition of equal dignity. Liberal democratic states, while granting civil rights to every individual, resist the recognition of differential ethnic and national rights because these are believed to undermine the equal rights of individuals. The nation-state is built on the premise that it is possible to associate a territorial state with a national community. Since this match is rarely perfect, national and ethnic minorities are always subject to the toleration of the majorities. Toleration is always something given conditionally, and without sovereign guarantees minority status communities will live, at best, an insecure existence. National autonomy addresses some minority concerns, but for the model to provide equitable conditions, it requires the dilution of the principle of the nation-state.

## Bibliography

Anaya, Sir James. 1996. *Indigenous Peoples in International Law*. Oxford: Oxford University Press.

Bauer, Otto. 1999. *The Question of Nationalities and Social Democracy*, with an introduction by E. Nimni. Minneapolis: Minnesota University Press.

Eriksen, Thomas. 1993. *Ethnicity & Nationalism*. London: Pluto Press.

Jackson-Preece, Jennifer. 1998. "National minorities and the international system," *Politics* 18, 1:17-23.

Kann, Robert. 1951. "Karl Renner," *Journal of Modern History* XXIII: 243-249.

Macartney, C. A. 1968. *National States and National Minorities*. New York: Russell & Russell, New York.

Nimni, Ephraim. 1994. *Marxism and Nationalism: Theoretical Origins of a Political Crisis*. London: Pluto Press.

Renner, Karl. 1994. "Staat und Nation" in *Karl Renner Schriften*. Vienna: Residenz Verlag.

Reynolds, Henry. 1996. *Aboriginal Sovereignty: Reflections on Race, State and Nation*. Sydney: Allen & Unwin.

Schlesinger, Rudolf. 1945. *Federalism in Central and Eastern Europe*. London: Kegan Paul.

Taylor, Charles. 1994. "The Politics of Recognition" in A. Guttman (ed.), *Multiculturalism: Examining the Politics of Recognition*. Princeton, NJ: Princeton University Press.

Ephraim Nimni

# National Identity

To have a "national identity" is to be conscious of, and act as if belonging to a nation. "National identity" is to be distinguished from "nationalism," which refers to an ideological project or movement on behalf of the nation. It is therefore possible to claim that a population possesses a national identity without it being nationalist, and nationalism may emerge in populations without a national identity (with the object of creating one).

How "national identity" is defined depends on one's understanding of "nation." It is a much contested concept. Among the debates are: is it a subjective or objective identity; is it ethno-cultural or political; is it a core identity or just one among others; and is it changing forms or being superseded because of globalization?

Since populations cite different criteria of their common membership (language, religion, race), many have concluded that a national identity is essentially subjective. Hugh Seton-Watson in despair of any "scientific definition" of a nation has proposed that a nation (and by extension a national identity) exists when a significant number of people in the community behave as if they formed one. The subjectivist approach tends to focus on identity-formation as an outcome of in-group-out-group differentiation. This has taken a variety of forms. Social psychological approaches, notably Henri Tajfel's "Social Identity Theory," in seeking to understand how individuals attach themselves to nations, employ universal principles of group identity formation. Nations are a form of individual categorization whereby members identify themselves with an in-group which is counterposed to an "OTHER" in order to develop a positive social identity. Stereotyping is employed to contrasting images of (good) self and (inadequate) "Other." A second version, influenced by the transactionalist model of FREDERIK BARTH, examines nations as groups of self-ascription whose identities are maintained by a continuous boundary marking with "Others," in which "SYMBOLS" are used as border guards (Barth 1969).

MICHAEL BILLIG has criticized such approaches for their individualistic assumptions and for their universalist focus on how members categorize. What is important is the nature of the group (its nationness) they categorize, and why they choose the nation (rather than another group affiliation). To explain this one needs to refer also to institutional factors. In other words, a national identity is a cognitive and sociological phenomenon, before it is a psychological phenomenon. Prior to identifying with a nation individuals have to know what such an entity is and what the qualities of their nation are. Moreover, since national identities are in the modern world stable collective formations, they are not dependent on the daily plebiscite of the individual will, cited by ERNEST RENAN, but on the institutional routines of social life.

But are these identities essentially ethno-cultural or civic and territorial? Those who plump for the ethnic dimension tend, though not invariably, to stress the historical rootedness of nations, for example, JOHN ARMSTRONG who discusses the role of *mythomoteurs* and symbols which are institutionalized and carried into the present by religious systems, languages, and urban architecture (ARMSTRONG 1982). PROPONENTS OF THE CIVIC (BENEDICT ANDERSON, ERNEST GELLNER, AND ERIC HOBSBAWM) emphasise the modernity of nations, novel in their political character, cultural homogeneity, and territorial consolidation, and their conception of membership as citizenship in a self-governing state (Anderson 1983; Gellner 1983; Hobsbawm 1990). Nation-states provide the frameworks of modern industrial societies, through whose meritocratic career structures, educational systems, cultural genres (novel and newspaper) and political institutions their members sustain a national identity. ANTHONY D. SMITH, however, argues that nations combine both ethnic and civic-territorial components, as is evident in his definition of the nation as a "named population sharing an historic territory, common myths and historical memories, a mass, public culture, a common economy and common legal rights and duties for all members" (Smith 1991). Although they vary considerably in the mix, he lays weight on the importance of ethno-historical myths for providing political communities with a sense of collective immortality and destiny as they navigate through the storms of modernization.

The relation between national and other identities is a third issue: is it a master identity (as nationalists assume) or merely one of many that individuals may hold? Michael Billig maintains that in contemporary societies such as Britain there is a core national identity, which is reproduced by "banal" (i.e., taken-for-granted) everyday practices. The answer may depend on the period one chooses, but many accounts assume a teleology at work in modernizing societies of an ever wider incorporation of social strata into the nation. This is true even of MIROSLAV HROCH who assesses the capacity of national identities to override class identities during the nineteenth and early twentieth centuries by the timing of their respective mobilizations. Partha Chatterjee, however, has questioned the homogenizing effects of nationalism, at least in Africa and Asia, claiming its co-existence in India with still vital and contending kinship, religious, gender, regional and communal allegiances. Walker Connor's suggestion that national identity formation is an unfinished and reversible process offers a useful starting point for a causal analysis.

Recent contributions by FEMINISTS (e.g., Nira Yuval-Davis 1997) have explored the gendered character of national identities, including the symbolic, reproductive and participatory roles of women in the nation. Post-modernists, including HOMI BHABHA, have questioned whether national identities are taking on a new hybrid, fluid and multicultural quality in an interdependent world marked by diaspora or transnational migrant communities, planetary-wide communications, and supranational economic and political institutions. As nations cease to be economic and political "power containers" for populations, is identity increasingly becoming a matter of choice, and will multicultural replace mono-ethnic conceptions of identity? Skeptics suggest that nation-states are not dying but diversifying in their functions as they pool sovereignty internationally. They could point to the rise of anti-immigrant movements in the advanced industrial societies, including the multicultural societies of the U.S., Canada and Australia, as well as national conflicts in Eastern Europe, the Middle East, the Asian sub-continent as indicators that national identities remain "hot."

### Bibliography

Anderson, Benedict. 1983. *Imagined Communities*. London: Verso.

Armstrong, John A. 1982. *Nations before Nationalism*. Chapel Hill: University of North Carolina Press.

Barth, Frederik (ed.) 1969. *Ethnic Boundaries*. Oslo: Norwegian University Press.

Bhabha, Homi (ed.) 1990. *Nation and Narration*. London: Routledge.

Billig, Michael. 1995. *Banal Nationalism*. London: Sage.

Chatterjee, Partha. 1993. *The Nation and Its Fragments*. Princeton, NJ: Princeton University Press.

Connor, Walker. 1994. *Ethnonationalism*. Princeton, NJ: Princeton University Press.

Gellner, Ernest. 1983. *Nations and Nationalism*. Oxford: Blackwell.

Hobsbawm, Eric. 1990. *Nations and Nationalism since 1780: Programme, Myth, Reality*. Cambridge: Cambridge University Press.

Hroch, Miroslav. 1985. *Social Preconditions of National Revival in Europe*. Cambridge: Cambridge University Press.

Hutchinson, John. 1994. *Modern Nationalism*. London: Fontana Press.

Mann, Michael. 1993. "Nation-States in Europe and other continents: diversifying, developing, not dying," *Daedalus* 122, 3: 115–40.

Seton-Watson, Hugh. 1977. *Nations and States*. London: Methuen.

Smith, Anthony D. 1991. *National Identity*. Harmondsworth: Penguin.

Tajfel, Henri. 1981. *Human Groups and Social Categories*. Cambridge: Cambridge University Press.

Yuval-Davis, Nira. 1997. *Gender and Nation*. London: Sage.

John Hutchinson

# National Stereotypes

The word "stereotype" was originally a technical term used in printing to refer to a page of metal type cast as a whole. In the 1920s the American journalist, Walter Lippman used the term metaphorically to describe fixed and exaggerated prejudices, which are held about members of other social groups. This notion of stereotype was rapidly adopted by social scientists, particularly social psychologists interested in the study of prejudice. The idea was that prejudiced people do not see members of out-groups as individuals; instead, when they think of, or encounter, a member of another group, they have a preset view, or stereotype, of the characteristics which the individual possesses by virtue of belonging to the group. In this sense, a stereotype is a prejudgment based on group membership. National stereotypes refer to the preset views about members of national groups.

The first major study of stereotypes was conducted by Katz and Braly (1935). They asked white American students to indicate which character traits described "typical" members of various ethnic and national group labels. They also asked other subjects to rate independently the favorability or unfavorability of the character traits. The main results indicated that the subjects readily applied character traits to the various groups. Moreover, different characteristics were assigned to different groups, so that, for instance, the set of traits, or stereotype, assigned to Japanese was very different from that assigned to Americans. The subjects tended to assign the most favorable set of traits to their own group, "Americans." Unfavorable characteristics were assigned to "Turks," "Negroes" (sic), "Jews," and so on.

One of the most important findings of the Katz and Braly study was that the subjects tended to agree in their assignment of traits. They regularly used the term "industrious" in relation to Germans, "shrewd" for Jews, "artistic" for Italians, and so on. Stereotypes are not *individual* prejudgments or prejudices, but they reflect culturally shared beliefs about out-groups. As later research was to demonstrate, people may persist in making stereotyped judgments about other groups even in the light of personal experience which contradicts the stereotype.

It should be added that Katz and Braly did not distinguish between ethnic and national groups. For instance, the subjects, in rating "Chinese," may have been judging Chinese in China or Chinese living in the United States. However, the readiness with which the subjects completed the task would indicate that they themselves were not concerned with such distinctions. The stereotype, thus, is a broad judgment, and, as subsequent social psychological studies have shown, it is a generalization. Respondents, even if not claiming that *all* Italians are "impulsive," will claim either that a majority are, or that, on average, Italians are more "impulsive" than members of other national groups. Moreover, stereotypes are often psychologically self-confirming. The person who believes that Italians are "impulsive" will interpret ambiguous behavior of Italians as evidence for their impulsivity. An experimental study showed that white Americans interpreted the behavior of a black male target figure as "aggressive" in accordance with the prevailing stereotype, but when a white figure behaved in exactly the same way the behavior was categorized as "playful" (Duncan 1976).

There has been much debate whether national and ethnic stereotypes have been fading in recent years. Some observers have found that respondents have been less willing to apply traits than were the subjects in Katz and Braly's original study. This has been attributed to the growing awareness that stereotyping is a form of prejudice and that it is socially unacceptable to be seen to be prejudiced. Nevertheless, research from laboratory studies and public opinion data, has shown that stereotypes, as measured in this way, have by no means disappeared. For example, Inglehart (1991), in examining European public opinion data, has shown how readily European publics will make judgments of "trustworthiness" about their own and other nations. Social psychological studies have shown how respondents will claim to be aware of the general stereotypes about various national and ethnic groups, even if they deny holding the stereotype themselves. It has also been shown that, under certain circumstances, even those who disclaim holding the stereotype themselves, can be subtly, even unconsciously, influenced in their judgments about members of other groups (Devine 1989).

The notion of stereotyping has been central to a number of psychological theories of prejudice, most notably personality theories such as that of the "authoritarian personality." Adorno *et al.* (1950), in an extensive investigation of prejudice conducted in the United States after the Second World War, proposed that a particular type of personality was predisposed to ethnic and national prejudices. Authoritarians, they suggested, have a fear of ambiguity and a need to categorize the world clearly. In consequence, authoritarians have a hierarchical view, which divides the world into superior and inferior nations. The authoritarian's thinking is dominated by stereotypes, most principally negative stereotypes about out-groups and positive ones about their own group. Authoritarians are said to project their own denied desires onto the image of the despised out-group. The result is that the authoritarian is deeply ethnocentric and nationalist. Although the original study of authoritarianism contained a number of methodological flaws, more recent investigations have shown the extent to which right-wing prejudices can be connected with stereotyping and authoritarianism (Altemeyer 1988).

Explanations of stereotyping in terms of authoritarianism contain limitations. In the first place, only a minority of people tend to have authoritarian personalities, whereas stereotypes, as the Katz and Braly study showed, can be shared by a majority of people within a particular culture or nation. Second, the theory of authoritarianism depicts a rigidly fixed way of thinking: the authoritarian is assumed to be someone who cannot change his or her pattern of thinking. However, national stereotypes have been shown to be volatile, changing according to political circumstance. In the Katz and Braly study, which was conducted before the Second World War, the image of Germans was positive. In fact, the Germans were the third most favored group, following Americans and English. Once the United States entered the Second World War, the stereotype of Germans became markedly unfavorable, while that of Russians, who were allies in the conflict, dramatically improved. However, after the war and with the advent of the cold war, the stereotype of Russians became markedly unfavorable.

One aspect of the authoritarian theory continues to offer insight. This is the idea that the image of the out-group may be a projection of characteristics which in-group members deny that their group, and themselves, possess. In Western Europe, immigrant groups are often seen as being "intolerant." It has been argued that members of the majority group deny, and simultaneously justify, their own intolerance by projecting this intolerance onto the image of the foreigner (Kristeva 1991).

There has been debate about the psychological status of stereotyping. Cognitive psychologists tend to see stereotypes as internal schemata, which process incoming information in standardized ways (Leyens et al. 1994). Thus, the stereotype is seen as a cognitive structure, which, for instance, would predispose Katz and Braly's subjects to process information about Germans as signs of efficiency. Discursive psychologists, however, have taken issue with the cognitive approach. They claim that cognitive psychologists in general overlook the importance of language

in constituting psychological states (Potter and Wetherell 1987). Stereotyping, according to discursive psychologists, above all involves verbal claims: the stereotyper is claiming that members of a social group tend to possess particular characteristics. Discursive psychologists argue that stereotyping is not best studied by the sorts of rather artificial methods used by Katz and Braly or by public opinion pollsters. Instead, stereotyping should be studied in naturally occurring discourse, in order to understand exactly what speakers are suggesting when they make stereotyped claims about groups (Wetherell and Potter 1992).

When stereotyping is examined in its discursive context, it has been shown to be rhetorically complex, as speakers use stereotyped phrases and judgments in a variety of ways (Billig 1996). This is particularly true in contemporary discourse, where speakers often wish to avoid the accusation of being prejudiced. A seemingly positive evaluation of a group's characteristics can carry subtle, implied criticisms. For instance, praise of an ethnic group's athletic prowess can be used to imply, without stating openly, that the group in question has less intellectual achievement.

The discursive approach has recast some of the traditional questions which have been asked about stereotyping. One question has been whether stereotypes contain a "kernel of truth" or whether they are completely inaccurate over-generalizations (Lee et al. 1995). This implies that the issue is essentially factual and can be determined by matching alleged traits to actual behavior. However, stereotyped judgments typically are not factual claims in any simple sense. The choice of words used to describe behaviors carries rhetorical implications. Different speakers may label the same behavior as either "determined" or "pushy"; "efficient" or "ruthless"; "lazy" or "easy-going," and so on. The chosen words bear evaluative implications. When national stereotypes change, as for instance the American stereotype of Germans during the Second World War, people do not necessarily believe that the members of the other nation have suddenly altered their patterns of behavior or their character dispositions. Instead, a different vocabulary is being used to talk about the group's behavior, with the new discourse carrying different evaluations than the previous one.

There is a further reason for studying stereotyping in natural discourse. Although respondents may show awareness that one should not appear prejudiced in answering formal questionnaires, stereotypes may still be used in spontaneous talk, sometimes subtly and sometimes more overtly. Teun van Dijk, in a series of studies, has shown how the publics of Western Europe and the United States, especially at elite levels, use stereotypes when talking about foreigners and immigrants. Speakers typically accompany their use of stereotypes with the disclaimer that their judgments are "factual," not evaluative or prejudiced. In this way, the speakers simultaneously display and deny their prejudices. O'Donnell (1994) has shown how sports reporters regularly employ national and geographic stereotypes. Across Europe, newspapers routinely contrast northern emotional "coldness" with southern "volatility." Implicit evaluations are bound up with these apparently "factual" assertions of sports performance.

Such stereotyping can be expected in the modern world of nation-states and mass communication. Publics have discursive frames-of-reference for understanding a variety of national groups, of which they have minimal, direct personal experience. The "volatile Southern European" is a familiar figure to Northern Europeans, who may have met few southerners, let alone any impulsive southerners. As such, the continually repeated clichés about national out-groups, which can be found in the mass media, are forms of "banal nationalism," by which "our" national identity and "their" otherness is repeatedly reproduced as a "fact" of life (Billig 1995).

### Bibliography

Adorno, T. W., E. Frenkel-Brunswik, D. J. Levinson and R. N. Sanford. 1950. *The Authoritarian Personality*. New York: Harper and Row.

Altemeyer, B. 1988. *Enemies of Freedom*. San Francisco, CA: Jossey-Bass.

Billig, M. 1995. *Banal Nationalism*. London: Sage.

Billig, M. 1996. *Arguing and Thinking*. Cambridge: Cambridge University Press.

Devine, P. G. 1989. "Stereotypes and prejudice: their automatic and controlled components," *Journal of Personality and Social Psychology* 56: 5–18.

Duncan, B. L. 1976. "Differential social perception and attribution of intergroup violence: testing the lower limits of stereotyping blacks," *Journal of Personality and Social Psychology* 34: 590–598.

Inglehart, R. 1991. "Trust between nations: primordial ties, societal learning and economic development," in K. Reif and R. Inglehart (eds.), *Eurobarometer*. Basingstoke: Macmillan.

Katz, D. and K. Braly. 1935. "Racial prejudice and racial stereotypes," *Journal of Abnormal and Social Psychology* 30: 175–193.

Kristeva, J. 1991. *Strangers to Ourselves*. Hemel Hempstead: Harvester/Wheatsheaf.

Lee, Y.-T., L. J. Jussim and C. R. McCauley (eds.). 1995. *Stereotype Accuracy*. Washington D.C.: American Psychological Association.

Leyens, J.-P., V. Yzerbyt and G. Schadron. 1994. *Stereotypes and Social Cognition*. London: Sage.

O'Donnell, H. 1994. "Mapping the mythical: a geopolitics of national sporting stereotypes," *Discourse and Society* 5: 345–380.

Potter, J. and M. Wetherell. 1987. *Discourse and Social Psychology*. London: Sage.

van Dijk, T. A. 1993. *Elite Discourse and Racism*. London: Sage.

Wetherell, M. and J. Potter. 1992. *Mapping the Language of Racism*. London: Sage.

Michael Billig

# National Symbols

Symbols are concrete images of meaning and identity. They are crucial in every sphere of human interaction: indeed social interaction presupposes and in significant part actually comprises symbolization (Mead 1934).

In the macro-sphere of the nation—which remains, along with the family, the most fundamental arena of human meaning and identity—symbols are especially important. Yet, remarkably, within the field of investigation of nations and nationalism, the study of national symbols is notably underdeveloped. For example, none of the recent excellent texts devoted to nations and nationalism includes any sustained analysis of the topic. Nor do any of the major examinations of symbolism and symbolization by social scientists address national symbols better than cursorily.

The general significance of symbolization in shaping social interaction and in solidifying the basis of social relationships at all levels from micro to macro has been widely recognized (Cassirer 1979; Douglas 1973). Language and culture, which mark off human beings as sharply as any biological differences from other species, are both essentially symbolic domains. Man is the symbol-making animal.

The significance of symbols—as representations and projections of national values—in the construction and re-construction of the "imagined communities" which nations comprise can hardly be overestimated. National symbols play key roles in at least six distinct spheres of national being:

1. In the recruitment of individuals and organizations into national movements.

2. In the consolidation of the commitment of individuals and organizations to national movements.

3. In legitimating nationalist political parties in post-dependency electoral competition.

4. In disseminating the image of newly independent nations on the global political and economic stage.

5. In sustaining the national identity of citizens of historical and new nations alike in the face of disruptive internal and external pressures.

6. In sustaining confidence and competitive advantage in international relations, ranging from trade, through diplomacy, to war.

In each of these symbolic functions, the imageries of the *flag* and the *currency* seem to be primary. The power of the Stars and Stripes, the Union Jack, the Tricolore, the Swastika, and the Star of David as representations of their respective historical or contemporary national communities is rivaled only by the Dollar, the Pound Sterling, the Franc, the Mark, and the Rouble. The burning of national flags of enemies, for example in Iran, Palestine, and Northern Ireland, has become an almost routine humiliation ritual. *Postage stamps* too have become a key arena of national symbolic imagery in recent years, as have export-oriented business *advertising* and *tourist material*. Nor should we ignore *maps*, which name national names from competing national perspectives (e.g., the Malvinas/Falkland Islands), and lay claim to preferred national boundaries (e.g., the disputed frontier between China and India).

A key role in national symbolization also seems to be played by paintings, sculptures and other public monuments, and by characteristic buildings.

Among *paintings*, the magnificent series of murals in Barry's House of Commons representing the pageant of British history is notable. Portrayals of Joan of Arc commissioned in the aftermath of the Franco-Prussian War, such as the 1880 depiction by Balze of the Maid of Orleans crushing France's enemies, seem calculated to promote *revanche*. More recent interesting examples include the decorations of the great flagship liners, such as Raymond Connard's interwar painting—twenty-six feet by fourteen—of "England" for the *Queen Mary*. The same artist also painted a famous picture of "St. George's Day, 1918" set on the deck of a ship of war as the fleet raided Zeebrugge and Ostend (Preston 1997).

Of *public monuments* the best known include the Statue of Liberty, Nelson's Column, the Arc de Triomphe, the Eiffel Tower, and more recently the massive crossed-swords monument erected by the Iraqi dictator Saddam Hussein in Baghdad. The collapse of Communism in the Soviet Union and Eastern Europe has provided many examples of physical destruction of symbols of the old regime, such as statues of Lenin and sculpts of "workers," and their replacement by images of newly retrieved national heroes such as Genghis Khan (Mongolia), Tamerlaine (Uzbekistan), and Count Jelacic (Croatia).

*Buildings* which either by original intention or in terms of subsequent interpretation serve as national symbols include Buckingham Palace, St. Paul's Cathedral, the White House, the Pyramids, the Taj Mahal, the Parthenon, and the Sydney Opera House in Australia.

Aspects of the *landscape*, such as the "White Cliffs of Dover," Mount Fuji, the American prairies, the Argentinean pampas, and the Russian steppes are also typically invested with symbolic national significance (Daniels 1992). A similar role is played by plants and animals, such as the Irish shamrock, the English rose, and the New Zealand Kiwi. These images figure prominently in paintings, poems, songs, and even dreams, all serving ex-patriates, including both exiles and "voluntary" emigrants and especially prisoners of war as symbolic mementos of "home" and "the old country." They represent that attachment to territory which is so central to national identity (Grosby 1995).

At a deeper level national symbols seem to be modernized versions of the totems whose socially solidary and psychologically protective functions have been examined by Durkheim (1915), Freud (1960), and others. At a still deeper level, they may attach to antique myths (Frazer 1915) and even to Jung's archetypes (Storr 1973), with national symbols projecting the ethno-racial dream world of the collective unconscious onto the public screen of political action.

In relation to this wide range of national symbols the task of analysis is complex and challenging (Leoussi 1998). It must include: photographic archiving, designed to provide a comprehensive data-base of national symbols; historical analysis of the contexts and roots of national images; comparative analysis designed to elucidate constancies and variations in national symbolism world-wide; iconographic analysis drawing on the concepts and skills of art history to investigate formal properties and deeper meanings and to establish typologies; statistical analysis of the patterning of images and of incidence, trends, and correlates of images of particular types; and not least sociological analysis exploring the functions of symbols in national movements and in the regional and global arenas of perennial competition and conflict between nations (Oppenheimer 1914).

This last task puts the analysis of national symbols into the theoretical context of what has come to be called *image engineering* (Bromley 1993). This is sometimes mistakenly viewed as a contemptibly trivial aspect of mere marketing. There can be no doubt, however, that images, symbols, and especially national symbols are of the first importance—not least when the new millennium is heralding an efflorescence of nationalism throughout the world, and when ancient, histori-

cal nations in Europe are faced with the threat or the promise of dissolution into larger state units (Kunczik 1997). At such historical junctures as these, the power of national symbols, rendering visible the invisible and speaking in a language deeper than words, can sway the fate of nations.

### Bibliography

Bromley, D. B. 1993. *Reputation, Image and Impression Management*. New York: Wiley.

Cassirer, E. 1979. *Symbol, Myth and Culture*. New Haven, CT: Yale University Press.

Daniels, S. 1992. *Landscape Imagery and National Identity in England and the United States*. Oxford: Blackwell.

Douglas, M. 1973. *Natural Symbols*. Harmondsworth: Penguin.

Durkheim, E. 1915 (first published in 1912). *The Elementary Forms of the Religious Life*. London: Allen and Unwin.

Frazer, J. G. 1915. *The Golden Bough*. London: Macmillan.

Freud, S. 1960 (first published in 1913). *Totem and Taboo*. London: Routledge and Kegan Paul.

Grosby, S. 1995. "Territoriality: the transcendental, primordial feature of modern societies, nations and nationalism," *Nations and Nationalism* 1, 2, 143–162.

Kunczik, M. 1997. *Images of Nations and International Public Relations*. New Jersey: Erlbaum.

Leoussi, A. S. 1998. *Nationalism and Classicism*. Basingstoke: Macmillan.

Mead, G. H. 1934. *Mind, Self and Society*. Chicago: Chicago University Press.

Oppenheimer, F. 1914. *The State: Its History and Development*. Indianapolis, IN: Bobbs-Merrill.

Preston, M. 1997. "On sensing an unseemly frolic," *Arts Club Journal* Spring, 8–11.

Storr, A. 1973. *Jung*. London: Fontana.

David Marsland

# Nationalism

Despite some early references in Herder and the Abbé Baruel (1798), the term "national*ism*" did not come into general usage until the mid-nineteenth century. In general, it came to signify feelings or doctrines about and on behalf of the nation, or movements for national self-determination. In fact, we can distinguish five main usages today:

1. a doctrine, or more broadly an ideology, of nations;

2. a movement on behalf of the nation and its citizens;

3. a language or discourse, and a symbolism, of the nation;

4. a set of sentiments on behalf of the nation;

5. a process or set of processes of nation-formation.

The last, and most general, usage which is sometimes equated with "NATION-BUILDING," covers the whole gamut of activities and processes by which nations have been formed across the globe, and thus clearly transcends what is normally meant by the term "nationalism." The penultimate usage, national sentiment, also needs to be distinguished from the first three usages; collective sentiments on behalf of the nation, its strength and well-being, may or may not be accompanied by ideologies, movements, and discourses of and about the nation. They may be clearly articulated or be fairly inchoate, they may be widely diffused in the population of the designated nation, even though there is no nationalist ideology or movement, as at some moments in English history, or they may be hardly diffused at all, when an ideology and movement of nationalism develops, as occurred in several sub-Saharan African states.

For these reasons, it may be advisable to reserve the term "national*ism*" for the first three usages. In most cases, the phenomena to which they refer occur together; only rarely do we find the ideology or language of nationalism articulated without an accompanying movement on behalf of the nation.

Scholars have defined nationalism, even in this restricted usage, in quite different ways. For some, it is the striving for statehood, that is, the desire to attain and immerse society and the individual in the STATE. But this is to confuse the nation as the object of nationalism with the state. Others regard nationalism as a movement that seeks independent territorial statehood for the nation. Here the nation is the object of aspirations, but nationalism is restricted to the drive to give every nation its own state, as well as to give to each state one nation, that is, making the national and political principles congruent and coextensive, and creating "nation-states." The difficulty here is that acknowledged nationalisms like the Catalan and Scots have not and do not strive for independent statehood in their homelands.

At the other end of the definitional spectrum are the "ethnicists," who tend to regard nationalism as an ideology or movement of the ethnic nation, whether it seeks cultural autonomy, home rule or independent statehood for the nation. This view is able to accommodate a purely cultural nationalism, which does not aspire to political independence, only moral regeneration and vernacular mobilization of the nation. The difficulty with this view is deciding whether every folklore revival, and every movement for equal ethnic rights, such as we find in immigrant societies like the United States or Canada, constitutes a case of "nationalism."

Both kinds of definition, statist and ethnicist, suffer from a certain essentialism, and for many scholars the term nationalism is simply too vague and loose to allow precise definition. A single definition of nationalism seems impossible, even if it were desirable. There are simply too many forms and types of nationalism to envisage a unified concept. However, while it is necessary to recognize the varieties of nationalism in clear typologies, we can nevertheless single out those characteristics of nationalism as ideology, movement and symbolic language that set it apart from other ideologies, movements and languages. What marks out "nationalism" are recurrent sets of (1) propositions, (2) ideals, and (3) SYMBOLS, to which nationalists everywhere subscribe and which they habitually invoke.

The main propositions to which nationalists subscribe may be summarized as follows:

1. The world is divided into nations, each with its own character, history, destiny and homeland.

2. Nations constitute the sole source of power, and individuals owe a primary loyalty to the nation.

# Nationalism

3. Individuals must identify with and belong to a nation, if they want to be truly free.

4. A world of peace and justice can only be founded on autonomous and territorially secure nations.

These are the tenets of what we may call the "core doctrine" of nationalism, which the founding fathers—Rousseau, Herder, Fichte, Mazzini—and their latter-day successors embraced. They focus exclusively on the nation, not the state, as the object of nationalist endeavors, seeking to turn it into the measure of history, society, and politics. They do not, of themselves, entail a commitment to securing a state for each nation and a nation for each state, even if in practice this has been the general thrust of the doctrine. But they do imply that every nation must have its own historic territory, or homeland. Of course, specific nationalisms add all kinds of secondary ideas and motifs, such as the Sun Language theory of the Turks espoused by Ataturk, or the American idea of Manifest Destiny, or the idea of Poland as the suffering and risen Christ. But none of these additions is part of, or entailed by, the core doctrine of nationalism, and should not be confused with it.

The specific goals for which nationalists strive are varied, but they all derive from three basic ideals: the autonomy, the unity and the identity of the nation. Nationalists everywhere seek to attain the maximum autonomy consonant with the circumstances, be it in the sphere of culture and social life, in the economy and infrastructure, or in politics and defense. To be autonomous is to listen only to the inward dictates of the nation and determine one's own national destiny, and to be free of every external influence which can interfere with the "natural" flow of the nation's inner "rhythms." Unity, likewise, is vital to the nation: it implies both territorial unification, the gathering in of all members as citizens of the ideally compact historic HOMELAND in its borders, and social solidarity, the integration of all citizens as real brothers and sisters on the soil of the mother- or fatherland. The nation is conceived here as an extended but close-knit family "at home," occupying a distinctive and bounded historic habitat. Finally, the nation has an individual identity and profile, a definite and distinctive "personality," which is clearly recognized by those outside its borders. This is based on its unique culture in which all members come to share by birth or naturalization over long periods; even if cultural homogeneity is only a distant ideal, the creation and reconstruction of a specific NATIONAL IDENTITY remains a paramount concern of all nationalisms.

What makes nationalism so unique and powerful as a movement, ideology and language is its self-reflexive quality, the celebration and commemoration of the collective "self," the community of one's own citizens, through symbols, myths, memories, rituals and ceremonials. Every nation must have its flag, anthem, national day, coinage, capital, assembly, borders, censuses, oaths, constitutions, laws and customs, parades and remembrance ceremonies, monuments to heroes and to the fallen, museums, academies and galleries, sports events, archaeological sites and much else. All of these symbolic resources are both unique in their content and commensurable in their forms. For nations exist in a world of nations; the celebration of one is the recognition of all. Worshipping itself through its panoply of symbols, the nation becomes for nationalists an abstract, transhistorical and transcendent, yet also an immediate and concrete "familial" community, powerful in suffering and glorious in self-sacrifice. In this respect, nationalism resembles a religious salvation drama, unfolding the history and destiny of the nation, its past vicissitudes and resplendent future.

From these propositions, ideals and symbols, we may tentatively propose the following definition of "nationalism": *an ideological movement for attaining and maintaining autonomy, unity and identity on behalf of a population deemed by some of its members to constitute an actual or potential "nation."*

What this working definition allows for is the possibility of having nationalism without nations, indeed of nationalisms creating nations by seeking autonomy, unity and identity for a designated population; just as it may be possible to find cases of nations without nationalisms, of populations sharing a national identity and language, but without any overt ideology, let alone a movement, of nationalism.

Nationalism, in the sense in which we defined it above, although it had important precursors in seventeenth-century England and Holland, first emerged in the late eighteenth-century Europe and North America—in the late 1780s, in the aftermath of the American War of Independence and at the outset of the French Revolution. Its power became plain in the Revolutionary Wars from 1792 and in reaction to Napoleon's invasions. It spread swiftly to Argentina, Chile and other Latin American countries, and also to the Balkans and Central and Eastern Europe during the mid-nineteenth century. After the demise of the 1848 revolutions, nationalism was appropriated by tsars and emperors in Austria-Hungary, Russia and Japan, but mobilized ethnic and linguistic communities in much of Eastern Europe and the Middle East by the turn of the century. Thence it spread to the Far East, the Indian subcontinent, southeast Asia, Central Asia and Western and Eastern Africa. Today, there are few parts of the world untouched by nationalism, either through the reconstitution of empires, kingdoms and tribal communities as nations and national states, or through the ravages of intrastate ethnic separatism and irredentism which spill over into bitter and protracted conflicts such as those in the Middle East and the Balkans. Nationalism remains, despite attempts to supersede it in supranationalist organizations and internationalist ideals, the cornerstone of the contemporary inter-state order. In an era of globalization, the fires of ethnic nationalism and the conflicts over national identities have become, if anything, more intense and stronger than ever.

### Bibliography

Breuilly, J. 1993. *Nationalism and the State*, second edition. Manchester: Manchester University Press.

Connor, W. 1978. "A nation is a nation, is a state, is an ethnic group, is a...," *Ethnic and Racial Studies* I, 1: 378–400.

Deutsch, K. 1966. *Nationalism and Social Communication*, second edition. New York: MIT Press.

Greenfeld, L. 1992. *Nationalism: Five Roads to Modernity*. Cambridge, MA: Harvard University Press.

Smith, A. D. 1983. *Theories of Nationalism*, second edition. London: Duckworth.

Smith, A. D. 1991. *National Identity*. Harmondsworth: Penguin.

Anthony D. Smith

# Nationalism: Evolution of Nationalism

The word "nationalism" has acquired a multiplicity of meanings which do little to clarify its inner quality. Further, because of the deeply negative connotations that the word has gained in the West—few would admit to being a nationalist—it has become hard to see the operation of nationalism in any detached way. The proper meaning of nationalism should be seen as having clear denotative limits and internal consistency. In sum, nationalism is a modern doctrine used to legitimate the nation (in the modern sense). Its main tenets are the proposition that the world is divided into nations and only into nations; that each individual is a member of a nation and only of one nation; that each nation is possessed of a shared past and future peculiar to it; and, possibly, that each nation is connected to a particular territory, which may be a symbolic territory.

It is generally agreed that nationalism is a modern doctrine that came to be formulated in the latter half of the eighteenth century (Kohn 1944; Kamenka 1976). However, there are some who argue that nationalism, at least in the sense of national sentiment, is either old or ancient (Smith 1986). It is said by these champions of nationalist antiquity that the Classical Greeks and Hebrews knew nationalism and/or that it existed in medieval times. This position appears to confuse group sentiment and, in medieval Europe, the use of the Latin word *"natio"* with modern nationalism. Crucially, membership of the pre-modern nation was restricted to the aristocracy and the proposition that all the inhabitants of a political unit should have equal access to political power was unknown.

This provides a clue to the evolution of nationalism as a modern phenomenon. The rise of the modern state, with its much improved organizational and rationalizing capacity, demanded a new power relationship between rulers and ruled.

# Nationalism: Evolution of Nationalism

The efficiency of state organization in the new mode was enormously enhanced when government was consensual. To attain this consent, it was necessary to redistribute power, so that all those affected by it should have a stake in it. The redistribution of power did not take place voluntarily, but was the outcome of pressure from the bourgeoisie and the intellectuals who were busy legitimating their demands by claiming that they too were members of the nation and as such rightfully entitled to share in power. And it was far easier to redistribute power to those whose attitudes and values were shared. That, in essence, was the basis of the modern nation.

The doctrine of nationalism was, therefore, formulated in parallel to the coming of democracy and, indeed, is inseparable from it. Furthermore, membership of the nation, in the CIVIC sense, was an integral part of CITIZENSHIP. This was the radical turning point of the French Revolution, the proposition that each individual in France was a member of the French nation and as such a citizen. A similar process was taking place in the United States, although under somewhat different conditions and slightly earlier.

Hence, the central significance of nationalism is that it is a legitimating doctrine that underpins the modern nation (Brass 1985). That in turn is the central political space of modernity, without which democracy and citizenship are hard to conceive. Nationalism, therefore, gained its extraordinary energies—and these are not denied even by the most determined anti-nationalists—because it contained a promise of liberty and emancipation. In its initial phase, the political movements fired by this promise targeted the privileges of birth, the remnants of feudalism, the obscurantism of the particular, all the obstacles that stood in the way of achieving the goal if universal freedom and equality. In this context, odd as this may sound to contemporary ears, not only was nationalism an emancipatory discourse, but it also contained the concept of a utopia—that expressed in Schiller's *alle Menschen werden Brueder*" ["all shall be brothers"] and set to music by Beethoven in his Ninth Symphony—because they would be liberated by the newly defined access to power.

The positive aspect of nationalism, however, came to be questioned when it emerged that while civic sentiment might be sufficient to provide consent to be ruled in relatively small communities, it would not work on its own in large, modern polities. Although the doctrine of democracy emphasizes the civic contract as its basis, reality is more complex. The doctrine of nationalism promises emancipation and does so on a consensual basis. What it does not do is to provide an answer to the dilemma of what happens when a group dissents, when it consistently claims that it wishes to be ruled by itself because it does not accept membership of the polity in which it finds itself.

This is a widespread problem and, indeed, it has affected virtually every European state in the twentieth century. When the claim to non-consent is articulated repeatedly over time and a number of other conditions are fulfilled—the most important of which probably being the loss of the will to rule on the part of the majority—a group of this kind will be permitted to secede. But no state likes this. The loss of territory especially is seen as quite traumatic, because it is experienced as damaging the coherence of the community. The claims of the would-be seceding minority are denied as long as possible, but when this fails, a democracy (founded as it is on consent through nationhood) must eventually accede by recognising the right of other nations to determine their own national destinies.

This is a central dilemma for the nation, because it marks a failure of the state and thus of the nationalism that legitimates it. As this danger became clearer during the nineteenth century, the quality of nationhood, and thus the content of nationalism, shifted imperceptibly. It began to acquire more explicit ethnic traits, a process that was encouraged by the evolution of nations with claims to statehood in Central and Eastern Europe. These nations had to define their existence not by citizenship—this was impossible as these national movements did not control a state—but by culture in the broadest sense.

The direction of the shift was to move from civic nationhood pure and simple to a mixture of civic and ETHNIC elements; correspondingly, nationalism acquired an ethnic coloring which it had not had in any very pronounced way beforehand. This was the transformation that has given nationalism a bad name, because once the nation came to be defined simultaneously by both civic and ethnic qualities, nationalism regularly spilled over into national exclusivism. Broadly speaking, the stronger the reliance on the ethnic elements of nationhood, the greater was the likelihood that national egoism would dominate. The process could be clearly observed in France, where the civic nationalism of the Revolution was gradually but inexorably transformed into a civic-cum-ethnic definition.

This is the type of nationalism which emerged in the twentieth century, and can be said to have reached its apogee with the First World War. This type continued to play a key role in legitimating the state *after* the First World War having, in a sense, become successful, if not too successful, as a principle of state formation.

The early twentieth-century state, based on the nation and underpinned by nationalism, had been more and more driven towards self-glorification, had established hard boundaries towards the rest of the world and, pushing the doctrine of state sovereignty to the limit, rejected any thought of interdependence. The role of nationalism in this development was palpable and, indeed, the doctrine could be properly interpreted in this way.

FASCISM and Nazism confused the picture. Both addressed themselves to the ethnic dimension of nationhood, but took its imperatives to new levels by using ethnic cohesiveness as the starting point for social revolution. That direction was certainly something that could be derived from nationalism, but was in no way a necessary consequence of it.

After 1945, nationalism was blamed for Europe's second Thirty Years War (1914-1945) and far-reaching moves were launched to prevent the excesses attributed to nationalism from recurring. ETHNICITY as a source of identity was severely frowned on and state powers were to be restricted by European integration (the most radical experiment) and by various other forms of international cooperation. The untrammelled power of the nation-state and thus the limitlessness of nationalism were over. Democratic nationhood sought to restrict itself to the civic elements of national identity,

without much explicit nationalism. At the same time, the ethnic elements remained in being as an implicit foundation for consent, as much as before, but without being given the space for self-articulation.

This period lasted until 1989 when the collapse of COMMUNISM appeared to give a far more traditional nationalism a new lease of life. The communist systems had attempted to eliminate all aspects of the nation, and to extinguish all expressions of nationalism—logically so, given the origins of Marxism-Leninism in an anti-national doctrine (Schöpflin 1991).

If nationalism can be said to have its origins in the demand that all members of, first, a political-cultural community and second, of an ethno-cultural community should have access to political power, then communism claimed that access to power should be based on economic identities. The two were not and are not reconcilable. What communism succeeded in achieving was the destruction of non-ethnic identities. Consequently, the collapse of communism left the post-communist states with the task of constructing a democratic order largely from ethnicity.

Predictably, when political action is underpinned primarily by ethnicity and seeks to exercise power by ethnic definitions of the nation, lacking the non-ethnic dimensions, it inevitably recreates the worst excesses attributed to nationalism, particularly in the eyes of those who have not undergone the communist experience. The war in former Yugoslavia was a powerful instance of what happens when the sole collective identity is ethnicity and each ethnic group becomes involved in the construction of a new state with insufficient materials to hand. Elsewhere in the world, where state and civil society have been weak or eroded, analogous patterns can be observed. Throughout the twentieth century nationalism maintained its position as the preeminent legitimating ideology of the nation. And as the character of the nation changed, so did the content of nationalism. But the basic principle was unchanged. Where the civic elements of nationhood were strong, ethnicity would be held in check and the causal nexus between democracy, citizenship, nationhood and consent remained unaffected.

## Bibliography

Brass, Paul (ed.) 1985. *Ethnic Groups and the State*. London: Croom Helm.

Kamenka, Eugene (ed.). 1976. *Nationalism: The Nature and Evolution of an Idea*. London: Edward Arnold.

Kohn, Hans. 1944. *The Idea of Nationalism*. New York: Collier Books.

Schöpflin, George. 1991. "National identity in the Soviet Union and East Central Europe," *Ethnic and Racial Studies* 14, 1: 3-14.

Smith, Anthony D. 1986. *The Ethnic Origins of Nations*. Oxford: Blackwell.

George Schöpflin

# Nationalism and the "Other"

In his influential book on nationalism, ELIE KEDOURIE highlights how "the excellence of diversity" (1992: 44–55) becomes one of the main features of the nationalist doctrine. Kedourie shows how the emphasis on diversity as a fundamental characteristic of the universe and, most importantly, as "willed by God" has led to the argument "not only that every culture, every individuality, has a unique incomparable value, but also that there is a duty laid upon us to cultivate our own peculiar qualities and not mix or merge them with others" (ibid.: 51). The application of this idea to politics, he argues, has transformed the conception of the nation into a "natural division of the human race," which should maintain its purity and further cultivate its own character separately from other nations. Kedourie's inquiry into the foundations of nationalism, thus shows that the doctrine not only defines the "we," the nation, to which the individual owes his/her loyalty, but also asserts that there is a "they," an out-group, namely other nations from which the in-group must remain separate. The quest for AUTHENTICITY of the national self is thus inseparable from the conception of Others.

The role of the Other in the emergence of nationalism is highlighted by ERNEST GELLNER too. He contends that cultural differences per se are not divisive; the deep cause of divisive nationalism is to be found in the uneven spread of industrialization and modernization. According to Gellner, when the discontent of the disadvantaged sections of the population of a backward region can find national expression because those privileged are culturally different, the shared nationality of the under-privileged becomes salient. In this context, differences in culture, language or physical appearance become important because they provide the means of exclusion for the benefit of the privileged, and also a means of identification, a set of common features among the underprivileged (Gellner 1964: 168). Thus, national identity comes into being in order to differentiate the in-group from an Other with whom the nation competes for the distribution of resources. The awareness of a shared nationality lies not in the cultural specificity and/or intrinsic uniqueness of the nation but rather in its providing for an identity contrasted to a specific Other. Indeed "the Ruritanian nation was born out of this contrast" (Gellner 1983: 62). In his book *Nations and Nationalism*, Gellner pushes the argument further suggesting that "if an industrial economy is established in a culturally heterogeneous society (or if it even casts its advance shadow on it), then tensions result, which will engender nationalism" (ibid.: 108–9).

The relationship between the nation and an Other is also the basis for the building of typologies of nationalism. Thus, SMITH's (1991: 82–3) distinction between pre- and post-independence nationalism indicates not only the political condition of a specific community, namely its autonomy or subordination to some other nation, but also the simple fact that each nation has to assert itself in contrast, and often in opposition, to another national community. Moreover, in the same typology, nationalist movements are distinguished between those that hold an ethno-genealogical conception of the nation and those that define it as a civic-territorial community. However, it is not made clear whether the goals of the movement are derived from the ethnic or territorial character of the nation or whether the nation is conceptualized as an ethnic or civic community, because of the specific context and situation in which the national movement develops. Thus, one wonders whether it is the need to integrate disparate ethnic populations into the political community of a post-colonial state that leads to a territorial conception of the nation or the civic and territorial features of the national community that dictate its goals (Geertz 1963). In other words, the question remains whether the ethnic or civic character of the nation defines who the Other is or whether it is the surrounding others that condition the nation's self-conception.

The arguments outlined above may not put into question the validity of the above mentioned theories. They show, however, that the notion of the Other is inextricably linked with nationalism as a social and political phenomenon. As Connor (1993: 386) argues, nationalism leads to a dichotomous conception of the world: it divides humanity into "us," fellow nationals, and the "others," non-members of "our" community. In other words, the opposition to the Other is taken as an intrinsic feature of nationalism.

The role of the Other in the formation and transformation of nations is investigated by psychologists who emphasize the role that Others play in strengthening the sense of belonging to the nation and promoting its cohesion in the face of a common enemy. Furthermore, the relationship between nationalism and the Other is discussed by scholars who address the issue of boundaries. An interesting work, in this field, is a book by Robin Cohen (1994) on British identity, which investigates the impact of interaction with Others on the formation of national identity. Cohen examines the formation of British identity "looking at the interaction of 'the British' with the Celtic fringe, the Dominions, the Commonwealth, Anglophone America, Europe and peoples described in immigration law as 'aliens'" (Cohen 1995: 35). Quite interestingly, he suggests that frontiers between identities tend to be fuzzy, that is, malleable and open to a certain extent, allowing Others a degree of penetration. Other works in this field include B.B. Ringer (1983), who studies the constitution of the American nation and its ethnic MINORITIES as Others, V.D. Volkan and N. Itzkowitz (1994), who provide for a psycho-historical account of the problematic relationships between Greeks and Turks and, last but not least, the work of cultural anthropologists such as FREDRICK BARTH (1969), Anthony P. Cohen (1995) and Thomas Hyland Eriksen (1992), who have analyzed the role of interaction with Others in the constitution of ethnic identity. Even though national identity as an analytical category is distinct from ethnicity, theories on boundaries between ethnic groups and on the role of the Other in ethnogenesis may be helpful for the study of nationalism as well.

## Bibliography

Barth, Frederick. 1969. "On ethnic groups and boundaries," in *Process and Form in Social Life. Selected Essays on F. Barth,* vol. 1. London: Routledge & Kegan.

Cohen, Anthony P. 1995. *The Symbolic Construction of Community.* London and New York: Routledge (first edition 1985).

Cohen, Robin. 1995. "Fuzzy frontiers of identity: the British case," *Social Identities* 1, 1: 35–63.

Cohen, Robin. 1994. *Frontiers of Identity: The British and the Others.* London and New York: Longman.

Connor, Walker. 1993. "Beyond reason: the nature of the ethnonational bond," *Ethnic and Racial Studies* 16, 3: 373–89.

Doob, Leonard. 1964. *Patriotism and Nationalism: Their Psychological Foundations.* Westport, CT: Greenwood Press.

Eriksen, Hyland Thomas. 1992. *Us and Them in Modern Societies: Ethnicity and Nationalism in Mauritius, Trinidad and Beyond.* Oslo: Scandinavian University Press.

Geertz, Clifford. 1963. "The integrative revolution: primordial sentiments and civil politics in the new states," in C. Geertz (ed.), *Old Societies and New States: The Quest for Modernity in Asia and Africa.* New York: Free Press.

Gellner, Ernest. 1964. *Thought and Change.* London: Weidenfeld and Nicholson.

Gellner, Ernest. 1983. *Nations and Nationalism.* Oxford: Blackwell.

Kedourie, Elie. 1992 (4th ed.). *Nationalism.* Oxford: Blackwell.

Ringer, B. B. 1983. *"We the People" and Others: Duality and America's Treatment of its Racial Minorities.* New York: Tavistock.

Smith, Anthony D. 1991. *National Identity.* Harmondsworth: Penguin.

Volkan, V. D. and N. Itzkowitz. 1994. *Turks and Greeks: Neighbours in Conflict.* Huntingdon: The Eothern Press.

Anna Triandafyllidou

# Nationalism and Patriotism (Minogue's Theory of Nationalism)

Since publishing *Nationalism* in 1967, Kenneth Minogue has taken an increasingly skeptical view of nationalism as an explanatory concept. The basic question, in his view, is not: "What is nationalism?," but rather, "What *kind* of thing is nationalism?" The suffix "-ism" suggests that it is a doctrine, but it is difficult to find much in common between the beliefs of Herder and Fichte, Mazzini and Cavour, Nkrumah and Nehru, Nasser and Zia Gökalp, to name only a few members of the nationalist pantheon. Hence it may be that nationalism is not so much a doctrine as a *phenomenon*—a drive or passion. But then the question arises: does the doctrine cause the phenomenon, or the phenomenon the doctrine? In other words, is nationalism to be understood in terms of social sciences (such as social psychology and political science) or in terms of intellectual history?

The eager student commonly opts for both, and with reason. But the combination of these methods causes many problems. Historical events and ideas are carved up according to some analytic schema distinguishing liberal, organic, integral, traditional, pan-movement, and a large variety of other types. Something can be learned from these analyses, but on Minogue's view, they mistake contingencies for categories. He follows ELIE KEDOURIE in thinking that we must understand nationalist episodes historically, in their own terms. And the initial identifying mark of nationalism is any movement within a state or an empire in which a set of people, claiming nationhood, seeks to establish a state of their own.

The source of many errors is the fact that the academic explanation of nationalism, as the theory of a theory, must either be history (how nationalist ideas "develop"), or philosophy (which judges the rationality of these ideas), and it cannot simultaneously be both. It is generally believed that nationalist doctrines are, intellectually, poor stuff. For example, the first question for any nationalist doctrine is how a nation may be defined, and the answer always favours the politically convenient over the intellectually coherent. Nations have been defined in terms of language, culture, religion, blood, race, will, and much else: anything goes, so long as it gets the followers out on the streets.

The problem with theorizing a theory is that the lower level theory (nationalism itself) will tend to infiltrate the higher level theory (the academic understanding of nationalism). This, notoriously, was a common corruption of many treatments of nationalism until about the 1960s. Many academics went along with the view that national allegiance, and hence nationalist passion, was a universal characteristic of politics down the ages; that Moses, Pericles, Joan of Arc, Henry V and so on, had been nationalists *avant la lettre*, and this helped to make contemporary nationalism respectable. But we must understand human action in terms of what the actors believe, and earlier figures thought in terms not of the nation, but of God, the *polis* and legitimate authority. As Elie Kedourie famously wrote in 1960, "Nationalism is a doctrine invented in Europe at the beginning of the nineteenth century" (Kedourie 1960).

Yet, even before students of nationalism had acquired clarity on this issue, another confusion had appeared. It emerged from the fact that nationalism, as an intellectuals' doctrine seeking mass support, was one of the dominant ideologies of recent times. It competed with Marxism and other forms of political enthusiasm for popular support, and in 1914 came what was thought a test case. Would social democratic parliamentarians support the war, or would they support international proletarian brotherhood? When, in France and Germany particularly, they supported their own governments, nationalism was judged (as the common formula has it) the "strongest political force" in the modern world.

However, if the formula had been true, Britain would have succumbed to Irish, Welsh and Scottish agitation, the Austro-Hungarian empire would have been incapable of a war effort because of the hostility of Czechs, Slovaks, Hungarians, Slovenes etc., and so on. What in fact the socialist vote demonstrated was that the established states of Europe had a patriotic cohesion which could, for the most, part subordinate nationalist movements within these states. Britain had trouble in Ireland, but this did not weaken the war effort.

# Nationalism and Patriotism (Minogue's Theory of Nationalism)

This confusion arises partly from the simple linguistic fact that the European states that went to war in 1914 were (slightly misleadingly) called "nation-states." They were not, indeed, nations in the classic sense, but whatever their national divisions, their subjects felt an overriding political loyalty to them. Semantically, English does not have an adjective from the noun "state," and we have to use "national" (as in "national loyalty" or "national interest") instead. But that does not mean that when Britain or France call on the loyalties of their peoples in war, they are "nationalist."

The linguistic confusion, however, is only one part of the story. The academic understanding of nationalism had again been infected by ideological contamination—and this time the source was not nationalism itself, but a movement in some ways directly hostile to nationalism. Minogue has called it "olympianism."

Olympianism is a state of mind in which individuals detach themselves from loyalty to their own state and identify with like-minded believers abroad in working for a world managed so as to guarantee universal human rights, peace and a safe environment. It is any belief in the superior wisdom of international institutions and arrangements. What Minogue called "olympianism" might be described as a form of negative nationalism; it is hatred for rather than love of one's native culture. It often involves feelings of superiority to one's fellow nationals, who are thought to be irrational and xenophobic. The fact that international organizations are remote from any electoral process reveals that olympianism mistrusts democracy. It belongs to an ideological style of politics in making its appeal to those whose political judgment flows from the abstract ideas they entertain rather than the interests they have. In a loquocentric society (Minogue 1986) opinion rules the world, and abstract opinions lack an anchor in the substance of day to day living.

Olympianism may be recognized in the use of "nationalism" to stigmatize as collective aggression or selfishness almost any pursuit of national interests. It has generated what Elie Kedourie has called "the dark gods" view of nationalism: namely, that it is an atavistic political pathology which reason must overcome. And it appeals to politicians as an all-purpose (because circular) explanation of conflict between peoples. It can cover everything from scepticism about the project of European Union at one extreme to ethnic cleansing at the other.

Minogue argues that the concept around which we must orient ourselves in understanding nationalism and competing ideologies is the modern state. States are commonly called "NATION-STATES" because *all* their subjects, as subjects, share the same kind of solidarity as is claimed for what we might call the "pure" nations of nationalist thought. States are always in some degree plural, most incorporating several nationalities. And what sustains them, especially in war, is the emotion called "patriotism" which must be clearly distinguished from nationalism.

Patriotism is (as Hegel notably argued in section 268 of *The Philosophy of Right*) the sentiment sustaining the public good. Whereas nationalism aims at a *future* civil state in which the *nation* will be self-governing, the patriot enjoys a *present* condition of civic involvement. Nationalism is always in some degree a condition of civil strife, sometimes of actual civil war, because there will be some in any nation who are loyal to the existing state or empire against which the nationalist struggles, or perhaps who have a quite different idea of the essence of the nation. The patriot on the other hand will always support the government and his fellow citizens even where he may not like specific policies, unless such policies outrage some deep moral or political principle.

It might seem that nationalism is an affirmation of the desirability of the nation-state, since it normally aims at creating a new one. This is misleading. In many cases, the nationalist aims to create some sort of true community based on race, blood, language, religion, or perhaps ideological affirmation. The nationalist often aims, that is, at an association very much more restrictive—shall we say totalitarian?—than the modern European state, whose essence is constitutionality. This is the reason why states emerging from nationalist movements have such trouble with MINORITIES.

Hostility to existing states, including liberal democracies, is where nationalism and olympianism, for all their hostility, come together. Each can, for its own purposes, be found arguing

# Nationality

that in a modern globalized world the nation-state is an anachronism, and the olympian will add— "and a dangerous one." The reason is that the olympian identifies the state with national sovereignty, and national sovereignty with nationalism, and nationalism with irrational and xenophobic tendencies towards aggression. The only final cure the olympian sees for this pathology is planetary unification. But in order to achieve world government, existing national states must be weakened or destroyed, and one device for such destruction is breaking them into the smaller and weaker regional autonomies where nationalists are calling for self-expression. Hence olympianism can be the ally of those nationalisms which seek to destroy existing states. It is for the same reason enthusiastic about MULTICULTURALISM where power is devolved away from the state down to the cultures.

Nationalism is thus, on Minogue's view, one term in the fundamental (and ultimately unresolvable) conflict in human affairs between universalism and particularism. The one takes off from our humanity, the other from our culture, and the relation between them is a perennial problem in politics.

## Bibliography

Kedourie, Elie. 1960. *Nationalism*. London: Hutchinson.

Minogue, Kenneth. 1967. *Nationalism*. London: B.T.Batsford.

Minogue, Kenneth. 1976. "Nationalism and the patriotism of city states," in Anthony D. Smith (ed.), *Nationalist Movements*. London: Macmillan.

Kenneth Minogue. 1985. *Alien Powers: The Pure Theory of Ideology*. London: Weidenfeld & Nicolson.

Minogue, Kenneth. 1986. "Loquocentric society and its critics," *Government and Opposition* 21, 3.

Minogue, Kenneth. 1993a. "Olympianism and the denigration of nationalism," in Claudio Veliz (ed.), *The Worth of Nations*. Boston: Boston University, The University Professors.

Minogue, Kenneth. 1993b. "Identity, self and nation," in Guy Laforest and Douglas Brown (eds.), *Integration and Fragmentation: The*

*Paradox of the Late Twentieth Century.* Queen's University Institute of Intergovernmental Studies.

Kenneth Minogue

# Nationality

Like many terms in the vocabulary of nationhood and nationalism, "nationality" is a complex term meaning several different things. It is thus not easy to offer a definition. According to Peter Alter,

> A distinction should be made between "nation" and the frequently encountered notion of "nationality," which generally has a dual meaning. Following the definition of nation offered here, a nationality is a social group which regards itself as an ethnic minority within a given state and desires no more than respect as a separate community. It does not seek to wield political power in its own state, but it does strive for cultural and political autonomy within a broader state framework. Most of the individual nationalities in the Habsburg monarchy, for example, did not begin to yearn for separate states until the nineteenth century. In addition, nationality is used, particularly in West European law, to mean citizenship: to which state one belongs (Alter 1994: 11-12).

Alter's definition is incomplete. Besides the two meanings offered above, "nationality" has also been used to refer to national sentiment, or nationalism; it has also been employed to designate the "national character" of a group; additionally, the existence as a sovereign nation, the attainment of political independence, statehood, by a national group (thus, in the nineteenth century, one could talk of the nationality achieved by Greece for example).

But when does the term appear? According to Gérard Noiriel, the word "nationalité" was first employed in 1807 in a novel by Madame de Staël (Noiriel 1995: 7). However, in English, it appears quite earlier, already in the eighteenth century. Thus, for instance, in his celebrated biography of Samuel Johnson (published in 1791), James Boswell reports several times Dr. Johnson's complaint (in reported conversations from the years 1773, 1775, 1783) that the Scotch "have...that extreme nationality" (Boswell 1980: 531). And, "Talking of the success of the Scotch in London, he imputed it in a considerable degree to their spirit of nationality" (ibid.: 1210). As far as Boswell was concerned, who was a Scotchman himself, Dr Johnson credited him for being "wonderfully free from that nationality" (ibid.: 599, 586).

In a thorough account of the uses of the concept of "nationalité" in France, Gérard Noiriel has described how it came to prominence especially among authors writing during the July Monarchy (1830-1848), and then was used in the plural as the "principe des nationalités" during the Second Empire (1852-1870) not least thanks to its use by Emperor Napoleon III himself (Noiriel 1995).

Thus, the nineteenth century was the heyday of the idea of nationality, which became a battle-cry after the revolutions of 1848. It was following the Revolution of February 1848 in Paris and the —diplomatic, yet controversial—declarations of the new Provisional Government of France to the effect that it would uphold the "legitimate" claims of certain nationalities of Europe if their attempts at self-determination were threatened by despotic powers that the most explicit denunciations of the "principle of nationality" were enunciated. In Britain, the Whig Lord Brougham took it upon himself to be the Edmund Burke of the French Revolution of February 1848, attacking almost everything the new revolution and the provisional government that had resulted from it had done or stood for. Thus, among other things, he vehemently denounced what he called

> That new-fangled principle, that new speculation in the rights of independent states, the security of neighbouring governments, and indeed the happiness of all nations, which is termed *Nationality*, adopted as a kind of rule for the distribution of dominion. It seems to be the notion preached by the Paris school of the Law of Nations and their foreign disciples, that one state has a right to attack another, provided upon statistically or ethnologically examining the classes and races of its subjects, these are found to vary (Brougham 1848: 126).

It was in reaction to this onslaught that JOHN STUART MILL articulated his first explicit vindication of the principle of nationality a few months later (Mill 1963-1991 XX: 340-348). But most scholars refer to Mill's later, classic definition of nationality, in chapter XVI of his now famous book, *Considerations on Representative Government* (1861). That chapter was entitled:

"Of Nationality, as Connected with Representative Government" (Mill 1963-1991 XIX: 546-52). Mill defined nationality as follows: "A portion of mankind may be said to constitute a Nationality, if they are united among themselves by common sympathies, which do not exist between them and any others - which make them co-operate with each other more willingly than with other people, desire to be under the same government, and desire that it should be government by themselves or a portion of themselves, exclusively." This feeling of nationality "may have been generated by various causes," none of which were "either indispensable, or necessarily sufficient by themselves" (ibid.: 546). It is well known that Mill went on in that chapter to assert that, whenever practically possible, the limits of government should coincide with those of nationality. A year after the publication of Mill's *Considerations*, another classic and oft-quoted treatise on "nationality" was published by Lord Acton. In an article entitled "Nationality," Acton offered a subtle and controversial analysis of the rise and consequences of the principle of nationality. In an oft-quoted statement he asserted:

> The greatest adversary of the rights of nationality is the modern theory of nationality. By making the State and the nation commensurate with each other in theory, it reduces practically to a subject condition all other nationalities that may be within the boundary. It cannot admit them to an equality with the ruling nation which constitutes the State, because the State would then cease to be national, which would be a contradiction of the principle of its existence. According, therefore, to the degree of humanity and civilisation in that dominant body which claims all the rights of the community, the inferior races are exterminated, or reduced to servitude, or outlawed, or put in a condition of dependence."

And Acton went on to assert, in another famous sentence:

> "If we take the establishment of liberty for the realization of moral duties to be the end of civil society, we must conclude that those states are substantially the most perfect which, like the British and Austrian Empires, include various distinct nationalities without oppressing them. Those in which no mixture of races has occurred are imperfect; and those in which its effects have disappeared are decrepit. A State which is incompetent to satisfy different races condemns

itself; a State which labors to neutralize, to absorb, or to expel them, destroys its own vitality; a State which does not include them is destitute of the chief basis of self-government. The theory of nationality, therefore, is a retrograde step in history. (Acton 1907: 273-300)

It is well-known that "the principle of nationalities" was evoked *par excellence* after the First World War as a criterion for the redrawing of the map of Europe according to the principle of self-determination. Many analysts, agreeing with Acton, believe that the consequences have been disastrous, due to the suppression of minorities that ensued and the never-ending claims and counter-claims to self-determination that were bound to arise.

In recent years the term "nationality" has come to prominence again in political theory and philosophy. The most important contributor to the revival of the idea of nationality is David Miller. In his celebrated book *On Nationality*, Miller used the notion to describe a version of particularistic national attachment which he also favors (Miller 1995). As he puts it, his book "neither celebrates nationalism nor writes it off as some kind of irrational monstrosity. It sets out to explore and defend what I shall refer to as 'the principle of nationality.'" Rejecting earlier analyses of national consciousness which had focused on nationalism and had tried to distinguish, more or less explicitly, between good and bad kinds of nationalism (distinctions such as those proposed by scholars like Hans Kohn or John Plamenatz, between "Western" and "Eastern" types of nationalism), Miller opts for a different term, less charged or tainted than "nationalism": "I prefer...to use the term 'nationality' for the position I want to explore and finally defend, following here in the footsteps of (among others) John Stuart Mill, who employed the term in a sense similar to mine in chapter 16 of *Considerations on Representative Government*" (Miller 1995: 10). Miller's views have given rise to a lively debate. Even his severest critics recognize his work as the most sophisticated of recent attempts by political theorists and philosophers to promote a sanitized version of national attachment which they consider to be compatible with liberal values (Benner 1997; O'Leary 1996).

234

## Bibliography

Acton, [Lord] John E.E. Dalberg-Acton. 1907 (1862). "Nationality," in *History of Freedom and Other Essays*. Salem, NH: Ayer Co. Pubs., Inc.

Alter, Peter. 1994. *Nationalism*, 2nd edition. London: Edward Arnold.

Bauer, Otto. 1995 (1907). "The Nationalities Question and Social Democracy," in Omar Dahbour and Micheline R. Ishay (eds.), *The Nationalism Reader*. Atlantic Highlands, NJ: Humanities Press.

Benner, Erica. 1997. "Nationality without nationalism," *Journal of Political Ideologies* 2, 2: 189-206.

Boswell, James. 1980 (1791). *Life of Johnson*. Oxford and New York: Oxford University Press.

Brougham, Henry Peter [Lord]. 1848. *Letter to the Marquess of Lansdowne, K.G., Lord President of the Council, on the Late Revolution in France*. London: Ridgway.

Mill, John Stuart. 1963-1991. *The Collected Works of John Stuart Mill*, 33 vols. Toronto and London: University of Toronto Press.

Miller, David. 1995. *On Nationality*. Oxford: Clarendon Press.

Namier, L. B. 1952. "Nationality and Liberty," in L. B. Namier, *Avenues of History*. London: Hamish Hamilton.

Noiriel, Gérard. 1995. "Socio-histoire d'un concept. Les usages du mot 'nationalité' au XIXe siècle," *Genèses: Sciences sociales et histoire* 20: 4-23.

O'Leary, Brendan (ed.). 1996. "Symposium on David Miller's *On Nationality*," *Nations and Nationalism* 2, 3: 407-452.

Georgios Varouxakis

# Nineteen-Eighty-Nine: Significance for Nationalism

In the 1989-90 issue of *Foreign Affairs* the distinguished British historian Michael Howard published "The springtime of nations," deliberately entitled to recall the 1848 springtime (Howard 1990). Perhaps Howard also wanted to caution readers that the startling rebirth of national movements might suffer new setbacks before it attained fruition. Howard placed the "miraculous year" in a series that began with the popular outbreak of the French Revolution precisely two centuries earlier, and included the Wilsonian emphasis on national self-determination, seemingly triumphant in 1919, and the widespread rebellion against Hitler's Europe in 1945. He might have added the somewhat similar revolt against Napoleon's order that culminated in 1813 at the Leipzig "battle of the nations."

Since the focus of this analysis is nationalism, the many factors that favored the re-emergence of independent nations in East Central Europe in 1989 will not be fully treated. Gorbachev's personal role after the passing (1982) of adamant defenders of the Communist *ancien régime* like Brezhnev and Suslov; the leadership's (especially the Soviet military) desperate search for economic revival; and the impact on the world balance of power have been discussed elsewhere (Armstrong 1994). To be most useful to students of nationalism, the presentation requires a thematic approach. First, though, it may be helpful to present a brief chronological outline showing how 1989 fitted - as all dramatic years must - into a longer span of nationalist upsurge.

Rebellion against totalitarianism based in Moscow had never wholly ceased. The Berlin uprising following Stalin's death (1952), the Hungarian revolution of 1956, and the suppression of the "Prague Spring" of 1968 all testify to this resistance, especially in their broad resonance within the Soviet Bloc. The most prolonged struggle, never quite reaching the level of widespread rebellion, occurred in Poland. Throughout the 1940s, 1950s, 1960s, and 1970s this disciplined resistance helped maintain a religious organization and a peasant agriculture that prepared Poland for a post-Communist society. At the end of the 1970s this relatively quiet resistance was emboldened by the election of a Polish Pope and, to a limited degree, the emergence of Polish national communist leaders such as Wojciech Jaruzelski. It is no coincidence that, a decade later, the boldest resistance within the USSR began in adjoining areas, once part of the Polish realm. In Lithuania (denunciation of illegal annexation under the Molotov-Ribbentrop pact) and in West Ukraine (mass demands for legalization of the Uniate Church) produced results as early as 1989. The real start of dominoes fall-

ing toward independence occurred, however, in East Germany, where demands for civil liberties and economic progress were sharper than national calls for re-unification. Under one of the strictest totalitarian regimes, yet open in many ways to examples set by German Federal Republic, East Germans could and did vote with their feet. By legally departing via Hungary, German "tourists" pushed the cautious legal and economic liberalization in that country to a climax. As the labor drain became crucial, the Pankow (East Berlin) regime believed it could humiliate deserters by exposing them to scorn as they were compelled to return, then permitted to proceed by train to the West. Instead of humiliating them, regime-sponsored crowds in Saxony and Thuringia loudly acclaimed their departing fellow-citizens. On November 10, 1989, in full view of the world press, dissidents dismantled the Berlin Wall, which became the symbol of popular (though still only partially national) triumph as it had, since 1961, been the symbol of totalitarian repression. In the few remaining weeks of 1989, not only the Pankow government, but Communist governments in Poland (where the nationalist Solidarity party had won an August election), Czechoslovakia, Bulgaria, and Hungary were replaced. In the very last days of December a Romanian uprising overthrew the dictator Nicolae Ceausescu, who was summarily tried and executed despite his "national communist" credentials.

Immediate pressures for national independence within the USSR were somewhat more cautious. Nevertheless, it became evident that 1989 would not be the only year of a "national springtime." As suggested above, the Baltic republics, notably Lithuania, led the way. As demands for independence were augmented by practical steps like installing customs controls at republic borders, Lithuania was again in the forefront, although it faced bloody reprisals by Moscow agents. After a series of elections that resulted in the victory, throughout most of the non-Russian Soviet Republics, of movements demanding "sovereignty" if not outright independence, Mikhail Gorbachev's cautious plan for a new Soviet confederation was met by an inept military coup in August 1991. Following dramatic resistance by leaders like Boris Yeltsin, the coup collapsed, while Gorbachev was too weakened to maintain his posts. Arguing that an independent Russia could still lead a confederation of independent republics, his *de facto* successor, Yeltsin, sanctioned independence for all republics of the USSR. During the next few years, these fifteen new independent states, all United Nations members, were joined by five former members of the Yugoslav federation and the two separated components of Czechoslovakia - Slovakia and the Czech Republic. In all, the Soviet Bloc and its sometime national Communist members in Europe, Yugoslavia, Romania, and Albania, were replaced by twenty-seven widely recognized members of the international concert, not including the "German Democratic Republic" which became a component of united Germany. On the other hand, no Communist state outside East Central Europe and the USSR fundamentally altered its regime, with the marginal exception of the Mongolian Republic. While opening their economic systems, China, Cuba, Vietnam, Laos, and Cambodia remained one-party dictatorships.

More significant for the observer of nationalism than these formal changes are the factors producing real independence. Nationalism played a part in all, but the themes and motivations behind nationalism varied greatly. By taking the twenty-seven newly independent states as a kind of sample, one can profitably analyse the impact of such factors behind nationalism. The following generalizations can be taken as hypotheses for future examination.

1. In most states, particularly in those that had been incorporated in the Bloc after 1939, *resentment* of foreign tyranny was a major force, as readers of works like Liah Greenfeld's discussion of the origins of nationalism might expect (Greenfeld 1994). Such resentment was, as indicated earlier, strongest in East Central Europe and its Soviet periphery, particularly in nations of the old Polish realm. It is nevertheless remarkable that a few nationalist movements rejected public resentment directed at Moscow. In 1992, for example, the Armenian Republic leadership, among the most strongly nationalist, urged that Russian troops remain on its territory. Clearly this decision was based not on Russophilia, but on the age-old principle, "the enemy (Russia) of my enemy (Turkey

and its Turkic allies) is my friend." For similar reasons neighboring Georgia has reluctantly admitted a Russian military presence. Moldavan nationalists are somewhat ambivalent toward the Russian-puppet "Dniester Republic" because the alternative of gradual absorption of Moldava in Romania is not without its drawbacks. Nor has resentment against Russians been an undiluted concern for the national Communist leaderships in the Asian republics, despite their religious and cultural aversion to Moscow.

2. The ethnoreligious factor in nationalist movements, strong after many decades of suppression. Orthodoxy remains a key element of Russian nationalism, and attracts not only Russian elements in the former USSR (the "near abroad"), but states where orthodoxy remains dominant as in Belarus and Moldava. But formal incorporation of the Armenian Gregorian Church in Orthodoxy has really not undermined national distinctiveness, although Armenians, like Russians, welcome support from Greece and other Orthodox states against Turkey. Similarly, Georgians, Orthodox for centuries, still reluctantly retain culturally Russian Orthodox monuments in their capital. The strong opposition to Moscow in western borderland, as discussed earlier, is intensified by the Catholic component ("Latin" or Uniate). As a result, Ukraine, unevenly divided among Uniates and Orthodox of several persuasions, has obstacles to overcome in establishing a united (*soborna*) state.

3. The Ukrainian case illustrates most clearly the ambiguities arising for any nationalist theme (Armstrong 1996). Reluctant to stress potentially divisive ethnoreligious themes, nationalists might turn to linguistic factors. Indeed, most intense nationalists in Galicia resent use of Russian, particularly "Russian-Ukrainian jargon," although communication in this mixture is usually feasible for urban people. Top national leaders like President Leonid Kuchma assiduously study Ukrainian, while (although Ukrainian by birth) privately employing Russian. Leaders' desire for a supra-ethnic civic culture requires full legal recognition for Russian and other languages in public discourse. In Yugoslavia, on the other hand, language became the overt requirement for citizenship in the new republics, at the price of eth-

nic cleansing. Yet, the minute distinctions in speech between Muslim Bosniaks, Catholic Croats, and Orthodox Serbs are really shibboleths rather than barriers to communication. In Estonia and Latvia, on the other hand, opposition to *exclusive* reliance on Russian arises from the imposed immigration of large minorities under Soviet rule. Even halting attempts to learn the local language are accepted, while for inter-Baltic communication persons like bus drivers continue (e.g., on the Estonian-Latvian frontier) to employ Russian. The well-established literary languages in East Central Europe, Lithuania, Armenia, and Georgia, where huge foreign minorities are absent, can be accepted as national characteristics without temptations for ethnic cleansing, except rarely on a religious basis. The same would be true of the Muslim republics of Central Asia, where centuries of religious usage have provided a reinforcement for non-European culture. But for technical subjects like economics, meetings of leaders from several of these countries are often obliged to resort to the Russian they learned in school—just as early Cominform meetings were reluctantly obliged to employ German.

4. Confronted by conflicting myth themes based on religion or language, Ukrainians frequently resort to *historical* topics like oppressive collectivization, or, "freedom-loving" Cossacks. But such myth themes pose difficulties in societies where peasants are a diminishing minority and revived Russian Cossacks are often anything but freedom-loving. Moreover, even in well-established national societies like Poland or Hungary, emphasis on history is likely to revive myth themes of an archaising nature impeding urbanization and economic development, or even reviving anti-Semitism.

5. Confronted with a recent history of shocking lags in economic well-being under Communism, nationalists often perceive the utility of stressing a link between independence and progress toward market economies. The difficulty of making this case undoubtedly has something to do, since 1992, with election successes of avowed national communists, experienced in management if not entrepreneurial activity. As indicated earlier, thirst for better living conditions was evidently the major source of East German rebellion. For newer independent states, the need for Western aid and investment, on the other hand, has acted as a major restraint on extreme ethnocentrism. Thus Slovenia, a promising candidate for European Community membership, has distanced itself from ethnic cleansing in the former Yugoslavia, while Estonia, another leading candidate, has moderated curbs on its Russian minority. Most former Yugoslav and former Soviet states are, however, far from meeting minimal economic requirements. Consequently, much of the claim for continued independence rests on the comparison with the even less promising Russian environment. Although income levels within the former USSR remain at roughly equal low levels, the larger units (Ukraine, Uzbekistan, Kazakhstan) have preserved a greater degree of domestic tranquility, thereby justifying a modest claim for independently advancing toward civil society. In turn, maintaining that claim requires tolerance of minorities and stable political circumstances.

6. Earlier one was able to note the importance, even at the peak of Soviet rule, of the diffusion effect in encouraging independence in East Central Europe and the USSR. It would be hard to identify a parallel effect from these areas, once they attained independence during 1989 and its 1991 sequel. There is no demonstrable impact on West European or American independence movements. The Québecois, the Catalan, the Basque, and the IRA, have apparently gained no strength, while the South Tyrolese, the Walloon, the Flemish, and the Occitan movements seem dormant compared to earlier years. The relative success of the Scottish movement needs more study. Spectacular as its initial results were, 1989 produced too many difficulties in establishing growing economies and stable governments to produce rapid emulation in distant areas. Undoubtedly, the extreme violence in former Yugoslavia and the Caucasian regions, while predictable in the light of the violent history and peculiar ethnic mixtures of those regions has also been offputting. On the other hand, 1989 and its sequel have produced the kind of tyranny and mass destruction which 1789 and 1919 eventually fostered. Hence while a sweeping victory for nationalist ideologies is unlikely, the oppor-

tunity for stabilizing newly independent members of the international community remains open.

## Bibliography

Altstadt, Audrey. 1988. "Nagorno-Karabagh," *Central Asian Survey* 7, 4:63-79.

Armstrong, John A. 1992. "Nationalism in the Former Soviet Empire," *Problems of Communism* 41, 1-2:121-37.

Armstrong, John A.1994. "National Liberation and International Balance," *Nationalities Papers* 22, 1:11-26.

Armstrong, John A. 1996. "Whither Ukrainian Nationalism?" *Canadian Review Studies in Nationalism* 23, 1-2 (1996):111.

Gagnon, V. P. 1991. "Yugoslavia: Prospects for Stability," *Foreign Affairs* 70, 3: 17-38.

Greenfeld, Liah. 1994. *Nationalism: Five Roads to Modernity.* Cambridge, MA: Harvard University Press.

Hayda, Lubomyr and Beissinger, Mark. 1990. *The Nationalities Factor in Soviet Politics and Society.* Boulder, CO: Westview Press.

Howard, Michael. 1990. "The springtime of nations," *Foreign Affairs* 69, 1: 17-32.

Khazarov, Anatoly M. 1995. *After the U.S.S.R.: Ethnicity, Nationalism and Politics in the Commonwealth of Independent States.* Madison: University of Wisconsin Press.

Kaiser, Karl. 1990-91. "Germany's Unification," *Foreign Affairs* 70, 1:179-205.

Laba, Roman. 1990. "How Yeltsin's exploitation of ethnic nationalism brought down an empire," *Transition* 2, 1:7-13.

Odom, William E. and Dujarric, Robert. 1995. *Commonwealth or Empire? Russia, Central Asia, and the Transcaucasus.* Indianapolis, IN: Hudson Institute.

Przeworski, Adam. 1991. "The East becomes the South?," *PS: Political Science and Politics* (March):20-27.

Woodward, Susan L. 1995. *Balkan Tragedy: Chaos and Dissolution after the Cold War.* Washington, DC: Brookings Institution.

John A. Armstrong

# P

## Patriotism

Patriotism is usually defined as "love of country," or, more literally, of fatherland, the land of the fathers. The term derives, etymologically, from the Greek words *patris* and *patriotés*, themselves derivatives from the Greek *pater*, meaning father. The term "patriotism" has acquired different meanings at different times and in different contexts. In eighteenth-century England "the title 'patriot' was one that all parties were eager to claim for themselves"(Viroli 1995: 60). It has been remarked by Quentin Skinner that "both the Whigs and Tories used the concept of patriotism to mean 'the ideal of acting in such a way as to defend and preserve the political liberties which their fellow-countrymen enjoyed under, and owed to, the constitution'" (Viroli 1995: 60). Early in the eighteenth century it referred more to a conservative, a Tory ideologue, as the Tory Party claimed to be the "Country Party." Quite characteristically, Robert Walpole's arch-enemy, Bolingbroke, wrote *The Spirit of Patriotism* and *The Idea of a Patriot King* (1749). Later in the century, however, the language of patriotism assumed increasingly radical connotations (Cunningham 1989). Thus, when Samuel Johnson wrote, for the 1775 edition of his *Dictionary*, his notorious dictum "patriotism is the last refuge of the scoundrel," he was censuring the Radicals (whom he considered populists), who were by then called "patriots" (Cunningham 1989; Breuilly 1993: 20). A few years later, the radical Richard Price received no less scathing attacks from conservative thinker Edmund Burke for his sermon celebrating the French Revolution and entitled, characteristically, *A Discourse on the Love of our Country* (4 November 1789). The *Discourse* was a celebration of a patriotism that was consistent with the Christian ethic of universal benevolence, and could be considered a precursor of late twentieth-century theories advocating "cosmopolitan" or "universalist" versions of patriotism.

No less interesting was the discourse on patriotism in France during the eighteenth century. The most articulate and probably most influential theorist of patriotism writing in French at that time was the "Citizen of Geneva," JEAN-JACQUES ROUSSEAU. In works such as *Considérations sur le Gouvernement de Pologne*, *Projet de Constitution pour la Corse*, *Discours sur l'Économie Politique*, and *Du Contrat Social*, Rousseau dedicated long passages to an analysis of patriotism and methods of promoting it through education as well as public ceremonies, children's games, and even through a "civil religion." This was in accordance with Rousseau's conviction that Christianity, and Catholicism in particular, could not serve the purposes of patriotism because it was too universalistic (Leliepvre-Botton 1996).

During the French Revolution "patriot" described a zealous revolutionary within France, as well as foreign supporters of the French Revolution, such as the notorious Prussian Anacharsis Cloots (O'Brien 1988: 36-42). But since the time of the French Revolution and the gradual emergence of the discourse concerning "nationality" or "nationalism" during the nineteenth century, patriotism has come to be either confused with, or sharply differentiated from "nationalism."

The most fundamental problem in any attempt to define "patriotism" today is to establish its relationship with "nationalism." Solutions to this problem have been particularly diverse. What bedevils attempts to offer a definition of patriotism is that such attempts tend to be partisan and normative rather than descriptive and objective. As a result of the negative connotations that "nationalism" acquired during the twentieth century, "patriotism" emerged as its acceptable twin. Those in favor of national or other particularistic attachments, of a "sense of belonging," or of the civic virtues associated with participation in, and concern for the affairs of one's polity, tend to assert the existential significance of such attachments.

# Patriotism

At the same time, they stress that these attachments do not need to entail all the aggressive, exclusionist or xenophobic connotations associated with "nationalism," "chauvinism," "jingoism," and so on. These thinkers thus redeem patriotism from its negative associations by claiming that "patriotism" is—or should and could be—very different from "nationalism." In this context, patriotism has been taken to be the acceptable, and moreover, commendable version of particularistic attachments, while nationalism has been regarded as aggressive and a degeneration or exaggeration of patriotic attachments.

Such distinctions became sharper and more frequent in the second half of the twentieth century, as a result of the discrediting of nationalism after the specific and traumatic experiences of two world wars. Nevertheless, attempts to distinguish between the two concepts were already made in the nineteenth century, again, quite characteristically, in contexts where nationalism was seen as taking extreme and aggressive directions. As Erica Benner has observed, "the 1866 edition of *Larousse* describes nationalism as a neologism meaning a 'blind and exclusive' preference for one's nation, a vice of immoderation afflicting the sound republican virtue of *patriotisme*" (Benner 1997: 190). According to Claude Nicolet, it was from the 1880s onwards, and especially after the rise of the populist nationalist Boulangist movement, that the republicans (especially those of the left) began to speak of "patriots" and "patriotism" rather than the "nation" and "nationalism" (Nicolet 1982: 17-18).

In the twentieth-century literature on nationalism we find a variety of divergent accounts of the differences between nationalism and patriotism. In a work published in 1960, based on a series of lectures given in 1940, Dutch historian Johan Huizinga defined patriotism as "the will to maintain and defend what is one's own and cherished." Huizinga defined nationalism as "the powerful drive to dominate, the urge to have one's own nation, one's own state assert itself above, over, and at the cost of others" (Huizinga 1960: 97). He also remarked that "The dividing line between patriotism and nationalism, however one may understand the latter, is in theory absolutely clear: the one is a subjective feeling, the other an objectively perceptible attitude. In the practice of the individual case the line dividing them is often very difficult to trace" (ibid.: 98-9).

Psychologist Leonard Doob has distinguished between patriotism as a group-oriented feeling or psychological predisposition which exists *universally*, wherever human beings are joined in societies, and nationalism as a much more complex, programmatic and historically conditioned elaboration of this simple feeling into *patterns of demands and actions* deeply affecting group policy (Doob 1964: 6-9).

Similarly, ELIE KEDOURIE distinguished "nationalism from patriotism and xenophobia with which it is often confused." According to Kedourie, "[p]atriotism, affection for one's country, or one's group, loyalty to its institutions, and zeal for its defence, is a sentiment known among all kinds of men; so is xenophobia, which is dislike of the stranger, the outsider, and reluctance to admit him into one's own group." Kedourie stressed that "neither sentiment depends on a particular anthropology and neither asserts a particular doctrine of the state or of the individual's relation to it." In contrast, "[n]ationalism does both; it is a comprehensive doctrine which leads to a distinctive style of politics. But far from being a universal phenomenon, it is a product of European thought in the last 150 years. If confusion exists, it is because nationalist doctrine has annexed these universally held sentiments to the service of a specific anthropology and metaphysic" (Kedourie 1985: 73-4).

ERNEST GELLNER has also asserted that one important factor in the persistence of the groups in which mankind has lived at all times has been "the loyalty men felt for these groups, and the fact that they identified with them." He remarked that "[t]his element in human life did not need to wait for some distinctive kind of economy. ... If one calls this factor, generically, 'patriotism,'" then "some measure of such patriotism is indeed a perennial part of human life." As far as nationalism is concerned, Gellner claimed "that nationalism is a very distinctive species of patriotism, and one which becomes pervasive and dominant only under certain social conditions, which in fact prevail in the modern world, and nowhere else. Nationalism is a species of patriotism distinguished by a few very important features..." (Gellner 1983: 138).

From the above it is evident that there exists a general tendency among scholars of nationalism to regard patriotism as a perennial feature of human affairs, a feature which is much older than nationalism, and, in most cases, much more legitimate or at least less harmful than nationalism.

During the 1990s, political theorists and political philosophers made important contributions to the analysis of the two concepts, patriotism and nationalism. They identified at least three varieties of "patriotism" which they distinguished from "nationalism." The first variety consists of adaptations of the old republican patriotism to the needs of contemporary multi-cultural societies. Maurizio Viroli's study *For Love of Country: An Essay on Patriotism and Nationalism* gives an excellent account and defense of this variety (1995). A second type of patriotism is what scholars have labelled "constitutional patriotism." This is a form of civic patriotism which is firmly attached to universalist and rationalist principles, and is regarded as an antidote to aggressive, xenophobic and illiberal nationalism. In constitutional patriotism the object of collective loyalty and reverence is the current constitution, the *Grundgesetz*, of the democratic state. The idea of constitutional patriotism (*Verfassungspatriotismus*) is usually associated with the German philosopher Jürgen Habermas who, in fact, advocated it during the early 1990s, although it had been championed by others a decade earlier (e.g., Dolf Sternberger) (Habermas 1992). A third variety of patriotism which is sometimes identified with the second, constitutional patriotism, and is sometimes distinguished from it, is the so-called "cosmopolitan patriotism" (Nussbaum 1996).

Some of these attempts to distinguish between a commendable patriotism from an unsavory nationalism have been severely criticized by a number of scholars of nationalism. These have criticized the normative implications of such distinctions which make patriotism good and nationalism bad, and especially the use of such distinctions to sanction the nationalism of certain nations by calling it "patriotism" while condemning that of others by calling it "nationalism"

(Breuilly 1993; Benner 1997; Canovan 1996). Nevertheless, the distinction between patriotism and nationalism remains in use among both scholars and intellectuals.

## Bibliography

Benner, Erica. 1997. "Nationality without nationalism," *Journal of Political Ideologies* 2, 2: 189-206.

Breuilly, John. 1993. "Nationalism and the State," in Roger Michener (ed.), *Nationality, Patriotism and Nationalism in Liberal Democratic Societies*. St Paul, MN: Professors World Peace Academy.

Canovan, Margaret. 1996. *Nationhood and Political Theory*. Cheltenham: Edward Elgar.

Cunningham, Hugh. 1989. "The language of patriotism," in Raphael Samuel (ed.), *Patriotism: The Making and Unmaking of British National Identity*, vol. 1. (3 vols.). London: Routledge.

Doob, Leonard W. 1964. *Patriotism and Nationalism: Their Psychological Foundations*. New Haven, CT and London.

Gellner, Ernest. 1983: *Nations and Nationalism*. Oxford: Blackwell.

Habermas, Jürgen. 1992. "Citizenship and national identity: Some reflections on the future of Europe," *Praxis International* 12, 1: 1-18.

Huizinga, Johan. 1960. "Patriotism and nationalism in European history," in J. Huizinga, *Men and Ideas: History, the Middle Ages, the Renaissance*. London: Eyre & Spottiswoode.

Kedourie, Elie. 1985 (1960). *Nationalism*. London: Hutchinson.

Leliepvre-Botton, Sylvie. 1996. *Droit du Sol, Droit du Sang: Patriotisme et Sentiment National Chez Rousseau*. Paris: Ellipses.

Nicolet, Claude. 1982: *L'Idée Républicaine en France (1789-1924): Essai d'Histoire critique*. Paris: Gallimard.

Nussbaum, Martha C. *with respondents* and edited by Joshua Cohen. 1996. *For Love of Country: Debating the Limits of Patriotism*. Boston: Beacon Press.

O'Brien, Conor Cruise. 1988. "Nationalism and the French Revolution," in Geoffrey Best (ed.), *The Permanent Revolution: The French Revolution and its Legacy 1789-1989*. London: Fontana Press.

Viroli, Maurizio. 1995. *For Love of Country: An Essay on Patriotism and Nationalism.* Oxford: Clarendon Press.

Georgios Varouxakis

# Perennialism and Modernism

One of the major dividing lines in the study of nationalism concerns the antiquity of nations. While most scholars would agree that nationalism as an ideology and movement is relatively modern, dating from the latter half of the eighteenth century, though with earlier harbingers in the seventeenth-century Dutch and English revolutionary nationalisms, there is considerable disagreement over the dating and provenance of nations.

Prewar scholars tended to assume that nations, which they often conflated with ethnic groups (*ethnies*) and races, were found throughout history. Indeed, many scholars were "primordialists," regarding nations as components of the natural order, existing, as the Abbé Sieyés put it, "outside time." Other scholars were more cautious; they preferred to stick to the historical record, and this suggested that nations had emerged from at least the late third millennium B.C. in the ancient Near East, and thenceforth were to be found in every period and continent. Indeed, present-day nations appeared to have existed over many centuries, if not millennia; they were, if not "primordial," certainly "perennial."

After 1945, many scholars began to question these assumptions. Not only were they able to show that nations were not elements of the natural order, that they possessed no logical necessity; they were also increasingly skeptical of the claim that nations were immemorial and perennial. After all, were not nations being created under their very eyes in the newly independent ex-colonies of Africa and Asia? Were not new immigrant societies in the Commonwealth and the Americas being forged into nations? From these observations, it was a short step to affirming that even apparently "old nations" in Western Europe were really relatively modern, that they had been constituted as nations rather than kingdoms as recently as the seventeenth and eighteenth centuries, and that they therefore were just as much products of modernity as were the later nations being formed in contemporary Africa and Asia.

In place of the earlier "perennialism" of the pre-War generation, post-War scholars like Karl Deutsch, ELIE KEDOURIE, ERNEST GELLNER and ERIC HOBSBAWM proposed a "modernist" approach which claimed that nations were not only relatively recent historical phenomena, they were also products of modernity. In this they relied to a considerable extent on the tenets of "modernization theory," with its assumption of a radical rupture between traditional and modern societies. Ernest Gellner put the "modernist" case most forthrightly (Gellner 1983). He claimed that traditional agrarian societies had no room for either nations or nationalism. Such societies were generally divided into a tiny class of ruling and specialist elites, on the one hand, and a vast mass of food-producers, on the other hand. A large social and cultural gulf separated the elites from the peasants, and while the elites saw no reason to spread their culture down to the masses, the latter were themselves divided into a mosaic of local cultures and societies. Modern societies, on the other hand, were oriented to economic growth and required a mobile, literate workforce educated in the "high culture" of a modern industrial society. Through the mass, standardized, public education system, the state was able to secure the necessary culturally uniform workforce bound by loyalty to the nation and its high culture.

Other modernists like Deutsch, Hobsbawm, and Anderson filled out this picture. They argued that economic development uproots populations and increases social communication among large numbers of people, especially in the anonymous cities (Deutsch 1966; Hobsbawm 1990; Anderson 1983). This in turn leads to the growth of a "public," able to communicate more intensively and over a larger range of topics with other members of that culture. For Anderson, this process was abetted by the dissemination of vernacular books and newspapers by print technology in alliance with commodity capitalism. With the decline of sacred monarchies and liturgical congregations, the new literate public looked to the sociological language community of the nation increasingly represented in texts and narratives for their salvation through posterity. Moreover, in an age of rapid industrialization and mass democratization, the public required, Hobsbawm argued, new forms of community underpinned by new "invented traditions" so that the ruling elites could channel their energies and control change through new status systems.

Whatever the mechanisms, the "modernists" all agreed on three points. The first was historical: the nation, as well as nationalism, was relatively recent, a phenomenon of the last two to three hundred years, and many individual nations were even more recent, some of them being created under our very eyes. The second point was sociological: the nation was a product, for many modernists, an inevitable one, of "modernity," that umbrella term for all the novel processes characteristic of the modern world, such as capitalism, industrialization, urbanization, secularization, democratization, and the bureaucratic state. The third point was methodological: rather than seeing nationalism, the ideology and movement, as the product of the nation, as nationalists assumed, we must view nations as the product of nationalism, not only as a means of defining the concept of the nation, but as the key to explaining its formation. It is nationalism that creates nations, not the other way round. In this essentially social constructionist (if not "inventionist") view, the nation is a product of social engineering on the part of elites, and more especially of the intelligentsia.

In many ways, modernism has become the current historical and sociological orthodoxy. This is attested by the many books and articles with titles and arguments for the "invention" and "construction" of nations. It would be a mistake, however, to assume that all modernists subscribe to the idea of the invented or constructed nation, even when they argue for the primacy of nationalism in the formation of nations. Nor are all modernists unaware of the premodern cultures that enter into the creation of modern nations, or of the very different historical trajectories of nation formation. This is evident in the investigations of Miroslav Hroch into the roots of nationalism among the small nations of Eastern Europe, or the distinction made by an historian like Hugh Seton-Watson between the "old, continuous nations" of Western Europe and the new nations of design created in large part by nationalists in nineteenth-century Eastern Europe and twentieth century Asia (Hroch 1985; Seton-Watson 1977).

It is exactly this distinction that has led others to question the historical basis of the modernist argument. If some nations have pre-modern roots, could it be the case that others, which have been categorized as recent creations, owed more than modernists have realized to these older ethnic ties and sentiments, and that popular ethnic beliefs and practices are necessary to the formation of viable nations? In other words, modernists may have been misled through their methodology and the assumptions of "modernization theory" into neglecting the pre-modern ethnic components of, and the popular basis for, the formation of modern nations.

This is a position adopted by John Armstrong. While conceding the importance of nationalist ideologies and movements in helping to create new nations, Armstrong claims that we can locate many nations in a process of national development over the *longue durée*. France and England offer examples of how nations may be formed over many centuries and through a variety of political, religious, linguistic and economic processes in roughly the same territory. On the other hand, we can also witness in other areas such as the Near East and Central Asia repeated processes of ethnic and national identity formation and dissolution which attest to the perennial existence of nations over the ages.

This kind of analysis suggests that "perennialism" can be used in either of two ways: as continuity and as recurrence. In the first sense, particular nations have a durability and continuity from their earliest mention in the historical record to the present, which implies some kind of longevity of nations and corresponds to the widespread sense of the immemorial nature of "our nation." Armenians, Greeks, Jews, Chinese and Japanese, as well as French, English, Scots, Catalans, and Basques can describe their nations as in this sense "perennial," despite all the changes in social life and cultural content undergone by the populations claiming these names, territories and national identities. In the second sense, the nation is regarded as a recurrent phenomenon. Particular nations come and go, emerge and decline, separate and are absorbed; but every epoch and every continent can boast some nations. In this sense, the so-called "modern nation," even if it has distinctive features of scale, size, density and political format, is simply a recent embodiment and development of an age-old and widespread phenomenon.

One may be skeptical of both kinds of perennialism, but remain equally unconvinced by the arguments of modernism. While conceding the recent vintage of "nations," as we know them today, scholars like John Hutchinson and Anthony Smith point to the importance of pre-modern ethnic ties for so many nationalisms and nations, as well as to the fact that in some (European and Far Eastern) cases the ethnic community was well developed long before the advent of the modern era and could therefore form the basis of the "modern" nation with relative ease. In these cases, to aver that nationalism creates the nation is at best a half-truth; its validity depends on regarding the nation as by definition not only relatively recent but sociologically wholly "modern," when the question of its modernity in this sense must remain open, not so much because either of the perennialist arguments may possess some validity, but because the so-called "modern nation" so often incorporates pre-modern features of name, memories, symbols, customs, language territory, religious denomination and the like, the kind of elements explored by "ethno-symbolists." These make it perhaps less "modern" in the sociological and methodological senses than modernists tend to believe.

## Bibliography

Anderson, Benedict. 1983. *Imagined Communities: Reflections on the Origin and Spread of Nationalism*. London: Verso.

Armstrong, John. 1982. *Nations before Nationalism*. Chapel Hill: University of North Carolina Press.

Deutsch, Karl W. 1966 (2nd ed.; 1953, 1st ed.). *Nationalism and Social Communication: An Inquiry into the Foundations of Nationality*. Cambridge: MIT Press.

Gellner, Ernest. 1983. *Nations and Nationalism*. Oxford: Blackwell.

Hobsbawm, Eric. 1990. *Nations and Nationalism since 1780*. Cambridge: Cambridge University Press.

Hroch, Miroslav. 1985. *Social Preconditions of National Revival in Europe*. Cambridge: Cambridge University Press.

Hutchinson, John. 1994. *Modern Nationalism*. London: Fontana Press.

Seton-Watson, Hugh. 1977. *Nations and States*. Boulder, CO: Westview Press.

Smith, Anthony. 1986. *The Ethnic Origins of Nations*. Oxford: Blackwell.

Smith, Anthony. 1994. "The problem of national identity: ancient, medieval and modern?," *Ethnic and Racial Studies* 17, 3: 375–99.

Anthony D. Smith

# Postcolonialism, Nations, and Nationalism

Postcoloniality is essentially the latest perspective in the debate over issues of culture and power. This perspective arose out of the comparative study of commonwealth literature and the question of cultural representation. Early postcolonial narratives had definite political significance, expressing the views of those deprived of their own voice, land, liberty, history, and culture, in other words, the colonized. Postcolonial "theory" at this initial stage was primarily literary, relating to language, genre, and text and addressed the need to assert and to account for difference from Eurocentric narratives which for so long had been dominant and regarded as universal (Darby 1997:13). However, expansion into cultural studies and the dominant influence of postmodernism radically transformed the discourse. It acquired a sharper theoretical focus, became equivocal as a formal political and historical condition, and moved from its third world mooring to globalized perspectives (Darby 1997).

Postcolonial discourses of nations and nationalisms are concerned with differences in perceptions about the nature of the contemporary nation-state and the relevance of nationalism in (post)modern politics. The type of discourse depends on the weight attached to either global capitalism or the nation-state as the locus of identity, and to geographic location. The global discourse emphasizes the idea of "postnationalism" which asserts that the nation-state is increasingly irrelevant, practically overtaken by other forms of allegiance and identity that are antinationalist. On the other hand, the nation-state discourse emphasizes the increasing global significance of ideological nationalism and the primacy of the nation-state as the locus of identity.

The postnationalism debate is located in the developed West where, it is claimed, regionalism, migration, and globalization are eroding the traditional authority and homogeneity of the nation-state. In this domain postcolonialism refers to the implications of postimperial conditions for the definition of identities in the West rather than to the identities of those who live in the actual postcolonial societies (Chabal 1996:37). Postcoloniality is thus about the West coming to terms with its colonial past, and another way of describing the racialization and ethnicization of Western societies by the in-migration of colonized subjects. The crisis of postcolonial identity in the West finds expression in the ideological and cultural discourses of Multiculturalism, antiracism, Hybridity, and Diaspora and the growing right-wing xenophobic movements across Europe whose Racism focuses on the necessity to return to some allegedly "real" but actually imaginary preimperial roots.

The equivocal nature of postcolonialism as a form of political and historical condition is demonstrated by First World nation-states and breakaway settler colonies like Australia, the United States, Canada, and New Zealand that have not undergone decolonization but were founded on the principle of transferring imperial power from the core to the colony itself (McClintock 1993:295). Here the debate about postcolonial identity is similar to that in Western Europe but the racism of the colonizer/settler is based on white supremacist ideologies, caught up with and defined against non-white settlers and immigrants, and against indigenous, especially autochthonous, claims by "tribal" peoples.

For the indigenous peoples of breakaway settler colonies (and Latin America) the "post" of postcolonialism is prematurely celebratory. However, the ideological discourse of purity (natural sovereignty, ancestral home, firstness on land) invests indigenous peoples with distinction, as the "original political nexus of colonizer and colonized relations is being decentred by the increasing presence of immigrant settlers from

around the world" (Jacobs 1996:23); the claim of primordial habitation becomes the political means by which indigenous peoples assert their difference and gain peoplehood. In claiming both autochthony and a specific transregional worldliness, new tribal forms preserve their peoplehood from inevitable destruction by modernizing forces such as emerging nation-states, colonialism and transnational capital (Clifford 1997:254). The indigenous national discourse is politically articulated through local First Nation movements and transnational Fourth World alliances forged by indigenous peoples across the globe. These alliances loop into the global ideoscape (Appadurai 1993:331) of environmentalism, deploying "diasporist visions of return to an original place—a land commonly articulated in visions of nature, divinity, mother earth and the ancestors" (Clifford 1997:254).

The pro-nationalist or nation-building discourse is located in the Third and ex-Soviet Worlds, where the legacies of colonialism and communism have both retarded and fuelled the impetus to build sovereign nation-states out of the ruins of empire (Joppke 1996:1). Here again the discourse of postcolonial nationalism is colored by location, the distinction being between the ethnonationalisms of Eastern Europe, and the ethnicities and religious nationalisms of the colonial-successor states.

In the colonial-successor states the developed forms of nationalism and nationalist ideology are not based on the unity of culture but on anti-colonialism. They are generally the opposite of the ethnically and linguistic homogenous forms that are the standard in the West. The postcolonial debate is essentially about the legitimation crisis of the state and the identity crisis caused by the failure of anti-colonial nationalism to deliver on its secular promise of a more progressive social order, and the impact of neocolonialism and its global capitalist and cultural forms. The debate is expressed in the challenge of Ethnicity, especially, behavioral ethnicity, and religious nationalisms in which Islam, especially Islamic fundamentalism, is the dominant type. Reformed Islam, as an ideology of national self-rectification, purification, and recovery, reinforces nationalism, notably in the context of the struggle against neo-

## Postcolonialism, Nations, and Nationalism

colonialism. Joppke (1996) organizes the postcolonial discourse of nationalism in the southern periphery into three phases: the first is the phase of anticolonial nationalism in which the concept of national self-determination is appropriated from the colonial power; the second is the phase of nation-state building, in which the consolidation of the colonial successor states is threatened by ethnic divisions; and finally, a second wave of anticolonial discontent, in which anti-western fundamentalist movements reject the very idea of a secular nation-state.

The East European discourse of postcolonialism, like its southern counterpart, is anti-Western, laden with "resentment," but stresses indigenous "folk" qualities (Joppke 1996:2). It is about ethnically, religiously, and linguistically homogenous nations acquiring their own state and the pathos attached to the idea of one's own state. The narrative of nation is "about the vindication and recovery of already established nationhood against a regime whose purpose had been to wipe it out" (Joppke 1996:19). Accordingly, it attests to the tenacity of nationalism against a strong antinationalist force like communism, and repudiates the antinationalist discourse of postnationalism. The national discourse is saturated by primordial sentiments that have the ability to inject intimacy into politics and "turn locality into a staging ground for identity" (Appadurai 1993:332), for example, myths of common origins, memories of past victimization, and ideologies of purity articulated through the now common metaphor of ethnic cleansing. The East European discourse has spawned a critical new form of popular nationalism, Ethnonationalism—an increasingly popular term used to denote the ideological nationalism of groups struggling for the formation of a national state. The key problem posed for ethno-nationalism is the tension between cultural homogenization and heterogenization. It is intolerant of multi-national states and national minorities, and thrives on a list of alternative fears of extinction by majorities and minorities (Joppke 1996:31). For the ethnonation-state, the external enemy, especially if it is a nearby polity of larger scale, is more real than the threat of its own hegemonic strategies.

Postcolonialism has opened up new ways of thinking about the nation state and the nature of nations and nationalism. It has enabled the rethinking of identity in terms of transnationalism, as a relational interaction between global and local processes. It calls attention to the need to sort out and specify the new nationalisms of the contact zones of nations, cultures, and regions.

The postcolonial discourse constitutes a much needed corrective to the Eurocentrism and conservatism of so much mainstream writing about nationalism, especially approaches that view Third World heterogenous nationalisms as poor reflections or copies of the European model, still regarded as the universal standard to emulate. Postcoloniality invests these marginal types with distinction and their difference becomes the means by which they assert their own authority in the debate on nations and states. For postcoloniality, nationalism studies is as much about the study of "authentic," hegemonic and plural nations and nationalisms as it is about subaltern and subversive forms caught up with and defined against the norms of nation-states.

Finally, postcoloniality enables us to examine representations and constructions of nations and nationalisms in the context of literary and cultural narratives, of all kinds. Texts from cultural media like music, the media, arts, sports, fashion, cuisine, and film, are ideal for rethinking the limits and possibilities of nations and nationalisms because they give expression to cultural and psychological forces which are seldom considered in sociological and political studies of nations and nationalism owing to disciplinary closures and conventions. And because such cultural texts are themselves part of the process of global exchange, the critical debate which they engender represents a new form of enquiry into the relationship between nations, nationalisms and the state in an increasing transnational present.

### Bibliography

Appadurai, Arjun. 1993. "Disjuncture and Difference in the Global Cultural Economy," in Patrick Williams and Laura Chrisman (eds.), *Colonial Discourse and Post-Colonial Theory: A Reader.* New York: Harvester Wheatsheaf.

Clifford, James. 1997. *Routes: Travel and Translation in the Late Twentieth Century*. Cambridge, MA: Harvard University Press.

Darby, P. 1997. "Postcolonialism" in P. Darby (ed.) *At the Edge of International Relations: Postcolonialism, Gender and Dependency*. London: Pinter.

Gellner, Ernest. 1983. *Nations and Nationalism*. Oxford: Basil Blackwell.

Igwara, Obi. 1993. *Ethnicity, Nationalism and Nation-building in Nigeria, 1970-1992*. Ph.D. Thesis: London School of Economics.

Jacobs, Jane M. 1996. *Edge of Empire: Postcolonialism and the City*. London: Routledge.

Joppke, Cristian. 1996. *Nation-Building after World War Two: Postcolonialism, Postcommunism, and Postfascism*. Florence: European University Institute.

McClintock, Anne. 1993. "The Angel of Progress: Pitfalls of the Term 'Post-Colonialism'" in Patrick Williams and Laura Chrisman (eds.), *Colonial Discourse and Post-Colonial Theory: A Reader*. New York: Harvester Wheatsheaf.

Obi Igwara

# A Postmodern Conception of the Nation-State

This article offers a brief reading of Homi Bhabha's conception of the phenomenon of the nation-state, as the dominant modern "space" of collective identity. National identity is a specific form of collective identity, which has been embodied in the political institution of the nation-state since the eighteenth century. Bhabha provides us with a postmodern analysis of national identity, which deconstructs a nationalistic representation of the nation-state as a unit in which people cohere around a historical and homogeneous common core which sets them apart from "others." According to Bhabha, we must understand nationalism as a discourse of power which, by unifying "us" against "them," conceals the heterogeneous nature of "us" and the contingency and intertwinement of "us" and "them."

Some postmodern theorists, such as Lyotard and Foucault conceptualize an essential opposition to modern meta-narrative discourses of identity (which also apply to national identity), and also to the Enlightenment's practices of establishing universal truths. Such discourses are regarded as invariably ideological and linked to power relationships in organizing and "normalizing" human identity. Now, if the nation-state is one of the dominant containers and organizers of a grand and homogeneous "national" identity, then, from a postmodern point of view, it can be perceived as an institution that is very similar to "the clinic," "the hospital," "the school," "the prison." It is, in a Foucaultian sense, a discourse of power, and a modern apparatus of both making and representing collective identity.

The Enlightenment conception of the human subject is that of a "fully centred, unified individual, endowed with the capacities of reason, consciousness and action, whose 'centre' consisted of an inner core, which first emerged when the subject was born, and unfolded with it, while remaining essentially the same—continuous or 'identical' with itself—throughout the individual's existence" (Hall 1992: 275-77). This conceptualization of the subject as sovereign and capable of reason, has been an important component of modernity.

The Enlightenment conception of the individual subject can also be applied to a collectivity, to a collective subject. The nation-state is a good example of such a collective subject. The nation-state can be understood by reference to an inner core within the collectivity, which is present ontologically, self-referentially and as an *a priori* in the thought and action of the collectivity. This inner core within human collectivities has the following functions: first, it distinguishes them from others; second, it articulates and gives value to the separation of "us" from "them"; and third, it assumes some kind of unquestionable cultural homogeneity or commonality within each collectivity. We may recognize in the Enlightenment's conception of the collective subjective the philosophy of nationalism which has dominated the world since the French Revolution of 1789. And it was this same vision which constituted the spirit of the League of Nations, founded in 1919. This spirit gave legitimacy to the attempts of national states to achieve cultural and political congruence. It also legitimized the aspirations and am-

## A Postmodern Conception of the Nation-State

bitions of all "ethnic groups" to have their own, national state.

A postmodern subject, on the other hand, is conceptualized by Stuart Hall as having no "fixed, essential or permanent identity. Identity becomes a 'moveable feast': formed and transformed continuously in relation to the ways we are represented or addressed in the cultural systems which surround us" (Hall 1992: 275-77). According to Hall, if we feel that we have a unified identity from birth to death, both individually and collectively, it is only because we narrate it as such; because we narrate it according to fundamental facets of the Enlightenment thought.

From a postmodern perspective, it can be argued, that the human subject has not only formed different collective identities in different times and places, but also, that these formed identities have a hybrid nature. There is no unified, coherent, completed "self," or an inner core that is spatially and temporally linear. The only "time" that is spatially and temporally linear is Benedict Anderson's "homogeneous empty time" of the "IMAGINED COMMUNITIES" in which the anonymity of the individual is linked to an "imagined community" of the nation.

A postmodern narration of the nation-state has the following components:

a. The nation-state, and "national" identity are essentially hegemonic, ambivalent and hybrid systems, whose formation, function and imagination should be analysed in the context of power relationships.

b. National imagination is formed by the incorporation of "other" spaces, times and characters. Thus the "other" is always part of the definition and conception of "us." The dichotomization of "us" and "them" and their hierarchical structure is a function and a discourse of power. The incommensurability of positions in the structure of power relationships is vital in the genesis of hegemonic systems such as a "national" culture.

c. A postmodern conception of the nation-state deconstructs the Enlightenment's perception of the individual and collective subject and its assumption of an ontological inner core within "national" boundaries.

These components are thoroughly examined in the analysis of the "nation-space" in Homi Bhabha's book, *Nation and Narration*. Bhabha combines and adopts a Saussurian/Freudian/Foucaultian approach in developing his analysis of the notions of "nation" and "national culture."

Homi Bhabha writes on the category of the nation-state from the position of late twentieth-century ex-colonized people and communities, who are gathered in exile as immigrants, refugees, foreigners, ethnic minorities, and diasporas, and who live in the margins of the imagined community. He writes about the cultural construction of nationhood, which, in the name of the "people," conceals their heterogeneities, and narrates the experience of those on the edges and margins of the nation. The nation is presented as an abstract, modern meta-narrative (similar to other Enlightenment meta-narratives). For Bhabha, the nation is a narrative strategy for the standardization of identity; an apparatus of power, a form of institutionalized political rationality in which the real individual is anonymous.

In *Nation and Narration*, Bhabha considers Anderson's concept of the nation as an imagined community and draws our attention to its two and rather contradictory meanings: first, the imagined community that constitutes the nation, originates in an immemorial past and glides into a timeless future; second, the nation has a historical newness, in the time and space of modernity. To Bhabha, this double meaning of the nation indicates that nations and nationalisms, by their very nature are ambivalent. Modern society, and the modern nation are "culturally ambivalent" (Bhabha 1990: 291-320). Nations are not only culturally ambivalent, they are also institutions that symbolize and perform the essential ambivalence of the human psyche.

The ambivalence of the nation happens at three levels: firstly, at the temporal and spatial representation of the nation of itself, which links its immemoriality to its historical newness; secondly, in its psychic ambivalence of love and hatred embodied in the form of "us" and "them"; and, thirdly, in the tension between, on the one hand, the nation's abstract representation of itself as an entity which is based on "unities" and "homogeneities," and the realities of cultural difference, on the other.

248

These three dimensions of ambivalence in the work of Bhabha can be better understood by reference to Saussure, Freud, and Foucault whose work, in my opinion, have influenced Bhabha's conception of the "nation-space." One way of establishing the ambivalence of the nation, for Bhabha, is to look at the narrative strategy of the nation. This strategy has two functions: a "pedagogical" and a "performative" function. These two functions link the nation's nationalistic conception of itself as immemorial and timeless, to its historical newness. The "pedagogical" function of the nation in Bhabha refers to the totality of social institutions and practices that teach, represent and signify the nation and national identity as immemorial and timeless. The education system is the prime vehicle of the pedagogical function. The "performative" function of the nation, on the other hand, refers to the unfolding and representation of the nation in its daily life as it lives out and performs its modern "national" life. In this sense, the nation is signified by its own daily activities in the present time.

By means of this strategy, the nation is "told" in a "pedagogical" narrative, and it also does the "telling" of itself in its "performative" narrative. The nation is thus both "signified" in its "pedagogical" dimension, and is a "signifier" of itself in its "performance"; the nation is both a category of immemoriality and of modernity; of both "past" and "present."

The intertwinement of performative/pedagogical, telling/told, signifier/signified, present/past notions of the nation is inspired by a Saussurian distinction between *"Langue"* and *"parole"* in language studies. *Langue* is the language of pedagogy and *parole* is the language of people. However, the unity of these functions in the name of "people" turns "people" into a linguistic "sign" which arbitrarily unites the signifier with the signified. As Saussure states, "I propose to retain the word 'sign' to designate the whole and to replace concept and sound-image respectively by 'signified and signifier'" (Saussure 1970: 45). The first principle that Saussure established about the nature of the sign is its arbitrary nature, by which he means that there is no innate relationship between the "signified" and the "signifier."

The implication of this for the nation is that there is no innate relationship between the pedagogical/performative, immemorial/modern dimensions of the nation. The nation-state as a modern container of collective identity has no natural relationship to immemoriality and real folk differences of human collectivities. However, this arbitrary connection is hidden in the name of "people," and in the "nation-space" of cultural signification. The link is a political one, and it lives in the sphere of national culture.

The absence of an innate relationship between the immemorial nation, signified by its pedagogues, and the modern nation that signifies itself in its performance, is precisely why Bhabha conceives the nation, and the "national subject" to be "split" in a "double-time." The reason is that the category of "people" is the "object" of narrating the nation in an immemorial sense by its pedagogues, and it is also simultaneously the "subject" of narrating the nation in a modern sense by its performers. These disjunctive narratives, according to Bhabha, indicate the ambivalence of the nation at the level of language and consciousness.

None of the above, however, explains why the "nation" is so enthusiastically performed; why people sacrifice themselves for the "nation"; how "national" figures, symbols, traditions, legends and legacies become part of the "nation's" memories and sentiments.

A Freudian reading of Bhabha provides some answers to these questions, and explain the ambivalence of the nation in a different light: psychically. For Freud, what binds people, communities and groups together, has always a libidinal essence. This libidinal essence can only be analysed by reference to primary instincts and the unconscious of the group. Love and hate have to go hand in hand in giving rise to solid bondings and communities. Freud says that it is always possible to bind together a considerable number of people in love, so long as there are other people left to receive the manifestation of their aggressiveness (Freud 1959).

According to Freud, ambivalence is a psychic phenomenon. Its roots are in the period of early childhood when, in the case of little girls, their initial total love and desire for the mother has to

# A Postmodern Conception of the Nation-State

be transformed into competition with the mother for the father's love. The little girl identifies with the mother, at the same time that she wants to replace her to gain father's love. In the case of the little boys, the original love for the mother also has to be followed by, first, a competition with the father for the love of the mother, and, eventually, by the abandonment of the mother as the original love object, and an identification with the father in the search for an external love object.

Ambivalence, that is, the psychic intertwinement of love and hatred in the unconscious and infantile processes of identification, means that, at the level of the group, individuals in their narcissistic search for the love of the group have to give up their egoism for altruism and, as Freud says, identify with the group. However, identification is always ambivalent. The psychic function of hatred is embodied in the group's distinction of itself from the "OTHER," and in the diversion of their hatred or aggressiveness towards the "other."

The most famous study that has taken place within this Freudian framework, is that of Theodor Adorno on "Freudian theory and the pattern of Fascist Propaganda." In this analysis, which is of FASCISM during the Second World War, a Freudian approach has been adopted. The psychic ambivalence of love/hatred is manipulated for political purposes by Hitler. Through the excitement and sensationalization of the "love for Germany," a very strong Fascist group emerges around Hitler as the father figure, whose aggressiveness and hatred is then diverted against the Jews in the form of ANTI-SEMITISM. According to Adorno, no system of rationality can explain the Fascist Propaganda and its barbaric GENOCIDES. Only the irrational, the unreason, the psychic can explain the mass psychological base of fascism (Adorno 1982: 118-137).

The Freudian discovery of "the unconscious" leads us to perceive human identity in terms of symbolic and contradictory processes of identification. Thus, when Bhabha talks about the intertwinement of "us" and "them" in the "liminality" (the collective unconscious) of the nation, he is in fact referring to this structure of the unconscious mind of the group. Bhabha's claim is that the nation's ambivalent psyche, automatically

constitutes the borders beyond which the "other" is posited, although the "other" is part of the psychic structure of the nation. The nation and its locality are neither unified nor unitary in themselves but reside beyond and outside themselves in their "others." Here, the other important concept in Bhabha, that of the HYBRIDITY of identity, is produced and anchored psycho-analytically. The nation and its "other" are located in the same psychic structure. The nation has a hybrid essence. The rhetoric of the nation in the hands of nationalism signifies an inner common core. However, Bhabha stresses, this rhetoric is always "incomplete in its signification," as it excludes the "other" from its own definition. The "other" is part of our definition even when we think and speak most intimately and indigenously between ourselves.

The Freudian scheme of psychic ambivalence, such as desire/disavowal, narcissism/projection, self/other, unconscious/conscious etc., is very much part of Bhabha's work. According to Freud, the narcissism of the group, the principle which binds the group can only happen if there is an "other" that can be hated and enemized. This unconscious ambivalence is the major psychic factor in any identification process. For Freud, doubling, dividing and interchanging of the Self is part of being and becoming a group.

Foucault is another theorist whose concepts have become important tools for analysing the nation-state. Foucault gives us an account of the modern subjects as "docile bodies" who are the agents of disciplinary power. "Disciplinary power" is the "panopticon" function of modern institutions whose technologies of, and concern with administration, regulation and surveillance of identity produce "normality" and maintain a particular order. The modern sites of "disciplinary power," according to Foucault, are the police, the school, the hospital, the clinic, the prison, psychiatry, the mental institution. To these, Bhabha has added the nation-state. "Disciplinary power" refers to a kind of regime that produces and maintains "normality," not so much by external force, but through its homogenising and regulating effects and by entering the subjectivity of its individual performers, in our case, in the form of "national" identity.

# A Postmodern Conception of the Nation-State

Homi Bhabha sees the nation-state as one of the modern apparatuses of "disciplinary power." The nation-state standardizes, homogenizes, and normalizes a "national" identity. The "disciplinary power" of the nation-state generates and preserves the rationality of "nationality" through the dominant state of "knowledge" of the time; its discourses, practices, and conceptual system, which together form the notion of "truth" in the modern age. According to the Foucaultian triangle of power, knowledge, truth which is the basis of all of Foucault's genealogical and archaeological investigations, no system of modern power can maintain itself, except on the basis of some form of "legitimation" which, in turn, must be endorsed by what is "known" at the time to be "true" and "correct." All power and its disciplinary procedures are, therefore, endorsed by "knowledge of the experts" and together claim truthfulness and legitimacy. The nation-state exercises its "legitimacy" and "truthfulness" on the basis of what is believed to be "true" subjectively.

The significance of this triangle, with all its regulatory functions, is that it does not function merely "objectively" and does not emanate merely from an external source. It enters into the very depth of human subjectivity, and his/her self perception. The triangle of power, knowledge, truth forms a mode of governing the soul and the body. It is in this light that Foucault presents the "modern subject" as the agency of the actualization of "disciplinary power" and the modern bodies as "docile bodies": "It does not matter who exercises power, any individual, taken almost at random, can operate the machine" (Foucault 1979: 202).

In this light, the homogenizing functions of the nation are facets of "disciplinary power." But then, the homogenized community of the nation is taken as an a priori in the narrative strategies of the nation, and this is precisely the way power lives. It lives in narrative strategies of the pedagogues of the nation, and it lives in the performative function of the nation. Power lives in the mind, heart and the body of each individual, in the way they perceive themselves, and in the way their mind and bodies are educated.

Bhabha conveys the same message, in his claim that power is embedded in the homogenising discourses and practices of the nation-state. Human subjectivity, the human mind and body constitute the first and last "stations" where these discourses and practices must live. Hence, the "disciplinary power" works towards the docility of the mind and the body. Goffman in his *Asylums* shows clearly how the treatment of the human body and mind must be transformed in the asylum centre, in generating and administering a different self-perception for the inmates (Goffman 1968). The "nation-space" in Bhabha represents the space in which docile nationalized communities are taught and performed.

We may conclude from the above that power is inseparable from the narrative strategies of the nation. The imagined communities are docile communities. Their soldiers, clergymen, military men, teachers, politicians, doctors, police, as well as their criminals, ill-socialized immigrants, and refugees actualize the nation. For Foucault, power is to be found in the processes of dispersion, dichotomization and marginalization. It is to be found in individual bodies and identities, and not in macro-structures. Power operates, not so much through physical force, but through the hegemony of norms, technologies of normalization; through the shaping of the body and soul, and through the shaping of the individual and group subjective identity. For this reason, Foucault, in *The History of Sexuality* calls this new mode of power "bio-power." "Bio-power" links the "technologies of domination" to the "technologies of self" through the dominant paradigm of knowledge and discourse (Foucault 1980).

Foucault's notion of the "technologies of domination" is similar to Bhabha's "pedagogical narrative" strategy of the nation. His "performative narrative" of the nation echoes Foucault's "technologies of self," where the nation performs its own discourse in a daily "national" life. The split between the two is conditioned by the structure of our psychic ambivalence, but in its external manifestation it is dichotomized and signified by the presence of the periphery, the marginal and the "other." The people of the nation-state are both the embodiment of the mechanism of power over, and the exclusion of the "other," while, at the same time, they *are* the "other," in the liminal structure of their national consciousness and language.

The most powerful modern institution that homogenizes and standardizes identity is the nation-state. The nation-state is a gigantic culture industry. A postmodern critique of the nation-state offers a radically different reading of the nation-state, by describing it as an apparatus of power that produces mega-narratives of identity in the name of "people." A postmodern theory of the nation-state deconstructs the nationalistic account of the nation-state, and anchors the question of "national" identity in the locus of the "other," and in so doing erases its totalising boundaries, challenges the political and ideological manoeuvres that assume an essentialist core in the imagined communities, and argues for the hybridity and ambivalence of national identity.

Bhabha looks at the "others" within the "nation-space" and locates them in the centrality of the "national" discourse. He thus describes collective identity as a hybrid and ambivalent system of cultural representation and signification which is formed in contexts of power relationships.

### Bibliography

Adorno, T. 1982. "On Freudian Theory and the Pattern of Fascist Propaganda," in A. Arat and E. Gebhart (eds.), *The Essential Frankfurt School Reader*. New York: Continuum.

Bhabha, Homi (ed.). 1990. *Nation and Narration*. London: Routledge.

Foucault, Michel. 1979. "Panopticism," in *Discipline and Punish*. New York: Vintage Books.

Foucault, Michel. 1980. *The History of Sexuality*. New York: Vintage Books.

Freud, Sigmund. 1959. *Group Psychology and the Analysis of the Ego*. London: Hogarth Press—Institute of Psychoanalysis.

Goffman, Erving. 1968. *Asylums*. Harmondsworth: Penguin Books.

Hall, Stuart. 1992. "The question of cultural identity," in S. Hall, D. Held, and A. MacGrew (eds.), *Modernity and its Futures*. Cambridge: Polity Press.

Saussure, Ferdinand de. 1970. "On the nature of language," in M. Lane (ed.), *Structuralism: A Reader*. London.

Fariba Salehi

# Primordiality

The primordial is an ideal-typical category of interpretative understanding of social action. Its justification exists in its heuristic utility as a descriptive classification for certain recurring relations (patterns) of social action formed, as are all social relations, around a particular meaning for those who participate in the relation through their acknowledgment of that meaning, and by which, as a consequence, the participants evaluate one another. The meaning characteristic of the social relation of primordiality centers on the significance attributed to the facts of birth. The beliefs conveying this significance are about the life-giving, life-determining, and life-ordering connections formed through birth to particular persons and birth in a delimited area of land of varying dimension. Thus, primordial beliefs are beliefs about relational modes of attachment constitutive of lines of descent, both familial and territorial. These beliefs about the creation, transmission, and ordering of life are the cognitive references to the objects—the actual or perceived biological connection and the locality—around which various structures of kinship—primordial relations—from the family to the nation are formed.

The empirical existence of primordial objects—the physical fact of biological connectedness and a delimited area of land—do not themselves account for the formation of primordial collectivities of kinship. Rather, it is when they become objects of attachment by being perceived as significant, when they become objects of shared beliefs (that is, referents in a collective self-consciousness) that primordial relations of kinship are formed. Thus, primordiality does not assert that the objects of primordial relations, for example, "blood" as in the belief in a putatively common blood-line, necessarily exist in the form that those who refer to them believe. It does say that human beings make classifications of the self and the other in accordance with their beliefs about such primordial objects as biological connection and territorial residence, and that, on the basis of such classifications, human beings form groups, membership in which influences their conduct.

Perhaps those social relations that are perceived to be vital to human existence also, precisely for that reason, arouse great passion. Certainly primordial relations elicit much passion. Often, these relations and the passion associated with them are expressed constructively as in the emotionally intense love for one's family or for one's country, patriotism. At times, primordial relations and the accompanying passion are warped so as to be destructive of other social relations such as friendship or civility, for example, as in nationalism. That intense emotional response often accompanies recognition of primordial objects is to be expected given that beliefs about such objects have to do with the generation of life and its continuity, whether it be through family, lineage, or nation. The metaphor "roots" refers to these primordial beliefs about what is essential in the generation and continuity of life: the flesh and blood transmitted through familial descent and the life-sustaining products of the land absorbed and transmitted through descent in a locality.

Everything known historically and anthropologically about human beings indicates that there has always been the perception of powers that are believed to determine human existence, and that these powers are further believed to inhere in primordial objects, hence the sacredness attributed to both those objects and the relations formed between human beings through the shared beliefs about them. In the pagan, primordial religions of antiquity, recognition of such powers was explicit: the worship of the god of the land whose power was responsible for the fertility of the land that nourished the lives of its inhabitants; the worship of ancestors whose power of creation was responsible for the life of the family or lineage. In the modern world, recognition of these powers has not been eliminated by the monotheistic world religions. Rather, in the Judeo-Christian Occident, recognition of telluric power continues to exist, but it has been redirected by virtue of being doctrinally subordinated to monotheism, for example, Catholicism's veneration of a nation's patron saint, or the national Christian churches of Protestantism and eastern Orthodoxy. An expression of the redirection today of ancestor worship may be seen in the wish, occasionally unacknowledged, of adult human beings to achieve immortality for themselves and their family through the transmission of their vitality in the creation of their (note well!) offspring.

Perhaps those social relations that are perceived to be vital to human existence also, precisely for that reason, evince greater persistence over time. The primordial relations attendant on nativity have certainly evinced persistence over time, albeit, as with all social relations, with variation. While recognizing this persistence, there is, nonetheless, nothing in the concept of the primordial that necessarily leads to the conclusion that the territorially extensive structure of nativity that we call nationality is perennial. However, because often smaller primordial collectivities of the past and the (not necessarily factually accurate) memories of them are constitutive elements of nationality, it runs counter to the nature of nationality to speak of its origin at any particular point of time. What primordiality does recognize is that everything known historically and anthropologically about human beings indicates that there have always been primordial attachments. Of course, the structural form of these attachments has varied: tribe, city-state, ethnic group, nation and so forth.

There are two things to say about this structural variation. First, such a variation is neither surprising, nor does it call into question the merit of the primordial as an ideal-typical category. All forms of social relation, for example the primordial collectivity of nationality, necessarily exhibit degrees of variation. That is because a social relation is a form of living human beings who must continually acknowledge, that is, make anew as their own, the meaning of the form. In this process of acknowledgment, the meaning of the social relation necessarily undergoes change in the face of the changing standpoints of the human beings who also make up the social relation. This necessary process of always acknowledging anew the meaning of the social relation as one's own was recognized by ERNEST RENAN (1882) when he characterized the nation as a "daily plebiscite." However, as Renan also properly recognized, this daily plebiscite on the traditions constitutive of the nation, has, among its many referents, two that are primordial: a temporally deep territory and those human beings who believe that they are

# Primordiality

related to one another by virtue of dwelling within the territory—even though how that location and its inhabitants are understood at any point in time, including how their past is understood, may change.

The second thing is to recognize that our interpretative categories of social relation remain imprecise; specifically, the boundaries separating diverse patterns of primordial collectivities from one another are not clearly demarcated. For example, the categorial problem of the tribe has been much discussed in the literature of the social sciences; but it is by no means an isolated example. Many difficulties exist in demarcating clearly a tribe or a confederation of tribes from a city-state or confederation of city-states, and both from either an ethnic group or a nation. In the tradition of the analysis of nationality, Friedrich Meinecke's (1928) distinction between *Kulturnation* and *Staatsnation*, and, more recently, Anthony D. Smith's (1986) use of "ethnie," indeed, the very category of ethnic group, are all indicative of this interpretative difficulty of demarcating the distinctive categorial boundaries of large primordial collectivities. No matter—what primordiality does assert is that human beings, *qua* humans, appear always to have been members of not only an immediate family, but also a larger primordial collectivity. Contributing to the difficulty in understanding these larger primordial collectivities is the characteristic "intermingling" or "conflating" of the image of biological connection with an image of territorial residence such that there exists the "fictitious" kinship of an ethno-geographic collectivity.

The most obvious instance of an ethno-geographic collectivity is the nation; but there are many other instances from different periods of time and civilizations, for example, the categorially fluid "house of the father" (or eponymous ancestor) in the ancient Near East. Of course, the very use of the adjective "fictitious" underscores the categorial difficulty in understanding larger primordial collectivities. Indeed, its use is illegitimate for it implies that only the primordial relations of the immediate family and its areal locus of the house are real, presumably because they are factually traceable. However, as has been observed, the individual human being has always

been a member of not only his or her family, but also a larger collectivity to which some variation of kinship among its members has always been attributed. Why there has been this persistent attribution of a kinship more extensive than that of the family is difficult to say. Perhaps elements of this attribution are a result of two factors: firstly, the referents of the larger collectivity contribute to the self-definition of the individual as he or she develops from infancy to adulthood within the conceptual horizon of the collectivity into which he or she was born; and secondly, the individual recognizes that his or her life is, to some degree, dependent upon the existence of the larger collectivity.

These elements of attribution, consequences of the compulsory relations attendant on birth, were emphasized by Clifford Geertz (1963) when he described primordial attachments as those that stem from the assumed, cultural givens of social existence: thus, not only are presumed blood-tie and areal contiguity the shared, primordial properties perceived in the other, but also, for example, is speaking a particular language. Such relations, as compulsorily constitutive of one's being, are thus seen to have an ineffable coerciveness in and of themselves.

Within the literature of the social sciences, primordiality, as a pattern of orientation of social action, achieved its initial formulation in the work of Edward Shils (1957; 1961), who designated as primordial objects the referents in the consensus, the collective self-consciousness, of Tönnies's (1887) relational category of *Gemeinschaft*, namely kinship and locality. Shils argued that kinship and locality are not merely preconditions for the formation of *Gemeinschaft*; rather, they are relational properties of the members of the *Gemeinschaft* that greatly influence the conduct of those members towards one another. By so doing, Shils extended WEBER'S (1922) recognition of the charismatic importance of the real and presumed biological connectedness of the blood relationship (*Sippen-* or *Erbcharisma*) as a relational property of social action and the constitution of society. The category was taken up by Geertz (1963), and defended and extended by Grosby (1994; 1995; 1996).

Influenced by Schmalenbach (1922), Shils recognized that various *Gemeinschaft*-like experiences of intense and highly integrative attachments—what Tönnies referred to as *Wesenwille*—were characteristic of many primary groups: not only the tradition-bound village as described by Tönnies, but also the religious sect, or a friendship. While the relations of all of these primary groups of relatively intense solidarity may be properly contrasted with those associated with the image of a highly individualistic, atomized and expediential *Gesellschaft*, it is clearly unproductive for understanding social action to bring together under one category the intense attachments characteristic of a family or a village community with those of a religious sect or a friendship. Thus, Shils distinguished the various modes of attachment that individuals form to one another—various structures of social relation—by differentiating the incommensurable properties or objects of those attachments, one of which centers on vitality, the primordial.

### Bibliography

Geertz, Clifford. 1963. "Primordial sentiments and civil politics in the new states," in C. Geertz (ed.), *Old Societies and New States*. New York: Free Press.

Grosby, Steven. 1994. "The verdict of history: the inexpungeable ties of primordiality," *Ethnic and Racial Studies* 17: 164–71.

Grosby, Steven. 1995. "Territoriality: the transcendental, primordial feature of modern societies," *Nations and Nationalism* 1, 2: 143–62.

Grosby, Steven. 1996. "The category of the primordial in the study of early Christianity and second-century Judaism," *History of Religions* 36, 2: 140–63.

Meinecke, Friedrich. 1970 (1928). *Cosmopolitanism and the National State*. Princeton, NJ: Princeton University Press.

Renan, Ernest. 1896 (1882). "What is a Nation?" in E. Renan (ed.), *The Poetry of the Celtic Races and Other Studies*. London: W. Scott.

Schmalenbach, Herman. 1977 (1922). "Communion—a sociological category," in *Herman Schmalenbach on Society and Experience*. Chicago: University of Chicago Press.

Shils, Edward. 1975 (1957). "Primordial, Personal, Sacred, and Civil Ties," in E. Shils, *Center and Periphery, Essays in Macrosociology*. Chicago: University of Chicago Press.

Shils, Edward. 1975 (1961). "Society: the idea and its sources," in E. Shils, *Center and Periphery, Essays in Macrosociology*. Chicago: University of Chicago Press.

Shils, Edward. 1995. "Nation, nationality, nationalism and civil society," *Nations and Nationalism* 1, 1: 93–118.

Smith, Anthony D. 1986. *The Ethnic Origins of Nations*. Oxford: Blackwell.

Tönnies, Ferdinand. 1940 (1887). *Gemeinschaft und Gesellschaft*. New York: American Books.

Weber, Max. 1978 (1922). *Economy and Society*. Berkeley: University of California Press.

Steven Grosby

# The Psychology of Nationalism

Among the many faces of nationalism as a social, cultural or political phenomenon one should not neglect its psychological aspects. Three main theoretical approaches may be identified in the study of the psychology of nationalism. First, there is a psychoanalytic approach which looks at the role of national identity with regard to both intra- and intergroup processes. Psychoanalysts subscribing to this school of thought suggest that group boundaries, and here, in particular, national boundaries, "exist to give cohesiveness to the group-self, to exclude its disavowed parts; to prevent fusion with others; and to keep disowned parts of the group-self at a safe distance, embodied by one's enemies" (Group for the Advancement of Psychiatry 1987: 89). Thus, the nation and nationalism are constituted through projection: the bad is expelled outside the nation's boundaries so that the good may be retained within it. This perspective has been particularly developed with regard to ethnic identity by anthropologists (Barth 1969; Leach 1964; Levi-Strauss 1963; 1967).

A number of scholars have identified the double psychological character of nationalism, namely one that comprises, on the one hand, a set of egocentric and ethnocentric values that are attributed to the nation and, on the other hand, one that emphasizes the role of hatred in bringing about the feeling of belonging to a nation (Doob 1964). Indeed, it seems that love of nation and hatred of its enemies are two sides of the same coin. This approach examines the role of the outsider, the enemy, in the establishment, functioning, and preservation of nationalism.

The third and perhaps most comprehensive approach to the psychology of nationalism is one that has been developed within Social Identity Theory and which sees social-psychological analysis of group identity as an essential part of the understanding of nationalism. This approach concentrates on the role of social identification of the individual with a group and also of in-group/out-group relations in the formation of nations and in the relations between different national communities. Moreover, some theorists have investigated the social-psychological dynamics of actual and potential divisions within a nation (Billig 1976). Research conducted within this approach is based on the assumption that neither the study of the "objective," historical conditions that brought about nationalism nor general psychological explanations, each taken on their own, can enable one to understand the phenomenon (Tajfel 1970: 140). Major themes within this perspective include the cultural and social background of national and ethnic attitudes (Le Vine 1965; Klineberg and Zavalloni 1969); the development of national/ethnic attitudes in children (Lambert and Klineberg 1967); the patterns of personal involvement in the national or ethnic community (Kelmàn 1969); and the cognitive processes involved in nationalism (Tajfel 1969).

## Bibliography

Barth, Frederick. 1969. "On ethnic groups and boundaries," in *Process and Form in Social Life: Selected Essays on F. Barth*. vol. 1. London: Routledge & Kegan Paul.

Billig, Michael. 1976. *Social Psychology and Intergroup Relations*. London: Academic Press in collaboration with the European Association of Experimental Social Psychology.

Doob, Leonard. 1964. *Patriotism and Nationalism: Their Psychological Foundations*. Westport, CT: Greenwood Press.

Group for the Advancement of Psychiatry. 1987. *Us and Them: The Psychology of Ethnonationalism*. New York: Brunner/Mazel.

Hamilton, J. W. 1981. Review of C. F. Keyes (ed.), *Ethnic Adaptation and Identity: The Karen on the Thai Frontier with Burma.*, *American Anthropologist* 83: 952–5.

Kelman, H. C. 1969. "Patterns of personal involvement in the national system: a social-psychological analysis of political legitimacy," in J. Rosenau (ed.), *International Politics and Foreign Policy: A Reader in Research and Theory*. Glencoe, IL: Free Press.

Klineberg, O. and M. Zavalloni. 1969. *Nationalism and Tribalism among African Students*. Paris and the Hague: Le Mouton.

Lambert, W. E. and O. Klineberg. 1967. *The Development of Children's Views of Foreign Peoples. Adapted from Children's Views of Foreign Peoples: A Cross-national Study*. New York: Appleton-Century-Crofts.

Leach, E. R. 1964. *Political Systems of Highland Burma*. Boston: Beacon Press.

Levi-Strauss, Claude. 1963. *Structural Anthropology*, vol. 1. New York: Basic Books.

Levi-Strauss, Claude. 1967. *Structural Anthropology*, vol. 2. New York: Basic Books.

Le Vine, R. A. 1965. "Socialisation, social structure and intersocietal images," in H. Kelman (ed.), *Inter-national Behaviour: A Social-psychological Analysis*. New York: Holt, Rinehart and Winston.

Tajfel, Henri. 1969. "The formation of national attitudes: a social-psychological perspective," in M. Sherif and C. W. Sherif (eds.), *Interdisciplinary Relationships in the Social Sciences*. Chicago, Ill: Aldine.

Tajfel, Henri. 1970. "Ethnic and national loyalties," *Social Science Information* 9, 3: 119–144.

Anna Triandafyllidou

# R

## Race

To the zoologist, a race is a subpopulation within a species whose members share with one another a greater degree of genetic inheritance than they share with individuals assigned to other such subpopulations. A key criterion in the classification of species, subspecies and races is that of interbreeding. Human races cannot be precisely differentiated because they interbreed freely.

This is not the sense in which the word features in popular usage. Nor is it the sense in which it was earlier used by zoologists and anthropologists. Possibly no other concept has been surrounded by so much bitter controversy or used in so many different senses.

### Race as Lineage

The word "race" entered West European languages around the sixteenth century when it was employed simply to denote the sharing of characters because of common descent. Though now somewhat antiquated, the word is still occasionally used in this sense. In 1986, for example, an exposition of Christian belief by the Church of England's House of Bishops stated that "Jesus is also the 'second Adam', the Head of a new race of God's children in the Spirit." In this usage, common descent is not necessarily genetic.

From the eighteenth century, natural historians classified plant and animal specimens, naming the least general classes as genera, species and varieties. Similar specimens were classed together as being of common descent. But specimens could be similar without being of common descent, or dissimilar despite common descent. If they were called a race, did this denote their appearance or their descent? The ambiguity inspired confusion, both in anthropological writing and among those who propounded the nationalist doctrines in which physical appearance, language, culture, and sometimes even religion, were seen as different aspects of the nation as a primordial entity.

### Race as Type

Up to the eighteenth century at least, the chief paradigm for explaining human differences was that of the Old Testament. This furnished a series of genealogies by which it seemed possible to trace the peopling of the world and the relations which different groups bore to one another. But it was difficult to explain how these differences could have developed in less than six thousand years, which was all that seemed to be allowed by the Bible's chronology. One hypothesis was that they had not developed at all, but the differences had been there, unchanging, from the beginning. Those who argued in this way included Charles Hamilton Smith in England, Robert Knox in Scotland, Arthur de Gobineau in France, J. C. Nott and G. R. Gliddon in the U.S. and Karl Vogt in Germany. They popularized a conception of race as permanent type and equated race with species. This has been called "scientific racism"; it underlay the Nazis' ideas about race.

Charles Darwin showed that there were in nature no permanent types. He wrote of "geographical races," or subspecies, as "local forms completely fixed and isolated." Their geographical isolation prevented interbreeding with other subspecies. For a time the theory of natural selection inspired a second kind of scientific racism, one which held that racial prejudice served an evolutionary function. It would eventually create pure races. Only in the 1920s did psychologists assemble evidence that such prejudices were learned rather than inherited. Then in the next decade the Darwinian revolution was completed by the establishment of population genetics. This demonstrated that it was not the species but the gene that was the unit of selection. It led to the conclusion that there could be as many races as there were genes. The typological mode of reasoning

# Racism

had been replaced by one of superior explanatory power.

## Race as a Social Construct

The pre-scientific senses of the word race were maintained in the popular historical writing of the nineteenth century. For example, Sir Walter Scott's best-selling novel *Ivanhoe* told the story of Robin Hood as that of a struggle between the Saxon and Norman races. In North America persons of African and European descent were distinguished as two races (whereas in early twentieth-century South Africa references to race relations were likely to concern the relations between the English-speaking and Afrikaans-speaking whites). In the United States a person with one African grandparent and three European grandparents was accounted black, indicating that the social definition prevailed over any scientific calculation. Ideas of race were used by the more powerful, white, section of the population to reinforce their position of privilege. In the 1960s, with the civil rights movement, this started to change. African-Americans used the idiom of race to mobilize support for their cause and to assert that they took pride in being black. Statistics classifying people by race were used when litigating for affirmative action as part of a campaign to see that they achieved equitable representation in the more desirable positions. Many members of the black minority in Britain have adopted a similar conception of race.

The use of the word "race" as part of a move to rectify wrongs can also be seen in legislation, such as the British Race Relations Act, which makes it unlawful for someone to treat another less favorably "on racial grounds." For an applicant to claim a remedy for indirect discrimination, he or she has to establish membership in a "racial group." Since this has to be "a group defined by reference to colour, race, nationality or ethnic or national origins," the link between race and nation lives on, albeit in quite a different context.

## Bibliography

Banton, Michael. 1998. *Racial Theories.* 2nd edn. Cambridge: Cambridge University Press.

Huxley, Julian S. and A. C. Haddon. 1935. *We Europeans: A Survey of Racial Problems.* London: Jonathan Cape.

Kohn, Marek. 1996. *The Race Gallery: The Return of Racial Science.* London: Vintage.

Michael Banton

# Racism

Up to the late 1960s it was customary in English usage to use the expression "race relations" to distinguish interracial relations from intraracial relations. Interracial relations were exemplified primarily by the relations between persons of different skin color or appearance, although, following nineteenth-century usage, the relations between persons of different nationality but similar appearance were sometimes accounted interracial. These relations were thought to have three dimensions: the psychological (prejudice), the behavioral (discrimination), and the ideological (racism). From the end of the 1960s "racism" was used in new senses. The changes in the meaning given to the word can most easily be understood if they are reviewed historically.

In the early 1930s the word "racism" came into use to identify the doctrine that race determines culture. This doctrine, fundamental to the political philosophy of Nazism, had its origins in the pre-Darwinian theory of racial typology. That theory held that blacks, browns, reds, yellows, and whites were distinct and permanent types (comparable to species rather than varieties) each of them suited to a particular region of the earth. They did not adapt or evolve and were endowed with different capacities for building cultures so that civilization was the product of racial determinism and prejudice against members of other races was an inherited characteristic. In the Nazis' elaboration of this theory Jews counted as sub-human rather than human.

Starting in the 1920s, psychologists demonstrated that racial and national prejudices were learned rather than inherited. Then in the 1930s population geneticists showed the gene to be the unit of evolution; ideas of race were transformed. Logically, the use of "race" as a name for a sociopolitical group should have been abandoned, but it was too well-established in popular usage for any such change. Because of the way they had been exploited for political ends, doctrines of racial superiority were fiercely condemned making it impossible to use the adjective "racist" in any neutral fashion. With the upsurge of the civil rights movement in the U.S. the black power activists Carmichael and Hamilton (1967: 19–21) seized on its rhetorical potential to define racism as the use of racial beliefs and attitudes to subordinate and control a category of people defined in racial terms. This excluded any possibility of a black person being accounted racist, but it appealed to the temper of the times and thereafter racism was often defined teleologically, that is, by its results. Marxist writers presented it as a historical complex, generated within capitalism, that facilitated the exploitation of categories of people defined in racial terms. In 1975 the U.N. General Assembly, by 72 to 35 votes, adopted a resolution declaring "Zionism is a form of racism and racial discrimination." This was part of an Arab-led campaign against the policies of the Israeli government which reverberated around the world. No distinction was drawn between racism and racial discrimination. In Britain some university students used the resolution as a justification for refusing to recognize Jewish student societies. Until the dissolution of the USSR, its representatives insisted that racism was a product of the socioeconomic structure of capitalist, and particularly imperialist, societies, and that it had been eliminated in their society by the revolution of 1917.

Because the adjective "racist" was so easily turned to political ends, it was overused. Robert Miles (1985) protested eloquently about the conceptual inflation that resulted and maintained that since the concept of race lacked scientific validity the expression "race relations" was misconceived. The political and scientific problems were those of racism and they could not be separated. Popular usage of the word followed a parallel course, so that "racism" came to supplant "race relations" and to serve as a name for what had earlier been seen as a three-dimensional phenomenon. The change implied that the task for scholars was to provide a historical interpretation of the growth and expansion of racism.

A dictionary of the English language will summarize the meanings attributed to "racism" in contemporary usage, but the purposes of scholarship may demand some more precise definition. For these purposes it is helpful to distinguish contexts in which racism is regarded as an *explanandum* (something to be explained) and those in which it is used as part of an *explanans* (that which explains). When racism is seen as a historical phenomenon it is usually presented as an *explanandum*. Those who seek to account for features of interracial relations find it advisable to separate the psychological, behavioral and ideological dimensions. If "racism" is then used as part of an explanans, it should be defined in a manner appropriate to the socioscientific problem rather than the political problem.

It may also be helpful to ask whether "racism" is being used to designate something resembling a social sickness or a crime. Usually people are not blamed for being sick, but they are held responsible for crimes. Those approaches which picture racism as a pathological form that changes in its expression as society changes therefore minimize individual responsibility. They may be contrasted with Durkheim's argument that crime (or deviance) is not a pathology because it is a characteristic of all human societies. Discrimination against persons defined as not belonging to the group is also a characteristic of all societies and, on this reasoning, a normal rather than a pathological phenomenon; the law now treats discrimination as resembling a crime.

One conclusion that can be drawn from the passionate debates about racism during the past thirty-five years is that since the word means different things to different people it is more than usually important to attend to the different ways in which it is defined.

## Bibliography

Banton, Michael. 1997. *Ethnic and Racial Consciousness*. London: Longman.

Carmichael, Stokely and Charles V. Hamilton. 1968 (1967). *Black Power: The Politics of Liberation in America*. Harmondsworth: Penguin.

Miles, Robert. 1985. *Racism.* London: Routledge.

Wieviorka, Michael. 1995. *The Arena of Racism*. London: Sage.

Michael Banton

# Rational Choice Theories of Nationalism

As a name for a kind of theory, "rational choice" has been used increasingly since the mid-1970s. It designates a kind of reasoning pioneered in Anthony Downs' *An Economic Theory of Democracy* (1957) and in Mancur Olsen's *The Logic of Collective Action* (1965). It has been applied chiefly in the study of voting behavior, the sociology of religion, educational choice, criminology, residential segregation, and gender-based occupational segregation, but it can cast some light on processes that are central to the study of nationalism, such as those of group solidarity and collective action.

There is no consensus at present as to which kinds of theory are properly to be called "rational choice theories," or, indeed, whether this is the best name to use. One set of theoretical writings may be called rational actor theories, since they concentrate on interpreting the intentions of actors and distinguish rational actions from nonrational actions. Usually it is actions which maximize the actor's net advantages, or utility, which are accounted rational. Another set of writings may have a stronger claim to be called rational *choice* theories because they pay more attention to the alternatives presented to actors, and between which they choose, but seek to explain only aggregate behavior. There is then a parallel with Durkheim's theory of the causes of suicide, which set out to account for differential rates of suicide and to predict how a rate would alter if particular circumstances changed, and did not claim to explain individual suicides. Rational choice theories seek to specify the costs of particular courses of action without distinguishing rational from nonrational actions. They rely upon a concept of procedural rationality, inferring that actors are rewarded if they adopt the most effective procedures to attain their goals. For example, after comparing several alternatives, a consumer may purchase something in the belief that it is the "best buy"; should it transpire that it was not the optimal decision, this does not mean that it was not a rational choice. The consumer will try to learn from the experience and do better next time.

Although there are differences between various versions of rational choice theory, there is a much greater difference between them and the currently conventional theoretical approaches to the study of nationalism. The rapid growth of interest in nationalism in the 1990s was inspired by the apparent upsurge in nationalist sentiment following upon (and presumably influenced by) the end of the Cold War. This gave the field of study a strongly historical orientation, to the detriment of social science theorising. The resulting orthodoxy adopted a "top-down" approach, starting from the ideas of "the nation" and of "nationalism" present in late twentieth-century English-language speech. It saw individuals as impelled to behave in particular ways by the strength of shared ideas of national belonging and opposition. Activist groups could propagate and intensify such feelings. The orthodoxy frequently failed to take sufficient account of the difficulties of translating between Arabic, Chinese, English, Russian, and other languages such words as "people," "NATION," "NATIONALITY" and "national MINORITY." It therefore ended as an attempt to impose current Western conceptions upon the interpretation of behaviour in other cultures and historical periods.

Rational choice theorists employ a "bottom-up" rather than a "top-down" approach and seek to develop concepts which are not culture-bound in either space or time. In this, as in some other respects, they have learned from the study of economics. For example, economists have fashioned the concept of inflation into a powerful explanatory tool and the public's understanding of inflation is based upon that developed by the theorists. In the study of nationalism, by contrast, theorists have started from, and attempted to refine, popular conceptions of national belonging. Rational choice theorists deny that there can be any special theory of nationalism; they try to identify the fundamental elements underlying the behavior that is classed as nationalist and to analyse them within a more general social science theory.

The strength of rational choice theory lies in the way it relates the analysis of the individual and collective levels of behavior (contrary to the strategy of separating them which is favoured by Anthony D. Smith [1986]). All social scientists should be able to agree that individual characteristics cannot be deduced from collective ones (or vice versa) and that there may at times be conflicts between social norms and individual interest, but this does not dictate any separation of levels. Individual actors are able to take account of any such conflicts and the degree of their conformity to norms is likely to be influenced by self-interest. From their earliest years humans are taught about the society into which they have been born and with which sorts of person they should identify themselves. Just as they learn whether they are male or female, so they learn that they belong to national or ethnic groups, that they should align themselves with fellow-members, and that others will treat them as members of such groups. The strength of this element in socialization varies from one society to another. Moreover, some individuals grow up more group-dependent than others. Those who are more group-dependent have a higher need for the approval of their peers, a stronger preference for within-group association, and a greater potential for prejudice against nonmembers. Despite such variations, all humans derive psychological rewards from conforming to the norms they have learned, so when rational choice theorists assume that actors seek to maximize their net rewards they include psychological as well as material rewards.

In the course of their socialization individuals acquire goals and ambitions. Some they can pursue by individual action, but other goals they can attain only by collective action. Collective action may be either voluntary, as by joining an association, or coerced. Nearly all humans grow up as citizens of a state which provides them with a variety of services, including, for example, armed defence forces and police. Public goods of this kind can be provided only by coercive collective action to which every citizen is forced to contribute, if only by taxation. In certain other circumstances, however, individuals may be free to choose whether to pursue their goals by individual action or collective action. For example, they may join together to create bargaining agencies, as employees create trade unions and employers create countervailing associations. Bargaining agencies attempt to secure maximum advantage for their members, though they do not necessarily

succeed and may even act in ways that damage their members' long-term interests. In some circumstances individuals can maximize their advantages by "free-riding," that is, by benefiting from the collective action of others without contributing their share. A trade union may attempt to prevent free-riding by creating a "closed shop," obliging all workers to participate in collective action. As exemplified in the work of Michael Hechter, the analysis of "free-riding," and of the kinds of controls that can prevent it, has been one of the successes of rational choice theory. Political parties can also serve as bargaining agents, and rational choice theories have been used to explain the rise and decline of ethno-nationalist movements within states.

Individuals identify themselves socially in many ways. National identifications can exist side-by-side with class, ethnic, familial, religious, and other identifications. Individuals have at times to choose whether they will align themselves on the basis of one of these identities rather than another. They may invest heavily in one of them, or identify themselves with one in only a token fashion, or try to ignore them all. The relative priority they accord to the various options will reflect their estimates of the likely costs and benefits (including the possibilities of free-riding). Whether people can be mobilized into collective action on the basis of a shared alignment is then a politically important variable. As is frequently observed, some sporting teams have higher morale than others and win more games as a result. A high degree of mobilization, or team-spirit, requires that individuals give priority to shared goals over individual goals and do not put short term rewards before possible medium and long-term rewards. Mobilization can be promoted by leaders when they are able to deploy rhetoric (the art of persuasion) to get individuals to work together. Communities which are distinctive on several dimensions (common descent, distinctive religion, shared territory, etc.) generate collective action and survive from generation to generation much more easily than single-interest associations.

The principles which explain the degree of collective action can be applied in the analysis of groups of all sizes, including states, providing due account is taken of historical circumstances.

# Rational Choice Theories of Nationalism

The industrial states of the West were able in the course of centuries to generate collective action on an ever larger scale. Much of their current power is generated by co-ordination (such as, to take a very simple example, the adoption of a rule to keep to one side of the road). Russell Hardin has usefully distinguished this from the power that is generated by processes of exchange. When in the post-1945 period the colonial powers withdrew from their overseas territories responsibility for those territories had to be assumed by new states because there was no other kind of organization to do the job. Because international politics were organized on the assumptions that humans belonged in states and that states had duties to other states, there was a top-down pressure on the new governments to promote national collective action of a kind comparable to that in other states. They had to cultivate among their populations a sentiment of belonging to a nation if they were to get the benefits that can flow from state organization. Many of these governments have found it difficult to achieve co-ordination and, because exchange depends upon trust, have been able to generate only limited exchange power in their dealings with their citizens. Hence their reliance on force, especially in states rent by sectional conflict. Particular interest groups (like the military, or distinctive elites) have treated the state and its institutions like a cow to be milked for their personal benefit. No other course of action could offer them short-term rewards as great as those deriving from control of the state apparatus. The pursuit of short-term and sectional advantage has led to actions, such as the expulsion of Asians from East Africa in 1967-72, which have had negative long-term effects for national economies. Decisions which result in everybody's being worse off are more likely when the decision-takers have insufficient information about the probable consequences of certain alternative courses of action and when they respond to the self-interested demands of their own section of the public.

Challenged to account for the rise in ethno-nationalism linked with the dissolution of the Soviet Union, the rational choice theorist would take over the evidence and arguments of Valery Tishkov. The assumption that there were dormant primordial entities only waiting for an opportunity to express themselves he decried as the "Sleeping Beauty theory of nationalism." According to Tishkov, the official recognition of nationalities in the USSR never depended on the existence of a name held in common, or on any sentiment of group identification. Recognition was conferred by elites for their own purposes. Ethno-nationalism arose in reaction to Soviet political practice; it was cultivated by those who bargained for resources and by activists seeking to mobilize supporters. The idea that they expressed a national will provided them with a new rationale for the totalitarian pretensions that had characterized the preceding era. Ordinary people did not use the word "nation" and it was empty of academic content. Had it not been for the vanities, ignorance and rivalries of the politicians, the dissolution could have been avoided.

The relations between individual and collective action can be illustrated from other recent historical events. Before 1990 there were Africans, sometimes of mixed ethnic origin, who identified themselves as Rwandans or Burundians rather than as Hutu or Tutsi, while in Europe they had counterparts who were committed to a Yugoslav rather than a Serb or Croat identity. The nature of commitment has been illuminated by Jon Elster's analysis of it—in *Ulysses and the Sirens* (1986)— as the deliberate exclusion of an alternative (as when the leader of an invasion has ordered the burning of the boats in which his company has arrived). Commitment to a shared goal can be important for collective action. Yet circumstances can sometimes be changed so as to enforce a re-alignment, eliminating previously viable alternatives and constraining choice. Terrorist groups have demonstrated that the perpetration of atrocities, by destroying trust, can quickly change the priorities of those willing to collaborate with members of the other group and lead many to believe that they can be safe only when they are together with others of the same ethnic or national origin as themselves. It is another kind of boat-burning. Given their values, a terrorist decision to commit an atrocity may represent a rational choice. The conflict in Northern Ireland was powerfully affected by terrorism; it could have changed into one of civil war had the London government been unwilling to maintain public order by armed force. The inauguration of majority rule in South Africa in 1994 could have led to a winner-takes-all scramble for resources, but did not do so because of enlightened leadership and political discipline within the black population. These last two instances show that a sequence of actions by influential leaders can shape the social structure by opening to other individuals options that the extremists are attempting to close off. This speaks against any analytical separation of individual and collective levels of behavior.

An account from a rational choice perspective of historical sequences after the events have occurred will appear a common-sense interpretation and no test of any theory, but it is no better to attribute events to the influence of nationalist sentiment without explaining what has evoked it or determined its strength. Individuals identify with groups using proper names, like Hutu and Tutsi, Serb and Croat, Catholic and Protestant, and persisting group conflicts are always multidimensional in character. When observers classify such conflicts as ethnic or national they select one dimension as being most important and imply that the conflict in question shares major characteristics with conflicts elsewhere that have been similarly classified. It is the historian's task to comprehend and interpret conflicts like these in their entirety. The social scientist's mission is to identify the links in the chain of causes and, by comparative analysis, to uncover regularities in the way they operate. Rational choice theory is a useful aid in this enterprise and it can contribute in significant measure to a better understanding of historical events.

### Bibliography

Banton, Michael. 1998. *Racial Theories*. Cambridge: Cambridge University Press.

Elster, Jon. 1986. *Ulysses and the Sirens*. Cambridge: Cambridge University Press.

Hardin, Russell. 1995. *One for All: The Logic of Group Conflict*. Princeton, NJ: Princeton University Press.

Hechter, Michael. 1987. *Principles of Group Solidarity*. Berkeley: University of California Press.

Smith, Anthony D. 1986. *The Ethnic Origins of Nations*. Oxford: Blackwell.

Tishkov, Valery. 1997. *Ethnicity, Nationality and Conflict In and After the Soviet Union: The Mind Aflame*. London: Sage.

Michael Banton

# Regionalism

Regionalism refers to the set of movements demanding the economic, political and cultural AUTONOMY of certain areas or "regions," which form part of one or more states. Since the early 1960s, there has been a revival of regionalist movements all over the world. Catalonia, Scotland, Quebec, Punjab, Chechnya, Kurdistan, and Tibet are good examples. The collapse of the Soviet Union in 1989 has contributed to the rise of regional movements in the former Soviet republics, some of which resulted in the creation of independent states as in the Czech Republic, Slovakia, Croatia, and Bosnia; others are still struggling for political autonomy or independence.

In Asia and Africa the rise of regionalist movements is associated with the processes of DECOLONIZATION. There, states were created by colonial powers which drew the frontiers of the new states quite arbitrarily from a cultural point of view. In so doing they divided indigenous communities some of which are currently challenging the legitimacy of the states of which they form a part. Consequently, most, if not all, of these states are heterogeneous, containing national and ethnic MINORITIES. The new, postcolonial states pursued a policy of cultural homogenization of its culturally diversified citizenry and this policy was in some cases quite successful, eliminating or, at least, substantially eroding cultural differences. In other cases, states only partially managed to homogenize their population.

In Europe, on which the present analysis will focus, strong regionalist movements have been observed in Flanders, Catalonia, Scotland, Corsica, and the Basque Country, among many others (Harvie 1994). Some of these movements employ peaceful means to advance their claims for self-determination while others have turned

# Regionalism

to the use of violence. There is no simple answer to explain why violence has emerged in some cases and is absent in others, but the study of the particular circumstances concerning each case are usually illuminating.

The constitution of the European Union (E.U.) as a novel political institution has opened up new possibilities for the development of regionalism in Europe. However, it is still unclear whether regions will become an essential unit of government in the E.U. The idea of a Europe of the Regions raises serious questions about which particular regions will qualify for such a privileged status. This is because there are significant differences between regions. First, not all of these regions are what I call nations without states: not all regions are culturally distinct from other regions or, indeed, from the metropolitan centre. Second, many regions have an economic or geographical basis rather than a cultural one. Thus, regions such as Catalonia, Flanders, and Wallonia have managed to maintain a powerful cultural distinctiveness. The E.U. does not distinguish between the two, and, in what follows, I shall employ the term "region" as containing both meanings. This will make it easier to refer to E.U. policies and attitudes. However, the reader should be aware of the crucial distinction that should be made between nations without states and regions based upon purely economic arguments.

I employ the term "nations without states" to refer to substate communities who have a strong cultural basis, a shared history, an attachment to a clearly delimited territory and the desire to determine their own political future (Guibernau 1999). In Europe, the importance of regional economies began to emerge in the 1980s. The dynamics of a Single Market and the rising significance of European regional policy have encouraged the emergence of a new kind of innovative, specialized economic region oriented towards the global economy. The 1988 reform of the Structural Funds, the new opportunities generated by the Single Act and the 1992 Programme have contributed to a general move towards reflexivity and indigenous growth at the regional level.

Poor regions have benefited from changes in the Structural Funds, while more prosperous regions have taken advantage of the new opportunities opened up by the implementation of the Single Act. The "Four Motors of Europe" (a cross-frontier collaboration involving Baden-Württemberg, Rhône-Alpes, Lombardy, Catalonia, and Wales) has proved successful in attracting both European funds and foreign capital to a joint venture based upon the use of their combined strength. Developments of this sort seem to have important implications for the character of relations between central state and regional levels of authority and structure: "The Europeanisation of policy-making means that regions both can and have to take more responsibility for their socio-economic destiny, a trend that has been identified in most countries." In my view, this requires greater political autonomy at a regional level. To this end, the nation-state must devolve some of its powers to the regions, and the regions must turn into political units of some sort. The Committee of the Regions was set up in 1994 by the Treaty on European Union. It aims to represent the interests of the regional and local authorities in the E.U. The Committee of the Regions is made up of 222 independent representatives of the regional and local authorities and the same number of alternates, who are appointed for four years by the Council of the Union. The mixture of regional and local representatives within the Committee undermines its character as a body representing the regions. This has sparked off great controversy among its potential and actual members especially since there are no rules about how the fixed number of representatives from each country have to be distributed between the various levels of authorities, regional and local.

The Committee of the Regions is an advisory body of the E.U. Its opinions have no delaying effects and are in no way binding on decision-making bodies. The policy areas in which the Committee must be consulted by the Council and the Commission are: health, culture, promotion of general and vocational training, trans-European networks, and structural and regional policy. It becomes evident that the Committee has a very limited scope and influence within the E.U. The Europe of the Regions which many nationalists in nations without states defend is far from being represented by the Committee of the Regions. In spite of this, the Committee stands as a first step towards greater recognition of the significance of a regional Europe. In the literature about regionalism there is no distinction between areas with a cultural and historical basis, and areas which are merely determined by economic or geographic factors. Patrick Le Gales and Christian Lequesne in their recent book *Regions in Europe* (1998) challenge the notion of a "Europe of the Regions" and argue that "the dynamics of particular regions and the discourse of the Europe of the regions, have led one to overlook the fact that regions are structurally weak in terms of government and governance." In their view, only a small number of regions (and cities) are on their way to becoming collective political actors in European governance. Most regions are weakly institutionalized or have limited political powers.

Nationalist movements in Catalonia, Scotland, the Basque Country, and Northern Ireland, among others, are favourable to the creation of a Regional Europe, and constantly emphasize the importance of E.U. development and membership in their manifestoes.

### Bibliography

Harvie, C. 1994. *The Rise of Regional Europe*. London: Routledge.

Le Gales, P. and Lequesne, C. 1998. *Regions in Europe*. London: Routledge.

Guibernau, M. 1999. *Nations without States*. Cambridge: Polity Press.

Montserrat Guibernau

# Religion and Nationalism

Nationalism and religion are two distinct elements of world history. Yet they are both so similar and so mutually related that to discuss one often involves discussing the other. Sometimes the two are fused as in Biblical Israel, where the idea of a people and a nation are embedded in the worship of Yahweh. Indeed, many scholars trace the origins of nations and nationalism to religion. Adrian Hastings, for instance, has argued that Christianity, and especially vernacular translations of the Bible played a decisive role in the emergence of nations and nationalism in Europe (Hastings 1997). On the other hand, for Steven Grosby, when

religion has certain referents like territory and lineage, which he calls "primordial," then religion can be a decisive factor in the constitution and persistence of a nation. These referents can be either explicit, as in the religion of ancient Israel and Judaism, or implicit, as in the case of eastern Orthodoxy and certain Protestant denominations (Grosby 1996).

Historically, the relationship between the two has often been precarious with changes in political institutions and the social structure influencing the degree of fusion and balance between the two elements. However, with the introduction of constitutional secularism by the Americans in late eighteenth century, the explosive relationship between the two was deemed to be finally resolved. Secularism was seen as allowing for their independent development but nations and nationalism continued to be shaped by religion, despite secularism.

The myth of secularization was finally exploded in 1979 by the Islamic Revolution which established a religio-political system in Iran. The success of the revolution raised the hopes of religious nationalists everywhere and demonstrated that it is possible and feasible to combine modern nation-building with a strong, pervasive, powerfully internalized religious conviction and identification (Gellner 1992:22). Religious nationalism, that is, the active use of religious ideas to challenge the status quo or nationalism based around a common religious belief system, has been on the increase since.

Contemporary religious nationalism is underscored by the idea that secular nationalism has failed individuals and communities who put their faith in its secular promise of a more progressive social order. Consequently, religion has become both a hopeful alternative and a base for criticism and change (Juergensmeyer 1993:2). In various parts of the world today alienated victims of maldevelopment are turning to religion to reinterpret their identity and to challenge the secular status of the state. Current religious nationalisms differ in terms of their religious values, structures, goals, political and historical settings. However, many of their concerns are similar. They are united by a common enemy, Western secular nationalism, and a common hope for the revival of religion in the public sphere. They are concerned about the moral basis of politics, and the reasons why a state should elicit loyalty (Juergensmeyer 1993:7). They reject the idea that nationalism can be defined solely in secular terms or that the unifying and legitimating principle of a political order is a rational understanding that unites individuals and communities in a geographical region through common laws and political processes, and see no contradiction in affirming the state structure as long as it is legitimized not by the secular idea of a social contract but by traditional principles of religion (Juergensmeyer 1993:7).

Islam, especially Islamic fundamentalism, features prominently in contemporary religious nationalisms, but not exclusively so. As Gellner (1992:15) observes, "identification with Reformed Islam has played a role very similar to that played by nationalism elsewhere. In Muslim countries, it is indeed difficult to distinguish between the two movements." In Africa, reformed Islam is the major force opposed to neo-colonialism, and it defines its adherents as culturally African nationalists (Igwara 1995). Reformed Islam is justified by the idea that the virtue of puritanism leads to prosperity. It is viewed by Muslim nationalists as an ideology of national self-rectification, of national purification, and of national recovery, and it reinforces nationalism, notably in the context of the struggle with neo-colonialism. It is seen as progressive, the reaffirmation of the best in national tradition and culture. Reformed Islam confers a genuine shared identity on the under-privileged and ratifies the social mobility of many contemporary Muslims, from peasants to urbanites (Gellner 1992:16).

The enduring interaction between religion and nationalism questions the validity of the sociological wisdom that they are mutually incompatible. Religion is always "positioned." In other words, the human reality explained by religion makes sense only in so far as believers are able thereby to understand the social, cultural and political environment in which they live. As Lease (1983:67) observes "religion defines reality; in so far as that definition of the reality becomes coextensive with the com-

munity in which it has taken shape, that religion becomes identical with that community," and "for a people to establish themselves as absolute in their world leads inevitably to an identification with the religious persuasions of that same community; that is, religion and nationalism in their final apex and development are the same." They both have totalitarian tendencies, and decree a way of life. As some commentators have observed nationalism is not a mere political programme but a religion, a creed which people live.

The great attraction of nationalism and religion for each other lies in their power of salvation. Nationalism—the political ideology to legitimate the struggle for and control of the state that protects the people and their culture—aims to redeem individuals and communities from bondage and suffering imposed by the dominant structure of power in a social order. National salvation focuses on the observable reality of land, that is the liberation of the land from the dominance of "evil" alien forces and the radical evil of progressive decline and disintegration. Most of the symbolism and mythology that go into the making of a nation are anchored in the land (O'Brien 1988). The underlying idea is that the right to the land is divine and the land is held in trust by the living for the unborn. Thus, the land links the dead, the living and the unborn. The link between the past, the present and the future explains the emotional attachment to the land and illuminates the idea of mystical participation involved in nationalism. As Steven Grosby has observed, the sacred and primordial attachment of human communities to the land is most evident in the veneration of the "god of the land" in the societies of antiquity (Grosby 1995).

Nationalism's special appeal as the means of salvation centres on the existence of national suffering and oppression. In difficult times, individuals and communities always devise new strategies to cope and many of these involve religion. The religious, according to Peter Berger (1969:27), emerges out of disorder and thus provides man's ultimate shield against the terror of anomie: "To be in a 'right' relationship with the sacred cosmos is to be protected against the nightmare of chaos. To fall out of such a 'right' relationship is to be abandoned on the edge of the abyss of meaninglessness." The sacred ultimately enables individuals and communities to endure the hardship around them. The expectations of religious ideologies do not disappoint, in the same way as material expectations offered by secular ideologies, because they are not expected to be fulfilled in this world (Juergensmeyer 1993:194). Religion thus provides both a sacred canopy against the threat of chaos and anomie, and raises new hopes for individuals and communities in crisis. Through the hope it raises, it offers salvation to the nation-state by sacralizing its identity and existence.

In the case of religious nationalisms, sacralization is the process of self-transcendence by which individuals and communities come to perceive their society as the result of a revelation or supernatural principle, not just the result of human construct, and their homeland as a setting for the divine destiny. Faith and hope in the land is transformed into practical and effective love of the nation in order to bring about a reintegration of life and goals for individuals and the society in which they live and interact. Such consciousness and knowledge, and the fellowship it generates, legitimates nationalism as ideology, and sacralizes its identity as English, German, Nigerian, and so forth. The nation is consequently a blend of nature, history, and grace, and nationalism, a blend of awareness, faith, and sacrament (Smart 1983:16).

Grace is symbolically represented by sacraments whose ultimate goal is to enable fellowship. National sacraments are signified in the everyday life co-nationals share with each other, the sharing together in the joys and sorrows of the land, whether it be food, literature, history, humor, belief in one God, whether such participation takes place in large assemblies, families, household, clubs, farm, factory, church. In other words every lived experience of a nation's people is sacramental, enabling individuals to have fellowship with each other. Consequently, birth rites, rites of passage into adulthood, marriage rites, gender roles, social norms, death rites, and shared taste in food, fashion, and style are all constitutive of the national sacraments, the outward signs of national salvation, of members' union with the land, and of the unity of the individuals constituting the nation.

### Bibliography

Berger, Peter L. 1969. *The Social Reality of Religion*. London: Faber and Faber.

Gellner, Ernest, 1992. *Postmodernism, Reason and Religion*. London: Routledge.

Grosby, Steven. 1995. "Territoriality: the transcendental, primordial feature of modern societies," *Nations and Nationalism* 1, 2:143-162.

Grosby, Steven. 1996. "The category of the primordial in the study of early Christianity and second-century Judaism," *History of Religions* 36, 2:140-163.

Hastings, Adrian. 1997. *The Construction of Nationhood: Ethnicity, Religion and Nationalism*. Cambridge: Cambridge University Press.

Igwara, Obi.1995. "Holy Nigerian nationalisms and apocalyptic visions of the nation," *Nations and Nationalism* 1, 3:327-355.

Juergensmeyer, Mark.1993. *The New Cold War? Religious Nationalism Confronts the Secular State*. Berkeley: University of California Press.

Lease, Gary. 1983. "The Origins of National Socialism: Some Fruits of Religion and Nationalism," in Peter H. Merkl and Ninian Smart (eds.), *Religion and Politics in the Modern World*. New York: New York University Press.

O'Brien, Connor Cruise. 1988. *God Land: Reflections on Religion and Nationalism*. Cambridge, MA: Harvard University Press.

Smart, Ninian. 1983. "Religion, Myth and Nationalism," in Peter H. Merkl and Ninian Smart (eds.), *Religion and Politics in the Modern World*. New York: New York University Press.

Obi Igwara

# Renan, Ernest (1823-1892)

French philosopher, scholar of Semitic languages, religious historian, essayist, and critic. Denounced by the Catholic Church and suspended from his professorial chair at the Collège de France for his book *Vie de Jésus* (1863), Renan went on to con-

## Rousseau, Jean-Jacques (1712-1778)

sider the nature of nations. His definition of a nation, the *sine qua non* for nationalism, is still widely discussed today. For Renan, a nation is an historical and purposive collectivity, a form of morality. It emerges from a community of will based on common experience and grief. This common experience draws upon past glories, heroism, and great leaders, and coupled with a common will, it provides a people with a continued desire to accomplish great things. More importantly, a common grief, (that is to say, past sorrows and sufferings) serves to bind a people by imposing obligations and demanding a common effort. A nation is a "daily plebiscite," in that it is based on the consent of the people to live together in light of sacrifices made in the past, and a willingness to make additional sacrifices in the future. Accordingly, it is not race, language, state, religion, economic interests, or civilization that makes a nation.

To quote from the famous lecture, "Qu'est-ce qu'une nation?" ["What is a Nation?"], which Renan delivered at the Sorbonne in 1882: "A nation is a soul, a spiritual principle. Only two things actually constitute this soul, this spiritual principle. One is the past, the other is the present. One is the possession in common of a rich legacy of remembrances; the other is the actual consent, the desire to live together, the will to continue to value the heritage which all hold in common. Man, sirs, does not improvise. The nation, even as the individual, is the end product of a long period of work, sacrifice and devotion..."

### Bibliography

Renan, Ernest. 1990 (1882). "What is a nation?" reproduced in Homi Bhabha (ed.), *Nation and Narration*. London: Routledge.

Rachel Monaghan

# Rousseau, Jean-Jacques (1712-1778)

Rousseau was born and educated in what was in his day the city-state of Geneva, to which, although he spent nearly all of his adult life in France and neighboring countries, he always maintained a kind of loyalty. His political ideas constituted the prime influence upon the thoughts and actions of the Jacobins in the 1789 French Revolution, and it was they who were the first or among the first to introduce what in the following century became typical characteristics of nation-states, such as, for instance, military conscription. In his *Discourse on Political Economy* he announced that "It is certain that all peoples become what government makes them," and the Jacobins did not scruple to employ all available means in order to reshape the people of France to their own ideals.

Rousseau himself normally speaks of peoples rather than of nations. But it is, surely, obvious that his ideal state would be a nation-state. Thus in *The Social Contract*, in concluding his discussion of the kind of people who would be ready and able to accept good laws, he says: "There is still in Europe one country capable of being given laws - Corsica. The valour and persistency with which that brave people has regained and defended its liberty well deserve that some wise man should teach it how to preserve what it has won" (11 [x]).

It was only in 1764 that Pasquale Paoli, the leader of the Corsican rebellion against Genoese oppression, sent a representative to ask Rousseau for his advice on shaping a constitution. Rousseau never completed more than a fragment of the *Project for a Constitution for Corsica*, and this was first published only in 1861. Its principal concern is with economic arrangements, although these are throughout subordinate to the political and social objectives that Rousseau believed that Corsica ought to be trying to achieve.

His *Considerations on the Government of Poland* was most emphatically not another attempt to play the legislator. Instead, the concern here is with the customs, tastes and prejudices (in Burke's sense) which give Poles a sense of themselves as a single distinctive nation aspiring to sustain a common national identity and, along with that, national independence. All these things Rousseau wants to maintain and intensify; for three reasons. First, because without them a country is vulnerable to foreign influence and invasion. Second, because without them people will place their private concerns, or their own and just a few others', above those of the rest of society. And, third, because he believes that love of country is a necessary condition for the maintenance and enjoyment of law and liberty for all. At times, Rousseau becomes quite lyrical about patriotism:

> Every true republican has drunk in love of country with his mother's milk. This love is his whole existence; he sees nothing but the fatherland, he lives for it alone; when he is solitary he is nothing; when he has ceased to have a fatherland, he no longer exists; and if he is not dead, he is worse than dead.

## Rousseau, Jean-Jacques (1712-1778)

### Bibliography

Rousseau, J. J. 1973. *The Social Contract and Discourses*. Translated and introduced by G. D. H. Cole, revised and augmented by J. H. Brumfitt and John C. Hall. London and Melbourne: J. M. Dent and Sons.

Nisbet, Robert. 1974. *The Social Philosophers*. London: Heinemann. (See the essays on "Rousseau and the General Will" and "The French Revolution and the Jacobins.")

Antony Flew

# S

## Secession and Irredentism

Although movements of ethnic protest and resistance can be documented since the ancient world, it is only in the modern world that there have been concerted attempts to redraw the political map to fit the unsatisfied aspirations of peoples and communities. The proximate cause of this worldwide trend has been the nationalist ideological drive for congruence between nation and polity, usually in the form of an independent state. Since the interstate system has clearly been unable, and often unwilling, to accommodate such widespread ethno-national demands, the world has witnessed successive waves of ethnic nationalisms seeking to alter existing state borders in line with their needs.

This worldwide movement has taken two basic forms. The first is *irredentist*, where a state seeks to unite to itself those "unredeemed" (*irredenta*) peoples and lands outside its borders which it claims are historic and ethno-cultural components of its nation. Examples would include the drive by the newly independent states of Greece and Italy to annex the territories and people outside its borders who were deemed to be culturally and historically Greek and Italian. In the contemporary world, the Argentinians manifest an identical desire to annex historic territories in the Malvinas, as do the Spanish in Gibraltar, while the Irish entertain similar claims towards their kinsmen in Ulster. While irredentist claims were sometimes conceded in the nineteenth century, the manipulation of such sentiments by the Nazis and the strengthening of the inter-state system in this century have meant that most irredentist claims have been unsuccessful.

A similar fate has befallen the larger-scale "pan" movements, which seek to unite several sovereign states and peoples on the basis of a wider cultural unity. Examples include the pan-Slav movement, championed by Dostoevsky, which sought to align the various Slavic peoples and states in virtue of an alleged spiritual and cultural sympathy and to unite them in a loose confederation. A similar project was entertained by scholars who discerned a pan-Turanian group of languages and peoples, including the Turks, Hungarians, and Finns; but this was later scaled down to a tighter pan-Turkic-speaking family of peoples and formed the ideological basis for the disastrous Young Turk policies in the First World War. In the contemporary world, both pan-African and pan-Arab projects are politically stillborn; while they may bring the leaders of the African and Arab states together, often against external enemies, and encourage some wider cultural projects, they have failed to mobilize Africans and Arabs to pool their resources, let alone unite in a confederation.

A more serious threat to the stability of the inter-state order is posed by the spate of ethnic *secession* movements in many parts of the world. By ethnic secession is meant the attempt to withdraw a part of the population from an existing polity in virtue of its possession of a separate ethno-cultural identity. From the revolts of the Serbs and Greeks against the Ottoman empire to the current wars of ethnic secession in Kosovo, Chechnya and Sri Lanka, submerged ethnic communities have demanded the right to secede from states into which they had been incorporated, often against their will. Such a drastic move generally takes place only where other options have failed. In the West European and North American states, ethnic communities and nations within poly-ethnic or multinational states, like the Bretons, Flemish, and Catalans, have generally been content with a much greater degree of AUTONOMY, in line with the nationalist goal of running one's own affairs without outside interference. But even here "home rule" may prove to be insufficient, as we are witnessing in Quebec and Scotland. Outside the West, more authoritarian regimes make few concessions to ethnic sentiment; the southern Sudanese, the Kurds in Iraq, the Karen and Shan in Burma, the Tamils in Sri Lanka, the Moro in the Philippines, even the Sikhs and Kashmiris in democratic India, have engaged in long-running conflicts which show no sign of early resolution, despite temporary lulls.

Two questions have dominated the study of ethnic secession. The first concerns its causes. Michael Hechter has proposed a "RATIONAL CHOICE" theory of secessionist movements, arguing that, given the right conditions, elites make a series of strategic choices in the light of their resources and information about the strength and will of dominant state elites. But his schema includes a good deal of what needs to be explained: the emergence of economic and cultural communities that provide the resources and aspirations for secession, with the result that only the strategies and tactics of secession become the products of rational choices. For Donald Horowitz, it is just these economic and cultural resources and communities that need to be examined, and he provides a typology of ethnic secession movements depending on whether the group in question is "advanced" or "backward" in terms of its economic and educational resources, and whether it inhabits an economically advanced or backward region. He then argues that secession is most likely among backward groups in backward regions, and least likely among advanced groups in advanced regions; even advanced groups in backward regions like the Ibo are hesitant to secede until prompted by violence.

While one could cavil at the specific predictions (for example, it did not take long for the "advanced" Latvians or Tamils to opt for secession), a typology along these lines offers considerable insights into the structural preconditions of secession among so many ethnic groups unequally incorporated into wider territorial states under colonialism. To which we need to adduce the role of ideologies of nationalism, and the cultural resources of ethnic symbolism, which also encourage and sustain worldwide ethnic protest and conflict.

The second question concerns the chances of success of secession movements. The power and hostility of the inter-state system to any redrawing of the political map, despite official if carefully circumscribed assent to the principle of national self-determination, made it extremely difficult to realize secession projects, at least from 1945 to 1990. Since that time, however, with the break-up of the Soviet Union and Ethiopia, and the fragmentation of Yugoslavia and Czechoslovakia, some twenty new ethnically based states have emerged, and have received grudging international recognition. Whether this has weakened, or paradoxically strengthened, the inter-state system is the subject of much dispute, as are the conditions under which it may be defensible to countenance a bid for ethnic secession. What seems certain is the endemic nature of the tension and conflict which an international system of political and cultural pluralism must generate, given the many unresolved ethno-territorial disputes and the many unsatisfied aspirations of ethno-nations left out of the world's political dispensation.

### Bibliography

Horowitz, Donald. 1985. *Ethnic Groups in Conflict.* Berkeley and Los Angeles: University of California Press.

Hechter, Michael. 1992. "The dynamics of secession," *Acta Sociologica* 35: 267–83.

Heraclides, Alexis. 1991. *The Self-determination of Minorities in International Politics.* London: Frank Cass.

Mayall, James. 1990. *Nationalism and International Society.* Cambridge: Cambridge University Press.

Sheffer, Gabriel (ed.) 1986. *Modern Diasporas and International Politics.* London: Croom Helm.

Anthony D. Smith

# Self-Determination

The principle of self-determination is closely associated with Woodrow Wilson who, in 1918, while President of the United States of America, contended that at the end the First World War:

> National aspirations must be respected; peoples may now be dominated and governed only by their own consent. "Self-determination" is not a mere phrase. It is an imperative principle of action, which statesmen will henceforth ignore at their peril.

# Self-Determination

In Wilson's view, self-determination had an external aspect (which might be realized in the attainment of independence as a sovereign state), and an internal aspect, for self-rule could not be fully achieved without meaningful participation in the processes of government, (implying that self-determination required democracy). Since he could not specify what constituted the relevant "self" whose consent was needed, nor the mode of determination of any dispute about the principle's application, his formulation was open to criticism as supporting claims to secession. His proposal that this principle be incorporated in the Covenant of the League of Nations was not accepted by other states.

In the 1919–39 period self-determination was regarded as applying to five kinds of "people": firstly, those living within a state ruled by another people (as the Irish before 1920); secondly, those living only as minorities in more than one state (as the Poles in Russia, Austria and Germany before 1919); thirdly, those living as a minority but understanding themselves as part of the people of a neighboring state (as Hungarians in Romania); fourthly, those obliged to live in separate states (as the Germans); and fifthly, those constituting a majority under foreign domination (as under colonial regimes). Groups of immigrants dispersed over a country (like African-Americans), indigenous peoples and Gypsies were not thought to qualify as peoples. The self-determination of peoples was thought to entail either international protection (as by a special treaty), or a degree of AUTONOMY within the state, or national independence.

Following the Atlantic Charter of 1941 there was a retreat from Woodrow Wilson's vision which limited the entitlement to self-determination to the fifth kind of "people." In 1960 the U.N. General Assembly adopted the Declaration on the Granting of Independence to Colonial Countries and Peoples (resolution 1514[XV]) which stated: "all peoples have the right to self-determination; by virtue of that right they freely determine their political status and freely pursue their economic, social and cultural development." In the same resolution it also recognized a principle of national unity which might well be in conflict with the former right: "Any attempt aimed at the partial or total disruption of the national unity and the territorial integrity of a country is incompatible with the purposes and principles of the Charter of the United Nations." In 1976 the two U.N. Covenants on Human Rights came into force, each containing in its first article a guarantee of the right of self-determination, without defining its content, or the beneficiaries, or establishing any procedure for its realization.

Legal difficulties remain. The 1960 Declaration was adopted as an interpretation of the U.N. Charter, Article 1.2 of which establishes only a principle, not a right. The General Assembly is not empowered to amend the Charter. Neither this principle, nor the right mentioned in the Covenants, qualifies as a human right in the technical sense since human rights are rights of individuals, not of collectivities. Some human rights may be exercised collectively when the individual consents to be joined with others, but it is difficult to ascertain consent to self-determination. The tension might be resolved by holding that just as self-determination is a prerequisite of the enjoyment of human rights, so the enjoyment of such rights is a prerequisite of self-determination.

In practice the principle of national unity has taken precedence over that of self-determination, except for decolonization and for the recognition of the state of Bangladesh, whose independence owed more to the Indian army than to the precepts of international law. Attention has turned towards possible forms of autonomy that stop short of independence, such as that negotiated in the case of the Åland Islands. An international committee of jurists appointed by the League of Nations determined that Finland (including the Åland Islands) had become an independent state in 1917, but that the vast majority of the population of the islands would choose union with Sweden were they were given the option. So Finland agreed to give the islanders cultural autonomy within the Finnish state. Their rights to maintain the use of the Swedish language were protected by measures which, for example, limited the rights of persons from outside the islands to reside there or purchase property.

Such a solution requires goodwill on both sides. Examples of the obstacles that may arise when this is absent can be found in the western

Pacific. Papua New Guinea, previously a U.N. Trust Territory administered by Australia, became independent in 1975. Two weeks beforehand the island of Bougainville (population 120,000) declared itself independent. The world's largest open cut copper and gold mine, generating 60 percent of Papua New Guinea's export earnings was in Bougainville, so the declaration was regarded as an unacceptable attempt to secede. Representatives of Bougainville took their case to the U.N. Working Group on Indigenous Affairs. They made reference to the U.N. Declaration of Principles of International Law concerning Friendly Relations and Cooperation among States in accordance with the Charter of the United Nations; this reaffirms the right to self-determination while stating that it does not authorize the dismemberment of states "possessed of a government representing the whole people belonging to the territory without distinction as to race, creed or colour." The islanders claimed that in history, in color, and in location, they belonged not with Papua New Guinea but with the western Solomon Islands. The government of Papua New Guinea objected, inter alia, that representatives of Bougainville had agreed to be part of their state in return for provincial autonomy. Such a dispute exemplifies the difficulties in applying the principle of self-determination.

### Bibliography

Hannum, Hurst. 1990. *Autonomy, Sovereignty, and Self-Determination: The Accommodation of Conflicting Rights*. Philadelphia: University of Pennsylvania Press.

Partsch, Karl Joseph. 1982. "Fundamental principles of human rights: self-determination, equality and non-discrimination," in K. Vasak and P. Alston (eds.), *The International Dimensions of Human Rights,* vol. 1. Paris: UNESCO, and Westport, CT: Greenwood Press: 61–86.

Michael Banton

# Sociobiological Theory of Nationalism

It is difficult to treat nationalism except in relation to the overlapping concepts of ETHNOCEN-TRISM, RACISM and XENOPHOBIA. Since these terms are related but not synonymous, we must begin with a brief set of definitions. "Ethnocentrism" is the seemingly universal preference of people for their own ethnie over all other ethnies.

Membership in an ethnie is usually validated by the possession of some cultural characteristics in comparison, such as language, dress, religion, cuisine, and shared symbols, traditions or myths. Sometimes, inheritable physical phenotypes, such as skin, eye and hair color, facial features, or stature, are used as markers of group membership, in which case the group is generally referred to as a "RACE" (socially defined, but on the basis of biological phenotypes), and claims of superiority for one's race are termed "racism."

Members of both ethnic and racial groups generally believe that they share a common history, destiny and biological descent, but while ethnocentrism is universal, racism is not, for reasons that will become clear presently.

When ethnocentrism becomes politicized, that is, when a sense of belonging to an ethnie is transmuted into a demand or a rationale for political autonomy, or independence, then we speak of nationalism. In its most classical form, nationalism is an ideology that supports or demands that STATE AND NATION should be coterminous, and which only grants nation-states the stamp of legitimacy. A nation is simply a politically conscious ethnie. Multinational states, like India, Nigeria, Congo, Switzerland, Belgium, Canada, Bolivia, and many others, which make up the great majority of the world's nearly 200 "sovereign" states, cannot be nationalist as defined here and feelings of loyalty towards multinational states are best called "statism" or "PATRIOTISM" to avoid confusion.

Finally, xenophobia is an active antipathy towards strangers in general, and especially towards members of other ethnies or races. As we shall see later, xenophobia is not simply the inevitable mirror image of ethnocentrism.

Students of nationalism, ethnicity, and race have fallen into or been assigned to broadly two camps, depending on whether they have viewed ethnic, racial or national groups as objective, stable entities into which individuals are fortuitously born, or as socially constructed catego-

# Sociobiological Theory of Nationalism

ries that are manipulated, and thus flexibly change-able according to circumstances and the interests of their members or elites. The first approach is often called "primordialist," while the second has been variously labeled "instrumentalist" or "social constructionist." (Banton 1977; Brass 1991; Francis 1976; Horowitz 1985; Schermerhorn 1970; Smith 1986; van den Berghe 1978, 1987). Like many debates in social science, this one rests on a false antinomy, as we shall soon see.

The sociobiological theory of ETHNICITY, race, and nationalism holds that there is indeed an objective, external basis to the existence of such groups, but does not deny that these groups are also socially constructed, manipulated and changeable (Reynolds et al. 1987; Shaw and Wong 1989; van den Berghe 1978, 1987; van der Dennen and Falger 1990). In simplest terms, the sociobiological view of these groups is that they are fundamentally defined by common descent and maintained by endogamy. Ethnicity, thus, is simply kinship writ large.

The innate and universal preference we show for kin (which biologists call "nepotism" or "KIN SELECTION") is extended to those super-families that ethnies, races, or nations either constitute, or, at least, are perceived as, by their members. The study of race, ethnic, or international relations is, most fundamentally, an extension of the study of these systems of kinship and marriage that form the basic building blocks of all human societies. Ethnies, races and nations are super-families of (distant) relatives, real or putative, who tend to intermarry, and who are knit together by vertical ties of descent reinforced by horizontal ties of marriage. In small, stable ethnies that have occupied the same area for centuries, this social web of kinship and marriage is very tight indeed, and the transition between kinship and ethnicity is continuous and imperceptible. In larger, industrial nations of millions of people, the web of solidarity is much looser and the discontinuities more evident, but unless a credible belief in common descent and historical continuity exists, there is no nation.

Sociobiology is the only model in social science that not only gives equal time to genes and culture, but that so intertwines heredity and environment in its evolutionary explanations as to

expose the folly of trying to oppose them. The social constructionists are not so much wrong as half-right. To use the phrase of one of the most distinguished representatives of social constructionism—Benedict Anderson (1983)—ethnies are, indeed, "IMAGINED COMMUNITIES," and ethnic sentiments can be manipulated by opportunistic elites for political or economic gain. Ethnies appear and disappear, coalesce and break-up. But all this construction, reconstruction and deconstruction of ethnicity does not happen in an empirical vacuum. It remains anchored in the reality of socially perceived, biological descent. To be sure, descent often has an element of fiction, but pure fiction seldom flies. Of course, groups can be formed on bases other than descent, but then they are not *ethnic* groups. Ethnic relations always involve the interplay of the objective reality of biological descent and the subjective perception, definition *and* manipulation of that objective reality.

There is, in short, nothing in the sociobiological view of ethnicity that leads one to the conclusion that ethnicity is a fixed, rigid, unchangeable concept or reality. Quite the opposite is true. Sociobiology is an individualistic model that seeks to explain the behavior of selfish maximizers in an ever changing environment. Clearly, an intelligent social organism like *Homo sapiens* that fine-tunes its conduct to the behavior of conspecifics must, of necessity, exhibit highly situationally variable and opportunistic behaviors. Ethnicity is only one of the bases of solidarity manipulated by humans for individual gain, and much deception is involved in this as in other bases of association. The point is that this situational variability is not only fully compatible with a sociobiological outlook; it is *inherent* in the model. Furthermore, sociobiology *explains* the variation better than competing social constructionist "theories."

Let me illustrate with the question of racism, in the sense of attribution of moral and cognitive superiority or inferiority to somatic phenotypes. "Explanations" of racism range from unqualified primordialism—a position fallaciously attributed to sociobiologists by many social constructionists—to narrow historicism. Racism is clearly not universal. In fact, it is rather exceptional, although it has spread during the last 500 years because of the rapid increase in international migration. Ethnocentrism is universal, but the vast majority of people attribute their superiority to cultural traits, such as morality, language, religion, manners, and technology. Only in a few societies do people link inherited physical attributes to categorical superiority or inferiority of character and intelligence. The primordial explanation of racism is clearly wrong.

Equally wrong are historicist accounts that make racism a unique Western invention, or that link racism to capitalism or slavery. Racism is found in some non-Western societies, long before European contact: the "heightism" of the Tutsi towards the Hutu in Rwanda and Burundi is an example. Capitalists may have exploited racism to divide the working class, but racism in former Communist countries (such as that shown to African students at ex-Soviet universities) show the independence of racism from the system of production. The same is true of slavery: racism helped buttress chattel slavery in the Western Hemisphere, but there are numerous cases of slavery without racism (e.g., in Greek and Roman antiquity and in many pre-colonial African societies), as well as racism without slavery.

The theory I proposed in 1978 involves both genes and culture, and specifies the conditions for the appearance and disappearance of racism (van den Berghe 1978, 1987). Like all social species, we have a genetic propensity to favor kin. As the most complexly gregarious of mammals, we form large social groups based on kinship and marriage, and in the course of our recent evolution (last 10,000 years), we have found it beneficial to form many groups of increasing size and complexity, of which ethnies have been the most ubiquitous. Ethnies are made up of intermarrying kin groups which, because of this network of affinal ties between them, become, in effect, a super-family. Our innate nepotism thus progressively extends from the nuclear family, to the extended family, to the lineage, to the clan, to the ethnie, to the nation. That is why ethnocentrism is universal.

However, we are not only highly gregarious animals. We are also intelligent opportunists. As the sphere of our nepotism extended, we faced an increasingly difficult problem of distinguishing in-group from out-group. The criteria we use for determining ethnicity are not fixed. Ethnic markers are highly situationally specific. We simply use those criteria that minimize information costs and maximize reliability and validity. Language, for instance, is a widespread criterion and a very useful one because ethnic affiliation can be quickly ascertained through speech and is not easily faked. Somatic phenotypes, on the other hand, are, in most cases, poor markers. In most cases and for most of human history, people have been interested in distinguishing themselves from neighbors who looked much like they did: Norwegians from Swedes, Zulu from Swazi, Flemings from Walloons, and so on.

We can now easily predict the circumstances that will foster racism with a theory anchored *both* in the biology of nepotism and in cultural adaptation to conditions of the social environment. Racism appears when substantial long-distance migration suddenly puts in contact *visibly* different populations, and put them in situations where they either compete for scarce resources, or where one group dominates and exploits the others (e.g., conquest, colonialism, slavery). Under such exceptional conditions physical markers of group membership suddenly become cheaper and more reliable than cultural ones. Skin color, for example, becomes a better marker than language, because it is visible out of earshot and because, unlike language, it cannot be learned. The Boer on the South African frontier could, with nearly perfect reliability, shoot first and ask questions later.

Our theory can not only explain and predict the emergence of racism, but also its perpetuation and its demise. Once established, a social system based on racism tends gradually to break down, unless concerted efforts are made to preserve it. That is, racial systems "naturally" tend to decay for a simple reason: nepotism seems to have little effect on sexual attraction and behavior, especially of males. Thus contact breeds interbreeding, and interbreeding by definition blurs racial boundaries. The more brutal forms of interracial contact, such as military conquest and slavery, even *favor* interbreeding as they expose conquered women to rape and impregnation by their male conquerors. The preference for ethnic en-

# Sociobiological Theory of Nationalism

dogamy applies to marriage, not to concubinage or rape, and is always sexually asymmetrical: it seeks to bar a group's women from contact with out-group men, but it seldom restrains dominant group men from access to subordinate group women. Frequently, this double standard is institutionalized in law. A Muslim man, for instance, can freely marry a Christian or Jew, but a Muslim woman cannot.

The few cases of enduringly racially stratified societies, such as the United States and South Africa, are the exceptions that prove the rule. Even there, considerable interbreeding took place and it took an institutionalized caste system to "save" racism. The aim of APARTHEID or Jim Crow was to pretend that interbreeding did not happen, and that everybody clearly belonged in a racial category. The ultimate fragility and artificiality of a racial caste system is now glaringly demonstrated by South Africa, a society that is becoming deracialized at a rapid rate, now that the underpinnings of apartheid have been removed. This is a lesson that North Americans have not yet understood, namely that it is futile to try to solve racial problems by obstinately using racial categories, even for purposes of redress. Race-based affirmative action continuously reinforces the categories it purports to undermine. That is why many "African-American" beneficiaries of affirmative action in the United States, for example, vigorously oppose the growing movement of millions of Americans who define themselves as being of "mixed race." They rightly fear the breakdown of race categories from which they now profit.

Ethnocentrism—a preference for one's own group—is universal, rooted as it is in the biology of nepotism. Racism—rooted in *social*, *not* biological categories—is exceptional and relatively ephemeral. It only arises under conditions that are not only unusual but self-destroying (van den Berghe 1995, 1996).

What about xenophobia? It is commonly assumed that xenophobia is simply the other side of the coin of ethnocentrism. If one is *for* one's own group, must one not, of necessity, be against all other groups? The answer, I think, is *no*, and that answer too, is deducible from a sociobiological perspective. All behavioral ecologists know that cooperative interaction is based not only on nepotism, but also on reciprocity, and, I would add, on coercion. The natural world is full, not only of nepotism, but also of mutualism and parasitism, frequently across species, genera, orders and even kingdoms.

The role of reciprocity in human interaction is especially large, as social scientists have long emphasized, and as biologists have more recently rediscovered. As Robert Trivers (1971) has suggested, the development of complex systems of reciprocity in humans may well have driven our rapid encephalization in our last million or so years of evolution, culminating in symbolic language and human-level culture in the last forty to 50,000 years.

If we are the clever, flexible opportunists that the study of human history reveals, and if we are constantly in contact with ethnic others, as has increasingly been the case over the last few millennia, then it follows that blanket, categorical xenophobia is a very sub-optimal strategy. Politics, and, by extension, self-interest, make for the strangest of bedfellows. Any student of politics knows that interests predict the formation and break-up of alliances much better than ideologies or professions of eternal friendship or hostility. The 1939 Nazi-Soviet pact to gobble up Poland should serve as a recent reminder, and indeed shocked only naïve communists.

Nepotism and reciprocity are *not* isomorphic. Nepotism is a *categorical*, albeit *graded*, imperative to co-operate, even at net cost to ego, if the ratio of benefit to alter over cost to ego is greater than the reciprocal of the coefficient of relationship between them (Hamilton, 1964). This simple Hamiltonian inequation maximizes ego's inclusive fitness, and neatly predicts much of sociality in tens of thousands of species (for the concept of "inclusive fitness" see KIN SELECTION). Reciprocity, on the other hand, is purely *conditional*, on whether *both* partners are better off co-operating, quite irrespective of other aspects of their relationship. Thus, categorical ethnocentrism ("my country, right or wrong"), internally graded by coefficient of relationship, as it invariably is, does not imply categorical xenophobia. A selfish maximizer would be foolish categorically to reject vast categories of potential partners in reciprocal exchanges. Non-kin require a higher threshold of acceptance than kin, but unqualified exclusion is not the best strategy, as indeed a mountain of empirical evidence shows.

The history of modern warfare, for example, is replete with episodes of fraternization between frontline enemy troops, or, at least, consensual truces and understandings not to shoot at each other, despite their officers' incitement to hatred. Indeed, it became almost the maxim of the German officer corps that soldiers had to be made more afraid of their officers than of the enemy! Xenophobia in warfare has to be constantly fanned by government propaganda to become effective, and, even then, it seldom survives conditions of common adversity where it pays to co-operate, as in trench warfare.

A study of ethnic or racial stereotypes also reveals the conditional nature of xenophobia. The conventional, canonical view of ethnic stereotypes in social science is that they reflect an irrational, categorical judgment by prejudiced individuals to satisfy their need to hate, to demean, to belittle, or to ridicule out-groups. This view is false. There are, to be sure, some pathological bigots, but any model of behavior that assumes that most people most of the time hold inflexible beliefs that resist contrary evidence, even at the cost of impeding potentially beneficial relationships, is highly problematic (van den Berghe, 1997).

Stereotypes, far from being inflexible, wrong-headed crutches for categorical xenophobia, are, in fact, for most people most of the time, low-cost, statistical guides to action in situations where transient encounters between strangers make better information costly, unavailable or risky. Take, for instance, the widespread fear of young black men among urban Americans of all "races." Does that fear reflect, as "authoritarian personality" theorists would have us believe, categorical racism, or simply a cautious avoidance strategy in the urban jungle of North America? I suggest the latter, because I hypothesize that most urban Americans, who are daily confronted with total strangers, have different fear thresholds for different categories of people whom they know to have statistically different probabilities of committing violent crimes. Even though they know that most young black men are harmless, they also know that men are more violent than women, that

violence decreases with age, and that blacks (for whatever reasons) have a higher rate of violent crime (mostly against other blacks, by the way) than members of other groups. Thus, it is hardly any evidence of racism that they should be more afraid of young black men, than, say, of old Irish-American women.

Nor is it true that stereotypes are resistant to contrary experience, or situationally insensitive. Even genuine bigots make exceptions for members of the out-group they know and profess to like. Or, to use the young-black-men example again, the fear threshold is lower at 2 A.M. than 2 P.M., in a bar than in a library, in a derelict slum district than on a golf course, in a prison than in a college classroom. In short, stereotypes are simply crude statistical devices that help us keep the odds in our favor while navigating the dangerous waters of an alien urban environment in which we simply do not know anything about 95 percent of the people we meet daily, except gross characteristics such as gender, age, skin color, or class. Given the information vacuum about individuals that urban *anomie* generates, we simply could not function without stereotypes. True, stereotypes are often not very accurate, but they are generally at least somewhat better than nothing in helping us to make predictions about the behavior of unknown others. The cost of using them is lower than that of ignoring them. Yes, it isn't fair, but, then, neither is life. And life is better than death.

Another contribution that sociobiology can make to the study of ethnicity is to look at it as a breeding system, or, more precisely, as a system of breeding preferences. Ethnies correspond closely to what geneticists call breeding populations. In cultural terms, ethnies are created and maintained through endogamy. It is important, however, to distinguish between mating and marriage, and between in-breeding and endogamy. Marriage is socially sanctioned and privileged pair bonding, and thus a much narrower concept than mating. Endogamy is marrying within a socially defined group, while in-breeding is the result of mating between individuals with a high coefficient of relationship.

There is much evidence that the best mating strategy involves a compromise between in-breeding and out-breeding. We best avoid mates who are too closely related to us because of the dangers of in-breeding depression. Very few human societies permit, much less favor, matings between first and second degree relatives, who share more than one eighth of their genes by common descent. Yet, many people (and perhaps other animals as well) seem to prefer mates who are much like themselves. Scores of societies (mostly small-scale tropical horticulturalists) prefer first-cousin marriages (r=.125), but many others avoid or even forbid them. The main endogamous unit in human societies, however, is the ethnie, although sometimes it is an ethnic sub-unit, such as a caste group, which is endogamous.

The modal societal arrangement in which this optimum compromise between in-breeding and out-breeding plays out is the endogamous ethnie subdivided into exogamous kin groups, at a minimum the nuclear family, but very commonly much larger groups such as lineages and clans in unilineal descent societies. Ethnies, then, are congregations of inter-marrying kin groups. Put more relativistically, the degree of ethnic cohesion is a direct function of the degree of endogamy. Beyond a certain threshold, say two or more generations of 25 percent or more out-marriage, ethnic boundaries erode, a fate which threatens, for example, American and European Jews, many small aboriginal groups of the Americas and Australasia, and numerous immigrant groups in their "host societies." Conversely, some highly cohesive ethnies such as the Hutterites, maintain nearly total endogamy, so that their kin network is coterminous with the ethnie, or, more precisely, with one of the three Hutterite sub-ethnies that constitute the main endogamous units. While highly in-bred, however, Hutterites avoid first-cousin marriage and seek to maximize out-breeding within their narrowly defined endogamous units.

As Joseph Whitmeyer (1997) has argued, the main factor of ethnic cohesion may not be direct nepotism as such, especially in large ethnies where the bond of common descent may be tenuously diluted. Rather, fellow ethnics are seen, at least in part, as prospective co-parents of one's descendants, as partners in a reciprocal breeding system. There is no need to choose between these two mechanisms of social cohesion in ethnic groups, for both are clearly at work. Ethnies incorporate

both biological kin and in-laws, and these two categories, in turn, overlap, the more so as endogamy is long-lasting and complete, and the ethnie small. Ethnies, then, are effective breeding systems, because they constitute networks of individuals creating between them ties of both kinship and marriage, of nepotism and reciprocity. They are, in fact, the most ubiquitous blueprint for creating a human society.

The social constructionists will, no doubt, object that this view of ethnicity as a breeding system is far too static and too "anthropological," meaning irrelevant to "modern" societies. One of their most quoted spokesmen, Benedict Anderson (1983), for instance, takes the view that nationalism (if not ethnicity) is a modern phenomenon created by literate elites who use the printed word to diffuse a standardized dialect among the many spoken vernaculars that existed before, and thereby create new nations, almost *ex nihilo*. This comes close to a spontaneous generation theory of ethnicity. What we have here is, in fact, not a theory of ethnicity at all, but simply a historicist account of the rise of national *consciousness* in the post-colonial world. It is not incompatible at all with the views presented here.

Nor is the sociobiological view of ethnicity static. Quite clearly, new ethnies emerge out of hitherto unrelated groups: new religions such as the Hutterites or the Mormons are cases in point. Related but distinct groups may develop a wider consciousness and merge into new super-ethnies: many African ethnies such as the Yoruba, the Ibo, the Kikuyu, the Luo and countless others are well-known cases. Disparate groups of immigrants may gradually fuse into new nations. Other ethnies may disintegrate and vanish through conquest, GENOCIDE, ASSIMILATION, or intermarriage: such was the fate of numerous aboriginal groups of the Americas and Australia. Ethnies, like other human (and other animal) populations are in constant flux. But ethnies do not appear or disappear instantaneously, capriciously and unpredictably. Ethnogenesis typically takes a minimum of two or three generations of intermarriage.

Equally significant are the glaring *failures* of most "modern" states to create new nations out of a grab-bag of ethnies. Belgium, after nearly two centuries of independence, is no closer to being a nation than it was in 1830. Indeed, Flemings and Walloons are almost exactly where their ancestors were in relation to each other just after Julius Caesar wrote *De Bello Gallico*: straddling an almost static linguistic frontier between more and less Romanized populations. Canada, some two and a half centuries after the British Conquest, is persistently trembling on the verge of political disintegration. It is not even a bi-national state, for only the Franco-Canadians (and many small indigenous nations) are true ethnies. The Anglo-Canadians are little more than a disparate batch of immigrants who find it convenient to use English as a *lingua franca*. The Swiss Confederacy, one of the world's most successful states, remains after nearly 800 years what it was at its birth: an alliance of convenience between Alpine hill tribes. How ludicrous, then, to expect "NATION-BUILDING" to work in the dozens of impoverished post-colonial states of Africa!

If nationhood could be conjured like a *deus ex machina* from a Tagalog translation of the Bible, or a ringing Declaration of Independence in Philadelphia, or a Pan-African Congress in London, then why has our century—supposedly that of triumphant nation-states—so signally failed to create new nations out of multinational states?

There was, of course, another school of social scientists—both capitalists and Marxists—who predicted that the rise of "modernity" would make ethnicity and nationalism obsolete. They, too, proved wrong—dead wrong in fact. One of the things that our century deserves to be remembered for is that it produced the metastasis of that deadliest of nationalist malignancies: genocide. The twentieth century has been the century of routinized genocide, from Armenia to Rwanda, from Germany to Iraq, from Tasmania to Wyoming, from Namibia to Cambodia, from high-tech gas chambers to low-tech machetes.

Who, in the light of these horrors, can deny that ethnicity is deeply rooted in the human condition? It is not unchanging, but it cannot be expected to vanish. States can organize it in genocidal orgies, but intellectuals cannot invent it out of printed paper. Individuals can escape ethnicity to some extent. Collectively, however, as a species, we cannot escape the persistent reality of ethnicity. What we can do is endeavor to mini-

mize its most lethal manifestations by depoliticizing it. To succeed, we must first understand it. And to understand it, we must look for it both in our genes and in our culture.

### Bibliography

Anderson, B. 1983. *Imagined Communities*. London: Verso.

Banton, M. 1977. *The Idea of Race*. London: Tavistock.

Brass, P. 1991. *Ethnicity and Nationalism*. New Delhi: Sage Publications.

Francis, E. K. 1976. *Interethnic Relations*. New York: Elsevier.

Hamilton, W. D. 1964. "The genetical evolution of social behaviour," *Journal of Theoretical Biology* 7: 1-52.

Horowitz, D. 1985. *Ethnic Groups in Conflict*. Berkeley: University of California Press.

Reynolds, V., V.S.E. Falger and Vine, I. (eds.) 1987. *The Sociobiology of Ethnocentrism*. London: Croom Helm.

Schermerhorn, R. A. 1970. *Comparative Ethnic Relations*. New York: Random House.

Shaw, R. P. and Y. Wong. 1989. *Genetic Seeds of Warfare*. Boston: Unwin Hyman.

Smith, A. D. 1986. *The Ethnic Origin of Nations*. Oxford: Blackwell.

Trivers, R. 1971. "The evolution of reciprocal altruism," *Quarterly Review of Biology* 43: 35-37.

van den Berghe, P. L. 1978. *Race and Racism: A Comparative Perspective*. New York: John Wiley.

van den Berghe, P. L. 1987. *The Ethnic Phenomenon*. New York: Praeger.

van den Berghe, P. L. 1995. "Does race matter?," *Nations and Nationalism* 1, 3: 357-68.

van den Berghe, P. L. 1996. "Racism," *The Encyclopedia of Cultural Anthropology*, New York: Holt, pp. 1054-57.

van den Berghe, P. L. 1997 "Rehabilitating stereotypes," *Ethnic and Racial Studies* 20, 1: 1-1 6.

van der Dennen, J. and V. Falger (eds.) 1990. *Sociobiology and Conflict*. London: Chapman and Hall.

Whitmeyer, J. M. 1997. "Endogamy as a basis for ethnic behavior," *Sociological Theory* 15, 2: 162-78.

Pierre L. van den Berghe

# Sport and Nationalism

While specialists in nationalism have paid a good deal of attention to central aspects of culture such as language and religion, they have paid remarkably little attention to that other aspect of culture around which nationalism so often coheres in the modern world, namely sport. Analysis of the relationship has suffered from ideological bias and inadequate conceptualization, and, in addition, there is an unfortunate tendency in the literature on this question to reduce sport to politics.

In realist international relations theory if nationalism permeates international relations then we should expect the conduct of sport at the international level automatically to reflect this state of affairs (Kanin 1981). From Marxist and Marxisant perspectives sport provides a ready vehicle for diffusing nationalist ideology to the masses and diverting them from their true interests. Thus the celebration of the American nation in the 1984 Los Angeles Games has been interpreted as promoting American ideals and values which reconcile class conflict (Lawrence and Rowe 1986). References to sport and the nation in the British mass media have been taken to represent the hegemony of "banal nationalism" (Billig 1995). Globalized sport is said to have legitimized British imperialism and nationalism in the late nineteenth and early twentieth centuries (Holt 1995) and to help foist Western values upon the non-West today (Houlihan 1994). Such accounts are deficient not only because they have no conception of sport as an autonomous cultural form, but because they have no clear conception either of nationalism as an autonomous political force.

The prevalence of loose conceptions of nationalism where sport is concerned is a major source of confusion. The term has come to signify ideas, sentiments and policies, including state policy, international conflicts and supportive public opinion. Often it means no more than an irrational, atavistic form of politics, or obnoxious and aggressive policies pursued by governments (Breuilly 1993). The nub of the confusion is a common failure to distinguish nationalist politics from other forms of politics, and a tendency to equate the policies pursued by "nation-states"

with nationalism. A vast diversity of cases of sport supposedly getting tied up with nationalism can thus be adduced making it difficult to formulate a theory which would encompass all of them and indeed, making it difficult not to find a connection between sport and nationalism. When it is claimed that cases as diverse as the role played by gymnastics clubs in German unification, the nineteenth-century British cult of athleticism, hooliganism among English football supporters today, the Nazi-organized Berlin Olympics of 1936, Olympic politicking between the U.S. and USSR during the Cold War, and John Major's public references to cricket when he was the British prime minister, all reveal the machinations of nationalism at work in sport, plainly, there is a need to be clear about what is meant by nationalism.

The first and most important step in achieving greater clarity here is to stop conflating the state with the nation, an elementary error which so often leads commentators into mistakenly attributing state policies and actions to the nation and nationalism. The state is that public institution which successfully wields the monopoly of legitimate physical force within a given territory (Weber 1948). Nations, on the other hand, are population groups held together by a particular kind of enduring identity that encompasses common myths of origin, historical memories, a common culture, conceptions of rights and duties and economic opportunities, and above all, an attachment to a sacred HOMELAND. Nations may be distributed over the territories of more than one state and states are frequently multinational. Despite the strenuous efforts that have been made by political elites to build "nation-states," the situation where the state is populated by a single homogeneous nation is relatively rare. Nationalism is a specific form of politics generated where political movements seeking or exercising state power justify their actions by attributing a specifically nationalist meaning to the symbol, "nation" (Brubaker 1996). Nationalist ideology hinges on the claim that there exists a nation with an explicit and unique character, one of a world of nations, each with its own individuality, history and destiny. The nation is the source of legitimacy and of all political power: loyalty to it overrides all other allegiances and its interests take priority over all other interests and values. Human beings must identify with the nation if they want to be free and secure: the nation should be as independent as possible, if not politically sovereign (Breuilly 1993; Smith 1991).

## Nationalist and Non-Nationalist Constructions of Sport Distinguished

With this more specific conception of nationalist politics one can determine which cases are genuinely nationalist constructions of sport and which are not. Let us illustrate this first with reference to the case of gymnastics and German nationalism. In the early nineteenth century Johann Friedrich Jahn, invented *Turnen*, from which German gymnastics, the modern form of competitive gymnastics developed, as a means of strengthening and directing the German national will in the cause of German unification. The *Turnen* movement advocated the superiority of everything German over the foreign. Immensely successful in creating a network of clubs throughout Germany, *Turnen* became a pillar of German nationalism, so much so that when football spread to the Continent from Britain, it was denounced in Germany as "the English Disease," as un-German, a symptom of Anglo-Saxon superficiality and materialism, a product of a land without music or metaphysics. English games were considered rational, international, and Semitic lacking "higher values," such as reference to *Volk und Vaterland* (Dixon 1986). Here we have an unequivocal case of sport helping to unify the separate German states (with the exception of Austria) into a single, new, modern, and highly nationalistic German state.

Contrast this with the cult of athleticism in Britain at the time. In Britain, it was during the second half of the nineteenth century that the cult of athleticism came to be promoted in the public schools, at the same time as the Empire grew, and Britain came close to achieving global hegemony. It was, to a significant extent, through this cult of athleticism, that a sense of national superiority, tinged later with jingoistic sentiment, was diffused, especially among the dominant classes (Hargreaves 1986). An important cultural aspect of the expansion of Britain's power was the export of sport to large areas of the world and especially to the Empire, where it provided a source of social solidarity for the British in an alien environment and a means of enculturing their subjects.

It has been argued that British nationalism thus concealed itself under the cloak of racist imperialism which, it is claimed, was a prominent feature of the cult of athleticism (Holt 1995). The cult of athleticism, as a child of its times, was, no doubt, permeated by imperialist sentiment, but the claim that it was racist is based largely on the fact that social Darwinist notions of racial superiority were currently in fashion. However, British Imperialism was not a unitary phenomenon: it was also driven by a variety of other ideal and material interests, such as religious conviction, strategic considerations, economic advantage, philanthropic motives, and liberal and progressive ideas. Even if we were to accept that racist imperialism inspired the cult of athleticism and that racism and imperialism can be equated with nationalism, there would still be a problem, because the cult of athleticism was restricted to the elite's sports, and so it could not possibly have been used to help mobilize a *mass* nationalist movement.

The promotion of sport in Britain differed fundamentally from the pattern in comparable countries like Germany and France at the time. There was no centralized state direction of sport or ambition to encompass the whole population, let alone a coordinated drive to promote sport for military preparation and national unity. Sport was firmly in the hands of elements within civil society—the public schools, the churches, and the voluntary associations—whose efforts to spread a suitably modified version of the cult of athleticism, through the rational recreation movement, were limited to targeting only certain sections of the population who were deemed to be in need of social order and discipline (Hargreaves 1986). Sporting activity in Britain before 1914 may often have had patriotic overtones but it hardly amounts to the kind of nationalistic mobilization we see at the time in Germany and France.

Today, great national sporting events like the FA Cup Final, enveloped in rather elaborate ritual and ceremonial activity, deploy powerful symbols of the nation—the presence of royalty, fly-

## Sport and Nationalism

ing the Union Jack, playing the national anthem, singing "Abide with me," etc.—thereby celebrate national unity, but this is far from constituting a mobilization of nationalist sentiment. Even where English football hooliganism today is concerned, such XENOPHOBIA and ETHNOCENTRISM as it exhibits hardly amount to a significant manifestation of English ETHNIC NATIONALISM as some have exaggeratedly claimed. There is no significant backing for a racist English nationalist construction of sport. Extremist right-wing, xenophobic groups like the British National Party have had little success with football, or any other sports fans.

Indeed, it is peripheral nationalism rather than British or English nationalism that has manifested itself in sport in the British Isles. Welsh and Scottish national sentiment is given vent during football and rugby matches against England, but such expressions are relatively mild and politically insignificant. The one really significant nationalist construction of sport here concerns Irish nationalism. The thinking of leading Irish nationalists like Archbishop Croke, lay behind the foundation in 1884 of the Gaelic Athletic Association. He complained of "the ugly and irritating fact that we are daily importing from England not only her manufactured goods...but her fashions, her accents, her vicious literature, her dances and her pastimes to the utter discredit of our grand national sports, and to the sore humiliation, as I believe, of every son and daughter of the old land" (Holt 1995: 45). The Gaelic Athletic Association which established itself as the most important sporting body in Ireland, pursued a policy of promoting exclusively Irish sports, like hurling and Gaelic football, and refused to play English sports on the grounds that they undermined Irish culture. It plays a prominent part in the Irish republican nationalist movement in Northern Ireland today (Sugden and Bairner 1986).

German nationalism was the ideological bedrock of National Socialism. The manner in which the Nazi regime staged the Berlin Olympics of 1936 probably represents a watershed in the relationship between sport and nationalism, in that it revealed how effectively internationalized sport could be used by a ruthless state nationalist machine (Mandell 1971). Communist regimes like the former German Democratic Republic and the USSR, and Cuba also brilliantly exploited sport. With the exception of the Cuban regime which, arguably, is as much nationalist as communist, it would be a mistake to categorize them as nationalist. In common with national socialism, such totalitarian regimes incorporate sport into the service of the state, but the meaning of the nation is different and such "national" symbols as are deployed in sport are better understood as state rather than as nation symbols, for the ideology is not fundamentally nationalist. Sport here is thoroughly integrated into the diplomatic armory and therefore its use in this context is best understood in terms of international relations theory rather than theories of nationalism.

In the same way we should understand the Cold War conflict around the Olympic Games which ensued from 1952 when the USSR entered the competition. Here, success in the medal table supposedly demonstrated the superiority of American capitalism or Russian communism. The culmination of this policy was the U.S. boycott of the Moscow Olympics in 1980 in response to the USSR's invasion of Afghanistan, and the USSR's boycott of the following Games in Los Angeles, in retaliation.

Indeed, many states favor the use of sport as an instrument of foreign policy in the name of the "national interest," largely because it is cheap and relatively risk-free, but implement it in a realist and pragmatic mode that has little, if anything, to do with nationalism. The objective may be to gain legitimacy internationally, for example, when Mexico's one-party state staged the Olympics in 1968 and Argentina's military regime staged the World Cup in 1978, these occasions were used to create an impression of political stability, whereas in reality the opposition was being violently repressed. The motivation may be partly to wrongfoot an opponent, as when South Korea used the Seoul Olympics in 1988 to demonstrate its economic and political superiority over the communist North. Or, it may be for a mixture of reasons that include nationalist sentiment. Smaller, weaker countries, like Kenya with its excellent record in distance running, can put themselves on the map through success in international sport, and this is often part of their "NATION-BUILDING" strategy.

Sport has played an important part in the development of African nationalism and particularly in the emergence of the new South Africa. Tolerance of South Africa's APARTHEID regime abroad up to the 1970s was achieved to a significant extent through its international sporting contacts, and whites' national identity cohered to a considerable extent around a more or less fanatical attachment to sports like rugby and cricket. Consequently, the international sports boycott of South Africa from the 1970s proved to be a potent weapon in the hands of the anti-apartheid movement, reinforced black nationalism and pan-Africanism, and eventually helped to bring the regime down. Today, the South African government regards sport as one of the main instruments for building a multi-ethnic nation. Nelson Mandela has endorsed South Africa's rugby and cricket teams, still dominated by whites, as representing the new South Africa; and football, the game with which blacks overwhelmingly identify, is promoted at national and grass roots level for its supposed integrative power. Actually, in this case there is little evidence so far that sport integrates the different races (Guelke and Sugden 1999).

The Spanish government saw the Barcelona Olympic Games of 1992 as an opportunity to enhance Spain's international prestige. However, the regional government of Catalonia and Catalan nationalists, fearing central government control and intervention in their affairs and an "*Españolisation*" of the Games, thoroughly Catalanized them and used the opportunities the Games offered to enhance the political, economic and cultural position of Catalonia vis-à-vis the centre and to legitimize Catalan nationalism internationally (Hargreaves 1999; Hargreaves and García Ferrando 1997). The Catalan NATIONAL SYMBOLS (the flag, the national anthem, and the language) played a prominent part in the ritual and ceremony of the Games and Catalan culture permeated the Games as a whole. In this case, although Spain's prestige was ultimately enhanced as well, this was not achieved through a state nationalist construction of the Games. On the contrary, it was the Catalan nationalists who achieved their objectives by casting them in a nationalist mould which was directed against the state.

## Explaining the Linkage between Sport and Nationalism

It is unlikely at this stage that any single theory of nationalism can satisfactorily explain all the aforementioned instances, let alone the many more that exist. Realistically, the most that can be expected is that a framework or approach at a relatively high level of generality can be formulated which can be appropriately modified and refined, as required, for the analysis of a given case or cases. Such an approach would require, at the very least, a synthesis of PERENNIALIST AND MODERNIST approaches to theorizing nationalism, as well as an adequate notion of sport as a modern cultural form.

A synthesis of the two major kinds of approach to nationalism is required because exclusive reliance on either one of them has its dangers: perennialism tends to downplay the importance of structural bases of nationalism and modernism to downplay the significance of its cultural antecedents. Perennialism stresses the ethnic origins of nations and the importance of cultural tradition and of cultural nationalism as a foundation of nationalism. Nations cannot be constructed, invented or imagined out of thin air as modernists and post-modernists imagine. Modernists stress that increasing state centralization, capitalist economic development, and an associated tendency to cultural homogenization tend to trigger nationalism as a response.

Sport and nationalism are interrelated through their anchorage in common cultural traditions that may undergo sharp transformations as modernization occurs. Sport functions as a point of coherence for national movements to the extent that it is central to the culture, or can be made so by a nationalist movement. Seen from a perennialist perspective, just as nationalism has pre-modern origins, so sport has its premodern origins in games, physical recreations and pastimes of all kinds that are an important part of the cultural life of all pre-modern societies. That is why sports so often have associations with rural life. A people's identity forms around such pursuits as an integral part of its attachment to place, territory or homeland, its myths of origin, its customs, its art and literature, its language and religion, its memories

# Sport and Nationalism

of great events in the past. Where civil society is very well developed, as in the case of pre-industrial England and some other parts of Britain, participation in a rich variety of popular sporting recreations was institutionalized—folk football and cricket, horse racing, cruel sports involving animals, pugilism and wrestling, bowling, foot racing, forms of golf, and so on—and sports more exclusive to the elite—tennis, shooting, fencing, hunting, and so on—flourished as well.

The sports we play and watch today, in contrast, are the result of MODERNIZATION processes in which such traditional recreational forms were reformed and restructured and in the process their meanings were transformed. They were "nationalized" in the sense that they largely lost their original local and social class associations as they were diffused in homogenized or standardized forms throughout the country, indeed, they were universalized in so far as Britain exported much of its sporting tradition to the rest of the world. In this modernization process sports came to occupy a central position in the popular culture of very different kinds of societies. Concomitantly, a sense of national identity cohered around popular sporting forms like football in Europe and Latin America, and around other sports like cricket in the white dominions, the Caribbean and the Indian sub-continent. In Britain, this process occurred to an extent spontaneously, but increasingly it occurred at the behest of the urban gentry, sections of the intelligentsia and astute politicians, who consciously engineered such an identity (Hargreaves 1986). Sport became part of the mythology of NATIONAL IDENTITY, to the extent that love of sports and the values of fair play they are supposed to inculcate are still thought to differentiate the British from other nations. Sport could not have acquired such status in the national consciousness had it not been so deeply rooted in the culture of premodern Britain, and had it not been thoroughly modernized in the nineteenth and twentieth centuries. On the whole, sport was not imbued with nationalist meanings, as such, in this particular case. Elsewhere, it clearly was, as some of our examples show, and an explanation can be found in the particular circumstances of each case. With more comparative work we should be in a better position to begin to formulate the necessary and sufficient conditions in which nationalism and sport become linked.

Any aspect of culture—music, literature, religion, architecture, and so on—may, in principle, be given a nationalist inflection depending upon its specific features and the political context. There are certain features of sport which enable it readily to represent the nation and function well as an adjunct of nationalist politics in given circumstances. At the most basic, primordial level, sport gratifies the play instinct by providing opportunities for acquiring and exhibiting valued physical qualities connecting man to nature and which are necessary for physical survival—skill, endurance, strength, speed, and so on. Crucially, it provides opportunities to acquire and display moral qualities—courage, aggression, leadership, self-control, initiative, will power, steadfastness in adversity, self-sacrifice, loyalty—qualities commonly perceived as essential for cultural and for national survival.

The contest element in sport is especially significant because it allows opposition, conflict and struggle to be experienced and represented in extremely dramatic and spectacular ways in which sports can be made to map national struggles. Sporting contests are liminal: they are conducted according to rules that suspend reality by equalizing contestants' chances of winning. If, on the whole there are no such rules ensuring equal competition between states and nations in the real world, the laws of sport allow them to compete equally by proxy, and in doing so a potential is generated which facilitates the articulation of nationalist sentiment. The ritual activity which now envelops the great sporting contests—dramatic openings and closings, victory ceremonies, and so on, in which the national symbols are prominently deployed—does, to one extent or other, draw on national cultural tradition, but what we witness in sport as a result, is a representation of the nation that is quintessentially modern. The increasing elaboration of rules and regulations, the application of science and technology to enhance participants' performances, state intervention and control, mass marketing, spectacularization, and globalization of sport, are aspects of a universal modernizing process. Far from eroding nationalism, the modernization of sport provides it with new opportunities to mobilize support, given the right conditions. Once sport is harnessed to nationalism, it constitutes a powerful cultural resource in its service. Through sport, highly condensed, instantly effective images of the nation can be diffused to mobilize the potential nationalist constituency and to legitimate the movement externally. The power of such images resides in their impact not only at the cognitive level but above all at the emotional level and in their appeal to the aesthetic senses.

### Bibliography

Billig, M. 1995. *Banal Nationalism*. London: Sage.

Breuilly, J. 1993. *Nationalism and the State*. Manchester: Manchester University Press.

Brubaker, R. 1996. *Reframing Nationalism*. Cambridge: Cambridge University Press.

Dixon, J. G.1986. "Pressure Politics and Physical Education," in P. McIntosh et al. (eds.), *Landmarks in the History of Physical Education*. London: Routledge.

Guelke, A. and Sugden, J. 1999. "Sport and the 'Normalising' of South Africa," in J. Sugden and A. Bairner (eds.), *Sport in Divided Societies*. Aachen: Meyer and Meyer.

Holt, R. 1995. "Contrasting nationalisms: sport, militarism and the unitary state in Britain and France before 1914," *International Journal of the History of Sport* 12, 2.

Hargreaves, J. E. 1986. *Sport, Power and Culture*. Cambridge: Polity Press.

Hargreaves, J. E. and García Ferrando, M. 1997. "Public opinion, national integration and national identity in Spain: the case of the Barcelona Olympic Games," *Nations and Nationalism* 3, 1: 65-87.

Hargreaves, J. E. 1999. *Freedom For Catalonia? Catalan Nationalism, Spanish Identity and the Barcelona Olympic Games*. Cambridge: Cambridge University Press.

Houlihan, B. 1994. *Sport and International Politics*. London: Harvester Wheatsheaf.

Kanin, D. 1981. *The Political History of the Olympic Games*. Boulder, CO: Westview Press.

Lawrence, G. and Rowe, D. (eds.). 1986. *Power Play*. Hale & Iremonger: Sydney.

Mandell, R. 1971. *The Nazi Olympics*. New York: Macmillan.

Smith, A. D. 1991. *National Identity*. London: Penguin.

Sugden, J. and Bairner, A. 1986. "Sport in a divided society," in L. Allison (ed.), *The Politics of Sport*. Manchester: Manchester University Press.

Weber, M. 1948. "Politics as a vocation," in H. Gerth and C. Wright Mills (eds.), *From Max Weber*. London: Routledge.

John Hargreaves

# "Springtime of Nations"

The metaphor of spring, a favorite among nineteenth-century nationalist movements, has retained much of its propagandist resonance throughout the twentieth century. The seasonal imagery, suggesting a climatic shift from a reactionary "winter of discontent" towards an emancipatory "summer of fulfilment," was tailored by the nationalist intelligentsia to promote a new political philosophy which promised the empowerment of the mobilizing masses through the historical inevitability of nationalist victory. Also implicit in the projected image of the "springtime of nations" was faith in an historic juncture when European nations would take a collective quantum leap forward in their national development.

The historical episode traditionally associated with the label of "springtime of nations" is the "Year of Revolutions" in 1848, which cruelly spotlighted the gulf between nationalist aspiration and political reality.The concrete constitutional and geopolitical achievements of "1848" were disappointingly derisory, with not a single nation-state precipitated by the much-vaunted nationalist challenge. Moreover, no communal continental "springtime" occurred : "1848" demonstrated that each nation would follow its own individual time-scale of development, effecting (at best) an historically unsynchronized "*échelon*" of national springtimes rather than a simultaneous, cataclysmic and irreversible shift towards nationalist global warming.

Even so, the historical importance of "1848" in the development of nationalism is irrefutable. A sense of critical turning point was shared by nationalist movements and defending establishments alike. "Eighteen-forty-eight" proved a traumatic rite of passage converting innocent "men of sentiment" animated by cultural proto-nationalism into seasoned "men of convictions" galvanized by political nationalism. "Eighteen-forty-eight" provided a crash course in practical politics for nationalist leaderships, in particular demonstrating the future need to integrate the low politics of "nationalism-from-below" with the high politics of the Great Powers. For a potential but previously unpoliticized constituency, "1848" comprised a dramatic consciousness-raising exercise, a morale booster which prompted a "revolution of the spirit" expressed in snowballing recruitment to the nationalist cause. A political epiphany for significant hitherto uncommitted classes of society, "1848" spawned a new generation of "forty-eighters" dedicated to the nationalist creed and insulated by heretical zeal against the cold snap of official reaction in 1849 and beyond.

Just how "natural," "healthy," or "inevitable" nationalism may be has naturally been a contentious issue ever since 1848. The ambivalence of "1848" is pointed up by the contrast between the retrospectively politically correct metaphor of "springtime" and the populist slogan of *Risorgimento* (resurrection) on display across Europe throughout the revolutionary year. If "springtime" implies naturalness, inevitability, and spontaneity, "resurrection" constitutes the patently miraculous raising of the dead, tacitly conceding that some "nations" might be beyond mere revival or resuscitation. Notwithstanding the contradictions of the legacy of the "Year of Revolutions," the conviction that the opening battle of 1848 may have been lost but that ultimate victory in the ongoing war was assured now prevailed, effecting a confidence trick in a dual sense. As the first (and arguably last) mass outing for idealistic or Romantic nationalism, "1848" marked a watershed in the overall development of nationalism. Although never planned as a publicity stunt, "1848" was subsequently exploited as the greatest nationalist propaganda coup of the later nineteenth century. To observe the metaphor, the failures of "1848" were put down to a revolutionary spring which may have been early to the point of premature but could never be dismissed as false; the success of "1848" lay in the inspirational and buoyant belief that the worst of the reactionary winter was past and a summer of triumphant nationalism was imminent.

### Bibliography

Namier, Lewis. 1992 (1946) *1848:The Revolution of the Intellectuals*. Oxford: Oxford University Press.

Pearson, Raymond 1994. *The Longman Companion to European Nationalism, 1789-1920*. London: Longman.

Sperber, Jonathan. 1994. *The European Revolutions, 1848-1851*. Cambridge: Cambridge University Press.

Raymond Pearson

# State and Nation

One of the main goals of nationalism has been the attainment of AUTONOMY; this has usually, but not always, been interpreted to mean the attainment of a sovereign state for each nation, that is, a "nation-state." The latter may be regarded as a special kind of a polity, a political community that is congruent and coextensive with a historic culture-community, or "*nation*." Not only are the boundaries of state and nation coextensive; within its borders there is a single nation, and its public culture and laws, as well as its myths and memories, encompass and pervade the whole population within its boundaries.

In practice, few contemporary polities can be characterized as "nation-states" in the strict sense of the term. Most must be regarded as "national states," states that aspire to become unified nations and are legitimated by the principles of *nationalism*. The reason is that such political communities are not culturally unified, let alone homogeneous; they usually include one or more ethnic minorities, and derive their origins from several ethnic and cultural sources. In this respect, one might contrast Portugal and Iceland as mono-ethnic "nation-states" with France, Kenya and Burma, poly-ethnic states dominated by a large, strategic ethno-nation (the French, Kikuyu, and Burmans) but including in their political communities sizable ethnic minorities like the Bretons and Alsatians, the Luo, and the Shan and Karen.

The definition of the "nation-state," as well as the chances of creating and managing nation-states, are largely functions of ETHNICITY or rather of the ethnic demography and ethno-history of a polity. This is not, however, the view of a sizable body of influential theorists from Charles Tilly to Rogers Brubaker. They argue that nations and nationalism are modern (recent and novel), and their creation, as well as their form, can be attributed to the institutions of the modern state. In Anthony Giddens' analysis of the "nation-state," the nation is clearly the subordinate element of the pair. Characterizing the nation-state as a "bordered power container," Giddens argues that it is best seen as a type of political community having jurisdiction over clearly demarcated stretches of territory and reflexively monitored on a continuous basis, with nationalism, the "cultural sensibility of sovereignty," providing vital psychological reinforcement, or opposition where state and nation fail to coincide.

Political modernism also characterizes the approach of Michael Mann. He distinguishes four phases in the rise of modern nations in Europe: a religious-literary stage which generates discursive frameworks; a commercial-political phase in which the operations of capitalism and an expanding bureaucratic state widen these frameworks; a military-fiscal phase where military revolution breeds fiscal crises and popular resistance to state penetration, especially after the French Revolution; and finally an industrial capitalist phase which encompasses most social classes through the vastly expanded economic and social role of the state. Later, Mann puts forward a more starkly "political" theory of nationalism, attributing its aggressive excesses to the role of military factors and the modern state, to produce either a state-supporting nationalism in France and Britain, or a state-subverting nationalism in Germany and Austro-Hungary.

That the modern state has played a major role in forging nations and nationalisms, both in Europe and in Asia, Africa and Latin America, can hardly be doubted. The state has hardened the nation's borders, endowed it with the weapons of bureaucratic power and military force, and helped to diffuse the culture of the dominant ethnic community throughout the territory by its growing control over mass education, as occurred so memorably in the French Third Republic. At the same time, this state-centered modernism fits some areas better than others, Western Europe better than Eastern Europe, the "state-nations" of Africa more than the ethnic nations of Asia and the Balkans. Even in the West, the state's expansion was premised on a certain degree of ethnic unity, with a dominant *ethnie* (the French, English, Castilians, Swedes) providing the cultural foundation for subsequent state expansion. Moreover, the experience of nations like The Netherlands, Switzerland, Slovenia, and Finland, whose states were either weak or nonexistent, suggests the limitations of an approach centered on the impact of the modern state.

The same difficulties beset the most comprehensive and rigorous state-centered modernist account, that of John Breuilly. He argues that nationalism should be seen as a political movement aiming for state power by using nationalist arguments to mobilize the people, coordinate various social groups and legitimize their political demands. A nationalist argument is a political doctrine that claims that "there exists a nation with an explicit and peculiar character," whose interests and values take priority over others, and which requires maximum autonomy, and usually political sovereignty. Nationalism is an exclusively modern movement, which seeks to overcome the split between an absolutist modern state and civil society consequent on the advent of capitalist modernity. Though nationalist intellectuals provide a spurious solution by using historicist arguments to equate the cultural with the political nation, and celebrating this union in ceremonials, myths and symbols, we should not regard nationalism as a primarily ideological movement nor as the politics of the intellectuals. However, by excluding all concern with cultural identity from his purview, Breuilly like other state-centered modernists denudes nationalism of much of its content and appeal. Cultural diversity has always been a prime value for nationalists, and nationalism, as a secular form of salvation drama, has always held a special attraction for intellectuals and artists. It is the nonpolitical re-

## State and Nation

generative dimensions of nationalism that account for its mobilizing power, especially when it taps into the preexisting ethnic ties and popular cultures of submerged peoples. State-centered modernists, for whom the primary focus is the "nation-state" and the rational activities of political elites, tend to omit this view "from below" and to neglect the role of cultural networks and ethnic memories, myths and symbols in the formation of nations.

### Bibliography

Tilly, Charles (ed.) 1975. *The Formation of National States in Western Europe*. Princeton, NJ: Princeton University Press.

Breuilly, John. 1993. *Nationalism and the State*, 2nd edn. Manchester: Manchester University Press.

Giddens, Anthony. 1985. *The Nation-State and Violence*. Cambridge: Polity Press.

Mann, Michael. 1993. *The Sources of Social Power*, vol. II. Cambridge: Cambridge University Press.

Mann, Michael. 1995. "A political theory of nationalism and its excesses," in Periwal, Sukumar (ed.), *Notions of Nationalism*. Budapest: Central European University Press.

Smith, Anthony D. 1998. *Nationalism and Modernism*. London: Routledge.

Anthony D. Smith

# T

## Tribalism

In contemporary, popular discourse about nations and nationalism "tribalism" is commonly used as a pejorative attribute of small nations and their struggles to win or to defend their AUTONOMY (Parkinson 1998).

Thus, media accounts of the wars in former Yugoslavia in the nineteen nineties have regularly referred to the allegiance of Slovenes, Croats, Bosnians and Kosovars to their respective national identities as "tribal," and their conflicts with Serbia as "tribal wars" (Malcolm 1994). Similarly, the resistance of Unionists in Northern Ireland to the Irish Republican Army's terrorist campaign is routinely dismissed as "tribal"—and therefore indefensibly unfit for the modern world—even by otherwise knowledgeable journalists and politicians (Bardon 1992; Bruce 1994).

This mistaken usage is a product of prejudice and ignorance combined. Prejudice in as much as it springs from paternalistic contempt for the presumption of small nations in disturbing the international status quo. Ignorance because tribalism is a mode of social organization with its own distinct and proper role at a much more primitive level of evolutionary development than that of incipient nations (Schapera 1956). Thus in its commonest contemporary usage tribalism refers merely to a nationalism to which one is antagonistic.

An equal and opposite conceptual error, which gravely underestimates the importance of tribalism, is also detectable in the literature of nations and nationalism. For some large and powerful tribally organized societies, such as that of the Zulus, straddling several states in Southern Africa, evidently do represent a genuine basis for potential national identity (Taylor 1995). Indeed, in sub-Saharan Africa in general the transformative significance of *bona fide* tribal nationalism seems quite likely to surprise over-sophisticated Western commentators. Developments during the nineteen nineties in South Africa, Congo/Zaire, Rwanda, Burundi, and Nigeria may be called in evidence.

### Bibliography

Bardon, J. 1992. *A History of Ulster*. Belfast: Blackstaff Press.

Bruce, S. 1994. *The Edge of the Union: The Ulster Loyalist Political Vision*. Oxford: Oxford University Press.

Malcolm, N. 1994. *Bosnia: A Short History*. Basingstoke: Macmillan.

Parkinson, A. F. 1998. *Ulster Loyalism and the British Media*. Dublin: Four Courts Press.

Schapera, I. 1956. *Government and Politics in Tribal Societies*. London: Watts.

Taylor, S. 1995. *Shaka's Children*. London: Harper Collins.

David Marsland

## Typology of Nation-Forming Processes in Europe

Even though modern nations were formed in all parts of Europe during the nineteenth century, the nation-forming process cannot be subordinated to any one general, explanatory model. Relevant typological differences have to be respected and incorporated into historical and sociological research. The key point of departure for explaining the basic typological difference is the concept of a nation as a large social group whose members are linked together by a combination of several kinds of ties emerging as the result of a long nation-forming process.

This process can be divided into two distinct stages, the second—since the end of the eighteenth century—being the decisive one. At the threshold of this second stage we observe two typologically different situations:

The first of these two typologically different situations is that of the state-nation. The

**289**

state-nation emerged during the Middle Ages and Early Modern period in the shape of an established state with a codified language and a homogeneous high culture. Its culture was shared and supported by its elites, who developed and maintained a powerful NATIONAL IDENTITY and worked hard at supporting the economy.

Under the conditions of a state-nation, the nation-forming process went forward as an organic component of MODERNIZATION. Thus, national identity and nationalism penetrated the masses hand in hand with consciousness of being members of an emerging civil society. Citizens of a state, they were, at once, also a nation.

Naturally, there were important differences in this process in different countries, and it is necessary to distinguish some sub-types, related to two ideal-typical opposing situations:

- The development of an almost mono-ethnic state, such as the northern Netherlands and Portugal.

- The development of a multi-ethnic empire, such as the British, Spanish, Danish, Russian, Austrian, and Ottoman Empires. These cases evince a culturally homogeneous ruling elite with a strong identity related to the empire as such. With modernization and secularization, they faced some difficulty in defining themselves in terms of a modern national identity. There were several different strategies:

a) Identifying the imperial identity with the national identity, or understanding the empire as a nation. This was managed successfully in the British case, less successfully in Spain, and failed entirely in the Russian case.

b) Redefining the imperial identity —after the failure of empire—as a narrow ethno-national identity. The Danes and Swedes offer examples.

c) Accepting the identity of a neighbouring example of strong nation-formation—as in the switch from Austrian to German identity.

d) Substituting the imperial identity with a newly defined, modern national identity, as with the case of the Turks.

As between the two situations mentioned above, the French and Polish cases could be regarded as transitional: a strong state-national identity among the ruling classes combined with an effort for homogeneity within an ethnically heterogeneous territory. This could succeed in centralist and absolutist France, but not in Poland, where the state broke down as a result of the second and third divisions in the 1790s.

The second of the two major typologically distinct situations within which modern states have developed is quite different. Ethnic groups (*ethnies*) whose members lived in the territory of multi-ethnic empires differed at the threshold of the modern era from state-nations in three important respects:

- Firstly, their nation-forming was not related to a state which could be regarded as "their own." In some cases, a previous, medieval statehood was partially or totally annihilated. In others, statehood never existed for them before at all.

- Secondly, these ethnic groups were not in possession of a high culture in their own standardized language. Or, alternatively, the previous development of their high culture and written language was interrupted, with the capacity of their cultural life significantly weakened.

- Thirdly, we find very few or no members of ruling classes belonging to these ethnic groups. Their social structure excluded some of the key social strata appropriate to their extant level of economic development.

Taking account of these three typological features, it seems to be legitimate to classify these ethnic groups which travel the second road towards modern nationhood as "nondominant" (Hroch 1985).

The basic difference between these two distinct types of nation-formation consists in the fact that national formation initiated in the situation of nondominant ethnic groups is carried through by an explicitly national movement—a process of organized endeavor to achieve all of the attributes of a fully-fledged nation. Historically, the goals of each national movement have corresponded to the absence of these attributes, and consisted in three groups of demands:

- The development of national culture based on the written language and the normal use of this language in administration, education, economic life, and so on.

- The achievement of civil rights together with some kind of political self-administration and ultimately of independence.

- The creation of a complete social structure from out of the ethnic group including an entrepreneurial class and educated elites, together with free peasants and organized workers.

The relative priority, combination and timing of these three sets of demands has varied in each case. Common to all national movements, however, there is one key developmental feature. Between the starting point of any given national movement and its successful conclusion, three characteristic structural phases can be distinguished.

During an initial period (Phase A), the energies of activists were devoted to scholarly investigation of the linguistic, cultural, social and historical attributes of the nondominant ethnic group—and to dissemination of the resulting knowledge. In a second period (Phase B), a new set of activists tended to emerge, who sought to win over their ethnic fellows to the project of creating a future nation, and to spread by patriotic agitation a modern national identity. Once the major part of the population came to set special store by their national identity, a mass movement was formed which ushered in a third period (Phase C), accompanied by a differentiated political program.

Despite these important common features of the "nondominant ethnic group" case, it also exhibits considerable diversity. This is occasioned, in the first place, by differences in social structure. A minority of national movements has started its Phase B under the leadership of "national" ruling elites: for example, the trading bourgeoisie and officials in Norway, aristocracy and gentry in the Magyar national movement in Hungary, and Phanariots in the Greek case. Symptomatically, national movements such as these—which included the participation of ruling classes—gave exclusive priority in Phase B to political demands as such. The majority of national movements, by contrast, concentrated their endeavors during

Phase B on linguistic, cultural and, subsequently, also social demands. This was the key difference between national movements which faced three sets of deficits—and formulated three sets of demands—and those which faced only two sets of them.

In this connection, it should be noted, that among European national movements there are three which formulated only one set of demands, corresponding to the fact that only one deficit distinguished them from the family of fully-fledged nations: they did not have a state of their own. These movements—in Germany, Italy, and Poland—sought the support of a society with a completed social structure. They had already an old-established tradition of national culture and language, and they concentrated purely on the fight for political independence or unification. In other words, their leadership tried to achieve a switch from cultural to political national identity. They cannot be included in the category of "nondominant" ethnic groups, and constitute therefore, a transitional case between the two basic roads of the nation-forming process.

National formation has not proceeded in a social and political vacuum. On the contrary, it has been closely connected with the process of social, economic and political modernization. Accordingly, a significant typology of national movements can be formulated, which is based on criteria concerning the interrelations between the three phases of national movements described above on the one hand, and the general process of social and political transformation on the other.

Combining these two series of changes, we can describe four types of national movements:

- National agitation (Phase B) occurred under the old regime of late absolutism, and the national movement acquired a mass character in a time of fundamental—sometimes revolutionary—changes in the political system and social relations. The national political programme developed in conditions of liberal and democratic upheaval. This was the case with the Magyars, the Norwegians, the Czechs, and with some delay, with the Finns and the Estonians.

- National agitation got under way, similarly, under the old regime, but the transition to a mass movement (Phase C) was delayed until the fundamental changes which abolished absolutist systems, were completed. As a result of this, the political program was formulated under conditions of a more or less established constitutional regime and sometimes in opposition to it. This shift of sequence could be caused either by uneven economic development, as in Lithuania or Croatia, or by insufficiency of internal coherence, as in the Slovene and Latvian cases, or by foreign oppression—Slovaks under Magyars, for example, and Ukrainians under Russian rule.

* The national movement was directed against the old regime and acquired a mass character early, before the establishment of a civil society and constitutional order. This pattern was favourable for armed insurrections, and was confined to the lands of the Ottoman Empire in Europe (Serbs, Greeks, Bulgarians, Macedonians).

* National agitation first began under constitutional conditions, in a more developed capitalist setting, characteristic of Western Europe. In these cases, the national movement could reach Phase C quite early, as in the Basque lands and Catalonia, while in other cases it did so only after a very long Phase B, as in Flanders, or not at all, as in Wales, Scotland, or Britanny.

Beyond these basic distinctions there are further sub-types which should be noted, based on criteria of somewhat lesser importance. They are primarily defined in terms of relations between pre-existing political "national" entities and national movements. There are three main sub-types:

* Firstly, those where the nondominant ethnic group could not be related to any state or administrative unit in the past: examples are, the Estonians, Finns, Latvians, Slovenes, and Slovaks.

* Secondly, those which could be related to a medieval state which was subsequently totally destroyed and survived only in the "collective memory" of some members of the group: for example, the Serbs, Greeks, Bulgarians, Lithuanians, Ukrainians, Catalans, and Flemish. In these cases the way was open to the spread of myths and deliberate invention.

* Thirdly, the medieval independence of a given state was lost, but several institutional relics, such as, Diets, frontiers, or church administration remained, together with some degree of political identity: for example, the Norwegians, Magyars, Czechs, Croatians, and Irish. Significantly, al-

most all of these belonged to the first, "integrated" type of national movement described earlier.

Corresponding to these differences, some kind of polarity in the role of history, historical argument, and historical consciousness can be observed. This role was obviously more relevant in the case of "nations" with a political history than in the cases where political history could not be adopted and used as national argument. In some cases, such as the Czechs, Magyars, and Croatians, the "historical right" became a central argument deployed in the national movement.

Another difference can be observed if we take into account cultural and literary traditions. We can distinguish ethnic groups with a rather rich tradition of literature in their written language, such as Czechs, Catalans, Greeks, and Magyars, and ethnic groups which, by contrast, had to create their own national culture and language.

How, we must ask, did these typological differences—both the basic distinction between state-nations and national movements, and the secondary typology of national movements—influence national programs and the character of national formation and nationalism? This question can, as yet, be answered only partially, since further comparative research in this field is required. Nevertheless, some links can be regarded as probable.

Above all, there are marked differences between the nationalist attitudes which can be observed among the members, and more particularly the elites, of the state-nations and attitudes among the members of nations which emerged as a result of a successful national movement. To the members of state-nations, national identity, and the existence of their nation seemed self-evident. They did not feel they had to prove it. By contrast, in the case of national movements, demonstration of their national identity was their primary goal.

State-national nationalism was obsessed with the idea of a national mission, civilizational, cultural, or political, which involved the integration and assimilation of weaker and less developed peoples. It implied the idea of conflicting interests with other state-nations. National movements, by contrast, focused on keeping their old ethno-national identity alive. This involved at the same time a defensive position against the political goals of state-nations. This perspective usually produced a feeling of being endangered and a call for national unity with national goals as such preferred to civic goals. As a result, internal political differentiation was later and shallower than in the case of established state-nations.

International politics was an obvious and important component of the existence of state-nations, with national interests defined in terms of state interests. This was not the case in national movements. In as far as national movements became involved in international relations at all, they were integrated not as a subject but as an object of political competition or collaboration between state-nations. The consequence was a lack of experience in international relations and a provincialism which remained a part of the political culture of nations which developed from non-dominant ethnic groups.

All the distinctions identified earlier also powerfully influenced the differentiation of national programmes and of NATIONALIST STEREOTYPES. Thus, the integrated type of national movement developed its image of national values more or less synchronously with the process of anti-feudal and civic revolutions—above all 1848 in Central and 1905 in Eastern Europe. Their participants regarded civil rights and constitutional and democratic principles as a self-evident part of national goals and demands. The ideals of civil society and of national community were integrated and regarded as fully compatible.

This was not the case with belated national movements, where the leaders of emerging mass movements often had to continue fighting for national rights even after the civil revolution. The struggle continued against the newly established liberal state elites of the ruling nation—Slovaks and Croats against Magyar elites, Slovenes against German elites, Ruthenes in Galicia against Polish elites. Even though these national movements did include civil rights in their political programmes,

they could not play a national mobilizing role because they were either recently realized and appropriated by the liberals of a ruling nation (Austria-Hungary) or ineffective in the face of political persecution (Russia).

Insurrectionist national movements subordinated everything to the struggle for what their leaders understood as national rights under conditions of a latent war with the Ottoman Empire and unfulfilled territorial claims. Moreover, these claims often clashed, and produced additional tensions between newly born nation-states. For these reasons, rather strong, indeed, decisive influence could be achieved by those politicians who gave an absolute priority to national interests and regarded the problems of civil rights and democracy as unimportant.

Disintegrated national movements experienced the opposite of this, but the results were similar. National agitation started under conditions of a rather polarized political life, and the space of political claims and programmes was occupied by the political programmes of liberalism, democratism, clericalism, or socialism. It was very difficult to enter this space with political claims made in the name of a nation, that is, to formulate specific national interests, different from state-national interests, in terms other than those of cultural or historical tradition. For this reason, all Western national movements, with the possible exception of the Irish, could be denounced as antimodernist and conservative, and they achieved Phase C of national development very late or not at all.

## Bibliography

Hroch, Miroslav. 1985. *Social Preconditions of National Revival in Europe: A Comparative Analysis of the Social Composition of Patriotic Groups among the Smaller European Nations*. Cambridge: Cambridge University Press.

Miroslav Hroch

# W

## Weber's Theory of the Nation

In the period before 1900 the highly patriotic thinking of the young professor Max Weber focused mainly on the political and structural facts and challenges of the contemporary German national state (Weber 1993). His concerns in this context, however, hardly went beyond Germany. Furthermore, in this context, his terminology was less scientific and more political and lacked the conceptual clarity of his later writings. Concise explanations of the central terms of nation (*Nation*) and people (*Volk*) were lacking. For him the "nation" embodied "the particular strain of humankind [*Menschentum*] we find within our own nature" (Weber 1994: 15), and he described his main task and that of his colleagues as "the *eternal struggle* to preserve and raise the quality of our national species" (ibid.: 16).

At that time, in German usage, the terms *Nation* and *Volk* meant a section of the human race with a common origin, language, custom, and education, the word *Volk* additionally describing the entire citizenry of a state (Koselleck et al. 1992; Weber 1988, 2: 922). One of the best German encyclopaedias—*Meyers Konversationslexikon* (vol. 19 of 1897)—explicitly equated the German words *Volk* and *Staatsvolk* with the English/French "nation," and the German *Nation* with "people"/ *peuple*."

In the German usage of the time it might have been correct to call the English, Irish, Scotch, and Welsh peoples "nations" and because the English dominated Great Britain, the Germans regarded Great Britain as the state of the English nation, the English national state (*Nationalstaat*). A completely different—and in that period singular—type of state which could not be regarded as the political instrument of one nation was represented by Austria. She had been multiethnic (*Vielvölkerstaat*) since the Middle Ages, and when her peoples began to regard themselves as nations her end was on the agenda.

It is very hard to decide whether Weber's usage of the terms is closer to their meaning in English or in German. His concept of the "nation" was already inherent in his early political writings. The starting point of his analyses was the process of ethnic, social, and economic change in the east provinces of Germany, where large-scale landholding dominated all structures of the polity. Modern capitalism, however, and world wide competition by overseas producers caused a deep social and economic change in the organization of the rural society in those regions. The living conditions of the rural workers deteriorated dramatically while the smallholders lost the market for their products. In Weber's analysis, this development resulted in a twofold migration: German smallholders and rural workers moved away from the east and were replaced by Polish smallholders and rural workers.

Weber explained this ethnic shift in the east as the result of an economic struggle of the German and Polish nations (I use the terms "Polish nation" advisedly because there was no Polish state at this time), and because the German state was a national state, he demanded that it should be on the side of the German nation (Weber 1994: 13). In his opinion, the *raison d'état* of the German Empire was to be derived from its quality as a national state, the national state being "the worldly organisation of the nation's power" (*weltliche Machtorganisation der Nation*) (ibid.: 17). Weber's analysis neglected the civil rights and the interests of the entire citizenry of the Empire which included some millions of citizens who were not German but Danish, French, Polish, or Serbian. He probably assumed that the German national state had to serve the German nation and no other.

Consequently Weber's concept of the nation strongly stressed the ethnic aspect. It was, however, focused on the capitalist order of the economy and the situation of the bourgeois upper middle class on whom that order rested. Weber thought that the German upper middle-classes lacked the inner power to direct national policy with the strength with which they were directing German economic development and that the lower middle classes as well as the proletarian workers lacked both the ability and maturity to undertake the leadership of state and nation. At the same time, the dominance of the agrarian aristocracy of the *Junkers* was dissolving under the pressure of the capitalist system (ibid.: 22-26).

But, supposing that the German national state were to be directed by the upper middle-classes, what policy did Max Weber expect in that case? Weber thought that the government would have to face two main challenges. It had to stimulate the cultural and economic development of the dominant nation, that is, the Germans, and it had to stabilize and develop the free constitutional structures of the "Fatherland" (Weber 1993: 673). Weber's concept of a national policy directed by the interests of the middle-classes combined the idea of liberal parliamentarianism with the program of economic strength and the growth of foreign trade. The combination of these factors would prepare Weber's nation for the eternal struggle of the nations world wide; it would contribute to the growth of its power, making it a "power state" (*Machtstaat*), and enabling it to pursue the politics of a world power (*Weltmachtpolitik*) (Weber 1994: 26-7). In addition, Weber expected that the growth of the world population would, in future, intensify "the struggle for existence, the universal contest of man against man" (*Kampf des Menschen mit dem Menschen*). From this, he deduced "the gospel of the struggle as the duty of the nation," which he declared to be "the only way to the nation's greatness" (Weber 1993: 638).

Quite surprisingly, however, despite its belligerent tone, Weber's concept of the power and greatness of his nation, related less to foreign and military affairs than to the education of people (*Kulturmenschentum*) and to the economy and trade policy. The "greatness of the nation" depended mainly on its cultural and economic potential, on its position among the "great capitalistically developed nations" and especially among the industrialized states. Weber expected "that among the leading nations the desire for

more stable trade relations would continuously strengthen" (Weber 1993: 629). Military force was mentioned only in so far as it could protect the nation's economic development. When he propagated maritime imperialism he mainly had in mind the military protection of Germany's foreign trade. His call for naval power, for the construction of a German fleet and for overseas colonies resulted from the need to protect the "powerful development of the middle-class commerce and industry" which represented "in the age of capitalism for the long term the only possible economic policy" (Weber 1993: 672-3).

No doubt, all those partly emotional and partly irrational thoughts on the topic of the nation had their equivalents in the thinking of the middle-class elites of all Great European Powers. Although Weber's thinking was rather nationalistic at that time, it represented neither a theory of the nation nor of nationalism. It was only on the eve of the outbreak of the Great War that he came closest to producing some explicit but still fragmentary theory of the nation. And even then Weber would not have admitted that his theory of the nation was simultaneously a theory of nationalism.

It was at the second meeting of the German Sociological Association in October 1912 and at a time when he was already working on his *magnum opus Economy and Society* (*ES*), that Weber spontaneously outlined for the first time his sociological reflections on the nation: "In so far as there is at all a common object lying behind the obviously ambiguous term 'nation,' it is apparently located in the field of politics. One might well define the concept of nation in the following way: a nation is a community of sentiment which would adequately manifest itself in a state of its own; hence, a nation is a community which normally tends to produce a state of its own" (Gerth and Mills 1948: 176). The complete version of Weber's theory is found in two different manuscripts written for *Economy and Society*. In the first of them (*ES* I: 385-398) Weber dealt with the nation in the context of the sociology of ethnic groups, and in the—fragmentary—second manuscript (*ES* II: 901-940) he examined the nation as a political community.

Surprisingly, both texts omit any discussion of such important subjects as the systematic linking of "nation" and "national state," the analysis of the interdependence between different types of nations and different types of states, or the analysis of the achievements of the modern national states in the fields of the social integration of their populations and the modernization of the state and the economy.

Weber's discussion of ethnic groups (*ethnische Gemeinschaften*) is located in the context of reflections on different types of social action (*Gemeinschaftshandeln*). One such type is the belief in common descent (*Abstammungsverwandtschaft*) or blood relationship (*Blutsverwandtschaft*), which can be frequently observed even in tribes that originate in an act of the political will of rulers or authorities (*ES* I: 389, 393-4). This belief—and also the common customs of people which originate, at least partly, in the necessity to adapt themselves to their natural environment and to the customs of their neighborhood—facilitates social actions on the part of the tribal members (*Volksgenossen*). It also contributes—especially by warlike actions—to the forging of tribal consciousness (*Stammesbewußtsein*) and consequently to the formation of continuous political communities (*Dauergemeinschaften*).

Thus, to the extent to which those customs (*Sitten*) conditioned by heredity and those determined by tradition—together with the particular content of custom (*Sitte*), and religious, political and linguistic commonality—produce the belief in affinity, a relationship of blood, they create what was nearly identical: tribes (*Stämme*) and peoples (*Völker*) (*ES* I: 392-4).

At the end of Weber's enquiry not only the relevance of racial identity for the making of tribes and peoples dissolved, but also "ethnicity" and finally even "nation" proved to be unusable sociological categories: "The concept of the 'ethnic' group, which dissolves if we define our terms exactly, corresponds in this regard to one of the most vexing, since emotionally charged concepts: the *nation*, as soon as we attempt a sociological definition." (*ES* I: 395) In the pages following this passage, originally entitled "'Nation' and 'people'" ("'*Nation' und 'Volk*'") Weber discusses some different types of contemporary nations and some patterns of the contemporary national iden-

tification of some populations. The only link of all of these passages was the aspect of political power: "Time and again we find that the concept 'nation' directs us to political power" (*ES* I: 395-8).

Weber examined the relationship between political power and the nation in a more detailed way in the section on "Political Communities" of *Economy and Society* (*ES* II: 613-926). In accordance with his normal procedure the first phrases of that section contain a definition: "The term 'political community' shall apply to a community whose social action is aimed at subordinating to orderly domination by the participants a 'territory' and the conduct of the persons within it, through readiness to resort to political force, including normally force of arms" (*ES* II: 901). Weber assigns to this community the readiness to use well-ordered force not only to compel the inhabitants of the territory to do their duty but also against external enemies. In short: "The individual is expected ultimately to face death in the group interest. This gives to the political community its particular pathos and raises its enduring emotional foundations. The community of political destiny, i.e., above all, of common political struggle of life and death, has given rise to groups with joint memories which often had a deeper impact than the ties of merely cultural, linguistic, or ethnic community. It is this 'community of memories' (*Erinnerungsgemeinschaft*) which ... constitutes the ultimately decisive element of 'national consciousness'" (*ES* II: 903).

But what is the essence of the nation as a distinctive type of human community and of that *Nationalbewußtsein*? For Weber, the concrete reasons for the belief in joint nationality and for the resulting social action vary greatly. A national community requires the existence of social action and of political community. But, finally, even the eloquent Max Weber had no definition: "If the concept of 'nation' can in any way be defined unambiguously, it certainly cannot be stated in terms of empirical qualities common to those who count as members of the nation. In the sense of those using the term at a given time, the concept undoubtedly means, above all, that *it is proper* to expect from certain groups a specific sentiment of solidarity in the face of other groups. Thus, the concept belongs in the sphere of values." Yet, there was no further agreement about the meaning of the term. Consequently, Weber tried to identify distinct types of contemporary nations: "In ordinary language, 'nation' is, first of all, not identical with the 'people of a state,' that is, with the membership of a given polity." For, as he observed, many groups, as, for example, in the multiracial and multinational state of Austria, emphatically asserted the independence of their respective nation in contrast to the other nations in the same state (*ES* II: 922).

Weber was aware that a shared common language was, at the time, "pre-eminently considered the normal basis of nationality" (*ES* I: 395). He knew that "the pretension to be considered a special "nation" is associated with a common language as a culture value of the masses (*Massenkulturgut*)." But the case of the multilingual Swiss nation, the English-speaking countries in Europe and overseas, or the neighbouring Serbs and Croats, who had a common language but were divided by different religions, led Weber to deny that there was any necessary link between nationality and linguistic community (*ES* II: 921-4). "National solidarity among men speaking the same language may be just as well rejected as accepted. Solidarity, instead, may be linked with differences in the other great culture value of the masses, namely, a religious creed... National solidarity may be connected with differing social structure and mores and hence with 'ethnic' elements ... .Yet, above all, national solidarity may be linked to memories of a common political destiny (*Schicksalsgemeinschaft*) with other nations." In this context, Weber made use of the striking example of the Alsatians who spoke German and identified with the French since the Revolutionary War, "which represents their common heroic age" (*ES* II: 923).

In conclusion, Weber's method of approaching a theory of the nation is a descriptive one. This is because of the sheer multitude of distinct realities that resisted his attempts to give a consistent definition or even to elaborate an ideal type of the nation. Nevertheless, we owe him the observation that, to the extent to which a nation is also a political community, a national state, all such nations have three features in common,

namely, the use of force, the desire for power prestige and the readiness—or obligation—of their members to face death in the common interest. "On the basis of this power, the members [of those political structures] may pretend to a special 'prestige,' and their pretensions may influence the external conduct of the power structure"—and, ultimately, they may play a part in the origin of wars. "The prestige of power means in practice the glory of power over other communities"(*ES* II: 910-1). It also means that those groups who hold the power to steer social action (*Gemeinschaftshandeln*) can effectively demand unqualified devotion (*ES* II: 922). It is thus that Weber explains the aggressiveness of nationalism.

The primary exponents of the desire for power prestige were those "strata living off the exercise of political power": feudal lords, modern officers, or bureaucrats. "Power for their political community means power for themselves, as well as the prestige based on this power," whereas the territorial expansion of their state meant "more office positions, more sinecures, and better opportunity for promotion"—interests that were not so far away from the capitalist interests of tax-farmers, state creditors, suppliers of the state, overseas traders privileged by the state, and of colonial capitalists, which "rest upon the direct exploitation of political power directed towards expansion" (*ES* II: 911, 917).

Soberly checking the risks of the desire for power prestige could calm down the upper classes' nationalistic enthusiasm: kings might lose their thrones, victorious commanders might supersede their rulers, the wealthy middle-classes might suffer from losses to their fortunes and earnings, and dignitaries were endangered by the revolution of the poor. Only among the masses of the lower classes who, in Weber's disdainful words, had "nothing concrete to lose but their lives," the valuation and effect of those dangers could easily be reduced to zero "through emotional influence," because, the "sentiments of prestige" often extended deep down to the petty-bourgeois masses who were rich only "in the historical attainment of power-positions." In some sense their emotional attitude was similar to that of Weber's own social strata of the intellectual elite. "They comprise especially all those who think of themselves as

# Weber's Theory of the Nation

being the specific 'Partners' (*Teilhaber*) of a specific culture." In some non-material sense they were somehow privileged (*irgendwie ideell privilegierte Schichten*) and pursued indirectly material as well as ideological interests. "Under the influence of these circles, the naked prestige of 'power' is unavoidably transformed into other special forms of prestige and especially into the idea of the 'nation'"(*ES* II: 921-2).

Enrichment, prestige, emotion, power, and war —or at least permanent readiness for war as well as the awareness of the risks of war—formed the main components of Weber's theory of the national state. And under the influence of the educated it was only a short step from there to the "idea of the 'nation.'" Thus, the final result of Max Weber's effort to develop a theory of the nation consisted in the identification of the specific force of emotion and power: "Time and again we find that the concept 'nation' directs us to political power. Hence, the concept seems to refer —if it refers at all to a uniform phenomenon—to a specific kind of pathos which is linked to the idea of a powerful political community of people,"— people who share a common language, or a common religion, or common customs, or common political memories. The more power is emphasized, the closer appears to be the link between those emotions, the power and the nation (*ES* I: 397-8).

## Bibliography

Beetham, David. 1985. *Max Weber and the Theory of Modern Politics*, 2nd edn. Oxford: Polity Press (especially pp. 119-150).

Gerth, H.H. and Wright Mills, C. (eds.).1948. *From Max Weber: Essays in Sociology*. London: Routledge & Kegan Paul.

Koselleck, Reinhard *et al.* 1992. "Volk, Nation, Nationalismus, Masse," in Otto Brunner, Werner Contze and Reinhard Koselleck (eds.), *Geschichtliche Grundbegriffe. Historisches Lexikon zur politisch-sozialen Sprache in Deutschland*, vol. 7. Stuttgart: Klett-Cotta.

Mayer, Jacob Peter. 1956. *Max Weber and German Politics.*2nd edn. London: Faber and Faber.

*Meyers Konversations-Lexikon. Ein Nachschlagewerk des allgemeinen Wissens.*1897. 18 vols. 5th edn. Leipzig and Vienna: Bibliographisches Institut.

Mommsen, Wolfgang J. 1984. *Max Weber and German Politics*. Chicago and London: The University of Chicago Press.

Weber, Max. 1922. *Wirtschaft und Gesellschaft* (Grundriß der Sozialökonomik III). Tübingen: J.C.B. Mohr (Paul Siebeck).

Weber, Max. 1968. *Economy and Society. An Outline of Interpretive Sociology*. Edited by Guenther Roth and Claus Wittich, 3 vols. New York: Bedminster Press (referred to as "*ES*" in the text).

Weber, Max. 1984- *Max Weber-Gesamtausgabe*. Abt. I: *Schriften und Reden*. Tübingen: J.C.B. Mohr (Paul Siebeck).

Weber, Max. 1984. *Zur Politik im Weltkrieg. Schriften und Reden 1914-1918*. Edited by Wolfgang J. Mommsen and Gangolf Hübinger, vol. 15 of *Max Weber-Gesamtausgabe*. Abt. I: *Schriften und Reden*. Tübingen: J.C.B. Mohr (Paul Siebeck).

Weber, Max. 1988. *Zur Neuordnung Deutschlands. Schriften und Reden 1918-1920*. Edited by Wolfgang J. Mommsen and Wolfgang Schwentker, vol. 16 of *Max Weber-Gesamtausgabe*. Abt. I: *Schriften und Reden*. Tübingen: J.C.B. Mohr (Paul Siebeck).

Weber, Max. 1993. *Landarbeiterfrage, Nationalstaat und Volkswirtschaftspolitik. Schriften und Reden 1892-1899*. Edited by Wolfgang J. Mommsen and Rita Aldenhoff, vol. 4 of *Max Weber-Gesamtausgabe*. Abt. I: *Schriften und Reden*. Tübingen: J.C.B. Mohr (Paul Siebeck).

Weber, Max. 1994. The Nation State and Economic Policy (Inaugural Lecture [1895]), in *Political Writings*. Edited by Peter Lassman and Ronald Speirs. Cambridge: Cambridge University Press.

Karl-Ludwig Ay

# X

## Xenophobia

Literally, the fear of strangers. The word has been coming into use in Europe to denote negative attitudes towards immigrant groups on account of their cultural difference; sometimes these feelings are distinguished from RACISM. The German word *Fremdenfeindlichkeit* (literally hostility to strangers) may be considered more accurate, since hostility towards strangers is not necessarily a phobia or irrational fear. Some individuals can be regarded as strangers in respect of their social status and not because of race or color. Some strangers are tolerated provided they stay at a distance, which is a reflection of a social convention rather than a psychological hostility.

### Bibliography

Wimmer, Andreas. 1997. "Explaining xenophobia and racism: a critical review of current research approaches," *Ethnic and Racial Studies* 20: 17–41.

Michael Banton

# Y

## Youth and Nationalism

For many decades the powerful significance of *young people as such* in political movements was cloaked by the influential tendency of Marxists such as Stuart Hall to conceptualize youth as a mere epiphenomenon of class forces (Frith 1984). This theoretical error is magisterially refuted in classic works such as Eisenstadt's *From Generation to Generation* (1956) and Feuer's *The Conflict of Generations* (1969).

It is now broadly accepted that youth is a perennial feature of the age structure of society. It is a universal age group whose boundaries are defined by the physical onset of puberty at between eleven and fourteen and the achievement of adult autonomy at between eighteen and twenty-five. Young people display basic characteristics which recur in most types of historical and cultural situations (Mitterauer 1992).

Primary among the structural characteristics of youth are the natural tendency of young people towards *rebellious opposition* and the *idealism* which their structural position protects from the influence of pragmatic expediency (Marsland 1993). On both counts young people are peculiarly disposed towards activist involvement in political movements. In modernizing and modernized societies their political activism is channeled and reinforced through their role in the student movement and, independently, through their participation in the youth wings of political parties.

Of course the political role of youth finds expression in internationalist movements antagonistic to nationalism, such as Communism, and in movements such as environmentalism and nuclear disarmament, unrelated either positively or negatively to nationalism. However, young people have long played and continue to play a crucial role in specifically nationalist movements.

This is no accident. Nationalist movements of most types, and nationalist ideology as a general phenomenon, proclaim above all renewal, *risorgimento*, resurrection. Young people routinely play a lead role in resistance to foreign oppression and in pointing the way forward towards a new and liberated national future. Their rebellious spirit and their unencumbered idealism combine—sometimes dangerously, always powerfully—to project them into the front rank of nationalist uprisings. This has been vividly evident in recent years across the globe.

For example, in Tienanman Square in 1989 many hundreds of young people supporting proto-nationalist opposition to Communism were slaughtered. In South Africa the movement of resistance to APARTHEID which is as much nationalist as socialist was driven through to victory in Soweto and elsewhere during the 1970s and 1980s by township risings of the young. And in anti-Serbian demonstrations in Kosovo in 1998, marches were led by young people draped in the double-headed eagle of the Albanian flag. From Mazzini's romantic "Young Italy," through the ruthless *Hitlerjugend* of National Socialism, to the stone-throwing mobs of young people in Ulster and Palestine, young people's part in national resistance and national liberation is manifest.

The concrete mechanisms and mundane dynamics of young people's involvement in nationalism is well illustrated by the prototypical case of Guinea-Bissau in West Africa (von Freyhold 1979). The revolutionary movement of young intellectuals which had in the 1960s initiated the anticolonial struggle against Portuguese rule found the peasants "too timid and conservative" and workers "too individualistic and petty bourgeois" for revolutionary commitment. Instead, they turned for successful recruitment to the national cause to the shifting masses of young people migrating from the villages into the towns.

"There," declared Amilcar Cabral, "we found our little proletariat." Moreover, the guerrillas and soldiers recruited by the initial youth cadres to fight on behalf of a new NATIONAL IDENTITY were themselves even younger—for the most part indeed teenagers.

This paradigm—rootless youngsters, angry with the past, eager for a new future of AUTONOMY—was prefigured in the revolt of the Maccabees against Rome and by the young outlaws who helped Alfred, himself King at twenty-two, to establish the English nation. It became firmly established in the nineteenth century in the nationalist movements of Europe and Latin America. Repeated across Africa and Asia in the twentieth century, it is symbolized in the nineteen nineties in the almost hackneyed televisual image of the child with a Kalashnikov. Nationalist uprising enfranchises the adolescent dream, capitalizes on the social dislocation of youth, and harnesses the zealous idealism of young people to a vision of liberty.

The key role of youth in national development was explicitly recognized long ago by Giuseppe Mazzini, who excluded persons over forty from membership in Young Italy (Moller 1972). "Place the young at the head of the insurgent masses," he declared. And again:

> You do not know what strength is latent in those young bands, what magic influence the voices of the young have on the crowd; you will find them a host of apostles for the new religion. But youth lives on movement, grows great in enthusiasm and faith. Consecrate them with a lofty mission; inflame them with emulation and praise; spread through their ranks the word of fire, the word of inspiration; speak to them of country, of glory, of power, of great memories.

It has to be admitted that young people can be manipulated by their elders (Hitler was a past master), and that the nationalist idealism of youth can be hijacked by darker forces—as exemplified by the sinister influence of the Serbian Black Hand on Gavrilo Princip and other members of the student group known as Young Bosnia (Van Maanen 1967; Kotek 1996).

The force and vigor of youth, however, cannot be manipulated to order or channeled reliably in just any direction. It stands preeminently at the service of nations oppressed or inchoate. It finds its most characteristic and psychologically satisfactory expression in the spiritual collective of national identity and the millennial dream of nationalist aspiration.

## Bibliography

Eisenstadt, S. N. 1956. *From Generation to Generation*. New York: Free Press.

Feuer, L. S. 1969. *The Conflict of Generations*. London: Heinemann.

Frith, S. 1984. *The Sociology of Youth*. Ormskirk: Causeway Books.

Kotek, J. 1996. *Students and the Cold War*. Basingstoke: Macmillan.

Marsland, D. 1993. *Understanding Youth*. St Albans: Claridge Press.

Mitterauer, M. 1992. *A History of Youth*. Oxford: Blackwell.

Moller, H. 1972. "Youth as a force in the modern world," section 6 in P. K. Manning and M Truzzi (eds.), *Youth and Sociology*. Englewood Cliffs, NJ: Prentice-Hall.

Van Maanen, G. 1967. *The International Student Movement: History and Background*. The Hague: International Documentation Centre.

von Freyhold, M. 1979. "Youth in the third world," chapter 6 in L. Rosenmayer and K. Allerbeck (eds.), *Youth and Society*. London and Beverley Hills, CA: Sage.

David Marsland

# Index of Entry Titles

# Index of Entry Titles

# Index of Subjects

The index of subjects lists the subjects which either constitute entries or are discussed inside entries. Readers may find useful to consult this index when looking for particular subjects or themes. This index also guides readers to the headings (entry titles) under which they may find specific subjects. For example, "civic nationalism" is treated under "ethnic and civic nationalism"; while "economic theories of nationalism" are discussed in the entry "modernization theories of nationalism". The instruction "*see*" in the second column beside a subject (which can be a person's name) directs readers to the entry in which that subject is discussed; while "*see also*" suggests to readers related entries.

# Index of Subjects

# Index of Subjects

# List of Entries With Contributors

# List of Entries With Contributors

# List of Entries With Contributors

## List of Entries With Contributors

racism                             Michael Banton
Bristol University, UK

rational choice theories        Michael Banton
Bristol University, UK

regionalism                 Montserrat Guibernau
Open University, UK

religion and nationalism       Obi Igwara
Hull University, UK

Renan, Ernest             Rachel Monaghan
University of Ulster, UK

Rousseau, Jean-Jacques    Antony Flew
University of Reading, UK

secession and irredentism     Anthony D. Smith
London School of Economics and Political Science, UK

self-determination          Michael Banton
Bristol University, UK

sociobiological theory       Pierre L. Van den Berghe
University of Washington, Seattle, USA

sport and nationalism        John Hargreaves
University of Brighton, UK

"springtime of nations"      Raymond Pearson
University of Ulster, UK

state and nation            Anthony D. Smith
London School of Economics and Political Science, UK

tribalism                   David Marsland
Brunel University, UK

typology of nation-formation  Miroslav Hroch
Charles University, Czech Republic

Weber's theory of the nation  Karl-Ludwig Ay
Weber Archive, Munich, Germany

xenophobia                 Michael Banton
Bristol University, UK

youth and nationalism       David Marsland
Brunel University, UK